PENGUIN BOOKS

THE NEW PELICAN GUIDE TO ENGLISH LITERATURE

4

FROM DRYDEN TO JOHNSON

THE EDITOR

Boris Ford is the General Editor of *The New Pelican Guide to English Literature* (in 11 vols.), which in its original form was launched in 1954. At the time it was being planned he was Chief Editor and later Director of the Bureau of Current Affairs. After a spell on the Secretariat of the United Nations in New York and Geneva, he became Editor of the *Journal of Education* and also first Head of Schools Broadcasting with Independent Television.

Following a period as Education Secretary at the Cambridge University Press, Boris Ford, until he retired in 1982, was Professor of Education at the Universities of Sheffield, Bristol and Sussex, where he was also Dean of the School of Cultural and Community Studies. He edited *Universities Quarterly* from 1955 until 1986. He is General Editor of *The Cambridge Guide to the Arts in Britain* (in 9 vols. 1988–91), retitled *The Cambridge Cultural History of Britain* (1992); and of a forthcoming series of 10 volumes on the arts and civilization of the Western world. He edited *Benjamin Britten's Poets* (1994).

HAVANT & SOUTH DOWNS COLLEGE

New Road
Havant
Hants PO9 1QL

**Study Central
Havant Campus**

Tel : 023 9387 9999 extension 5005.

Email : library@hsdc.ac.uk

*Please return by the last
date stamped below or
contact the us to renew.*

PENGUIN BOOKS

Published by the Penguin Group
Penguin Books Ltd, 27 Wrights Lane, London W8 5TZ, England
Penguin Books USA Inc. 375 Hudson Street, New York, New York 10014, USA
Penguin Books Australia Ltd, Ringwood, Victoria, Australia
Penguin Books Canada Ltd, 10 Alcorn Avenue, Toronto, Ontario, Canada M4V 3B2
Penguin Books (NZ) Ltd, 182–190 Wairau Road, Auckland 10, New Zealand

Penguin Books Ltd, Registered Offices: Harmondsworth, Middlesex, England

First published in *The Pelican Guide to English Literature*
in Pelican Books 1957
This revised and expanded edition published 1982
Reprinted, with revisions, in Penguin Books 1991
Reprinted with a revised Appendix 1995
Reprinted with a revised Appendix 1997
1 3 5 7 9 10 8 6 4 2

Copyright © Boris Ford, 1957, 1982, 1991, 1995, 1997
All rights reserved

Illustrations by
Albany Wiseman, pp. 427, 429, 431, 435, 437, 440, 441, 443

Printed in England by Clays Ltd, St Ives plc
Filmset in Monophoto Bembo

CONTENTS

CONTENTS

PART IV

GENERAL INTRODUCTION

The publication of this *New Pelican Guide to English Literature* in many volumes might seem an odd phenomenon at a time when, in the words of the novelist L. H. Myers, a 'deep-seated spiritual vulgarity ... lies at the heart of our civilization', a time more typically characterized by the Headline and the Digest, by the Magazine and the Tabloid, by Pulp Literature and the Month's Masterpiece. Yet the continuing success of the *Guide* seems to confirm that literature – both yesterday's literature and today's – has a real and not merely a nominal existence among a large number of people; and its main aim has been to help validate as firmly as possible this feeling for a living literature and for the values it embodies.

The *Guide* is partly designed for the committed student of literature. But is has also been written for those many readers who accept with genuine respect what is known as 'our literary heritage', but for whom this often amounts, in memory, to an unattractive amalgam of set texts and school prizes; as a result they may have come to read only today's books – fiction and biography and travel. Though they are probably familiar with such names as Pope, George Eliot, Langland, Marvell, Yeats, Dr Johnson, Hopkins, the Brontës, they might hesitate to describe their work intimately or to fit them into any larger pattern of growth and achievement. If this account is a fair one, it seems probable that very many people would be glad of guidance that would help them respond to what is living and contemporary in literature, for, like the other arts, it has the power to enrich the imagination and to clarify thought and feeling.

The *Guide* does not set out to compete with the standard Histories of Literature, which inevitably tend to have a lofty, take-it-or-leave-it attitude about them. This is not a *Bradshaw* or a *Whitaker's Almanack* of English literature. Nor is it a digest or potted-version, nor again a portrait gallery of the Great. Works such as these already abound and there is no need to add to their number. What it sets out to offer, by contrast, is a guide to the history and traditions of English literature, a contour map of the literary scene. It attempts, that is, to draw up an ordered account of literature as a direct encouragement to people to read widely in an informed way and with enjoyment. In this respect the *Guide* acknowledges a considerable debt to those twentieth-century writers and critics who have made a determined effort to elicit from literature what is of living value to us today: to establish a sense of literary tradition and to define the standards that this tradition embodies.

The *New Pelican Guide to English Literature* consists of ten volumes:

1, Part One. *Medieval Literature: Chaucer and the Alliterative Tradition* (with an anthology)

1, Part Two. *Medieval Literature: The European Inheritance* (with an anthology)

2. *The Age of Shakespeare*
3. *From Donne to Marvell*
4. *From Dryden to Johnson*
5. *From Blake to Byron*
6. *From Dickens to Hardy*
7. *From James to Eliot*
8. *From Orwell to Naipaul*
9. *The Literature of the United States*

A Guide for Readers.

Though the *Guide* has been designed as a single work, in the sense that it attempts to provide a coherent and developing account of the tradition of English literature, each volume exists in its own right and sets out to provide the reader with four kinds of related material:

(i) *A survey of the social context of literature* in each period, providing an account of contemporary society at its points of contact with literature.

(ii) *A literary survey* of the period, describing the general characteristics of the period's literature in such a way as to enable the reader to trace its growth and to keep his or her bearings. The aim of this section is to answer such questions as 'What *kind* of literature was written in this period?', 'Which authors matter most?', 'Where does the strength of the period lie?'.

(iii) *Detailed studies* of some of the chief writers and works in the period. Coming after the two general surveys, the aim of this section is to convey a sense of what it means to read closely and with perception; and also to suggest how the literature of a given period is most profitably read, i.e. with what assumptions and with what kind of attention. This section also includes an account of whichever one of the other arts (here architecture) particularly flourished at the time as perhaps throwing a helpful if indirect light on the literature itself.

(iv) *An appendix of essential facts for reference purposes*, such as authors' biographies (in miniature), bibliographies, books for further study, and so on.

Thus each volume of the *Guide* has been planned as a whole, and the contributors' approach to literature is based on broadly common assumptions; for it was essential that the *Guide* should have cohesion and should reveal some collaborative agreements (though inevitably, and quite rightly, it reveals disagreements as well). They agree on the need for rigorous standards and have felt it essential not to take reputations for granted, but rather to examine once again, and often in close detail, the strengths and weaknesses of our literary heritage.

BORIS FORD

NOTES

Notes designated by an asterisk, etc., and glosses by a
letter, are given at the foot of each
page. Numbered notes are given at
the end of each chapter.

PART I

THE SOCIAL SETTING

ARTHUR HUMPHREYS

Writer and Public

To give a clear account in a single chapter of a period as long, even though as comparatively straightforward, as the Augustan* is anything but simple. The difficulty is not lessened by the fact that the age is often misrepresented by two prejudices – the one that it was decorative and elegant, a hundred years of costume drama; the other that it was an age of prose and reason, unadventurous and dull, commendable but unimaginative. Some limitations were certainly necessary for the consolidation of its very constructive achievement, but the intention of this chapter is to stress how interesting were its activities in the normal ways of life and its determination to make an enlightened best of human existence. This aim was a worldly one, but the term is not used in any bad sense, for its worldliness was guided by such qualities as imagination, zest, and the devotion of moral and religious responsibility. It is the first age in which we recognize the ordinary man as the norm, but the ordinary man here is not that dreary abstraction the statistically average citizen but a variety of living persons – the merchant energetic in business, the divine addressing his fellow Christians with faithful good sense, the politician busy with elections and votes, the traveller observing life at home and abroad, the country gentleman directing his farms and estates, the engineer designing his roads, canals, and bridges, the lady in her social calls, the doctor, lawyer, soldier, sailor, shopkeeper, servant, and labourer in their occupations, and the writer comprehending all these as his public. None of these classes or activities of course was new; what was new was that the whole of life in its ordinary aspects be-

* 'Augustan', a term deriving from the prestige of Latin literature in the age of Augustus, and 'applied to the period of highest refinement of any national literature' (*Oxford English Dictionary*), normally refers in England to the years from about 1680 to 1750. It is here stretched from 1660 to 1780 in so far as the outlook of the central period is evident.

15

came a source of interest and generally of comedy. Whether the record of this life seems prosaic or not depends partly on the writer and partly on the reader; the writer may fail in vigour or perceptiveness, and the reader may fail in sympathy for normal men and women. But a good deal of Augustan writing does not fail in vigour or perceptiveness and there will always, one may hope, be a sufficiency of readers ready for a while to forgo the headier passions in favour of an imaginative sense of the normal. It is necessary first to examine the conditions under which the normal came to be expressed.

Not the least important subject in literary history is the writer's sense of his public.[1] What social conditions bore mainly on the writer's mind? And why did those conditions produce a literature so predominantly of social record? Apart from the drama, pre-Augustan writing does little to call to mind any extensive public. Sidney's *Arcadia*, Spenser's *Faerie Queene*, Bacon's *Advancement of Learning*, Donne's *Songs and Sonets*, Herbert's *The Temple*, Browne's *Urn Burial*, and Milton's *Paradise Lost* appear to be written partly for their own sakes and partly for the reader as a single person, a private auditor, not one of a wide community. On the other hand Restoration comedy, the satires and prefaces of Dryden, the prose of pamphleteers, essayists, and novelists, the addresses of philosophers and divines, and the verse of almost all Augustan poets call up an inescapable notion of an extended public, though not always the same public. They are addressed rather to general than to individual reception – though their immediate recipient may be a patron, as representative of cultured taste – and their writers are choosing subjects which will strike readers as a record of what they themselves know. Why the ordinary reader was interested in the normal rather than the abnormal will be discussed shortly: the present point is that a considerable public was coming into view.

The process was gradual and the Augustan period covers its essential phases. In the last decades of the seventeenth and the first decades of the eighteenth centuries, the writer wishing to profit by his writing generally fixed his eye on a patron; he hoped less to make his living professionally by his books than to recommend himself to someone eminent in Church or State who would support him directly or appoint him to civil or ecclesiastical office. This system had its drawbacks. The writer sometimes humiliated himself (John-son's refusal to be humiliated led to his famous letter to Lord Chester-field, in February 1755, declaring his independence of patronage): the patron was sometimes – like Pope's 'Bufo' (Halifax-*cum*-Dodington) – 'fed with soft dedication all day long'.[2] But it did also mix the worlds of letters and society intimately together, and this intimacy is appropriately reflected in Kneller's Kit-Cat Club portraits in the National Portrait Gallery. The debt was not all from writer to patron: Godolphin begged Addison to write *The Campaign* (supporting, and dedicated to Marlborough) for the Whigs, and Bolingbroke was glad to entertain John Philips, the author of the rival Tory eulogy *Blenheim*. The poet Prior entertained the politician-patron Lord Harley; so did Pope the Prince of Wales. Halifax first, then Harley and Bolingbroke, sought the friendship of Swift; and Bolingbroke, Lyttelton, Peterborough, Chesterfield, Burlington, and Bathurst were as favoured by Pope's esteem as he by theirs. Under this system the interests and aims of art and letters were largely those current in the patron's circle, though since he was probably himself interested in politics, economics, philosophy, the Church, or the arts, those aims were not themselves narrow. The general public was in the back-ground; taste was established in circles where social distinction, political importance, and classical reading predominated, and Dryden counted it one of the disadvantages of his Elizabethan predecessors that 'Greatness was not then so easy of access, nor conversation so free, as it now is'.

There were still patrons through much of the eighteenth century, from Queen Charlotte downwards (she took an interest in divines and philosophers like Berkeley, Butler, Sherlock, and Whiston, and also helped some struggling writers like Richard Savage and Stephen Duck, 'the thresher poet'). But in 1709 a Copyright Act had secured to authors certain rights in the publication of their works and so given them an improved chance of bargaining with the book-sellers (the counterparts of modern publishers). At the same time the first signs of a wide popular market began to show themselves in a large sale for the more flamboyant sermons and pamphlets of Queen Anne's reign, and the circulation of the early periodicals. There were soon more writers than the market could stand, and these early and middle decades of the eighteenth century are the years of 'Grub

Street', of those 'caves of poverty and poetry' Pope describes in *The Dunciad*, and of the hand-to-mouth hack-writing Fielding displays in *The Author's Farce* and in the story of Mr Wilson in *Joseph Andrews*. Thomas Amory's curious novel *John Buncle* relates how Edmund Curll the bookseller had his hacks sleeping in relays, three in a bed; Johnson in the *Life of Savage* and elsewhere gives a first-hand account of literary poverty in sombre and moving terms.

But slowly the profession established itself. From the late seven-teenth century certain kinds of writing proved lucrative; on Arch-bishop Tillotson's death (1694) his unpublished sermons brought in 2,500 guineas, and early in the eighteenth century the more popular sermons and plays could bring their authors £100, a sum which, in the case of plays, benefit nights might raise to £1,000. In 1712 Addison and Steele sold half their rights in the collected *Spectator* for nearly £600; in 1716, according to Johnson's *Life*, Prior's *Poems* reaped him 4,000 guineas, which the younger Lord Harley doubled. Circulations increased, and periodicals like *The Spectator* both fostered and benefited from wider circles of readers. Addison in particular took seriously his task of educating the public in morality and criticism, as well as amusing it by satire and portraiture. The fact that he could run eighteen *Spectator* papers on Milton and eleven on 'The Pleasures of the Imagination' is a sign of some literary maturity common to a considerable public. The Press began to have its publish-ing successes, the most famous of which were Pope's translations of the *Iliad* (1715–20) and *Odyssey* (1725–6). These translations were dedicated – it is a sign of the times – not to a noble patron but to Congreve, a fellow-writer, and their popularity was such as to make them the most notable landmarks on the way to professional success, bringing Pope money enough to give him independence and being recognized as striking evidence of the support which, in favourable circumstances, literature could mobilize.

Gradually the taste for reading, and the ability to read, spread with the spread of charitable foundations, Sunday schools, dissenting academies, and the Methodist movement, and circulating libraries and better roads made the procuring of books much easier, even in the country. From the founding of *The Gentleman's Magazine* in 1731 onwards there were periodicals reviewing and popularizing current literature. Johnson commented in the seventh *Idler*, in 1758, that 'the knowledge of the common people of England is greater than that of any other vulgar' (a fact which visiting foreigners corroborated), and in the *Life of Addison* he remarked that the knowledge 'which now [1779] circulates in common talk was in his [Addison's] time rarely to be found'. The public in view during the Restoration decades had been a special and sophisticated circle, with the important exception, however, of the many who bought works of devotion – a large number of titles in the publishers' Term Catalogues are religious and theological.[3] In the late seventeenth century it extended to include merchants and the better-off citizens, mainly of London, and during the eighteenth it stretched widely, until from the 1740s onwards the heady influences of popular enthusiasm could spread literary reputations with unprecedented contagion. Richardson's success with *Pamela* and *Clarissa*, Sterne's with *Tristram Shandy* and *A Sentimental Journey*, and Macpherson's with the Gaelic romanticism of *Ossian* were portents of an age of popular taste.

The Normal as Novel

This period, then, saw the author facing a radical change in his public and prospects. But this would not in itself make his work what in fact it preponderantly was, a social record; it would merely incite him to provide what his public wanted. The question remains, then, why the public of the time was so interested in its own doings, why it asked less for substitutes for real life than for the recognizable facts of its own existence, not only in the greater part of its literature but in most of its art too. In the best Augustan work social fact is being not only described but felt with a particular reality; its substance, variety, and interests are perpetually being recorded, and social behaviour is both recorded and corrected in the interests of good sense. Indeed, the essence of Augustan literature is that it is integrated with social life, and treats, in their natural idiom, the interests of social men and women. In so far as it is modified by some other fashion – for classical or Miltonic diction, for Spenserian or Shakespearian imitation – and in so far as its substance is not the interested acknowledgement of social life, it is the less Augustan.

Why was society so interested in itself and so disposed towards the everyday stuff and proportion of life? Why were its dominant literary forms those of the essay, novel, and social poetry? Why, of the classical poets, was it the civilized sensible Horace whom it most read, re-read, translated, and re-translated? The answers lie in historical circumstances: political, economic, and intellectual conditions were favourable to a practical humanism. English society had crossed a watershed in the middle seventeenth century; dynamic and explosive conceptions of religion and politics, and complex but unstable fashions in prose and poetry, had, experience proved, to be abandoned in favour of modes which would unite rather than divide men, and unity would come most obviously on that common ground where men overlap, rather than on the frontiers of individualism where they differ. Englishmen had suffered so much from intellectual fission that they wanted amalgamation. Their sentiments were expressed by Burke when, in the *Reflections on the Revolution in France*, he defended England's mistrust of novelty:

> We are afraid to put men to live and trade each on his own private stock of reason; because we suspect that this stock in each man is small, and that the individuals would do better to avail themselves of the general bank and capital of nations and of ages.

The Civil War, and subsequent tragedies like the persecution of Dissenters after Monmouth's futile rebellion in 1685, provoked a wish for harmony. Moreover, economic expansion in town and country was encouraging confidence and co-operation; and in philosophy what Hume calls 'the science of man' was emerging as the focus of attention. As the convalescent invalid (or, say, Cowper recovering from his religious frenzies) sees the very ordinariness of life as blessed, so, one feels, the Augustans received the steady processes of social order almost as a revelation. In normality lay novelty. They were often satirical, since they contrasted the enlightenment men might well achieve with the folly they in fact commit; there are no more scathing comments on unreason than in Rochester's *Satyr Against Mankind* or Swift's greater satires. But what they satirized was departures from the 'general bank and capital' of reason, of decent responsible humanity. This, though it restricted originality, was in the circumstances a source of strength.

Enterprise and Development

If, of many possible strands, we follow first the economic, it is not in deference to current fashion but because economic progress entered deeply into the national consciousness. Defoe's *Tour Thro' the Whole Island of Great Britain* (1724–7) mentions the difficulty of recording this progress adequately, 'from the abundance of matter, the growing buildings, and the new discoveries made in every part of the country'. The medieval and Elizabethan idea of organic harmony between the parts of the body politic was reinforced and reinterpreted in terms of economic interdependence. Much was still said about the hierarchy of superior and inferior ranks, but more began to be heard about that 'secret concatenation of society which links together the great and the mean, the illustrious and the obscure' (*The Adventurer*, No. 67, 1753). 'The grand affair of business', in Defoe's phrase, was not only, as it always must be, the main occupation of life: it came prominently to the forefront of conscious attention, largely because the old conventions of limited enterprise were increasingly dislocated by new opportunities which technical developments and the expansion of trade afforded. 'Not sufficiency to the needs of daily life', it has been said, 'but limitless expansion became the goal of the Christian's efforts'.[4] The start of this process cannot of course be dated; trade and industry have always been a social concern and doubtless some men have always wanted as much wealth as possible. Certainly the Middle Ages and the Tudor and Caroline periods have their usurers and monopolists. Yet the degree to which economic life was respected was something new. From about 1660 the nation's conscious concern was the organization of its practical affairs. Following Bacon, Locke desired man to be

well-skilled in knowledge of material causes and effects of things in his power; directing his thought to the improvement of such arts and inventions, engines and utensils, as might best contribute to his continuance with conveniency and delight.

Robert Boyle, one of the founders of the scientific Royal Society (1662), wrote to a friend in Paris, François Marcombe, about the practical aims of

natural philosophy, the mechanics and husbandry, according to the principles of the new philosophical college, which values no knowledge but as it has a tendency to use.

Important elements of business organization too came into being – the Bank of England (1694), insurance and trading companies in-

cluding Lloyd's coffee-house from which sprang the great shipping
agency, and the 'Society for the Encouragement of Arts, Manufac-
tures and Commerce' (1754). Encyclopedias of the arts and sciences
began to appear, and periodicals ran advisory columns about useful
projects. On to this busy stage stepped the man of business, in the role
of public benefactor – in life the bankers, industrialists, and agricultural improvers,[5] in literature Defoe's traders and merchants, and
characters in periodicals and plays like Sir Andrew Freeport (*The
Spectator*), Mr Charwell (*The Guardian*), Mr Sealand (Steele's *Conscious Lovers*), and Mr Thorowgood (Lillo's *London Merchant*). No
longer an uncouth money-grubber to be wittily cheated by impudent
rakes (which is his role in Restoration comedy), the merchant
becomes a figure of honour evincing the 'indefatigable industry,
strong reason, and great experience' of a Sir Andrew Freeport, who
defends trade as a liberal pursuit. Far from being incompatible with
gentlemanliness, Defoe contends in *The Complete English Tradesman*,
the wealth of business sustains high place and distinction. 'In this
great commercial country', Boswell remarks, 'it is natural that a
situation which produces much wealth should be considered as very
respectable.' This is the strongest assertion of the middle class, and it
profoundly colours the age; that class's emergence has been called an
outcome of the Puritan spirit in its energy of self-justification, and
works like *The Tradesman's Calling* (1684) by Richard Steele (a nonconformist divine, not the essayist),[6] Defoe's novels and pamphlets,
and Benjamin Franklin's *Autobiography* (written 1771–90) have
indeed the true Dissenting flavour. Yet it was characteristic not
only of Dissent but of the whole nature of the time: men of all
sects and creeds were, in fact, taking to business as to a philosophy of
life.

The Eminence of London

The economic and cultural heart of England was London, whose
predominance is a commonplace of social history. This predominance, as will be suggested later, was not absolute, yet no reader of
Augustan literature can overlook how much London meant in the
literary world. Its growth during the eighteenth century, from
500,000 to 900,000, was thought extraordinary; even the ebullient
Defoe found it 'a great and monstrous thing', sprawling seven miles

from Limehouse to the Earl of Peterborough's mansion at the western end of Westminster. Between 1660 and 1780 London was transformed from a late medieval into an early modern city, not only by the fire of 1666 but by the steady replacement of medieval brick and timber by neoclassic brick and Portland stone, which translated a city in touch with Ben Jonson into one in touch with Thackeray.[7] Yet despite the speed of its change and growth it remained a healthy centre for literature because, while large enough to provide the desirable social and intellectual opportunities, its scale and character were still comprehensible and, in a way, intimate. Journalists, poets, and novelists dealt with this world of coffee-house and tavern, of church, theatre, and club, of book- and print-shop, of street-market, pleasure-garden, and residential square, until no territory seems more familiar; here, and in many a personal record like the *Journeys* of Celia Fiennes, Boswell's *London Journal* and *Life of Johnson*, Horace Walpole's letters, and William Hickey's *Memoirs*, is the portrayed personality of an amply felt place. Such works deal less with individualistic glimpses of life than with communal knowledge, with a participated spirit

London's special significance was as the symbol of national life; the popular pulse beat strongest there, in the turbulence of mobs, the enterprises of trade, the schemes of politics, the curiosity of intellect, the pursuit of amusement. Celia Fiennes's *Journeys* has pages of lively description which are worth consulting, but the indispensable guide is Defoe's *Tour*. As a government propagandist Defoe was out to make the best possible showing for the existing state of things, and one learns somewhat to discount his superlatives, yet the enthusiasm for the great city rising with its churches, mansions, and commercial houses is much more captivating than any cooler account could be. London was for him, as two centuries before for Dunbar, the flower of cities all – 'the most glorious sight, without exception, that the whole world at present can show'. His eulogies were not unsupported: Marvell had earlier written, in his *Last Instructions to a Painter* (1667), of the multiplying ships which –

> Unloaded here the birth of either Pole:
> Furs from the *North*, and silver from the *West*,
> From the *South* perfumes, Spices from the *East*,
> From *Gambo* gold, and from the *Ganges* Gems.

A succession of writers recited praises not less eager, and Smollett, prefacing his *Continuation of the History of England* (1761), signalized a high tide in the nation's affairs – 'such a fortunate assemblage of objects as never occurred in any other era of English history'.

Worlds Overseas

Commercial prosperity, then, centring on London and extending its activities thence throughout the world, inspired confidence which the protests of moralists and satirists against luxury and indulgence only slightly chequered and we may glance at the interest in practical life it afforded the Augustans. Here was the evidence that Britannia had emerged on to the world stage, that in war and peace she was likely to rule the waves, as James Thomson's patriotic poem urged her to do. Thomson, the poetic epitome of the time, elsewhere (in *Liberty*, 1736) expressed the mood of enterprise:

> For Britons, chief,
> It was reserv'd, with star-directed prow,
> To dare the middle Deep, and drive assur'd
> To distant nations thro' the pathless realm.

Robinson Crusoe, to be followed by Defoe's other novels of foreign ventures, is the first, and the supreme, masterpiece of this spirit, little though Defoe shows himself aware of his novel's symbolic significances.

Augustan horizons were wider and more exotic than we sometimes remember. In Pope's *Rape of the Lock*, Belinda's dressing-table, with 'all Arabia' breathing from perfume-boxes, tortoise-shell and ivory uniting in combs, 'the various off'rings of the world' assembled for her adornment, reflects the enrichment of commercial ventures just as, in its ornate pattern of luxurious products from all the continents, does Addison's *Spectator* paper (No. 69) on the Royal Exchange. The interest in remote lands, of which Defoe's novels are a symptom and Swift's *Gulliver's Travels* a satiric reflection, was greatly heightened by Captain William Dampier's *New Voyage Round the World* (1697, dedicated to Lord Montague as President of the Royal Society – Defoe drew on it in *Robinson Crusoe*), followed by his *Voyages and Descriptions* (1699) and the *Voyage to New Holland* (1703). Throughout the eighteenth century interest in the East was keen: the

South Sea Company was launched in 1711 (and the South Sea Bubble burst in 1720): Commodore Anson circumnavigated the globe in 1740–44, Byron's grandfather, Commodore John Byron, in 1764, and Captain Wallis in 1766–8. Captain Cook made his great expeditions in 1768–71, 1772–5, and 1776–9. Eastern trade was only a small part of economic life; the American was far greater (Burke's speeches refer admiringly to its extent and the rapidity of its increase), and the European far greater still. But the imaginative effect of the Orient's luxuries and of its reported wisdom and virtue was much more influential than its actual economic importance; trade was the channel for a wave of Oriental interest which overflowed Europe, bringing fascinating and unusual aesthetics, and (it seemed) a more enlightened morality (whether of the wise Chinese or of the paradisally-innocent Tahitians) than Europe could show outside the works of the ancient philosophers. But that is a digression.

Provincial Life

When the Englishman looked around at home he was not less gratified; for most of the century rural England seemed busy and prosperous. It is the sense of local vigour that to some extent counterbalances the dominance of London and gives Augustan culture a healthily wide basis. Again it is the practical Defoe who in his *Tour* gives the richest sense of the countryside's occupations. Much of the land, it is true, was still unimproved; much was still far from complete in that process of development and enrichment which went forward throughout the century (and which Swift satirized in *Gulliver's Travels* when, in 'A Voyage to Laputa' (chapter 4), he described the ravages caused by 'new rules and methods of agriculture' – Swift was no advocate of novelty). It is not wildness that Defoe likes: upland Derbyshire he finds 'a howling wilderness', the Lakeland hills are 'most barren and frightful', and the Pennines, with an 'inhospitable horror', lack not only pleasant valleys but even lead-mines and coal-pits and so have no attraction for him whatever. But in better circumstances Defoe exuberates; he celebrates the great houses which were the economic and cultural centres of local life, and a whole series of country towns, with particular praise for their social advantages. His particular forte is the theme of agricultural prosperity – Kent flourishing with hops, pastures, and 'abundance of large bullocks'; the South Downs covered with sheep; Leominster, Lincoln, the Midlands famous for wool; 'innumerable droves and flocks of sheep' at Boston and on the Yorkshire wolds; 'the land rich, the grass fine and good, and the cattle numberless' along the East Anglian rivers; rich Cheshire pastures, Evesham fruit-orchards, and everywhere 'most fertile rich country'. Defoe's statistics rarely stand analysis, but the important point is the spirit, the belief, of his writing, and it is a spirit which rises also from many other quarters, from Thomson's *Seasons*, Gay's *Rural Sports*, Dyer's *Fleece*, and many an essayist, novelist, and diarist. At the end of the century the quizzical and sophisticated Horace Walpole was as pleased as the serious and plebeian Defoe had been at its beginning; in a letter of 1793 he wrote to his cousin, George Montagu, of 'the felicity of my countrymen' and of —

such a scene of happiness and affluence in every village and amongst the lowest of the people... New streets, new towns, are rising every day and everywhere; the earth is covered with gardens and crops of grain.

This picture, it may be admitted, was a partial one, drawn at harvest-time in a good summer. Goldsmith's *Deserted Village* (1770) mourns the lost happy peasantry of his youth (a lament partly but only partly justified); Crabbe's early poems like *The Village* (1783) are revelations of rural poverty; and economists like Arthur Young were not lacking to point out, as Goldsmith did, the misery caused by the enclosure system, by which the old communally farmed open fields were being replaced by enclosed private estates, and a great many labourers dispossessed, to become an urban proletariat. The major results, however, were happier; farming stock and methods greatly improved, and many a dreary landscape was transformed into fertility and prosperity. The result was to consolidate the pattern of landed aristocracy, well-to-do squirearchy, and substantial yeomanry which forms the bucolic background to much Augustan literature (and later to Jane Austen, Thackeray, and Trollope),[8] to produce that scenic change from large featureless fields to the detailed beauty of enclosed meadows and hedgerows, accompanied by an enthusiasm for landscape-gardening and rural beautifying which was perhaps the most fruitful of all aesthetic fashions in England, and finally to improve the countryside with the seemliness of new manors, parsonages, and farms, and with the palatial beauty of great houses which still in their hundreds dominate, with classical porticoes and far-spreading symmetrical wings, the serene beauties of their undulating park-lands.

All this is not so remote from economic life or from literature as it may appear. The development of the countryside was a great eighteenth-century interest; the skill which devised new industrial processes and the development of commerce went also into the draining and fertilizing of land, its organization into efficient units, and the improvement of livestock: the eighteenth century is one of practical adventure, not the less adventurous for being practical. As Mr Christopher Morris observes in his introduction to Celia Fiennes's *Journeys* (1949), there was widespread interest in development:

> It must be remembered that a new discovery of England was in progress. Aristocratic house-parties would sometimes go to watch a river being made more navigable or a fen being drained. Treatises were written on Stonehenge and poems on 'the wonders of the Peak'. A new edition of Camden's *Britannia*, brought up to date by Bishop Gibson, seems to have lain on the parlour tables of most well-to-do people... Ogilby's wonderful road-book had appeared in 1675, and there were also surveys, comparable with modern directories and gazeteers.

A comparison of Adam Smith's *Wealth of Nations* (1776) with a modern economic treatise throws this sense of man into relief. Everything in Adam Smith is personal activity; the 'nations' whose wealth is his subject are gatherings of men and women. Economics, he knows, can get out of human control; indeed, behind the façade of what man proposes he sees the 'invisible hand' of a disposing God, contriving a result superior to anything intended by short-sighted humanity. But there is no alarm in this, no sense that an economic juggernaut is crushing the individual. In the eighteenth-century world of farming, small business, and a merely embryonic stock-market (though there were already some City magnates, mostly Whigs, in the chartered companies), we are still amidst the personal efforts of the single man or woman making his or her livelihood. Indeed, though Adam Smith's style is more urbane, his world is still that of Defoe, and of all English writers it is Defoe who best gives the human side of economic life, interested as he is in the economic side of human life. His characters keep themselves alive: if women, they exploit their sex, and after each spell as mistress or wife they count gains and losses ('As for me', says Moll Flanders of one inamorato, 'my Business was with his Money, and what I could make of him'); if men, they sail the world, outward-bound with bays and druggets, inward with silks and spices. It is this Defoe world, of traders abroad or citizens and farmers at home, that Adam Smith welds into economic philosophy. His main doctrine, at the end of his fourth book, leaves trade (as he feels God meant it to be left) to 'the industry of private people'. The fatal flaw in this is the non-existence of any wise 'invisible hand', but the point is that this outlook preserved the traditional scale of man in society while allying it with the opportunities of an expanding economy and with traditional notions (reinforced by science) of providential harmony. In its economic as well as its moral philosophy the age was eager to unite 'self-love and social'. Its practical emphasis differed (to generalize with dangerous brevity) from the medieval theological reading of life, the Elizabethans' heroic passion, and pre-Commonwealth religion-and-royalism, but was by no means a mere dehumanized materialism. If literature dealt so much with normal activities, it was because these seemed to take on a new air of constructive vigour and compulsion.

Before economic themes are finally left there is something more to be said on country life (even though its bearing is not strictly economic: a mixed subject cannot be completely disentangled), since an interest in its prosperity was widespread, and since the Augustans are sometimes thought to have limited their horizons to town life, and even to London. Country life provided them with bucolic pleasures and occasionally with some approach to 'the divinization of Nature'. Even in Restoration comedy, indeed, the town is not allowed to have everything its own way; Bellamy, in Shadwell's *Bury Fair*, is an admirable supporter of country life. And later, Swift writes to Stella of his willows at Laracor, his Irish retreat near Dublin, and the beauty of cherry-blossom and fine days; Steele, in the 118th *Spectator*, speaks of a fine scene as inspiring 'a certain transport which raises us above ordinary life, and yet not ... inconsistent with tranquillity'; Mr Ironside, the pseudonymous author of *The Guardian*, prefers bird-song to the best Italian singers, and likes 'to rise with the sun, and wander through the fields'; Pope evokes the pleasures of moonlight on water, with summer breezes stirring the leaves, and nightingales singing, in the 425th *Spectator*; and Sophie von la Roche, a visiting German lady, writes in 1786 of how –

Nature and man both enjoy noble freedom; the landscape over which hundreds and hundreds of fertile hills extend is set with splendid country houses of the great, and charming well-built farms.

Such pleasures the Augustans were by no means too urbanized to feel. More deeply, however, country life was an assertion of stability, and Augustan literature is that of a pre-industrial society. Many of its concerns are admittedly, as Gay observes, those of the town –

> Where news and politics divide mankind,
> And schemes of state involve th' uneasy mind,
> Faction embroils the world, and every tongue
> Is mov'd with flattery, or with scandal hung.

But the slow steadiness of a country economy may be felt behind many a praise of rural retirement, deriving ultimately perhaps from Horace and Martial but felt to be corroborated in contemporary circumstances – in Cowley's *The Wish*, Pomfret's *The Choice*, Lady Winchilsea's *Petition for an Absolute Retreat*, Matthew Green's *The Spleen*, Goldsmith's *The Deserted Village*, Shenstone's and Cowper's letters, in Cowper's poetry, in the patient naturalism of Thomson's *The Seasons*, Dyer's *The Fleece*, and many a country diary like those of William Cole of Bletchley or the more famous James Woodforde and (more sensitive and skilful) in Gilbert White's *The Natural History of Selborne*. Most Augustans had largely extricated themselves from theological and political fears, and they were not yet seriously under the shadow of industrial or international fears. They inherited a social order (agriculture supported four Englishmen out of five) which linked them as firmly to the past as their spirit of enterprise led them to the future. On this settled agricultural foundation (despite passing dearths and gluts) they might instinctively sense that nothing fundamentally would go wrong.

Temperate Politics

A comparable, and more conscious, double sense of order and progress arises from the Augustan philosophy of politics. 'Great Britain', the 1708 edition of Edward Chamberlayne's *Magnae Britanniae Notitia* observes, 'is of all countries the most proper for trade, as well from its situation as an island as from the freedom and excellency 'of its constitution'. That 'freedom and excellency', consequent on the Revolution of 1688, was a fundamental of post-revolutionary faith;[9] its spirit is that for which the astute statesman Halifax pleaded in his *Character of a Trimmer* (1688) – impartial law, latitude in faith, and a middle way between absolute monarchy and mob-republicanism. James II's Roman Catholicism and exercise of royal authority over universities, judiciary, and the Church had threatened constitutional tradition: 'our great Restorer', as Locke called William III, appeared to rescue that tradition and safeguard it for the future. The 1689 Convention Parliament settled the political system on what Burke describes as 'that ancient constitution formed by the original contract of the British state' – that is, the balanced powers of the realm. By its initiative in restoring that tradition, however, Parliament had asserted its supremacy, and the Court-centred society which prevailed up to 1688 (except during the republican Commonwealth between the execution of Charles I (1649) and the accession of Charles II (1660)) yielded to that Parliamentary predominance by which membership of either House bestowed peculiar prestige and privilege.

The new system, indeed, evolved amid violence. There was the anti-Catholic 'Popish Plot' (1678) of Titus Oates, devastatingly satirized in Dryden's *Absalom and Achitophel*; there were subsequent attempts to block James II's succession (during which the nicknames of Whig and Tory emerged), and explosive episodes like Shaftesbury's manoeuvres against James which Dryden counter-attacked in *Absalom and Achitophel* and *The Medall* (1681–2); there were the executions of Algernon Sidney and Lord William Russell (1683), and Monmouth's revolt (1685) and its suppression. Even when the century turned, the Tory Occasional Conformity Bill (1702) led to anti-Dissenter riots, violent sermons from High Church fanatics, and Defoe's parody of this fury *The Shortest Way with the Dissenters* (1702), which brought him to the pillory. There was a bitter Tory campaign against Marlborough, in which Swift's *Conduct of the Allies* (1711) contributed to the idol's fall; there were party intrigues, on the verge of civil war, leading to the Whig replacement of the Stuart line by the Hanoverian in 1714; there were the Jacobite invasions of 1715 and 1745; there were strong personal animosities during Walpole's long prime ministership (1721–42), and again over John Wilkes's disputed election to Parliament (1763, 1769), and over the American War of Independence and the French Revolution. Yet against this the concern for social order was strong enough to avert disaster. Of many moderating voices there might be said what Johnson said of Addison's *Spectators*, that 'to minds heated with political contest they supplied cooler and more inoffensive reflections'. If a ruling Augustan interest is political understanding, the reason lies in seventeenth-century experience of disaster. The politics of the age could be bitter – bitterest perhaps in the years closely (though partisanly) documented in Swift's *Examiner* papers (1710–11) and *The Four Last Years of the Queen* (written 1713), the years first of the Whigs and Marlborough's triumphs, then of the Tories and Marlborough's fall. But though the invitation to George of Hanover might have precipitated civil war, it did not do so; a peaceful succession inaugurated the long constitutional stability of the Hanoverian royal line. Weaknesses abounded in eighteenth-century politics – hostility to reform, electoral violence and corruption, the spoils system, ignorant high-handed justices – but they were weaknesses within a general acceptance of the rule of law and the autonomy of judges. By a happy circumstance, Locke's political philosophy, long maturing against the absolutism of Hobbes's *Leviathan* (1651), and Filmer's *Patriarcha* (1680), issued in his *Treatises of Government* (1690), a work which so well expounds the balance of constitutional power and the maintenance of the subject's rights that it has become a classic.[10] If political philosophy, even in such opposed writers as Godwin and Burke at the end of the eighteenth century, breathes rational enlightenment, if the great claims made for the normal man in the American and French revolutions are now the dogmas of Western thought, the reason largely is the way Locke's treatise crystallized a long, sensible tradition.

Since the theme of this chapter is the Augustan ethos of normal life, and since the political thought of the age is characteristically concerned with the needs of the normal man (as that useful fiction is envisaged in Britain), Burke (1729–97) earns a place alongside, and in amendment of, Locke.[11] He earns it too in a literary study not only because his ample and animated style is a great accomplishment in prose, but also because he represents an evolution of ideas closely reflected in literature; the evolution from the prestige of reason to that of feeling is exemplified in the way Burke supplements Locke. For (ruthlessly to compress a complex matter) Locke considered man as predominantly a reasoning creature, and both in political and moral philosophy the Augustans came to find this view not so much wrong as incomplete. Burke's is the most compelling voice speaking for the political importance of instinct, and for the sentiment of history which was becoming immeasurably powerful. In his later works he often seems an oracle of reaction, distrusting any reform, even of admitted wrong. But that was not the central Burke; the central Burke noted the organic growth of political institutions, wanted equally to preserve and develop ('a disposition to preserve, and an ability to improve', he asserted, 'would be my standard of a states-man'), and studied human behaviour in the nexus of its place and time. His great speeches on American affairs (1774–5) and his attack on the oppression of India are true historical understanding, whereas his profound antipathy to revolution, rather than evolution, led him to play down the reasons for the French Revolution in horror at its excesses. But despite this late inflexibility Burke is of all English political thinkers the one most sensitive to growth and adaptation, to a richly organic conception of society. The Burke who, in his *Enquiry into the Origin of our Ideas of the Sublime and the Beautiful* (1757), analysed the emotional effects of grandeur, darkness, and mystery, and so enriched the modes of aesthetic analysis, deepened in politics that psychology of emotion which was to be the spirit of Romanticism.

The politics of the period were not, of course, mainly philosophical. They must figure in accounts of social life because they interested so many men so much. From 1660 to 1800 few notable writers were not actively concerned; to run through the roll-call from Samuel Butler and Dryden to Tom Paine, Godwin, and Burke would be to recite many of the major and minor names. They attended on the whole less to philosophical principles than to current political practice, particularly when religion and politics intermingled. Party business, election contests, foreign policy, Church and State, Church and Dissent, the prevalence of corruption – such topics were the perpetual agitation of news-sheets and pamphlets. And, it hardly needs saying, those out of power viewed the conduct of those in with a perennial sense of imminent doom. Yet under the flurry of protesting gesticulation there ran a general sense that a sober and practical political order had been achieved, by what was held to be British reasonableness, and this was not to be forfeited. As Dr Johnson observed, on the very first occasion of Boswell's meeting him (16 May, 1763), 'When a butcher tells you that *his heart bleeds for his country*, he has, in fact, no uneasy feeling.' Such was the general assumption. Britain was free both negatively (from absolutism) and positively (to exert herself and enjoy the fruits of exertion). This was the liberty rooted (so the belief went) in tradition, and bearing fruit in art and knowledge, though admittedly felt more confidently by Whigs than by Tories. Richard Savage celebrated its past and present triumphs in his *Epistle to Sir Robert Walpole*:

> From Liberty each nobler science sprung,
> A Bacon brighten'd, and a Spenser sung;
> A Clarke and Locke new tracts of truth explore,
> And Newton reaches heights unknown before.

It was liberty with a divine sanction: ordered freedom was what God ordained for man. Its guardian was Parliament, the nation's focus ('to be out of Parliament is to be out of the world,' said Admiral Rodney), with its nobility-gentry-professional membership not split by any great division of interests.[12] All in all, political affairs were a typical function of Augustan life, with their practical bent, their basic assurance, and their reference to the normal man's frame of mind, reflected incidentally in the numerous (though seldom good) patriotic verses in any collection like Johnson's *Poets*.

The Sense of Society

There was, then, much in the Augustan background that gave a sense of freedom and harmony. A sociologist, no doubt, could easily deny that Augustan society was free and harmonious; indeed, as the eighteenth century advanced and for various reasons (including the ministrations of the Methodists) the actual circumstances of the poor came to light, many consciences were deeply disturbed. The conditions that hackwriters knew, that are glimpsed in Johnson's life, that Hogarth drew in many of his cartoons, and that his friend Fielding saw as a magistrate and revealed in his sociological pamphlets and

Amelia, began to press more strongly on the world of letters, though with nothing like the force they were to exert in Dickens and Mrs Gaskell. But our concern here is less with social fact than with what writers from Dryden to Johnson felt about their world, and generally they considered that the standards of the well-to-do were the natural codes of literature, the expressions of sense and civilization, provided that a perpetual corrective of satiric criticism was played upon them. This was on the whole a reasonable and not a snobbish attitude; the Augustans were not foolish enough to equate human worth with social station, and some of their most stinging criticism (the satires of Dryden, Swift, Pope, and Churchill) was directed against those unworthy of the responsibilities of place and privilege. But it was on society's upper levels that economic, political, and intellectual circumstances seemed to have liberated energy for partnership in a sane world, building bulwarks of good sense against tyrants, pedants, and fanatics. Here were most observable what the distinguished French exile Saint-Évremond, whom Restoration society so warmly received, calls 'that natural cheerfulness ... that readiness of wit and freedom of fancy, which are required towards a polite conversation', and that knowledge of philosophy, politics, and polite learning which, he assures us, 'particularly deserve[s] the care of Gentlemen'.

Indeed, gentlemen began, in their well-bred way, to become rather prominent in the Augustan scheme of things.[13] If their attributes are displayed in Addison's *Spectators*, and embodied in Richardson's Sir Charles Grandison, with too much unction they were at least a creditable discipline in behaviour, the more so in that much actual social conduct was boorish and heartless. Gentlemanliness was not mere outward decorum or the show of courtesy; it included all the qualities, including religious faith, moral and physical courage, and mental and physical energy, which make up the force of social life, as well as the culture and considerateness which give it grace. The gentleman, we are informed in the 34th *Guardian*, is 'the *most uncommon* of all the great characters of life', 'a Man completely qualified as well for the Service and Good, as for the Ornament and Delight, of Society'. It was to such a person, in so far as an imperfect world could produce him, that the Latitudinarian divines preached, and journalists, poets, and philosophers directed their works. He was

34

the recipient of Locke's religious *Letters on Toleration*, his political *Treatises of Government*, and his psychological *Essay Concerning Human Understanding*, which seem to be merely the enlightened social man making those practical adjustments to faith, politics, and his own mind which men of sense approve. Locke's pupil, Shaftesbury, the third Earl (1671–1713), took an airier flight; his *Characteristicks of Men, Manners, Opinions, Times* (1711) was the main source of that fashionable refinement in art and morals which became an Augustan code. Yet patrician though his tone, Shaftesbury's aim was to encourage in his fellows the companionable disposition and enlightenment which are 'natural' to man. And Hume's felicitous considerate style equally clarifies his own mind and engages the reader's by its admirable tone.

Gentlemanliness, even when the word has a responsible rather than a merely refined connotation, is doubtless an inadequate ideal; in any case it would hardly cover such Augustan figures as Swift, Defoe, and Johnson (though it would Fielding). But it recognized the value of social decency, and in literature it imposed its discipline. An essential element in its art of expression was consideration for the reader, together with such harmony of phrase and effectiveness of image (misleadingly referred to as 'polish' and therefore wrongly seeming superficial) as would best recommend the meaning. The writer's sense of his public has already been discussed, and even as the circles of that public widened its core still remained as his court of appeal – the reliable minority of experienced persons, active and shrewd in the affairs of the world, of sound social standing, and fairly seasoned in classical literature.

To enter on the related theme of education would be to broach too large a subject here. What may briefly be said is that in all its reaches beyond the elementary it served and strengthened the same ideals by instilling a reasonable knowledge of Latin authors and probably some modest skill in Latin composition. Its canons of careful metrics, chosen phrasing, and orderly structure, and its sense of writing as a craft and of the reader as a judge of craftsmanship, bore markedly on the ways the Augustans wrote English. The results were bracing in some ways and enervating in others.[14] Gentlemanliness and a classical training conduced to good prose; their influence on poetry was less happy, though (in view of Dryden, Pope, Johnson, and Gray) not so unhappy as is sometimes supposed. In a kindred spirit the Augustans did much of their reading; they went to the major authors of antiquity (in original or translation) and to those of the Renaissance who best understood human nature (Chaucer, Shakespeare, Cervantes, Rabelais, Molière) or moral truth (Milton). Much else they ignored, so avoiding (at the price of a limited range) the confusions of omnivorous cosmopolitanism. They took their good where it suited them, and they simplified their search by going to the most likely places. If their reading was selected ('All ancient authors, Sir, all manly', Johnson said of his own education), it did at least reinforce their responsible sense of life and their care for an enlightened coherent civilization. This is the education of human-ism; it selects its tradition to produce social man according to the canons of the past's enlightened best: it adopts as models those who have shown how to live well in the world.[15]

Faith and Morals

The pursuit of social and literary amenity, of classical reading, of agreeable style and 'polite conversation', looks from the outside like dilettantism. The suspicion is not baseless; many of the Augustans have no adequate defence against those accusations of shallowness which it is almost a routine to bring against them. On the other hand there is another routine charge, that of didacticism, which points to a very different quality, and that didacticism, though often tedious, reflects something far removed from dilettantism. For basically the hold of moral and religious faith was still very strong; even the ideal gentleman was incomplete without his Anglican orthodoxy, and lower down in society there were religious impulses cruder but more fervent, where 'enthusiasm' survived from the seventeenth century and Methodism caught hold earliest, where sects splintered apart and zealots saw by an inner light. At many levels religion still provoked intellectual though no longer physical combat; indeed, the second quarter of the eighteenth century has been declared more vigorously controversial than any equal period in English history. What is more important is that (except in some fashionable circles angrily spotlighted by the devout) religion was a continuing concern of life, deeply represented in the work not only of the divines like Archbishop Tillotson, Swift, Law, Bishop Berkeley, and Bishop

Butler, but also of laymen like Dryden, Pope, Addison, Johnson, Burke, Cowper, and many others, respectfully deferred to (with few exceptions) by scientists and philosophers, and served with an architectural passion by Wren, Hawksmoor, Gibbs, and their fellows.

'In the last analysis, it is the ultimate picture which an age forms of the nature of its world that is its most fundamental possession.'[16] That ultimate picture depends not only on what an age makes explicit about itself but also, more deeply, on what lies implicit. The Augustan age is not one of metaphysical distinction (except in Locke, Berkeley, and Hume), yet a metaphysical fact – its belief in a moral and intellectual Absolute, which it is simplest to call God, establishing moral laws and requiring man to discover and obey them, by revelation or reason or both, is the deepest thing in the Augustan intellectual world. In this the Augustans were continuous with the Middle Ages and deeply divided from the twentieth century: they were, even when deistically inclined, believers.[17] For believers, God has embodied in man that spiritual being which is the supreme fact of life, making him the crowning phenomenon of the created (or evolved) universe, its florescence into spirituality. Juxtapose with this belief, which both Christians and humanists would endorse (and *a fortiori* a Christian-humanist ethos such as the Augustans inherited from the Renaissance), such a statement of the modern 'ultimate picture' as Bertrand Russell once provided in *A Free Man's Worship*, and the difference is seen to be fundamental:

> That man is the product of causes which had no prevision of the end they were achieving; that his origin, his hopes and fears, his loves and his beliefs, are but the outcome of accidental collocations of atoms; that no fire, no heroism, no intensity of thought and feeling, can preserve an individual life beyond the grave; that all the labours of the ages, all the devotion, all the inspiration, all the noonday brightness of human genius, are destined to extinction in the vast death of the solar system, and that the whole temple of Man's achievement must inevitably be buried beneath the debris of a universe in ruins – all these things, if not quite beyond dispute, are yet so nearly certain that no philosophy which rejects them can hope to stand. Only within the scaffolding of these truths, only on the firm foundation of unyielding despair, can the soul's habitations henceforth be safely built.

However Russell's formulation may be disputed, a world view maintaining an impersonal universe, the merely relative nature of truth, and a general meaninglessness of existence (in any sense involving a spiritual end) is the characteristic, though not the universal, modern philosophy. The notion of man as created to obey a divine moral reality through his free will is, though widely accepted, apt to seem rather a mirage in a desert of materialism than a certain truth.

The Augustans were not unaffected by the modern earthquake; they had the materialism and virtual atheism of Hobbes's *Leviathan* to contend against. But they did contend against it, as so blind an error that its refutation could be a matter only of time and energy; there was an absolute truth of things against it. It is easy to quarrel with them for their conformity, for not pursuing their inquiries with more sceptical rigour, for reasserting the old moral and critical commonplaces. But this was not laziness; it reflected the prestige that accepted truths gained by being demonstrable, in the sense that heterodoxy, far from being laudable, was as eccentric a divergence from tried experience as if a man denied that the three angles of a triangle make two right angles. This should not be put too sweepingly; there is plenty of mental independence among the Augustans, and anything but enervation in the way orthodoxy is accepted. Englishmen, and Protestants, were proud of their opinions; Dryden, Locke, Swift, Addison, Berkeley, Shaftesbury, Pope, Butler, Johnson, and Burke were not diffident about offering intellectual leadership. But even when, as with the Deists, the conclusions were unorthodox, they were virtually bound to include a supreme moral authority: the Mosaic laws might be suspect, but those of Nature and Reason would, it was felt, produce a sound and right philosophy of life and were, moreover, demonstrably sanctioned by the existence of God.[18]

Moreover, natural laws were the evidence of God's beneficence. They were not merely statements of verifiable phenomena, such as that bodies fall at specific speeds, that the heavenly globes move by predictable courses, or that certain economic causes will produce certain economic results. They were laws in seeming not only to impose such speeds, courses, and results but also to bear the imprint both of intelligent direction and good will, to be the means by which a benevolent God directs his universe towards the best results. The notion of cosmic laws as designed for the best ends occurs in the thought of the time with significant frequency, and Augustan literature draws a deep moral assurance from its certainty as to fundamental spiritual goodness, accessible to man through his conscience and intelligence as well as through Revelation. The point may be illustrated from Colin Maclaurin's *Account of Sir Isaac Newton's Discoveries* (1748), which was efficient and popular (1,300 copies of a large quarto edition were subscribed for). This declares that 'natural philosophy' is to be 'subservient to purposes of a higher kind' (as a 'sure foundation for natural religion and moral philosophy'), and is to lead 'in the most satisfactory manner' to the knowledge of God:

> Our views of Nature, however imperfect, serve to represent to us, in the most sensible manner, the mighty power which prevails throughout, acting with a force and efficacy that appears to suffer no diminution from the greatest distances of space or intervals of time; and that wisdom which we see equally displayed in the exquisite structure and just motions of the greatest and subtlest parts. These, with the perfect goodness by which they are evidently directed, constitute the supreme object of the speculations of a philosopher; who, while he contemplates and admires so excellent a system, cannot but be himself excited and animated to correspond with the general harmony of Nature.

There (and similar quotations offer themselves from scores of writers after about 1650) is the new, confident, natural philosophy reasserting the medieval belief in omniscient, infinitely wise, divine superintendence. In a sense the Augustans had all the advantages; with traditional confidence in God's purposes they could enjoy a new intellectual technique of inquiry (science) which seemed progressively to reveal those purposes as more convincingly admirable.

But why, if the Augustan bases were so traditional, did they provide a foursquare assurance more evident than before the Restoration? There is indeed no more metaphysical certainty in Locke and Berkeley than in St Thomas Aquinas and Dante, no more confidence in natural law than there had been in stoic philosophy or in Hooker's *Laws of Ecclesiastical Polity* (1594), no more theory of an ordered universe than the Elizabethan world-picture had afforded. In Dante or St Thomas there is a complex structure of faith, for the formulation of which reason has been intensively mobilized and tradition deeply drawn upon. In Shakespeare and Milton there is a poetic sense of life in its context of moral order and disorder. The Elizabethan universe was one of cosmic law. But these systems, it came to be felt, were unsatisfactory because not based on demonstrable fact: they were symbolic inventions of man's mind, myths elaborated to provide life with purpose and relationships but essentially matters of theory, and, moreover, of theory encrusted with superstition. 'Natural philosophy' seemed to make impressively for clarification and rational conviction based on fact. Whatever the technical complexities of Newtonian physics or of biological science (with all the wonders of the microscope), a wilderness of apparently miscellaneous phenomena seemed to be rectified by the co-ordinating power of laws objectively and demonstrably true. These were far more comprehensible, trustworthy, and indeed astonishing than the methods of Aristotelian science (which Joseph Glanvill's *Vanity of Dogmatizing* (1661) calls 'inept for new discoveries'), or of medieval theology, or of pre-Restoration pseudo-science. The old philosophies had left so much, so enormously much, obscure; life had remained, despite all arguments of divine wisdom, so extraordinarily mysterious and incomprehensible that irrationality and superstition could flourish in the absence of evident criteria by which they could be refuted. The new sense of things is expressed in Mulgrave's *Essay on Poetry* (1682):

> While in dark ignorance we lay, afraid
> Of fancies, ghosts, and every empty shade,
> Great Hobbes appear'd, and by plain reason's light
> Put such fantastic forms to shameful flight.

Hobbes's alleged atheism was repellent to the Augustans; his cool reason was not. Under the new dispensation much was still mysterious: the Augustans were not so immodest as to suppose the human mind capable of omniscience. But what was discovered – in particular, gravitation, the nature of light, and the beauties of microscopic biology – seemed to prove a universe so intelligent in cause and effect as to be admirable and reassuring. The scholastic philosophers, it may be said, were as certain of this as the Augustans; God's laws, directing each thing according to its nature, were a supreme witness to divine order. But the novelty lay in the proofs of experiment rather than those of scholastic logic; the metaphors of dawn, of enlightenment breaking on darkness, often applied to this process both then and now are justified. The process was perhaps less revolutionary than it seemed at the time: the 'New Philosophy' would still agree with the tenor of St Thomas Aquinas's pronouncement that:

The first [stage of God's schooling] is the enlightenment of intellect by faith, and this is the most excellent lesson. It is a greater thing that a man have a

modicum of faith than that he should know everything that all the philosophers have discovered about the universe.

(Sermon on the Feast of St Martin)

But faith seemed progressively to be a matter less of taking the universe on trust than of understanding it. The Augustan enlightenment
was no more rational, no more convinced of divine goodness and
wisdom, than medieval or Elizabethan cosmogony, but it still broke
like a flood of light across a confused sky because the cherished
faith in that goodness and wisdom seemed confirmed by such evidence, macroscopic and microscopic, as no man with eyes could fail
to see and accept. This was what faith seemed to have been waiting
for

Faith, of course, came not only through the new science but also
through religious tradition. To speak of an Augustan tradition in
religion may seem perverse, since what first strikes the eye is either
apathy or sectarian dissension. The faith of the time is quiet compared
with that of the century before or after, but this is not because the
tide has ebbed away to nothing but because it runs with a steadier
current.[19] It would be a complicated business to describe the structure
of religion, with the mutual relations of Church and Dissent, or the
divisions of these each within itself; in the briefest compass it may
be said that Anglicanism, which had a High Church phase under the
Stuart kings (persisting after 1688 with Non-jurors loyal to the divine
right of the exiled line), became thereafter Low Church and latitudinarian in the spirit of rationalism, and preached a reasonable faith and
the social virtues instead of dogma, or the conviction of sin, or the
ecclesiastical privilege. Though inspired by Christian charity, its
characteristic flavour is ethical: 'our business here', Locke asserted, 'is
not to know all things but those which concern our conduct.' Being
unfanatical and comprehensive it is apt to seem dull, and above all
it feared 'enthusiasm', that ardent sense of divine stimulus which had
fired the sects of the seventeenth century. But in its own circumstances it was a sign of maturity and understanding, an honourable
attempt to unite rather than divide the Christian faith, and it engaged
the assent of the majority of divines and laymen, who had, on the
whole, no less serious a sense of their moral responsibilities than their
predecessors and successors.

Yet it came to need the force of a new spirit, and it found it (without entirely liking it) in Methodism, the one great movement of eighteenth-century religion, originating inside the Church and only reluctantly parting from it. John and Charles Wesley, influenced by their father's High Church devotion, and by the passion of William Law's *Serious Call to a Devout and Holy Life* (1728: one of the century's great books), instilled into their followers in England and the American colonies an urgent sense of religious experience, a sense which shocked more sedate believers by manifestations of frenzy and physical convulsions. Since the Church had subsided into plain sense and reason, and since Dissent now tempered with sobriety its former righteous and godly zeal, there was indeed a psychological need for Methodism and for certain other similar evangelical movements, just as the whole social-reasonable temper of the time was coming to need the deeper emotions of the nineteenth century. The optimistic confidence described a few pages earlier was not general enough to save many Christian believers from anguish over their sins. The Methodist and other forms of religious revival stirred crowded congregations into paroxysms of soul-searching and the dread of damnation. Many deeply thinking individuals – Johnson and Cowper among the most notable – suffered from an appalled sense of God's wrath. Many, too, of the most famous hymns of the century express the passion of feelings of unworthiness and of inadequate faith. Such things belong to the age-old tradition which fears an omnipotent judge who demands from his creation entire obedience to his laws. Methodism broke like a sudden storm across the relatively placid sky of Anglicanism, reminding men of fundamental power, and of sin and salvation. One side of it was Calvinistic, and worked through dread (this, unfortunately, was the side of Evangelicalism which afflicted Cowper), but the Wesleys' own message was Arminian, the doctrine of salvation for all, bringing a sense of sin but in the very process a simultaneous sense of divine mercy.

The religion of the age is relevant to literature in various ways: firstly, because its conviction of moral truth and moral law, to be found by faith and good sense, was a source of assurance; secondly, because its latitudinarian charity had much to do with the eighteenth century's social sympathies; thirdly, because more than any other subject it deepened the writing of men like Law, Berkeley, Johnson, and Cowper; and fourthly, because the insurgency of Methodism was a sign of something profoundly evolving in the temper of the time, the passing of the phase of reason and judgement in favour of that of passion and 'possession'. To call the Methodist and kindred movements parallels to Romanticism is to beg some large questions but is not really untrue. Eighteenth-century religion has many faults – an episcopate wedded to party politics, an impoverished lower clergy, dull orthodoxy and Dissent, a sceptical world of fashion, and an hysterical evangelical resurgence. Yet with all its faults it contributed much more valuably to the outlook of the time than has been customarily allowed; it inspired much scholarly and pastoral devotion, and much in the way of Christian apologetics. Sermons and theological works abounded, and many of the most popular and impressive hymns date from the period from Bishop Ken to William Cowper.

Reason and Feeling

It remains, finally, to trace an aspect of mental evolution already touched on, under which many miscellaneous phenomena can be, and indeed must be, subsumed – that is, the transition from the dominant prestige of reason to that of feeling. It is true that no sensible Augustan at any time doubted that man is actuated by his feelings – there had been throughout the seventeenth century, and there were throughout the eighteenth, treatises analysing the symptoms of 'the passions'. Yet the triumphs of science, and the clear advantages of being reasonable rather than fanatical in the discussion of religion and politics, invested reason with a high renown. This involved a fresh investigation, on the lines inaugurated by Bacon, of the mind's powers, and, as in politics and religious thought, the stage was set by Locke, in his *Essay Concerning Human Understanding* (1690). He analyses human capacities in a way dictated by his own thoughtful and practical temperament and by his subject which is, avowedly, 'understanding', the function not mainly of imagination but of reason.[20] It is the rational mind which receives most of Locke's attention: he is alert for sources of intellectual confusion; he elevates judgement (which analyses and distinguishes ideas) over 'wit' (which unites them by their resemblances, as in a wider sense does what we now call imagination); he is concerned for the clear definition of words and ideas so that the mind can work properly, and his pleas for a more exact use of language were reinforced by the scientists and the admirers of French criticism.

One important result was to produce a basic Augustan style of exemplary clarity, and a confidence that in any context the words mean what at first sight they appear to mean. This is not precisely to say that the Augustan grasp of verbal meanings is supremely accurate; no writers have used words more exactly than Shakespeare or Donne, Keats or Hopkins. But while in these cases the exactness is complex and perhaps inexhaustible, the Augustan exactness is that of clear equivalence of word to thing or notion, an exactness by limitation of range. It may still, as in Swift and Pope, have subtle and complex implications, but that is not frequent; normally it works as Locke recommended, lucidly and without mystifying aura.[21] 'Reason', then, is a powerful talisman in the Augustan understanding of the world, in the critical establishing of clear expression, and in the control of ideas and feelings which might otherwise be extravagant. In such contentions 'Reason' is, implicitly or explicitly, 'Right Reason' – reason, that is, guided in moral matters by conscience and in physical matters by the ordered laws of the universe. That other kinds and uses (or rather, misuses) of reason could lead to abominations the Augustans were well aware; that is what *Gulliver's Travels* is largely about. As for the management of words and the mode of style in discourse, these were to obey the sanity and intelligence which God has offered to each thinking human being. The characteristic Augustan prose discussion (Dryden's *Essay of Dramatic Poesy* is a signal example) is much better than the characteristic Elizabethan or Caroline, its ideas being pruned of excess, its tone steadier, and its mode much more persuasive. Bacon, Donne, Milton, Browne, and Jeremy Taylor are magnificent prose artists but as advocates leave much to be desired, not because they were less anxious than the Augustans to sway by the pen, but because the whole apparatus of reasonable argument – a sceptical disposition, a civilized attitude to the opponent, a sense of the audience, an appropriate prose, and the very conception of language itself – needed half a century of development.

If Locke, for his particular purposes, gave reason his predominant attention, he did at least also stimulate psychological analysis, and 'the science of man' is a leading topic of Augustan philosophy. Wherever one looks there are discourses on human nature – in *The Spectator* and other periodicals, in the *Essay on Man* and other poems, and in scores of moral treatises. What is remarkable, particularly as time passes, is the recognition increasingly given to feeling – in Steele's *Christian Hero* (1701), which upholds the generous emotions; in Shaftesbury's *Characteristicks* (1711), which puts 'our passions and affections' in the centre of attention; in Addison's 'Pleasures of the Imagination' *Spectators* (Nos 411–21); in the Shaftesburyan portions of Thomson's *Seasons* (1726–30); and in the moral philosophy of Francis Hutcheson, Hume, Burke, and Adam Smith. In critical theory, too, whereas the fashion of Hobbes and Locke is to apply standards of intellectual judgement, the fashion of Dryden and Dennis, of Addison, Shaftesbury, and Welsted, is to transcend rules and rational criteria for the 'grace beyond the reach of art', which only instinct can achieve or appreciate.[22]

In other words, Augustan criticism knows, as well as does moral philosophy, that we react to letters as to life by intuition, instinct, and impulse rather than by reason. And Augustan literature, whose allegiances in the Restoration had been predominantly intellectual (not in a palely logical sense of the word, but one strong and vigorous, whether heartlessly witty or severely thoughtful), became after 1740 predominantly a matter of sentiment (as in Richardson and Sterne, and partly in Fielding too; and as in Gray, or Goldsmith, or Cowper), exaggerated at times into a luxuriant indulgence of sentimentality, which Henry Mackenzie exploited in *The Man of Feeling* (1771), and Goldsmith, Sheridan, and Jane Austen satirized. It is time to put the rationalism of the Augustans into its place, as a discipline, a process indispensable in the evolution of English civilization, but only subsidiary to the motivating passions of life. If the Augustans sang the praises of reason, it is partly because of reason's intellectual triumphs, and partly because their feelings were strong enough to require control.

Social Benevolence

Within that general evolution from the prestige of reason to that of feeling there were many related aspects of social morals and literary taste. In social morals the main relevant phenomenon is the

Augustans' growing humanitarianism: in literary taste it is their increasing admission of emotions and interests which go beyond sense and reason. In respect of the former, the eighteenth-century's characteristic philosophy is 'utilitarianism', whose famous principle is 'the greatest happiness for the greatest numbers'. This phrase, often attributed to Jeremy Bentham (who himself attributed it to Joseph Priestley or Cesare Beccaria) in fact goes back to Francis Hutcheson's *An Inquiry into the Original of our Ideas of Beauty and Virtue*, Part II, Section 3, 'Inquiry Concerning Moral Good and Evil' (1725): the basic idea was expressed in Richard Cumberland's *De Legibus Naturae* (1672). The rights of 'life, liberty, and the pursuit of happiness', written into the American Declaration of Independence, were man's due expectations, as Locke had defined them: they might be, and often were, pursued in the spirit of selfishness, but they were often seen also to involve help to others – the attainment of social good on earth was a preliminary to eternal happiness earned by virtue and charity. Since the great concern of Augustan moral philosophy was the individual's relations with his fellows, the major theme was that of general wellbeing and interdependence:

> Heav'n forming each on other to depend,
> A master, or a servant, or a friend,
> Bids each on other for assistance call,
> Till one Man's weakness grows the strength of all.
> (POPE: *Essay on Man*, II, 249–52)

Society fulfils its purpose in ensuring the welfare of all. In *The Religion of Nature* (1722) William Wollaston saw maximum happiness as 'the end of society and laws', and in his *Political Maxims* George Washington, echoing the American Declaration of Independence, laid it down that 'the aggregate happiness of society, which is best promoted by the practice of a virtuous policy, is or ought to be the end of all government'. Many writers in similar secular terms reaffirmed the Christian message of mutual good, as, for instance, did Samuel Clarke the philosopher–theologian, who in his *Discourse Concerning the Unalterable Obligations of Natural Religion* (1706) reminded his readers that every man 'is bound by the law of his nature ... to think himself born to promote the publick Good and Welfare of all his Fellow-creatures'. As Pope put it,

Self-love thus push'd to social, to divine,
Gives thee to make thy neighbour's blessing thine.
Is this too little for the boundless heart?
Extend it, let thy enemies have part:
Grasp the whole worlds of Reason, Life, and Sense,
In one close system of Benevolence.

(Essay on Man, IV, 353–8)

A social conscience, propagated through poems, periodicals,
novels, sermons, and philosophy, bore fruit in works of welfare – the
foundation of charity schools, of dispensaries providing medicine for
the poor, and of bodies like the Marine Society (1756: founded to prepare poor boys for a seafaring life) and the Royal Humane Society
(1777); the investigation of prison conditions (the devoted life-work
of John Howard); the assistance of debtors (the great name here is that
of James Oglethorpe, the founder of the colony of Georgia where
debtors might make a new start); the rescuing of poor children and
particularly of chimney-sweeps. The humanitarian philosophy with
its concern for personality involved, too, a growing respect for
women (Steele distinguished himself in this respect). As the years
passed, women played an increasingly important part in social life,
which improved markedly in moral tone and politeness, and in the
constitution of the reading public. The later eighteenth century is
noted for the expression of feminine taste through the Blue-stocking
salons of ladies like Mrs Vesey, Mrs Boscawen, and the famous Mrs
Montagu, and the literary activities of others like Elizabeth Carter
(who translated Epictetus to general admiration), Mrs Thrale (Dr
Johnson's hostess and friend), and Fanny Burney. The long road that
female emancipation had still to travel is the theme of Mary Woll-
stonecraft's revolutionary *Vindication of the Rights of Woman* (1792)
where, perhaps for the first time, eighty-seven years before *A Doll's
House*, we perceive the lineaments of the Modern Woman, demand-
ing in the spirit of Ibsen and Shaw a full share of civic and domestic
rights and duties. Still, social consideration and intellectual respect had
advanced as much since the Restoration as libertinism and grossness
had declined; ideologically, society in 1800 was in many respects,
sexual and sociological, more humane than that of 1700.

47

Cultural Variegation

The last word must be for that other aspect of the century's emotional evolution, its growing sensitiveness to those moods which lie on the periphery of rationalism. An increasing pleasure in natural landscape, outmoding the geometrical French and Dutch gardens of the late seventeenth century; a reviving interest in Gothic architecture, given prestige from 1747 onwards in Horace Walpole's Strawberry Hill; sensitiveness to the moods and atmosphere, over and above the human activities, of the country, of which the first landmark is Thomson's *Winter* (1726); a fashion of twilight or graveyard poetry; a taste for pre-Restoration styles, like the Spenserianism of Thomson's *Castle of Indolence* (1748) or Shenstone's *Schoolmistress* (1737–42), or the pseudo-medieval 'Rowley' poems (1777) by the precocious Chatterton (1752–70), or the more-or-less-genuine balladry of Thomas Percy's *Reliques of Ancient English Poetry* (1765); a prepossession for the primitive, such as Gray showed in *The Bard* and his interest in Celtic and Norse verse, and the public at large in the sensational Ossianic poems bestowed upon it by James Macpherson in the 1760s; a cultivation of solitary pleasures, as reflected in Akenside's *Pleasures of Imagination* (1744), and of picturesque scenes, as George Morland's paintings show and William Gilpin's travelbooks describe them; a curiosity about exotic and particularly Eastern cultures, and a general responsiveness to those aesthetics of gloom, sublimity, and mystery of which Burke's thesis on *The Sublime and the Beautiful* (1757) is an interesting example – all such things chequer what might otherwise be the too-simple pattern of Augustan sense and assurance, and witness to the complexity of human moods. 'Romantic' curiosities which in the progressive confidence of early Augustanism were scarcely admitted, like an interest in medieval art and letters, became respectable, even the rage; and that tide which set away from predominant daylight and reason carried the English, and the European, mind towards the social and cultural complexities of the nineteenth century.

After so miscellaneous a survey it is not easy to sum up. Augustan life is so unspecialized that any social movement may impinge on literature, and, indeed, it is hard to name a single aspect of social concern which literature ignores. The erudite learning of the seventeenth century had gone and the nineteenth century's intellectual specializations had not yet arrived: economics, politics, religion, philosophy, criticism, the arts, and social and natural science were available as the natural interests of the normal intelligent man, to be discussed in the confident vocabulary of sound sense. Inevitably this state of affairs could not long persist; knowledge accumulates and the standards of expertness rise. But in the lively participation of normal minds in the interdependent intellectual life of the age, and in the interaction of self- and social-love which still enabled men to feel their society as an organism of human proportions, there lies an integration of literature and society so natural that one responds to Augustan idiom as to the active speech of social life rather than as dream or introversion, and looks upon Augustan letters in the healthy terms of a useful rather than a fine art.

NOTES

I should like to express my gratitude to Messrs Methuen & Co. Ltd for allowing me to use in abbreviated form, in this and other essays in this volume, material on social, political, philosophical, and architectural history more fully presented in my book *The Augustan World,* of which they are the publishers; to Messrs Allen & Unwin Ltd for permission to quote from Bertrand Russell's *Mysticism and Logic*; and to the Cresset Press for the passage from Mr Christopher Morris's introduction to *The Journeys of Celia Fiennes.*

1. For treatment of the reading public, see particularly Q. D. Leavis, *Fiction and the Reading Public* (1932), 118–50; also A. S. Collins, *Authorship in the Days of Johnson* (1928); F. A. Mumby, *Publishing and Bookselling* (1930); A. Beljame, *The Public and Men of Letters in the Eighteenth Century* (1948); and R. W. Chapman, 'Authors and Booksellers', in *Johnson's England* (1933), ed. A. S. Turberville.

2. See *Epistle to Arbuthnot*, lines 231–48, for the sham virtuoso.

3. J. L. Lowes, *Of Reading Books* (1930), 8–10.

4. R. H. Tawney, *Religion and the Rise of Capitalism* (edn of 1933), 248.

5. For the 'vertical mobility' of eighteenth-century society, see T. S. Ashton, *The Industrial Revolution* (1948), 17, and A. R. Humphreys, *The Augustan World* (1954), ch. ii.

6. For Richard Steele, see Tawney, *Religion and the Rise of Capitalism,* ch. iv, 'The Puritan Movement'.

7. See J. Summerson, *Georgian London* (1945), for building developments.

8. See H. J. Habakkuk, 'English Landownership 1680–1740', *Economic History Review*, X, No. i; G. M. Trevelyan, *English Social History* (1944), 267–9, 273–82, 298–302, 306–10.

9. See G. M. Trevelyan, *The English Revolution 1688–9* (1938), *passim.*

10. For Locke, see H. Laski, *Political Thought from Locke to Bentham* (1920), C. H. Driver, 'Locke', in *Social and Political Ideas of Some English Thinkers of the Augustan Age*, ed. F. J. C. Hearnshaw (1928); *The Second Treatise of Civil Government*, ed. J. W. Gough (1946); B. Willey, *The Seventeenth-Century Background* (1934), 246ff.

11. For Burke, see B. Willey, *The Eighteenth-Century Background* (1940), 240–52; P. Magnus, *Edmund Burke* (1939); J. Morley, *Burke* (1882).

12. The best studies of eighteenth–century politics are L. B. Namier, *The Structure of Politics at the Accession of George III* (1929); R. Walcott, *English Politics in the Early 18th Century* (1956). See also G. N. Clark, 'The Augustan Age', in *Social and Political Ideas of . . . the Augustan Age*, ed. Hearnshaw; R. Lodge, *Political History of England 1660–1702* (1910); I. S. Leadam, *Political History of England 1720–60* (1912); W. Hunt, *Political History of England 1760–1801* (1905). There are some pleasant contemporary pages by the visiting C. P. Moritz, *Travels in England* (1924), 52–65, 219–20.

13. See F. R. Leavis, *The Common Pursuit* (1952), 103–4; J. R. Sutherland, *Preface to Eighteenth-Century Poetry* (1948), 65ff.

14. For the influence of Latin verse composition, see A. R. Humphreys, 'A Classical Education and Eighteenth-Century Poetry', *Scrutiny*, VIII, 2 (1939), and for general classical background, Sutherland, *Preface*, 51ff.

15. For the prestige of moral philosophy, see W. J. Bate, *From Classic to Romantic* (1946), 2ff.

16. E. A. Burtt, *The Metaphysical Foundations of Modern Science* (1924), 3.

17. For continuity of cultural tradition and faith, see C. S. Lewis, *De Descriptione Temporum* (1955).

18. See C. Becker, *The Heavenly City of the Eighteenth-Century Philosophers* (New Haven, 1932), 7ff., 21ff., 45ff., 62ff. For moral uniformity, see Bate, *From Classic to Romantic*, 13ff.

19. For Augustan religious life and its relationship to literature, see A. R. Humphreys, *The Augustan World* (1954), ch. iv.

20. See Willey, *The Seventeenth-Century Background* (1934), 290–95.

21. Though it may have overtones and allusions; see Sutherland, *Preface*, 61–2.

22. See J. E. Spingarn, *Critical Essays of the Seventeenth Century* (1908), I, xcii–ci; J. W. H. Atkins, *English Literary Criticism: 17th and 18th Centuries* (1951), 146–85; Bate, *From Classic to Romantic*, (1946), 44–8.

PART II

THE LITERARY SCENE

ARTHUR HUMPHREYS

The Critical Background: 'First follow Nature'

The vigour and variety of Augustan literature are commonly under-rated. Often supposed to be uniform over a century and a half, it in fact reflects the enormous process by which the late Renaissance becomes the onset of nineteenth-century modernity, a psychology of reason and the conscious mind turns into one of subtle intuitions, a cosmos of stable revealed truth changes to subjectivity and agnosticism, and verbal habits sharing the experimenting exuberance of Jacobean speech moderate into the sensible, well-directed idiom of social amenity. Far from reflecting an unadventurous worldliness, it is the utterance of intelligent men concerned to make the most of human nature, and facing always new problems which compel the continual evolution of idea.

Basically, the critical injunction which gained the widest, indeed almost universal, acceptance was the call to 'follow Nature'. This call the Augustans did not invent; the classical stoics had expressed through it man's duty of following moral law as the central cosmic reality, and Renaissance critics had repeated it, in a variety of senses, according as they interpreted 'Nature' as the normal course of the world or as ideal truth by which art should be guided. In Augustan criticism there are almost as many interpretations as there are critics, but beneath them the prevalent sense has been defined as 'the universe conceived of as governed by law, with general human nature as the microcosm of this mechanical order'[1] – in other words, the notion (reinforced by science) that there is a divinely appointed right way for the universe to work and, with respect to man, there is a permanent (as opposed to local or temporary) truth of human behaviour and also a principle (of reason) which man should obey. 'Follow Nature' might mean 'portray the world as you see it' – in that sense Restoration comedy followed Nature and was true to life.

It might mean 'show the permanent truths underlying the individual varieties of man' – in that sense Homer and Shakespeare, Chaucer and Molière, were poets of Nature. It might mean 'obey reason; seek order and harmony in life and art' – in that sense the higher forms of philosophy, art, or science (the classical philosophers, the great Renaissance painters, and such moderns as Milton and Newton) had followed Nature, and in accordance with it Rymer claimed that poetry should express the 'constant order, harmony, and beauty of Providence' and Dennis desired the arts to 'restore the decays that happened to human nature by the Fall, by restoring Order'. Clearly an injunction that sets up as a goal the ordinary realism of life, the permanent truth of humanity, and the mind's achievement of transcendent order, is anything but precise; nevertheless, in all senses it directs the study of mankind to man, and to man in his recognizable, representative, normality. Following Nature becomes following life, and following life means recording it as one's good sense and wide knowledge tell one that men in general experience it. 'The manners of men' is how Hobbes defines the subject of poetry, and even critics less swayed by the Renaissance prestige of epic agree. According to Pope, 'the best employment of human wit' is to present human nature interestingly. Such concepts as universality (what has always, of all men, been true), reason as a guide to 'Nature' and as 'common to all people' (Rymer), and the art of writing as the accomplished technique whereby the mind most clearly and acceptably communicates its ideas – these are the signs of Augustan humanism. Properly to write in this way a large equipment is needed (though the untaught genius like Shakespeare may manage without), an equipment of classical scholarship, history, general reading, and critical principles:[2] new writing is to be supported (though not smothered) by the lessons of inherited experience. Yet its substance should be the first-hand knowledge of life. Denham summed up the ideal in praising Cowley – 'To him no author was unknown, But what he writ was all his own.' Following Nature – understanding life, and expressing the lasting truth about it in civilized and convincing words – was a highly responsible ideal.

The Responsibilities of Literature

Literature, then, was a responsible art. The *Essay on Poetry* (1682) by John Sheffield, Lord Mulgrave, reflects this responsibility; it came naturally, even to a fashionable amateur in letters, to express such ideas –

> Of all those arts in which the wise excel,
> Nature's chief masterpiece is writing well;
> No writing lifts exalted man so high
> As sacred and soul-breathing Poesy.
> No kind of work requires so nice a touch,
> And, if well finished, nothing shines so much.

With prestige of that kind, deriving from classical and Renaissance tradition, literature must be perpetually criticized in the interests of good communication, just as social habits must be perpetually satirized in the interests of good conduct, and so the theory and practice of criticism, as of satire, become unusually important. Prefacing his *Sullen Lovers* (1668), Shadwell writes of 'this very critical age, when every man pretends [i.e. claims] to be a judge': Swift's *Battle of the Books* (1704) calls criticism a 'malignant Deity': the 12th *Guardian* (1713), by Pope, assumes that any new poem will be severely scrutinized since 'most men, at some time of their lives', set up for critics. This criticism was often mere angry pedantry or pedestrian common sense or personal spite – 'a man seldom sets up for a poet', *The Spectator* (No. 253) declares, 'without attacking the reputation of all his brothers in the art'. But basically it was rooted in a sense of literature as 'Nature's chief masterpiece', man's greatest intellectual achievement, the treasury of his creative power, the standard of his civilization.

The desire for order, then, was a prepossession to which the Augustans were moved both by the disorder, the eccentricity, and the extravagance of much preceding literature, and by the belief that it has a divine sanction, that, as Dennis asserts, 'there is nothing in Nature that is great and beautiful without rule and order'. Yet order was even then recognized to be secondary, particularly in poetry, to the energy of creative genius. The most important classical influence on Augustan criticism after (perhaps even before) that of Horace was that of Longinus's treatise *On the Sublime*, which praises passion and ecstasy. The terms in which Pope extols Homer, in the preface to *The Iliad*, are typical; only 'common critics', lacking inspiration, will prefer 'a judicious and methodical genius to a great and fruitful one'. 'Invention [that is, imaginative creation] is the very foundation of poetry.' In this, Homer is unrivalled; his 'unequalled fire and rapture' make his epic 'a wild paradise', in which everything is animated. Shakespeare and Milton, too, though not so supremely, share 'this poetical fire, this *vivida vis animi*'. The same exultance in creative force, as the spirit of life's drive, Pope expressed in *An Essay on Man* (1733):

> In lazy Apathy let Stoics boast
> Their Virtue fix'd; 'tis fix'd as in a frost,
> Contracted all, retiring to the breast;
> But strength of mind is Exercise, not Rest;
> The rising tempest puts in act the soul,
> Parts it may ravage, but preserves the whole.
> On life's vast ocean diversely we sail,
> Reason the card, but Passion is the gale;
> Nor God alone in the still calm we find,
> He mounts the storm and walks upon the wind.
>
> (II, 101–10)

Dryden's praise of Shakespeare in the *Essay of Dramatic Poesy* (1668) had already stressed the same quality; it strikingly admits that Shakespeare has 'the largest and most comprehensive soul' of all modern and perhaps of all ancient poets, and presents his images so vigorously as to affect the reader like the very experience of life itself. Other critics were no less definite about the prime requirement of creative force. Mulgrave demands 'e'en something of divine, and more than wit'; Edward Phillips in his *Theatrum Poetarum* (1675) prefers energy to 'wit, ingenuity, and learning in verse, even elegancy itself'; Thomas Sprat praises the 'masculine' qualities in Cowley; and Roscommon's *Essay on Translated Verse* (1684) elevates 'the sterling bullion of an English line' over the elegant gilding of the French. One may sometimes feel that the Augustans used the snaffle and the curb too mu6ch, yet there was undoubtedly meant to be a horse – Pegasus they would call it – beneath the harness. The very experience of writing proved, if common sense did not, that rule and order must be the rule and order of something energetically alive.

'Wit' and its Functions

That being axiomatic, the critical aim was to express this grasp of living reality as well as possible. This is where 'wit', in its most important Augustan meaning, came in. The basic, though not the only, Augustan concern was to understand things and express them plainly. 'We love plain truth,' said Saint-Évremond, 'good sense has gained ground upon the illusions of fancy, and nothing satisfies us nowadays [about 1690] but solid Reason.' Away with the conceits of metaphysical poetry, the freaks of Caroline sermon-style, the 'fantastic fairy-land' of romance which Cowley rejects from English epic (*To Sir William Davenant*), the 'monstrous, singular fancy' which Rymer deplores, the 'gigantic forms and monstrous births' which Lansdowne condemns in his *Essay upon Unnatural Flights in Poetry* (1721; it is based on Bouhours' significantly-named *Manière de bien penser*). These must yield before the true function of 'wit', which is 'to copy out ideas in the mind' (Lansdowne) with an exact correspondence. The ideas themselves are to be objectively true to life. Cowley's *Ode to Wit* (1663) protests against the stylistic acrobatics of puns, quibbles, and encrusted imagery; true style is the power of expressing a truth with the clarity which serves it well, instead of the showiness which obscures it. Dryden defines wit as 'deep thoughts in common language', and Robert Wolseley as 'a true and lively expression of Nature' (*Preface to Valentinian*, 1685). 'Wit' has other meanings, certainly, some damagingly near to irresponsible fancy, some like the 'occult resemblances in things apparently unlike' that Johnson defined in metaphysical poetry, some resembling our own sense of piquant surprise. But that the Augustans should so often have linked it with perspicuity ('a propriety of words and thoughts adapted to the subject' – Dryden) indicates their desire to define life well and express enduringly the truth about it. Incidentally, Pope's definition of wit as 'what oft was thought but ne'er so well expressed' is criticized by Johnson for reducing wit from strength of thought to happiness of language; Johnson prefers to describe wit as that –

which is at once natural and new, that which, though not obvious, is upon its first production acknowledged to be just; . . . that which he that never found it wonders how he missed it.

Wit is the clear and fresh comprehension and expression of representative truth.[3]

The General and the Original

Augustan criticism praises the general, the familiar, the traditional, because the truth of human nature (the basic quest of literature) lies not in idiosyncrasies but in common humanity. 'Human nature is ever the same': so, Pope argues in the 12th *Guardian*, the moderns are bound to describe life much as the ancients had done. Richard Hurd's *Discourse Concerning Poetical Imitation* (1751) describes the passions as 'constant in their effects', and for Hume the aim of history is 'to discern the constant and universal principles of human nature' (*Essays*, 1758). Basically this goes back to Aristotle and Horace but it suits the Augustans so well as to seem their own property. Yet wit does not merely recite the familiar truths; it finds fresh ways of impressing them and it also discovers new truths. Johnson condemns Gray's *Eton College* because it contains nothing that every reader does not already realize; he praises Gray's *Elegy* because it 'abounds with images which find a mirror in every mind'. He is not being inconsistent: the former, he feels, does not bring the familiar to life while the latter does – a difference which is a common experience in reading, though often hard to account for. With its fresh perceptions wit may indeed go further than the familiar, especially with non-human subjects, and discover unprecedented methods and subjects. Pope enthusiastically admitted such creative boldness into the *Essay on Criticism* (1711; lines 150–55):

> Thus Pegasus, a nearer way to take,
> May boldly deviate from the common Track.
> Great Wits sometimes may gloriously offend,
> And rise to Faults true Critics dare not mend;
> From vulgar Bounds with brave Disorder part,
> And snatch a Grace beyond the reach of Art.

Denham admires Cowley for novelty; Rochester praises Etherege as 'a sheer Original'; Swift's *Proposal for Correcting the English Tongue* (1712) speaks of the genius as being 'one who is able to open new scenes and to discover a vein of true and noble thinking'; and Johnson commends Savage for being individual in style and Denham for inventing 'local poetry' with *Cooper's Hill*, and so earning 'the rank and dignity of an original author'. The idea that originality is anathema to the Augustans is quite false – but originality is not endorsed unless it extends our sphere of true experience, either by revivifying the old or by profitably widening our view of life.

The Canons of Style

John Hughes's essay *Of Style* (1698) defines the Augustan aims – 'propriety, perspicuity, elegance, and cadence'.[4] These seem superficial until their purpose is remembered; their value lies in the intelligent, ordered, and appropriate expression of what has been clearly grasped. Horace's *Ars Poetica* and Boileau's *L'Art poétique*, with their counsels of critical care and the adjustment of means to ends, were written gospels, but no less effective was the influence of good conversation and good manners, which Swift describes as 'the Art of making those people easy with whom we converse' (*A Treatise on Good-Manners and Good-Breeding* (*c*. 1728)). The ideal was that 'gracious and dignified simplicity ... the mean between ostentation and rusticity' which the preface to Pope's *Iliad* (1715) prescribes, the 'strength and grace united' which Goldsmith's *Account of the Augustan Age in England* (in his periodical *The Bee*, 1759) sees accomplished in the days of Queen Anne the 'eloquence by wisdom taught,/The graceful vehicle of virtuous thought,' praised in William Cowper's *Epitaph on Dr Johnson* (1785). Literature kept, on the whole, to those emotions which could be expressed in public; it considered its reader's convenience and echoed Sprat's approval of 'a natural easiness and unaffected grace, where nothing seems to be studied yet everything is extraordinary' [i.e. unusually well-expressed]. Dryden's *Defence of the Epilogue* (1672) thinks Restoration styles better than Elizabethan because of 'the last and greatest advantage of our writing, which proceeds from *conversation*'. There was general, though not universal, agreement that the language was less faulty than ever before and more suitable to be the medium of literature, and that what Pope calls 'the present purity of writing' was born from the stylistic needs of the new philosophy and from the happy alliance of literature and polite society.[5] Clarity, coherence, polite idiom, and a gentlemanly and sociable tone were the ideals appropriate to the effective expression of truth, though actual discourse and manners often failed to realize them.

French Precedents

The influences forming the new styles were mostly, and most deeply, home-bred, yet they were given extra authority by classical and French precedent to a degree which at times, though not in general, suggests subservience. Even for this there was some excuse; as Voltaire was to say, those who love the arts are fellows of one commonwealth. Ancient Rome, Louis XIV's France, and Augustan England, it was widely, almost unquestioningly, believed, embodied the ideals of civilization, expressing in manly good sense and urbanity the best elements of human nature. The French contribution, for reasons of space and because it goes less deep than the Latin, must be treated tersely:[6] it amounted, especially during the first half of the Augustan era, to a strong influence of Corneille on Dryden (the explanatory *Discours* and *Examens* prefixed to Corneille's plays begot Dryden's critical prefaces), and to a general admiration for Boileau and a more transient one for other critics. Lord Mulgrave's *Essay upon Poetry* (1682) adapted, and Sir William Soames's *Art of Poetry* (1683) translated, Boileau; Rymer translated Rapin's *Réflexions sur la Poétique d'Aristote* the year it appeared (1674) and Dryden, in *An Apology for Heroic Poetry* (1677) coupled Rapin and Boileau as 'the greatest of this age'. A lot of this criticism – on the dramatic unities, for example, or the nature of dramatic characterization, or rules of various kinds – has lost its interest, but the general importance of French thought was to encourage sceptical instead of dogmatic discussion and to strengthen the ideals of energy and clarity. On this point Addison's tribute to Bouhours and Boileau is worth quoting, since every phrase has the hallmark of its age:

> Bouhours, whom I look upon to be the most penetrating of the French critics, has taken pains to show, that it is impossible for any thought to be beautiful which is not just and has not its foundation in the nature of things; that the basis of all wit is truth; and that no thought can be valuable of which good sense is not the groundwork. Boileau has endeavoured to inculcate the same notion ... This is that natural way of writing, that beautiful simplicity, which we so much admire in the compositions of the ancients; and which nobody deviates from but those who want strength of genius to make a thought shine in its own natural beauties.
>
> (*The Spectator*, 62)

The French pioneered the way the English wished to go; their mistakes could be avoided, their successes could be a model for the new styles. They were allies rather than masters.

Classical Precedents

The masters, though by no means the tyrants, were the ancients. To resemble them was not only desirable – it was, since they had so expressed the civilized mind, almost inevitable. This had its drawbacks; some kinds of writing, Cowley remarks in the *Preface* to his poems (1656), could only be '*Cold-meats* of the *Antients*, new-heated', and charges of plagiarism were easy to bring. Pope faces this situation in the 12th *Guardian*, and also in prefacing his poems in 1717; voluntary or involuntary borrowing is inevitable, but the classically versed reader's enjoyment will be increased rather than diminished by his remembrance of an original. Over and above its clarity and definiteness Augustan language often had its enriching echoes, and Augustan literature could gain in confidence by a family resemblance to the classics. 'Those who say our thoughts are not our own because they resemble the Ancients,' Pope observes, 'may as well say our Faces are not our own because they are like our Fathers'.' Devotion to the classics fostered some faults, such as an external conception of literary graces, some loss of linguistic subtlety, an obtrusion of unassimilated Latin diction, and (in poetry) a heavy or artfully deliberate composition. But then each age has its own reasons for writing poorly. On the credit side it encouraged a vigorous grasp of social themes, a concern (which was certainly laudable) for discipline and verbal skill, and a range of literary 'kinds' (epic, ode – Pindaric or Horatian – epistle, epigram, and so on) into which the order-seeking Augustan mind liked to fit.[7] They provided too the perspective of a successful and honoured tradition.

It is easy to overstress the Augustans' debt to the past. They lived their own lives, thought their own thoughts, and developed their own styles. Yet a respect for the way things had been done before, by those who had done them well, was part of their sense of responsibility, no more to be deplored than their addiction to classical architecture. They felt themselves part of a majestic ideal of humanity, emulating but not rejecting 'the masters'. 'Those great men' (Dryden quotes Longinus, in the Preface to *Troilus and Cressida*, 1679) –

whom we propose to ourselves as patterns of our imitation, serve us as a torch which is lifted up before us, to enlighten our passage, and often elevate our thoughts as high as the conception we have of our author's genius.

In terms as little obsequious do Sir Joshua Reynolds's *Discourses*, delivered between 1769 and 1790 to art students at the Royal Academy, recommend antique and Renaissance models (though at times these might result in tedious academicism – Blake was to reject Reynolds's doctrines outright, and the artist Constable to complain of ' "high-minded members" who stickle for the "elevated and noble" walks of art'). The intention was to benefit from the past, to discipline but not subdue individuality, and to capture either in ideal or real terms that human nature which Pope pronounces 'the most useful object of human reason'. The ancients were, says the 86th *Guardian*, 'fountains of good sense and eloquence': familiarity with them was considered the source of 'that good and manly taste which distinguishes so many English writers' (the phrase is that of a German visitor, Friedrich August Wendeborn), and Burke's *Letter to a Member of the National Assembly* (1791) credits England's disdain of Rousseau-istic anarchy to her reverence for 'sound antiquity'.

Not all this reverence was first-hand; translations abounded and so, more significantly, did adaptations, classical originals adjusted to the latitude of London with a sense of kinship. Yet whatever may have been the readers' case, many writers were well-grounded in Latin; indeed, as Leslie Stephen remarks, since they held most earlier English literature to be obsolete, where else could they find sustenance? A classical allegiance had its faults; Eachard's witty *Contempt of the Clergy* (1670) deplores the neglect of English studies, and there was a cant of classicism which Johnson, stalwart classic though he was, rejected.[8] Yet the ancients provided so much that the moderns needed – the discipline of central style, the stimulus of models, the fire of Homer, dignity of Virgil, energy of Juvenal, eloquence of Cicero, pith of Seneca, and urbanity of Horace, Terence, and Petronius – that no influence could better have co-operated with the concrete and vigorous native styles to produce the sense of living civilization.

The Life of Augustan Styles

Yet there remains an important critical question. Augustan intellectual habits had revolutionary effects on poetry and prose, hailed with enthusiasm then but with cooler feelings ever since. Much Augustan prose, by being plain and reasonable, much Augustan verse, by being trim and disciplined, is dull. How far do Augustan styles still live for us?

A current commonplace is that they lack the intimate life which animated the rich 'metaphysical' technique of language, and that the prestige of judgement and reason killed something which, until the death of Cowley (1667), had been alive and imaginative. This commonplace gained its fame from T. S. Eliot's diagnosis of a 'dissociation of sensibility', the loss of that power which could feel a thought as immediately as the odour of a rose, and whose literary expression was the 'direct sensuous apprehension of thought, or a recreation of thought into feeling, which is exactly what we find in Donne'.[9] If before 1660 language could, and afterwards could not, express this 'sensuous apprehension', something perhaps invaluable had been lost. What, in fact, is the case?

One might answer, as Bonamy Dobrée did – 'Is it really better to write like Sir Thomas Browne than to write like Swift, or to write like Nashe than to write like Defoe?' One might further note that not only other scholars but indeed Eliot himself later found the theory not at all satisfactory. Restoration and later styles show a plainer mental process than some (but not all) Jacobean styles, arising from a world of ideas more familiar to us and from what seems a more straightforward organization of mind. But any split between thought and feeling is slow to operate, and the best post-Restoration writing does not at all suggest schizophrenia. Dryden, Swift, and Pope are obvious examples; in Sterne a fantastic complexity emerges again, based on self-consciousness, wit, and immediate connexions between intellect and sense. Hardly less is this the case with Horace Walpole. Even when complexity is not evident, there can be an absolutely firm impact of language, as in Fielding and Johnson, which shows the full integration of personality, and of feeling with thought.

The fact that styles were simplified is obvious, the more so since such a simplification is stated repeatedly as a critical aim and a need of the time. Yet that still leaves Augustan styles with a great fund of strength, which critical reiteration of 'polish' and 'elegance' tends to obscure. The higher imagination may be suspect in the period, but the imagination which grasps the material of life and embodies it in concrete images and a vigorous speech drawing on the vernacular is there in abundance. To write Pope's *Epistle to Arbuthnot* (1735) requires as much imagination as to write Wordsworth's *Tintern Abbey* (1798), though of a different kind. The reason the dissociation-of-sensibility theory seems misleading (despite the arguments based on the Augustan divorce of wit-imagination from judgement) is that the best Augustan writing is strongly personal and is, if any writing be so, 'thinking in images', images which strike the mind as the projections of other minds in immediate contact with social realities. Augustan literature gives us fact, variously patterned and ordered, but fact none the less. And this fact is conveyed in a vigorous vernacular which expresses its reality. The impact of Restoration comedy, for instance, comes largely from the graphic force with which deportment, gesture, expression, and social habit are seized: even the cosmopolitan Saint-Évremond preferred its grasp of manners and its satirical social force to the mere gallantries of the Spanish and French. It derives from Ben Jonson and the 'character' tradition and, though far less vital than the comedy of Jonson, is still alive with keen curiosity and vehemence. The signs are its concrete imagery, vigorous metaphor, and picturesque phrases; Shadwell, Etherege, Wycherley, Congreve, Vanbrugh, and Farquhar abound in them. So, in general, do the novelists. Semantic vitality and metaphoric invention overflow in Aphra Behn (for instance, in the elaborate-fantastic portrait of the fop, in *The Fair Jilt*, 1688); even a minor writer like Mrs Manley (in *The New Atalantis*, 1709) has a vivid and full natural idiom which is clearly her uninhibited whole personality. Defoe writes with all his practical nature, with a speaking voice and the energy of gossip; much the same is true of Smollett, and Sterne's feeling, thought, and style are all one. Nor is Swift's sensibility noticeably dissociated in the *Journal to Stella* (1710–13): flaccid idiom he scarifies in his *Genteel and Ingenious Conversation* (as the comic playwrights often do also), but he is himself idiomatic and personal. Lady Mary Wortley Montagu's *Letters* (1709–62) give the very pulse both of herself and of the thrusting social scene she describes; so, in their own ways, do Boswell's personal papers. As for verse, Butler's tumbling octosyllabics in *Hudibras* (1663–78), Oldham's ferocious *Satires upon the Jesuits* (1681: provoked by the 'Popish Plot' of 1678 and gaining him the title of

'English Juvenal'), and supremely Dryden's satires, whose brilliance is that of bold wit working through the concrete vigour of contemporary vernacular – these have no split personality; thought in them cannot be distinguished from feeling. Nor, indeed, can it in Defoe's *True-Born Englishman* (1701), vehement with rough witticism, or in Ned Ward's anti-Defoe-and-Dissenter *Hudibras Redivivus* (1707), or in Swift's *Death of Dr Swift* (1731), or in Johnson's *London* (1738) or Goldsmith's *Deserted Village* (1770) or much of the work of Crabbe. To say that they feel their thought as immediately as the odour of a rose would be to introduce an analogy from a realm of experience other than that most Augustan writers work in, but they *do* feel their thought immediately. In Pope this is clear. 'Vivid *and* abstract', F. W. Bateson called *The Dunciad*, since it unites concreteness and thought, components which in one sense – but with violence to the poem – might be dissociated but in another and truer completely coincide. A similar conclusion arises from Maynard Mack's Twickenham edition of the *Essay on Man* (1950);[10] far from this poem's being a speciously-felt versification of borrowed ideas, it fuses into a passionately-apprehended whole a tradition-charged philosophy; thought in it is indistinguishable from feeling – each prompts and reflects the other. As for the *Epistle to Arbuthnot*, no more 'un-dissociated' poem exists; fluctuating moods, varying tones, shifting stress and speed, attitudes from venomous to pathetic – these are only the most obvious of the vitalities which make the *Epistle* both completely social (in its references, communicative skill, and demeanour) and completely personal (in its dramatic expression of one man's thought-and-feeling). While not precisely in the 'metaphysical' mode, Pope is in that which makes a man write in the full context of all his interests, with the literary undivided from the non-literary sides of life. Imaginative daring is less prominent in the eighteenth century than in the centuries before or after, and not much of the poetry, consequently, penetrates to the imaginative inwardness of experience. But the notion that even the better Augustan writing is merely a well-bred art suffering from a split personality is as mischievous as it is common.

One argument that might be added to refute it is that of verbal vitality. This is widespread until Addison spreads his ideals of urbanity, and even then it survives for a while. Congreve is a virtuoso of the vivid word and surprising simile. 'He was once given to scrambling with his hands and sprawling in his sleep,' Mellefont says of Sir Paul Pliant in *The Old Bachelor* (1693), 'and ever since she [Lady Pliant] has had him swaddled up in blankets, and his hands and feet swathed down, and so put to bed, and there he lies with a great beard like a Russian bear upon a drift of snow.' 'An she should [frown],' Sir Wilful declares of Lady Wishfort in *The Way of the World* (1700), 'her forehead would wrinkle like the coat of a cream-cheese.' Proper discussion of comedy-styles would take too much space; one can only state summarily that Congreve's image-finding and graphic phrase has its kinship with Shakespearian comedy, that Etherege has the precise sharp flavour of vernacular, and that Wycherley's close-wrought language with its mordant Jonsonian strength has a peculiarly sensory life – 'the canonical smirk, and the filthy clammy palm of a chaplain', 'this toad, this ugly, greasy, dirty sloven', 'Well madam, now have I dressed you and set you out with so many ornaments and spent upon you ounces of essence and pulvilio; and all this for no other purpose but as people adorn and perfume a corpse for a stinking second-hand grave' (*The Country Wife*, 1675). There is something of Webster in Wycherley, something of Wycherley in Swift. Much Restoration prose shows this sensory quality; Shadwell writes of 'rejected authors, who will strut, and huff it out, and laugh at the ignorance of the age', and Vanbrugh of hypocritical 'saints – your thorough-paced ones, I mean, with skrewed faces and wry mouths'. Eachard's *Contempt of the Clergy* (1670) has an Elizabethan nut-cracking virtuosity in satirical extravagance. Sir Roger L'Estrange's *Observator* papers (1681–7) – 'the chief manager of all those angry writings', he is called in Gilbert Burnet's *History of My Own Times* (1724–34) – and a great deal of miscellaneous political and critical polemic have the hammering colloquial scorn which was the idiom of controversy until well into the eighteenth century and which invigorated if it did not refine the written language. The greatness of Dryden in prose is partly that he so well unites the raciness of such writing (going back to the Elizabethans – Oldham's grotesque *Character of an Ugly Old Priest*, c. 1680, is akin to Nashe) with the new ideal of clarity and coherence. Both in verse and prose Dryden is, though immeasurably more civilized than Oldham or Butler, rooted in image-making vernacular inventiveness and immediacy, and so, strikingly, is Swift. There is a passage in *A Tale of a Tub* (1704) beginning –

> When a Man's Fancy gets astride on his Reason, when Imagination is at Cuffs with the Senses, and common Understanding, as well as Common Sense, is Kickt out of Doors; the first Proselyte he makes is Himself.

If with this one compares Johnson's own meditation in *Rasselas* (1759) on 'The Dangerous Prevalence of Imagination', it is clear what prose has forgone to gain greater decorum. Still, Johnson's lucid and intelligent gravity has an enduring quality not to be sacrificed for any alternative; though Swift's highly charged vivacity fascinates, Johnson's is the mind the discipline and considerateness of which one can sit down with, certain that it will deal rightly with its material, and its reader. The hey-day of racy invention is over by about 1720, though much remains in Defoe. The politer work of the age rejects it, as it rejects the 'Senecan' (pithy) kind of sentence for the 'Ciceronian'(formally evolving, rhythmically balanced), or at least the Addisonian, with its easy sequences.[11] Much verse becomes too insipid or too Miltonic, much prose too suave or (sometimes with Johnson or Gibbon) too grandiose. Yet though squibs and explosions may cease, there is health in the later Augustan styles – in epistolary vigour (Lady Mary Wortley Montagu, John Byrom, Gray, Cowper, and Walpole), unadorned cogency (Smollett, Captain Cook's *Voyages*), athletic discipline (Fielding), flexibility and immediacy (Sterne), precision and order (Berkeley and Hume), and a considerate gravity (Gray's *Elegy*, Johnson). Art gradually gains on vivacity, but when the results include Hume's philosophy, Goldsmith's verse, Gibbon's history, and Johnson's discourses, any losses are well compensated and by no means to be regretted. The eighteenth century in effect made literary proficiency second nature.

Finally, there is the formal side of Augustan style, which the modern reader does not always find interesting. The concern for verse- and prose-form, for literary species and kinds, was, however, reasonable and sound; an obvious need, in the early years, was for technical skill. The Sedleys and Dorsets, Pope's 'mob of gentlemen who wrote with ease', were often careless; popular anthologies like *The Covent-Garden Drollery* (1672) show that tone and technique had coarsened since Elizabethan and 'metaphysical' days and needed civilizing (though it is true that the best Restoration lyrics had learnt grace, poise, and limpidity from the example of Ben Jonson). Shadwell's plays, Rochester noted, show 'great mastery with little care'. Marvell's and Oldham's satires are rough, and though Dryden admires the vigour of Butler's thought he finds his helter-skelter verse and double rhymes unsatisfactory – 'we are pleased ungratefully'. Improved technique is a corollary of an ordered language and civilized ideals. It is not formal for formality's sake; Augustan patterns – decasyllabic or octosyllabic couplets, anapaests, *Elegy*-quatrain, and prose-balances – are not mere docility to rule (though complaints were heard even then of over-discipline); they aim at effective transmission of sense. The rhymes in Dryden's satires are both the bases of sound-pattern and the bearers of the satiric barb; no form but the couplet, enlivened with alliterations, functionally varied pauses, and paragraph continuity, would serve the purpose so well.* But the couplet had other resources; Oldham and Defoe tore into it with straightforward colloquial syntax, rough rhythms and rhymes, and demagogic vocabulary. Pope is quite different – his nicely-calculated-less-or-more adjusts sound and movement to a more complex correspondence with sense than anyone else in his century achieved (indeed, than anyone else save Shakespeare), and his couplets are the frame which by its limiting edges and gleam of gilding sets off the lively tonal relationships within the picture. For Gay again the couplet is different, is richly coloured, and mockingly grandiloquent within the fortifying expected rhythm; a burlesque elegy on a drowned pippin-seller is to be –

> Soft as the breath of distant flutes, at hours
> When silent evening closes up the flow'rs;
> Lulling as falling water's hollow noise,
> Indulging grief, like *Philomela's* voice.
>
> (*Trivia*)

* The decasyllabic couplet (iambic pentameter) is often known as the 'heroic' couplet since it was the main form for Restoration 'heroic' tragedies (see p. 95). It was often the medium for un'heroic' subjects, either as mock-heroic satire (as in Dryden's *MacFlecknoe* and *Absalom and Achitophel* or Pope's *The Rape of the Lock* and *The Dunciad*), for moral or meditative rumination (as in Johnson's *The Vanity of Human Wishes* or Goldsmith's *The Deserted Village*), for social portrayals, and for many other purposes, the firm form of its decisive rhymes serving to sharpen and define its subjects.

Lady Mary Wortley Montagu's pastoral parody *Town Eclogues* (1716) has, less skilfully, a similar light mockery and elegant tune. Johnson is slow and momentous, with Dryden's weight and his own darkness of mood; Goldsmith and Cowper can shade the couplet with a dying fall conveying the poignancy of loss; and Crabbe, by subtly sensory language, regulation of pause, and careful placing of image, evolves again another character from the same form. In all this, however, the decasyllabic couplet retains its power to shape its content into symmetry, definition, and controlled progression. Octosyllabics were freer, lighter-footed in social verse, more of a holiday (Congreve's *An Impossible Thing*, Swift's *Death of Dr Swift*, Green's *The Spleen*, Gay's and Cowper's *Fables*, and Thomas Warton's comic stories), or else galloping-grotesque following *Hudibras* (Mandeville's *The Grumbling Hive*, Ward's *Hudibras Redivivus*, Hughes's *Hudibras Imitated*, Mallet's *Tyburn*, and Churchill's *The Ghost*). The triple rhythm of anapaests served for badinage or easy sentiment, the irregular Pindaric ode for the higher raptures (generally a calamitous failure), and blank verse turgidly imitating Milton for discursive meditation. In prose, symmetries patterned the sense into phases the mind could methodically grasp. Augustan order was not really a superficiality; it came as fugue- or sonata-form comes to the musician, not without practice but bringing the reward of craftsmanship in the effective display of its material. Technical command is no more over-polish than the brilliance of Augustan visual arts is over-refinement; it includes the functional formlessness of Swift's doggerel verse and Defoe's or Richardson's prose as well as the formality of Johnson, with many middle styles between. To display life widely and well, to command general acceptance in forms which symbolize the high morality of order, was the philosophy of Augustan letters.

Literary Outlines: Prose

The Restoration's prose ambition was to ally traditional vivacity with emergent discipline and evolve a medium for reasonable discourse. Its realization was a fight against ingrained habits of colour and passion, and for a long time the older modes fought a rearguard action. Puritans and their like, for instance, still recorded their struggles in a characteristic idiom of Biblical phrase crossed with the speech of the market-place – Bunyan is full of it, and so are Baxter's vigorous *Life and Times* (1696) and George Fox's formless but vivid *Journal* (1694). Much Anglican oratory was not very different; Glanvill's *Essay on Preaching* (1678) objects equally to erudite incomprehensible divines and to emotional popular preachers with their 'Roll upon Christ, close with Christ, get into Christ'. Picturesque oratory passed by slowly. When Jeremy Taylor died in 1667 Robert South, Prebendary of Westminster, wittily contrasted his elaborate style with the apostles' simplicity, yet South himself, if not as convoluted as his predecessors, is still surprising; he likes fantastic, grotesque, or homely detail (wherefore Fielding is sarcastic about him in the *Voyage to Lisbon*; 1755), is eloquent, alert, and dramatically varied in tone. Isaac Barrow, his graver contemporary, is more logical and coherent but still has the Caroline weight, and so, outside the pulpit, has Clarendon in his great *History of the Rebellion* (1646–71, printed 1702–4). After Clarendon the most impressive of these writers of the older styles is Thomas Burnet, in his *Sacred Theory of the Earth* (1684), a long-breathed majestic argument explaining the Deluge, sombrely passionate in its contemplation of the ruined world. Burnet responds to his vast matter with vast grandeur; themes of Eternity, the beauty of Paradise, the tragedy of the subsequent cataclysm, and the changes of the earth throughout millennia stir in him a rich sense of mystery and a heightened tone consonant with his majestic topics. Great and theological matters can still arouse sublimity.

If darker themes are still resonant, the lighter can still be opulent. In *Oroonoko* and *The Fair Jilt* (published 1688), Aphra Behn tilts a shapeless style towards the heroic-romantic and achieves a huddle of vivid detail, an exuberant and exotic life. She has the good sense of the Augustans brightened with an enriched manner and a happy credulity in romantic wonders. *The Fair Jilt*, though its theme is the crimes of an impassioned courtesan, conveys by its imagery of wealth a valid stateliness and splendour of living. This one might call Stuart literature in its florid worldliness, its bold colour and feeling for the heroic.

But soberer fashions were encroaching. The later *Essays* (1668) of Cowley, though mildly intoxicated with wit, show this: they are landmarks in alert discourse, with a Montaigne-like self-analysis in neat short rhythms, though still here and there ingeniously pointed. The great virtues of Dryden (1631–1700) in this respect have already been mentioned; in this as in other forms without precisely innovating he knew how to make the best of current modes, and his critical essays (the best are *Of Dramatic Poesy*, 1668, and the *Preface to the Fables*, 1700) have a ranging personal manner, encouraged by Montaigne and Corneille, and a racy sense of phrase typical of his century from Bacon and the character-writers downwards. His style is the more satisfactory in that he shares it with others – for instance, with Halifax (1633–95), whose *Character of a Trimmer* (1688) is witty political persuasion, or with Richard Bentley (1662–1742), whose *Boyle Lectures* (1692) and preface to his *Epistles of Phalaris* (1697–9) are trenchant and firm polemic, not unlike Swift. Swift himself, Bentley's mocker in *The Battle of the Books* (1704), makes the style his own, and with Arbuthnot and Mandeville provides the early decades of the eighteenth century with much of its most searching and enviable prose. It is prose addressed, though not to the erudite, yet to men of wit and knowledge, who do not need the easy manner and predigested substance which Addison and his fellow-journalists necessarily devised for their wider circle, and who enjoy strong idiom rather than undue refinement. In this same phase of style, incidentally, Peter Motteux completed Sir Thomas Urquhart's translation of Rabelais, in 1693–4, in a cogent style adequate to his vigorous precursor.

But still plainer prose was on the way, encouraged both by the scientists and their supporters like Locke, and by the religious seriousness of this supposedly cynical age. Discussions of pulpit oratory, such as Joseph Glanvill's *Essay on Preaching*, insisted earnestly on the forging of a style fit for those great purposes of faith which are above ornament or ostentation. Religion even more than science had truths to announce too sincere for tinsel, and the clearest Restoration writing comes from the Latitudinarian divines, and eminently from Archbishop Tillotson (1630–94), whom Gilbert Burnet praises as 'a man of a clear head and a sweet temper', with 'the brightest thoughts and the most correct style of all our divines'. Tillotson's prose now seems to lack flavour, yet without any spectacular qualities it is free from affectation and in a restrained way is equal to its themes of charity and reason. Goldsmith's praise in *The Bee* (24 November 1759) shows how exactly it served Augustan ideals of expression:

71

There is nothing peculiar to the language of Archbishop Tillotson, but his manner of writing is inimitable: for one who reads him wonders why he himself did not think and speak in that very manner.

Dryden, Addison, Steele, Johnson, and many others praised him, and rightly found impressive his lucid dignity and his fortifying alliance of reason and religion. Gilbert Burnet (1643–1715), also a Whig Latitudinarian, follows the same road; his account of *Some Passages of the Life and Death of John, Earl of Rochester* (1680) has a grave charm, in prose clear but not cold. As for the philosophers, the style of Locke, though steady and methodical, is all that is meant by prosaic – his matter is much more impressive than his manner – but both Berkeley (1685–1753) and Hume (1711–76) are masters of as much civilized skill as is to be found in English.

By the time of Addison (1672–1719) the new prose was completely naturalized, and was getting used to its wider public. The periodical essay not only benefited from, it was created by, the new manner. A kind of writing which in Cowley's essays had been a private meditation enlivened with wit developed into a generalized medium of social commentary, eagerly sought by middle-class readers and moderated in style to the highest common denominator of taste. The smoothing-out which went with the social motive reduces the present interest of most Augustan essays; a century after Addison, Alexander Chalmers, prefacing *The Spectator* in his series of *British Essayists* (1817), admitted a general triteness, though he excused it on the grounds that the essays had been too much imitated and in their own time had been valuably popular. This popularity was indeed important; it broadcast the civilizing influences of literature, philosophy, and the arts, engaged men's thoughts not towards the separatist tendencies of sects and individualism but towards a harmonious corporate life, and provided a mild but effective current of criticism. At first a vehicle for news, the periodical developed a commentary on social life – the first, and popular, steps were taken in John Dunton's *Athenian Mercury* (1690 onwards, soon imitated by other *Mercuries*) – and Defoe's *Review* (1704–13) contained 'a weekly history of Nonsense, Impertinence, Vice, and Debauchery'. The essay gradually relegated the news to a minor role, and because it so well cultivated the general body of readers it was largely responsible for evolving the characteristic eighteenth-century style.[12] Restoration prose is pithy but often moves jerkily by galvanic impulses; Shaftesbury the philosopher (1671–1713) declared that his age had 'scarce the idea of any other model' than the epigrammatic 'Senecan', priding itself on sharp flashes and isolated points rather than on continuous discourse. (There were, however, many exceptions to his generalization.) Addison distinguished between two essay-methods, that of spontaneous sallies and that of careful order, and while the former was more animated he preferred the latter as being easier to follow. His great achievement, accomplished in *The Tatler* (1709 11) and *The Spectator* (1711–14), was, even at the expense of dilution, to simplify prose, so that the reader need never retrace his steps or query an unfamiliar word, to organize his ideas and to carry them forward on sentence-rhythms with an onward undulation instead of momentary sparkles, and never to vary from the tone of good manners. 'Propriety, perspicuity, elegance, cadence' are here attained infallibly. In an age of uneasy technique and of strong animosities his style and matter were healthy, the more influential in that he was widely admired for himself; Swift speaks of his pleasant conversation, and Lady Mary Wortley Montagu thought him, of all contemporary wits, the best companion. Garth, Tickell, Young, and Pope (despite the Atticus satire in the *Epistle to Arbuthnot*) admired him, and Steele told Congreve that a night in his company was like 'conversing with an intimate acquaintance of Terence and Catullus', who had 'all their Wit and Nature heightened with Humour more exquisite and delightful than any other man ever possessed' (Prefatory letter to Addison's *Drummer*). Frequently republished in book form, *The Spectator* essays (largely though not wholly Addison's) did as much as any literary work to shape the Augustan ethos.[13]

Of many kinds of wide appeal the periodical essay chose that which best combined amenity and responsibility, and it mediated between the common reader and the best thought of the day. The other important papers of the century are the *Guardian* (1713: the best essays are from Steele, Addison, and Berkeley), Steele's *The Englishman* (1713–14), Addison's *Freeholder* (1715–16), Fielding's *Champion* (1739–42) and *Covent-Garden Journal* (1752), Johnson's *Rambler* (1750–52) and his 'Idler' essays in *The Universal Chronicle* (1758–60), Moore's *World* (1753–7: the liveliest of mid-century papers), Colman and Thornton's *Connoisseur* (1754–6), Goldsmith's *Bee* (1759), and his

'Citizen of the World' essays in *The Public Ledger* (1760–61). In all these there is much that is trivial or repetitive, but there is much too that is a true focus of Augustan thought, both light and serious.

Making the easy transition from essayists to 'occasional' writers, one observes Swift (1667–1745) as the most powerful, and his friend Arbuthnot (1667–1735) – 'the most universal genius', Johnson thought him, of Queen Anne's reign – as one of the most interesting. With Pope, Gay, and Parnell (and the approval of Congreve, Addison, and Lord Oxford), they constituted the Scriblerus Club (1713), intending, Pope said, 'to have ridiculed all false tastes in learning'. Its monuments are Pope's own *Dunciad* and Arbuthnot's *Memoirs of the Extraordinary Life, Works and Discoveries of Martinus Scriblerus* (written *c.* 1714 published 1741; comprehensively satirical on educational, philosophical, and scientific theories), which forms a link in the chain of the learned wit popularized by Rabelais and continued later by Sterne. Arbuthnot's vigorous manner and dialogue resemble Swift's, but the eccentric theories by which 'Martin's' father educates him are rooted in the extravagances of Renaissance polymaths. Arbuthnot's other main works, the *John Bull* pamphlets (1712) and *The Art of Political Lying* (1712: Swift's 15th *Examiner* paper in 1710 has the same subject), have much of Swift's sardonic power, and *The Humble Petition of the Colliers* is a Swiftian absurdity against the scientists. This kind of writing is among the Augustan best – firm in rhythm, assured in tone, in vital but not vulgarizing contact with current idiom, and satirical with a controlled extravagance. Its supreme exponent is, of course, Swift himself. *The Battle of the Books* and *A Tale of a Tub* (pub. 1704) show his genius in image-making on the scale of allegory. Each is a concrete fiction of an abstract situation – a literary dispute, and the prevalence of fanaticism. His 'sensuous apprehension of thought' works in images which are not only metaphors as the passing mintage of imagination but also whole symbolic situations. His favourite tone is ironic, and his favourite intellectual exercise is the ingenious protraction of the link between idea and image; his wit lies less in the initial conception than in the inimitable follow-through, so that Johnson was merely obtuse in complaining, of *Gulliver's Travels*, that anyone might think of big and little men. Swift's mind moves among real things and promptly embodies abstractions; his fable is metaphor at its most vital. In a long series of satires and political pamphlets – *An Argument Against Abolishing Christianity* (1708), *The Examiner* papers (1710–11: a Tory weekly), *The Conduct of the Allies* (1711), *The Public Spirit of the Whigs* (1714), a momentous succession of Irish pamphlets (especially *The Drapier's Letters*, 1724, the *Short View of the Present State of Ireland*, 1728, and *A Modest Proposal*, 1729), and *Gulliver's Travels* (1726) – he wielded a prose unequalled for pungent short rhythms, lively images and analogies, and the subversive deceptions of its honest-citizen reasonableness. In a not-dissimilar kind is the series of essay-commentaries which Bernard de Mandeville (1670–1733) appended to his satirical poem *The Grumbling Hive* under the title of *The Fable of the Bees* (1714); Mandeville's prose is clear, forceful, and sardonic, and his matter – a realistic appraisal of social behaviour – is meant to shock the idealists. 'Shavian', one might call its methods.

After 'occasional' prose, the personal: diaries, memoirs, letters, travels, biography, and autobiography. These were peculiarly congenial to the Augustan mind, and from being previously a minor interest took on a major importance. Social life was being fertilized by wealth and leisure, by better transport (Horace Walpole carried on one of his longest correspondences with Sir Horace Mann, as far away as Naples), and also, no doubt, by the satisfaction of using an easy and civilized prose style; there is a sensuous and intellectual pleasure in the very form of good Augustan writing, regardless of its content.

Diaries and journals are not always intended as communication, and art is often less prominent in them than spontaneity. Foremost in any enumeration must be the name of Pepys (1633–1703), whose diaries are so famous that any comment is superfluous except, perhaps, a reference to their almost hallucinatory vividness and their maturity and intelligence. They are supreme in an absorbing but diverse species. This embraces also the devotion of religious enthusiasts (Bunyan's *Grace Abounding to the Chief of Sinners* (1666), George Fox's *Journal* (1694), Thomas Ellwood's *History of His Life* (1714), and John Wesley's *Journal* (published 1827)), the quieter Anglican character emerging variously in the records of James Woodforde and William Cole, and Gilbert White's *Natural History of Selborne* (1789). The Augustan temperament is characteristically reflected in the ironic gravity and formality of Gibbon's own *Memoirs* (1796), and the

Augustan variety of character in the miscellaneous interest of John
Evelyn's *Diary* (published 1818), Colley Cibber's *Apology* (1740),
John Byng's *Torrington Diaries* (published 1934–8), William Hickey's
Memoirs (published 1913–25), Fanny Burney's *Diary and Letters* (published 1842–6, 1889), and, with effusive self-display, in Boswell's
various journals (the *Tour to Corsica*, 1768, *Tour to the Hebrides*, 1785,
The London Journal 1762–3, 1950, *Boswell in Holland 1763–4*, 1952,
Boswell on the Grand Tour, 1764, 1953; with continuation for *1765–6*,
1955, and others). No more engaging or lively records exist than
these Boswellian self-revelations, the comic-touching eagerness and
intimacy of which, along with Boswell's vivid responsiveness to
others, conduct the reader intimately through the human comedy of
the years he covers.

The transition from journals to letters is a small one; indeed,
Swift's *Journal to Stella*, a commentary in his most personal idiom
from the centre of affairs in the years of his greatest power (1710–13),
is in fact a series of letters to Stella and Mrs Dingley. Unlike Swift
in scope and intensity, but still deeply coloured by the Augustan
world, are two correspondents in differing spheres of life, Lady Mary
Wortley Montagu (1689–1762) and John Byrom (1692–1763). Alike
in their dates, they are not unlike in lively, economical styles, close
to the realities of persons and places. Byrom translates his family
motto – 'Frustra per plura' – as 'the less ado the better', and the
phrase would suit either Lady Mary or himself. When the former's
letters appeared in 1763, *The Critical Review* spoke of 'the spright-
liness of her wit, the solidity of her judgement, the elegance [i.e.
critical intelligence] of her taste, and the excellence of her real character'. Her honest mind and vigorous phrase are refreshing after
Addisonian amenity; in some ways they suggest Jane Austen's strong
wit, a control of head over heart which is not coldness but a frank
judgement of the world. Her interests are intelligent; she maintains
her style without lapses. Like Lord Byron she responds to romantic
scenes (the most interesting of her letters are those about her expedi-
tion to Turkey), but unlike him she sees them not as an orchestration
of her own adventurousness but for their own colour and interest. As
for Byrom's *Journals and Papers*, they have been ably re-edited
(1950, by Henri Talon) and revealed as a good record of London and
provincial life. The stamp of the period shows in the plain vocabulary,

the accurate manner, the clear grasp of subject. Vigorous in the normal events of life, Byrom is as sound as a bell on a harder occasion; his letters on his daughter Ellen's death (November 1729) are models of firm but not unfeeling sense.

Letter-writers better-known than Byrom, must be briefly recorded. Shenstone (1714–63), writing to country clergy, comfortable gentry, and literary amateurs, luminaries of the fourth rather than the first magnitude, recounts his landscape gardening, reading, small dissatisfactions and pleasures, in a sensitive manner which reflects the tastes of the time the better for lacking the force, prominent in Horace Walpole, necessary to transform them. Cowper (1731–1800) does still better than Shenstone the things Shenstone does well; his 'enjoyment of country air and retirement' comes through a style quietly perfect in tone, lucid, and not a whit insipid; the subdued but real vivacities which gleam in his verse appear also in the prose. As for Horace Walpole (1717–97), his vivacities are anything but subdued; his world seems to have existed in order to be written about, with appreciative wit, enthusiastic knowledge, and marvellously intent animation. His phrases move quickly, and their subjects are caught not motionless but in those moments of amusing self-expression which suggest a successful mime. He exaggerates, sometimes subtly, sometimes flagrantly, is malicious, is sentimental, but always alert and vivid. For their vitality, agility, and brilliant social panorama Walpole's letters are unrivalled in English; in deeper qualities – scholarship, poetic sensitiveness, and subtle humour – they are surpassed in their own time by those of Gray (1716–71), which have, if any English letters have, the true note of friendship. Page after page, rich in comment on literature, history, art, building, and landscape (which he sees not in raptures but in full and careful detail), Gray reveals a personality whose depth and variety not even the poems quite prepare us for.

Lastly, as personal prose, there is biography, with Izaak Walton's *Lives* of Herbert (1670), and Sanderson (1678), Aubrey's *Lives* (written before 1697), Sprat's *Cowley* (1668), and Gilbert Burnet's *Rochester* (1680), and then waiting for its next triumph in Johnson's *Life of Savage* (1744), a small masterpiece which, though possibly too lenient to an obstinate Bohemian and certainly too generous to his verse, is an example not of exculpation so much as of sympathy and charity, careful in its 'placing' of both Savage and his acquaintances, and finally dignified in exorcising any condescension to the dead man. This and the later *Lives of the Poets* (1779–81) have an abundance of human interest, and much of their century's most stimulating criticism. But, of course, the supreme biographical achievement of the age, indeed of this whole tradition of biography in English, is Boswell's *Life of Samuel Johnson* (1791), unprecedented in scope and detail, and unequalled in recording the substance of life. Here, as with Pepys's *Diary*, comment is superfluous; the *Life* is an unimpeachable triumph.

Biography is a form of history, and history is a growing Augustan passion. Among the major examples are Clarendon's *History of the Rebellion* (written 1646–71, published 1702–4), penetrating in character-study, judicious in analysis, and carried on a strong-shouldered prose, and Gilbert Burnet's *History of My Own Times* (written before 1715, published 1724–34), expounding a Whig interpretation of history. As for minor history, it is the more abundant as the Augustans the more closely examine their society; Swift's pamphlets on *The Conduct of the Allies* (1711), *The Barrier Treaty* (1712), and *The Four Last Years of the Queen* (published 1758) have even more than Swift's usual serried marshalling of fact and argument, though their aim (to vindicate Tory policy) has lost its interest. The same eclipse has overtaken the miscellaneous Whiggism of Defoe and Steele, the Toryism of Johnson, and Bolingbroke's above-party *Idea of a Patriot King* (1749), but emphatically not Burke's American and Indian speeches and the *Reflections on the Revolution in France* (1790). History proper was among the most widespread of serious literary interests in the age of Johnson; Hume, Smollett, and William Robertson made once-popular though now outmoded contributions to it, but the supreme monument of Augustan historiography is Gibbon's *Decline and Fall of the Roman Empire* (1776–88), whose patterned style allots to every fact in an intimidating multitude its due shape and relationship, as a great civilization dwindles into anarchy. The major part of Gibbon's life went into the gathering and ordering of his material and the evolution of his ample manner, and the result is a panorama of majestic and melancholy magnitude. Besides history in large perspective the Augustans provide also history as men lived it, not often better recorded than in Defoe's and Arthur Young's tours (social history, these), Horace Walpole's *Memoirs* (of the reigns of

George II and George III; published between 1822 and 1859), and Nathaniel Wraxall's *Historical Memoirs of My Own Time 1772-1784* (1815).

The particular new continent conquered for literature by Augustan prose is, however, the novel. By comparison the development of the essay was the cultivation of a garden plot, slight when contrasted with the energy by which wide stretches of life were subdued to ordered narrative – an exertion comparable in significance with the development of Elizabethan drama or of seventeenth-century spiritual poetry.

Fiction was anything but a new invention. Even if legend and myth be omitted (since their religious or symbolic bearing differs from that of ordinary narrative) and the enquiry be confined to invented prose stories, abundance of them is to be found in the Middle Ages. The Renaissance has its classical translations, pastoral-Arcadian romances, allegories, character-studies, and records of rascality. Yet then the main channels ran elsewhere; fiction's relation to life was peripheral, as idealization or moral doctrine, anecdote or satire. For the central current to carry it, certain conditions were required – a reliable prose, sufficient readers ready to follow the long evolutions of an organized rendering of life, and, above all, a belief that prose fiction was artistically and intellectually worthy of major talent. Abroad it had been proved so, with Rabelais and Cervantes and, as an influential but passing fashion, with French heroic romances and (more lastingly) Scarron's realistic *Roman comique* (1651). The novel might clearly be important, though in England its growth was less a matter of Continental discipleship than apparent accident – Bunyan spontaneously inspired to *The Pilgrim's Progress* (1678), Defoe transforming travel narrative or artless biography, Richardson stumbling from model letters into the epistolary story, Fielding reacting from Richardson's prudential morality. The Augustan achievement was the use, on a large coherent plan, of real social material, amplified and varied by following a considerable stretch of the hero's life story, and by allowing a good deal of coincidence and digression. Its important technical innovation was its understanding of character and of plot – not as mere episodes (though in all the novelists these still abound, and in Defoe and Smollett predominate), but as cause and effect artistically unifying a particular phase of life. Such a conception is not, in itself, realism; life is generally casual, not organized to a logical end, and Defoe's and Smollett's haphazard progress is, strictly, more realistic than the organized sequence of Richardson or Fielding. Yet in general the mind prefers the order of plot to the disorder of episode: human significance is heightened when human experience has a coherent shape.

Bunyan's work, great as it is, belongs to an older mode and, as allegory, differs from the strict novel. Aphra Behn hardly survives save for the remarkable and moving *Oroonoko* (c. 1678), the story of a Noble Savage enslaved by white tyrants. There is a miscellany of fiction before Defoe – Congreve's *Incognita* (1692) is piquant and pert, as we should hope from him – but it is only with Defoe (1660–1731) that the novel becomes something more than a minor accomplishment. He raises the adventure story to greatness, seemingly by a mere desire to exploit the commercial possibilities of travellers' tales and picaresque realism. 'Adventure' here has its double meaning; the episodes occur by chance, and their substance is self-preservation in danger. For his characters, as for Defoe himself, to live is to struggle. He was nearly sixty when, apparently casually, *Robinson Crusoe* appeared (1719). Prolific pamphleteering and journalism – mercantile, political, religious, and social – had preceded it from his own and from others' hands, and this with its originating commercial and political experience had established his points of reference as the material and practical conditions of life. *Robinson Crusoe* and the other novels – *Captain Singleton* (1720), *Moll Flanders* (1722), *Colonel Jack* (1722), *A Journal of the Plague Year* (1722), and *Roxana* (1724) – are as much the spirit of their age as are Pope's satires, though in a different way. They seem less works of literature than products of sheer unminded natural process, the rough reality of the time expressing itself. While Pope's interests are those of society's upper levels (though not snobbishly so), Defoe's are those of economic man. The main characters are unprotected by social advantages – Colonel Jack the waif, living like a small animal on his wits, yet feeling things as a child; Moll Flanders, Newgate-born, orphan-reared, living by intermittent matrimony; Crusoe on his island. Life is chance, though with elements of coincidence which can be interpreted (as the characters themselves point out) as destiny and retribution. Chance is the main thing; 'my ill Fate push'd me on now with an obstinacy that nothing could resist,' Crusoe remarks, 'I hurried on and obeyed blindly the Dictates of my Fancy, rather than my Reason.' It is by their exertions in this state of life that we know the characters; they represent the struggle to live. Consequently the best of the novels have a symbolic power and an extraordinarily broad significance. Superficially bound to their time and place, they have (*Robinson Crusoe* above all) a universality beyond any other Augustan work. 'The writer,' Coleridge observed, 'who makes me sympathize with his presentations with the *whole* of my being is more estimable than the writer who calls forth and appeals to but a part . . .; and again, he who makes me forget my *specific* class, character, and circumstances, raises me into the universal man. Now this is Defoe's excellence.'

With the *Pamela* (1740) and *Clarissa* (1747) of Richardson (1689–1761) the full experience of plot-compulsion seized the public; the sexual dangers which Moll Flanders and Roxana had taken as the inevitable conditions of survival were immensely concentrated and made matters of life and (in Clarissa's case) death. To us these novels are far too long, and they were so even to some of his leisured contemporaries, like Shenstone. Yet to others the length was not a deterrent, and the reason for the length (the protraction of suspense) was hypnotically magnetic. The same may be said of Richardson's epistolary method – what he called 'writing to the moment'; often improbable, it can be startlingly immediate – it comes directly from those engaged and almost in the very moment of engagement. Any way of conveying material without loss is justified, and for many Augustan readers that is what the urgent voluble letters of Richardson's heroines (considerably less of his heroes) did. He experimented, from limited comedy of victorious virtue (*Pamela*) to extended tragedy of seduction (*Clarissa*) and extended comedy of social ethics (*Sir Charles Grandison*, 1753). His intensity (he is both intense and prolix) comes from his exploiting of the strongest natural feelings – the pressure of family influence, the magnetism of filial ties, pity for helpless innocence, the fear of outrage. His emotional world rose out of sexual peril or (in *Grandison*) sentimental beneficence, it is true, but this all the more invited the reader's apprehensive or admiring participation, heightened by Richardson's instinct (a partial foreshadowing of Sterne) for the minuter expressiveness of behaviour, each look and phrase telling. There is a deep and novel significance in this unprecedented interplay of personal tempers. Elizabethan drama has wars of nerves as intense, but they are briefer, are shared (by the playgoer) in a communal response, and invite nothing like so sentimental an indulgence. Richardson's achievement is a large one, even though its length and sentimental basis make it on the whole a historical landmark rather than a surviving pleasure; he had an electrical sensitiveness to the inner world of impulse which philosophy and psychology also were exploring.

The achievement of Fielding (1707–54), as all critics have remarked, is different. His novels are a kind of parallel-in-inverse to Richardson's: *Joseph Andrews* (1742), vivacious itinerant comedy, follows *Pamela* which it sketchily parodies; *Tom Jones* (1749), full-length comedy of unvirtuous man, follows *Clarissa*, full-length tragedy of virtuous woman; and *Amelia* (1751), near-tragedy of. virtuous woman, precedes *Grandison*, sentimental comedy of virtuous man. Richardson puts one at the heart of a situation to feel its emotional luxury; Fielding derives his method from the tradition of mock-heroic whose essential quality is that the narrator preserves his separate status as dramatic presenter and manipulates his material for comic effect. Besides the novels there are *Jonathan Wild* (1743), a sardonic portrayal of flourishing villainy, and the *Journal of a Voyage to Lisbon* (published 1755), which despite his ill health (he died shortly after reaching Portugal) has much of his flavouring of human comedy.

Smollett (1721–71) is, in a sense, more elementary than his great contemporaries in that until *Humphry Clinker* (1771) he deals in episodes rather than plots; there is, again until *Humphry Clinker*, least evidence of intellectual control or, save for a strong infusion of satire, any purpose superior to the primal impulse to go on with a yarn. *Roderick Random* (1748), partly disguised autobiography, is, like *Peregrine Pickle* (1751) and *Ferdinand Count Fathom* (1753), one of the century's tough novels (its toughness amply paralleled in real life); it has the shape to some extent of Smollett's own life, and its hero, though less markedly than the later two, is unappealing. *Sir Launcelot Greaves* (1760) is mellower – Smollett was influenced by Cervantes – and *Humphry Clinker* shows his extending humanity; the characters are presented, with lively illuminations of humour, for themselves and not as projections of their author's self-assertion. Smollett here presents his material in letter-form, and since the correspondents comment on events from complementary points of view the resulting synoptic view of life and scene makes this the novel in which the later eighteenth century most abundantly embodies itself.

Laurence Sterne (1713–68) is among the most controversial of writers, the controversy centring on whether the experience of reading him is rewarding or not: in fact, it most certainly is, though the reader must be prepared for a disconcerting (entertainingly disconcerting) encounter, even after several readings. In both *Tristram Shandy* (1760–67) and *A Sentimental Journey* (1768) Sterne plays all imaginable tricks with one's sense of fictional (and sexual) conventions, bringing into play a startling range of intimacies, subversions, indirections, indulgences, and revelations. Interspersions of sly and demure prurience are a game played against the conventional proprieties, proprieties which gained strength throughout Sterne's century, strengthened further in the following century, but have largely relaxed in our own, so that for most readers the jokes are a source of fun, not of disturbance. Likewise Sterne's cultivation of his 'dear Sensibility! Source inexhausted of all that's precious in our joys, or costly in our sorrows' (*A Sentimental Journey*) now comes over less as the rhetoric of emotional dissipation and more as the language for those 'generous joys and generous cares beyond myself' which, like others in his time, he wished to recognize. In fictional technique he provides an extraordinary complex of speech, thought, and action, in prose often reduced to syntactic minimum with startling vagaries of punctuation, which sometimes serves for laughter alone, but sometimes, more functionally, suggests the quick slipping of thought from subject to subject (he made play with Locke's theory of the association of ideas). His allegiances are to something older and less rational than the Augustan vogue – to Cervantes as master of the noble-minded absurd, to Elizabethan satirists, to the great prose extravagants of the seventeenth century like Browne and Burton (though since he had also absorbed Tillotson and Swift there is a plainer manner in the *Sermons of Yorick*, 1760–69), and to Rabelais as the liberator in morals and style, the celebrant of Nature's joyful proliferations as against narrowness and sterility. Yet for the future too he had his significance, in showing new possibilities by which the novel might become not a simple mirror held up to Nature but a complex of nuances, associations, and apparent irrelevances. Fielding has the typical *ordonnance* of his time: Sterne's structure is that of a world where the fringes of the mind encroach on its central clarities.

It would be wrong to suggest that from Defoe to Sterne the novel was solely in the hands of five major practitioners. There were many others who, their works being dead, have no memorial, a few who are still readable, and two or three who are in fact read. In the second category come that ominous portent of Gothic sensations, Walpole's *Castle of Otranto* (1764), Henry Mackenzie's ultra-sentimental *Man of Feeling* (1771), an exercise in the well-meant pathetic which reflects the ravages of 'sensibility', and Richard Graves's more satisfactory fun with Methodism, *The Spiritual Quixote* (1772). In the third category there is Johnson's *Rasselas* (1759), discussed in a later chapter, Goldsmith's *Vicar of Wakefield* (1766), with its mellow style and sympathetic comedy, Fanny Burney's *Evelina* (1778), a narrative with the liveliness of youth, which Johnson praised unreservedly and which Reynolds and Burke read in a night and Gibbon in a day, and finally Beckford's *Vathek* (1786), a fantastic result of the eighteenth century's interest in Eastern story. Some of these works, Goldsmith's particularly, deserve more comment than a phrase or two, but their reputations are safe and they may be left for 'the common reader' to take his pleasure in.

Verse

As for verse, its general evolution is similar; first, disentanglement from complexity (though still with wit and force); then the main Augustan manner; then, or concurrently, new or revived modes of feeling. In general the 'life and sharpness' that Ben Jonson liked, and the eccentricities of metaphysical conceits, were moderated to a manner which sought (as Gray said of his own aims) 'extreme conciseness of expression, yet pure, perspicuous, and musical'. Here, as in prose, 'wit' became not fantastic surprise but the cutting edge of reason, surprising only by the fresh clarity with which it carved out true perceptions. Poets and painters alike, Lansdowne's *Essay Upon Unnatural Flights* (1721) informs us, copy what is really in Nature, in its due proportions. Poetry is truth, and metaphors are admissible only to clarify, poetic figures only to 'grace, illustrate, and adorn':

As veils transparent cover, but not hide,
Such metaphors appear, when right apply'd,
When thro' the phrase we plainly see the sense.

Allied thus to the intellectual revolution, poetry observes the real world, its social intercourse, its ethics, and its temper.

The Augustan stock is now lowest, perhaps, in lyric. The standards of comparison are the supreme ones of the flanking pre-Restoration and Romantic periods. Yet the Augustan lyric should be more esteemed than it is, for there is much to be said for poetry's being widely welcome in social life. This wide welcome included (though it spread far beyond) lyric, the more so that the lyrics of the time were easy to read and not hard to write. In brief and often pleasant verses poets expressed little perhaps of poignancy or rapture (good manners forbade the intensities) but much civilized compliment, morality, and even fun, the quantity of which in Augustan verse is surprising and not at all to its discredit.

The Restoration lyric has indeed been praised, though with a natural regret for lost pre-Restoration felicities. Briefly, it is remarkable for its poised movement, its private content conveyed in public expression as though (as was indeed the case) the personal thought was being adduced for the pleasure of a lively and sophisticated circle. The mode derives ultimately, though with decreasing power, from Jonson and his Cavalier followers like Carew and Lovelace, and predominantly from verse like that of Waller (1606–87). His *Go, lovely Rose* is in a straight syntax carrying a straight plea, with a beautifully 'hanging' rhyme which gratifies the ear and distracts attention from some banality of phrase ('How sweet and fair she seems to be'; 'In deserts where no men abide'). The sway of movement comes through sensitive alternation of longer and shorter lines, and the same qualities of trim form and movement characterize his lines *On a Girdle*. With Dorset's *To all you ladies now at land* we are in the Restoration world; the tone is gay, the language that of badinage, the syntax neat, and the persons (revealingly) plural. In other words, the social mode is here. In it there cannot be much artistic seriousness, and in comparison with the pre-Restoration lyric there is a blunted feeling, a loss of imaginative and intellectual power. 'The last and greatest advantage of our writing which proceeds from conversation' was not always an advantage. Still, the conversational self-possession behind many Restoration lyrics is not without appeal; it remains on the surface but it shows how integrally verse with spirit and point was a part of social life. Characteristically, many lyrics were written for plays, and have the gallantry or artful poignancy of their setting, just as many later lyrics were written for (or appear in) periodicals or middle-class miscellanies and so have a more domestic air.

In the best Restoration work, however, the note is more serious and the rhythmic poise finer – in Cowley (though he belongs rather to the declining mode), Rochester (1647–80), and Dryden particularly. Rochester's *Love and Life* has a fine movement, an ostensibly insouciant argument, a hyperbole of light cynicism, yet its sense of transience is haunting and colours the professed inconstancy. The sense is more striking still in *Absent from Thee*, where the lilt and the decisive phrasing bear an overtone of world weariness that anticipates Byron. It is not surprising that Gilbert Burnet commented on Rochester's 'strange vivacity of thought' and his 'subtility and sublimity both, that were scarce imitable'. Dryden's lyrics are among the Restoration's most impressive: thought moves in them (as in so much of his best work) without intricacy but with beautiful management and haunting gravity. *I feed a flame within*, from *Secret Love* (1668), has a grave movement with a yielding regret in the breaking-away of double rhymes, the emotion contained and not extravagant, the imagery subdued save for one perfect tremulous moment:

> Not a sigh, nor a tear, my pain discloses,
> But they fall silently, like dew on roses.

The wonderful *Farewell, ungrateful Traitor*, from *The Spanish Friar* (1681), is a dramatic lyric from the woman betrayed; it carries its thought on a firm rhythm with falling rhymes in plangent succession. The best lyrics of Sedley (1639–1701) are almost as good in careful thought and earnest phrase – *To Cloris, Constancy, Ah Cloris that I now could sit, Love still has something of the sea*, and the exquisite *Not Celia that I juster am*.

Of other Restoration lyric qualities there is room only for two – for the moral lyric deriving through Jonson from Horace (Waller's *When we for age could neither read nor write* is a famous example), and for bravura-fancy deriving from an older magic, like Aphra Behn's

Love in fantastique Triumph sate, from *Abdelazar* (1677), with bleeding hearts, love's 'strange tyrannic power', and a paradoxical idea (woman providing love's weapons, man his passive yearning). The Restoration liked its Elizabethan drama, after all, and witnessed the last years of the 'last' Elizabethan (Shirley, 1596–1666) and of Carolines like Vaughan, Cowley, and Traherne. A fine and late example of the richer fashion is Congreve's *On Mrs Arabella Hunt, Singing* (1692).

The eighteenth century lowers the lyric to the level of prose sense, and draws its style from conversation, from Dryden's disciplined grace, and from the spareness of the moral lyric (as in Dryden's exequy for the Restoration years, *The Secular Masque*, or Pope's *Happy the Man*, both 1700). But if less piquant the species still ranges widely, as an art-form co-extensive with social life: there are ballad-opera verses (wedded, often, to folk-tunes), like those in Gay's *Beggar's Opera* or *Acis and Galatea*; there are patriotic songs – *The National Anthem*, *The British Grenadiers*, Thomson's *Rule, Britannia*, Garrick's *Heart of Oak*, or Cowper's *Loss of the Royal George*; there are bucolics – *A-hunting we will go*, *The Roast Beef of Old England*; there are ballad-imitations – Carey's *Sally in our Alley*, Goldsmith's *An Elegy on a Mad Dog*, and Cowper's *John Gilpin*; there are mock-heroics, social chitchat, domestic vignettes, compliments, satires – light like *The Vicar of Bray*, or severe in Swift, and in Johnson's *A Short Song of Congratulation*; and there is controlled meditation like Dodington's *Love thy Country, wish it well*, Johnson's *On the Death of Dr Levet*, and (its climax) Cowper's *The Castaway*, which combines terror and economy in one of the century's great poems. The Augustan lyric covers normal experience too; in Prior (1664–1721) it has a virtuoso in the easy and witty vernacular of the fashionable world, in that truly Augustan social use of the living language, and in Cowper (1731–1800) it has, outside the moments of tragedy, a modest master of domesticity, amusing or poignant.

The Augustan verse a modern reader usually hears about first is satire. This is not altogether a happy circumstance, since the satiric detail often eludes him in proportion as it came home to its contemporaries: the immediate appeal of *The Rape of the Lock* is unique. Still, satire was the ally of civilization, and its vogue was to the age's credit, since it was the ally of civilization; as Mulgrave wrote:

> Of all the ways that wisest men could find
> To mend the age, and mortify mankind,
> Satire, well-writ, has most successful prov'd.

Its first triumphs were political, particularly in Butler's *Hudibras* (1663–78), and Dryden's *Absalom* (1681–2), *Mac Flecknoe* (1682), and *The Medal* (1682). Butler's art is the satiric grotesque with much strength of idea, in hurtling and humorous octosyllabics to which the later Augustans looked back as a change from the discipline of more respectable forms. But whereas Butler is a stimulating curiosity, Dryden is a great poet, for the reason that makes great poets great – a genius for verse-rhythm and an exceptional expressiveness of language, generally good-tempered, but capable at times of devastating scorn. With the satires go the discourse-poems *Religio Laici* (1682) and *The Hind and the Panther* (1687), where satire is incidental. The ruling qualities are decisive wit, good-tempered scorn, and vernacular energy. The poems are public utterance, emphasized by assonance and alliteration, varied in speed and pause, impudently reminiscent of such dignified precedents as the Bible and Milton, and tightly managed in thought.

Yet there are degrees of greatness, and Dryden, though often more easily enjoyable than Pope (1688–1744), cannot really contest the supremacy of his successor, whose range of interest and vitality of expression are much greater than his own. Pope is the greater poet in virtue not of immediate accessibility (one must grow into much of his work in a way unnecessary with Dryden) but of his crystallization of the Augustan world in a style not less animatedly vernacular but more subtle in its complex of sense-and-feeling. *The Rape of the Lock* (1712–14) not only recounts a social frivolity but acts its scenes and emotions, conveys colour and texture of materials, light and warmth of summer, airy substance of sylphs, sheen and whisper of their wings, pride and passion of the outraged lady – and all this by multiple activity of words in which sound, meaning, movement, sensory qualities, and feelings are evoked simultaneously, the total situation being given immediately, as very rarely elsewhere in poetry. The same is true of the other great poems – the best *Moral Essays* (1731–5), the *Epistle to Augustus* (1737), *The Epilogue to the Satires* (1738), parts of *The Dunciad* (1728–43), and, best of all, the *Epistle to Dr Arbuthnot* (1735), that clear and complex poem in which the poetasters can be seen, felt and heard, their tempers high and desperate, their voices strident, their scribbling frenzies symbolized by a madman's charcoal squeaking on his whitewashed cell.

Not all Pope's work is satire, yet to include the rest of it here is convenient. There are delicate *Pastorals* (1709), whence Handel composed 'Where'er you walk'; the extremely intelligent discourse-poems the *Essay on Criticism* (1711) and *Essay on Man* (1733–4); the *Verses to the Memory of an Unfortunate Lady* (1717), where gleams of metaphysical wit link up with heroic rant on one side and on the other with clarity foreshadowing Collins and dignity foreshadowing Gray; simulated passion in *Eloisa to Abelard* (1717 – his venture into medieval-picturesque); pleasant *Epistles* – *To Miss Blount, with the Works of Voiture, To Miss Blount, on her leaving the Town, after the Coronation, To Robert Earl of Oxford, To Mr Jervas, To James Craggs;* and finally the *Imitations of Horace* (1733–8), in which Pope adapts to Augustan England his predecessor's commentary on Augustan Rome. One obstacle to the modern reader is Pope's dependence on contemporary references; another is the worldliness of his interests (save, he might properly protest, in the *Essay on Man*, where the theme of human life related to God and society is as highly conceived as possible). Experienced readers often admire him profoundly, but to others he must be introduced with inducements unnecessary in the case of the great nineteenth-century poets. Indeed, argument about his poetic status started almost with his death (to neglect the personal enemies who questioned it even earlier): deeper veins were available in the always-admired Shakespeare and the increasingly-admired Milton, and as early as 1726 James Thomson's preface to *Winter* (2nd edition) called for poetry's rescue from social satire, by the choice of 'great and serious subjects' such as arise in 'wild romantic country'. Pope's greatness lies elsewhere, in a deeply responsible concern for taste, intelligence, and humanity, expressed with an artistic intensity and personal passion which fuse into vividness, and often into beauty, the raw material of contemporary life. Once Pope's vitality, vividness, range of interests, and centrality to his alert and rich civilization are appreciated there can be no doubt about the wealth of poetic experience he offers. He shares with the finer writers of the time, and with its great architects and artists, an original force, a power and daring of conception, a genius of expression, and a richness of feeling which compete with those of any other era of the national culture.

Pope by no means monopolizes satire and social verse; other poets have their own voices. Swift can be racy in doggerel (*Mrs Harris's Petition*), journalistic in songs and ballads, tart, friendly, angry, or wittily nasty in squibs and narratives. The best of him is in the verses *On the Death of Dr Swift* (1731), a sardonic apologia as much in the manner of Augustanism as any poem could be, sheltering behind no artificial convention but crackling with worldly witty reality in a mordant vernacular idiom. Swift never quits reality an inch; he recites the spirited substance of life. Gay's is another personal voice: *The Fan* (1714) is interesting mainly as showing how inimitable is *The Rape of the Lock* from which it derives; still, its melody is lithe and continuous, and its imagery has Gay's heightened gleam. *Trivia* (1716) is intimate comedy of town life; in the dignity of heroic couplets it maintains an affectionate mockery and sometimes attains a beauty which transforms the commonplace. The town reappears in Johnson's *London* (1738), vigorous and severe, full of epigrams in that mode by which epigram is the moral passion of a deeply-experiencing mind. The same, more decidedly, is true of *The Vanity of Human Wishes* (1749), imitating Juvenal's tenth satire as *London* the third, evoking a crowded scene not of the ambitiously futile insect-nuisances of the *Epistle to Dr Arbuthnot*, bound to Grub Street in place and time, but more symbolic of general human life with its named and nameless figures pressing towards fatedly elusive or unattainable goals. Of succeeding satirists (*The Vanity* is satire not as ridicule but as moral rectification) the major names are those of Churchill (1731–64) and Crabbe (1754–1832). The former is too attached to his time now to be much read, yet his energy reminds one that that was a prized Augustan quality and his bite of phrase is not outdone by Dryden or Byron. Crabbe's best poems (*The Parish Register*, 1807, and later works) fall outside this volume, but even the early *Inebriety* (1775) and *The Village* (1783) have exact observation and bold attack, later modulated to subtle correspondences with sense and psychological skill in realistic narrative. *The Village*, a hit at Goldsmith's pastoral sentiment, records his Suffolk scene with grim and graphic mordancy, and uses its couplets to sharpen details and incise them on the consciousness.

A mode as characteristic of the Augustans as satire was the discourse, the reflection of personal interests and observations. In its aspect as a dream of country retirement it goes back to Martial and Horace; Cowley translated Martial in that poem praising moderate life which he included in his essay *Of Myself*: in the same mode he wrote *Of Solitude* in verse and *The Garden* in prose. As for Horace, translating him was an Augustan pastime; he appealed through his praise of the golden mean, his sober morality of human life, his desire for pastoral retirement, and his enjoyment of friendship; he encouraged that praise of gentry-pleasures which the Augustans made their own. Swift translated the sixth satire of his second book –

> I've often wished that I had clear
> For life, six hundred pounds a year,
> A handsome House to lodge a Friend,
> A River at my Garden's end –

and Pope added lines of his own (*Imitations of Horace*). Pomfret's *The Choice* (1700) is an alert significant poem in the same manner; so, in parts, are Lady Winchilsea's *Petition for an Absolute Retreat* (1713) and Matthew Green's witty and sensible *The Spleen* (1737). This cheerful mode in which the Augustans relaxed is in Cowper, though he transforms it as much as Goldsmith's *The Deserted Village* transforms the pastoral. His leisurely blank-verse ruminations in *The Task* (1785) and many of his letters record the quiet pleasures of his retirement. Their placidity does not wholly conceal the religious torments from which he sought refuge; his observation of friends, pets, village life, and the countryside is the escape of a man who has looked into hell and whom hell may still await, as he recognizes in his lines *On the Receipt of my Mother's Picture* and, terrifyingly, *The Castaway*. *The Task*'s concealed frame of reference is anything but Horatian amenity.

In another sense *The Task* is more than the ripe fruit of gentry-contentment; it is a long meditation on life, perambulating agreeably through quiet landscapes and personal reflections. James Thomson's *The Seasons* (1726–30) had been the first triumph in this genre, elaborated in successive editions and losing much of its early fresh flavour yet still offering much of sensitive and delighted attention to natural effect, and long remaining a much-loved poem.

The Seasons is important, indeed seminal, in revealing the pictorial and emotive possibilities of natural scenes. With absorbed and delicate (though often, too, heavy-handed) care it looks at and records its countryside subjects. The Romantic poets of the next century, it hardly needs saying, greatly outdid Thomson; too often he smothered his subjects in the dense embroidery of style and overlaid his vignettes with moral exhortation. Yet at his best he vividly and rightly catches, whether in small scale or large, the exact truth of the scenes he renders with a fresh quality of vision. Except to the professed student, however, one would recommend Thomson only at his selected best; the true life of Augustanism runs in less congested channels. The same applies more strongly still to Akenside's *The Pleasures of Imagination* (1744), even though it foreshadows Wordsworth; to Somerville's *The Chace* (1735 – source of the phrase 'the sport of kings'), though it has the charm of sporting prints; and to Dyer's *The Fleece* (1757), though it sings the wool-trade with honest observation and amiably rotund diction. Dyer's *Grongar Hill* (1726), however, is an agreeable landscape-poem which will survive, as will the amusing Spenserian imitations of Shenstone's *The Schoolmistress* (1737–42) and Thomson's *The Castle of Indolence* (1748), signs of a more indulgent literary taste.

Goldsmith, Gray, Smart, and Collins are other poetic ornaments of Johnson's age. Goldsmith's *The Traveller* (1764) is a true and thoughtful poem; *The Deserted Village* (1770) is much more. Goldsmith's gift is a pure style, lucid and gently effulgent; his feelings are simple but haunting, for the lost years of youth and the vanished 'innocence and ease' of country life, banished by oppressors. To them the reader easily and rightly yields unless he is too distrustful of the thin partitions dividing sentiment from sentimentality. About Gray's *Elegy* (1751) there is not even that qualification to make; it is rich in effect, harmonious in mood and substance. The richness comes from the ranging of the theme (the simple country burial ground) through perspectives of literary reminiscence, historical greatness, 'the boast of heraldry, the pomp of pow'r', Nature's laws which ordain that gems shall be hidden in ocean-depths and flowers in deserts, and finally time's inevitability which parts man from the loved familiarities of life. Round the humble theme Gray amasses a large potency, but balances it so that nothing of strain or melodrama enters; this is that troubling and familiar commonplace of mortality given the steadiness of acceptance, the fortifying breadth of universal relevance, and the music of phrases evolving with grave decorum. Each line, less decently handled, might touch off sentimentality, but Gray carries a full tide of feeling without letting it overflow. The best of his other work is the *Odes* (1747–57) – *On the Spring, On a Distant Prospect of Eton College, The Progress of Poesy, The Bard*, and *The Pleasure Arising from Vicissitude*. These are remarkable among Augustan odes for the rhythmical impetus which bears them along, and for phrase after phrase that dwells in the mind with happy finality; yet they remain at a distance, rhetorically splendid but personal neither to the reader nor on the whole, it would seem, to the writer, impressively devised, yet essentially artefacts of elaborated show and conventional gesture. Into the *Elegy* went the ordering, the literary memories, the thoughtful though conventional moralizing, the generalized but communicative phrasing, the modulated sound and movement which the *Odes* abound in, and in it they were transformed from the 'cumbrous splendour' that Johnson deprecated there into the measured thought and phrase that drew from him the tribute that

The *Church-yard* abounds with images which find a mirror in every mind, and with sentiments to which every bosom returns an echo... Had Gray written often thus, it had been vain to blame, and useless to praise him.

(*Life of Gray*)

As for Smart (1722–71), he lives virtually by one poem, the *Song to David* (1763). He is often spoken of as a poetic oddity, a kind of 'sport' in inappropriate surroundings. The only odd thing, critically speaking, is his brilliance and passion, for he has behind him a long tradition, by no means dead in the eighteenth century, of Biblical inspiration, and the shorter but powerful one of hymnody. Augustanism was not restricted to drawing-rooms and coffee-houses, and its churches and chapels were not always prosaic. Line by line in shining and urgent phrases the poem sings David's virtues and through them creation's manifold duties of praise. It ranges the world partly with the enriching imagery of the Bible to express the urges of religious adoration, but partly also with a strong independent vision of living things in their beauty and power. This would be an astonishing poem at any time; it is not really the more astonishing for being written when it was.

To end this survey of Augustan poets with Collins (1721–59) is not to climax them (indeed, they are too varied to submit to any single figure), but is certainly to leave them with one whose quality outshines nearly all of them and whose best work, though minute in bulk, is movingly imaginative. Often coupled with Gray, Collins has a different, indeed subtler, imagination: where Gray is dignified and melodious but not precisely *inward* in sensing his subject, Collins penetrates it by what seems sheer intuition. A good deal of his work was put carefully together of the approved Miltonic echoes and allegorical personifications, but those few poems which are his best – *How sleep the brave*, the *Dirge in Cymbeline*, and the odes *To Simplicity, The Passions, On the Death of Mr Thomson, On the Popular Superstitions of the Highlands*, and above all *To Evening* – have a purity and delicacy which sound Shakespearian even through the Miltonic reminiscence. That Collins shares certain new interests – crepuscular landscape, ghosts, fays, and Highland mythology – is significant, but not so significant as the fact that he has a shifting grace of phrase, a fragility almost, which in delicacy and imaginativeness has no equal in his century.

Drama

For the brevity of this section the excuse must be that Augustan drama is less important than prose or poetry, and that it lends itself less to reading. Both serious and comic plays were, of course, mainly opportunities for acting, for the delivery of animated speech, the playing of strong situations, and the creation of a direct relationship with an audience. Much that in print is awkward (elaborated wit, elementary psychology, open ironies and asides, crowded plots, and stilted 'refined' dialogue) is acceptable, indeed effective, on the stage, and to apply standards other than stage-effectiveness is to miss the main point. Dramatic conditions gave the actor pre-eminence. Audiences and players could know each other well: a close relationship was further encouraged by prologues, epilogues, and the apron-stage (though the latter was foreshortened in the eighteenth century as the auditorium was enlarged). Type-casting encouraged expert acting in expected roles; and resounding tragic bombast or comic repartee was meant to dominate unruly pits and galleries.

The main Restoration forms are heroic drama (often rhymed), 'humour' comedy, and comedy of manners. In his essay *Of Heroic Plays* (1672) Dryden derives heroic drama particularly from Davenant's *The Siege of Rhodes* (1656), defends rhyme as exalting the tone, and claims that his own tragedies are modelled on epic as 'the most noble, the most pleasant, and the most instructive' way of writing in verse, 'the highest pattern of human life'. The heroic drama's themes of superhuman love and honour came to be satirized in Buckingham's *The Rehearsal* (1672), robustly and farcically in Fielding's *Tom Thumb* (1730), and sketchily in Carey's *Chrononhotonthologos* (1734). Yet heroic plays were an assertion of human splendour made, not altogether incongruously, by a court circle whose libertinism did not exclude flamboyant devotion and courage. Roger Boyle (1621–79) and Sir Robert Howard (1626–98) really set them going, Settle (1648–1724), Lee (1653–92), and Otway (1652–85) developed them, but their best exponent is Dryden in *Tyrannic Love* (1670, with the heaven-defying Maximin), *The Conquest of Granada* (1672, with the astonishing Almanzor and Lyndaraxa), and *Aurengzebe* (1676, his last rhymed play). It is outside the heroic fashion, however, that the best Restoration tragedy lies, in Dryden's well-modelled *All for Love* (1678), Otway's domestic tragedy *The Orphan* (1680) and vigorous *Venice Preserved* (1682), and later Southerne's *Oroonoko* (1696), and Rowe's *Fair Penitent* (1703) and *Jane Shore* (1714). The psychological climate of the eighteenth century was not favourable to the poetic force required to generate real tragedy, though it could prompt some high-minded literary drama like Addison's classical and sententious *Cato* (1713), which died quickly after a brief *succès d'estime*, and Johnson's *Irene* (1749), which died even more quickly after an even briefer success. It was favourable to melodrama and pathos, such as gave Lillo's *London Merchant* (1731) and Edward Moore's *The Gamester* (1753) a long-continued hold on the stage; both these plays are vehemently histrionic, with strong villains and weak victims, effective for their age but certainly not for all time. But at least they remind us that the eighteenth century was, in its own way, almost naïvely susceptible to emotion.

'Humour' comedy and comedy of manners are not always separable; most playwrights indulge themselves in a caricature or two drawn after Jonson's formula of 'one particular quality', and they all display social behaviour though not always in that witty fashion that 'comedy of manners' implies. Shadwell (1642–92) is the best 'humorist', in the old sense of caricaturist, owing debts to Molière and to Jonson, 'whom I think all dramatic poets ought to imitate' (*The Sullen Lovers*, preface). In speech often strong and picturesque he ranges from cheerful farce to coarse verisimilitude: in *The Sullen Lovers* (1668), *Epsom Wells* (1673), *The Squire of Alsatia* (1688) with its urban turbulence, and *Bury Fair* (1689) with its country pleasures, his prosaic but vigorous mind plants the reader in Restoration life more faithfully than does the wit and intrigue-comedy of Dryden, Etherege, and Congreve.

About wit-comedy, the Restoration's speciality, opinions differ. Condemned as immoral, vindicated as amoral, or praised as moral (since it satirizes folly), it has been found cheaply cynical or brilliantly gay, factitious and dull or sparkling with wit. Its pedigree is from Beaumont, Fletcher, and Shirley, through Dryden's early comedy to Etherege (1634–91). After his unremarkable *Love in a Tub* (1664), the latter came nearer to comedy of manners in *She Would if She Could* (1668) and achieved it in *The Man of Mode* (1676), with the debonair cynicism of Dorimant (drawn from Rochester), the affectation of Sir Fopling Flutter, and amatory intrigue presented in repartee and witty extravagance. Such close recording of sophisticated society was considered a new style; it was, he claimed, 'the modern way of writing' and a contemporary remarked that 'What he writes is but translation From Dog-and-Partridge conversation' (i.e. fashionable tavern-talk). The master of witty comedy was Congreve (1670–1729) in *The Old Bachelor* (1693), *The Double Dealer* (1694), *Love for Love* (1695), and, most famous, *The Way of the World* (1700).

The flavour of Wycherley (1640–1716) is different. His contemporaries admired his mordant satire; 'in my friend,' wrote Lansdowne, 'every syllable, every thought, is masculine,' and his nickname of 'Manly' was not merely a nominal transfer from the hero of *The Plain Dealer*. His plays are *Love in a Wood* (1672), *The Gentleman Dancing-Master* (1673), *The Country Wife* (1675), and *The Plain Dealer* (1677): the two latter in particular make a formidable impact, since a complex intrigue is carried on (as already mentioned) in language with a strong sensory charge and a flurry of satiric violences. The ferocity of Wycherley's moral judgements belongs to the Jonsonian tradition of corrective comedy; prefacing *The State of Innocence* (1677), Dryden wrote that *The Plain Dealer* was 'one of the most bold, most general, and most useful satires' ever shown on the stage.

Morally speaking, the general heartlessness of all the plays mentioned (except *The Way of the World*) and the triviality of what is so elaborately displayed are innutrient. But they stand or fall not on such grounds but on their virtuosity as stage entertainments, by characters which for stage-purposes are bold and actable, and by speech which, if often tedious to close scrutiny, electrifies the ear with unexpected simile, realistic imagery, and pungent vernacular.

Succeeding comedies must be enumerated cursorily. Vanbrugh (1664–1726) wrote *The Relapse* (1697), *The Provok'd Wife* (1697), *The Confederacy* (1705), and the lively fragment *A Journey to London* which Colley Cibber completed as *The Provok'd Husband* (1728); he provides clear plots, good cues, easy cynicism and sentiment, and energy rising to strong satire in *The Provok'd Wife*'s Sir John Brute. Farquhar (1678–1707) produced genial comedy of provincial humour in *The Recruiting Officer* (1706) and *The Beaux' Stratagem* (1707). To venture into the comedy of Cibber, Mrs Centlivre and Steele is to descend too far into the second-rate; it is more necessary to note how Restoration wit-cynicism modulated, through a more extended and sober taste, into virtue and didacticism (Cibber made a small contribution and Steele a larger one here), and by the 1750s into sentimentality, against which Goldsmith's comedies of humour – *The Good-Natured Man* (1768) and *She Stoops to Conquer* (1773) – are reactions, and Sheridan's *The School for Scandal* an anti-hypocrisy satire. Of all the dramatists mentioned, Sheridan (1751–1816) is deservedly the best known; to name *The Rivals* (1775), *St Patrick's Day* (1775), *The School for Scandal* (1777), and *The Critic* (1779) is to recall clear plot, excellent cueing, captivating stage-situations managed with deceptive ease, and agile wit and fun. The 1770s, which contain these plays as well as *She Stoops to Conquer*, are a most fruitful decade in comedy.

Nearly all writers attempted a play or two; Gay's *The Beggar's Opera* (1728), Colman's *The Jealous Wife* (1761, indebted to *Tom Jones*), and Colman and Garrick's *The Clandestine Marriage* (1766) have proved their vitality in modern revivals. Moreover, the eighteenth century is rich in dramatic ephemera – farces, ballad-operas, and entertainments – which are not literature but serve as a reminder that the theatre is not primarily a literary medium. The stage was a centre of attraction in London (the platform for a succession of famous players – Cibber, Quin, Macklin, Garrick, Mrs Oldfield, Kitty Clive, Mrs Siddons, and others) and a provincial pleasure too (Garrick organized a celebrated Jubilee at Stratford in 1769 and many provincial towns had theatres for the reception of touring actors). Theatrical taste reflects the evolution from satire to sentiment, and the increasing appeal of Shakespeare; but except for Goldsmith and Sheridan most eighteenth-century plays lack the final vitality.

NOTES

1. See J. E. Spingarn, *Critical Essays of the Seventeenth Century* (1908), I, lxviii. For the whole idea of following nature, see Spingarn, lxviiff.; B. Willey, *Eighteenth-Century Background* (1940), *passim*.

2. For intellectual equipment, see J. R. Sutherland, *Preface to Eighteenth-Century Poetry* (1948), 58–9.

3. For 'wit' see J. W. H. Atkins, *English Literary Criticism: 17th and 18th Centuries* (1951), 40–41, 56, 63, 99, 163; W. Empson, *The Structure of Complex Words* (1952), 84–100; Spingarn, *Critical Essays*, xxix–xxxi.

4. For comment on these aims, see F. W. Bateson, *English Poetry and the English Language* (1934), 47–58; Spingarn, *Critical Essays*, xxxiiff.; Sutherland, *Preface*, chs v and vi; J. Lannering, *Studies in the Prose Style of Joseph Addison* (Uppsala, 1951), 131–2.

5. See Bateson, *English Poetry and the English Language* (1934), 47ff.

6. For French influence, see Spingarn, *Critical Essays*, introduction, *passim*; W. P. Ker, *Essays of John Dryden* (1900), introduction, sections i–vi.

7. On the kinds, see Sutherland, *Preface*, 121–30.

8. See *Johnsonian Miscellanies*, ed. G. B. Hill (1897), I, 201–2 fns.

9. See T. S. Eliot, *Selected Prose* (1953), 'The Metaphysical Poets', and Willey, *Seventeenth-Century Background*, 87; also the discussion in *Essays in Criticism* (ed. F. W. Bateson), July 1951 and April 1952.

10. See the introduction to this edition, and especially xlvii–lxxx.

11. For the differences between pre- and post-Addisonian prose, see J. Lannering, *Studies in the Prose Style of Joseph Addison*, 85–94.

12. For details of the periodicals, see A. Beljame, *The Public and Men of Letters, 1660–1744* (1948), 248ff.

13. For Addison's personal influence, see Beljame, *The Public and Men of Letters*, 275–300.

PART III

JOHN DRYDEN

FRANCIS NOEL LEES

In 1649, while still at school, Dryden wrote a poem for a collection
of elegies on the death of Lord Hastings, a collection to which
Marvell, Herrick, and Denham also contributed. This was his first
published work.

> Must noble Hastings immaturely die,
> The honour of his ancient family,
> Beauty and learning thus together meet,
> To bring a *winding* for a *wedding* sheet?*

it begins, and very typical it *looks*. Here are the decasyllabic couplets
– a form which he was to develop as his own favourite and establish
as that of a whole age; and here is the 'public' theme – no less
prophetic of Charles II's Poet Laureate and a writer who was to be a
professional[1] in quite a new degree. But as one really reads the lines it
becomes evident that these are *not* the couplets of the mature Dryden,
not, in fact, post-Waller, Restoration couplets at all.

> Must Virtue prove Death's harbinger? must she,
> With him expiring, feel mortality?

it continues:

> Is death, sin's wages, grace's now? shall art
> Make us more learned only to depart?
> If merit be disease; if virtue death;
> To be good, not to be; who'd then bequeath
> Himself to discipline? Who'd not esteem
> Labour a crime? study self-murther deem?

These are couplets reminiscent of those of Donne, with the poet
struggling to bend the form to the shape of the dramatic blank verse
of the age just passed – and the couplet has, as it were, grown strong

---

* Original italics. Other italics by present author, except where indicated.

enough to put up a fight. The result is unfortunate; cumbrous throughout, at times ('Is death, sin's wages, grace's now?') a positive feat of awkwardness; and it shows plainly Dryden's metrical relationship with the poetry of the century. The hint of a late 'metaphysicality' in the wit of 'To bring a *winding* for a *wedding* sheet' is only too fully confirmed in the conceits of some forty lines farther on:

> Was there no milder way than the small pox,
> The very filth'ness of Pandora's box? ...
> Blisters with pride swell'd, which thro' 's flesh did sprout,
> Like rosebuds, stuck i' th' lily skin about.
> Each little pimple had a tear in it,
> To wail the fault its rising did commit ...

(note the tight squeeze of 'thro' 's' and 'i' th''); and in the lines, near the end:

> But thou, O *virgin-widow** left alone, ...
> With greater than Platonic love, O wed
> His soul, tho' not his body, to thy bed:
> Let that make thee a mother; bring thou forth
> Th' *ideas* of his virtue, knowledge, worth ...

This is writing of the metaphysical decadence, what Dryden himself would later call Clevelandism, the kind of 'wit' that was to arouse Dr Johnson's disapproval in his *Life of Cowley*. To see it attempted so conscientiously by the young Dryden not only fixes his point of contact with the poetry of his time, but throws into relief the qualities of his later work. As here, for example, from *To the Memory of Mr Oldham* (1684):

> Farewell, too little, and too lately known,
> Whom I began to think and call my own:
> For sure our souls were near allied, and thine
> Cast in the same poetic mould with mine ...
> O early ripe! to thy abundant store
> What could advancing age have added more? ...

with its easy, yet firm, verse-movement, and its natural simplicity of expression, combining in a due solemnity of tone which is sincere and moving. This time the natural quality, the spontaneity, of speech – the speech movement, is caught by working *with* the couplet and its pause, not against it. In the lines on Hastings there is, it is true, some

---

* Hastings's betrothed. Original italics in this passage.

promise of a characteristic conciseness and decisiveness of expression, as in

> His Native soil was the four parts o' th' earth;
> *All Europe was too narrow for his birth,*

but it is to show what Dryden grew from, grew out of, that the poem is worth quoting here.

Not that Dryden's later elegiac touch is always as in the *Oldham* lines. He could in 1685 produce the superficial ornateness of the ode *To the Pious Memory of the accomplish'd young lady, Mrs Anne Killigrew*, grandiose in idea and form (that of the loose 'Pindaric' ode made fashionable by Cowley – though, interestingly, a great part of it consists of heroic couplets), artificial in a damaging sense, not much less exaggerated in its hyperbole than the lines on Hastings but without the concentration of idea and conceit, the 'metaphysical' energy:

> Thy brother-angels at thy birth
>> Strung each his lyre, and tun'd it high,
>> That all the people of the sky
> Might know a poetess was born on earth.
>> And then, if ever, mortal ears
>> Had heard the music of the spheres!

– and showing the persistence in Dryden of a certain coarseness of taste and insensitivity, with its melodramatic and intrusive

> O gracious God! how far have we
> Profan'd thy heav'nly gift of poesy!...
> O wretched we! why were we hurried down
>> This lubric and adult'rous age,
>> (Nay, added fat pollutions of our own,)...

and its almost comic closing stanza:

> When in mid-air the golden trump shall sound,
> To raise the nations underground...
>> When rattling bones together fly
>> From the four corners of the sky:
> When sinews o'er the skeletons are spread,
> Those cloth'd with flesh, and life inspires the dead;
> The sacred poets first shall hear the sound,
> And foremost from the tomb shall bound,
> For they are cover'd with the lightest ground.

And the *Oldham* lines, of course, give no idea of the interests and vitality of his mature work as a whole.

Dryden himself at a late date in his life wrote in a letter to the Earl of Abingdon (prefaced to *Eleonora*, 1692): 'They say my talent is satire'; and few today would disagree with that judgement. 'If it be so,' he continued, ''tis a fruitful age, and there is an extraordinary crop to gather.' These remarks lead straight to the part of Dryden's voluminous work that most compels attention today – and first to the poem written, it seems pretty certain, at the request of Charles II, to turn opinion against Shaftesbury and the Whigs, *Absalom and Achitophel* (1681). His couplets had taken most of their true shape as early as 1660, as his piece on 'the Happy Restoration', *Astraea Redux,*[a] or *To my honour'd friend Sir Robert Howard*, both of that year, will show; and before 1681 he was to exercise his versification strenuously in the heroic drama, and in his numerous prologues and epilogues – these latter bringing into play also his turn for the pithily mocking. He came, then, to his first considerable undertaking in non-dramatic poetry since *Annus Mirabilis* (1667) with a highly developed technique.

The poem begins with a swing, a good-humoured satiric irony accompanying the placing of Charles II, as David, in Biblical times:

> In pious times, ere priestcraft did begin,
> Before polygamy was made a sin:
> When man on many multiplied his kind,
> Ere one to one was cursedly confined, . . .
> Then Israel's monarch after Heaven's own heart,
> His vigorous warmth did variously impart
> To wives and slaves; and, wide as his command,
> Scatter'd his Maker's image thro' the land,

the verse moving with conversational ease while the interest is engaged by the series of preparatory clauses in the paragraph, alliteration working to promote significant emphasis, the diction plain yet with body, and the metre really *used* in the expression. One notices how the repeated 'v' gives point to 'variously', and how the rhythmic plunge into 'Scatter'd' animates the word and thence the line, and strengthens the end of the paragraph. Or again:

a That is, 'Astraea – virgin goddess of Justice – brought back'.

> The Jews[a], a headstrong, moody, murm'ring race,
> As ever tried th'extent and stretch of grace;
> God's pamper'd people, whom, debauch'd with ease,
> No king could govern, nor no God could please;
> (Gods they had tried of every shape and size,
> That god-smiths could produce, or priests devise:) . . .

the first line of which shows a control of and freedom within the couplet which should disprove any idea that variety is in the keeping of a single caesural pause. Dryden's vibrant language and gift for expressing assured contempt shows already, and something of the power of narration which was to make his adaptations of Boccaccio in the *Fables* (1700) so attractive to Keats. But the poem has not a genuine 'action', and it is in the individual character-sketches that Dryden achieves most. First, of Shaftesbury himself:

> Of these the false Achitophel was first;
> A name to all succeeding ages curst:
> For close designs and crooked counsels fit;
> Sagacious, bold, and turbulent of wit;
> Restless, unfix'd in principles and place:
> In pow'r unpleas'd, impatient of disgrace:
> A fiery soul, which, working out its way,
> Fretted the pigmy body to decay,
> And o'er-informed the tenement[b] of clay,

in which a figure simply described in moral terms is created concrete, positive, enough to survive as a character in the poem by the sheer precision of the language, the energy, the capability of the words. Without such positive emergence, satiric comment on actual persons will rapidly fade to something of interest only as a record, hardly to be revivified by even the fullest explanatory footnote. Giving this terse sketch added life and increased value is its acknowledgement of the powers of Shaftesbury, an admiration for them, and, even so early in the portrait, the beginnings of a distinct personal feeling of regret at the perversion and waste of talents; particularly when they are turned to the upsetting of that 'common quiet' which, as he says in *Religio Laici*, is 'mankind's concern'. The humanizing sense of regret gets plain statement soon after:

a The English, b body.

> O, had he been content to serve the crown,
> With virtues only proper to the gown.*
> Or had the rankness of the soil been freed
> From cockle, that oppress'd the noble seed;
> David for him his tuneful harp had strung . . .

(These lines first appear in the second edition but are thought to have been in the first draft.) Dryden's attitude varies from character to character, of course, and with it his methods of presentation. Zimri (Buckingham) receives a much tarter treatment:

> A man so various, that he seem'd to be
> Not one, but all mankind's epitome:
> Stiff in opinions, always in the wrong;
> Was everything by starts, and nothing long;
> But, in the course of one revolving moon,
> Was chymist, fiddler, statesman, and buffoon:
> Then all for women, painting, rhyming, drinking,
> Besides ten thousand freaks that died in thinking . . .

'Nothing long' though '*always* in the wrong'; the insinuation in 'revolving moon'; the juxtaposing of 'chymist', 'fiddler', 'statesman', and so on; there is not much respect here, but there is a trace of pity. For Shimei (Bethel, Sheriff of London), a very fourth-rate personage is created by a brilliant comic use of a kind of bathos:

> Shimei, whose youth did early promise bring
> Of zeal to God and *hatred* to his king,
> Did wisely from *expensive* sins refrain,
> And never broke the Sabbath, but for gain; . . .
> The city, to reward his pious *hate*
> Against his *master* chose him magistrate.
> His hand a vare*a* of justice did uphold;
> His neck was loaded with a chain of gold.

(It is remarkable how 'loaded' is given both physical and moral weight.)

> During his office, treason was no crime;
> The sons of Belial had a glorious time;
> For . . .

and he relentlessly resumes the account,

* Shaftesbury was a judge.
a Wand or staff.

> For Shimei, tho' not prodigal of pelf,
> Yet lov'd his *wicked* neighbour as himself...

In the depiction of Corah (Titus Oates), to aid in the effect of sheer contemptibility, he employs a direct insulting language – though wittily embodied in a play of word and idea – and finally drops to rough physical description (in lines which provide one of his strikingly few reminders of Chaucer):

> Yet, Corah, thou shalt from oblivion pass:
> Erect thyself, thou monumental *brass*,
> High as the *serpent** of thy metal made...
> Ours was a Levite, and as times went then,
> His tribe were God Almighty's gentlemen.
> Sunk were his eyes, his voice was harsh and loud,
> Sure signs he neither choleric was nor proud...

– and what in contrast with the other sketches is not far from mere abuse takes on something of a positive character. His share in the sequel, *The Second Part of Absalom and Achitophel* (1682) (mostly by Nahum Tate), and his own piece *The Medal* (1682), offer nothing of the same positive moral creation as does *Absalom and Achitophel*, Part I, but they show again his command of expression and his power of caricature. In *The Medal*, for instance, we have Shaftesbury:

> Bart'ring his venal wit for sums of gold,
> He cast himself into the saintlike mold;
> Groan'd, sigh'd, and pray'd, while godliness was gain,
> The loudest bagpipe of the squeaking train...;

in *The Second Part of Absalom and Achitophel* there is Shadwell:

> Round as a globe, and liquor'd ev'ry chink,
> Goodly and great he sails behind his link.
> With all his bulk there's nothing lost in Og,
> For ev'ry inch that is not fool is rogue:
> A monstrous mass of foul, corrupted matter,
> As all the devils had spew'd to make the batter...
> But tho' Heav'n made him poor, (with rev'rence speaking,)
> He never was a poet of God's making.
> The midwife laid her hand on his thick skull,
> With this prophetic blessing: *Be thou dull*...†

* The serpent of brass made and set up by Moses to save the Israelites from the fiery serpents. See Numbers, XXI, 6–9.
† Original italics.

Mac Flecknoe, published first in 1682, but now accepted as written in 1678, though a highly entertaining lampoon on Shadwell, with passages of fine comic description, is light in weight and too often merely topically allusive; but its mock-heroic framing, which suggested Pope's *Dunciad*, is skilful. *Absalom and Achitophel* is, of course, genuinely 'heroic' (it is entitled 'a Poem', not, as *The Medal*, 'a Satire'), and in it Dryden is at bottom making another attempt at what his age so desired, epic poetry, as a form of which he and others had been cultivating the fantastic 'heroic play'. The confident, unfaltering zest of the poem surely owes much to the concurrence of his long developing weariness with the theatre, and his sense of a waiting public, thirsty for the political literature that the licensing authority denied them, with the pressure of this deep-rooted urge to produce an epic. The reminiscences of *Paradise Lost*, then, are not without significance – the reference to Adam and the Temptation in the preface, and such phrases as 'Him staggering so when hell's dire agent found' or 'Some had in courts been great, and thrown from thence, Like fiends were harden'd in impenitence.' The poem is witty, but not at all in a 'metaphysical' manner now – the power behind the 'conceitedness' has been schooled into one of clear analysis and epigrammatic expression; yet it is the same intelligence in the anticlimaxes of the Shimei portrait as in the 'metaphysical' notion of:

> How shall I then begin, or where conclude,
> To draw a fame so truly circular?
> For in a round what order can be shew'd
> Where all the parts so equal-perfect are?

from the *Heroic Stanzas* of 1658. His previous attempt at a heroic poem, *Annus Mirabilis* (1667), achieves nothing of the order of *Absalom and Achitophel*, though it contains in an assortment of styles a good deal of promise and some passages of distinct quality. Its quatrains (copied from Davenant's *Gondibert*) are monotonous, its actions (sea-fights with the Dutch, the Great Fire of London) are insufficiently interesting in themselves, are incapable of the moral development of the later poem.

In *Absalom and Achitophel* there is much evidence of the author's gift and liking for clear, summing statement, for telling exposition; and we should not be surprised, therefore, to find that his two other major *original* poems, *Religio Laici; or, a Layman's Faith* (1682) and *The*

Hind and the Panther'(1687), are works very largely of exposition and argument, and that he translated – and impressively – parts of Lucretius. The preface to the former, written before he (in 1685) became a Roman Catholic, concludes with remarks on style which well suggest the judicious, workmanlike approach of Dryden and the 'age of Reason' then beginning:

> The expression of a poem design'd purely for instruction ought to be plain and natural, and yet majestic . . . The florid, elevated, and figurative way is for the passions . . . A man is to be cheated into passion but to be reason'd into truth.

There is a sense of calculation, of concoction, in reference to the 'passionate', and a separation of it from the 'truthful', which it is hard to imagine in Shakespeare or Donne or, in general, their contemporaries. And Hobbes's philosopher's distrust of metaphorical language in argument has evidently become a commonplace. All the more seriously, then, must we take the purport of the imagery in the rather surprising opening lines of the poem:

> Dim as the borrow'd beams of moon and stars
> To lonely, weary, wand'ring travellers,
> Is Reason to the soul; and, as on high
> Those rolling fires discover but the sky,
> Not light us here, so Reason's glimmering ray
> Was lent, not to assure our doubtful way,
> But guide us upward to a better day.
> And as those nightly tapers disappear,
> When day's bright lord ascends our hemisphere;
> So pale grows Reason at Religion's sight;
> So dies, and so dissolves in supernatural light.

Some feeling emerges from the imaginative expression here, enough to draw attention to Dryden's restriction of the authority of Reason in an increasingly rationalistic age – (which is not incompatible with the truly Cartesian Adam of *The State of Innocence* (1673–4), his rhymed dramatization of *Paradise Lost*, who rises, 'as newly created', with: 'What am I? or from whence? For that I am I know because I think . . .'). Yet, of course, the imagery is 'plain' enough, 'natural', and, to use Dryden's word in the preface to *The Hind and the Panther*, 'perspicuous': neatly analogous and explanatory above all. The perspicuity elsewhere in the poem may be testified to by continuing a little our quotation:

> Some few, whose lamp shone brighter, have been led
> From cause to cause, to nature's secret head^a;
> And found that one first principle must be:
> But what, or who, that UNIVERSAL HE;
> Whether some soul incompassing this ball,
> Unmade, unmov'd; yet making, moving all; ...

The brevity, conciseness, and exactness in the sixth line, its precision of tone and rhythm, make a piece of perfect expression, and show not merely a satisfactory versification of ideas, but verse functioning positively to create lucidity.

The Hind and the Panther is a very differently constituted work. It is of great, indeed excessive, length, and sets out to express the now Catholic Dryden's altered views by means of a beast fable, the 'milk-white Hind, immortal and unchang'd' standing for Dryden's new Church, 'the Panther, sure the noblest, next the Hind' for his old one. Other beasts represent various sects — 'The bloody Bear, an *Independent* beast ...', 'Among the timorous kind the *Quaking* Hare ...', 'Next her the *buffoon* Ape ...', 'The bristled *Baptist*★ boar, impure as he, (But whiten'd with the foam of sanctity,) ...'; but they are given no parts to play in the action, or, truer, there is no action for them to have parts in. The poem soon develops into a disputation between the Hind and the Panther, enlivened by occasional satirical characterizing touches, and couched in Dryden's most accomplished eloquence; but the allegory does little more than set the scene for the conversation piece and give opportunity meanwhile for a little satire on the other animals which is not susceptible of development in relation to their human parallels. The cautionary tale of the Martlets, presented with some narrative brilliance, is obscure in its point, and that of the Doves and the Chickens, though vividly told, has only the final interest of the contemporary allusion it makes. The poem is very deficient in narrative interest, but in eloquence, ease, and command of expression it is unsurpassed in his works. An autobiographical passage may be quoted here as a rarity:

> My thoughtless youth was wing'd with vain desires,
> My manhood, long misled by wand'ring fires,
> Follow'd false lights; and, when their glimpse was gone,

My pride struck out new sparkles of her own.
Such was I, such by nature still I am;
Be thine the glory, and be mine the shame.
Good life be now my task: my doubts are done:
(What more could fright my faith, than three in one?)*

– and how much less individually, less sharply, is this expressed than
where he is not concerned with himself! The repetition in 'misled
by wand'ring fires' and 'Follow'd false lights', the weakness of meaning in 'thoughtless' and 'new', the stock adjective–noun pairs that
the couplet form encouraged, are all involved in this comparative
debility of effect, all indicative of uncertainty with the intimately
personal, all contributory to the unexpected tinge of emotionalism.

His adaptations of Boccaccio and Chaucer in the *Fables* should be
mentioned. They have a narrative interest he never created in his
original poems. Of the former Wordsworth wrote to Sir Walter
Scott, 'I think his translations from Boccaccio are the best, at least
the most poetical, of his poems' – but it will be well to recall Wordsworth's Romanticism and to note that he has just previously said
that 'Whenever Dryden's *language* is poetically impassioned, it is
mostly upon unpleasing subjects, such as the follies, vices, and crimes
of classes of men, or of individuals.' He rightly observes that Dryden
has coarsened Boccaccio considerably, a coarsening which appears
too in his adaptation of Chaucer. Of the odes *Alexander's Feast* (1697)
and *A Song for St Cecilia's Day* (1687) and his many songs, one can
admire the complete assurance and ease of execution, but it is in
much inferior modes. The verse is unsubtle; the substance, the
thought and feeling, in the odes is trivial yet portentous, and in
the songs is of a now happily outmoded archness and, often, a
clever, superficial indecency typical of the Restoration drama from
which they mostly come. One finds a refreshing quality in a very
early song from *The Indian Emperor* (1665), written before the hardness and the smartness of the Restoration had set in:

Ah fading joy, how quickly art thou past!
　　Yet we thy ruin haste.
As if the cares of human life were few,
　　We seek out new:
And follow fate, which would too fast pursue.

* Refers to the doctrine of the Trinity.

> See how on every bough the birds express
>   In their sweet notes their happiness.
>   They all enjoy, and nothing spare;
> But on their mother Nature lay their care:
> Why then should man, the lord of all below,
>   Such troubles choose to know,
> As none of all his subjects undergo? . . .

– where with all the slightness there is a modesty of manner befitting that slightness, a delicacy and point in the rhythm, not to be found in his later lyric verse: the curious melodic reminders of Marvell's *Garden* certainly do not recur. Dryden was not a lyric poet, has nothing to offer in the way of illuminating or moving states of mind. His attention is directed outward and it is rather on states of things, on events and the people in them, that he brings his strong and mobile intelligence to bear, his wit, his feeling for language, and his highly trained verse-technique.

Our greatest debt to his years of work in the theatre is for no play or part of a play of his, but for what they did to develop this verse-technique. It was in the 'heroic' play that the couplet took 'possession of the stage', to use Dryden's own words in the preface to that arch-example, *The Conquest of Granada* (1670). The dramatic blank verse of the Elizabethans and Jacobeans, by the time of the closing of the theatres in 1642, had arrived at a slack and poetically empty facility, which would hardly do for a genre of 'greatness and majesty' whose laws, Dryden suggests in the same place, demand the 'drawing all things as far above the ordinary proportions of the stage, as that is beyond the common words and actions of human life ...' The couplet succeeds in these plays in conferring something of ceremony, an invitation to elocution, to declamation, which suggests a certain grandeur; but they are not endowed with any sufficient quality of feeling and imagination, and their poetry is negligible, even, surely, the passage on life in *Aurengzebe* (1676) – in the prologue to which Dryden declares that he 'grows weary of his long-loved mistress, Rhyme' and 'would quit the stage':

> When I consider Life, 'tis all a cheat;
> Yet, fool'd with hope, men favour the deceit;
> Trust on, and think tomorrow will repay:
> Tomorrow's falser than the former day;
> Lies worse; and, while it says, we shall be blest

> With some new joys, cuts off what we possess.
> Strange cozenage! None would live past years again,
> Yet all hope pleasure in what yet remain;
> And, from the dregs of Life, think to receive,
> What the first sprightly running could not give.
> I'm tir'd with waiting for this chymic gold,*
> Which fools us young, and beggars us when old.

A commonplace sentiment issuing in language which is characteristically clear and fluent, and given apt metrical movement, yes — but hardly entitled to the considerable amount of praise that it has received. Its meaning is thin, yet it strikes an attitude, gives itself unwarranted airs. Dryden's habit of easy intelligibility, his taste for and knack of philosophizing in verse in these plays is clearly enough suggested here. *All for Love*, however, his treatment of the story of Antony and Cleopatra, with which he made a return to the drama in 1677, is his only serious play which has much claim upon modern attention, and in this, as in later plays, he uses blank verse, coming back to the verse-form as well as the material of Shakespeare, and thereby to a closer concern with reality. To have laid aside so completely the heroic couplet and to have produced such eloquent blank verse is a considerable achievement, but the poetry rarely rises above eloquence, and then never far above it. Consider, for instance, Antony's

> How I loved,
> Witness, ye days and nights, and all ye hours,
> That danced away with down upon your feet,
> As all your bus'ness were to count my passion.
> One day passed by, and nothing saw but love;
> Another came, and still 'twas only love;
> The suns were weari'd out with looking on,
> And I untir'd with loving.

Pretty in its way certainly, but merely fanciful, and in meaning tenuous in the extreme. Or his:

> ... my eyes
> Are open to her falsehood: my whole life
> Has been a golden dream of love and friendship;

---

* Refers to the never-ending quest of the alchemists.

> But now I wake, I'm like a merchant, roused
> From soft repose, to see his vessel sinking,
> And all his wealth cast o'er. Ingrateful woman!
> Who follow'd me, but as the swallow summer,
> Hatching her young ones in my kindly beams,
> Singing her flatt'ries to my morning wake;
> But now my winter comes, she spreads her wings,
> And seeks the spring of Caesar ... ,

where one gets a little set piece of 'delightful' imagery which fails of any immediacy of expression because of the presumably decorative repetitious extensions of idea. 'But now I wake' is elaborated with the merchant simile, there are 'young ones' 'hatched', and so on. Neither Antony nor Cleopatra attains much stature; and such things as Antony's

> 'Tis time the world
> Should have a lord, and know whom to obey.
> We two have kept its homage in suspense,
> And bent the globe, on whose each side we trod,
> Till it was dinted inwards,

certainly do not increase it for him; while Cleopatra's

> Nature meant me
> A wife, a silly, harmless, household dove,
> Fond without art; and kind without deceit ...

merely softens the sentiment and makes Cleopatra an unconvincing mixture. It is an Antony that can say to the downright Ventidius, on receiving a gift sent by Cleopatra:

> What, to refuse her bracelet! On my soul,
> When I lie pensive in my tent alone,
> 'Twill pass the wakeful hours of winter nights,
> To tell these pretty beads upon my arm,
> To count for every one a soft embrace,
> A melting kiss at such and such a time ...

(*To Alexas, her messenger*)

> ... We soldiers are so awkward – help me tie it.

The neo-classic Unities of Time and Place are closely observed, and this further impedes the creation of anything like the sense of power and grandeur which heightens the tension and increases the significance of Shakespeare's play. The result is a talented but unconvincing treatment of these 'famous patterns of unlawful love' whose 'end accordingly was unfortunate'; and it is both impossible and, surely, pointless not to bring into blasting comparison that *Antony and Cleopatra* which it confessedly imitates.[2]

Clarity, ease, intelligibility are obviously present in a high degree in the passages quoted here, after the very earliest, and with them there is vigour and variety. These are features of his prose, too; and it is as a prose writer with these qualities that Dryden's genius has never been questioned – not even by Matthew Arnold, whose description of him, however, as a 'classic of our prose' had reference to his verse.[3] In his discussions of drama, heroic poetry, translation, satire, and other topics Dryden shows a seldom flagging interest in often strenuously detailed consideration of literary principles, techniques, examples; and the clearness of his exposition, the vivacity of his style, render surprisingly palatable discussions on matters of intrinsically little interest to the general reader of today; matters, too, which, although he was rightly distinguished by Johnson as 'the father of English criticism', are of some remoteness, as they stand, from the concerns of modern critics. They have an historically important and permanently refreshing freedom of judgement, a generous responsiveness (except in the niggling and patronizing *Defence of the Epilogue*), and an infectious zest. Historically, of course, they are most informative, not least the *Defence* just mentioned.[4] The *Essay of Dramatic Poesy* (1668) and the preface to the *Fables* (1700) are justly his most celebrated essays, the one discussing in dialogue form the main dramaturgic questions of the day, the other containing his tribute to Chaucer: quotation here, however, will be of passages from the *Dedication* of *The Spanish Friar* (1681) which show his characteristic easy free manner present in both a vivid expression of feelings towards a particular play and a lucid statement of principle:

But these false beauties of the stage are no more lasting than a rainbow; when the actor ceases to shine upon them, when he gilds them no longer with his reflection, they vanish in a twinkling. I have sometimes wondered, in the reading, what was become of those glaring colours which amazed me in *Bussy D'Amboys* upon the theatre; but when I had taken up what I supposed a fallen star, I found I had been cozened with a jelly; nothing but a cold, dull mass, which glittered no longer than it was shooting; a dwarfish thought, dressed up in gigantic words, repetition in abundance, looseness of expres-

sion, and gross hyperboles; the sense of one line expanded prodigiously into
ten; and, to sum up all, uncorrect English, and a hideous mingle of false poetry,
and true nonsense; or, at best, a scantling of wit, which lay gasping for life,
and groaning beneath a heap of rubbish ...

... as 'tis my interest to please my audience, so 'tis my ambition to be
read: that I am sure is the more lasting and the nobler design: for the propriety of thoughts and words, which are the hidden beauties of a play, are
but confusedly judged in the vehemence of action: all things are there beheld
as in a hasty motion, where the objects only glide before the eye and dis-
appear. The most discerning critic can judge no more of these silent graces in
the action than he who rides post through an unknown country can distinguish the situation of places, and the nature of the soil. The purity of phrase,
the clearness of conception and expression, the boldness maintained to
majesty, the significancy and sound of words, not strained into bombast, but
justly elevated; in short, those very words and thoughts, which cannot be
changed, but for the worse, must of necessity escape our transient view upon
the theatre; and yet without all this a play may take. For if either the story
move us, or the actor help the lameness of it with his performance, or now
and then a glittering beam of wit or passion strike through the obscurity of
the poem, any of these are sufficient to effect a present liking, but not to fix
a lasting admiration; for nothing but the truth can long continue; and time
is the surest judge of truth.

There is interest, too, in the verdict upon Chapman, and the terms
in which 'hidden beauties' and 'silent graces' are defined; and the
figurative language is typical in its neat, sufficient, illustrative quality,
and its accession of immediacy and expressiveness when, in the
'cozened with a jelly' sentence, his satiric humour is touched. The
looser articulation of the sentences, the disappearance of a strong
sense of Latin construction or vocabulary, the easier, more relaxed,
good-humoured, more conversational tone – these are the marks of
his prose; and it is from the loosening of structural habits derived
from the Latin and the incursion of ways of informal talk that Dryden's variety comes, and in them his modernity resides.

A writer, too, of comedies, of a life of Plutarch, a great translator
of Virgil,[5] Juvenal and others, Dryden was a professional man of
letters of rare versatility. Not surprisingly, much of his work has come
to be of only specialist interest; but at its best, in both verse and prose,
there is a completeness of expression, a feeling for language and a
sureness of technique, which any reader should find exhilarating and
educative.

NOTES

1. For a full treatment of this point, see *Men of Letters and the English Public in the XVIIIth Century, 1660–1744* (1948), by Alexandre Beljame, translated from the French by E. O. Lorimer and edited by Bonamy Dobrée.

For discussion of the intellectual background to Dryden's work, see L. I. Bredvold, *The Intellectual Milieu of John Dryden* (1934), and Basil Willey, *The Seventeenth-Century Background* (1934).

2. A higher opinion of *All for Love* is expressed in *Restoration Tragedy* (1930) by Bonamy Dobrée; from which F. R. Leavis dissents vigorously in '*Antony and Cleopatra* and *All for Love*', in *Scrutiny*, V (1936), 158ff.

3. For Arnold's views on Dryden, see 'The Study of Poetry' and 'Thomas Gray' in his *Essays in Criticism: Second series*.

4. A full discussion of Dryden's critical views will be found in the Introduction to *The Essays of John Dryden*, edited by W. P. Ker (1900). See also Barbara M. H. Strang, 'Dryden's Innovations in Critical Vocabulary', *Durham University Journal*, II (1959), and *A Glossary of John Dryden's Critical Terms*, by H. J. Jensen (Minneapolis, 1967).

5. See L. Proudfoot, *Dryden's 'Aeneid' and its Seventeenth-Century Predecessors* (1960).

RESTORATION COMEDY

P. A. W. COLLINS

> ... The stage but echoes back the public voice;
> The drama's laws the drama's patrons give,
> For we that live to please, must please to live.
>   (JOHNSON)

Of all literary forms, the drama is the most dependent upon and sensitive to its immediate audience. Shakespeare's achievement was born of a happy cross-fertilization between the man and the moment; such moments, like such men, occur perhaps only once in a nation's dramatic literature. English drama since then has been a poor thing. Restoration drama sparkles by comparison with the virtual nullity which followed it, but it is clearly inferior, in range and depth, to the Elizabethan. The course and causes of the deterioration of drama during the seventeenth century show the extent to which the individual talent is dependent upon the external forces of environment and tradition. Of course, like most ages, the Restoration could see gain rather than loss when it compared its life and literature with those of 'the last age'; the Elizabethans seemed 'barbarous' or 'Gothic' compared with 'our refined age'. The Restoration age was highly self-conscious, particularly about those social practices which distinguished it from pre-Commonwealth England, and Restoration comedy provided the main literary expression for this self-consciousness. A new form of comedy – later called the 'Comedy of Manners'[1] was evolved in response to these new habits and values. No such forces and convictions supported the tragedy of the age, and that is one reason why so little of it survives. For most readers, a sufficient sample of its heroics can be found in the 'tragic' plots of such tragicomedies as Dryden's *The Spanish Friar*, but the more serious student of Restoration culture should read and ponder more of the Heroic tragedies, remembering that the same audiences enjoyed these ridiculous displays of incredible loyalty and undying passion as applauded

Restoration comedy, with its very different ethos and conventions.

The tragedies reflect the sentimentality of cynicism: the comedies reflect the cynicism itself. Bishop Burnet remarked of Charles II that 'His private opinion of people was very odd. He thought no man sincere, nor woman honest, out of principle; but that whenever they proved so, humour or vanity was at the bottom of it.' Charles's love-life, wrote another contemporary, Halifax, manifested 'the effects of health and a good constitution, with as little mixture of the seraphic part as ever a man had'. Charles notoriously differed from his entourage rather in the scope than in the nature of his private activities, and as the most illustrious and one of the most assiduous of the drama's patrons he was not without influence on the drama. 'During the forty years that followed the Restoration, English literature, English culture was "upper-class" to an extent that it had never been before ...'[2] On the re-opening of the theatres in 1660, two companies, sometimes only one, sufficed for London, though the smaller Elizabethan London supported six. The tendency of the drama to appeal less generally, and more specifically to the Court, had been noticeable before 1642;[3] by the Restoration period, the audience had become much more limited and homogeneous than the Elizabethan. This audience prided itself on being critical, and certainly there was a good deal of discussion about dramatic theory among the readers, as well as the creators, of drama; but the taste of the audience was not nice, and least of all was this audience critical of itself. That the comic dramatists depicted this society without attempting to disturb its self-complacency aroused, of course, much protest at the time (Collier's famous attack, *A Short View of the Immorality and Profaneness of the English Stage*, 1698, was the most comprehensive and influential[4]), and many later critics have been equally scandalized. Macaulay's emphatic essay is well known; Leslie Stephen echoes him in saying that this is a comedy 'written by blackguards for blackguards'; Dr Johnson gives to this common attack on 'the wits of Charles' his usual weight and finality of phrasing:

> Themselves they studied, as they felt they writ;
> Intrigue was plot, obscenity was wit.
> Vice always found a sympathetic friend;
> They pleas'd their age, and did not aim to mend.
> (*Prologue spoken ... at Drury Lane*, 1747)

Some did 'aim to mend', Wycherley's attitude was ambiguous, and Dryden was unhappy with both the ethos and the form of current drama; but, as a professional, Dryden had to comply with popular taste, so he contrived his 'mechanical obscenities' and continued writing in the loose dramatic form inherited from the Elizabethans, though he could not believe in it himself. Similarly, Shadwell, another professional, began his career with protests against the bawdy and repartee so popular in the comedy, as in the life, of the period, but he soon succumbed to the pressure of the times, and provided the conventional characters, situations, dialogues, and attitudes. The authority of the social mode is apparent when we find Dryden assuming that repartee is 'the very soul of conversation', and Steele asserting that 'the chief qualification' of a dramatist is 'to be a very well-bred man'.

These professionals, Dryden (1631–1700) and Shadwell (?1642–92), wrote copiously (twenty-eight and seventeen plays respectively). They have generally, and rightly, been considered inferior to the Big Five of Restoration comedy – Sir George Etherege (?1634–?91), William Wycherley (1640–1716), William Congreve (1670–1729), Sir John Vanbrugh (1664–1726), and George Farquhar (1677–1707). Of these, only Farquhar was a professional, and he only intermittently; in his short life he produced seven plays. The others wrote only three or four original comedies apiece, and those when they were fairly young. They belonged by birth to at least the fringes of the society they depicted. Etherege and Wycherley wrote themselves into the inmost circle of Court wits; Dryden, Shadwell, and Congreve acknowledged in various Dedications the help they had received from enjoying the conversation of noble gentlemen. They knew the world they reproduced with such vividness; the world of their plays was not the 'Utopia of gallantry' which Lamb professed to find it, but a heightened version of contemporary life. (It was the Heroic drama, rather than the comedy, which presented an Utopia; as Evelyn's wife innocently wrote of Dryden's *The Conquest of Granada*, '... love is made so pure and valour so nice, that one would imagine it designed for an Utopia rather than our stage'.) The most common setting for these comedies was London (Shadwell and Farquhar provide notable exceptions, and it is worth noting that both 'gloried' in acknowledging Jonson as master), and the action was generally seen through the eyes of the Metropolitan wit, who was the hero. Commonly, the hero was a projection of the dramatist himself, who accepted the assumptions that the Countryman was a boor, the Puritan a hypocrite, and the Citizen the husband of a wife who might be tempted. The presence of the upper-class Wit – impoverished though he often was – at the centre of the comic action marked off Restoration comedy from its predecessors. Traditionally, comedy dealt with lower-class persons, and one of the limitations which the Restoration found in Elizabethan comedy was its poor showing in 'gentlemen'. Dryden complains that the Elizabethan dramatists' wit 'was not the wit of gentlemen'.

Nevertheless, it was from Elizabethan comedy that Restoration comedy derived.[5] Not from Shakespeare, for, like Jonson, the Restoration looked askance at his romantic comedy; but rather from the more realistic comedy of Jonson (the descriptive surnames for the characters remind us of him), and above all from Beaumont and Fletcher. Dryden noted in 1668 that they were more popular than the other Elizabethans:

... they understood and imitated the conversation of gentlemen much better; whose wild debaucheries, and quickness of wit in repartee, no poet before them could paint as they have done.

It was Fletcher, wrote Flecknoe four years before, who had introduced and popularized 'witty obscenity' in English drama. Their popularity is significant. A recent critic has said that their work 'indicates the collapse of a culture, an adult scheme is being broken up and replaced by adolescent intensities'.[6] This may, perhaps, suggest the central criticism of Restoration comedy: not only or chiefly, that it is limited in the social class it portrays, but that its attitudes towards experience are immature. The preoccupation with love (in both tragedy and comedy), the stress on sex-antagonism, the common conventions that marriage is a bore and love primarily or exclusively a physical appetite – all these are as typically immature attitudes as is the complementary love-idealism of Restoration tragedy. Here, perhaps, may be suggested a critical approach to the 'immorality' of Restoration comedy. Henry James, in a famous passage, asserted 'the perfect dependence of the "moral" sense of a work of art on the amount of felt life concerned in producing it'. The amount of life *felt* by Restoration dramatists was severely limited, and the feeling too often at the level of cliché. One important limitation is suggested by Wordsworth's remark on Dryden (it applies to his contemporaries), that his language becomes impassioned 'mostly upon unpleasing subjects, such as the follies, vices, and crimes' of men, and that he rarely succeeds in 'the amiable, the ennobling, or the intense passions'. An instance from a minor dramatist, one therefore largely dependent upon the common stock of contemporary achievement, may be illuminating. Colley Cibber (1671–1757) amazed audiences in 1696 with *Love's Last Shift*, a comedy in which the rakish hero is strikingly reclaimed by his faithful wife. Cibber absorbed enough from his contemporaries to give pungency to the speeches of the unregenerate Loveless, but the speeches of the faithful Amanda and the repentant Loveless are preposterously unconvincing.

Restoration comedy, then, has conspicuous limitations, the extent of which may be seen by a comparison with Elizabethan comedy. But, inside this limited range, certain situations and character-types are seen sharply and amusingly; the dramatists' keen interest in the social achievements and follies of their extraordinary society is communicated down the ages. If, for example, sex-antagonism and physical appetite are not the whole of love, they are important phases of it, and the Restoration dramatists had the honesty, or the nonchalance, to display these manifestations more adequately than many subsequent ages have done. Similarly, one may disagree with Dryden, that repartee is 'the very soul of conversation' but acknowledge that it can be an agreeable ingredient. If the 'wit' of the Restoration quickly palls (one sees with Keats, the 'lover of fine phrases', that to strike off fine passages is not enough), still this wit often has the element of truth and perception one may expect of an epigram, and certainly it is stage-effective. Indeed, the most conspicuous quality of Restoration comedy is the witty exchange of words, and one of the best books on this comedy has traced its rise, fullness, and decline in the handling of the most frequent participants in these exchanges – the 'gay couples' of heroes and heroines.[7] Wit and repartee were, of course, highly prized qualities in the 'conversation of gentlemen'; verbal cleverness and intellectual agility of this kind were comparative novelties in English social life, and if like most novelties they were overrated, they still remain attractive elements in the comedies which reproduce them. No comedies, however, rely entirely on wit-exhibitions. Dryden most approved 'the mixed way of comedy; that which is neither all wit, nor all humour, but the result of both'; and though it is convenient to adopt the scholars' categories of Comedy of 'Manners', of 'Humour', and of 'Intrigue', most plays contain elements of all three, partly because they had to please all sections of the audience – the Wits of the Pit, the ladies of the Boxes, and the servants and wenches of the Gallery.[8]

Every dramatist mixed these and other elements in varying proportions, but a glance at early Restoration comedy shows clearly that the strength lies in the witty scenes; contemporary dramatists realized this, and there is a steady increase in and refinement of this 'Manners' element. The early plays of Dryden and Etherege are a hotchpotch of gay-couple adventures, low farcical intrigues and humours, and romantic-heroic love-and-honour plots in verse, but the vitality clearly belongs to the gay couples, Etherege's Sir Frederick Frolick and Widow Rich in *The Comical Revenge* (1664), Dryden's Loveby and Constance, Celadon and Florimel, Wildblood and Jacintha, in his *Wild Gallant* (1663), *Secret Love* (1667) and *An Evening's Love* (1668).* The recent introduction of actresses on to the English stage contributed, of course, to the success and popularity of these sharp encounters between the sexes. One prominent element in Dryden's plays was the 'Proviso-Scene', in which hero and heroine bargained about the conditions under which each might contemplate matrimony; Dryden's success with these scenes established them as a stereotype, and they were much imitated and burlesqued, the bargaining of Congreve's Mirabel and Millamant being the most brilliant of the series. Dryden's gay couples begin from such premises as these:

FLORIMEL (a Maid of Honour): But this marriage is such a bugbear to me! much might be if we could invent but any way to make it easy.
CELADON (a Courtier): Some foolish people have made it uneasy by drawing the knot faster than they need; but we that are wiser will loosen it a little.

(Secret Love, or, The Maiden Queen, V, i)

The couple traverse some familiar grounds for marital discord:

* Plays are dated in this essay by their first production, not by publication.

Florimel hopes that Celadon may find 'marriage as good as wench-ing', if they are married, not into the damning titles of 'husband and wife', but 'by the more agreeable names of mistress and gallant' This, like Dryden's fuller examination of *Marriage à la Mode* (1672), is bright and shrewd rather than penetrating; the premises about human nature, and about the satisfactions and frustrations of marriage, are too narrow. One cannot, for instance, imagine any set of 'provisos' that would make marriage 'easy' enough to be endurable to persons of such shallow character and roving disposition as the quartette in *Marriage à la Mode*: nor can one agree with Professor Dobrée that there is 'health and sanity in every phrase' of that play. Professor Dobrée maintains that Restoration comedy expressed 'not licentiousness, but a deep curiosity, and a desire to try new ways of living'; but experiments at this level of understanding are not very significant. *Marriage à la Mode* is successful at the level of light comedy, and Dryden acquired considerable expertise in this kind, un-congenial though he personally found it. His *Sir Martin Mar-All* (1667), based on Molière, is one of the gayest farces of the period, if one ignores the nauseous subplot which Dryden added to the French original. (It is noteworthy that Restoration adaptations of Molière were always made both more coarse and more complicated than their originals.)

Marriage à la Mode is a 'mixed' play, of a kind which Dryden continued to write all his life; scenes from a half-length love-and-honour verse play are interspersed with scenes from a half-length comedy. Sometimes, as in *The Spanish Friar* (1680), the two plots are mechanically interdependent, but they remained two plays 'tacked together . . . for the pleasure of variety', and Dryden later admitted that it was 'an unnatural mingle', done to meet the audi-ence's 'Gothic' taste. 'This critical age', indeed, was like Polonius: 'he's for a jig, or a tale of bawdry, or he sleeps.' The popular demand for multiplicity of plot – one Elizabethan habit which survived new fashions and theories – was a bane of Restoration drama. Although most comic dramatists abandoned the mixture of verse and prose, it is rarely that any unity of impression is achieved. Often, as in Dickens, there is 'rotten architecture, but wonderful gargoyles'.[9] Wycherley and Congreve are extreme in retaining melodramatic plots in *Love in a Wood* and *The Double Dealer*, but most plays have at least three plots of various kinds, connected in so bewildering a way that one too often asks, as Granville-Barker does of *Love in a Wood*: 'How could an audience both be clever enough to understand the story, and stupid enough to be interested by it when they did?'[10]

Etherege, in his second play, *She Wou'd if She Cou'd* (1668), and his third and last, *The Man of Mode, or, Sir Fopling Flutter* (1676), does not err in this respect: they were, as contemporaries remarked, 'two talking plays without one plot'. Etherege drops the romantic elements present in *The Comical Revenge*, though in *She Wou'd* he retains some rough humour and farcical situations: he now concentrates on witty persiflage. He has learned to catch the atmosphere of his times, to 'shoot folly as it flies, And catch the manners living as they rise'. This is the 'modern way of writing' which he proclaims in the Prologue of his first play, and now refines. The heroines of *She Wou'd*, Ariana and Gatty, are an admirably high-spirited and witty pair (their first encounter with their partners in II, i is a delight), and, in Lady Cockwood, Etherege gives impetus to a character-type which became excessively familiar on the Restoration stage – the superannuated amorous lady, usually in love with the hero. (This type survives in Gilbert and Sullivan, and in the Pantomime Dame.[11]) In *The Man of Mode*, Etherege attains a unity of tone, by excluding plots and situations of discordant kind, and was thus credited with having written 'the pattern of genteel comedy'. The plot is slight; it concerns the amorous adventures of Dorimant, who is simultaneously casting off one mistress (his '*pis-aller*', or 'convenient'), seducing another, and courting a third. The diverting fop who provides the title has little part in this plot, and indeed first appears in Act III; he is in part a glorious sideshow, and in part a contrast to the hero. Dorimant is a credible, memorable, and highly disagreeable figure; one recalls Professor Krutch's remark that Restoration fine gentlemen 'were gentlemen in everything – except essentials'. But Dennis's *Defense of Sir Fopling Flutter* (1722) against such aspersions innocently reveals the temporary degradation of the chivalric ideal, by asking:

What indeed can any one mean, when he speaks of a fine gentleman, but one who is qualified in conversation, to please the best company of either sex?

Some of Dorimant's affections are nicely undermined by his witty Lady Harriet (his 'grave bows', for instance), and her rejoinder, when he declines to look foolish by paying unsuccessful court to her in public, is shrewd:

> When your love's grown strong enough to make you bear being laughed at, I'll give you leave to trouble me with it: till then, pray forbear, sir.
>
> (IV, i)

Harriet admirably justifies Dorimant's description of her – 'wild, witty, lovesome, beautiful, and young' (as in the excellent scene when she and the pleasant Young Bellair parody the conventional love-birds of the period), and she has the sense not to expect too much from Dorimant's promises of reformation. Yet, despite all the evidence of his faithlessness and 'ill-nature', she clearly regards him – and Etherege seems to intend us to share her view – as a desirable mate: the crucial criticisms of him have been left unsaid, or have been made by jealous, angry, or foolish characters (one might contrast Henry James's placing of the charming, but heartless, Gilbert Osmond in *Portrait of a Lady*). For Etherege, as John Palmer has written, 'there was form: and there was bad form. The whole duty of man was to find the one, and to eschew the other.' Etherege's insight and values are restricted; there is an emotional inadequacy which corresponds to the hardness of the surface and the mechanical quality of the polished witty dialogue. Yet there are suggestions of a delicacy and tenderness which are never made central in the fable or the dialogue: as in the often-quoted final speeches of Harriet, when she warns Dorimant that he must leave London to find her in

> ... a great rambling lone house, that looks as it were not inhabited, the family's so small; there you'll find my Mother, an old lame Aunt, and myself, Sir, perched up on chairs at a distance in a large parlour; sitting moping like three or four melancholy birds in a spacious vollary. Does not this stagger your resolution?

One recalls that Dryden thought Etherege 'the undoubted best author' of prose in English. This charming and imaginative vision remains peripheral, however: Etherege in general suffers (actually or by modish affectation) from emotional constipation.

By the time Etherege wrote his last play, Restoration comedy had its favourite character-types and situations. There were, of course, individual modifications of the pattern. Marriage remains a joke, but Vanbrugh and Farquhar see how bad a joke it can be; country remains a stock butt, though again Vanbrugh and Farquhar are less shy of it, less arrogantly Metropolitan; the rake-Heroes persist, until they are gradually ousted by Virtue and Sense after 1700, though Farquhar again produces an interesting variant, a warmer-hearted rip, belonging to that 'School of Good Intentions' which holds that 'a good heart will cover a multitude of sins'.[12] The similarities, however, are as striking as the divergencies; Congreve's *Way of the World*, commonly considered the finest of Restoration comedies, is also their quintessence, hardly an incident or character or dialogue being original. Congreve perfects the common mode, adding to it a nicety of feeling and phrasing. His main contemporaries are individual in their divergencies from the mode.

Shadwell is uneven; he aspired to a Jonsonian breadth and seriousness, but was easily deflected by need or whim. He is gaily bawdy in *Epsom-Wells* (1672), virtuously didactic in *Bury Fair* (1689); his *True Widow* (1678) has some amusing satire, and his *Squire of Alsatia* (1688) is a lively play, providing a vivid evocation of London's underworld, but ballasted with some well-meant discussions on the theory of education. Shadwell is not always the dullard his fame would suggest; his better plays are at least as worth reading as the lesser plays of his greater contemporaries, and, if his high Jonsonian ideal remained only an aspiration, at least his admiration for Jonson led him to explore social classes which his contemporaries ignored.

Vanbrugh's plays are an unsatisfactory mixture of personal gaiety, some conventional adultery and intrigue, and a persistent but inconclusive interest in two human plights – the unhappy marriage, and the penurious younger son of good family.[13] Vanbrugh was a dilettante in the drama: this is clear in the uneven quality of the dialogue and in the construction of his plays – none is satisfactory as a whole, except *The Confederacy* (1705), an adaptation from the French, though all contain good scenes and successful stage-characters. He lacked the power or the will to organize the materials he gathered or the ideas he started. In *The Relapse* (1696), the treatment of the marriage-theme is half-sentimental, half-realistic (or, as the Mermaid editor solemnly pronounces, 'Some very noble sentiments' and characters largely 'redeem ... whatever may be considered immoral in the

piece'); but Vanbrugh becomes more interested in the quite irrele-
vant sub-plot concerning Lord Foppington, the most finished and
reflective of fops. Vanbrugh is more interested in the unhappy
marriage of the Brutes in *The Provok'd Wife* (1697), he treats infidelity
farcically in *The Confederacy*, and his fragment *A Journey to London*
contains the most serious and convincing sketch of a marriage between incompatibles.

Farquhar perhaps derives from Vanbrugh his similar presentation
of the Sullens' unhappy marriage in his last and best play, *The Beaux'
Stratagem*: certainly, although fortified by a reading and rehash of
Milton's Divorce-pamphlets, he uses a Vanbrugh device for evading
the logic of the situation, by having the unhappy wife's seduction
by a lover fortunately, if accidentally, prevented by an interruption.
This play ends with an amusing anti-Proviso-Scene, in which the
Sullens at least agree with one another – to separate. But marriage is
not a main theme for Farquhar. His brief career is more varied than
the others'. He starts with high-spirited and morally incurious plays,
Love and a Bottle (1699) and *The Constant Couple* (1699); moved,
perhaps, by the Collier controversy, he moralizes ingenuously if
intermittently in *Sir Harry Wildair* (1701), and in *The Twin-Rivals*
(1703) writes moral melodrama. Finally, in *The Recruiting Officer*
(1706) and *The Beaux' Stratagem* (1707) he moves his scene from
London to the provinces, and presents convincingly and without
being patronizing sets of characters more varied in type and origin
than was usual. He is less self-consciously moral here (though he spoils
the end of *The Beaux' Stratagem* by the implausible and sentimental
confession of Aimwell); his heroes and heroines are good-natured,
'natural', and lively, rather than cynical, sophisticated, and brilliant,
or tearfully good. If these plays lack the nicer insights of Congreve
and the mordancy of Wycherley, they are more generously human
than theirs, and are the most attractive (as they were long among the
most popular) of Restoration comedies.

Wycherley is unmistakably the most individual of Restoration
dramatists. He impresses by the sheer vehemence of his language and
the energy of his characterization – the manifestations of a moral
passion which even made Collier acknowledge him 'an author of
good sense'. But this he certainly is not: he is too narrow and confused in his apprehension of moral issues. He satirizes the stock butts

of Restoration comedy – fops, lawyers, country-folk, the over-forties – but his distinctive gifts only appear when he can exercise his indignation against 'that heinous, and worst of women's crimes, hypocrisy'. His first play, *Love in a Wood* (1671), is a confused mixture of various stock situations and characters; the strength lies in the scenes involving the hypocritical Alderman Gripe and Lady Flippant. His second, *The Gentleman Dancing Master* (1672), does not engage his major talent. It is an amusing, if trivial, farce, and is characteristic of Wycherley only in its main fault – that of iteration. Here it is a joke, not a moral or a hatred, that is repeated and made over-obvious, but Wycherley never learned discretion or economy in dramatic projection. The lengthy asides which occur so implausibly and undramatically in all his plays are one sign of this unwillingness to leave anything to the audience's imagination, this inability to subsume into the fable and dialogue the full significance which he wishes to express. In his two next, and final, plays Wycherley finds himself: *The Country Wife* and *The Plain Dealer*[14] have a force, a bitterness and scorn unique in Restoration comedy. One can understand, if not fully share, the enthusiasm Dryden felt for 'the satire, strength, and wit of Manly Wycherley', who, in his *Plain Dealer*, had 'obliged all honest and virtuous men by one of the most bold, most general, and most useful satires which have ever been presented on the English theatre'.

Wycherley's dramatic talents are deployed best in *The Country Wife*; the characterization is assured, the dialogue incisive, and the management of situation (as in the 'china' scene, and the finale) masterly. The play has a theme, too, which gives it force and something approaching unity: the hypocrisy which underlies female 'honour'. The best scenes are those which expose the frailty and dishonesty of the ladies; but, beyond this, the moral scheme of the play is chaotic. Horner should perhaps be accepted as the almost impersonal assumption of the play, its means of providing a test-situation for female honour; certainly the play invites no judgement upon him – rather admiration for the audacity, ingenuity, and unashamed zest with which he satisfies his insanely omnivorous appetite for fornication. Conscious deceit, such as Horner practises on the husbands, is accepted, while the less self-aware hypocrisy of the ladies is derided. Similarly, Wycherley fails to focus the contrasts between the hypocritical 'honour' of Horner's victims and the true but fatuous honour of Alithea, and between Pinchwife's brutal jealousy and Sparkish's foolish superiority to jealousy. Wycherley, complained Pope, was 'always studying for antitheses'. The opening remarks of this play exhibit this well, and the trick of style is paralleled by the patterning of the play; and, in both style and pattern, there is something mechanical and ill-considered in Wycherley's grab at the half-truth.

The strengths and weaknesses of *The Country Wife* recur in exaggeration in *The Plain Dealer*. Again, the opening lines show Wycherley's energy, and his lack of control over it:

Enter Manly, surlily, Lord Plausible following him.

MANLY: Tell not me, my good Lord Plausible, of your decorums, supercilious forms, and slavish ceremonies! your little tricks, which you, the spaniels of the world, do daily over and over, for and to one another, not out of love or duty, but your servile fear.

LORD PLAUSIBLE: Nay, i'faith, i'faith, you are too passionate...

Indeed, Manly is too passionate, but it is only the tainted witnesses – Lord Plausible, Olivia, Freeman, and Novel – who say so. Wycherley is indulgent towards Manly: we need not look at his Dedication (signed 'The Plain Dealer'), or recall how the cognomen stuck to him, to realize how thoroughly he identifies himself with his naïvely and brutally 'honest' hero. (A profitable comparison can be made with D. H. Lawrence's treatment of his misanthropic hero Somers, in *Kangaroo*. Somers is largely a projection of Lawrence himself, but Lawrence makes the reader, and even sometimes Somers, see the elements of self-indulgence, subjectivity, and sheer folly in his 'diabolic' misanthropy.) There is some validity in both Manly's and Somers's violent rejection of their worlds; but the worth of Manly's criticism of life is impaired by the self-centred and adolescent quality of his splenetic contempt for social forms. 'Is railing satire?' Manly asks Novel. The question should have been asked of Manly and his creator, who both too obviously enjoy railing; they have an obsessed attraction towards the subjects on which they may exercise their verbal aggression.

'Since the *Plain-Dealer*'s Scenes of Manly Rage,' wrote Congreve, 'Not one has dar'd to lash this Crying Age.' Congreve – 'friendly Congreve, unreproachful man', as Gay called him – did not try to.

The Old Bachelor (1693), his first play, is like Wycherley's first, a medley, of unequal interest; the opening dialogue, however, suggests where his talent lies. *The Double Dealer* (1693) is a mixture of different, and more discordant, kind – of melodrama with romance and light comedy; but again Congreve shows his individual talents, his 'prodigious sense of human absurdity'[15] in Lady Plyant, and an uncommon tenderness and sensitivity in the love-scenes between Mellefont and Cynthia. Congreve's most popular comedy was *Love for Love* (1695), and it has justly remained a perennial stage-favourite. Even the minor characters have moments of dramatic life; they belong to familiar types, but are vivified and individualized by the excellence of dialogue which Congreve gives to them as well as to his Wits. The Nurse, for instance, replying to Angelica's playfully monstrous accusations about her relations with old Foresight:

> Marry Heav'n defend – I at midnight practices – O Lord, what's here to do? – I in unlawful doings with my Master's Worship – Why, did you ever hear the like now – Sir, did ever I do anything of your midnight concerns – but warm your bed, and tuck you up, and set the candle and your tobacco-box, and your urinal by you, and now and then rub the soles of your feet? – O Lord, I! –
>
> (I, iii)

Valentine's 'mad' speeches, if not the 'pure poetry' some assert, are an admirable artefact. Angelica is delightful, though she remains a 'riddle' to the audience as well as to Valentine, whom she urges –

> Never let us know one another better; for the pleasure of a Masquerade is done when we come to shew our faces.
>
> (IV, xx)

Perhaps Professor Dobrée is right in finding here and elsewhere in Congreve 'a strong element of wistfulness, ... a constant fear of disillusion'; perhaps it is merely the case that Congreve, like his fellow-dramatists, is unable fully to imagine and present, without sentimentality, a permanent affection or relationship.

The Way of the World (1700) was not, and has not proved, so successful a stage-piece, though it contains some of the best scenes and acting roles in Restoration comedy, even the severest critics of which have been charmed by Millamant. Actresses, from Mrs Bracegirdle in the first performance to Dame Edith Evans and Miss Pamela Brown in our day, have excelled themselves in portraying this mixture of gaiety, mockery, and genuine affection. As a contemporary critic said of a recent production, justice must be done to the quality of Congreve's dialogue, and he rightly criticized the Lady Wishfort of that production for failing to project with exactness the phrases given to her: 'Comic business is not enough here.' Congreve's phrasing is nice, often surprising: indeed, this strength is too consistently and exclusively exploited. He delights the style-fanciers, such as Hazlitt, but he works too much in terms of the fine phrase, the dazzling or more robustly amusing scene. This play, like his others, lacks coherence; the parts are more important than the whole. There is, in fact, no whole of any importance: the plot is intricate, but meaningless. Congreve has a sharp eye for certain situations – the gross self-deception of Lady Wishfort, the back-biting of Witwoud, the inability of Millamant, who loves Mirabel 'violently', to say more to his face than that she 'might by degrees dwindle into a wife', or the love that Mirabel feels for her:

... for I like her with all her faults; nay, like her for her faults. Her follies are so natural, or so artful, that they become her; and those affectations which in another woman would be odious, serve but to make her more agreeable.

(I, iii)

But Congreve's perceptions are not extensive; they remain the perceptions of a dramatist who abandoned the stage at the age of thirty, and whose primary inspiration was literary. Dr Johnson noted this of his first play, and it is true of his last. He answers to the description commonly given of Jane Austen, as the amusing but superficial observer of a superficial and restricted society: 'Miss Austen is only shrewd and observant,' said Charlotte Brontë. But Jane Austen is, as Virginia Woolf has remarked, 'mistress of much deeper emotion than appears on the surface'. Congreve sometimes has these depths of implication (Millamant's love is the best example), but he lacks the understanding of and concern for human values which make Jane Austen a major, while he remains a minor, writer.

'Congreve quitted the stage in disdain, and Comedy left it with him,' wrote Dennis in 1717. 'What plays! What wit!' wrote Byron a century later. '*Hélas!* Congreve and Vanbrugh are your only comedy. Our society is too insipid now for the like copy.' The best period of Restoration drama, as of Elizabethan, was brief:

the plays which followed, though informed by higher moral intentions, were dull, un-lifelike, fundamentally insincere (Steele's are the typical example). Byron's instinct was right: the strengths of Restoration comedy, like its weaknesses and limitations, were to a great extent dependent upon a particular social situation. No equally adequate dramatic form was discovered when Sense, and later Sensibility, joined and replaced Wit as the social ideal.

NOTES

1. On the meaning and evolution of this term, see F. W. Bateson's note in *Essays in Criticism*, I, 1, 90–3.

2. See L. C. Knights, 'Restoration Comedy: the Reality and the Myth', in *Explorations* (London, 1946). Contemporary reports of and rumours about the Court will be found in the *Diaries* of Pepys and Evelyn, *The Memoirs of Grammont*, and Bishop Burnet's *History of His Own Time* (abridged edition in the Everyman Series). See also John Harold Wilson, *The Court Wits of the Restoration* (Princeton, 1948), and Harold Wendell Smith, 'Nature, Correctness and Decorum', in *Scrutiny*, XVIII, 4 (1952).

3. See Alfred Harbage, *Cavalier Drama: An Historical and Critical Supplement to the Study of the Elizabethan and Restoration Stage* (New York, 1936), and Leslie Hotson, *The Commonwealth and Restoration Stage* (Harvard, 1928).

4. See J. W. Krutch, *Comedy and Conscience after the Restoration* (New York, 2nd edn, 1949), and extracts from Collier in *Critical Essays of the Seventeenth Century*, III, 253–91, ed. J. E. Spingarn (1908). Alexandre Beljame's *Men of Letters and the English Public in the Eighteenth Century, 1660–1744* (English translation, 1948) amasses a formidable amount of evidence of the 'immorality' complained of.

5. The contention that Restoration comedy owed anything substantial to French comedy has now been discredited; see, e.g., John Wilcox, *The Relation of Molière to Restoration Comedy* (New York, 1938).

6. John F. Danby, 'Beaumont and Fletcher: Jacobean Absolutists', in *Poets on Fortune's Hill* (1952), 165. See also John Harold Wilson, *The Influence of Beaumont and Fletcher on Restoration Comedy* (Ohio, 1928). Useful comments on the transition from Elizabethan to Restoration Comedy will also be found in Leslie Stephen's 'Massinger', in *Hours in a Library* (1892), II, 141–76; Kathleen M. Lynch, *The Social Mode of Restoration Comedy*, II–V (New York, 1926); Bonamy Dobrée, *Restoration Comedy*, IV (London, 1924).

7. See J. H. Smith, *The Gay Couple in Restoration Comedy* (Harvard, 1948).

8. See Clifford Leech, 'Restoration Drama: the Earlier Phase', in *Essays in Criticism*, I, 2 (Oxford, 1951), and George Farquhar, *Discourse upon Comedy* (1702), in *Critical Essays of the Eighteenth Century*, ed. W. H. Durham (Yale, 1915).

9. The likeness to Dickens is not accidental, nor the comparison unillumi-

nating: see R. C. Churchill, 'Dickens, Drama and Tradition', in *Scrutiny*, X, 4 (1942).

10. See his stimulating attack on Restoration drama, *On Dramatic Method*, IV (London, 1931).

11. Sir Arthur Quiller-Couch's essay on W. S. Gilbert, in *Studies in Literature: Third Series* (Cambridge, 1929), can usefully be read in relation to Restoration comedy.

12. F. W. Bateson, *English Comic Drama, 1700–1750* (London, 1929), 93: a useful introduction to this later period.

13. See Paul Muesche and Jeanette Fleisher, 'A Re-Valuation of Vanbrugh', in *P.M.L.A.*, XLIX (1934), 848–89.

14. Published 1675 and 1677, and probably first performed in 1673 and 1676 respectively. But the dates, and the order of compositions, are disputed; for a summary of the evidence, see xv–xxvii of the Introduction, by George C. Churchill, to his excellent Belles-Lettres Series edition of these two plays.

15. Virginia Woolf, 'Congreve's Comedies', in *The Moment, and other Essays* (London, 1947), 36.

LITERATURE AND SCIENCE

C. J. HORNE

Literature written after 1600 is markedly more modern in style and spirit than much that was written only a few years earlier. This modernity, as also a depression of the poetic imagination that went with it, is to be explained in part by the remarkable advance of science in the seventeenth century and the growing dominance of the scientific attitude throughout the eighteenth. The change in literature reflects that larger shift in thought which raised the seventeenth century as the frontier between the modern world and all the preceding ages. That probing of the physical world by sensory observation and experiment, by mathematical measurement and inductive reasoning, the process that we now shortly label as science, had been effectively established by the bold activities of men like Galileo the astronomer and Kepler the mathematician. This first eager age of science culminated in England in the work of Sir Isaac Newton (1642–1727), with his demonstration of the laws of gravitation and motion by which the planets move in their orderly courses.

These early achievements in science were not the work of specialists alone; they were, moreover, intelligible to most educated men and philosophical thought generally was soon involved with the new materialist view of the universe. The clear legal mind of Francis Bacon (1561–1626) promulgated the method of inductive reasoning, based on observation and experiment, and the versatile Frenchman Descartes (1596–1650) applied the same method to metaphysics in an attempt to prove the existence of God and the soul. The schism between science and traditional Christian humanism, a gulf so wide open in our own day, was for much of this period still capable of being bridged by men whose education fitted them to reconcile the new learning with the old. The revolutionary new branch of knowledge was still known as 'philosophy', or more specifically, 'natural philosophy', that part of the integrated discipline of all learning directed to the understanding of Nature.

There were, of course, big changes in the attitude to older beliefs. Without rejecting the Christian faith or the refinements of classical culture, these men broke finally with the authority of Aristotle and medieval Scholasticism, subjecting all beliefs and all knowledge to a rational examination based on the evidence of fact as supplied by the senses. For Galileo, Descartes, Hobbes, the only real truth was that discoverable by inductive and mathematical methods. On this view the universe appeared as a great machine and the principles on which it worked were taken as a demonstration of the ultimate rationality of creation; all was capable of explanation.

There were obvious advantages in the new attitude. A great burden of fear and superstition was lifted off the minds of men. Hobbes, it was justly claimed, had put 'Fancies, Ghosts, and every empty Shade' to shameful flight. Men had now more confidence in their own unaided and unrestricted intellect, and with increased understanding of the ways of Nature felt better able to control and dominate their environment; though some, it is equally true, felt that man's importance lessened when measured against the newly-discovered systems of Nature, so vast and intricate after the comfortably delimited Ptolemaic cosmogony and the macrocosm of older thought.

On the whole, however, self-confidence, eagerness about the world of wonders opened up before them, and a belief in human progress, now thought to be nearing a splendid culmination, were the predominant effects of scientific thought throughout the eighteenth century. Its upholders worked in a plain daylight world of fact and reason, and anything lurking in the shadows, too insubstantial to be snared by observation and dragged out into the light by rational processes, was derided and dismissed as fanciful. Conceptual thinking found an apparently solid basis in physical reality; the natural world seemed to provide an objective touchstone for speculation and hypothetical thought.

It was a climate unfavourable to religion and poetry. Bacon, Locke, and Newton, while wishing to preserve religion (though inevitably it was trimmed to natural theology and deism), had no use and little respect for poetry. Poetry, said Newton, is 'a kind of ingenious nonsense'; at the best it was a pleasing cheat, supplying 'pleasant pictures and agreeable visions', as Locke admitted without intending greatly to praise it. The imagination was distrusted and its value depreciated, an attitude reinforced by the disgust with zeal and enthusiasm that the religious disputes of the seventeenth century had provoked. From such disquiets the eighteenth century was thankful to have escaped. The effect on prose was salutary, forcing order and distinctness upon it and extending its usefulness as a medium both of common intercourse and learned discussion. Poetry, on the other hand, was circumscribed and poets were on probation. Strangeness, mystery, 'metaphysical' exuberance, were dropped, and the poet often fell into line with the prose writer as a sensible instructor who, though perhaps less reliable, could temper his instruction with pleasing adornments. At the same time it was not a bad thing that poetry had to take on a new precision and apply it in the study of man. A new and often rigid distinction between intellect and feeling, reason and imagination, fact and fiction, prevailed throughout the eighteenth century and it was more favourable to prose than to poetry.

The early history of the Royal Society of London for the Improving of Natural Knowledge illustrates the inclusiveness of the new philosophy. Beginning in Oxford in the middle of the seventeenth century as an informal association of like-minded individuals, the Society received public recognition with its royal charter in 1662 and became at once the centre for scientific studies. The first members were men of diverse talents and interests, but all united by the common bond of a classical education and an implicit acceptance of humanist culture, as much as by their interest in the new inquiries. They included, besides many dilettanti noblemen, persons as distinguished as the Honourable Robert Boyle, John Evelyn, Samuel Pepys, Sir William Petty, John Ray, and Christopher Wren. One of the first books issued with the support of the Society was Evelyn's *Sylva* (1664), an elegant and charming discourse on forestry. Along with his other writings on horticulture, it was designed for 'the benefit and diversion of gentlemen and persons of quality', who had throughout the century shown an increasingly practical interest in the arts of planting and gardening. There were poets in the Society too, notably Denham, Dryden, and Waller; and Cowley, the most admired of poets in his time, hastened on the Society's schemes with his *Proposition for the Advancement of Experimental Philosophy* in 1661, and honoured it with an Ode.

The Society was careful not to give any countenance to the atheistical tendencies of the new philosophy, and at first even tried to maintain a distinction between its own predilection for experimental science and the mechanistic philosophy of Descartes. For this reason Hobbes was kept out of the Society, and clergymen and bishops enrolled among its Fellows without any scruples of conscience. Its first History (1667) was, in fact, written by a future Bishop of Rochester, Thomas Sprat. His view, and it was fairly representative, was that this 'learned and inquisitive age' could move forward most freely in its pursuit of true knowledge by not attempting to meddle with the spiritual and supernatural part of Christianity. Instead, the Society would direct men's energies away from futile religious disputes to the fruitful inquiries of natural philosophy. Reason, after all, was the best support religion could have.

Sprat also gives us more distinctly than any other writer of the time the new attitude to literature. Poetry could be of no assistance in scientific inquiries; on the contrary, its deceitful fables, apt enough for primitive ages, must now be banished with the fairies. Poetry was commanded to cease its correspondence with the slavish passions and, in style, to retrench 'this abundance of Phrase, this trick of Metaphors, this volubility of Tongue'. Reason must be its rule, and science could supply it with better matter and imagery than the outworn lore of the Ancients.

With poetry, however, promoters of the new learning like Sprat were not much concerned. Prose was their instrument and they were early determined to discipline it for their needs. They required a clear and unequivocal instrument of expression, and to this end the Society set up a committee in 1664–5 to examine and 'improve' the English language. At a time when the vernacular prose had undergone a century of exuberant development, it was trimmed and redirected by these new demands and given a new importance in intellectual commerce by the decision of the Royal Society to make full use of their native English for recording their experiments and conclusions, matters that had previously been as often expressed in Latin, the international language of learning. Already in 1663, it was reported,[1] French scholars were learning English in their eagerness to read the scientific works of Boyle before the Latin translations were ready. Thus science was in some measure repaying the debt that England owed to French culture after the Restoration.

In this new prose no flourish was to be permitted to obscure reason and plain sense. The Society, therefore, to quote from Sprat, was most rigorous in applying the only remedy for past extravagances:

... and that has been, a constant Resolution, to reject all the amplifications, digressions, and swellings of style: to return back to the primitive purity, and shortness, when men deliver'd so many *things*, almost in an equal number of *words*. They have exacted from all their members, a close, naked, natural way of speaking; positive expressions; clear senses; a native easiness; bringing all things as near the Mathematical plainness, as they can: and preferring the language of Artizans, Countrymen, and Merchants, before that, of Wits, or Scholars.

(*History of the Royal Society*, 113)

The decision was not entirely novel; the plainer new prose had been maturing throughout the century and its seeds are to be found earlier in Bacon, Jonson, and Hobbes. Science, of course, was not the only influence shaping it, though it has been demonstrated that the prose of writers such as Joseph Glanvill and Abraham Cowley, and many of the preachers, changed markedly as they became more interested in the new science.[2] The style of Dryden, the master of Restoration prose, harmonized with the new requirements from the start, his clear-headed and calmly debated *Essay of Dramatic Poesy* (1667) appearing in the same year as Sprat's *History*, having been written even earlier. That individuality was not abolished along with 'the luxury and redundance of speech' is evidenced by the vigour of Dryden's prose. It reads like the distinguished and easy talk of a clear, independent, and inquisitive mind, sensitive to the tastes and prejudices of his audience, whose judgement he directs without dictation.

The most eminent of English scientists in this period before Newton was the Honourable Robert Boyle (1627–91). Recognized in his day as 'one of the Deepest and Most indefatigable searchers of Nature', he provides the most representative view of the accommodation at this time between the old thought and the new. A devout theologian and an eager scientist, he seemed quite unaware of any possible clash between Christian tenets and the mechanistic philosophy. Likewise, as a tireless experimenter and a creative thinker in science, he was 'the sceptical chymist' who demolished the lingering medieval belief in the four elements of earth, air, fire, and water, and the three principles of salt, sulphur, and mercury; and yet he was also a professed alchemist, clinging to a belief in the possibility of the transmutation of matter. In rejecting the vague theories of 'the hermetick Philosophers' and the Schoolmen he appealed for lucid expressions and factual arguments, even if in his own prose the aim to divert and recreate his readers as well as excite them was defeated by his wearisome manner. Though he aims, like Dryden, to write as a cultured man would talk, his style is hurried and careless, and his sentences rattle on without form or elegance.

The excitement that we miss in the prose of Dryden almost as much as in Boyle is to be found in Thomas Burnet's *Theory of the Earth* (1684–90), written first in Latin and then in English. Addison compared Burnet with Cicero for eloquence, and it is in the magnificently sonorous prose of an older generation that he presents his imaginative view of the earth as an awesome ruin. The methods of science are on this occasion employed to justify the older theology. In his travels Burnet had been startled by the Alps, 'those wild, vast and undigested heaps of stones and earth', and became convinced that Nature was in chaos. This he attributes to man's sin, and with an almost Miltonic cast of imagination unfolds his striking quasi-scientific explanations of the processes by which God's anger has wrought catastrophic changes in an originally smooth and perfect globe.

Burnet's prose remains something of a curiosity for this period, though affinities may perhaps be traced later in William Law and Edmund Burke. The main trend in style was otherwise. Clear statements and settled sentence forms, with a simple vocabulary (though more extensive in its simplicity than formerly), became the rule. English was at last provided with a plain, direct, and workaday prose that offered the right tools for writers so different in their trade as Defoe, Addison, Swift, and Goldsmith, in addition to all the host of lesser men who wanted to write clearly and correctly without aiming at literary distinction. It was not solely a literary gain; verbal communication was everywhere improved and extended.

Newton's *Philosophiae Naturalis Principia Mathematica* was published in 1687 and immediately put science in the top ranks of learning. John Locke's *Essay Concerning Human Understanding* followed in 1690 and applied the scientific method to the empirical study of the human mind, suggesting that mind is a form of matter, that human knowledge is strictly limited, and that knowledge comes initially only through the senses, innate ideas being an impossibility. Together, Newton and Locke were to dominate eighteenth-century thought and find their echo, often indistinctly, in much of the literature of the period. Newton was praised almost without exception.[3] Addison and Thomson were whole-hearted in their admiration of both the man and his discoveries. To Addison he was 'the Miracle of the present Age', and it was Addison who, in the popular homilies of *The Spectator*, gave the lead to a succession of popularizers of science in filtering the ideas of Newton and Locke for the understanding of an inquisitive public, insisting always on the wisdom and piety to be gathered from them. On Newton's death in 1727 Pope devised for his tomb in Westminster Abbey the witty epitaph:

> Nature, and Nature's Laws lay hid in Night.
> God said, *Let Newton be!* and All was *Light*.

Newton became for the eighteenth century its godlike sage and folk hero. As his fame increased he was lauded by a succession of poets in the heroic terms formerly reserved for epic warriors. Eighteenth-century poetry is littered with the failed attempts to write a Newtonian epic.

But that is not the whole story. During these same years at the opening of the eighteenth century a sharp and scornful challenge to the new science came from some of the men of letters. In part the objection arose from a distrust of the irreligious tendency of the modern philosophy, an attitude complicated by the eagerness with which the Puritans and Dissenters had taken up these studies and sought to impose them as a reform upon the Universities.[4] A conflict with religion was not, however, in England as distinct from France, the most serious issue in this period, partly because of the impeccable piety of men like Boyle and Newton, and even more because of the conviction with which the teaching of 'physico-theology' was received. Initiated in part by the Cambridge Platonists, this hybrid study was established mainly by John Ray (1627–1705), the greatest of English naturalists, in *The Wisdom of God Manifested in the Works of Creation* (1691) and was promulgated in the Boyle Lectures for 1713 by the Reverend William Derham (1657–1735). Ray's book was a serious and informed survey of scientific knowledge, often making original contributions, and in it he laid the foundations of all future biological studies (botany and zoology having hitherto lagged behind the physical sciences), thus preparing the ground for the work of eighteenth-century naturalists such as Gilbert White. Derham's published lectures were a more popular compendium. In vindicating and stimulating scientific inquiry, both Ray and Derham were concerned above all to provide through science a 'Demonstration of the *Being* and *Attributes* of an infinitely wise and powerful Creator',[5] who had not, as Burnet contended, given Nature over to the corruption of sin but still worked actively through 'some intelligent *plastick Nature*' to maintain his perfect design and purpose. The views of the physico-theologists happily suited the ordinary needs of the age and stilled much of the religious doubt that science was suggesting. They were commended, and their teaching promulgated even beyond the end of the century, by clergymen and moralists as diverse as Addison, Wesley, Johnson, and Paley.

More effective opposition to science in the first half of this period came from those wits and scholars who found much of the work of the Royal Society intellectually contemptible and culturally subversive. In an age much given to ridicule it provided a fertile subject for burlesque and satire. In the first place the virtuosi, or gentlemen scientists, were derided for triviality, pedantry, and lack of practical usefulness in their studies. Their self-regarding seriousness seemed grotesquely disproportionate to the mean and vulgar objects of some of their inquiries, 'useless experiments upon Flies, Maggots, Eels in Vinegar, and the Blue upon Plumbs', as Shadwell described them in his play *The Virtuoso* (1676). These were unusual subjects for learned study, and those who embraced them were marked down as gullible triflers and enemies of true learning. This was the attitude taken up by Samuel Butler in *The Elephant in the Moon*, and it recurs in the essays of Addison and Steele, and in the elaborate burlesques written by Dr William King, *The Transactioneer* (1700) and *Useful Transactions in Philosophy* (1709). These last probably provided some suggestions for the papers of the Scriblerus Club (1713), in which Swift, Arbuthnot, Pope, and a few others joined in their leisure hours to make fun of the excesses of the new learning. King may even have provided the suggestion for Swift's Academy of Lagado in *Gulliver's Travels*, where the author's disgust with many of the projects of the virtuosi culminates in that wild nightmare of ridicule. Several of Swift's works demonstrate how closely he had read many of the scientific writings of his day, and *Gulliver's Travels* is shot through and through with allusions to them. The technological benefits of science were slow in appearing, and it was Swift again who summed up a very general attitude about the apparent uselessness of scientific inquiry when he applauded the Brobdingnagians because with them the study of mathematics 'is wholly applied to what may be useful in Life; to the Improvement of Agriculture and all mechanical Arts; so that', Gulliver naïvely comments, 'among us it would be little esteemed'.

These men of letters, moreover, were perturbed by the way many scientists were misusing the English language. On the whole, the style of the *Philosophical Transactions* of the Royal Society in the eighteenth century was a poor return for the hopes Sprat had entertained when he wrote his manifesto. In attempting a factual plainness and conciseness, many writers had avoided the old sins of eloquence only to fall into the opposite errors of a stilted bareness, a conventional phraseology, and a low poverty of expression. The jargon of science was already proliferating and men of taste found it entirely disgusting.

It was in such matters that the rift between science and the humanities first openly appeared. Behind it all was something more than an itch for carping or the exuberance of a witty burlesque. Men educated in the older tradition of learning were genuinely repelled by the apparent aberrations of intellect and the pedantry of the times ('dullness' was their comprehensive term for it), and Pope's *Dunciad* is the greatest literary monument to their concern. In that poem, it may be recalled, the lesser breed of scientists, 'A tribe, with weeds and shells fantastic crown'd', find their dishonourable niche. The rejection of the complacent claims of the natural philosophers and their optimistic belief in human progress gave an urgent interest to the controversy about the comparative merits of Ancients and Moderns, set going in England by Sir William Temple's essay, *On Ancient and Modern Learning* (1690). The deeper extension of the contest is seen in the work of Swift and Pope when they seek to expose the pretensions of scientific optimism by making a rational study of the nature of man and recalling attention to the science of morality; for a science Locke claimed it to be, more exact than natural philosophy and more proper to mankind.[6] Pope's own philosophy in *An Essay on Man* (1733–4), half-baked as it may be, was a restatement of traditional concepts to harmonize with the Newtonian evidence for a rational and orderly universe. If that leads Pope to the glib deism of his *Universal Prayer* and the belief that 'Whatever is, is RIGHT, he also makes it a cause for rebuking the pride that man's new sense of his own importance has generated. Though in the 'Vast chain of Being' man is immeasurably raised above the lowest creatures now revealed by the microscope, he is still, Pope duly reminds him, infinitely below the wisdom and goodness of God.

It is ironical that Newton, himself so contemptuous of poetry, was the one scientist whose work the poets appropriated with delight and admiration. The reason is obvious. In an age when inner revelation (as necessary to poetry as to religion) was generally distrusted, it was some relief for poets to be able to turn to the physical evidence of God in Nature. Newton's revelation of a limitless but systematic universe, where God in Nature appeared by all the evidence the greatest of artists, gave a much needed stimulus to the repressed poetic imagination by providing poets with something vast and sublime to contemplate. In their response to Newtonian theory, eighteenth-century poets were unconsciously striving to fill the gap in the creative imagination left by the exhaustion of classical and Christian mythology. Newton became a quasi-mythological figure. In similar manner the prevalence of personification in eighteenth-century poetry may be explained as a less successful attempt to keep up some human warmth among the depersonalizing forces of science: Thomson's handling of Newton's theories frequently suggests that he imagined the natural elements as having a conscious will and purpose in performing their part in the great scheme of universal Nature. Furthermore, it was Newton's *Opticks* (1704) that helped to bring descriptive power back to English poetry by giving a new fascination to the play of light and colour in the landscape and a metaphysical interest in what has been called a 'symbolism of the spectrum'.[7] Description was added to moral and philosophical discourse in poetry, though the intention remained didactic rather than joyous surrender to the purely aesthetic delight of the natural world.

In this attempted rehabilitation of the imagination Addison once more gave the lead with his notable series of essays on 'The Pleasures of the Imagination' (1712) in *The Spectator* (Nos 411–21), and again his argument is a popular blend of Newton and Locke. Sight was regarded as the most important of the senses, the one to which all the discoveries of philosophy, or science, were due, and sight, Addison begins his discourse, is the 'Sense which furnishes the Imagination with its Ideas'. But when we read on, it is difficult not to be disappointed by the limited conception of imagination that he holds. It is no more than the awareness of visible objects, present or absent, along with the secondary ideas that they call up in the mind, and the whole argument is applied to show that Art is inferior to Nature, and the imagination limited and defective because on an empirical view it is inadequate to follow where Reason and the understanding lead. This is by no means the view of Francis Hutcheson in his *Inquiry concerning Beauty, Order, etc.* (1725), where he insists that the poet has a finer perception of the objects of natural beauty than the man of science; but Addison's is the more representative view for his age.

How closely Newton and the astronomers were read, how eagerly accepted, is apparent from the poetry of Blackmore, Thomson, Mallet, Young, Savage, Akenside, and others. All of them make interesting applications of Newton's theories and, missing the Miltonic sublimity at which in some measure they aim, fall back on grandiose invocations of divine glory and goodness, and admonitions to man to conform to the dictates of natural piety and reason. They failed to reconcile their two most admired geniuses, Milton and Newton. The modern view of creation could not be dressed in Miltonic style. They do however exhibit in varying degrees a new awareness of the beauty of Nature made manifest in light and colour. Akenside, a medical man, besides giving a blank-verse account of *The Pleasures of Imagination* (1744), wrote also a *Hymn to Science*; but of all these poets James Thomson (1700–48) was the most responsive to the advance of science. He had a good layman's knowledge of its findings, and the scientific matter which permeates his poetry was carefully brought up to date in successive revisions of *The Seasons*. The philosophy of Nature, so learnedly documented with encyclopedic thoroughness in his poetry, leads to a rosy and even complacent view of life, in which the beauty of Creation and the beneficence of the great Creator are seen as one harmonious whole. He is less than convincing in his pious attempt to locate the sources and sanctions of morality in a meaningful pattern of the universe. Nevertheless his was the influence that shaped all the subsequent scientific poetry, though the enduring effects were to be seen in the poetry of nature and description rather than in the grand philosophical endeavour to glorify the Wisdom of God in Creation.

The advance in scientific knowledge went on steadily during the remainder of the eighteenth century, with new discoveries about the nature of gases, the separation of the component elements of matter, experiments with electricity, and the introduction of the Linnaean system of classification in botany. None of these advances was as spectacular as the earlier discoveries in astronomy, so that the mental climate of the age was much less sharply affected by them. The effects were to be seen rather in a widening of the public interest in science and in technological improvements in industry. From Dyer's *The Fleece* (1757) onwards, the new machinery and industrial processes were celebrated in minor verse. Public lectures accompanied by scientific demonstrations were a favourite diversion of the time, the Lunar Society was founded at Birmingham in 1766, and though the Royal Society became less the workshop of science than a comfortable club, less distinguished bodies of enthusiasts founded Philosophical Societies in several provincial centres. While the number of popular compendiums of science multiplied, amateur activity shifted to the delighted observation of birds and flowers and insects. This enthusiasm for 'natural history' is reflected in the proliferation of nature images in poetry. The world of the naturalist became as wonderful as the remoter glory of the planetary systems.

Science subjects were given an important place in the curriculum of the Dissenting Academies, the most active educational institutions of the day. The two Universities were still apathetic and that partly explains the declining enthusiasm for the new discoveries among creative writers. They were, of course, interested. Dr Johnson intermittently carried out minor chemical experiments, and John Wesley studied the effects of electricity on the human body. Johnson in fact, as might be expected of such a polymath and devourer of knowledge, appears to have been acquainted with the whole range of scientific writings. His main concern, however, is with the relation of science to the total human complex and the perennial moral and spiritual issues.[8]

But writers were no longer excited by new prospects, and in *Rasselas* (1759) Johnson made a further assault on the optimistic view of human happiness that materialistic philosophies had encouraged. The increasingly cautious attitude was expressed by Joseph Priestley (1733–1804), the Unitarian minister and political philosopher, himself the discoverer of oxygen in 1774 and a notable writer on science, when he declared that 'a taste for science, pleasing and even honourable as it is, is not one of the highest passions of our nature, that the pleasures it furnishes are even but one degree above those of sense'.

The effects of scientific activity are to be observed in other ways, often less directly, in the later writers of the period. The sharpened powers of social observation in the novelists may be taken as one instance. More obviously the influence is reflected in vocabulary and imagery. A large number of technical and scientific words are recorded and precisely defined in Johnson's *Dictionary* (1755), and many of them, especially colour words, were finding a wider currency.[9] Johnson's style, in its diction, imagery, and analogies, reflects the matter of his scientific reading; its precision and concreteness are likewise consonant with scientific method. Gibbon records of himself that courses in anatomy and chemistry, together with a taste for books on natural history, contributed to the ideas and images in his *Decline and Fall of the Roman Empire* (1776–88). More crucially, Christopher Smart (1722–71), it has been claimed, 'was probably as well qualified in science as any poet before or since'.[10] Vying with the Psalmist in his paean of natural history that encompasses even such prosaic objects as the air pump, he extends the poetry of science into the lyric mode. At the same time he anticipates Blake in his reprobation of the Newtonian model of the universe as cold, mechanistic, and abstract. There is a similar if less intense revulsion from a hardening in the mechanistic view of the universe in the poetry of Cowper (1731–1800). As a palliative he exalts the restorative charm of natural objects as cherished by a gentleman amateur retired to the country.

The prevalence of stock poetic diction can, in the context of science, be explained as a mistaken attempt to provide for poetry a set vocabulary, as exact and appropriate as that used in scientific writings.[11] Dryden had early abandoned the attempt to employ correct technical terms for description in poetry, though the scientific images remained, as when he drew an analogy between the nature of tragedy and the laws of motion. Others, Pope and Thomson most importantly, tried to substitute more poetic equivalents for scientific jargon, stilted phrases like 'scaly breed' and 'feathered race' being in their day a novel method of designating the particular class of creature by characterizing it with a precisely descriptive epithet. It was a procedure significantly akin to the binominal system of classification that was being developed during the same period in natural history.

The scientific study of Nature had at first tended to lead poetry away from particular experience and individual insight into abstractions and generalizations. All knowledge is useful to a poet, says Johnson's Imlac in *Rasselas*, but, he continues:

> The business of a poet ... is to examine, not the individual, but the species; to remark general properties and large appearances. He does not number the streaks of the tulip, or describe the different shades in the verdure of the forest ...

Such a view, and it was prevalent, reflects in literature the overriding concern of eighteenth-century science with those universal laws in which can be comprehended all the diversity of individual phenomena.

The pleasing novelties of descriptive detail that we should expect from scientific observation are more often met with in the prose than in the poetry. This is notable in the travel books. Some of them are accounts of voyages undertaken, like those of Captain James Cook between 1768 and 1779, with a scientific purpose, others being records of tours in the homeland by such naturalists as Thomas Pennant (1726–98), who, as Johnson said, 'observes more things than anyone else does'. It was likewise the enthusiasm of field naturalists in the eighteenth century that nurtured the belief in the recuperating joys and interest of the English countryside and pointed the way to the intenser harmony between man and Nature in the Romantic poets. There is a more delightful description and a finer natural sensibility in the correspondence of Gray (1716–71), who was a keen botanist, than in his poetry, and before Wordsworth and Coleridge the most truly poetic response to the life of the plant and animal world is to be found in Gilbert White's *Natural History and Antiquities of Selborne* (1789).

The distinction of Romanticism at the end of the century, though for Blake it entailed the anathema of Bacon, Descartes, Locke, and Newton, was not its rejection of scientific knowledge but its full recovery of the sense of mystery and spirituality in Nature. Paradoxically, the way had been prepared by the practice of science. The absorbing observation and description of the external world had increasingly fostered a new aesthetic dimension in poetry. This and the unflagging emphasis throughout the period on the wonder of God in Creation had powerfully contributed to the ultimate resurgence of imagination. The Romantics transformed the philosophy of the five senses by the recovery of a sixth sense that transcended all, the creative imagination. That ended the dominance of the rational attitude so far as literature was concerned.

NOTES

1. By Henry Oldenburg in 'The Publisher to the Reader', prefaced to Boyle's *Experiments and Considerations Touching Colours* (1664)

2. See R. F. Jones, 'Science and English Prose Style in the Third Quarter of the Seventeenth Century', in *P.M.L.A.*, XLV(1930), 977 Joan Bennett, 'An Aspect of the Evolution of Seventeenth Century Prose', in *The Review of English Studies*, XVII (1941), 281–97.

3. The chief exception is Swift, who in addition to his contempt for mathematicians in general had a political prejudice against Newton.

4. When the Puritans came to power in the middle of the seventeenth century, they not only appointed experimental scientists to important posts in the universities but proposed to reform the universities by introducing the new sciences in place of the traditional studies as more conducive to 'the general good and benefit of mankind'. There was even a proposal to turn Christ Church into a scientific institute; which partly explains why that college became the centre of opposition to the new science. See further, R. F. Jones, 'The Background of the Attack on Science in the Age of Pope', in *Pope and His Contemporaries* (1949), ed. J. L. Clifford and L. A. Landa.

5. W. Derham, *Physico-Theology: or, A Demonstration of the Being and Attributes of God, from His Works of Creation*, 5th edn (1720), 3.

6. John Locke, *Essay concerning Human Understanding* (1690), IV, iii, 18, 26;

IV, xii, 10–11. Mathematics, he held, was the most exact science, and morality could be classed with mathematics 'among the sciences capable of demonstration'.

7. For a study of the effect of the *Opticks* on poetry, see Marjorie Hope Nicolson, *Newton Demands the Muse. Newton's 'Opticks' and the Eighteenth Century Poets* (1946). The distinction Miss Nicolson makes between the equation of colour with beauty, and light with sublimity, is disputed.

8. See R. B. Schwartz, *Samuel Johnson and the New Science*, 1971.

9. See A. D. Atkinson, 'Dr Johnson and Newton's " Opticks"', in *The Review of English Studies*, New Series, II (1951), 226–37; C. S. Emden, 'Dr Johnson and Imagery', in *R.E.S.*, New Series, I (1950), 30; and W. K. Wimsatt, *Philosophic Words: A Study of Style and Meaning in the 'Rambler' and 'Dictionary' of Samuel Johnson* (1948). Wimsatt traces the growth of scientific vocabulary from Bacon to Johnson and studies its effect on prose style. He demonstrates that Johnson collected specimens for his *Dictionary* from all the major scientific writers.

10. See D. J. Greene, 'Smart, Berkeley, the Scientists and the Poets. A Note on Eighteenth-Century Anti-Newtonianism', in *Journal of the History of Ideas*, XIV (1953), 327–52.

11. This attempt began as early as Sylvester's translation of Du Bartas (1592–9). See J. Arthos, *The Language of Natural Description in Eighteenth Century Poetry* (1949).

DEFOE AS NOVELIST

IAN WATT

Defoe was nearly sixty when his first novel, *Robinson Crusoe*, appeared in 1719. He had been well known to his contemporaries as a journalist and pamphleteer, however, long before he took overtly to fiction. The first work which brought him fame was *The True-Born Englishman* (1701), probably the most influential political verse satire in English after Dryden's *Absalom and Achitophel*. The poem defended William III against those who hated the idea that a Dutch king should govern 'trūe-born Englishmen'. Defoe retorted that there was no such thing:

> We have been Europe's sink, the jakes where she
> Voids all her offal outcast progeny.

Defoe, then, was no poet, although his rough vigour of expression cannot be denied. Elsewhere in the poem he handled the couplet better, as in:

> But English gratitude is always such
> To hate the hand which doth oblige too much,

and in the famous opening:

> Wherever God erects a house of prayer,
> The devil always builds a chapel there:
> And 'twill be found upon examination,
> The latter has the largest congregation.

Defoe used verse because that, since Dryden, was the favoured mode for public polemic; but earning literary glory was not his concern. Thus, in the Preface to *The True-Born Englishman*, Defoe anticipated critical objections with engaging jocularity:

Without being taken for a conjuror, I may venture to foretell, that I shall be cavilled at about my mean style, rough verse, and incorrect language, things I indeed might have taken more care in. But the book is printed; and though

I see some faults, it is too late to mend them. And this is all I think needful to say ...

Defoe could be cavalier because his main audience cared little for such niceties; they were not the cultivated patrons to whom so much of previous literature had been primarily addressed, but plain middle-class folk who constituted an important new force in the reading public, and were strongly asserting their independence, cultural as well as political. They felt, and Defoe agreed, that

> Fate has but small distinction set
> Betwixt the counter and the coronet,

and that the tastes of shopkeepers who worked behind the counter must also be served.

So if the great Augustans, Swift and Pope, sneered at Defoe as an outsider, he took little notice. With more than his share of the truculent self-reliance of the trading classes, Defoe was less an artist than a literary tradesman; and in a career that was as much devoted to business and politics as to literature, he produced over five hundred separate works, as well as a vast amount of journalism, including the whole of his thrice-weekly newspaper, *The Review*, which ran for nine years, from 1704 to 1713.

Defoe's novels – which are certainly the works that interest us most today – were among the greatest concessions he made to the tastes of the reading public. His own preference seems to have been for more factual and expository forms – for the political, economic, social, and moral improvement of his countrymen. As editor of *The Review*, however, he had learned that his readers often needed to be 'wheedled ... in to the knowledge of the world'; and, to 'carry out this honest cheat and bring people to read with delight', he had added to the usual fare of a newspaper a lighter section called 'Advice from the Scandalous Club' which dealt humorously with controversial aspects of the social life of the day. This feature was very popular and paved the way to *The Tatler*'s more polished presentation of similar matter; it also taught Defoe much about this side of the public's interests and gave him practice in catering to them.

In any case, Defoe was a professional writer, and always ready to supply whatever the printing press could use. Pope might attack what he called Grub Street and the Dunces that wrote for it; but Defoe saw Grub Street as merely an application of commercial principles to the manufacture of literary goods. As he wrote in a letter signed 'Anti-Pope', published in the popular *Applebee's Journal* in 1725:

> Writing, you know, Mr Applebee, is become a very considerable Branch of the English Commerce ... The Booksellers are the Master Manufacturers or Employers. The several Writers, Authors, Copyers, Sub-writers, and all other Operators with pen and Ink are the workmen employed by the said Master Manufacturers.

It was in the spirit of an 'operator with pen and ink' that Defoe turned to supplying the needs of the booksellers (or publishers as we should say now) for fiction. But, as in everything else he wrote, Defoe informed his fiction with so much of his own personality and outlook that it became something quite different from anything that the world had seen before: a form of prose narrative which, if not quite the novel in our sense, was in many respects much closer to it than what had been written before in English. It is, of course, highly appropriate that the rise of the novel – then regarded as a sub-literary form – should begin with a sub-literary figure like Defoe, a writer responsive to a wider reading public and largely independent of patronage and the critical standards of the literati.

Defoe's most important innovation in fiction was his unprecedentedly complete narrative realism. There is little doubt that it springs directly out of his long practice of journalism. Leslie Stephen long ago described[1] how his early pamphlet, the famous *A True Relation of the Apparition of one Mrs Veal, the next day after her death, to one Mrs Bargrave at Canterbury, the 8th of September, 1705,* contains all the hallmarks of Defoe's later narrative style, including 'the manufacturing of corroborative evidence' and the deflection of attention from weak links in the chain of evidence. Stephen thought that *The Apparition of Mrs Veal* was a work of fiction, but it has since been discovered that Defoe was merely reporting a popular news item of the day in his own characteristic manner. He was to use exactly the same technique when he came to write fiction, and even there we are never quite sure how much is pure invention. *Robinson Crusoe* itself was widely regarded as authentic at the time of publication, and it is still not certain to what extent some of Defoe's works, such as the *Memoirs of a Cavalier,* are fictitious or genuine.

It was certainly Defoe's overriding intention that readers should be gulled into thinking his fictions true. If he did not already know that the illusion of authenticity was his forte, he could have learned it from one of his journalist rivals who wrote in 1718 of 'the little art [Defoe] is truly master of, of forging a story, and imposing it on the world for truth'. Defoe never admitted that he wrote fiction; and it is typical of him that his greatest success, *Robinson Crusoe*, is prefaced with a statement by the 'Editor' that he 'believes the thing to be a just history of fact; neither is there any appearance of fiction in it'.

This claim to historical truth is false. For, although Defoe took a good deal from the accounts of Alexander Selkirk and other cast-aways, the story and the character of Robinson Crusoe are very largely of Defoe's invention. But the narrative is presented with so much circumstantial detail that the reader does not think of the book as fiction; and later generations have accorded it a semi-historical status.

Consider, for example, the way in which the famous finding of the green barley sprouts is told:

In the middle of all my labours it happened, that rummaging my things, I found a little bag, which, as I hinted before, had been filled with corn for the feeding of poultry, not for this voyage, but before, as I suppose, when the ship came from Lisbon. What little remainder of the corn had been in the bag was all devoured with the rats, and I saw nothing in the bag but husks and dust; and being willing to have the bag for some other use, I think it was to put powder in, when I divided it for fear of the lightning, or some such use, I shook the husks of corn out of it on one side of my fortification, under the rock. It was a little before the great rains, just now mentioned, that I threw this stuff away, taking no notice of anything, and not so much as remembering that I had thrown anything there; when, about a month after, or thereabout, I saw some few stalks of something green shooting out of the ground, which I fancied might be some plant I had not seen; but I was surprised, and perfectly astonished, when, after a little longer time, I saw about ten or twelve ears come out, which were perfect green barley of the same kind as our European, nay, as our English barley.

The main aim of the writing is clearly to keep as close as possible to the mind of the narrator as he struggles to make exactly what actually happened clear to himself and to us. Nothing but the exclusive pursuit of this aim, we feel, would have brought about such abrupt dislocations of rhythm and syntax as are found in the first sentence; no other reason could excuse the repetitions, the parentheses, the stumblings. The final result is that the little bag takes its place with all the other objects of Crusoe's life which have fastened themselves on our imaginations – the first clay pot, the climatically inept fur garments, the umbrella, the boat, the grindstone.

Defoe's style obeys more fully than ever before the purpose of language as his great contemporary John Locke redefined it: 'to convey knowledge of things'. Defoe concentrates his attention on the primary qualities of objects as Locke had defined them: especially solidity, extension, and number; and he presents them in the simplest language – Defoe's prose contains a higher percentage of words of Anglo-Saxon origin than that of any other well-known English writer except Bunyan. His sentences, it is true, are often long and rambling, but Defoe somehow makes this a part of his air of authenticity. The lack of strong pauses within the sentence gives his style an urgent, immediate, breathless quality; at the same time, his units of meaning are so small, and their relatedness is made so clear by frequent repetition and recapitulation, that he nevertheless gives the impression of perfect lucidity.

Defoe had been exposed to all the influences which were making prose more prosaic in the seventeenth century: to Locke's philosophy; to the Royal Society's wish for a language which would help its scientific and technological aims by keeping close to the speech of 'artisans, countrymen, and merchants'; and to the plain unadorned style of later seventeenth-century preaching which obtained its effects by repetition rather than by imagery or structural elaboration. Most important of all, Defoe's twenty years of journalism had taught him that it was impossible to be too explicit for the audience of 'honest meaning ignorant persons' which he kept continually in mind. As a result, Defoe's natural prose style is not only an admirable narrative vehicle in itself: it is also much closer to the vernacular of the ordinary person than any previous writer's, and thus admirably adapted to the tongues of Robinson Crusoe, Moll Flanders, and his other characters.

But the effect of the passage quoted is not just a question of clear description; there is also the effect of Defoe's emphatic pressure forcing us to accept the truth of his narrative. For instance, Crusoe seems to demonstrate his scrupulous care with the truth by admitting that he cannot be absolutely certain about some trivial details – when and where the bag had originally been filled with corn, or what he had actually wanted the bag for later. As readers we reflect that our memory has its little lapses too, and we think the better of Crusoe for frankly confessing his weakness. In this case Defoe is 'manufacturing' not so much the 'corroborative evidence' that Leslie Stephen spoke of, but the character of a corroborating witness whose fastidious concern for complete veracity authenticates every word he writes. And this particular reminder of the narrator's reliability, we notice, is strategically placed; for it deflects our attention from the weakest link in the chain of evidence – the fact that, as Crusoe admits, 'the climate ... was not proper for corn'.

We have been programmed by the way of writing to accept a miracle. The miracle itself reflects Defoe's religious background and his didactic intention. The Puritan tradition saw the whole world, and every incident of individual experience, as alive with secret indications of divine intervention or intention. Crusoe instinctively interprets his experience in this way; he looks for signs of Grace or Reprobation not only in the ears of corn, but in everything else that happens to him. *Robinson Crusoe* is not just – or even primarily – a travel story; it is also, in intention at least, one of what Defoe called his 'honest cheats', a sincere attempt to use fiction, a godless form of literature, to the purposes of religion and morality. Crusoe's story is supposed to demonstrate how God's Providence saves an outcast who by leaving his family and forgetting his religious training has sinned against the divine will out of a 'secret burning lust of ambition for great things'.

The book we know was called *The Life and Strange Surprising Adventures of Robinson Crusoe*. It was a phenomenal success, and to cash in on it Defoe wrote two continuations: *The Further Adventures*, and *The Serious Reflections of Robinson Crusoe*. In the latter Defoe repeats the moral and religious aim he had avowed earlier; his book 'is calculated for, and dedicated to, the improvement and instruction of mankind in the ways of virtue and piety, by representing the various circumstances to which mankind is exposed, and encouraging such as fall into ordinary or extraordinary casualties of life, how to work through difficulties with unwearied diligence and application, and look up to Providence for success'.

We tend to interpret *Robinson Crusoe* rather differently today; we are able to do so because Defoe's was a much secularized puritanism, and it relied more on 'unwearied diligence and application' than on faith. Defoe's heroes habitually seem to act on the assumption that it is prudent to keep your powder dry so that you won't have to put the imponderable effects of your trust in God to the test. Crusoe's religious ruminations are like bouts of benign malaria, easily shaken off; they indicate no organic spiritual change. Thus, as soon as Crusoe remembers that previously he had 'shook a bag of chicken's meat out in that place ...' his wonder ceases; and, as a result, he confesses that '... my religious thankfulness to God's Providence began to abate too, upon the discovering that all this was nothing but what was common'. The same operative primacy of non-religious considerations is evident in the book as a whole. For, of course, Crusoe is well rewarded for his sins: without them he would hardly have risen above the 'middle station of low life' to which he had been born, and become a wealthy merchant, plantation owner, slave trader, and colonizer.

If today we are sceptical about the book's religious significance, we see much else in it which was no part of Defoe's intention. We see Robinson Crusoe as the symbol of economic man,[2] who, by recapitulating on his island all the basic productive processes, provides the economists with their favourite example. We see him too as the very prototype of the empire builder, leaving a crowded homeland for the wide-open places where he establishes a little city in a tropical forest and converts the heathen. We may notice too that, just as economic individualism in general stands in the way of harmonious personal and social relations, so Crusoe's radical ego-centricity leads him to sell the Moorish boy Xury, who has saved his life, to the Portuguese trader for sixty pieces of silver, and later to treat Friday in the manner of a benevolent slave owner rather than in that of a friend. Defoe, it seems certain, was not conscious of the prophetic nature of his tale; but he had experienced the crucial social and economic processes of his time more fully and deeply than anyone, and, as an experienced reporter, without illusions, he revealed their effects on human behaviour and mental habits with unthinking fidelity.

Not that Defoe was unaware of the symbolic quality of Crusoe's experience. In the preface to the *Serious Reflections* he hints that the story is an allegory of his own life: and though this assertion is mainly an afterthought to defend himself against the critics who had charged that *Robinson Crusoe* was fiction, his plea has a certain essential truth. Defoe tends to identify himself with all his protagonists and most fully perhaps with Crusoe; his own life, too, had been one of solitary and heroic achievement against great odds. In an eloquent chapter, 'Of Solitude', which begins the *Serious Reflections*, Defoe converts Crusoe's island existence into an image of man's perpetual aloneness. This springs from his basic egocentricity:

> ... it seems to me that life in general is, or ought to be, but one universal act of solitude. Everything revolves in our minds by innumerable circular motions, all centering in ourselves ... we love, we hate, we covet, we enjoy, all in privacy and solitude.

Robinson Crusoe is one of the great myths of modern civilization; the story celebrates Western civilization's material triumphs and the strength of its rational will to conquer the environment: and it also prefigures the spiritual loneliness and social alienation which have accompanied its progress.

Some of this loneliness is itself a reflection of a force which did much to build modern civilization – Puritan individualism. The Puritans saw the activities of the world as a diversion from man's proper spiritual purpose, which was the scrutiny of his conscience for signs of his probable destiny in the divine plot of redemption and damnation. So Defoe makes Crusoe write in his *Serious Reflections*: 'It is the soul's being entangled by outward objects that interrupts its contemplation of divine objects'; and he concludes that 'the business is to get a retired soul'. This can be done anywhere, and so Crusoe affirms

> that I enjoy much more solitude in the middle of the greatest collection of mankind in the world, I mean, at London, while I am writing this, than ever I could say I enjoyed in eight and twenty years' confinement to a desolate island.

We must not underestimate Defoe's dissenting background. If he is not as serious as Bunyan, he has many of his qualities; if he does not convince us that considerations of piety are really the controlling factors in his stories, at least they are there, and their presence gives Defoe's novels a real, though problematic, moral dimension.

Indirectly, Puritanism also helped to develop Defoe's literary realism. Defoe shares its hatred of fiction, as he tells us in the *Serious*

Reflections: 'This supplying a story by invention is certainly a most scandalous crime, and yet very little regarded in that part.* It is a sort of lying that makes a great hole in the heart, at which by degrees a habit of lying enters in.' Pressure of circumstances led him to write novels: but one feels that, with a curious obliquity, Defoe resolved to make his lies as like truth as possible so that his scandalous crime would escape detection.

If Defoe's Puritan forebears need not have turned too often in their graves at *Robinson Crusoe*, their slumbers must have been more seriously incommoded by the major works of fiction which succeeded it. Their protagonists were not merely successful sinners, like Crusoe, but successful criminals, whores, and pirates. The best of these later works are probably *Moll Flanders* (1722), *Colonel Jack* (1722), and *The Fortunate Mistress* (1724), usually called *Roxana*; all three are closer to being novels than *Robinson Crusoe*, which is too little concerned with personal relationships and has too restricted an emotional scope. But all Defoe's other narratives are worth reading, especially *Captain Singleton* (1720) and *A Journal of the Plague Year* (1722), which are closer to the quasi-historical mode of *Robinson Crusoe*.

The earlier pages of *Colonel Jack* are perhaps Defoe's finest piece of writing; they have all his characteristically vivid reporting, his penetrating sociological understanding of the conditions which make children into criminals; and they also have an insight into the whole moral world of a young waif which he hardly equalled elsewhere. The final scenes of *Roxana* have a powerful dramatic interest unique in Defoe: the desperate expedients of the heroine to avoid discovery by the daughter she has abandoned have great psychological and narrative tension; they also – and this is rare in Defoe – embody the story's moral theme in the action; we see how Roxana's life of prostitution is exacting a terrible punishment on both mother and daughter.

But it is *Moll Flanders* which, at least since the praise of E. M. Forster and Virginia Woolf, has been generally accepted as the best of Defoe's novels.[3] It is richer in range of feeling than *Robinson Crusoe*; it is full of Defoe's best-written episodes; the heroine is per-

---

*'in that light', as we would say.

haps Defoe's most successful piece of portraiture; the theme is concerned, not with a fight against Nature, but with something more typical of the novel, the individual's struggle against society; and the plot, though rambling and confused, is based on a pattern of personal relationships which is finally rounded out with a degree of unity by the restoration of Moll to her husband and her son, and a final curtain closing on a peaceful old age of penitence and prosperity.

Much of *Moll Flanders* is concerned with plain reporting of the heroine's loves and larcenies, often brilliantly done in a narrative manner very similar to that in *Robinson Crusoe*. No novelist can succeed unless he is a good reporter, and there is a long and honourable tradition in the novel which makes the depiction of social reality its main aim. But there is more than this in *Moll Flanders* – much humour and drama, and some genuinely novelistic presentation of personal relations.

The humour is often of a blunt cockney variety, as when Robin quiets his sister who opposes his marriage with the penniless orphan Moll: 'Prithee, child, beauty's a portion, and good humour with it is a double portion; I wish thou hadst half her stock of both for thy portion.' And Moll adds: 'So there was her mouth stopped.' We also get more complex effects, sometimes ironical in their psychological point: as when Moll, having robbed a child, reflects that she had 'given the parents a just reproof for their negligence, in leaving the poor lamb to come home by itself, and it would teach them to take more care another time'; or when, giving her son a gold watch '... I desired he would now and then kiss it for my sake. I did not, indeed, tell him that I stole it from a gentlewoman's side at a meeting house in London. That's by the way.' There are also examples of a more polished wit that recalls Addison or Swift: Moll comments of her first lover, the elder brother, that 'though he had levity enough to do an ill-natured thing, yet had too much judgement of things to pay too dear for his pleasures'.

Moll Flanders has more conscious craftsmanship than *Robinson Crusoe*, and its orientation to the social and emotional world brings it much closer to the novel. The account of the first seduction and many of the episodes with the Lancashire husband combine vivid reporting with a command of character and emotion that foreshadow the later triumphs of the novel form. Such a scene occurs when, after a long absence, Moll Flanders is reunited with her Lancashire husband:

> He turned pale, and stood speechless, like one thunder-struck, and, not able to conquer the surprise, said no more but this, 'Let me sit down'; and sitting down by a table, he laid his elbow on the table, and leaning his head on his hand, fixed his eyes on the ground as one stupid. I cried so vehemently, on the other hand, that it was a good while ere I could speak any more; but after I had given some vent to my passion by tears, I repeated the same words, 'My dear, do you not know me?' At which he answered, 'Yes', and said no more a good while.

This passage, and a few others, have a supremely evocative quality; they show how powerful Defoe's narrative manner could be when focused on human feeling. But such passages are rare. Selected quotations normally give us a much more favourable opinion of Defoe than reading the whole work would; and *Moll Flanders* is no exception. Its pages contain a great deal of uninspired filling-in; and this is one reason for believing that Defoe's stature as a novelist has tended to be overestimated of late.

His central defect is a lack of serious order or design, a lack which is manifested, not only in the development of the story, but in the psychological and moral aspects of his work. What little narrative unity there is comes from the fact that it is Moll Flanders who is the chief character throughout; but this unity is largely submerged in an undiscriminating attempt to tell all that happened in a busy and eventful life.

The moral disunity of the work is even more striking. The purported moral does not tally with the plot. Defoe says in his preface that 'there is not a wicked action in any part of it, but is first or last rendered unhappy'; yet actually the heroine does not have to disgorge her ill-gotten gains, and they are the basis of her final prosperity. Even if Defoe had avoided this contradiction, the quality of his moral would have little to commend it, since it amounts to little more than telling the reader to look to his silver and be on his guard against pickpockets. The actual moral which emerges is even worse: the story suggests that honesty may not be the best policy, and that if you want to live in a genteel style, prudent and enterprising crime may prove more effective than plying your needle; you can always settle your spiritual account when the one at the bank has been taken care of.

This crassly material perspective is revealed in the moral reformation scene which occurs when Moll brings home to her husband all the wealth from her mother's plantation,

... the horses, hogs and cows, and other stores for our plantation; all which added to his surprise, and filled his heart with thankfulness; and from this time forward I believe he was as sincere a penitent and as thoroughly a re-formed man as ever God's goodness bought back from being a profligate, a highwayman, and a robber.

Reformation by cows and hogs. The book is indeed an example of 'mercantile morality that Defoe has apparently neglected to measure'.[4] So much so that many modern readers have assumed that the whole moral aspect of the book must be consciously ironical.

The psychological defects of the book are less obvious and could not be demonstrated without lengthy analysis. It can only be suggested, therefore, that Moll Flanders is not seen objectively by Defoe as a character in the round; like many of his characters, she is at times indistinguishable from her author, despite the various 'feminine' traits she is given, particularly in her first love-affair with the elder brother, and in her regular concern for genteel lodgings, clean linens, and the creature comforts of her males. But the autobiographical form, which Defoe always uses in his fiction, makes it particularly difficult for him not to identify himself with the heroine; it certainly makes it difficult for his picture of her to have much depth, since we do not know what the other characters think of Moll Flanders, and see her only as she sees herself. It is certainly suspicious that nearly all the other characters are shown treating her with adoring and selfless de-votion, whereas she is never completely honest with anyone. If we try to get deeper, and ask whether she or her author are aware of her duplicity, we find that Defoe has not told us enough of the relevant facts for an opinion to be possible. It seems that Defoe did not ask such questions himself, or conceive that his readers would. Defoe keeps us informed, as no other novelist does, of his heroine's holdings in cash and personal effects: he does not bother to make clear her emotional development, or to take stock of her real character.

Nor, apparently, does Defoe consider the nature of her personal relationships any more seriously. We are told nothing about most of her lovers or her children: it appears she had a dozen or so of each, but it is impossible to be sure, because most of them are treated very cursorily. She is properly maternal on being reunited with one son, Humphry, in Virginia; but what of the remaining seven children whose deaths have not been indicated? The answer is surely that all these are mentioned merely as items of realistic detail, and that after they have served that purpose Defoe does not give them another thought, and does not intend the reader to; we are certainly not meant to draw the conclusion that she is a heartless mother, nor, indeed, any conclusion, but only to forget as easily as she does. Everything in the narrative seems real, but most of it has no existence once it is off-stage: for Defoe, convincing the reader of the reality of the story is not only the means, but the end. There is no developing personality in Moll to be observed, no moral or psychological pattern to the loosely-strung-out network of personal relations. Defoe is too intent on getting away with the reality of his characters to try to get into them.

Defoe's forte as a writer is the brilliant episode. His imagination creates events and characters, and sets them solidly in their background; in that respect his narrative is much in advance of anything that fiction had seen before; but the novel as a literary form could be considered established only when realistic narrative was organized into a plot which, while retaining Defoe's lifelikeness, also had some intrinsic unity of development; when the novelist's eye was focused on character and personal relationships as essential elements of the continuity of the novel and not as incidental matter to be used in furthering the verisimilitude of the actions described; and when all these things were related to a unifying theme, a controlling intention. It was left to Richardson and Fielding to take these further steps.[5]

They did so, and very consciously. But now that later novelists have gone so much further than they did, and in so many ways, we tend to read Richardson and Fielding in the perspective of the novel tradition as a whole, and they may suffer in comparison. Defoe, on the other hand, does not really compete, and thus history has lent his artless veracity an adventitious charm: we rejoice to see a writer so innocently unaware of how novels are supposed to be written, and we are tempted to find irony and moral sophistication because we cannot credit that so remarkable a writer and so amazing a man could have produced so many contradictions in a spirit of genuine naïvety.

That, at least, is the main problem his novels pose for readers today.

It was not a problem for his contemporaries; and after his death, on 24 April 1731 the few belated obituaries concerned themselves with quite other aspects of his life: *Read's Weekly Journal*, for instance, wrote of 'Mr Defoe, Sen. [ior]' that 'He had a great natural Genius; and understood very well the Trade and Interest of this Kingdom ...'; no obituary mentioned the novels which were to make his name live.

NOTES

1. In his excellent essay, 'De Foe's Novels', in *Hours in a Library*, I (London, 1874).

2. See my '*Robinson Crusoe* as a Myth', in *Essays in Criticism*, I (Oxford, 1950), for a treatment of this aspect of the book.

3. Their judgements, and much else, are conveniently available in the Norton Critical Edition, *Moll Flanders: An Authoritative Text, Backgrounds and Sources*, ed. Edward Kelly (New York, 1973).

4. See Mark Schorer's Introduction to *Moll Flanders* in the Modern Library College Edition, Random House (New York, 1950).

5. See my *The Rise of the Novel: Studies in Defoe, Richardson and Fielding* (London , 1957). Its interpretation of *Robinson Crusoe* and *Moll Flanders* has been challenged by many, perhaps most, subsequent critics. On the economic interpretation of *Robinson Crusoe*, see especially Maximilian E. Novak, *Economics and the Fiction of Daniel Defoe* (Berkeley and Los Angeles, 1962). Sixty or so contributions to the debate about *Moll Flanders* are discussed in C. J. H. O'Brien, *Moll Among the Critics* (Armidale, N.S.W., 1979). George A. Starr, *Defoe and Spiritual Autobiography* (Princeton, 1965), and J. Paul Hunter, *The Reluctant Pilgrim* (Baltimore, 1966) have made important contributions to our understanding of the religious aspect of Defoe's fiction. The coherence and subtlety of Defoe's art have found many defenders; one notable recent study is John J. Richetti, *Defoe's Narratives, Situations and Structures* (Oxford, 1975). A recent, comprehensive, and balanced critical assessment, as well as a very attractive and reliable account of the life, is provided in James Sutherland, *Daniel Defoe: A Critical Study* (Cambridge, Mass., 1971). Pat Rogers, *Robinson Crusoe* (London, 1979) gives – among much else in the way of reliable historical and literary introduction – an up-to-date and acute analysis of the economic and religious interpretations of *Robinson Crusoe*.

LANGUAGE 1660–1784

A. S. COLLINS

The development of the English language in the period from Dryden to Johnson inevitably harmonized very closely with that of the literature and ideas of the age. When men desired stability in politics and society, they advocated stability in language. Since correctness and elegance became the ideals in literature, words and their usage had to be submitted to the same criteria. Order and harmony in life and thought must be reflected in the clear and graceful structure and cadence of sentences. The good breeding of a gentleman was impossible without well-bred speech free from affectation, pedantry, rusticity, and crudeness. As both the upper and professional classes and the growing mercantile middle class became increasingly conscious that material prosperity was a prime ideal to be pursued, language was required to be primarily useful, a clear, easy, precise means of communication. Science too demanded direct, unelaborate expression. The expanding journalism of newspapers and periodicals likewise favoured an easy, but dignified, use of words. The coffee-houses of Dryden's and Addison's days put English to a refining conversational schooling whereby Dryden's Prefaces and the *Spectator* papers could be entertainingly discussed. As women helped to swell the numbers of the reading public, authors kept their books freer from 'hard' words. The new literary form, the novel, called for a good central English to attract the general reader. In fact, the English language from Dryden's day through the eighteenth century developed steadily away from the rich individual freedom and variety of the earlier seventeenth century, with its licence, excess, obscurity, and crudity, until it became an instrument fully adapted to the needs of a broad-based society which valued, above all, order, discipline, good manners, common sense, prosperity, and a comfortable ease of communication. Probably in no other period in our history has English been so well written in the middle manner by all ranks of society, even in the diaries and letters of the least literary.

From about 1660 there gradually developed a conscious anxiety about the stability of the language and a sense of the need both to reform it and fix it. If the language could not be rendered stable, then modern poets would in their turn become as hard to read as was Chaucer with his then obsolete English, which justified Dryden, as he declared in the Preface to his *Fables* in 1700, in presenting Chaucer in a modern version despite the protests of such as held there was 'a veneration due to his old language'. What could arrest such change? How could a standard of correctness be attained and enforced? How could the vocabulary be pruned of the undesirable excesses which for many years had been entering it by borrowings, adaptations, and coinages from foreign sources and from the jargon of political and religious fanatics of the Commonwealth era? For half a century it seemed to many that the answer lay in the setting up of an Academy on the model of the several Italian Academies and of the French Academy, which had been founded in 1635. Dryden in his Dedication to *The Rival Ladies* in 1604 wrote: 'I am sorry, that (speaking so noble a language as we do) we have not a more certain measure of it, as they have in France, where they have an Academy erected for the purpose.' In the same year Dryden was a member of a small committee set up by the recently founded Royal Society to consider means 'for improving the English language'. The committee met only a few times and nothing resulted, but the idea remained in Dryden's mind. Roscommon thought similarly. An Academy was one of the proposals in Defoe's *Essay upon Projects* in 1697. In 1712 Swift addressed to Harley, the Tory Lord Treasurer, the last notable plea for an Academy in *A Proposal for Correcting, Improving and Ascertaining* (i.e. fixing) *the English Tongue*, but whatever prospects lay in his powerful advocacy were ruined no doubt by the collapse of the Tories in 1714. Sir Robert Walpole was not the man to spend good public money on an Academy.

That the idea of an Academy failed to take shape was due to various factors. For one thing, an Academy with any real authority over the language hardly seems a natural institution to grow in the soil of that practical, common-sense, and individualistic age, even though that age exalted the virtues of order and correctness. It was natural enough for an Academy to be advocated by Dryden, who was something of a literary dictator, by Defoe, whose bent was for planning, and by Swift, a dictator at heart, but one may well imagine that to most of the Augustans the answer lay in common-sense efforts by all who were concerned for the well-being of the language and the future of literature. That, at any rate, was how the reform of the language was largely achieved. From many quarters came the plea for 'correctness', for easy, direct, and perspicuous communication of meaning. Sprat in his *History of the Royal Society* (1667), while himself strongly in favour of an Academy ('such a project is now seasonable to be set on foot, and may make a great reformation in the manner of our speaking and writing'), told how the Royal Society was already doing its utmost to reform the writing of English by exacting

from all their members, a close, naked, natural way of speaking; positive expressions; clear sense; a native easiness; bringing all things as near the Mathematical plainness, as they can: and preferring the language of Artizans, Countrymen, and Merchants, before that of Wits, or Scholars.

In the schools Locke's earnest plea, in *Some Thoughts Concerning Education* (1693), for the exercising of children in English must have encouraged a better attention to the task in the following generation and have helped to lay a sound foundation: his book was steadily reprinted. And Locke further declared that

whatever foreign languages a young man meddles with (and the more he knows the better), that which he should critically study, and labour to get a facility, clearness, and elegancy to express himself in, should be his own, and to this purpose he should daily be exercised in it.

Dryden was influential not only by what he said about good writing in Prefaces, and surely in Will's coffee-house, but by the contagious example of all he wrote. Addison too preached good English by the very success of his own style, and no doubt orally too to his 'little senate'. Swift by example and precept taught that good style was no more and no less than 'proper words in proper places'.

Reference, however, to lesser rather than major writers perhaps conveys best how the campaign for a reformed English was fought and won. One such was John Hughes, who in 1698 wrote an essay, *Of Style*, at the request of a friend whose 'inquiry seems more particularly concerning the language'. Hughes therefore spoke mainly of prose style 'as being that which is most necessary'. Summing up all the qualities of a good style in Propriety, Perspicuity, Elegance, and Cadence, he recommended to his friend as

the best direction ... a diligent and careful perusal of the most correct writers of the language in their various kinds, with the conversation of people of fashion, that speak well and without affectation. The most correct writers that I know are Sir William Temple, Dr Sprat, and Dr Tillotson for prose, and Mr Waller for verse.

His friend must consider that for purity of language 'the rule ... is modern use'. Formal rules Hughes did not favour, especially for writing letters and essays; rules there must be, but his friend should furnish himself with rules deduced from the example of correct writers. Thus those who took the advice of a man like Hughes and were influenced too by the leading writers of the day, went a long way towards achieving a reformed English without the help of an Academy. Chesterfield, writing to his son in 1749, still spoke with contempt of his countrymen for not studying their language as carefully as the Italians and French studied theirs ('Witness their respective academies and dictionaries, for improving and fixing their languages'), but in urging the lad to 'make [him]self a pure and elegant English style' he admitted 'it requires nothing but application'. So, indeed, experience was proving that an Academy was unnecessary, and Dr Johnson in his Preface to his *Dictionary* (1755) went further, declaring such an institution un-English. The English in fact now turned to dictionaries and grammars as the best way of advancing that reform of the language which had already gone far, and the idea of fixing the language was generally given up. Johnson held that the inevitable mutability of language evidenced by history could be stopped neither by dictionaries nor by academies.

But before discussing dictionaries and grammars it is necessary to say something more of the Augustan vocabulary, and particularly of the 'poetic diction' which often comes between the Augustan poets and the modern reader, though rarely in the best poems. Gray remarked in a letter to his friend West in 1742 that 'the language of the age is never the language of poetry', and it was a view generally held, but the kind of language used by the poets depended largely on the kind of poem to be written. In satire the poet could and often did keep to the simplest language of everyday use: a scribbler 'at his dirty work again', 'pride that licks the dust', the soul that 'sits at squat, and peeps not from its hole', the 'painted child of dirt that stinks and stings' – for such themes Pope used the most direct vernacular. But as epic, pastoral, and ode were different in 'kind', and the Augustans were convinced of the virtue of observing difference of literary 'kind', a different poetic vocabulary was considered necessary for them. Pope remarked in the Preface to his *Homer*:

> To throw the language more out of prose, Homer seems to have affected the compound-epithets. This was a sort of composition peculiarly proper to poetry, not only as it heightened the diction, but as it assisted and filled the numbers with greater sound and pomp, and likewise conduced in some measure to thicken the images.

Similarly, when attempting themes epical or of high seriousness or the loftier lyric, the Augustans sought 'to throw the language more out of prose' by a special vocabulary to which a study of Virgil and Milton contributed much. In this kind of diction Dryden, a close student of the Latin poets and of Milton, led the way; Pope brought it to perfection in his translation of Homer, and then it became for many years the normal diction of the average serious poet. Hence arose such Latinisms as the constantly used *purple* in the sense bright, and *horrid* as rough, *gelid, mellifluous, turgent, irriguous, concoctive, diffusive* (view), *protended* (spear), *ovarious* (food). Thomson's *The Seasons* is full of such words, though he could often be simplicity itself: indeed, the contrasts jostle oddly, as in his description of a stag-hunt, where we read of the huntsmen 'adhesive to the track', while of the stag he writes simply 'the big round tears run down his dappled face'. The more ordinary or utilitarian the subject, the more needful the poet generally felt it to avoid the prosaic word at which his sophisticated readers might laugh. So Dyer in his *The Fleece* may let his sheep 'with busy mouths ... scoop white turnips', but he quickly changes the vulgar turnip to 'the watery juices of the bossy root'. Poetry indeed stood on its dignity when it could not on its inspiration. Cowper, very capable of simple English, felt still that the tobacco in a woodman's pipe required dignifying as 'the fragrant charge of a short tube that fumes beneath his nose'. Such efforts may to us seem verging on parody, but they were in part due to fear of the Augustan parodists to whom the natural often appealed as the ridiculous.

What perhaps particularly offends the modern reader is the constant use in Augustan poetry of terms like 'the feather'd choir', 'the wingy swarm', 'the finny tribe', 'our fleecy wealth', and 'the foodful brine'. Yet they had the merit often of being both precise and concise, and they came into existence for that end, carrying normally a fuller meaning than superficial reading detects. Thus 'feather'd choir' was not merely an evasion of 'birds' but a semi-scientific statement that these particular singers were birds, and 'fleecy wealth' conveys at once the physical and economic with verbal thrift. Moreover, this use of language harmonized with the Augustan belief in generalization, which Johnson famously expressed in *Rasselas*, where it is laid down that 'the business of the poet is to examine, not the individual, but the species: to remark general properties and large appearances'.

It was an attitude to poetry which appealed to and sprang from the eighteenth-century's love of order and its desire for intellectual clarity, and from this pursuit of the abstract and generalized idea there followed naturally two other characteristics, the constant use of certain 'poetic' words and of personification. The stock of poetic words and phrases included *gales*, which commonly *blow*, *vales* often *verdant*, *train* perhaps *glittering*, *swain* and *nymph*, *lawn*, *azure main*, *tender tears*, *melt* ('pity melts the eyes'), *smiling* (land), *blooming*, *genial*, *frantic*, *solemn hour*. The list could be a long one. Many of these words – for example, *gale, blow*, and *swain* – were, by virtue of their long vowels, especially useful for rhymes, but on the whole the significance of this choice of certain words in preference to many others available lies in their general nature. *Gales* are merely the air in movement, *vales* a broadly conceived aspect of landscape. Formal epithets like *smiling* or *solemn*, *verdant* or *azure*, with 'decent' grace supported the generalization. It was all Propriety, conforming to the now established tradition of the reformed and refined language, which, as Johnson said, had been transformed from brick to marble. Similarly, personification was a 'decent', but rarely successful, attempt to give animation to the marble of the abstract nouns with which eighteenth-century verse was inevitably overladen. Partly following Milton's example, it was as near as the Augustans generally felt justified in approaching concrete treatment of ideas. For them it was vivid enough to conceive 'Youth at the prow and Pleasure at the helm'.

Poetic diction also favoured compound adjectives. Homer, as Pope said, showed the example, and so did Milton. Welsted in *A Disser-*

tation Concerning the Perfection of the English Language, the State of Poetry, &c. (1724) considered one virtue of English to be 'that it is capable of finely compounding the words often times, like the Greek'. Hence came such compounds as Gray's *'rosy-bosomed Hours'* and *'incense-breathing* morn'. Outside his *Homer*, Pope hardly used them at all, but Thompson in *The Seasons* made free use of them, often agreeably – *blood-happy* hounds, *romp-loving* miss, *lovely-shining* leopard, and *thick-nibbling* sheep are typical instances. Adjectives ending in *-y* also became prolific in the poetic language. This suffix had, from the earliest stages of the language, been of the greatest use, and Elizabethans had used such words as *paly* and *steepy*, but with the Augustans the use and coinage of such adjectives became monotonous, partly for the value of the extra syllable, partly for poetic elevation and for conciseness. So, in addition to such favourites as *plumy, wingy, finny, gloomy, dewy, balmy*, there occur everywhere such formations as *spiry, stenchy, sleeky, lawny*, and *brooky*. *Downy* could apply to snowflakes, fleece, or even an orchard, such was the virtue of its typical lack of definition. Then, too, there were the Spenserian words. Earlier the imitation was deliberately humorous. *Ween, wight, mickle, perdie, withouten*, participles like *y-covered* and infinitives like *grieven* were an amusing colouring. A later Spenserian like Thomas Warton with his *paynim, orison, besprent*, and *emprise* was quite serious. In between, Thomson in *The Castle of Indolence*, truest Spenserian poem of the century, both smiled and worshipped as he used words like *replevy, swink*, and *bedight*.

The prose of this period invites less detailed comment. As in the poetry, a limitation of vocabulary was exercised. In the long run the general tendency was towards greater formality, as can be seen in the passage from the easy conversational style of Dryden to the balance and dignity of Johnson. As the aristocratic supremacy in life and letters of the Restoration period yielded to the middle class in the next century, the language naturally conformed to the change. The colloquial and easy, as well as the coarse, were avoided for fear of being 'low'. The free sparkling wit of Restoration drama was not to the taste of the later audiences who were addicts of the genteel sentimental drama; they might let Goldsmith and Sheridan laugh at their taste, but those dramatists had to observe greater propriety of speech than Wycherley and Congreve. A sense of literary 'kinds' was

felt in prose too, though with less force. Thus No. 25 of the
Guardian (1713) declared an historian's 'style must be majestic and
grave, as well as simple and unaffected; his narrative should be animated, short, and clear, so as even to outrun the impatience of the
reader, if possible. This can only be done by being very sparing and
choice in words' – a remark followed by disapproval of Bacon's style
in his *Henry VII*, for Bacon 'lived in an age wherein chaste and correct writing was not in fashion'. Hughes, similarly, in *Of Style*, held
Philosophy to require a grave style, while Morality and Divinity
'were capable of all the ornaments of Wit and Fancy' and History 'is
content with a plainer dress'. Probably the novel exercised the
strongest levelling influence on the prose vocabulary. Richardson's
middle-class sense of what was decent and suitable to be read especially by women reinforced the example of Addison's essays for
women. Fielding had Eton and the Classics behind him, but a wider
and less educated public to win. Smollett, ex-naval surgeon and prolific hack writer, employed a broad average vocabulary. All the
novelists indeed, Sterne excepted, in their different ways kept to the
middle kind of English, avoiding affectation and pedantry. Moreover, it should be remembered that the institution of circulating
libraries dates from 1740.

On the whole, the eighteenth century soon became satisfied with
the current state of English. Welsted in his *Dissertation* claims that English has reached 'the Perfection, which denominates a Classical Age':

[having] trafficked with every country for the enriching of it, we have laid
aside all our harsh antique words and retained only those of good sound and
energy; the most beautiful polish is at length given to our tongue and its
Teutonic rust quite worn away.

The time for extensive 'trafficking' had certainly passed. The foreign
language that continued to contribute most to English was French,
but even in the Restoration period, though there was a fashion for
using French words in conversation and in plays, the number of
French words that were adopted into English was not large. They
include *ballet, nom-de-plume, group, tableau, champagne*, and *reservoir*,
and in *envoy, aide-de-camp*, and *commandant* successors to military
terms like *dragoon, platoon*, and *brigade* borrowed before 1640. Military terms indeed continued to come in during Marlborough's campaigns, and Addison in No. 165 of *The Spectator* mocked at the

'modish' use of such 'modern military eloquence' as *gens d'armes, corps de reserve, carte blanche,* and *cartel,* and wondered whether 'superintendents of our language' were not required to prevent the entry of foreign, and especially French, words. *Enfilade, bivouac,* and *corps,* however, entered in Queen Anne's reign, and there was a trickle of French words throughout the century, increasing slightly at the French Revolution. Among these were *envelope, salon, bureau, canteen, roulette, connoisseur, coterie, glacier, chenille,* and words of cooking and social life, such as *casserole, croquette, picnic, etiquette, sangfroid,* and *gauche.*

In fact, the process of borrowing was now limited to taking a few words belonging to the arts or sciences or describing special things. Thus from Italian in the later seventeenth century came the architectural terms *dado* and *rotunda,* the musical *sonata, solo, spinet,* and *vivace,* and the artistic *mezzotint, cartoon, caricatura,* and *chiaroscuro,* and these were followed in the eighteenth century by *colonnade, arcade,* and *loggia, soprano, trombone, pianoforte, cantata, oratorio, libretto, adagio,* and similar terms, and by *picturesque, portfolio,* and *dilettante,* together with *malaria, influenza, lava,* and *bronze, conversazione* and *alfresco, poplin,* and the word *firm* for a trading company. Many a country indeed throughout this period made a small contribution through the medium of trade and travel books. Of such were *vanilla, caramel, cigar,* and *quadrille* from Spanish, *verandah* from Portuguese India, *shawl* and *carboy* from Persian, *albatross* and *candy* from Arabic, *mongoose, bungalow,* and *shampoo* from India, *mammoth* and *knout* from Russian, and from China *tea* itself, together with *pekoe, hyson, souchong,* and *ketchup* and *kaolin.* From nearer home came Scandinavian *to run the gauntlet, cosy,* and *muggy,* and the old terms *saga* and *skald,* the High German *cobalt, shale, quartz,* and *iceberg,* the Dutch *smuggle, schooner,* and *Geneva* (shortened to *gin* in 1714), the Irish *Tory* and *banshee,* and the Scotch *whisky, pibroch,* and *claymore.* Latin, not so long before a prolific source, now contributed only a few words, including *pendulum, nebula, fulcrum,* and *calculus* before 1700, and *nucleus, propaganda, ultimatum,* and *insomnia* later, while the Greek contribution was smaller still, as with *botany* (1696) and *bathos* (1727). Of all such borrowings the foreign origin is generally clear enough at sight, except for such words from Germanic languages as *smuggle* and *muggy,* but all borrowings quickly received an English pronunciation, and one may note that even foreign personal names were anglicized as in a rhyme like that of *Racine* with *line*.

But, if, with Welsted, satisfaction could be felt about the language itself, there was a growing realization that the use of the English language left much to be desired. There was often uncertainty about the correct meaning of words, and spelling, pronunciation, and grammar were all subject to variation according to the class and education of the writer or speaker. Hence arose the work of lexicographers and grammarians. The former were much concerned to register the correct spelling, and some dictionaries, such as J.K's *A New English Dictionary* (1702) and Dyche's *Spelling Dictionary* of a little later date, made that their principal aim. Nathaniel Bailey advanced further with his *Universal Etymological English Dictionary* (1721), which went into several editions and was recommended by Mrs Western in *Tom Jones* as the book to consult in order to learn 'a proper use of words'. Bailey was the first lexicographer to aim at including all English words.

But there was still no authoritative dictionary in existence when Johnson issued his Plan in 1747, and when his *Dictionary* itself appeared in 1755 his achievement was considered, as indeed it was, prodigious. He aimed to include all good English words, excluding only technical or vulgar words, though he did admit many scientific words, particularly medical and botanical, and in respect of learned words his scope was too wide, for he gave many such words as *cynegeticks* ('the art of hunting'), *enubilate, favillous,* and *geoponical.* Some words he allowed in only with a warning, such as 'a cant word' (*fiddlefaddle*) or 'an old word' (*gim* = neat). Above all, he sought to fix the meaning or meanings of words, and to this end he added illustrative quotations ranging forward from Sir Philip Sidney. Each word, where possible, was provided with an etymology, and though many of his etymologies are even absurd in the light of modern philological studies, Johnson did make good use of the growing work of Anglo-Saxon scholars. Further, one of his aims was, of course, to fix the spelling, for, though spelling had largely been stabilized by 1660 by the efforts of the printers, a standard authority was still desirable: here Johnson tended to be conservative. Of giving pronunciation Johnson fought shy, holding that there existed such variations even among good speakers that it was impossible to indicate more than the accentuation of words – which he did. Not that accentuation was without its variations still (in 1721 Isaac Watts had printed a list of words differently accented by differently educated speakers), but Johnson felt more scope for his authoritative verdict in that matter. And, the tendency running by 1780 strongly in favour of authority, in that year Thomas Sheridan, father of the dramatist, in his *Complete Dictionary of the English Language* ventured beyond Johnson in laying down the pronunciation too.

The grammarians especially yielded to the growing temptation to impose order. Apart from the eighteenth century's desire for uniformity in language as in society, the utilitarian middle-class order of the day increasingly justified it, for, as men of trade and commerce made themselves more prosperous, they felt it essential that their children should live up to their rising social position. Their sons particularly, but their wives and daughters too, must speak and write genteelly and not betray themselves by vulgarisms of grammar. One of the earliest grammarians was the scholarly John Wallis, a founder of the Royal Society, with his *Grammatica Linguae Anglicanae* in 1653, but it was not till after 1700 that the attempt began to be made to teach English grammar, and then not in the grammar schools, which kept to Latin, but in the Dissenting academies and private schools. Locke was a pioneer in advocating the teaching of English grammar. He declared in 1693:

> It will be matter of wonder why young gentlemen are forced to learn the grammars of foreign and dead languages, and are never once told of the grammar of their own tongues: they do not so much as know there is any such thing, much less is it made their business to be instructed in it. A gentleman ought to study grammar amongst the other helps of speaking well … since the want of propriety and grammatical exactness is thought very misbecoming one of that rank, and usually draws on one guilty of such faults the censure of having had a lower breeding and worse company than suits with his quality.

Soon, largely from such motives of class distinction and from that of business success, the task was undertaken. In 1700 a schoolmaster called Lane wrote a grammar under the title, *A Key to the Art of Letters*; in 1711 John Brightland produced *A Grammar of the English Tongue* and James Greenwood *An Essay Towards a Practical English*

Grammar; in 1721 Isaac Watts, the hymn-writer, published his *Art of Reading and Writing English*. There were others, and Johnson prefaced his *Dictionary* with a brief grammar.

From the beginning a problem which faced the grammarians was whether the rules of English grammar were deducible from good current usage, or whether there was a grammatical absolute ('according to the unalterable rules of right reason', as Lane declared). Wallis had based his grammar on the study of good usage. Locke believed that good grammar was the usage of good writers and speakers. We have noted the dislike by Hughes of rules for writing in general. Dr Johnson, in the matter of language as a whole, as witness in particular his attitude on pronunciation, favoured usage rather than rule; indeed his treatment of syntax in his grammatical preface was almost contemptuous – 'our language has so little inflection or variety of terminations that its construction neither requires nor admits rules'.

But other grammarians favoured rule above usage, and, worse still, in contempt of the quite different nature of the English language, they sought to force English grammar into the mould of Latin grammar. For rule there undoubtedly was a case, for, whereas an aristocrat could speak confidently in the assurance of his breeding, the new middle class would be happier if safeguarded by a grammarian's rule. For the assimilation to Latin grammar the schoolmasters were largely responsible. Locke had asserted, 'I know not why any one should waste his time and beat his head about the Latin grammar, who does not intend to be a critic, or make speeches and write despatches in it', but in this freedom of view he was not followed, and it was not unnatural that, when it was thought desirable to teach children English grammar, the drill book for that exercise should be as close as possible to the Latin. Moreover, schoolmasters, then at any rate, were lovers of rule, and so it was on the side of grammatical logic and of rule as against custom, idiom, and variety, of a Latin formalism as against English freedom that this period ended. Nor should it be forgotten that the historical study of the English language had not yet proceeded far enough to influence the grammarians of whom we are speaking, so that they worked in a real ignorance of the true nature and principles of the language they were presuming to formalize and 'correct'.

As late as 1761 Joseph Priestley, the scientist, still kept an open mind on the question of custom and use versus rule, and indeed favoured practice, for he held 'the general prevailing custom ... the only standard for the time that it prevails'. But in 1762 Robert Lowth, later Bishop of London, came out definitely on the side of logical 'correctness' as against practice, and his *English Grammar* was very influential. Lowth employed the method of giving examples of wrong usage in order to inculcate the 'correct', and, to him, even such writers as Addison and Pope were guilty of incorrectness. From about this time, in fact, the grammarians came forth as lawgivers, claiming to decide all questions of doubtful usage and giving their verdicts in favour of a neat and logical uniformity. Lindley Murray's *English Grammar* of 1795 followed Lowth's example, and it achieved such pre-eminence with its repeated editions that the victory for formal rules was won for a century. *It is me, you was, who did you meet, these sort of, I object to him coming*, double negatives, a plural verb with a collective subject, a singular verb with a double subject, superlatives like *perfectest*, preterites as past participles as in *An Elegy Wrote in a Country Churchyard* – such idiomatic usages and anomalies were to be no more, though they had been common in the practice of some of the best eighteenth-century authors. The rules for the correct use of *shall* and *will* were laid down. Murray, who wrote his grammar for a Quaker girls' school at York, included in it exercises in parsing as well as in correction of all kinds of errors. So far had 'the teaching of English' advanced in the course of the eighteenth century.

But it is time to consider the sounds of the spoken language. Our vowel sounds, which had undergone in the fifteenth century the great shift by which Modern English is mainly differentiated from Middle English, had by the first half of the seventeenth century approximately reached those of today. But, as is immensely noticeable from the rhymes of the poets, there were some important differences between the pronunciation of Dryden and Pope and our own. Thus we find Pope rhyming *speak* and *take* and Lady Winchilsea rhyming *day* and *tea*. Here, while present-day English has the same vowel sound in *take* and *day*, the sound commonly spelt *ee* has replaced the earlier sound represented by *ea*. In the early eighteenth century it would seem that the sound common to these three types of word (*speak, take, day*) was a long front vowel (slack, or more probably tense *e*) which was developing towards the diphthong now heard in *fate* and *day*. That the same sound is not heard now in words like *speak* indicates that a different development replaced that responsible for the long tense *e* in such eighteenth-century rhymes. This modern *ee* sound had clearly been developed in some areas by Elizabethan days, for Spenser could rhyme *stream* with *seem*. What happened was that gradually the speech of those who pronounced *ea* words with the sound represented by *ee* replaced in the standard speech the regularly developed long tense *e*. Pope could use either type (he also rhymes *seat* and *fleet*); by Johnson's time most words with *ea* were pronounced with the present-day *ee* sound. Again, there is the difference indicated by the frequent occurrence of such a rhyme as *line* with *join*. Here, too, one sound (that in *line*) had not quite reached the present-day stage, and the other has been replaced by a different sound from that of its normal development – modern dialect pronunciations like *bile* for *boil* show what the regular development would have been. Cowley, Dryden, Swift, and Pope readily illustrate this kind of rhyme. The stage at which these sounds rhymed in this period was that of a diphthong of which the first element was the sound in the modern *but* and the second short *i*: the first element was later retracted to give the present-day sound, but the words in which the sound was represented by the spelling *oi* gradually came to be pronounced as their spelling was considered to indicate, a process accomplished by 1800. This influence of spelling upon pronunciation grew only too rapidly with the growth of education from print.

Other differences of pronunciation revealed by the rhymes of poets include those arising from the shortening of long vowels. At least as late as the middle of the eighteenth century there existed a good deal of variety in pronunciation among the good speakers and it was often possible to use a long or a short vowel. This is particularly noticeable in words containing the vowel spelt *oo*. Dryden, for instance, rhymes *food, blood*, and *wood*. Here each word contained in Middle English a long tense *o*, which was raised to the present-day sound in *food* in the fifteenth century: our sound in *blood* is due to an early shortening, and that in *wood* to a later one, but certainly until 1700 no one type of pronunciation had become received standard – indeed, by some good speakers *soot* was pronounced with the vowel in *but* as late as 1900. Again, when Dryden rhymes *great* and *yet*, and Pope *beat* (as past participle) with *set*, we see that words with the long vowel spelt *ea* could also be pronounced with the vowel shortened. In addition, there were many variants which have since been levelled out, but which are all regular developments of certain linguistic tendencies. Thus the rhyme of *Rome* with *doom* found as late as Collins, those of *God* with *road* and with *unawed* by Pope, Dryden's *sense* with *prince* and *lost* with *boast*, and the rhyming of *have* with words like *crave* and *wave* by many poets are only a few examples of pronunciations which had full historical justification. It should indeed be taken as a general rule that the rhymes of the poets of this period represent pronunciations both genuine and linguistically explicable as variants naturally persisting in a time when a received standard was still far from being as fixed as it is today.

Many other details deserve mention. Everyone knows the fashionable *obleege* of Pope's day, aping the French pronunciation, and the ousting of the regularly developed *sarmon*, etc., by our *sermon*, partly perhaps as being nearer the French but chiefly from the influence of the spelling. Here it must suffice to state the general truth that in pronunciation, as in all the other aspects of language, this period was characterized by a steady approach to uniformity. Invaluable guides to the sounds of the period, in addition to the rhymes of the poets, are books like the *Practical Phonography* (1701) of John Jones which attempted to describe current pronunciation, and, most important perhaps of all, collections of letters and documents like the *Verney Memoirs*, covering 1639–96, and the *Wentworth Papers*, covering 1705–39, in which the writers often spelt words as they spoke them and not according to the conventional spelling fixed by printers, which was often remote from the writer's own speech. From such evidence it is clear that, well into the eighteenth century, these people spoke their sounds as they had developed on the lips of their forebears and not as teachers or print would prescribe. The difference in the treatment of vowels in unaccented positions is striking: *ow* in words like *narrow* was normally pronounced *er*; *fortune* was *fortin* and *picture* was *pikter* (even the scholarly Gray rhymes *venture* with *enter*); *value* and *nephew* were *valy* and *nevy*. Consonants too were treated with disrespect to the spelling: thus Jones in his book of 1701 lists *neglect*, *strict*, *corrupt* and many such words as being pronounced without the final *t*, and *beyond*, *scaffold* and a large number of similar words without the final *d*. Pope rhymed *neglects* with *sex*. *Ridin* not *riding* was the normal pronunciation of words with final *ing*, and Swift shows this frequently in rhyme. In the eighteenth century *Lunnon* was the usual pronunciation of *London*. Gradually, however, just as the formal grammarians put themselves forward as lawgivers, so those who wrote of pronunciation began to declare what the pronunciation *ought* to be. A good example was John Walker, author of a popular *Rhetorical Grammar* (1785), who, after abandoning the stage, lectured on elocution from about 1770. Such instructors were in general in favour of pronunciation close to the spelling, and, where words had two pronunciations, a careful one of formal speech and a slurred one of easy conversation, they insisted on the careful one. Since neither they nor those who required their teaching were of the higher class, the tendency naturally was towards a conscious refinement. In fact, we see again the joint effect of the eighteenth-century's desire for correctness, elegance, and uniformity and that of the middle class to be genteel. By the end of our period laxity in pronunciation was generally deprecated.

Even if such an important aspect of language as, among many others, change in the meaning of words has to be omitted in this brief survey (as, for instance, *sensible* was to lose such an ordinary eighteenth-century meaning as that of being capable of sensory or emotional reactions, and *awful* was to degenerate from its meanings of feeling or inspiring awe), the dawn of Anglo-Saxon studies deserves a place. Much honour is due to a small group of scholars at Oxford. The Dutchman Francis Junius, who printed the so-called Cædmon MS. in 1655, spent several years at Oxford. Somner published the first Anglo-Saxon dictionary in 1659, and George Hickes the first Anglo-Saxon grammar in 1689. Wanley made an invaluable catalogue of Anglo-Saxon manuscripts, published as Part II of the famous *Thesaurus* of Hickes. Thomas Hearne, the antiquary, printed the *Battle of Maldon* in 1726, five years before the manuscript was destroyed in the fire at the Cottonian library. And there was the remarkable young woman, Elizabeth Elstob, who in 1715 produced the first Anglo-Saxon grammar written in English, for that of Hickes was in Latin. She too began an edition of Aelfric's Homilies. With the death of Hickes in 1715 Anglo-Saxon studies ceased to advance and failed to reach a wide audience, but an enduring foundation had been laid, on which nineteenth-century scholars proceeded to build, so that with our fuller knowledge of our language we can see it in a truer perspective than could the eighteenth-century grammarians.

In conclusion, it is well to remember that the language of any age was always heard more upon the lips than it was set upon paper. Therefore, though we must rely for our evidence mainly upon the written word, upon which the eighteenth-century's tendency to formalism had its fullest effect, we must not exaggerate the extent to which that formalism permeated all classes and restrained all individuals. There surely survived that freedom which Sterne suggests by his phrase 'the sportability of chitchat'. Again, there were the diarists and letter-writers too much at ease to be formal – even like Gray from whose letters his friend Mason felt it necessary to prune the slang before he published them.

THE PERIODICAL ESSAYISTS

JANE H. JACK

It is not often that the appearance of a new literary form can be dated as precisely as that of the periodical essay, which was virtually invented by Steele in April 1709. 'The world has been obliged to an author of distinguished merit, now living, for having been the inventor of a manner of writing no less entertaining than any which had been established by the practice of the most celebrated ancients,' Sir Richard Blackmore remarked a few years later in the preface to a 'sequel to the *Spectators*' called *The Lay Monk*, and Boswell, writing towards the end of the heyday of the form, was no less certain of the modernity than of the merit of 'one of the happiest inventions of modern times'. 'A periodical paper of instruction and entertainment is truly of British origin,' he remarked in the first number of his 'Hypochondriack' essays (1777):

> It first appeared in London; and from the great lustre with which it was produced to the world by the constellation of wits in Queen Anne's reign, it would at any rate have for a time had eminence and imitators ... But from the long esteem and public favour with which a periodical paper has been attended, and the several successful works of that kind; nay, the many unsuccessful attempts of which there might be a large catalogue given, we must be convinced that this mode of writing has intrinsic excellence, and that mankind are fully sensible of its value.

It will be convenient to take our cue from Blackmore and Boswell and to leave aside what might be termed the prehistory of the periodical essay. What concerns us is the remarkable proliferation of this type of essay in the years following the first number of *The Tatler*. At least in the first half of the eighteenth century it might well be said to be the 'dominant form', if that term were not a trifle pretentious for a mode of writing which belongs essentially to the minor key. It is evidence of the adaptability of the periodical essay that it presented itself as an eligible medium to men of the most varied talents. Writers as different as Steele, Johnson, and Goldsmith wrote some of their finest work in it. It may be said to be the only literary form used by every major author of the century: it would not be easy to name many writers of the first or second rank who never used it at all. From the days of Queen Anne – who had *The Spectator* taken in with her breakfast – to the time of the French Revolution and beyond, periodical essays on the lines laid down by Steele and Addison flooded the country and met the eye in every bookseller's shop and coffee-house. If they had the slightest merit they found a ready public. It follows that a modern reader who wishes to breathe the atmosphere of the eighteenth century can hardly do better than spend a few hours with *The Tatler, The Spectator, The Connoisseur*, and *The Citizen of the World*. He will not find in them the spiritual peaks or abysses of the age, the scarifying satire of *A Tale of a Tub* or the eloquent political insight of Burke; but he will find a faithful and well-composed portrait of the age.

The first numbers of *The Tatler* (which originally came out on Tuesdays, Thursdays, and Saturdays, the days on which the post left London) are particularly interesting because in them one sees the new form shaking off the trammels of its origins. From the first, news was not the primary concern of the paper, and padding was particularly disclaimed: 'we shall not upon a dearth of news, present you with much foreign edicts, or dull proclamations.' Yet in the first few issues 'St James's Coffee-House' (from which Steele proclaimed his intention of dating foreign and domestic news) makes numerous appearances. Several reasons soon combined drastically to limit the space given to political news, however. The first was the fact that the culminating victory of Malplaquet presaged the end of Marlborough's long campaigning. In his first contribution Addison ironically commiserates the writers of news-sheets. After mentioning the plight of discharged soldiers, he comments:

There is another sort of gentleman whom I am much more concerned for, and that is the ingenious fraternity of which I have the honour to be an unworthy member; I mean the news-writers of Great Britain ... The case of these gentlemen is ... more hard than that of the soldiers, considering that they have taken more towns, and fought more battles ... Where Prince Eugène has slain his thousands, Boyer* has slain his ten thousands ... It is impossible for this ingenious sort of men to subsist after a peace: every one remembers the shifts they were driven to in the reign of King Charles the Second, when they could not furnish out a single paper of news without lighting up a comet in Germany, or a fire in Moscow.

He goes on to suggest that apartments in Chelsea Hospital should be set aside 'for the relief of such decayed news-writers as have served their country in the wars', and points out that he is not thinking of himself.

I cannot be thought to speak this out of an eye to any private interest; for as my chief scenes of action are coffee-houses, play-houses, and my own apartment, I am in no need of camps, fortifications, and fields of battle to support me; I don't call out for heroes and generals to my assistance. Though the officers are broken [discharged], and the armies disbanded, I shall still be safe as long as there are men or women or politicians, or lovers, or poets, or nymphs, or swains, or cits, or courtiers in being.

(No. 18).

While the refusal of the House of Commons to renew the Licensing Act in 1695 led to the increase in journalism of which *The Tatler* was a by-product, politics − as Steele was shortly to discover − was still not a safe subject for writers. Addison, who was less interested in politics than Steele and less impulsive, saw that it would be more profitable as well as safer to exclude the subject from the new periodical altogether. So it happened that within six months of its first appearance *The Tatler* was almost wholly devoid of political news and comment. It soon became common form with the essayists to disparage the appetite for news. 'Is it not much better to be let into the knowledge of one's self, than to hear what passes in Muscovy or Poland,' Addison asks in the tenth number of *The Spectator*, 'and to amuse ourselves with such writings as tend to the wearing out of ignorance, passion, and prejudice, than such as naturally conduce to inflame hatreds, and make enmities irreconcileable?'

News being excluded, what was to be the scope of the essayists? They might have replied, with Fielding in *Tom Jones*, 'The provision then which we have made is no other than HUMAN NATURE' (Bk I, introd.). 'The general purpose of this paper,' Steele wrote in the dedication which accompanied the first volume of *The Tatler*

*Abel Boyer issued *The Postboy*, *The Political State of Great Britain*, and other similar publications.

when it was published as a book, 'is to expose the false arts of life, to pull off the disguises of cunning, vanity, and affectation, and to recommend a general simplicity in our dress, our discourse, and our behaviour.' The essentially moral intention of the essayists obtains equal emphasis in the tenth number of *The Spectator*, where Addison echoes Cicero's description of the mission of Socrates:

> It was said of Socrates, that he brought philosophy down from heaven to inhabit among men; and I shall be ambitious to have it said of me that I have brought philosophy out of closets and libraries, schools and colleges, to dwell in clubs and assemblies, at tea-tables and in coffee-houses.

The exclusion of political news was not only safer: it also made for a larger circulation. When Pope was first coming into prominence, Addison gave him a piece of advice which shows how conscious he himself had been of this consideration. He advised Pope 'not to be content with the applause of half the nation'. What he meant was that Pope should refrain from throwing in his lot with either the Whigs or the Tories. 'There cannot a greater judgement befall a country,' he had written in *The Spectator*, No. 125,

> than such a dreadful spirit of division as rends a government into two distinct peoples and makes them greater strangers and more averse to one another than if they were actually two different nations. The effects of such a division are pernicious to the last degree ... This influence is very fatal both to men's morals and their understandings; it sinks the virtue of a nation, and ... destroys even common sense.

After emphasizing the particular harm this spirit does in literary matters (in a passage with which Matthew Arnold would have been in decisive agreement), Addison goes on:

> For my own part, I could heartily wish that all honest men would enter into an association, for the support of one another against the endeavours of those whom they ought to look upon as their common enemies, whatsoever side they may belong to. Were there such an honest body of neutral forces, we should never see the worst of men in great figures of life [positions in life], because they are useful to a party; nor the best unregarded because they are above practising those methods which would be grateful to their faction.

In the preface already quoted, Blackmore lays particular stress on Steele's 'invention' of 'introducing a set of persons of different humours and characters, acting on some imaginary occasion, which might draw out a variety of incidents and discourses'. The significance of the club which appears in *The Spectator* and many of its imitators should now be clear. The invention of the characters of Sir Roger de Coverley, Captain Sentry, Sir Andrew Freeport, and the rest was once a rhetorical or literary device, a symbol for the English people as it struggled to coalesce, and a flattering portrait of the reading public that the writers had as their aim. The Spectator Club forms an appropriate introduction to the literature of the eighteenth century – the century in which Parliament (the 'talking-shop') was rejoicing in its new powers, the great century of talk and talkers. Discussion had brought about the 'Glorious Revolution' and shown itself more useful than the blows of civil war. In the *History of the Royal Society* Sprat had rejoiced in the fact that scientific discussion, being now 'admitted into our Exchange, our Church, our palaces, and our Court', had begun to keep 'the best company'. It was time that encouragement should also be given to discussion of the great common question of how to live. To promote this was the chief object of the periodical essayists.

One of the main trends in the eighteenth century – it had begun much earlier – was a trend towards secularization. Although the Church remained much more powerful than it is today, it had retreated a long way from the position of predominance which it had occupied in the early seventeenth century. One cannot read far in the periodical essayists without realizing that they were taking over many of the functions earlier fulfilled by the Church. In this Addison made a suitable leader, a sort of lay Archbishop of Good Taste. Indeed, his quasi-episcopal characteristics were noticed by everyone, not only by the philosopher, Bernard Mandeville, with his sneer about a 'parson in a tye-wig', but also by Tonson the publisher. 'Old Jacob Tonson did not like Mr Addison', Pope once told Spence. 'He had a quarrel with him: and ... used frequently to say of him: "One day or other, you'll see that man a bishop! I'm sure he looks that way; and indeed I ever thought him a priest in his heart."' It is certain that Addison did at one time think of seeking high position in the Church. He wrote a work called *The Evidences of the Christian Religion*. And although he did not take the final step of seeking Orders, it might be said that the 'discourses against Atheism and Infidelity, and in defence of the Christian Revelation' contained in this book received stronger support from his periodical essays than they could have received from any sermons he could have written. In fact, many of the *Tatlers* and *Spectators* are very close to sermons. Avoiding alike the rigorous dialectic of Lancelot Andrewes and the argument from terror of John Donne, Addison's style of lay-preaching derives rather from the well-bred apologetics of men like Tillotson (from whom Dryden said that he learned to write English prose). His message is summed up in the motto to *The Spectator*, No. 112: 'Honour the gods according to the established modes.' His approach is readily suggested by the title of a widely read book of the time, *Christianity Not Mysterious*. What he wanted to promote was not wild and ungovernable religious feeling, 'enthusiasm' of the sort that had led to so much trouble in the previous century, but rather a cheerful and 'rational' faith. Addison would have agreed with many of his contemporaries that too much argument about religion was dangerous; but he would not have approved of the practice of some later essayists in excluding religion as well as politics from their pages. 'To say truth,' Edward Moore wrote in the first issue of *The World*, 'I have serious reasons for avoiding the first of these subjects. A weak advocate may ruin a good cause. And if religion can be defended by no better arguments than some I have lately seen in the public papers and magazines, the wisest way is to say nothing about it.' To avoid religion altogether in this way would not have been acceptable to Addison, who wished to 'recommend' Christianity. This he did by discussing the subject 'in a clear and lively manner, without unseasonable passions' (as he once said in commendation of a piece by Swift). He excelled in suggesting that not to be a Christian was slightly ridiculous, a breach of good manners. This set the tone in which most of the essayists (with the notable exception of Johnson) were to deal with religion.

What Addison and Steele and their successors were doing was to carry on at a much higher and more intelligent level the work of the people to whom Steele referred as 'my friends and fellow labourers, the Reformers of Manners'. Perhaps there was an absurd side to their work: in some ways they point forward to the strained 'gentility' of the Victorian age. But one has only to read the letters and memoirs of the time to see that some reformation of manners was highly desirable. There is a revealing passage in one of the notebooks of Mrs

Thrale: 'How great a change has been wrought in female manners within these few years in England!' she wrote. 'I was reading the letter in the third volume of *The Spectator* [No. 217] where the man complains of his indelicate mistress: I read it aloud to my little daughters of 11 and 12 years old, and even the maid who was dressing my hair burst out o' laughing.' This was written towards the end of the century by a woman who had put up with the manners of Samuel Johnson, which would horrify most people today. It suggests that a revolution of manners did really take place in the course of the century, and helps to make intelligible Jane Austen's objection to the 'coarse' language of *The Spectator* (*Emma*, chapter iv). Clearly there was room for reform at the beginning of the eighteenth century.

The strength of Steele and Addison lay in their ability to take a middle course, and they refused to go to the lengths advocated by many members of the Society for the Reformation of Manners, whose spiritual ancestors were the Puritans of the previous century. They gave strong and effectual support to the campaign against heavy gambling and duelling, but they did not share the distrust of plays which was still widespread in the middle and lower classes of society. Among Steele's earliest literary ventures were plays in which he tried to meet the objections levelled by Jeremy Collier against the moral effect of the drama. Steele would have been pleased with Parson Adams's remark that there were passages in his plays 'almost good enough for a sermon': it was his contention that 'a good play acted before a well-bred audience must raise very proper incitements to good behaviour, and be the most quick and most prevailing method of giving young people a turn of sense and breeding'. Nothing illustrates more clearly the reconciliatory course steered by Addison and Steele than their attitude to the drama. It gives definition to their famous objectives 'to enliven morality with wit, and to temper wit with morality'. They were always mindful of the cleavage in the English mind which had most recently and most dramatically been demonstrated in the Great Rebellion, but which went back farther and did not simply correspond to the two sides in that strange conflict. Behind Addison's phrase lies the whole history of the Reformation. Was 'wit', and perhaps art itself, dangerous to morality? Was not the Bible alone literature enough to teach a man to lead a good life? Attacks on 'wit' abounded in the seventeenth century, and they had more justification than is often admitted now. The great work of *The Tatler* and its successor was a work of civilization through conciliation. It is not surprising that the highest standards in literature and morality and religion too were sometimes compromised. It was the price that had to be paid for keeping Freeport, de Coverley, and Wimble together in one club.

If it had been necessary to placate also a Mrs Wimble and a Lady de Coverley, the difficulties would have been much greater; but one has only to play with the idea to realize that the society represented by the Spectator Club is essentially a masculine society. The fact that no woman is a member is a true reflection of the position of women in English society at the beginning of the century. A little later, the 'blue-stockings' were to attract attention and raise the question of the status of women; but at the point when *The Tatler* began to appear, the prevalent literary attitudes to women were not flattering. The accession of a woman to the throne made the time propitious for a change of attitude, however, and Steele – who had always stood out stoutly against the 'wenching' attitude which lingered on as a legacy from the Restoration – was the man to seize this opportunity. It became an important part of the *Tatler* and *Spectator* 'platform' to stress that the authors were writing for women as well as men, and to emphasize that women must play a large part in the process of civilizing which they were striving to promote. 'There are none to whom this paper will be more useful than to the female world,' Addison wrote in the tenth number of *The Spectator*. 'I have often thought there has not been sufficient pains taken in finding out proper employments and diversions for the fair ones. Their amusements seem rather contrived for them as they are women, than as they are reasonable creatures; and are more adapted to the sex than to the species.' Most people now agree with Swift, who found the tone in which Addison 'fair-sexed it' intolerably condescending. But it is clear that few women shared this feeling, for they made up a large proportion of his readers from the first: this general (though not universal) absence of irritation speaks volumes on the position of women before this time. Attention to the interests of 'the fair sex' became one of the invariable conventions of the periodical essay, and there can be little doubt that the essayists did much to improve the status and education of women. Within forty years it had become possible for

Johnson to comment that 'whatever might be the state of female literature [literacy, education] in the last century, there is now no longer any danger lest the scholar should want [lack] an adequate audience at the tea-table' (*The Rambler*, No. 173).

It should have become clear by now that one principal reason for the success of Addison and Steele was the fact that they kept the tastes and requirements of their readers, male and female, constantly in mind. Not the least of the attractions of their new form was its brevity. The seventeenth century had been the century of long books. A seventeenth-century reader seems to have been able to read anything. The only brief forms with any literary pretensions were stiff with 'wit'. The increasing 'reading public' of the eighteenth century brought a demand for easier reading. As Blackmore pointed out in the Preface to his *Essays*, 'The disrelish of ... diffusive pieces in these times is ... carried so far, that great books are looked on as oppressive ..., while those in which the principal end, as well as the sentiment of the author, are contracted into a narrower compass, if well writ, meet with general approbation.' It may seem paradoxical to claim that the century of *Clarissa* and *Tom Jones*, Boswell's *Life of Johnson* and Gibbon's *The Decline and Fall of the Roman Empire* was a period of short books; but so it was, by comparison with the preceding century. It was a time when writers paid more attention to the human frailty of their readers, and treated them with greater consideration. As in the format of books folios with double columns in small print were dying out and reputable publishers were paying more attention to clear type, so more care was devoted to presentation and style in the manner of writing. The periodical writers prided themselves on being 'nearer in our styles to that of common talk than any other writers' (*The Tatler*, No. 204), and there can be little doubt that the ubiquity of these essays had a good effect on the prose style of the century as a whole. A writer who had undergone the discipline of writing a few periodical essays was the less likely to have recourse to unnecessary pomposity or meaningless jargon in his other writings. The influence of the periodical essay made for clarity, simplicity, and literary good manners.

In nothing is this more evident than in the essays in literary criticism which were from the first a feature of the periodicals. It is as true today as it was in 1780 that the word 'critic' is 'a name which the present generation is scarcely willing to allow [Addison]'. But as Johnson pointed out in his *Life of Addison*,

his instructions were such as the character of his readers made proper. That general knowledge which now circulates in common talk, was in his time rarely to be found. Men not professing learning were not ashamed of ignorance; and, in the female world, any acquaintance with books was distinguished only to be censured.

It followed that 'an instructor like Addison was now wanting, whose remarks being superficial might be easily understood, and being just might prepare the mind for greater attainments'. His two series of essays on *Paradise Lost* and on the imagination are favourable examples of high-class popularization, and he wrote essays which deserve attention on such subjects as stage-comedy, the ballad of *Chevy Chase*, verse-epistles, and the style proper to tragedy. To explore any of the periodicals of the century is to come on numerous essays of this sort: they are brief, unpretentious, and sometimes surprisingly good (not least when they deal with some minor subject such as letter-writing or the composition of songs). One of the essayists was a great critic. Johnson used the form for some of his finest criticism, such as the essays in *The Rambler* on biography, the dramatic unities, and 'low' words in poetry (Nos 60, 156, and 168). But the sovereign merit of Johnson's best criticism quite apart, the fact that the essayists habitually devoted a proportion of their work to literary topics had important results. It made it clear that knowledge of a few great writers was not a matter for professional scholars only, but a part of general culture, almost of good manners. The same is true of the papers devoted to the English language, to points of style that concern anyone who tries to speak or write correctly. A critical interest in the spoken language is a mark of literary maturity: it may still be found in France, but since the eighteenth century it has not been an outstanding characteristic of our own country.

In spite of the excellent literary criticism which it contains, Johnson's *The Rambler* did not sell at all well in periodical form. It is said that only the number written by Samuel Richardson sold more than 500 copies. In volume form, however, it came to rival every other series of essays except *The Spectator*. It was not Johnson's instructional purpose (pronounced as that was) that was an innovation, but his refusal to insinuate his instruction in an agreeable and easy form. There will always be a few readers who agree with the talented Anna Seward in becoming easily bored with Addison's 'water-gruel style' – 'nothing wearies me like [his] prosing about and about the good cardinal virtues in their old robes' – and preferring 'the bright armour of Johnsonian eloquence'. But the average reader of the periodical essay found Johnson stiff going. Johnson's choice of subjects may be indicated by quoting some of the titles appended to the essays in the collected editions: 'Happiness not Local'; 'The Miseries of an infirm Constitution'; 'The Voyage of Life'; 'The frequent Contemplation of Death necessary to moderate the Passions'; 'Religion and Superstition, A Vision'; 'The Luxury of vain Imagination'. The staple topics of *The Rambler* are those which form the warp and woof of *Rasselas*: the inevitability of disappointments in human life, the dangers of excessive leisure, all the difficulties attending 'the choice of life'. The Prince of Abyssinia who travels about the world to see the manners and ways of many men is an image of Johnson's own ambition: perhaps this is one reason for his choice of 'The Rambler' as a title. His periodical essays form one of the principal repositories of his reflections on 'the various conditions of humanity'. It is noticeable that not only do moral subjects preponderate: even subjects which might seem to belong to the domain of manners, and would have been treated by Addison or Steele with a light touch, tend to be treated by Johnson in the same way as papers on fundamental moral duties. There are flashes of humour here and there; but were it not for *The Idler*, which (like Boswell's *Hypochondriack*) was a 'column' in a larger periodical and not an independent publication, the reader might conclude that Johnson was devoid of humour.

These briefer and more amusing papers also show a dramatic power which might have remained unsuspected. Instead of the characters in *The Rambler*, derived too obviously (with their ponderous Latin names) from classical models and the 'characters' of the seventeenth century, we find Dick Minim and a number of other characters in *The Idler* who are described with a much lighter touch. On the whole, however, the merits of *The Rambler* and *The Idler* are less those proper to the periodical essay as a form than those characteristic of all Johnson's writing. Every paper exhibits the sovereign merit of Johnson's work as a whole: he closes with his subject and grapples with it with all his strength, bringing to bear all his experience of human life. *The Rambler* and *The Idler* form a storehouse of mature reflections on human life and perceptive literary judgements.

The sixth decade of the century, which saw the appearance of Johnson's periodical essays, was the decade also of *The Adventurer, The World, The Connoisseur*, and Goldsmith's delightful *Citizen of the World*. This was the second great period of the periodical essay. Not that there was any notable diminution in the flood after 1760. Essayists consoled themselves with the reflection of Fielding in *The Champion*, that 'there is a sort of craft attending vice and absurdity; and when hunted out of society in one shape, they seldom want address to reinsinuate themselves in another: hence the modes of licence vary almost as often as those of dress, and consequently require continual observation to detect and explode them anew'. It is particularly noticeable that periodical essays tended to appear in other centres where there was an approximation to the conditions of London at the beginning of the century. The Edinburgh *Mirror* (1779–80) and *Lounger* (1785–6) were among the best examples of these: less important periodicals appeared in Dublin, Newcastle, and other provincial towns. But it is not surprising that the periodical essay began to exhibit the characteristics of a decadent form. The same conventions were repeated with less and less effect. Writers mistook the externals for the essence. The remorseless literary law of diminishing returns made itself felt. Then, as now, the essay attracted people who were anxious to 'commence author', but had nothing new to say. If Theobald had lived about the middle of the century he would have had more reason for the complaint he had made near the beginning: 'This period may well be called the Age of Counsellors, when every blockhead who could write his own name attempted to inform and amuse the public.'

The form was wearing out, with the society which had sustained it. The peculiar blend of seriousness and lightness of touch which was (in spite of Johnson) the essence of the periodical essay did not sort with the new age, and has never been possible since. That sureness of tone which characterizes so much of the literature of the eighteenth century was to go under in the Romantic flood. The Romantic essayists learned a good deal from their predecessors, indeed: Coleridge's *Friend* has many of the characteristics of the old kind. But two influences were incompatible with the old tradition: the tendency to autobiography and to the 'putting over' of the essayist's own idiosyncrasies which marks Romantic essay-writing and Romantic literature as a whole; and political events on a scale which made it impossible to live any longer in this temperate zone of literature. By a strange chance the inventor of the form made a remark about the situation in 1713 which was undoubtedly true in the years following the French Revolution. 'It is not now a time to improve the taste of men by the reflections and railleries of poets and philosophers,' Steele had written in the first number of *The Englishman*, 'but to awaken their understanding by laying before them the present state of the world like a man of experience and a patriot. It is a jest to throw away our care in providing for the palate when the whole body is in danger of death, and to talk of amending the mien and air of a cripple that has lost his legs and arms.' After the French Revolution a writer who wrote in the old form was being as consciously archaic as a man who wore a full-bottomed wig; the periodical essay passed away with the world into which it had been born.

SWIFT AND THE TRADITION
OF WIT

D. W. JEFFERSON

Too much emphasis, perhaps, has been laid on the simplicity of Swift's prose style. It is to this virtue in particular that Herbert Read draws attention in his remarks on Swift (1667–1745) in *English Prose Style*: 'however widely his vision might extend, however deep his insight, his mode of expression remained simple, and single, and clearly comprehensible'. And it was to this virtue that Swift himself drew attention in various places; for example, in his remarks on preaching in the *Letter to a Young Gentleman*, where he refers to 'that Simplicity, without which no human Performance can arrive to any great Perfection'. Yet the habit, in critics and teachers, of referring to it as the first and foremost of his qualities needs to be resisted. Swift's remarks on prose style, though of great interest, bear very little on the secret of his own greatness in that medium. The student, influenced by the emphasis on simplicity, is liable to get a limited impression of Swift's powers. It is a case of association of ideas. Simplicity of style suggests plain statement and a straightforward approach; qualities which, as it happens, are found together – or so it seems – in some frequently quoted passages of Swift; for example, in the description of Gulliver's arrival on the shore of Lilliput, so often produced as a classroom illustration by lecturers on the advantages of plain prose. But what ought to be said, whenever it is so used, is that the author has a special ironical motive here for cultivating the matter-of-fact narrative style of contemporary books of travel. It is essential to the effectiveness of *Gulliver's Travels* that its hero should seem to be a plain man telling a plain tale, and it is what Swift achieves under cover of this assumed manner that is interesting. The early pages of each of the four books, where a brief account is given of the commonplace circumstances leading to the strange adventures, are written in a dry and pedestrian manner which borders on parody. In the many roles which Swift adopts as a writer it sometimes suits his purpose to deal plainly and straightforwardly with his subject, but often he only appears to do so or does so only in part. His simplicity in syntax and diction is liable to be a camouflage for insidious intentions.

To emphasize his simplicity is to emphasize the differences between his art and that of the early seventeenth-century writers, and hence to deflect attention from the qualities which he shares with them. Both the differences and the affinities need to be recognized, but literary historians have been far too much preoccupied with the former. The demand for a simpler prose is historically related to the requirements of the new science and philosophy and the rejection of the old, fanciful type of speculation associated with Sir Thomas Browne; and Swift's style tends to be regarded, in some imperfectly defined way, as expressive of the new intellectual virtues; as the style of one who followed what Basil Willey refers to as 'the plain path of Nature and Reason'. This is not the place for a discussion of his attitudes to contemporary philosophical developments, but it may be suggested that in stressing his indebtedness to the intellectual habits of the earlier period we should do more justice to the richness and variety of his art. In his brilliant play with the old modes of learned speculation, his imaginative fertility in developing concretely an absurd pseudo-scientific conception, his dialectical resourcefulness and effrontery, Swift is of the world of Rabelais, Donne, and Ben Jonson. There are two clear reasons for giving priority to this aspect of him. First, the imagination is by nature conservative; it flourishes most when it has old forms and techniques and procedures at its disposal, and it is by adapting and modifying these rather than by discovering new ones that even the most original artist meets the demands of the contemporary world. The immediate contemporary influences upon a writer, though in one sense the most important, are in another sense secondary, because they can operate only on an inherited equipment, and will operate feebly if the equipment is inadequate. The Augustan economy of Swift's prose is not a quality to be isolated. It must be studied in relation to the arts which he inherited from earlier periods, which it modifies and which modify it. Secondly, the earlier period is the greater period, and by realizing his link with it we acquire a more generous sense of his greatness.

Plainness and simplicity in themselves are not sufficiently interesting qualities to be given first place in our account of such an artist.

It is in the earlier works, such as *A Tale of a Tub* (published 1704), that the more exuberant side of his art is most apparent. There are some delectable examples here of his ability to play with learned ideas, exploiting them ingeniously to build up a comic conception. One of his masters in this art was Rabelais, the English translation of whose work was completed in the 1690s, not long before Swift wrote these satires. A pleasant example, in the third book of Rabelais, is Panurge's celebrated defence of his own improvidence (he has just run through three years' income in a fortnight) in which arguments are drawn from astronomy, physiology, and other branches of learning to prove that borrowing and lending are the basic principles governing the universe. A witty misapplication of learned ideas in support of an audacious conclusion was one of the arts of the metaphysical poets. We should not expect such effects to occur in literature long after the seventeenth century, for they involve a parody of the pre-scientific methods of speculation which were discredited by the new scientists; and parody demands a certain nearness to the thing parodied. But Swift is not the last writer to make lavish use of them. They are abundantly present in Sterne's *Tristram Shandy*.

It is not enough to say that Swift is ridiculing the old ideas and intellectual procedures. To make such superb comic use of them he had to be imaginatively at home with them. The ideas he uses are *his* ideas, so far as his art is concerned.

One of his arts, much in evidence in the early works, consists in inventing a theory based on learned or pseudo-learned ideas in order to explain the phenomenon which is the object of his satire; for example, the fanaticism or 'enthusiasm' of the nonconformist sects. He begins with a suave, apparently innocuous, statement of the theory, and then proceeds to develop a series of grotesque images showing the theory in action. In *A Tale of a Tub* (ch. viii) this treatment is applied elaborately to a sect called the Aeolists, the believers in direct inspiration:

The Learned *Aeolists* maintain the Original Cause of all Things to be *Wind* ...

For two paragraphs he dwells solemnly on the different names for wind (*spiritus, animus, afflatus, anima*) and on the learned theories concerning the various kinds of wind with which man is endowed. Apparently there are four kinds, but man brings with him into the world:

... a peculiar Portion or Grain of Wind, which may be called a *Quinta essentia*, extracted from the other four. This *Quintessence* is of a Catholic Use upon all Emergencies of Life, is improveable into all Arts and Sciences, and may be wonderfully refined, as well as enlarged, by certain Methods in Education. This, when *blown* up to its full Perfection, ought not to be covetously hoarded up, stifled, or hid under a Bushel, but freely communicated to Mankind. Upon these reasons, and others of equal Weight, the wise *Aeolists* affirm the gift of BELCHING to be the noblest Act of a Rational Creature. To cultivate which Art, and render it more serviceable to Mankind, they made use of several Methods. At certain Seasons of the Year, you might behold the Priests amongst them, in vast Numbers, with their *Mouths gaping wide against a Storm*.

He then goes on to describe how a crowd of the faithful would blow each other up, and

... when, by these and the like Performances, they were grown sufficiently replete, they would immediately depart and disembogue, for the Publick Good, a plentiful Share of their Acquirements, into their Disciples' Chaps.

The Aeolists apply this principle to learning. 'Learning puffeth men up', and there is a syllogism to support this: 'Words are but wind; and learning is nothing but words; *ergo*, learning is nothing but wind'; hence, the philosophers of this school deliver all their teachings by eructation.

In the Introduction to *A Tale of a Tub*, Swift discusses the desirability of an elevated position for an orator, if he is to secure the attention of the public. Again, as in the passage about the Aeolists, he puts forward a learned theory and then a grotesque concrete demonstration of it:

The deepest Account, and the most fairly digested of any I have yet met with, is this, That Air being a heavy Body, and therefore (according to the System of *Epicurus*) continually descending, must needs be more so, when loaden and press'd down with Words, which are also bodies of much Weight and Gravity, as it is manifest from those deep *Impressions* they make and leave upon us; and therefore must be delivered from a due Altitude, or else they will neither carry a good Aim, nor fall down with a sufficient Force ...

And I am the readier to favour this Conjecture, from a common Observation; that in the several Assemblies of these Orators, Nature herself hath instructed the Hearers to stand with their Mouths open, and erected parallel to the Horizon, so that they may be intersected by a perpendicular Line from the Zenith to the Center of the Earth. In which Position, if the Audience be well compact, every one carries home a Share, and little or nothing is lost.

I confess there is something yet more refined, in the Contrivance and Structure of our Modern Theatres. For, First; the Pit is sunk below the Stage, with due regard to the Institution above-deduced; that, whatever *weighty* Matter shall be delivered thence (whether it be *Lead* or *Gold*) may fall plum into the Jaws of certain *Criticks* (as I think they are called) which stand ready open to devour them. Then, the Boxes are built round, and raised to a Level with the Scene, in deference to the Ladies; because, That large Portion of Wit, laid out in raising Pruriences and Protuberances, is observ'd to run much upon a Line, and ever in a Circle. The whining Passions, and little starved Conceits, are gently wafted up, by their own extreme Levity, to the middle Region, and there fix and are frozen by the frigid Understandings of the Inhabitants. Bombast and Buffoonry, by Nature lofty and light, soar highest of all, and would be lost in the Roof, if the prudent Architect had not, with much Foresight, contrived for them a fourth Place, called *the twelve-peny Gallery*, and there planted a suitable Colony, who greedily intercept them in their Passage.

In another early work, *The Mechanical Operation of the Spirit* (1704), Swift pretends to examine scientifically the physiological means whereby preachers produce a spiritual response in their congregations. The following passage is concerned with the part played by the members of the assembly:

The Methods of this *Arcanum* is as follows: – They violently strain their Eye balls inward, half closing the Lids; Then, as they sit, they are in a perpetual Motion of *See-saw*, making long Hums at proper Periods, and continuing the Sound at equal Height, choosing their Time in those Intermissions while the Preacher is at Ebb.

He then adds that this trick with the eyes is a secret of the Indian Yogis and accounts for their visions, and he makes learned comments of a similar kind on the origin of the other part of the performance. A concrete scene follows:

Now it is usual for a Knot of *Irish*, Men and Women, to abstract themselves from Matter, bind up all their Senses, grow visionary and spiritual, by Influence of a short Pipe of tobacco, handed round the Company, each preserving the Smoak in his Mouth, till it comes again to his Turn to take it in fresh: At the same Time there is a Consort of a continued gentle Hum, repeated and renewed by Instinct, as Occasion requires, and they move their Bodies up and Down, to a Degree, that sometimes their Heads and

Points lie parallel to the Horizon. Mean while, you may observe their Eyes turn'd up, in the Posture of one who endeavours to keep himself awake; by which, and many other Symptoms among them, it manifestly appears that the Reasoning Faculties are all suspended and superseded, that Imagination hath usurped the Seat, scattering a thousand Deliriums over the Brain.

What is notable in all these passages is the imaginative play between the idea and the concrete detail, the one always enhancing the other. Here and there the illusion is created that the fantastic posturings embody something significant, like ritual. The absurdities take on a mysterious piquancy, and at the same time a mathematical sharpness. The ability to give a pointedness to the concrete particulars of a description, to achieve a certain flavour by the ordering of them in relation to an extraordinary intellectual pattern, is one of the characteristic arts of Ben Jonson, while the assimilation of image to idea is especially associated with the Metaphysical poets. Swift is in their tradition. An admirable example of the metaphysical art of 'arguing through images' occurs in *The Battle of the Books* (1704), where the quarrel between the Bee and the Spider serves, by a nice manipulation of terms, as the embodiment of the dispute between Ancients and Moderns. The difference between the two intellectual types is stated by the Spider, who intends the comparison to favour himself, but achieves the opposite effect:

Your Livelihood is a universal Plunder upon Nature; a Freebooter over Fields and Gardens; and, for the sake of Stealing, will rob a Nettle as readily as a Violet. Whereas I am a domestick Animal, furnisht with a Native Stock within myself. This large Castle (to shew my Improvements in the Mathematicks) is all built with my Own Hands, and the Materials extracted altogether out of my own Person.

A play of idea and image may seem not to be characteristic of Swift's work in his later period. The fantastic exploitation of learned materials was, for the most part, abandoned, and his subjects were often such as called for a more or less straightforward factual treatment. But Swift never lost his power of charging concrete details with a peculiar intensity, of using them to give an unexpected force and nuance to an argument. His art, in pamphlets like the *Drapier's Letters* (1724), of marshalling squads of particulars into menacing patterns of monstrosity, so that the idea he is illustrating

(Wood's halfpence,* for instance) takes on an appalling proliferation of life, should be recognized as akin to the art of *A Tale of a Tub*.

If there is less play with learned ideas after this earlier period, there is no diminution but rather an intensification in the use of the arts of argument. The witty use of these techniques in literature belongs historically to the age when dialectic was still important in education, when the ability to dispute on either side of a question was an accepted accomplishment in schools and universities. The English masters of ratiocinative wit, of the art of developing a plausibly outrageous argument, are Donne, Dryden, and Swift, of whom the latter is, surely, the most astonishing. But dialectical dexterity declined in importance, the new philosophers and scientists of the seventeenth century having no use for the traditional logic, and English writers after this period show much less skill in these arts.

An analysis of Swift's dialectical technique in one of the more wonderful pamphlets would be a formidable and lengthy task. His capacity to see all the possibilities for wit in a situation, and to achieve a series of surprises as he moves from position to position exploiting each possibility, can be illustrated adequately neither by a summary nor by selection, but we must make the best of these means. His basic strategy in a number of works is to write in the character of someone from whose standpoint the facts he is satirizing can be stated with disconcerting freedom. This freedom depends on the ignoring of certain considerations, but trouble is in store for anyone who insists on them. The imaginary reader who is the victim of the manoeuvre is so placed that protest only leads to further embarrassment. Thus, in *A Modest Proposal* (1729) – perhaps the most tremendous pamphlet ever written – the horror of the proposal, which is that the children of the poor should be sold as food for the tables of the rich, can be stated with impunity in all its shocking details; for it is no more than commensurate with the horror actually existing and permitted by the social group which Swift's readers, roughly speaking, represent. His technique is to develop the one by continual reference to the other, so that every statement is double-edged:

*Swift, writing in the character of a Dublin draper, published a series of letters denouncing the project to provide Ireland with copper coins, the patent for which was held by an Englishman, William Wood. Largely as a result of his efforts the scheme was abandoned.

I have already computed the Charge of nursing a Beggars Child (in which
list I reckon all *Cottagers, Labourers*, and four fifths of the *Farmers*) to be about
two shillings *per Annum*, Rags included, and I believe no Gentleman would
repine to give Ten shillings for the *Carcass of a good fat Child* ...

The horrors are all the more effective in that they are not presented
as such. They are just introduced casually as part of the evidence for,
or in illustration of, his project. The tone of most of the pamphlet
is easy and matter-of-fact; the appeal is to the reader's practical
reasonableness, any attempt to excite pity or indignation being excluded. It is only towards the end that he finds a pretext for a change
of tone and an overwhelming frontal attack. Replying to the timid
objection, that under this scheme 'the Number of People will be
thereby much lessened in the Kingdom', he admits that,

... it was indeed one Principal design in offering it to the world. I desire the
Reader will observe, that I calculate my Remedy *for this one individual Kingdom of IRELAND, and for no other that ever was, is, or, I think, ever can be
upon Earth. Therefore let no Man talk to me of other Expedients: Of taxing our
Absentees at five Shillings a pound: Of using neither Cloaths, nor household Furniture, except what is of our own Growth and Manufacture: Of utterly rejecting the
Materials and Instruments that promote Foreign Luxury: Of curing the Expencive-
ness of Pride, Vanity, Idleness, and Gaming in our Women: Of introducing a Vein
of Parcimony, Prudence and Temperance: Of learning to Love our Country, wherein
we differ even from LAPLANDERS, and the inhabitants of TOPIN-
AMBOO* ...

In the *Abolishing of Christianity* pamphlet (1708), which is more
elaborate, the fictitious assumption is that there is a general unanimity
in favour of abolition, and he writes in the character of one who
thinks, but is conscious of his temerity in so doing, that the step may
be 'attended with some inconveniences'. From the opening page or
two we are led to expect an attack only upon the irreligious, but he
turns the tables on the conventional Christians among his readers by
announcing that it is only 'Nominal Christianity' that he proposes to
defend:

I hope no Reader imagines me so weak to stand up in the Defence of Real
Christianity, such as used in Primitive Times (if we may believe the Authors
of those Ages) to have an Influence upon Mens Belief and Actions: To offer
at the restoring of That would indeed be a wild Project; it would be to dig
up Foundations, to destroy at one Blow all the Wit, and half the Learning of
the Kingdom; to break the entire Frame and Constitution of Things, to ruin
Trade, Extinguish Arts and Sciences with the Professors of them; In short, to
turn our Courts, Exchanges, and shops into Deserts ...

As in *A Modest Proposal*, the imaginary victim is caught. Faced with the alternative of defending 'real' Christianity, he is in no position to protest. 'Nominal' Christianity proves a fruitful idea for exploitation from a variety of angles. It seems that its observances, considered as obstacles to business and pleasure, are hardly worth the fuss of abolishing; for example, church-going:

> I readily own there hath been an old Custom time out of mind, for People to assemble in the Churches every *Sunday*, and that shops are still frequently shut, in order as it is conceived, to preserve the Memory of that antient Practice; but how this can prove a hindrance to Business or Pleasure, is hard to imagine. What if the Men of Pleasure are forced one Day in the Week to Game at Home instead of the *Chocolate-House*. Are not the *Taverns* and *Coffee-Houses* open? Can there be a more convenient Season for taking a Dose of Physick? Are fewer Claps got upon *Sundays* than other Days?

As for the objection that religion endangers freedom of thought, the truth is that people are free to scoff and blaspheme to their hearts' content, and it is a good thing that they should have a religion to scoff at:

> Great Wits love to be free with the highest Objects, and if they cannot be allowed a God to revile or renounce; they will speak Evil of Dignities, abuse the Government, and reflect upon the Ministry, which I am sure few will deny to be of much more pernicious Consequence ...

Confining himself to the humbler advantages of established Christianity he makes surprisingly effective use of them as a stick to beat the world of fashion and free-thinking:

> It is likewise urged, that there are by Computation in this Kingdom above Ten Thousand Parsons, whose Revenues added to those of my Lords the Bishops, would suffice to maintain at least Two Hundred Young Gentlemen of Wit and Pleasure, and Free-thinking, Enemies, to Priest-craft, narrow Principles, Pedantry, and Prejudices, who might be an Ornament to the Court and Town: And then, again, so great a Number of able (bodied) Divines might be a Recruit to our Fleet and Armies. This indeed appears to be a Consideration of some Weight: But then on the other side, several Things deserve to be considered like-wise: As, First, Whether it may not be thought necessary that in certain Tracts of Country, like what we call Parishes, there should be one Man at least, of Abilities to Read and Write. Then it seems a wrong Computation, that the Revenues of the Church throughout this Island would be enough to maintain Two Hundred Young Gentlemen, or even half that Number, after the present refined way of Living, that is, to allow each of them such a Rent, as in the modern Form of Speech, would make them Easy.

But still there is in this Project a greater Mischief behind; And we ought to beware of the Woman's Folly, who killed the Hen that every Morning laid her a Golden Egg. For, pray what would become of the Race of Men in the next Age, if we had nothing to trust to besides the Scrophulous consumptive Productions furnished by our Men of Wit and Pleasure, when having squandred away their Vigor, Health and Estates, they are forced by some disagreeable Marriage to piece up their broken Fortunes, and entail Rottenness and Politeness on their Posterity. Now, here are Ten Thousand Persons reduced by the wise Regulations of *Henry* the Eighth, to the necessity of a low Dyet, and moderate Exercise, who are the only great Restorers of our Breed, without which the Nation would in an Age or two become but one great Hospital.

This is a paragraph to marvel at as an example of Swift's extraordinary fertility and vigour in argument. But perhaps the most withering stroke of irony occurs in the following passage, where he has shifted to an entirely different position and is aiming at a different target:

Nor do I think it wholly groundless, or my Fears altogether imaginary, that the abolishing of Christianity may perhaps bring the Church in Danger, or at least put the Senate to the Trouble of another Securing Vote. I desire I may not be mistaken; I am far from presuming to affirm or think that the Church is in Danger at present, or as Things now stand, but we know not how soon it may be so when the Christian Religion is repealed.

Swift's virtuosity in works like this transcends anything that a mere textbook of rhetoric or dialectic could have taught him on the subject of 'invention', the traditional name for the art of opening up a topic and finding all there was to be said about it; but a tradition of formal training is to be reckoned with if we are to account for the existence of this quality in him and in other writers like Rabelais, as compared with writers of later periods. Although there is no trace in his work of pedantic methodicalness, such as Rabelais delighted in parodying, Swift's capacity to seize every advantage that a situation offered has behind it something of the old discipline. When he has done, to quote Dryden on Juvenal, 'the wit of man can carry it no further'.

The effects of his manoeuvrings, of the general strategy of his pamphlets, depends very largely on certain uses of language. Swift's habit of writing in the character of a fictitious person allows him freedoms in the choice of idiom from which he is always ready to profit. The *Drapier's Letters*, for example, are written in the character of a plain-spoken citizen, who expresses his indignation in round terms, and illustrates his point with common-sense arithmetic. That is the fiction, but under cover of it Swift writes with a studied baldness and an ominous mathematical explicitness, the effect of which is far different from that of plain, homely exposition. The idiom appropriate to the assumed character is manipulated as an artistic medium and applied with an intense deliberateness. In *A Modest Proposal*, the scientific approach, the easy tone with which the problem is reduced to one of agricultural economics, permits him occasionally to use an appalling phrase:

It is true a Child, *just dropt from its Dam*, may be supported by her Milk, for a solar year with little other Nourishment, at most not above the Value of two Shillings ...

And the fact that, in the *Abolishing of Christianity* pamphlet, no higher principle than political expediency is invoked, gives him a pretext for expressions like, 'if the Gospel should be repealed'. Significant variations in tone and diction often occur within the same work, sometimes within the same sentence. Of these the long paragraph from the *Abolishing of Christianity* quoted above is quite rich in examples. Swift was a master of destructive juxtapositions of words: 'Young Gentlemen of Wit and Pleasure, and Free-thinking, Enemies to Priest-craft, narrow Principles, Pedantry, and Prejudices'. From these ironical phrases at the beginning of the paragraph he moves to the openly ruthless 'Rottenness and Politeness' of the later part. The double-edged phrase 'able-bodied Divines' echoes a callously secular view of the usefulness of the clergy, but is unexpectedly applied to their advantage. It is a typical stroke on Swift's part that they should be proved indispensable without reference to the things for which they primarily exist. 'Certain Tracts of Country, like what we call Parishes' conveys, beneath the innocently 'helpful' tone, the suggestion that the reader's familiarity with the elementary organization of Christianity is not beyond the need of a reminder. More drastic variations than these, involving sudden violence after suavity and polite detachment, are favourite devices of Swift, occurring more frequently in the earlier works.

It is generally admitted that the earlier works abound in imagery, but the view that the other works are altogether deficient in this respect is not quite just. He occasionally uses a destructive image to enhance an argument, as in this passage from the *Abolishing of Christianity* pamphlet:

If the Quiet of a State can be bought by only flinging Men a few Ceremonies to devour, it is a purchase no Wise Man Would refuse. Let the Mastiffs amuse themselves about Sheepskin stufft with Hay, provided it will keep them from Worrying the Flock.

Wood's halfpence provided endless stimulus to Swift's imagination, perhaps the most piquant example being the comparison between himself and David fighting Goliath. Goliath is Wood, he is wearing five thousand shekels of brass (Wood's halfpence), 'and he defied the Armies of the Living God'. A very pleasing sequence of images appears in a work of which Swift's authorship has been queried by Dr Herbert Davis: *A Letter to a Young Poet*. This is not the place for an examination of the evidence, but if the paragraph below is not by Swift, historians of literature are going to have an extremely brilliant anonymous satirist on their hands. The development of the idea in physical terms is, surely, very close to Swift's technique in *A Tale of a Tub*. The subject is the literary life of Dublin:

Seriously then, I have many Years lamented the want of a *Grub-street* in this our large and polite *City*, unless the whole may be called *one*. And this I have accounted an unpardonable Defect in our Constitution, ever since I had any Opinions I could call my own. Every one knows, *Grub-street* is a Market for *Small-Ware* in WIT, and as necessary considering the usual Purgings of *Human Brain*, as the *Nose* is upon a Man's *Face*. . . and truly this Defect has been attended with unspeakable Inconveniences; for not to mention the Prejudice done to the Common-wealth of *Letters*, I am of opinion we suffer in our Health by it: I believe our corrupted Air, and frequent thick *Fogs* are in a great measure owing to the common exposal of our *Wit*, and that with good Management, our Poetical *Vapours* might be carried off in a *Common Drain*, and fall into one Quarter of the Town, without infecting the whole, as the Case is at present, to the great Offence of our *Nobility*, and *Gentry*, and *Others* of nice *Noses*.

One becomes so accustomed to piquancies and nuances of phrasing in Swift that the habit of looking for them is liable to be carried over into the reading of works like *The Conduct of the Allies* (1711), where he is arguing a straight case and such subtleties would seem not to be called for. In such writings he sometimes succeeds in conveying the impression, which adds much to the effect, that he is acting a part, and that it is trying his patience a little; that he is stating mere facts, and trying only to place them in the clearest light, but that behind this restraint, which is a matter of expediency, is a consuming exasperation. In his sermons, which are not among his greater works, he really writes 'straight'. He would have scorned to use a sermon as an opportunity for virtuosity or for the indulgence of temperament. The role of preacher is not one in which he is especially happy; he has no remarkable insight into religion, and is unable to state his convictions feelingly; but there is an impressiveness in the rigid integrity with which he abides within his sometimes rather disconcerting limits. But if we turn to another piece of straight writing, *On the Death of Mrs Johnson*, we find restraint without the inadequacy of the sermons; through the perfect decorum of the style he gives the right public expression to his great regard for a woman towards whom his private feelings must very largely remain a mystery.

That Swift uses a number of styles, varying according to his theme and purpose, is one of the facts that deserve to be emphasized. Some of the works not discussed in this essay, like *Directions to Servants* (1745), present further variations, and in a complete survey it would be necessary to consider also his parodies, such as *A Meditation upon a Broomstick* (1710), and the specimens of vapid social talk in *A Compleat Collection of Genteel and Ingenious Conversation* (1738). Swift was a connoisseur of the different uses of language. If it is true that throughout all, or most, of these variations, the virtues of simplicity and conciseness remain as constants, is this the point which deserves priority, the aspect of his art most likely to lure a beginner on to enjoy the prodigies of wit that await him?

There is no work by Swift over which such revealing and significant differences of opinion occur as the last book of *Gulliver's Travels* (1726). To the kind of reader who inclines towards the 'Augustan' view of him, this book is a straight attack on the filthy degradation of the human species in the name of 'Nature and Reason'; and, in so far as Gulliver (who is Swift) rejects humanity, it is the work of a misanthropist. 'Jonathan Swift aimed at mankind the most venomous arrow that scorn has ever yet let loose,' writes Carl van Doren, whose very readable biography is marred by the excessive prominence given to the misanthropic and tormented side of his nature. But if we see

Swift first and foremost as a wit, skilled in the elaboration of ideas which do not directly represent his own beliefs, we may arrive not only at a more satisfactory interpretation of this book, but also at a more acceptable view of its author.

In this book a piquant situation is presented to us, which may be stated as follows: 'In the real world the gift of reason is bestowed upon human beings and withheld from animals. In the land of the Houyhnhnms reason has been given to horses and withheld from—.' Here we naturally pause, but we are intended to continue: '... withheld from human beings.' The Yahoos are human beings, without the gift of reason. Into this world comes Gulliver, different from both in that he is a human being with reason. An important factor is that everything is seen and judged from the Houyhnhnms' angle: it is their country and their point of view imposes itself. Gulliver is alone and unique. Anxious to make his hosts understand that he is not a Yahoo, he must abide the test of the physical evidence, which is against him, and here Swift, by a peculiarly inhuman detachment in his use of detail, makes us see him as the Houyhnhnms see him:

... he then stroked my Body very gently and looked round me several Times, after which he said it was plain I must be a perfect *Yahoo*; but that I differed very much from the rest of my Species, in the softness and whiteness and smoothness of my Skin, my want of Hair in several parts of my Body, the Shape and Shortness of my Claws behind and before, and my Affectation of walking continually on my two hinder Feet.

(ch. III)

Gulliver's superiority in the matter of reason is, however, recognized; but this leads to graver embarrassment. He is obliged to give an account of the uses to which reason is put in those lands where human beings dominate. Swift takes advantage of the fact that the Houyhnhnms know nothing of wickedness, so that everything has to be explained in detail. This device, of presenting the facts as they would have to be presented to an uninitiated listener, must be regarded as one of the modes of artistic distortion. It enables Swift to order his details in an ominous way, to secure heightening and emphasis. What purports to be a cold, purely matter-of-fact statement becomes a fearful concentration of images:

What you have told me (said my Master) upon the Subject of War, does indeed discover most admirably the Effects of that Reason you pretend to: However, it is happy that the *Shame* is greater than the *Danger*; and that

Nature hath left you utterly incapable of doing much Mischief: For your Mouths lying flat with your Faces, you can hardly bite each other to any Purpose, unless by consent. Then as to the Claws upon your Feet before and behind, they are so short and tender, that one of our *Yahoos* would drive a Dozen of yours before him. And therefore in recounting the Numbers of those who have been killed in Battle, I cannot but think that you have *said the Thing which is not.*

I could not forbear shaking my Head and smiling a little at his ignorance. And, being no Stranger to the Art of War, I gave him a Description of Cannons, Culverins, Muskets, Carabines, Pistols, Bullets, Powder, Swords, Bayonets, Battles, Sieges, Retreats, Attacks, Undermines, Countermines, Bombardments, Sea-fights; Ships sunk with a Thousand Men; twenty Thousand killed on each Side; dying Groans, Limbs flying in the Air: Smoak, Noise, Confusion, trampling to Death under Horses' Feet; Flight, Pursuit, Victory; Fields strewed with Carcases left for Food to Dogs and Wolves, and Birds of Prey; Plundering, Stripping, Ravishing, Burning, and Destroying. And to set forth the Valour of my own dear Countrymen, I assured him that I had seen them blow up a Hundred Enemies at once in a Siege, and as many in a Ship, and beheld the dead Bodies come down in Pieces from the Clouds, to the great Diversion of the Spectators.

(ch. V)

Human beings are superior to Yahoos, then, mainly in their capacity for mischief. We are obliged to consider the Yahoos in a new light. They are more primitive than human beings, more openly filthy; but are not human beings, with their complicated diseases, capable of even worse physical nastiness? Swift presents us with a number of descriptions of Yahoo behaviour, provokingly reminiscent of human behaviour but cruder; more contemptible in one sense, and yet more harmless. For example, Yahoo avarice:

... in some Fields of his Country, there are certain shining *Stones* of several Colours, whereof the *Yahoos* are violently fond; and when part of these *Stones* are fixed in the Earth, as it sometimes happeneth, they will dig with their claws for whole Days to get them out, and carry them away, and hide them by Heaps in the Kennels; but still looking round with great Caution, for fear their Comrades should find out their Treasure. My Master said, he could never discover the Reason of this unnatural Appetite, or how these *Stones* could be of any Use to a *Yahoo*; but now he believed it might proceed from the same Principle of *Avarice*, which I had ascribed to Mankind; that, he had once, by way of Experiment, privately removed a Heap of these *Stones* from the Place where one of his *Yahoos* had buried it: whereupon, the sordid Animal missing the Treasure, by his loud lamenting brought the whole Herd to the Place, there miserably howled, then fell to biting and tearing the rest; began to pine away, would neither eat nor sleep, nor work, until he ordered a Servant privately to convey the *Stones* into the same Hole, and hide them as before; which when his *Yahoo* had found, he presently recovered his Spirits and good Humour; but took Care to remove them to a better hiding Place; and hath ever since been a very serviceable Brute.

(ch. VII)

There are similar pictures of the Yahoo treatment of a fallen favourite and a Yahoo female sexually excited. It is the human equivalent that we are continually confronted with in these descriptions. The Yahoo is a mirror in which human nature must see itself. Swift's technique here may be regarded as an extended example of the device of 'arguing through images'. The Yahoo is the image of man, but distorted: man with a difference. Each picture of the Yahoo reminds us of the odious resemblance, but if we try to escape from it by insisting on the difference we come up against another set of images, of human behaviour, which show us what the difference really amounts to. Between the two sets of images we are caught, much as Swift's imaginary victim is caught in the two pamphlets discussed earlier.

The conclusion which Swift has forced us to entertain – that man is virtually a Yahoo or worse – is impossible and outrageous. Clearly some trick of logic has been practised upon us, and we must try to find out what it is. Where has Swift deviated from a true view of human nature to achieve this distortion? What is the relevant fact about man which he has succeeded in misrepresenting or suppressing? The answer will vary according to whether we resort to Christian orthodoxy or not. To a Christian, which Swift was, the relevant facts would be man's moral weakness owing to the Fall and the need for Christian charity in judging him. A modern, non-theological answer might be that man, in his development from primitive forms of life, has achieved only a limited rationality and morality, so that a measure of failure in all human beings must be expected.

Swift's strategy is to cause man to be judged by creatures who are unequipped to understand him sympathetically. The Houyhnhnms, living the placid life of reason, neither troubled nor inspired by irrational forces, know nothing of the indignity or the glory of the human state. They are on a different metaphysical level from man: there is no equivalent to the Fall in their history. But, as we have seen, it is their sense of values which imposes itself. The great mistake, surely, is to suppose that Swift seriously intended the Houyhnhnm standard to be applied to man. The Houyhnhnms are a device for embarrassing mankind. That Gulliver, the plain man who seems to represent average human nature, should be converted to the Houyhnhnms' standpoint is simply a part of Swift's strategy. It is also part of the strategy that Gulliver, in giving an account of the human race, should omit important truths which would have explained the more disgraceful side of the picture.

What do the Houyhnhnms represent? They may perhaps remind us of the impossible and inhuman standard of perfection which people sometimes apply to their fellow-men when they are feeling unreasonable. It is part of Swift's witty purpose here to be unreasonable. Can they represent his ideal of moral perfection? To say so is to bring his sense of values seriously into question, for the Houyhnhnms are in several respects unsympathetic, even repellent. They feel no sorrow at the death of their relatives; they marry according to the wishes of parents and friends, knowing nothing of love and courtship; and they seem depressingly deficient in urges and enthusiasms such as make life exciting, if less orderly, for human beings. As F. R. Leavis wittily expresses it, 'they may have all the reason, but the Yahoos have all the life ... The clean skin of the Houyhnhnms, in short, is stretched over a void.' He identifies them with, 'Reason, Truth and Nature, the Augustan positives', but claims that, 'it was in deadly earnest that Swift appealed to these'. This would imply that Swift's art is at fault, that he fails to make his point with us because his positives are thinner and less satisfying than he realizes. But is there not some injustice here? To a sensibility as much outraged by disorder and dirt as Swift's, mere order and cleanliness must have had an appeal, but this does not mean that they were his 'positives', any more than incidental, even frequent, exasperation at human behaviour is to be labelled 'misanthropy'. One has to distinguish here between the beliefs and attitudes to which the author, as a responsible moral being, commits himself, and those very different, sometimes livelier, reactions which are a matter of temperament, and which often lend themselves irresistibly to artistic treatment. It was easier in Swift's period than later for the author to step down from one level of attitude to the other, and it is the healthier state of affairs that this should be natural. The need to distinguish between the two levels is very important for readers of

Swift, and the failure to do so is a frequent occasion for misunderstanding. The Houyhnhnms were an idea to be played with, offering scope for the indulgence of temperamental animus, but not to be taken too seriously. Is there not a slight humorous awareness in the suavity with which he dwells on their solemn simplicity and innocence?

Some modern critics think that the Houyhnhnms embody the self-sufficient ethics of contemporary Deist or neo-Stoic thinkers, to which Swift was hostile. Kathleen M. Williams, in an interesting paper,[1] suggests that they represent 'an inadequate and inhuman rationalism', and that 'the negativeness of their blameless life is part of Swift's intention'. This view, whether we accept it or not, is certainly valuable as a corrective to the view that they represent Swift's ideal.

If the foregoing analysis of *Gulliver's Travels*, Book IV, is accepted, it reveals that Swift's techniques here are fundamentally similar to those which were pointed out in the earlier works. There is an outrageous thesis to be proved, an ingenious exploitation of logic for that purpose, and a translation of the ideas into concrete conceptions ('arguing through images'); and in the development of the concrete elements there is a significant ordering of detail to produce a tendentious distortion of the truth.

To the critics who complain of Swift's negativeness, of his lack of positives or their inadequacy, part of the answer is that his capacity to accommodate so much negativeness within an artistic pattern, often transforming it into comedy, is the sign of an heroic digestion. And an heroic digestion is what Swift, condemned to more than his share of unpleasantness in life, most certainly had. The immense freedom, which is also a consummate control, with which Swift handles his material is evidence of a liberating experience for him akin to that which it affords the reader. Perhaps we have become too reluctant to admit to the satisfaction which satirical expression provides. 'He gives me as much pleasure as I can bear,' writes Dryden of Juvenal. 'His spleen is raised and he raises mine.' Swift was, in curious ways, inhibited about positives, suffering perhaps from certain forms of emotional impotence. This may be regarded sympathetically as an infirmity, giving a strange aloofness, but also a certain distinction, to the very real goodness in his nature. For an expression of his attitude to the good life, reserved yet with more feeling than was usual with him, the composition *On the Death of Mrs Johnson* may again be cited. Sometimes he masked true benevolence beneath the cloak of curmudgeonliness, as in *A Letter to a Very Young Lady* (1727).

Both as man and as artist Swift gains by being studied in relation to a tradition of wit which provided for a free play of fictitious attitudes. Too 'straight' a reading of certain works has led to an exaggeration of the grimmer sides to the man, and emphasis on the element of frustration and tragedy in his life has deflected attention from what must have been an immense delight in successful artistic creation.

NOTE

1. 'Gulliver's Voyage to the Houyhnhnms', *A Journal of English Literary History* (December, 1951).

BOOKS, READERS AND PATRONS

PAT ROGERS

The circumstances in which books are written, published and read are not in themselves matters of direct literary concern. However, it happens that the period between 1660 and 1780 saw the growth of an identifiable and, compared with the past, almost an organized profession of letters. Moreover, it chances that certain of the greatest writers – Dryden, Pope and Johnson above all – played a crucial role in the evolution of this profession. The process we shall be discussing involves a number of distinct agents: authors, patrons, publishers, printers, booksellers, critics and reviewers, readers, book-buyers, subscribers and so on. Some of these roles overlap on occasions; but they may be broadly divided into three main categories. First, the producers: creative artists, but also editors, translators, compilers, right down to the humble index-makers. These are the people who 'generate' a text, that is to say provide the words on the page. Second, the middlemen: those who are responsible for the transmission of the message which has been generated. They might include scribes or printers who multiply copies; salesmen and advertisers who promote the sale of the book; commercial intermediaries who stock, warehouse and distribute the work. In the period under review, the most important figure here, at the centre of the whole web of book-trade operations, was located the so-called 'bookseller', equivalent in his central capacity to the modern publisher. Third, the consumers: those who handle the book after it has been duly replicated and broadcast by the previous group. This means the reader above all; the critic, except when he is engaged in puffing the work as part of its promotion; the polemical opponent who writes another book in reply; and any person at the far end of the process, who had no part in the creation or dissemination of the work, and simply responds to its appearance before the world.

In all these categories there was a growth in absolute terms during the period from Dryden to Johnson. The increase is not precisely quantifiable, but it indisputably occurred in each case, and we must be cautious lest we make too facile a causal connection between them. It is best to consider each group separately.

Logically, we should start with the authors. The number of separately published items appearing in Britain stood at an average of about six hundred items annually throughout the period. A high proportion of these were pamphlets, especially around the peak year of 1714 – in this year of the Hanoverian accession, over one thousand separate items appeared. But a slow and steady rise in the average can be discerned, with the lowest annual totals concentrated in the earliest span up to 1700.[1] A more clearcut and spectacular rise can be traced in the case of newspapers and periodicals: virtually non-existent in the time of Dryden, they have attained an annual average of forty or more by the time of Johnson's death in 1784. Now it is true that the authors of many books were anonymous, and so these raw statistics might possibly hide an alternative explanation – not more authors, but the same number of authors each writing more titles.

Samuel Johnson favoured the more straightforward explanation. In a celebrated *Adventurer* paper, dated 11 December 1753, he defined the 'peculiar character' of the age in which he was living in these terms:

> The present age, if we consider chiefly the state of our own country, may be styled with great propriety *The Age of Authors*; for, perhaps, there never was a time in which men of all degrees of ability, of every kind of education, of every profession and employment, were posting with ardour so general to the press. The province of writing was formerly left to those, who by study, or the appearance of study, were supposed to have gained knowledge unattainable by the busy part of mankind; but in these enlightened days, every man is qualified to instruct every other man: and he that beats the anvil, or guides the plough, not content with supplying corporeal necessities, amuses himself in the hours of leisure with providing intellectual pleasures for his countrymen.

And Johnson goes on to speak of the 'dogmatical legions of the present race'. For these 'legions' the arrival of the *Dictionary* was a major event.

The two resplendent folio volumes of the *Dictionary* which appeared in 1755 were followed by four more folio editions in the author's lifetime, and others just after his death. But already the *Dictionary* was available in other forms: as a quarto, in abridged versions, as the basis of bilingual dictionaries. Within a few weeks of its first appearance, the mountainous book was sliced up into one hundred and sixty five weekly parts at 6d. a time. In years to come the *Dictionary* found itself expanded and contracted. Noah Webster's celebrated *American Dictionary* (1828) was in several important respects a reply to Johnson. The copy of the work which Becky Sharp flung from the coach into Chiswick Mall was of course an abridgment not the bulky original. But even by 1848, when *Vanity Fair* appeared, the English public had not yet thrown the *Dictionary* aside. It remained authoritative and almost unrivalled. Its impact on the English mind, for generations, was astounding, and one could only chart this influence with any degree of accuracy if one were to follow the production of each new edition and recension aimed at a slightly different market.

The second category, that of the middlemen, undoubtedly grew within the period, and whilst complete accuracy cannot be guaranteed, reliable orders of magnitude are attainable. If we limit the term 'bookseller' to the narrow sense already defined there were perhaps no more than fifty London firms at the height of Dryden's career. By the time Pope started to write, early in the eighteenth century, there were perhaps a hundred; by the time of his death in 1744, more like a hundred and fifty; by the time Johnson died in 1784, over two hundred. A more than proportionate increase in the number of provincial booksellers occurred over the same interval: they came almost to equal the London tally. However, this does not mean that the whole of England (let alone Britain) was equally well served. At the very end of this period, the bookseller Lackington reports a journey to Edinburgh and back in the year 1787. According to his account, 'nothing but trash' was to be found in the sprinkling of shops he encountered on his route. Only Leeds and York were adequately covered, outside the two capitals: towns as large as Glasgow, Manchester and Newcastle could produce only an exiguous stock of reading matter.

Lackington it was who did most to improve matters, by his innovatory method of buying in bulk and selling large quantities of second-hand volumes. Up to this time, literature had been largely the property of the London book trade, and their title lay in the copyright of *new* books. As a result, the distribution system was geared to the commercial needs of a relatively small group of conservative businessmen. It was this monopoly power which irked some authors, among whom laments for a lost system of private patronage found a ready response. But Samuel Johnson took an opposite point of view, which may appear paradoxical at first sight.

Johnson was the son of a Staffordshire bookseller, and he therefore knew the ins and outs of the trade from firsthand experience. He was able to define the exact standing of a member of the trade, as he understood it. Witness a conversation reported by Boswell on 7 April 1775:

> Davies, zealous for the honour of *the Trade*, said, Gardner was not properly a bookseller. JOHNSON. 'Nay, Sir; he certainly was a bookseller. He had served his time regularly, was a member of the Stationers' company, kept a shop in the face of mankind, purchased copyright, and was a *bibliopole*, Sir, in every sense.'

There are several notable features in this definition. Johnson rightly emphasizes the need to serve a proper apprenticeship and to become 'free' in the city company. Though the Stationers were less powerful than a hundred years earlier, it was still true in the eighteenth century that an individual's legal and social position in the world of commerce was bound up with his place in the corporate structure. Secondly, the bookseller in the full sense is required both to have a 'shop' (which might be an ordinary retail outlet, or a wholesaling centre) and to buy authors' copyrights, the essential act in publishing. Thirdly, there is the strange word '*bibliopole*', which does not even occur in the *Dictionary*. One place it did turn up regularly, as Johnson would be aware, was in the indictments of booksellers prosecuted by the Secretary of State. The information laid against members of the trade, when they were suspected of producing a seditious, obscene or libellous work, would be given in English, but an official warrant would describe the individual as *bibliopola*.

With this detailed knowledge, Johnson brought to the subject a measure of affection for certain figures in the trade with whom he had been closely associated. So when he told Boswell that the booksellers were 'generous liberal-minded men' and 'patrons of literature' or that he 'uniformly professed much regard' for the profession, there may be a small element of special pleading. On the other hand, he was careful to make distinctions. Goldsmith called the booksellers, not without reason, his best friends. Clearly, those who profited from the system were not inclined to hark back to some mythical Golden Age under Queen Anne. But the myth of benevolent patronage persisted. It could not be scotched by Johnson's superbly scornful letter to Lord Chesterfield: though written in 1755, this did not appear in print until Boswell seized the opportunity to 'enrich [his] work with a perfect transcript' of that which 'the world has so eagerly desired to see'. This was in 1791, by which time the Augustan dispensation may be said to have passed for good. A generation earlier the dream of enlightened patronage was still alive and well. A few well-heeled men of affairs attempted to preserve the tradition of Dorset, Halifax and Somers, and to catch reflected glory from those they subsidized. There are dozens of dedications addressed to Lord Burlington right into the 1740s: Pope had cast his noble friend as a sort of unofficial Minister of the Arts in one of his *Moral Essays* (1731), and authors continued to hope that he would favour their slim volumes of miscellaneous verse or their ponderous architectural folios. Other would-be patrons survived longer, and so did their flock of followers.

In the late seventeenth and early eighteenth centuries, patronage had usually meant a direct subsidy for political support, or at the least a kind of cultural boosting of the patron. After the Hanoverian accession, there was less straightforward political support. The reasons for this have been debated: one popular view is that Walpole's government machine made bribery of M.P.s a more productive exercise than the promotion of good public relations through payments to authors. In its simplest form this argument cannot be correct, for Walpole *did* pay authors to churn out publicity on his behalf – though not the authors we should regard as the best qualified laureates which a regime might attract. Indeed, the Prime Minister's largest subsidy was discovered on inquiry to have been made to a near-anonymous hack called William Arnall, who has achieved a dubious niche in history as the recipient of almost £11,000 from government funds in the course of only four years. Pope gave this denizen of Grub Street a properly symbolic role among the muckrakers who take part in *The Dunciad*. Pope's note specifies his offences with prim accuracy, stating that Arnall 'writ for hire, and valued himself upon it'. The text freezes his characteristic posture more graphically:

No crab more active in the dirty dance,
Downward to climb, and backward to advance.

If this was patronage, it is not surprising that writers of honour were
disposed to turn their back on the whole exercise. Johnson's quest for
dignity and self-respect was typical of a wider movement affecting
the social position and psychological self-perception of writers at
large.

We can now turn to the third class, that is the readers and other
'consumers' of literature. At the start of the period there was no kind
of reviewing, as we should understand it. The major form of response
to books was a tract or pamphlet in reply, often scurrilous in tone. In
the middle of the period, civilized discussion of literature becomes a
more feasible undertaking. The largest contribution here was that
made by the hugely influential *Spectator*: Addison and Steele did not
spend much time discussing contemporary books, but their urbanity,
good humour and tolerance made for an atmosphere in which it
gradually seemed possible to take sensible note of current publications
without too much regard to personalities. Admittedly, the first important literary journal, *The Gentleman's Magazine* (from 1731), still
had little to contribute along these lines. It printed verse, the titles of
books published monthly, and other snatches of information concerning doings in the world of letters, along with births, marriages
and deaths, the latest bankrupts, prices of the funds, newspaper controversies and so on. However, with the *Monthly Review*, from 1749,
and the *Critical Review*, from 1756, we reach the beginning of mature
discussion of topical books. Goldsmith contributed to the former, and
Smollett to the latter. The articles are by no means totally free from
bias or personal rancour, but they do attempt something nearer an
objective survey of the ideas canvassed in new books.

As to the size and composition of the wider audience, this can only
be a matter of approximation or educated guesswork. It was generally
believed at the time that there had been a steady increase in the
volume of readership through the eighteenth century, and this is
probably true, though impossible to quantify with great exactitude.
In his life of Swift, Johnson commented on a sale of some eleven
thousand copies which *The Conduct of the Allies* (1711) attained in a
few weeks. He regarded this as a notable feat, for 'we were not yet
a nation of readers'. In this context we should note another famous

observation, reported by Boswell on 29 April 1778: 'It must be considered, that we have now more knowledge generally diffused; all our ladies read now, which is a great extension.' The latter contention has been widely accepted, and it has been applied to such matters as the increasing importance which the novel acquired among literary genres. The truth is that our evidence for this belief is almost wholly anecdotal. Only a few objective tests are available, such as subscription lists and inventories of deceased persons; and they most probably understate the proportion of female readers. One cannot be sure. Women of the upper classes were unlikely to have any more time on their hands in 1750 than in 1650 or 1550: indeed, newer child-rearing practices tended to involve them more rather than less in the day-to-day supervision of their family. Even women with an adequate supply of domestic servants, such as Mrs Thrale, devoted a substantial portion of their day to children. However, it may well be that, a few rungs down the social ladder, women had their lot eased by the alleviation of some domestic tasks. Middle-class women (the phrase is an anachronism, but a harmless one here) did not perform domestic tasks so much as supervise servants in their performance. A taste for reading presupposes a degree of leisure, and as the ordinary business of life became less brutal and penurious more and more people – both men and women – could begin to count on some time as their own.

Literacy is a subject on which we can be less vague. It appears certain that two-thirds of the male population, one-third of the female, had attained basic literacy by the middle of the eighteenth century – the evidence comes from wedding registers in the years following the passage of the Marriage Act in 1754. At the lower end of the social scale people may not have been able to do very much more than sign their name, which is the test applied. In country districts, especially the more remote, the number of the functionally illiterate would be higher. Labourers and servants would be among the groups scoring lowest, although even in this category about half the males probably had basic reading equipment. This would apply to only a quarter of the women in similar categories; as Lawrence Stone has pointed out, 'The education of the daughters of yeomen was confined to a very little reading and writing, barely enough for religious and functional use.'[2] More important to the spread of the habit of reading were the urban artisans and journeymen. One estimate suggests that this group achieved a 'literacy plateau' of seventy-five to eighty-five per cent around 1675, and did not achieve a higher proportion for another hundred years. At the time of revolutionary fervour this group became voracious consumers of the pamphlet wars of the 1790s: Burke's estimate of 400,000 regular readers may therefore not be excessive, though it should be remembered that a disproportionate share in this number would be accounted for by the residents of London.

The sharp increase in the scale of the periodical press within the eighteenth century does seem to point to a growth in readership. This process follows the appearance of the first regular daily newspaper, the *Daily Courant*, in 1702, and the first provincial newspapers, starting with the *Norwich Post* at about the same date. By the middle of the century there were papers in all considerable cities and towns, with places a small as Kendal, Cirencester and Bury St Edmunds capable of supporting their own local journal. Outside Edinburgh and Dublin, there were few organs to inform or entertain the citizens of Scotland and Ireland; but the proviso is an important one, since these capital cities led a vigorous journalistic life. Wales lacked a centre of population of any size (the only significant town with a Welsh sphere of influence was Shrewsbury, with a population of around 12,000 in the early eighteenth century), and so it fared even worse: there were no newspapers either in English or in the native language. Meanwhile the English provincial press flourished, and brought a spread of ideas and material culture to distant parts of the kingdom: advertising began to play a major role, not least in the sphere of book promotion.

In London, weeklies, bi-weeklies, tri-weeklies, dailies, evening papers and other varieties of newspaper sprang up – quite apart from monthly, quarterly and annual reviews. Compared with the modern array of periodicals, only the Sunday paper was missing; and with journals such as the *British Gazette and Sunday Monitor*, from 1780, that deficiency was remedied. In the case of newspapers we have, too, a reliable index to circulation. Government figures on the returns yielded by successive stamp duties prove conclusively that circulation did edge up as the century progressed. Pedlars distributed country newspapers, and also a significant portion of reading matter for the ordinary people: chapbooks, ballads and broadsides.[3] These were short, badly printed and evilly illustrated with crude woodcuts; they cost a penny or two, and generally concerned folk-heroes or demons, with the characters of fairy tale and legend occasionally joined by modern figures such as Robinson Crusoe or Moll Flanders.

It is fair to conclude that there was a marked development in reading during the period, with the market on the increase for good and bad literature alike. Adventurous publishers such as Edmund Curll risked the disapproval of their staider brethren in the trade (as well as the eternal infamy of *The Dunciad*) by pioneering new forms of advertisement and promotion. Curll's vulgar appeals to prurience and curiosity provide a distressing episode in the history of taste, but they do so because they were, to all appearances, *successful*. His activities as plagiarist and pirate, his prosecution for obscene libel, his blasphemous and mendacious ragbags thinly disguised as works of literature – all these manifest a new commercial confidence. His career is highly representative historically. His freedoms were only possible because of the lapse of the Licensing Act in 1695; up until then, an absolutist monarchy had censored all printed matter that might come before the public. Again, Curll was the first person to realize that literature could be *news*, and to capitalize on notoriety. His bold advertising methods were themselves reliant on the greater currency of newspapers. Later in the century, advertising techniques were developed by men such as John Newbery who produced a chapbook version of *Goody Two-Shoes* in which the heroine's father died 'miserably' when he was seized with a violent fever in a place 'where Dr James's powder was not to be had'. As was then not unusual, Newbery held the concession for proprietary medicines along with his book-stock. About the same time, packets were sent out to all parish clerks in England, containing advertisements for Smollett's serialized *History*. Each packet contained a half-crown and an invitation for the clerk to place the advertisements in every church pew. By such dubious means did the cause of literature advance.

More readers, then, to go with more writers and more middlemen. Johnson, we have seen, referred to an 'age of authors'; more cautiously, he wrote in *The Rambler* (6 August 1751) that 'the authors of London were formerly computed by Swift at several thousands, and there is not any reason for suspecting that their number has decreased.' But evidently this supply of prolific authors was satisfying a well-established demand – both from booksellers alert to the profit motive, and from readers hungry for fresh literary experience.

In their different ways, the careers and destinies of Dryden, Pope and Johnson were exemplary. Dryden's mission has been seen as that of first preparing 'an assault on the outworks of influence', with a view to infiltrating himself at the centre of power. A slow starter as a poet, he yet managed to become laureate by the time he was thirty-six: this carried the then considerable emolument of £200 per annum. Two years later the post of Historiographer Royal augmented Dryden's dignity, if not his salary. His plays brought him at least as much again. When he ultimately lost his court appointments, following the Glorious Revolution, he suffered a considerable financial setback, and promptly set about repairing the damage through literary production. It is noteworthy that his quarrels with Jacob Tonson were generally about money, whereas Pope's with his publishers were generally about copyright, confidentiality or quasi-moral issues. Dryden's biggest single coup involved his translation of the works of Virgil, which Tonson issued by subscription in 1697. This venture was planned over a number of years, and both poet and bookseller gave as much attention to financial arrangements as to its sumptuous physical appearance and grand stylistic gloss. Calculations as to Dryden's profit from the translation vary between £1,200 and £1,400. This was a high sum, particularly bearing in mind that the total number of subscribers was no more than three hundred and fifty and of these only one hundred paid five guineas instead of two, so that they might be commemorated with special engravings within the text. Three years later, two months before Dryden's death in 1700, Tonson issued his notable series of *Fables* from various sources. This time Dryden was paid 250 guineas, in return for which he supplied 12,000 lines of verse. Pope is supposed to have made this a rate of 6*d.* a line: it is in fact a little less. One might compare this with the rate of 1½*d.* a line which a genuine Grub Street denizen, John Oldmixon, was able to claim from Tonson for translations, exactly twenty years later.

Publication by subscription was a practice employed by many of the greatest writers of the age, Pope and Johnson following Dryden in this respect. It was a way of attracting support in advance of publishing (and frequently of writing) the book. Intending purchasers put down a deposit, commonly half the full price, with the balance paid when the work appeared. This system possibly made for a less sycophantic relationship between authors and the prominent sponsors of literature who led public taste. It certainly gave writers a better idea of their audience, or some parts of the audience; though subscriptions were managed by booksellers, authors generally had to take some share in mounting the venture if they wanted it to achieve wide circulation.

The practice of subscription began, as a publishing device, in the early 1600s, but it was Tonson's edition of *Paradise Lost* (1688) which really awakened the trade to its possibilities. Some five hundred and forty subscribers to this volume included many of the greatest figures in the land. Dryden's translation of Virgil followed within a decade, and the scene was set for the great burst of activity in the first quarter of the eighteenth century. Collected editions of *The Tatler* and *The Spectator* circulated almost as widely as the original periodical parts, and of course the subscription volumes survived longer in libraries and drawing-rooms. Major collections by John Gay, Matthew Prior and Addison appeared in this form. But it was the triumph of Pope's incursions into the subscription market which astounded the age and transformed the public notion of a professional author.

In fact, Pope undertook three main subscription campaigns.[4] His translations of the *Iliad* (1715–20) and the *Odyssey* (1725–6) were carried out in conjunction with the bookseller Bernard Lintot, and both parties stood to gain from the venture. On the other hand, Pope's edition of Shakespeare (1725) was mounted for the private benefit of the poet; the publisher, Tonson this time, did not put much effort into promotion, and the results were much less spectacular than was the case with Homer. Up to the time of the *Iliad* Pope had not made very much money although he was already famous. None of his early poems, *The Rape of the Lock* included, had yielded even as much as £40 for their copyright. Pope decided to take things into his own hands: as a crippled Roman Catholic, lacking any substantial private income, it was vital for him to capitalize on his only resource if he was to attain financial independence and social recognition. He enlisted the aid of prominent people, chivvied his friends and kept

Lintot busy. The result was that five hundred and seventy five subscribers were found, including some of the greatest men in the land – Sir Christopher Wren, Sir Isaac Newton and the Duke of Marlborough – adding the lustre of human achievement to the serried ranks of aristocrats and politicians. Pope extracted particularly good terms from Lintot, and he made more money than a subscription of this size would normally have ensured an author. In fact he earned something like £5,000. He did almost as well from the *Odyssey* (where he had the help of two collaborators in the translation): an equally vigorous promotion campaign produced a total of more than six hundred subscribers. It is possible that this latter venture was to some unascertainable degree a front for a Jacobite fund-raising exercise, but that does not alter the fact of its striking success.

Together, these two Homer subscriptions have been regarded as a turning-point in the fortunes of the man of letters. Leslie Stephen wrote that Pope

received a kind of commission from the upper class to execute the translation ... Every person of quality has felt himself bound to promote so laudable an undertaking; the patron had been superseded by a kind of joint-stock body of collective patronage.[5]

Moreover, Pope's decision to inscribe his *Iliad* not to the normal aristocratic name but to dedicate it instead to a fellow-professional, the dramatist Congreve, has been hailed as equally significant. Strictly speaking, Congreve had given up professional writing for some years and was by this time living as a sinecurist and rentier – but the point holds. It was one more step along the road to a declaration of authorial independence from the traditional system of patronage.

Pope did not use the method again on a large scale, though some work by himself and by Swift came out in this form in Ireland during the 1730s. The poet turned to new ways of exploiting his name and literary potential. But meanwhile, others had learnt from Pope the possibilities of publication by way of subscription. Thomson's *The Seasons* appeared in this form (1730), as did Fielding's *Miscellanies* (1743). During the 1760s Sterne employed this method for his sermons, and his European reputation is shown by the presence on his lists of names such as Crébillon, d'Holbach, Diderot and Voltaire. At the end of the period Cowper obtained seven hundred subscribers for his translation of Homer (1791), designed to supplant Pope's. Fanny Burney, who had received only twenty guineas for *Evelina* (1778), although it was the craze of the circulating libraries, decided to issue *Camilla* (1796) by subscription: she netted £3,000. In this she was following the example of her father, Johnson's friend Dr Charles Burney. He had issued the first volume of his *History of Music* by this method in 1776: eight hundred and fifty subscribers included many distinguished persons.

Even Johnson, not the most musical of men, was persuaded to enter his name for Burney's *History*. He was indeed a regular subscriber to works covering a wide range of subjects. However, his only exploitation of subscription publishing was restricted. Outside an Irish edition of the *Dictionary*, it seems to have been confined to the great edition of Shakespeare, and there his procedures were somewhat unorthodox. Boswell reports the scene when a young bookseller visited Johnson at a time when the project was reaching fruition:

> '*I shall print no list of Subscribers;*' said Johnson, with great abruptness: but almost immediately recollecting himself, added, very complacently, 'Sir, I have two very cogent reasons for not printing any list of subscribers; – one, that I have lost all the names, – the other, that I have spent all the money.'

It is not surprising that Johnson should elsewhere have given his opinion that 'He that asks subscriptions soon finds that he has enemies.' Johnson's contribution to the profession was to lie in a different direction. He was above all the true professional, capable of accepting a commission on almost every subject, willing to take up initiatives mounted by the booksellers, responsive to the demands of the market as mediated by the trade. Insofar as he achieved the dignity of hero as man of letters (which Carlyle was to bestow upon him), this can be attributed primarily to his reliance on the suffrage of the public. Even his acceptance of a state pension could not outweigh the fact that he wrote, not for a private circle or a privileged coterie, but for the growing number of readers willing to put down money in exchange for reading matter. Dryden had been the laureate of a court; Pope had been the careful manipulator of a wider, but still highly selective, audience. But Johnson was a servant of the reading public at large. His superb *Lives of the Poets* was generated, not by the whim of any individual taste, but out of the calculations and profit-estimates of a team of thirty-six booksellers.

His most important single work, the *Dictionary*, resulted from a plan by another collective group: nine booksellers are named on the title-page, with giants of the trade among them – Dodsley, Longman and Millar. In this respect, as in so many others, the career of Samuel Johnson was truly symbolic. He *lived* the life of a writer, and in his search for a livelihood he experienced at first hand the changes, big and small, which affected the world of letters in the eighteenth century.[6]

NOTES

1. Figures from I. Maxted, *The London Book Trades 1775–1800* (1977), supplemented by my own counts.

2. L. Stone, *The Family, Sex and Marriage in England 1500–1800* (Penguin, 1979), 144.

3. V. Neuberg, *Chapbooks* (2nd edn, 1972), is the major source.

4. For a detailed analysis, see P. Rogers, 'Pope and his Subscribers', *Publishing History*, III (1978).

5. Leslie Stephen, *English Literature and Society in the Eighteenth Century* (1904), 51.

6. I have not attempted to give details of payments to authors, edition sizes, book prices, etc., since they vary within such wide limits as to be incapable of summary. Details will be found in the works listed in the Appendix by Beljame, Chapman, Saunders and Collins. P. Rogers, 'The Writer and Society', 49–56, sets out some representative examples in each category, but it would be possible to provide different cases. The evidence does, however, suggest that books were printed in larger editions as time went on, and that the returns of authorship (insofar as we can compare like with like) roughly doubled between 1680 and 1780.

POETRY IN THE
EIGHTEENTH CENTURY

T. S. ELIOT

There is an essay to be written on the quotations which Sir Walter
Scott used for the chapter headings of his novels, to illustrate the wide
reading and critical good taste of that novelist. It is a great many
years ago — about thirty years ago* — that I was struck by a quotation
of four lines; I cannot now remember at what chapter of which of
Scott's novels it is placed:

> His fall was destin'd to a barren strand,
> A petty fortress, and a dubious hand;
> He left the name, at which the world grew pale,
> To point a moral, or adorn a tale.

It was not for a good many years after, that I read *The Vanity of
Human Wishes*, but the impression which the whole poem made upon
me was only a confirmation of the impression which the four lines
had made upon me long before. These lines, especially the first two,
with their just inevitable sequence of *barren, petty*, and *dubious*, still
seem to me among the finest that have ever been written in that
particular idiom.

It is dangerous to generalize about the poetry of the eighteenth
century as about that of any other age; for it was, like any other age,
an age of transition. We are accustomed to make a rough tripartite
division between the poetry of the age of Pope, the poetry of
sentimental philosophizing – Thomson, Young, Cowper – and the
early Romantic movement. What really happened is that after Pope
there was no one who thought and felt nearly enough like Pope to
be able to use his language quite successfully; but a good many
second-rate writers tried to write something like it, unaware of the
fact that the change of sensibility demanded a change of idiom.
Sensibility alters from generation to generation in everybody,
whether we will or no; but expression is only altered by a man of

*Thirty years before 1930, when this essay was originally written.

genius. A great many second-rate poets, in fact, are second-rate just for this reason, that they have not the sensitiveness and consciousness to perceive that they feel differently from the preceding generation, and therefore must use words differently. In the eighteenth century there are a good many second-rate poets: and mostly they are second-rate because they were incompetent to find a style of writing for themselves, suited to the matter they wanted to talk about and the way in which they apprehended this matter.

In such a period the poets who are still worth reading may be of two kinds: those who, however imperfectly, attempted innovations in idiom, and those who were just conservative enough in sensibility to be able to devise an interesting variation on the old idiom. The originality of Gray and Collins consists in their adaptation of an Augustan style to an eighteenth-century sensibility. The originality of Goldsmith consists in his having the old and the new in such just proportion that there is no conflict; he is Augustan and also sentimental and rural without discordance. Of all the eighteenth-century poets, Johnson is the nearest to a die-hard. And of all the eighteenth-century poets, Goldsmith and Johnson deserve fame because they used the form of Pope beautifully, without ever being mere imitators. And from the point of view of the artisan of verse, their kind of originality is as remarkable as any other: indeed, to be original with the *minimum* of alteration is sometimes more distinguished than to be original with the *maximum* of alteration.

Certain qualities are to be expected of any type of good verse at any time; we may say the qualities which good verse shares with good prose. Hardly any good poet in English has written *bad* prose; and some English poets have been among the greatest of English prose writers. The finest prose writer of Shakespeare's time was, I think, Shakespeare himself; Milton and Dryden were among the greatest prose writers of their times. Wordsworth and Coleridge may be cited, and Keats; and Shelley – not I think in his correspondence, but certainly in his *Defence of Poetry*. This is not a sign of versatility but of unity. For there are qualities essential to good prose which are essential to good verse as well; and we may say positively with Mr Ezra Pound, that verse must be at least as well written as prose. We may even say that the originality of some poets has consisted in their finding a way of saying in verse what no one else has been able to say except in prose written or spoken. Such is the originality of Donne, who, though employing an elaborate metric and an uncommon vocabulary, yet manages to maintain a tone of direct informal address. The talent of Dryden is exactly the same: the difference is only that the speech which he uses is that of a more formal age. Donne makes poetry out of a learned but colloquial dialogue speech, Dryden out of the prose of political oratory; and Pope out of the most polished drawing-room manner. And of Goldsmith and Johnson we can say the same; their verse is poetry partly because it has the virtues of good prose.

Those who condemn or ignore *en bloc* the poetry of the eighteenth century on the ground that it is 'prosaic' are stumbling over an uncertainty of meaning of the word 'prosaic' to arrive at exactly the wrong conclusion. One does not need to examine a great deal of the inferior verse of the eighteenth century to realize that the trouble with it is that it is not prosaic enough. We are inclined to use 'prosaic' as meaning not only 'like prose', but as 'lacking poetic beauty' – and the Oxford and every other dictionary give us warrant for such use. Only, we ought to distinguish between poetry which is like *good* prose, and poetry which is like *bad* prose. And even so, I believe more prose is bad because it is like bad poetry, than poetry is bad because it is like bad prose. And to have the virtues of good prose is the first and minimum requirement of good poetry.

If you look at the bad verse of any age, you will find most of it lacking in the virtues of prose. When there is a period of good verse, it has often been preceded by a period in which verse was bad because it was too poetic, too artificial; and it is very commonly followed by such another period. The development of blank verse in the hands of Shakespeare and some of his contemporaries was the work of adapting a medium which to begin with was almost intractably poetic, so that it could carry the burdens and exhibit the subtleties of prose; and they accomplished this before prose itself was highly developed. The work of Donne, in a lesser form, was the same. It has prose virtues, and the heavy toil of his minor imitators was wholly to degrade the idiom of Donne into a lifeless verse convention. Speech meanwhile was changing, and Dryden appeared to cleanse the language of verse and once more bring it back to the prose order. For this reason he is a great poet.

The idiom of the Augustan age could not last, for the age itself could not last. But so positive was the culture of that age, that for many years the ablest writers were still naturally in sympathy with it; and it crushed a number of smaller men who felt differently but did not dare to face the fact, and who poured their new wine – always thin, but sometimes of good flavour – into the old bottles. Yet the influence of Dryden and Pope over the middle of the eighteenth century is by no means so great, or so noxious, as has been supposed. A good part of the dreariest verse of the time is written under the shadow of Milton.

> Far in the watery waste, where his broad wave
> From world to world the vast Atlantic rolls,
> On from the piny shores of Labrador
> To frozen Thule east, her airy height
> Aloft to heaven remotest Kilda lifts.
> (MALLET: *Amyntor and Theodora*)

> Thus far of beauty and the pleasing forms
> Which man's untutored fancy, from the scenes
>   Imperfect of this ever changing world
> Creates; and views, enamoured.
> (AKENSIDE: *Pleasures of the Imagination*)

But besides this Miltonic stuff, which is respectable only because Cowper, Thomson, and Young made this line the vehicle for reflection and for observation of nature which prepared the way for Wordsworth; and besides the innumerable Odes, of which none but Gray's and Collins's are remembered, there was a considerable output of five-foot couplets of which one can only say that this form of verse is hardly more unsuitable for what the man had to say than any other would have been. Of such is the *Botanic Garden* and its competitors.

> Who that beholds the summer's glistening swarms,
> Ten thousand thousand gaily gilded forms,
> In violet dance of mixed rotation play,
> Bask in the beam, and beautify the day ...
> (BROOKE: *Universal Beauty*)

This is decadence. The eighteenth century in English verse is not, after Pope, Swift, Prior, and Gay, an age of courtly verse. It seems more like an age of retired country clergymen and schoolmasters. It is cursed with a Pastoral convention – Collins's Eclogues are bad enough, and those of Shenstone consummately dull – and a ruminative mind. And it is intolerably poetic. Instead of working out the proper form for its matter, when it has any, and informing verse with prose virtues, it merely applies the magniloquence of Milton or the neatness of Pope to matter which is wholly unprepared for it; so that what the writers have to say always appears surprised at the way in which they choose to say it.

In this rural, pastoral, meditative age Johnson is the most alien figure. Goldsmith is more a poet of his time, with his melting sentiment just saved by the precision of his language. But Johnson remains a townsman, if certainly not a courtier; a student of mankind not of natural history; a great prose writer; with no tolerance of swains and milkmaids. He has more in common in spirit with Crabbe than with any of his contemporaries; at the same time he is the last Augustan. He is in no way an imitator of Dryden or Pope; very close to them in idiom, he gives his verse a wholly personal stamp.

The two Satires which follow are Johnson's only exercises in this genre. *London* appeared in 1738; *The Vanity of Human Wishes* in 1749. To my mind the latter is the finer poem; but both of them seem to me to be among the greatest verse Satires of the English or any other language; and so far as comparison is justifiable, I do not think that Juvenal, his model, is any better. They are *purer* satire than anything of Dryden or Pope, nearer in spirit to the Latin. For the satirist is in theory a stern moralist castigating the vices of his time or place; and Johnson has a better claim to this seriousness than either Pope or Dryden. In the hands of Dryden the satire becomes almost the lampoon; and Dryden had a special gift for farce. Pope also is more personal than the true satirist. In one way, Johnson goes back to an earlier tradition; however inferior as satires Marston's or even Hall's may be to Johnson's, they are surely much nearer to the spirit and intention of Juvenal than are those of Dryden or Pope. Dryden is, in the modern sense, humorous and witty; Pope is in the modern sense witty though not humorous; Johnson, neither humorous nor witty in this sense, has yet 'the proper wit of poetry' as the seventeenth century and the Augustan age had it also. I can better expose this by a few quotations than by a definition.

There mark what ills the scholar's life assail,
Toil, envy, want, the patron, and the jail.

Condemned a needy supplicant to wait,
While ladies interpose, and slaves debate.

Fate never wounds more deep the generous heart,
Than when a blockhead's insult points the dart.

Some fiery fop, with new commission vain,
Who sleeps on brambles till he kills his man;
Some frolick drunkard, reeling from a feast,
Provokes a broil, and stabs you for a jest.

The precision of such verse gives, I think, an immense satisfaction to the reader: he has said what he wanted to say, with that urbanity which contemporary verse would do well to study; and the satisfaction I get from such lines is what I call the *minimal* quality of poetry. There is much greater poetry than Johnson's; but after all, how little, how very little, good poetry there is anyway. And the kind of satisfaction these lines give me is something that I must have, at least, from any poetry in order to like it. It is the certainty, the ease with which he hits the bull's-eye every time, that makes Johnson a poet. The blundering assaults of his contemporary Churchill — a man of by no means poor abilities – do not make poetry; Churchill gives us an occasional right line, but never a right poem.

And the verse of Johnson has the good qualities of his own best prose, and of the best prose of his time. Bolingbroke, for instance, at his best, has some of the same merit.

Those who demand of poetry a day dream, or a metamorphosis of their own feeble desires and lusts, or what they believe to be 'intensity' of passion, will not find much in Johnson. He is like Pope and Dryden, Crabbe and Landor, a poet for those who want poetry and not something else, some stay for their own vanity. I sometimes think that our own time, with its elaborate equipment of science and psychological analysis, is even less fitted than the Victorian age to appreciate poetry as poetry. But if lines 189–220 of *The Vanity of Human Wishes* are not poetry, I do not know what is.

NOTE

This essay first appeared, under the title 'Johnson's *London* and *The Vanity of Human Wishes*', as the Introduction to the Haslewood Books edition, 1930. It is reprinted in *English Critical Essays, Twentieth Century*, selected by Phyllis M. Jones (The World's Classics, Oxford University Press, 1933), and is reproduced here by permission of Mrs Eliot and the publishers.

ALEXANDER POPE

NORMAN CALLAN

Pope's first and most important claim to greatness is the fact that he is pre-eminently the poet of his age. As with the work of Chaucer and Shakespeare, his poetry 'dates' sharply and vividly: it crystallizes in memorable speech the emotional and intellectual attitudes of his day, and the reader who is going to receive the full effect of his poetry must be aware of him as speaking not solely for himself but for the age and society in which he lived.

If we sometimes fail to recognize this, one of the reasons is the relatively narrow appeal of Pope's culture when compared with that of Chaucer or Shakespeare. The culture of Chaucer's age, and even Shakespeare's, is more than half non-literary; it is made up of folk-tales, proverbs, ballads, and much else which belongs to oral tradition. When it is embedded in the literary art of a poet, the emotional overtones which go with the oral tradition persist, adding their strength to the effect of the poet's art. Thus Portia's words –

> How far that little candle throws his beams:
> So shines a good deed in a naughty world –

have fixed themselves in the memory of succeeding generations not simply because of the associations encircling the image of 'candle' on the one hand, or the exquisite modulation of phrase on the other: it is the inclusion within a single poetic statement of both a mature, sophisticated outlook and one which is traditional and unsceptical that gives the words their remarkable power. One senses that a harmony has been achieved between two different ways of looking at things, and the effect is therefore one of completeness.

Such an effect – surely one of the signs of great poetic utterance – is present in Pope's poetry too: but because the attitudes which are harmonized in, let us say, the opening lines of the *Epistle to Arbuthnot* –

> Shut, shut the door, good John, fatigued I said,
> Tie up the knocker, say I'm sick, I'm dead.

The Dog Star rages, nay, 'tis past a doubt,
All Bedlam, or Parnassus, is let out –

are less easily recognizable than those in Portia's words, the full effect
of such a passage is often missed. By Pope's time, for good or ill, our
culture had become pervasively literary; except for ridicule, poets had
dismissed from their repertoire the vernacular phraseology which
often makes the poetry of Shakespeare or the Authorized Version so
telling; and critics, when they met it (particularly in the plays of
Shakespeare), did not always recognize its effectiveness. Therefore,
since Pope is a child of his time, we shall not find in his poetry that
harmonizing of naïveté and self-consciousness which is so satisfying
and so easily recognized in earlier writing. His harmonies are more
subtle, their components more tenuous and less clearly contrasted.

The passage from the *Epistle to Arbuthnot* (1734) makes a starting-
point, for it illustrates an irony which is typical of much of Pope's
later verse. A learned reference is being deliberately set off against a
casual conversational tone. The 'dog star', which in Spenser would
have suggested traditional astrology, is now a conscious reference to
Horace, while the phrasing is effortlessly colloquial. Thus two attitudes are still combined, but both are sophisticated. In Portia's speech
childlike acceptance and adult self-awareness are fused: in Pope both
the component attitudes are adult and fully conscious.

A moment's reflection will show that the passage could never have
been written, let alone written with such devastating assurance, without certain clearly recognized assumptions. First, it assumes a cultivated audience with a literary field of reference; secondly, an
audience alive to subtle shades of manner and tone; and thirdly, an
audience with whom the poet can safely be on friendly terms. In this
case, of course, the 'audience' is Pope's close friend John Arbuthnot,
himself a literary man; but the fact that a poem of this kind could be
made public without incongruity emphasizes the nature of the
readers for whom Pope was writing. They are in some measure a
panel of experts, capable by training of appreciating, though not, of
course, of emulating, virtuosity. This brings us face to face with two
important considerations, the one relating to Pope's poetry itself, the
other to our appreciation of it.

To succeed before a panel of experts demands not only innate
genius but also the highest degree of acquired skill; and Pope was

born with the one and acquired the other at a remarkably early age. The rigorousness of his artistic training is evident in everything he published: one is conscious of standards meditated first and then kept continually in mind. In this way it may be said that the stringency of contemporary criticism contributed somewhat to that exquisite poise of judgement which is the mark of all Pope's work. But in writing to satisfy a limited and homogeneous audience there is the risk of accepting their standards as the only possible ones. Because Pope is so much of his age, his limitations tend to be those of the culture of that age:

> Be sure yourself and your own reach to know,
> How far your genius, taste, and learning go;
> Launch not beyond your depth, but be discreet,
> And mark that point where sense and dullness meet.

By comparison with Shakespeare's *The heavens themselves, the planets and this centre*, or Milton's *Things unattempted yet in prose or rime*, these limitations may seem narrow. They were made so largely by social considerations, for literature in Pope's day was, above all, a social art, and those poets who overstepped the conventions of art overstepped the social conventions also. Such poets as Christopher Smart and William Blake are sometimes solitary voices speaking unearthly things to an unearthly audience. Pope is never that: he is a professional speaking to professionals. His achievement lies in the perfection of what his age called 'judgement' – a sense of fitness so exquisite that it transcends all mere calculation. It is from this that the excitement of Pope's poetry derives.

The second point to remember is that Pope's writing for a specialized audience in his own day presents something of a challenge for readers in ours. His awareness of his audience is important not solely, or even preponderantly, for historical reasons, but because it forms an outstanding characteristic of his poetry. In all he wrote, even in the early pastorals and 'heroic' poems, there is a sense of something shared. The nature and strength of this implied relationship varies from poem to poem. In the verse-letter to Teresa Blount 'On her Leaving the Town after the Coronation' we come as near to personal tenderness as Pope ever reached in a poem:

> In some fair ev'ning, on your elbow laid,
> You dream of triumphs in the rural shade:
> In pensive thought recall the fancied scene,

See coronations rise on ev'ry green;
Before you pass the imaginary sights
Of lords, and earls, and dukes, and garter'd knights,
While the spread fan o'ershades your closing eyes;
Then give one flirt, and all the vision flies.
Thus vanish sceptres, coronets, and balls,
And leave you in lone woods, or empty walls!

In the epistles to Arbuthnot and Harley we are sensible of a dual relationship; the personal one between the poet and the recipient, and the wider one between the poet and an audience made up of people not unlike Arbuthnot and Harley. In *The Dunciad* (1728–43) and the *Essay on Man* (1732–4) Pope comes nearest at times to what may be called solitary utterance:

All nature is but art, unknown to thee;
All chance, direction, which thou canst not see;
   All discord, harmony not understood;
All partial evil, universal good:
And, spite of pride, in erring reason's spite,
One truth is clear, Whatever is, is right.

Yet even in this passage from the *Essay on Man* he assumes sufficient understanding on the part of his audience to prevent them from taking his words as an outburst of personal complacency. That the words have been so often quoted as evidence of Pope's 'facile optimism' demonstrates clearly enough how lack of such understanding can destroy the effect of his poetry.

Pope, in fact, presents a remarkable example of the poet who is topical without being ephemeral, and it is the business of his readers therefore to make something of an imaginative leap, to put themselves in something of the frame of mind of Pope's contemporaries. The nature of this leap is easier to understand than to define. On the one hand, it is obvious that much of the detailed contemporary reference in a poem like *The Dunciad* has lost its immediacy; historical research, though very necessary for the scholar, will not bring it back. On the other hand, the reader who fails to recognize its literary, and especially its Homeric and Virgilian, background, will never come within range of its full effect. What is required is not primarily the ability to recognize echoes of earlier poetry: that is a valuable talent for those who have it, and for those who have it not there are always footnotes. Rather, it is the knack of recognizing and relishing what the Augustans called 'imitation', the art of re-creating *in strictly contemporary form* something that had been written by a poet of an earlier age.

That the Augustan age was the first to define imitation critically and practise it systematically is not surprising. Poets like Dryden and Pope are intensely aware of the traditions of European literature, and by imitating Horace or Juvenal or Donne they regard themselves as both preserving and continuing the tradition. Secondly, they and their readers are delighted to see something old and well known given a suddenly new significance by being placed in a new context. The advice which Horace gave about using words –

> dixeris egregie notum si callida verbum
> rediderit iuctura novum –[a]

applies to poems as a whole. Almost all Pope's poems are 'imitations', and the ability to recognize at least some of the resemblances is necessary for an adequate response to his poetry. These imitations are not in any sense antiquarian efforts to write in the style of some earlier poet: that he would have regarded as mere pedantry. Rather, they are attempts to re-create the effect of a poem (or type of poem) as a whole in contemporary terms.

For the newcomer to eighteenth-century poetry the term 'imitation', with its suggestion of an intellectual *tour-de-force*, may prove something of a stumbling-block. In point of fact, the framework enabled Pope to organize within the context of a single poem a remarkable diversity of appeal. The following passage from the *Pastorals* (some of Pope's earliest work published in 1709) will show clearly what happens:

> Resound, ye hills, resound my mournful strain!
> Of perjur'd Doris, dying I complain.
> Here, where the mountains less'ning as they rise
> Lose the low vales, and steal into the skies:
> While lab'ring oxen, spent with toil and heat,
> In their loose traces from the field retreat:
> While curling smokes from village tops are seen,
> And the fleet shades glide o'er the dusky green ...

[a] 'You will advance your reputation if, by skilful placing, you give an old word a new meaning.'

Pope is here imitating the Virgilian eclogue, and the skill with which
he has suggested the atmosphere of the original without recourse to
archaic vocabulary or syntax is remarkable. The sense of reverence
and affection for Virgil and the Virgilian tradition which descends
through Spenser, Milton and Dryden forms, as it were, the groundwork on which the other levels of feeling lie. On further analysis the
passage is seen as a texture of specific echoes, each carrying its own
charge of emotion – the third line a direct borrowing from Virgil's
ninth eclogue,[1] the fifth and sixth from Milton's *Comus* and (less
directly) from *The Faerie Queene*, the last two from Dryden's translation of the first eclogue:

> For see, yon sunny hill the shade extends,
> And curling smoke from cottages ascends.

Thus within a short passage Pope has managed delicately to hint the
main line of English pastoral in a way which his readers will quickly
recognize.

And when we turn from the literary aspects of the piece to its more
obvious visual ones we meet this same combination of emotion and
conscious allusion. Pope is quite clearly 'composing' a landscape. Here
is a picture suggestive of the countryside in the Thames valley; but
suggestive also of the paintings of Claude Lorraine (whom Pope, one
feels, must have had in mind). Thus even the direct visual appeal is
in some measure derivative, and one begins to wonder how the piece
avoids frigidity. The answer is undoubtedly in the language which
Pope uses, again with astonishing restraint. Regarded separately the
words 'less'ning ... rise ... lose ... steal ... curling ... fleet ... glide'
are in no way remarkable: together they produce a subtle effect of
mobility which keeps the lines stealthily alive and stirring. It would
be absurd to load a fragment such as this with critical implications
out of all proportion to the gravity of the poetic occasion: nevertheless, one may glimpse, even here, below the urbane and charming
surface, forces at work which would not be suspected at first
reading.

To tease out the strands of a poem will not, of course, explain its
effect on the reader: but analysis of this kind is worthwhile partly
because it may give the beginner with Pope some idea of the interweaving and counterpointing of strains of feeling to be found almost

everywhere in his poetry, and partly because it is only by some such illustration that one can rebut the assertion that Pope's poetry is un-emotional – the product (as Matthew Arnold thought) of an age of prose and reason. Let us, then, examine two more instances: one a short extract from Pope's translation of the *Iliad* (1715–20) which has come in for much ill-considered abuse since Coleridge cited it as an example of pseudo-diction, the other a poem of some length, *Eloisa to Abelard* (1717), which raises in an acute form some difficulties connected with the approach to Pope's poetry.

First, then, the lines which close the eighth book of the *Iliad*:

> So many flames before proud Ilion blaze,
> And lighten glimm'ring Xanthus with their rays:
> The long reflections of the distant fires
> Gleam on the walls, and tremble on the spires.
> A thousand piles the dusky horrors gild,
> And shoot a shady lustre o'er the field.
> Full fifty guards each flaming pile attend,
> Whose umber'd arms, by fits, thick flashes send.
> Loud neigh the coursers o'er their heaps of corn,
> And ardent warriors wait the rising morn.

To anyone looking impartially at this passage, with its brilliant lights and deep shadows, it will occur that Pope is thinking as much about painting (and perhaps about Rembrandt's 'Night Watch' in parti-cular) as about Homer. It is, in fact, an essay in interpreting a certain style of painting in terms of poetry. Again it is the language – 'glimmering ... umber'd arms ... thick flashes ...' – which reveals the excitement underlying the more formal elements of the composi-tion. Coleridge[2] mistook the nature of the passage because he was thinking about Homer more than about Pope; and certainly there is no strong tie between the Greek and the English. But what matters is that a notable passage in Homer has released in Pope this spring of imagination which fuses the emotional associations of the original with feelings closer to his own time.

Eloisa to Abelard is an imitation of the Ovidian heroic epistle. It is a poem whose difficulties are more specifically those of the eighteenth century than any other work of Pope: yet it cannot be ignored, since it shows in a unique and vivid way certain important qualities of Pope's mind. The theme of *Eloisa* is frustrated passion; and for an age in which the novels of Richardson were best sellers, Pope's elaborate

and explicit analysis of the feelings of a woman torn from her lover
and forced to recant against her will had a strong appeal. That the
poem is brilliantly executed there can be no doubt. Pope is master of
the rhetoric of passion throughout its range, from –

> Still as the sea, ere winds were taught to blow,
> Or moving spirit bade the waters flow;
> Soft as the slumbers of a saint forgiven,
> And mild as opening gleams of promis'd heav'n . . .

to –

> When from the censer clouds of fragrance roll,
> And swelling organs lift the rising soul,
> One thought of thee puts all the pomp to flight,
> Priests, tapers, temples, swim before my sight:
> In seas of flame my plunging soul is drown'd,
> While altars blaze, and angels tremble round . . .

and his manipulation of the antithetic couplet is masterly in its sustained variety. Yet such considerations are only partly satisfying, and
for two reasons. First, because it is difficult for us who live in an age
in which the emotion of poetry is almost invariably private, to
project ourselves into one in which it was almost invariably public.
This is something about which one can do very little, and it is by no
means an absolute obstacle to appreciating the poem. The second is
more fundamental. It concerns the nature of the emotion in the poem.
Usually both those who like *Eloisa* and those who do not assume
that Pope's feeling (or lack of it) must focus on the central figure of
the heroine. In fact, it focuses on Ovid – or rather the kind of poetry
which Ovid first created.

Eloisa to Abelard is an astonishing evocation of an earlier poet's way
of writing: an evocation which goes far beyond the copying of man-
nerisms, or the hinting of a manner. Ovid becomes literally alive in
eighteenth-century verse: to such an extent that for anyone who is
well acquainted with Pope's poem it is impossible to read the
Heroïdes without thinking of it. Pope responds to the 'story' of Eloisa
by seeing her in terms of an Ovidian heroine. From the vividness and
appositeness of this response arises the poem's intensity.

When we realize this we have in our hands a key to the emotional
range of Pope's poetry. He responded to different kinds of theme
with remarkable variousness, and both the excitement and the

variety in his poetry derive from the perfect adjustment of style to feeling in such widely differing poems as *The Rape of the Lock* and *The Dunciad*, or *Eloisa* and the verse-letter to Teresa Blount quoted on pp. 237–8.

It is, of course, true that all considerable poetry depends partly on the relationship between style and content; but poetry like Pope's is more dependent on our recognizing this relationship than, let us say, poetry like Wordsworth's. Moreover, there are two kinds of relationship possible: that in which the poet seems to gain his effect by triumphing over his material, and that in which he seems to suggest that no difficulties exist because the medium is so perfectly suited to the theme. Donne's poetry, Milton's and perhaps Wordsworth's belongs to the first kind; Pope's to the second. Inevitably the first is more spectacular: it conveys a greater sense of power, if only because it calls attention to its own emotional urgency. The second calls for far greater perceptiveness on the part of the reader. If we fail to notice the exquisite judgement with which theme and tone are linked in 'To a Young Lady' or *The Rape of the Lock*, or the imaginative power with which the epic possibilities of the theme have been exploited in *The Dunciad*, we shall see little to attract us but technical virtuosity.

Moreover, unless we recognize in this term 'judgement' something more than an ability to know when to stop, we shall certainly miss most of the overtones in Pope's poetry. In Pope's case 'judgement' is rather the intuitive perception of the fitness of means for an end. It is from this perception and from the fusion of materials produced in its application that the emotional force arises.

It is axiomatic, then, that all Pope's poems have their roots in some original of an earlier period, and that this original is of greater importance in his poetry than in that of most English poets. It is, in fact, by the use of this original as a point of reference that associations, both emotional and intellectual, and shades of tone can be controlled. The method is economical and of a kind which one would expect from a poet who wrote his poems on the backs of his friends' letters: it is subtle, compressed, and allusive. It makes stringent demands on the reader's mental and emotional alertness.

The Rape of the Lock and *The Dunciad* are both mock-heroic poems, depending on the three great classical epics. As they are both satirical poems, however, the function of such reference is different from anything we have seen so far. Primarily it is to establish a scale of values whose extreme limits are epic sublimity and human pettiness, and whose point of equilibrium is the 'good sense' which conditions the outlook, social, moral, and artistic, of the period. It is as a philosophic rather than an emotional denominator that the 'original' is mainly employed.

As most people know, *The Rape of the Lock* (1712) is now a familiar poem ridiculing the fashionable world of Pope's day, its immediate aim being to laugh two families of his acquaintance into making up a quarrel over a somewhat trivial incident. This quarrel is presented in terms of the great epic contentions (Greeks and Trojans, God and Satan), and the effect of the poem, which for brilliance of conception and consistency of execution is unsurpassed in our literature, lies in the exquisite adjustment between the epic and mundane planes on which it moves. Nothing could better illustrate Pope's power of bearing in mind at one and the same time general design and particular detail. Everything is kept in proportion, from the comparative importance of the quarrels themselves to the physical measurements of armour and costume. Thus the gods, whose Olympian indifference to the human predicament so heightens the pathos of the *Iliad*, become, in Pope's poem, the sylphs and gnomes of Rosicrucian mythology[3] derived from a frivolous French romance. Even their names (Zephyretta, Momentilla) are suitably diminished. When the Homeric Zeus summons the assembly of the gods at the opening of the eighth book of the *Iliad* he threatens all who disobey with appropriately massive penalties:

> Back to the skies with shame he shall be driv'n,
> Gash'd with dishonest wounds, the scorn of Heav'n:
> Or far, oh far from steep Olympus thrown,
> Low in the dark Tartarean gulf shall groan;
> With burning chains fix'd to the brazen floors,
> And lock'd by Hell's inexorable doors; ...

The Miltonic echoes in this passage are suitably paralleled by echoes from *The Tempest* when Ariel summons an assembly to brief his subordinate sylphs in the second canto of *The Rape of the Lock*:

> Whatever spirit, careless of his charge,
> His post neglects, or leaves the fair at large,
> Shall feel sharp vengeance soon o'ertake his sins,

> Be stopp'd in vials, or transfix'd with pins;
> Or plunged in lakes of bitter washes lie,
> Or wedg'd whole ages in a bodkin's eye ...

The bite of this mock-heroic comparison lies in the social criticism it achieves so adroitly. It is not simply a display of literary virtuosity, but a superb example of what Dryden called fine raillery, which tickles while it hurts. Pope's description of the passage as 'parody' must not be taken too strictly in our modern sense of the word, which implies that the entrenched past is being made to look ridiculous in terms of the enlightened present. Here it is the trivial present which is being mocked in the light of the past.

Other poets of Pope's day made effective use of this mock-heroic scale, but it is the measure of Pope's genius and of his superiority over his contemporaries that he alone never allows it to become rigid. By a continual adjustment of the two planes he is enabled to move without apparent effort from ridicule bordering on farce (as in the last passage) to something like direct moral comment (as in the one which follows):[4]

> Say, why are beauties prais'd and honour'd most,
> The wise man's passion, and the vain man's toast?
> Why deck'd with all that land and sea afford,
> Why angels call'd and angel-like ador'd?
> Why round our coaches crowd the white-glov'd beaux,
> Why bows the side-box from its inmost rows?
> How vain are all these glories, all our pains,
> Unless good sense preserve what beauty gains:
> That men may say, when we the front-box grace:
> Behold the first in virtue, as in face ... &c. &c.

This derives from a *locus classicus* of the *Iliad*, the speech of Sarpedon to Glaucus in the twelfth book:

> Why boast we, Glaucus! our extended reign,
> Where Xanthus' streams enrich the Lycian plain;
> Our num'rous herds that range the fruitful field,
> And hills where vines their purple harvest yield,
> Our foaming bowls with purer nectar crown'd,
> Our feasts enhanc'd with music's sprightly sound?
> Why on those shores are we with joy survey'd,
> Admir'd as heroes, and as gods obey'd?
> Unless great acts superior merit prove,
> And vindicate the bounteous Pow'rs above.

'Tis ours, the dignity they give, to grace;
The first in valour as the first in place ... &c. &c.

It will be seen at once that whereas the parallels in the previous pair
of passages depend on outrageous fantasy, here they gain their effect
by a closer and more sober approximation. In this way the tone is
deepened without being distorted, and Pope is able, as he says, to
'open more clearly the moral of the poem'. The skill with which he
has succeeded will perhaps be more evident if we recall the violence
which Coleridge had to do to *The Ancient Mariner* when faced with a
similar problem.

The Dunciad is not so perfect artistically as *The Rape of the Lock*.[5]
It began as a 'brief sketch', which Swift may have saved from the fire
in 1726, and grew by a process of accretion until it reached its final
form as *The Dunciad in Four Books* in 1743. It lacks, therefore, the
precision of form to be found in *The Rape of the Lock* or in that other
formally exquisite poem *An Essay on Man*. But the fact is that the
accretive method of composition was the one which suited Pope, as
it has suited many other fine writers. *Clarissa*, for all its volubility, is a
more satisfying novel than the carefully planned *Charles Grandison*;
Pickwick Papers than *Little Dorrit*. And *The Dunciad*, though its
method of growth undoubtedly makes difficulty for the reader, has
always seemed to me most representative of Pope's poetic genius.[6]

The most obvious, though not the most troublesome, aspect of
the poem is its personalities. These were, perhaps, its starting-point,
and it is all too easy, if we take them out of relation to the rest, to
see *The Dunciad* as an arbitrary and ill-natured attack on those who,
whether living or dead, had offended Pope. In the final form of the
poem, however, they fall into place as symbols of moral and intellectual obtuseness, much as the personalities of the *Purgatorio* epitomize
particular aspects of sin, and not merely Dante's private enemies.

Of its kind, *The Dunciad* may fairly be called Pope's vision of
torment. From the laborious annotator –

> There, dim in clouds, the poring scholiasts mark,
> Wits, who, like owls, see only in the dark.
> A lumber-house of books in ev'ry head,
> For ever reading, never to be read ...

to the vulgar spectacles of pantomime –

All sudden, Gorgons hiss, and dragons glare,
And ten-horn'd fiends and giants rush to war.
Hell rises, heaven descends, and dance on earth:
Gods, imps and monsters, music, rage and mirth,
A fire, a jig, a battle and a ball,
Till one wide conflagration swallows all ...

Pope sees them all as part of a spiritual and intellectual decay which, in this long passage from the third book, he pictures as overwhelming England. Whether he was justified in taking this gloomy view is debatable. Today we accept as inevitable an appalling gulf between literature and other kinds of writing; and both worlds suffer because of it. Pope has not learned to make this dichotomy – indeed, it was just this he was fighting against – and one cannot fully appreciate the poem until one recognizes the genuine moral indignation behind it.

An index of this indignation is the way he uses the mock-heroic technique. In *The Rape of the Lock*, Belinda, the Baron, Sir Plume, and the rest are dwarfed, and so rendered harmless, by their epic counterparts: in *The Dunciad*, the Burnets, Oldmixons, and Cookes, themselves petty and contemptible, are inflated to epic proportions in the gargantuan caricatures of the first two books.

The use of the mock-heroic scale is thus the reverse of that in *The Rape of the Lock*, where Pope's vision of the pretty, if absurd, world of fashion has all the delicacy of a landscape seen through the wrong end of a telescope. In *The Dunciad*, meanness is magnified until it becomes as grotesque as a Daumier cartoon. This method makes it easier for Pope to move from the level of mockery to that of prophetic commination; and since the indictment of the poem is so much graver than that of *The Rape of the Lock*, such transitions are both more frequent and more moving. Pope's own favourite was the fourth book, but throughout the work, and especially in the third book where Dullness is generalized in terms of history, one meets passages where the poetry becomes the physical manifestation of desolation:

Lo! Rome herself, proud mistress now no more
Of arts, but thund'ring against heathen lore;
Her gray-hair'd synods damning books unread,
And Bacon trembling for his brazen head.
Padua, with sighs, beholds her Livy burn,
And ev'n th' Antipodes Virgilius mourn.

> See, the Cirque falls, th' unpillar'd temple nods,
> Streets paved with heroes, Tyber choak'd with gods:
> Till Peter's keys some christen'd Jove adorn,
> And Pan to Moses lends his pagan horn.

We have so far observed peculiarities of Pope's work as they are to be seen in particular poems. These, however, arise from something which is to be recognized in all his poetry – the remarkable integration of the world in which his imagination moves. The concept of unified (or dissociated) sensibility has been of great value to our understanding of seventeenth-century poetry. Unluckily, however, we have come to regard a unified sensibility as the perquisite of a small group of writers: we are too ready to say with Falstaff, 'Who hath it? He that died before 1660.' Pope's poetic universe is no less closely integrated than that of (say) George Herbert, as I hope will appear. But we must also beware of making another mistake by claiming that it is the *same* universe, and that the approach to the poetry of Pope is not essentially different from the approach to that of a seventeenth-century metaphysical. The terminal points of Herbert's universe or Donne's are God and Man: Pope's begins and ends with Man. But granted the limitation this imposes, there remains between that beginning and end the almost infinite scope of human activity. And it is the way his poetry expresses one aspect of this multifariousness in terms of another that makes it ultimately so satisfying. Pope does not, like Homer's steeds, leap from heaven to earth in one bound; but he can move from Augustan to Aztec civilization without apparent effort, or from the exploration of literature to the exploration of the Sahara and back again without seeming to stir:

> One simile, that solitary shines
> In the dry desert of a thousand lines ...

and it is difficult to say which seems more vivid – thought or image. He may not see a world in a grain of sand, but the ceaseless industry of the insect and of the scribbler become inseparable:

> Who shames a scribbler? Break one cobweb through,
> He spins the slight, self-pleasing thread anew;
> Destroy his fib, or sophistry; in vain,
> The creature's at his dirty work again,
> Throned in the centre of his thin designs,
> Proud of a vast extent of flimsy lines ...

In all such passages – and Pope's poetry is crammed with them – it is possible to see, when we pause to notice it, an exquisite sense of equivalence between thought and image. We are not at one moment talking about scribblers and the next about spiders; we are speaking about both at once.

If we fail to recognize the unified sensibility inherent in Pope's poetry it is probably for two reasons. The first is the astonishing ease and speed with which the identification of thought and image is reached:

> Something, whose truth convinced at sight we find.
> That gives us back the image of our mind ...

This second couplet of Pope's definition of wit in general admirably describes the process of his own. It is a process different altogether from, let us say, an image of Donne:

> While thus to ballast Love I thought,
> And so more steadily to have gone,
> With wares that would sink admiration,
> I saw I had Love's pinnace overfraught,
> Every thy hair for Love to work upon
> Is much too much, some fitter must be sought ...

In this passage from *Aire and Angels*, Donne enumerates all the details of his image, not because he has a laborious mind but because the details are all important. Like many of his images, this is a developing one: and it is the development quite as much as the total image that is significant. Now take a couplet from Pope's *Epistle to Augustus*:

> Authors, like coins, grow dear as they grow old;
> It is the rust we value, not the gold ...

The identification has been achieved 'at sight': the 'image' has been given back to the thought without any perceptible interval. We do not dwell on the nature of old coins and writers, because Pope does not require us to do so. He has made his point with economy and restraint; with the result that he leaves us meditating the thought itself rather than the image which has driven it home.

The object of such comparison is not to belittle one poet at the expense of another – a fruitless, though popular, form of criticism. Donne's image is aimed at making apprehensible a metaphysical experience, Pope's at rendering vivid and active 'a known truth that has been suffered to lie neglected'. Both aims are important and both are difficult. Donne moved from *a* to *b* and from *b* to *c* because the process by which he reaches the conclusion is as important as the conclusion itself. With Pope it is the terminals which matter: the greater speed of the spark between them, the greater the shock administered to the reader.

The second reason why we tend to neglect the fine qualities of Pope's imagery is that the distance to be travelled, as it were, between thought and image is seldom so great as to give the reader pause. Even if it is considerable, as when we are whisked from the emendations of scholars preserved in a poet's text to fossils preserved in amber –

> Pretty! in amber to observe the forms
> Of hairs, or straws, or dirt, or grubs, or worms!
> The things, we know, are neither rich nor rare,
> But wonder how the devil they got there –

we are not asked to go beyond the range of human observation. Pedants and desiccated bugs are both part of the social world; both odd, and both equally worthless. However he may develop an image, as, for instance, in the following lines:

> A little learning is a dangerous thing;
> Drink deep, or taste not the Pierian spring:
> There shallow drafts intoxicate the brain,
> And drinking largely sobers us again –

the same holds good. Here the activities of the expert poet and expert drinker meet on the level of social experience and without derogation to either term of the equation. And that they are able to do so is due to the integration of the world of Pope's poetry: the refinements of the mind are not things apart from daily existence, they are a means of enjoying the existence more fully.

The *Essay on Criticism* (1711) from which these lines come is a poem that has been somewhat spoiled by attempts to use it as a text illustrating the critical opinions of the period. Most of the material derives from the great critics of former ages – Aristotle, Horace, Quintilian, Boileau – but it is material which had been handled by almost every critic of the day, and of which all educated readers would have been aware. What we miss (and Pope's contemporaries

assuredly did not) by treating the poem in this way is the life which
informs the aridities of literary criticism:

> First follow Nature, and your judgement frame
> By her just standard, which is still the same:
> Unerring Nature, still divinely bright,
> One clear, unchang'd, and universal light,
> Life, force, and beauty must to all impart,
> At once the source, and end, and test of art.
> Art from that fund each just supply provides,
> Works without show, and without pomp presides:
> In some fair body thus th' informing soul
> With spirits feeds, with vigour fills the whole,
> Each motion guides, and every nerve sustains;
> Itself unseen, but in th' effects remains . . .

The ultimate derivation of this is probably Aristotle's assertion that a
work of art must be a living organism; but if we can ignore the critical dicta we see that a passage which sets out to instruct us in how to
form our literary judgements develops into something of much wider
significance. From abstract assertion we move to an unobtrusive
but telling political image, and from the body politic to the body
human in the last four lines. The *Essay on Criticism* is early work;
in fact, it is the first poem of any length which Pope published. Thus,
as we should expect, the fusion between thought and image is less
instantaneous and less complete than in a passage such as the following
from the first of the *Moral Essays*, published more than twenty years
later in 1733:

> Nor will life's stream for observation stay,
> It hurries all too fast to mark their way:
> In vain sedate reflections we would make,
> When half our knowledge we must snatch, not take.
> Oft, in the passion's wild rotation tost,
> Our spring of action to ourselves is lost:
> Tir'd, not determin'd, to the last we yield,
> And what comes then is master of the field.
> As the last image of that troubl'd heap
> When sense subsides, and fancy sports in sleep,
> (Though past the recollection of the thought)
> Becomes the stuff of which our dream is wrought:
> Something as dim to our internal view
> Is thus, perhaps, the cause of most we do . . .

Here material from Horace, Shakespeare, and Hobbes is so closely interwoven with the imagery that it is scarcely distinguishable. But in the *Essay on Criticism* we see what Coleridge called the esemplastic power of a poet's imagination beginning to function, fusing, though not quite perfectly, such disparate things as literary criticism, the human microcosm, and the administration of public money.

If we can rid our minds of the preconception that Pope's poetry is 'intellectual', the strongest impression we shall gain is that of a constant interchange between various sorts of human activity and experience. It is a restless effect, like that of sunlight on disturbed water, and one cannot fix one's eyes on it for too long. One is not, of course, meant to. It is on the central clue of thought that the reader is asked to concentrate, allowing the flash and interplay of image and allusion around him to act as stimulus to sharper perception. Nevertheless, if for a while we allow ourselves to forget the conceptual element of the poetry and watch, as it were, the medium in which it is suspended, we find ourselves in a world as unexpected and varied as a kaleidoscope, never knowing quite what form the pattern will take next or what pieces will compose the pattern; yet recognizing certain shapes as belonging distinctively to Pope's poetry. To call this medium Pope's 'illustration' or Pope's 'wit' and to distinguish it from his thought would be entirely misleading. In a passage such as this (from the first of the *Moral Essays*) –

> Know, God and Nature only are the same:
> In man, the judgement shoots at flying game,
> A bird of passage! gone as soon as found,
> Now in the moon, perhaps, now underground …

the imagery, which embraces partridge shooting, natural history, and *Orlando Furioso,* is the thought – or perhaps one might better say 'is the way Pope has this kind of thought'. Or again, take a simpler passage from the *Essay on Man* –

> What nothing earthly gives, or can destroy,
> The soul's calm sunshine, and the heart-felt joy
> Is virtue's prize. A better would you fix?
> Then give humility a coach and six,
> Justice a conqueror's sword, or truth a gown,
> Or public spirit its great cure, a crown.

Once more the passage is fascinating as a reflection of the poet's mind, not primarily as a philosophic aphorism.

The fact is that in the first couplet of his definition –

> True wit is Nature to advantage dress'd;
> What oft was thought, but ne'er so well express'd –

Pope is far from just to Pope: it suggests, as Johnson indicated, the mere verbal elaboration of an accepted commonplace. Had he said 'what oft was thought, but ne'er so well thought', English literature would have wanted one immortal couplet, but Pope would have come nearer to describing his own poetic processes. The Augustan age delighted in the great simplifications of philosophy and science, because it seemed to them that the universe itself was simple. It is Pope's distinction that in his poetry these commonplaces emerge not as abstractions relevant only to the rarefied atmosphere of science or philosophy, but as operative in the concrete and highly detailed day-to-day life of his age.

NOTES

1. The reader of Augustan poetry should not be unduly daunted by the field of classical reference. In Pope's time most of the major poems of classical literature had been rendered into English: the *Iliad* and *Odyssey* by Chapman (and, of course, by Pope himself); the whole of Virgil by Dryden; Ovid (in part) by George Sandys, and by a host of occasional translators (among them Dryden and Pope). These versions formed as much part of the Augustan literary background as the original poems, and the reader who will take the trouble to study them will be well equipped for eighteenth-century literature.

Horace was (and still is) an insuperable problem. A passable verse translation appeared in 1747 (republished by Unit Books with the Latin text in 1902). But the best reference for the hesitant Latinist is the Loeb edition of Horace's works with a prose translation by Fairclough.

2. *Biographia Literaria* (London, 1894), 19 (footnote). Coleridge misquotes the passage from Pope.

3. The first version of *The Rape of the Lock* (1712) contained no reference to the sylphs and gnomes, which were added in the final version (1714). For the two versions and a valuable introduction, see the edition by Geoffrey Tillotson (1940).

4. This point has already been made by John Butt in his essay 'The Inspiration of Pope's Poetry' (*Essays Presented to David Nichol Smith*, 1945).

5. For the growth of the poem, and an indispensable introduction, see the

edition by James Sutherland (1943). I should like to take the opportunity of acknowledging the debt this chapter owes to the assistance of Professor Sutherland.

6. See Ian Jack, *Augustan Satire* (1952). Dr Jack dissents from this view.

INTEGRITY AND DRAMATIC LIFE IN
POPE'S POETRY

S. L. GOLDBERG

In the Preface to his edition of Shakespeare, Pope remarked that Shakespeare's work was 'inspiration indeed; he is not so much an imitator as an instrument of Nature; and 'tis not so just to say that he speaks from her, as that she speaks through him'. It is easy to see what he meant. One mark of a very great writer is to present us with not so much a particular view of the world, as a 'world' itself – an imagined reality so large, so substantial, so free of any merely personal bias, that it seems continuous with our own. Things, places, actions, people assume an independent density and vigour; every particular seems alive; and the whole seems at once self subsistent and yet everywhere animated by the same protean energy. As Pope said of Homer, 'What he writes is of the most animated nature imaginable; everything moves, everything lives and is put in action.' It is what we call 'dramatic' power in its highest manifestation; and it is this 'dramatic' power that ought most to concern us in Pope's poetry. Whatever Pope's conscious moral or philosophical intentions, he did not merely reflect his world, represent or 'imitate' it artistically, and comment critically on it. As he matured, he also came (as I think he saw) to 'represent' it in the other sense of embodying its ideal possibilities of self-awareness and self-criticism. His world really 'speaks through him', and like all great 'dramatic' writers, Pope makes his world conscious of itself and thereby (as he suggests of Shakespeare) he partly re-creates it. In fact, I think Pope re-creates his world more substantially, ranges in it more widely, and engages with it more profoundly, than any English writer between Shakespeare and Dickens. It is a remarkable achievement for one who wrote so much formally in his own voice (Chaucer's is perhaps the only comparable case in English).

Pope is not only an intensely 'dramatic' poet; he is also an intensely self-conscious one. By this I do not mean merely that he was a deliberate craftsman (though of course he was), nor that he deployed his various self-images with masterly skill (though he did), nor even that references to himself form part of a quite remarkable number of his poems (though they do). More than that, he was so serious about being a poet that he obviously had something like a sense of vocation about it – a consciousness from first to last that his destiny, his very self, was essentially that of a poet and Wit. He knew the power of genius in himself; it was only half a joke, for example, to assert that *The Dunciad* 'was not made for these Authors, but these Authors for the Poem'. But as we might expect, the degree to which he actually understood himself corresponded exactly to the degree of his understanding of other people and of the ways in which their lives were also fated. His view of himself and his view of the objective world corresponded; and he clearly came to see this himself. But I think he also increasingly sensed that to realize the objective world was simultaneously to realize, to fulfil, and thereby to define himself – and vice versa.

These may sound odd terms to apply to Pope, for it is more usual to regard his art, like so much else in his age, as strictly – indeed, consciously – impersonal, and to talk of his use of artistic personae rather than different manifestations of his self. His age is supposed to have rested upon a commonly accepted, stable, comprehensive, and objective order of moral values, natural laws, and social institutions, in which no man needed to be much perplexed about who *he* really was or where *he* properly belonged; and Pope, it is assumed, simply adopted a number of recognized traditional personae – the social Wit, the easy Horatian Moralist, the philosophic Sage, the happy and virtuous Recluse, the dignified Poet and Critic of life, and so on – which are taken as devices, impersonal techniques, whereby Pope could get his personal self out of the way and bring traditional and impersonal values to bear on the present.

However much truth there may be in this view, it is not really adequate to Pope. For one thing, while it is obviously true that each of his poems is a created object in its own right, not a direct personal confession, it is also true that it is created by, and embodies, a particular mind, not some impersonal rhetorical process. In the second place, a term like persona suggests that he was more assured of the certain certainties of his age, and more self-possessed in confronting his material, than he really was. His 'wit' constantly played over those certainties; real self-possession – a full, measured, and secure self-understanding as a poet – was something he had continually to strive towards and win. And for a mind like his, as Johnson so well describes it, 'active, ambitious, and adventurous, always investigating, always aspiring', every success could be only partial and temporary. In any case it is Pope the 'dramatist' that matters, and the relevant kind of impersonality to seek in his work is that manifested in the greatest dramatic masterpieces – an integrity and plenitude of dramatic *and* personal realization.

The impulse towards such self-possession appears long before the obvious cases of the 1730s and 40s. In every one of his major poems up to 1717, Pope tries, more or less successfully, to locate the self who writes the poem by defining it in relation to his own personal experience on the one hand, and to the particular subject of the poem on the other. The reference to himself at the end of the *Essay on Criticism*, for example, hardly warrants even the term persona: it is little more than a conventional gesture imitated from Boileau, a tactful claim to modesty and moral integrity. But the actual spirit of the poem is much less conventional. It corresponds rather with the pervasive Longinian strain in its argument. Words like *life, force, vigour, motion, fire, ardent, teeming*, and so on, play against two other sets of words. One comprises such terms as *glittering, chaos, gaudy*, and the like. The other is an even more significant group: *dull, malignant, slow, creep, sleep, lumber, dust, dullness.* Pope once remarked that 'of the two extremes one could sooner pardon frenzy than frigidity'; and the similarly contrasting terms of the *Essay on Criticism* point forward to his explicit understanding later on in *The Dunciad*: that it is essentially the 'Elasticity' and 'Fire' his own verse represents that is the measure of the fools and dunces.

The consciousness of a power in himself less sedate, less controllable, less socially amenable, and far less modest, than a young man could fully understand, let alone express, is clearly part of the self that writes these early poems. It peeps out in *The Temple of Fame* (1711), for instance, where Pope measures the personal cost of seeking poetic fame. Once again, the opposition he sees there – between seeking a conscious moral integrity (which might well necessitate a psychic *retreat* from the world) and a conscious claim to public recognition (which is virtually the need to *master* the world) – is still rather crude, rather notional, in comparison with his later sense of the strains and difficulties involved. The finest of his early poems, *The Rape of the Lock* and the epistle to Miss Blount, 'On her leaving the Town after the Coronation', do realize their conflicting values with real vivacity and a delicate, even tender, sharpness; and Pope does hold them in a fine balance. All the same, he achieves that balance only because his sense of the opposing forces, and of what must be sacrificed in balancing them, is limited, limited in ways that Marvell's sense of them in *The Garden*, for instance, is not. 'Annihilating' is not a word Pope seems to need in either poem; nor does Clarissa's 'good humour' quite answer to the fate of those wretches who hang that jurymen may dine.

Where Pope does reach out in these early poems towards harsher, less tractable aspects of life, his sense of them inevitably corresponds to the extent and coherence of his self-understanding. In both *Eloisa to Abelard* and the *Verses to the Memory of an Unfortunate Lady*, for instance, his obvious self-identification with both unfortunate ladies suggests that he is trying not only to express the centre of their fates, the centre of each self as it confronted the world, but also to explore how far it is also a centre to which his own sense of himself could cohere. Certainly he now realizes the distinction between the self and the world is more complex than it appeared in *Windsor Forest*. But both poems remain merely rhetorical because what Pope realizes, at their centre and in his own self, is less the need and the capacity to commit one's life to a genuine passion than the *consciousness* of that need and capacity. He sees his subject-matter with a constricting kind of self-consciousness, as though it were enough to indulge in emotional rhetoric about it rather than to take emotion and rhetoric as means to discover it. His sense of himself has a correspondingly external pathos – a not very engaging mixture, in fact, of self-pity and self-congratulation on being a poet. And once again it hardly encompasses the harsher, more hostile feelings which give the poems such life as they have, and which spring from a quite different part of himself. One of the most revealing sentences in the Preface to his 1717 volume contains a metaphor that often recurs in his work: 'the life of a Wit,' he remarks, 'is a warfare upon earth.' The word 'life', we may notice, is as significant as 'warfare'. Clearly, the simple integrity of innocence, retirement, identification with the conventional ethical virtues, was impossible to one whose genius had to take him into the world. Eventually, the losses he had to accept as the other side of this destiny prompted a fuller, if more difficult, understanding both of the world and of himself, rather than driving him to moral retreat or emotional indulgence.

Such integrity did not come just from Pope's wanting it, however, nor was he always right in thinking he had achieved it. He was only the first to think (as some scholars still do) that his mature work is really animated and shaped by the values to which he consciously attached himself: reason, good sense, taste, nature, order, and so on. But as a number of critics have pointed out, his imagination draws most of its vigour from the disorder, folly, irrationality, dullness, grotesque and fantastic distortions and extremes, that it realizes as active forces in the world around him. If Pope eventually came to see this himself, he was not very clear about it at first. His confusions in the *Essay on Man*, for example, are most revealing. In so far as the *Essay* has any poetic life, it does not lie in Pope's repeated and rather strident assertions of a cosmic plan, or his attacks on 'pride', or even in his occasional perceptions of a scale of being in nature. His mind most fully realizes itself in realizing the strange forms, the ambivalent energies, the self-entangled contradictions of the world: the realities he tries to fix within the bounds of a single cosmic idea. The vehemence with which he tries in the *Essay* to assert an objective order – tries, that is, to possess all possible experience and thereby secure both the world and himself within one self-sufficient and demonstrable object of thought – seems to be the reaction of a mind made insecure, even anxious, by its very capacities. In beating down 'pride' he seems to be beating down an uneasy (and never quite acknowledged) sense of the restlessly active, various, outflying, *centrifugal* force of his own imagination. He seems determined to rope the self down within the confines of a single, recognizable identity, and to find in large, indisputable abstractions an imposing bastion, an impregnable centre, from which to command all the confusions of life.

What I am suggesting is that Pope cannot help responding to a *value* in the disorder he sees. Its energy and substance remain for him an irreducible part of life; but if it prompts, it also seems to withstand, every formal paradox, every set of opposing terms, in which he tries to comprehend it in a larger whole. Consequently he is driven to seek a centre within himself where sympathetic responsiveness, as well as true understanding, authoritative judgement, and virtuous intent, all coincide. The search for objectively 'real' values in the world is also the search for 'real' identity – for a self that can and must and should acknowledge the impersonal authority of those values.

He therefore had to resist on one side the temptation to suppose order and value are merely data in the world, obscure but given facts of life to which the individual consciousness must submit, rather than possibilities of the world realized by the mind *in* its activity, forms in which the individual realizes his identity as at once an individual, an inhabitant of a particular society, and a member of the human race. On the other side, he had to resist the temptation to equate an integral wholeness of being with a visible, objective simplicity. It is all too easy to think we have located our 'true' self when we have only lopped our experience back to some 'essential' or 'natural' pattern supposedly underlying all complexities: locating it, for instance, in the consciousness of our continuous and sincere attachment to a number of basic virtues. Pope's struggle to get free of both these temptations marks his artistic development through the 1730s and 1740s.

It is interesting to see the change from the *Essay on Man* in the *Imitations of Horace*. All of these Horatian poems, and both the *Epistle to Arbuthnot* and the *Epilogue to the Satires*, are built, more or less securely, on an interplay between the public self (in his various forms – the Wit, the Critic, the Sage, the Moralist, and so on), the private 'real' self beneath that (in his various forms – lisping in numbers, stooping to truth, practising virtue, or piddling along with broccoli and mutton), and the writer of the actual poem in which the other two are portrayed and defended. One common mistake with these poems is simply to equate all three figures, which unfortunately tends to make Pope look something of a hypocrite at times, or rather priggish, or pompously self-important. Another is to separate the three figures altogether, which unfortunately tends to leave him with no specific identity at all. But it is not always clear just how the three figures are related to one another – largely because Pope the writer was not always clear about it either. The *Epistle to Arbuthnot* is a case in point, where the end of the poem seems quite at odds with the rest.

As a personal apologia, the *Epistle* really depends on the brilliant 'fire' of its poetry and the protean but steady 'force' of its insight and judgement: on an imaginative wholeness, that is, of which only a part consists in the 'wit' and honesty of the public self, and another part in the conscious moral intent of the private self. This is clear enough even in lines not directly about himself:

> You think this cruel? take it for a rule,
> No creature smarts so little as a Fool.
> Let Peals of Laughter, *Codrus!* round thee break,
> Thou unconcern'd canst hear the mighty Crack.
> Pit, Box and Gall'ry in convulsions hurl'd,
> Thou stand'st unshook amidst a bursting World. (83ff)

The writer of these lines is obviously not one who could stand unshook amidst a bursting world; indeed, he demonstrates his lack of folly in his very responsiveness to Codrus's nature. His 'wit' lies in seeing that the ability to stand in unshaken self-possession in all circumstances and *not* to feel threatened or excited by the outside world, is the mark of an ultimate lack of spirit and intelligence. Obviously the writer here is not the public figure, whose only wish is to 'maintain a Poet's Dignity and Ease'. Nor is he the private man, who in the final section of the poem claims that he only wishes to 'live my own! and die so too!' and to be like his 'innoxious' father, who 'held it for a rule /It was a Sin to call our Neighbour Fool'. This latter self is quite sincere, of course, in wanting only to 'rock the Cradle of reposing Age,/With lenient Arts extend a Mother's breath'; but in the final section of the poem, the writer has come simply to identify himself with the private man; and in doing so, he has stamped flat all the vital antitheses in his own being – the being who could respond with such insight and such controlled, 'unlenient' art to Codrus, for instance, or to Atticus, or to Sporus who is merely a '*vile* Antithesis'. The last section of the poem fails to sustain the bite and integrity of passages like those.

Pope's impulse to 'fix' an identity that he could *know* was continually at odds with his very capacity to know anything – with his appetite for life, his mobility, and his vivacious intelligence and wit. On the other hand, he could not simply define himself as a bundle of contradictions either: he was conscious of a more significant kind of coherence than that. Thus, although he was often led to identify himself in rather conventional terms, this does not mean that the impulse to do so represented something merely conventional in him. It does mean, however, that he is not reducible to any one of the self-images he projects in his verse. In his satires of the 1730s, for instance, he is not 'really' the virtuous Horatian Recluse, standing aside from a corrupted society and opposing to it his ideal vision of social life. Pope's poetry represents that world too, quite as much as (if not more than) those who corrupt it. As a matter of biographical fact, Pope's retirement from the city in the 1730s was obviously sincere, nor was there anything ignoble in wanting to withdraw from a corrupt society and to denounce its corruption. The long tradition of such 'retirement' to some simpler and loftier bastion of the spirit testifies to the perennial need behind it. But it is also important to notice that Pope denounces that society *to itself*. To identify him with any one aspect of him is to mistake only one aspect of his poetry for the whole. It is also to miss what his critical imagination achieves at its greatest moments. Because the cast of Pope's imagination is so thoroughly dialectical, the impulse to 'fix' his true character is not merely a misguided attempt to identify himself with some consciously chosen persona or image, nor even a wish to play every role in the text like Bottom the weaver. It is the necessary reaction to the *out*going imagination, an attempt to find the centre in himself from which the imagination darts forth and to which it returns, the point where the personal fuses with the impersonal, each giving life, definition, and authority to the other.

The full integrity of his own life was something Pope could realize only 'dramatically' (as he does in most of *Arbuthnot*, for example, or in the ending of the *Epilogue to the Satires*), but I think his greatest poetry is dramatic in a more direct sense: where his imagination, his 'whole soul', turns completely outwards to the lives of other selves, and realizes its own integrity only in realizing that of its object.

I have deliberately used the word 'integrity' because it embraces various inter-related meanings, which we need to be clear about in order to understand Pope's real achievement and importance. In its most obvious sense, 'integrity' refers to *moral* wholeness or consistency. An individual has 'integrity' in possessing a single, unyielding ethical core. That is, the word pertains to the understanding and the will: to lack integrity in this sense is to be insincere, or weak, or just morally stupid. With an eye to Pope's rather confused ideas on the subject, we might also notice that the word 'character' can have pretty much the same meaning as 'integrity' here: 'a man of integrity' is 'a man of character'.

In the second sense, 'integrity' refers to *psychological* wholeness or consistency – the particular pattern of motives and causes that determine the individual's feelings, attitudes and behaviour. Even a villain may have a human 'integrity' in this sense; to lack it is to be mad, or unstable, or an incomprehensible mystery. And once again 'character' can have much this same meaning too: as in Pope's line, 'Most Women have no Characters at all'.

In yet a third sense, 'integrity' refers to the realized *identity* of an individual – the completeness with which he is the particular human being he is, his coherence, his total disposition, as a single being. Since this comprises all of his particular ways of being alive in the world, as distinct from those of any other person, the word now includes what is meant by the existentialists' term 'authenticity'. To lack this kind of integrity is to fail in some vital respect to be an individual at all, or to be oneself only incompletely, to live (as the existentialist would put it) in 'bad faith'. What makes the corresponding sense of 'character' hard to define is that sometimes we regard a person's disposition as something he chooses, the effect of an unconscious will in him to be what he is, while at other times we regard his capacity to choose as finally dependent on his disposition, so that his 'character' seems less the visible effect of his choice than the visible sign of his fate or destiny. Nevertheless, there is a relevant sense of 'character' here: if, for example, a man acts gratuitously, he negates his 'character' in the first sense I mentioned, and in another way the second sense too, but he affirms it in this third sense. Thus Macbeth's 'character' (or 'integrity') lies in *everything* he chooses his fate to be – although, as we see it, this is also everything he is destined to choose.

But of course in the last analysis we cannot separate destiny and choice, constancy and freedom. We therefore give 'integrity' or 'character' a composite meaning to embrace all the ways that impersonal facts and forces and values shape the individual person, and are in turn given visible shape and significance by the whole, integral activity of the person. At the very roots of consciousness, and so of self-consciousness, impersonal causes seem both to determine and yet to be transformed into, personal motive and choice; impersonal social traditions and pressures seem to condition, and yet to be subject to, the personal will that accepts or rejects them; the possibilities of an impersonal order in the objective world seem to be realized only in the personal activity of apprehending them. In the end, the 'integrity' of any individual is nothing less than his 'whole soul' in active and passive engagement with the whole of the not-self. It is the complex but elusive sense of 'character' corresponding to this that Shakespeare was concerned with (as in *Macbeth* or *King Lear*); so, in different ways, have the great novelists of the nineteenth and twentieth centuries been concerned with it too, as in some of Dickens's so-called 'caricatures', for instance, or (more consistently) in *The Brothers Karamazov*, or *Daniel Deronda*, or *Nostromo*, or in *Women in Love* and *Ulysses*. The tragic writer is most aware of how *much* a man may choose to experience in order to be what he is; the comic writer (and theories of 'humours' or the like are very much to the point) is most aware of how *little* a man need choose to experience in order to be what he is; but obviously these are not mutually exclusive points of view: indeed, in Pope it is almost impossible to distinguish them at times. But it is finally in Pope's concern with human 'character' in this sense that I see the basis of his stature and importance.

His rather muddled theory of the 'Ruling Passion' is his attempt to explain this essentially 'dramatic' insight. He tries to explain his theory in the first of the *Moral Essays*, and it is not hard to see why so few readers have taken him seriously. All of Johnson's objections, for example, are thoroughly justified: Pope's argument is confused, and does look like 'a kind of moral predestination' doubly confused with an absurdly simplified psychology. Nevertheless, it is worth asking if Pope was not driving at something rather different from what he seems to be saying, or even from what he thought he was saying. He talks about both causes and motives, but muddles them together; he talks about inconsistencies both of behaviour and of valuation but muddles these together too; claims that social forces condition the individual's 'manners', but he also claims that social phenomena are shaped and coloured by the 'manners' of the individual perceiving them. But if I have rather laboured the meaning of the term 'integrity' or 'character', it is because it may help us see Pope's confusion here as the result less of incompetence than of an insight he could not quite express in the conceptual vocabulary available to him. The real point of the theory is not to reduce human behaviour to a single psychological cause, nor (like Shaftesbury, and even Montaigne perhaps) to try to reduce all the individual's ethical activity to a single centre where it assumes rational consistency. Nor is he merely after a formula for depicting an individual's unique identity. His own principle, that for any observer 'all Manners take a tincture from his own', applies to *his* analytic 'manner' here. The awareness of his personal inconsistencies and fluidity impelled him to try to 'fix' his full integrity in some concept of himself; just so, his very responsiveness to others' inconsistencies impels him to try to fix their full integrity: to fix the point at which men's 'Manners with Fortunes, Humours turn with Climes', which is also the point where those fortunes and climes become destinies men choose for themselves in choosing to obey their pressure. The 'ruling passion' is the term Pope gives the point at which the individual is most intensely, most passionately, alive *as* himself; and since it also *delimits* his being, it is like the 'lurking principle of death' he receives at 'the moment of his breath'. Thus the term includes all its psychological, moral, and even philosophical meanings, since it is what we might call a 'dramatic' principle: for Pope, the 'ruling passion' is the shaping and animating principle of an individual life as a dramatist would conceive it, simultaneously from within and from outside. Not surprisingly, Pope's meaning emerges far more clearly in the way his imagination actually sees particular cases (even in the first *Moral Essay*) than in the way his intellect tries to expound the idea. And his finest 'Characters' – Atticus, say, or Sporus, or Villiers, or the main figures in the fourth Book of *The Dunciad* – are distinguished from those of any writer of 'Characters' before him precisely by this kind of integrity: the integrity of his imagination comprehending (and so also judging) the integrity of the individual as at once an ethical being, a social or psychological type, and a unique consciousness, sensibility, and will.

Pope's judgements are therefore far more complex and searching than any reference to conscious Augustan norms would suggest. Some of the finest examples come in the second *Moral Essay*, on 'the Characters of Women' – examples all the more interesting for the hints here and there of a conscious relationship between the subject and Pope himself. Flavia, the 'Wit', whose whole being desires 'while we live, to live', has so much fire and force that she can only 'die of nothing but a Rage to live'. She has authenticity, we might say, but no moral centre. The cases that immediately follow have a moral centre, a 'fixed' character, but lack a necessary mobility or 'fire'. With Atossa, Pope actually echoes the phrase he had used of himself: 'with herself or others', she 'finds all her life one warfare upon earth.' She

> Shines, in exposing Knaves, and painting Fools,
> Yet is, whate'er she hates and ridicules.
>
> (117–18)

'*Madame Atossa, c'est moi.*' It is as if Pope is realizing in himself the *self*-laceration he sees as Atossa's 'character'. Again, at some points he tends to think of women (rather simplistically) as 'chameleons' that cannot be accurately painted in 'white and black' – with the clear implication, of course, that he has to be something of a chameleon himself to get them 'right'. At the end, however, turning to Martha Blount, he sees not a chameleon, but a 'blend' of the best (but opposing) qualities of each sex: 'Fix'd Principles, with Fancy ever new', and so on. Heaven 'shakes all together and produces – You'. Once again the self-implication is clear. If Heaven gave her sense and good humour, it also gave her a poet whose own character – chameleon-like, but not without 'fixed principles' – can realize the nature and value of hers. Pope makes the point about himself very delicately – and of course long before Keats used the same word, chameleon, for the 'dramatic' poet's lack of a fixed identity.

Nevertheless, oppositions like that between 'chameleon' and 'fixed principles' are hardly adequate to Pope's very greatest poetry, here or elsewhere: for example, the passage here that begins, 'Yet mark the fate of a whole Sex of Queens!', and ends with 'Alive, ridiculous, and dead, forgot'. At first, the lines do turn on the opposition between the 'foreign glory, foreign joy' that women seek – the outgoing movement of life, against its integrating movement inwards towards a stable centre: 'Peace or Happiness at home', a 'well-tim'd Retreat' from the world, and so on. Yet (as always with Pope) the word 'fate' introduces a more profound kind of insight and judgement, which transcends such polarities: 'As Hags hold Sabbaths' ... 'their merry miserable Night' ... 'Ghosts of Beauty' ... 'haunt the places where their Honour dy'd' ... 'See how the World its Veterans rewards'. Compared with the way Pope saw human 'fate' in *The Rape of the Lock*, this passage is not only more substantial, more deeply observed, felt, and considered; his object here, in all of its personal, social, and even metaphysical dimensions, wholly contains his response to it in all of *its* dimensions. Here, 'fixed principles' *are* 'fancy ever new', and 'sense' and 'good humour' the other side of horror and compassion. To know that the life of a Wit is a warfare upon earth can amuse him, but it can also lacerate him with the consciousness of his being not just an elusive chameleon but a scarred and vulnerable veteran of the world too. But it is the *life* of the Wit, wholly realized in seeing what it means for these women to be no more than veterans of the world, that finally prevents him from also being 'alive, ridiculous, and dead, forgot'.

A comparable passage is the ending of the third *Moral Essay* (to Bathurst), 'Of the Use of Riches'. Whatever argumentative function the story of Sir Balaam has in the Essay as a whole, I think Pope's instinct was right to end with it, for it collects and fuses together all the various attitudes towards money and the power of money that go before. The Balaam passage is at once a 'life', a tale, a criticism of society, a brilliantly funny tragedy, a religious parable – a whole drama, one might say, or rather a whole novel, concentrated under intensely creative power into a mere sixty-four lines. It is surely one of the greatest things in the language; certainly, it is characteristic of nobody but Pope. In theory, of course, his account earlier in the poem of the Man of Ross represents his ideals – the norm against which he claims to be judging the commercialization of society. In fact, it represents only what he thought his central norm was. The difference in actual effect between that passage and the account of Sir Balaam could hardly be more striking: with the Man of Ross, rhetorical questions and vaguely general nouns, the verse deliberately flattening out its characteristic tensions and antitheses to correspond with an ideal peace, and ideal singleness of purpose, and a human identity so ideally simple that it is no more than the sum of its virtuous deeds – and £500 per annum; with Balaam, verve, spirit, a tone responsively alive to every manifestation of life – 'an added pudding', 'farthings to the poor', 'his gains were sure', 'rouz'd by the Prince of Air, the whirlwinds sweep/The surge', 'lo! two puddings smoak'd upon the board', 'Behold Sir Balaam, now a man of spirit', 'Things change their titles, as our manners turn'. All through the passage, the rhythms evoke and comment simultaneously; the nouns are specific, and they gather metaphoric generality like an electrical charge. Pope's attitude is no less complex than the complex relationship he sees between having one's soul 'secured', and being 'a man of spirit' and 'wit'; between being acted upon and choosing to be acted on; between 'biting' and being 'bit'; between 'manners' and names and 'titles'. The energy of the verse is that of the world it evokes, even that of the Prince of Air who enters this society through the soul Balaam opens to him. Pope really *enjoys* Balaam. His detachment includes a certain complicity; his contempt is mixed, though not diluted, with pity. The writing is more buoyant, less compassionate than the passage on women; but the same edge of dismay under the precision, the bitter taste of loss and futility that gathers under the moralist's relentless logic, make the last few lines on Balaam's end far more adequate a response to this society than all the talk about moderation, general use, reconciled extremes, and the 'thrice happy' Man of Ross. Here, the choices and deeds and understanding of men (including Pope's own) are seen as conditioned by inescapable forces — psychological, social, moral, and metaphysical — and conversely those forces are seen as manifesting themselves for good or evil only in the individual's life — in personal choices, deeds, and understanding.

The greatness of the final *Dunciad* lies in this kind of dramatic insight and power, much more than in its forceful application of Augustan norms to Augustan society and culture. Not that the two features are wholly distinct, of course: like Balaam's life, the life of Pope's poetry obviously depends on the norms to which he gives real (not merely notional) assent. It is significant, for instance, that *Dunciad* IV harks back (sometimes in a seriously ironic way) to some of his earlier works; the poem itself announces the personal implications right at the start. The poet prays to the mysterious powers he celebrates and to which Time is also taking him: 'Suspend a while your Force inertly strong, / Then take at once the Poet and the Song'. As he sees it here, Dulness is not just a possibility in the world he inhabits, a 'Seed of Chaos, and of Night', but an actual reality: it is the buzzing energy, the inert power, the weird and crazy forms of the life Pope also shares. It is the operatic singer, for example:

> Joy to great Chaos! let Division reign:
> Chromatic tortures soon shall drive them hence ...
> One Trill shall harmonize joy, grief, and rage,
> Wake the dull Church, and lull the ranting Stage ...
>
> (54ff)

It is the bard and blockhead marching side by side; the schoolmaster transforming boys into pedants; pedants transforming verse into prose again; the chef transforming 'Hares to Larks, and Pigeons into Toads'; the florist transforming the flowers of nature (including its human flowers: 'Each Maid cry'd, charming! and each Youth, divine!'); the fop transforming the education of taste into the mere eduction of tastes; and so on. The verse is alive with their activity, dense with their mental 'density', and integrated by their creation of 'one mighty Dunciad of the land'.

Obviously, part of the joke is that Pope (and we) realize perfectly well what he is doing here in transforming the Dunces' life into something else. The poet's creative 'character' is realizing itself in realizing theirs. His wit pounces on their activities as the material of its own. It too is buzzing with energy, vivacious, gaily – indeed, hilariously – responsive to every crazy object, exultant in its power to dart forth anywhere and everywhere so quickly and accurately. But it realizes 'madness' and 'chaos' for what they are only because it sees them by the light of its own sanity and order, its own integrity. Pope, we should notice, does not now suppose that sanity and order are objective realities outside himself, divinely given facts merely obscured by a 'maze' of appearances. The world he sees and recreates here is not one of mere appearances, any more than the values by which it is judged are absolutes shining clearly behind the clouds. The sun itself is 'sick'; it is precisely because Dulness is real and alive that it is so much of a threat to the fullest realization of life. Moreover, it is a double threat. On the one side, the chaotic plenitude of 'madness', its ever-multiplying forms, its 'bursting world', draw the mind (Pope's mind, our minds, the Dunces' minds) outwards, spinning the wits away from any stable integrity, any morally coherent, psychologically whole, personally authentic being. On the other side, its force is that of inertia; it continually pulls the wits back, in towards the single, fixed, impregnable centre of rest, of *inaction*.

In Pope's whole sense of it, the threat of Dulness lies in the 'one trill' that 'harmonize[s] joy, grief, and rage' as much as in its 'chromatic tortures', in the 'dull Church' as much as 'the ranting Stage'. The hour in which Dulness triumphs is quite properly the 'all-composing' hour. Peace, concord, and unity are achieved in the 'one mighty Dunciad of the land'. If Dulness is the necessary element of the poet's life as a Wit, and all the figures in the poem like parodies of himself (and of the understanding reader), it is also a 'resistless' power, one the Muse must also 'obey'. It is the power that finally composes everything in an all-inclusive unity, in imperturbable self-possession, in absolute integrity: in short, in the undivided, unviolated chaos of boredom, sleep and death. The final joke – and Pope clearly appreciates it to the full – is that (like any man, but more objectively than most) he realizes his own life, his own 'character', in triumphing (with the fullest and most passionately committed activity of his 'wit') over the 'resistless' triumph he proclaims. Although the poem portrays the 'all-composing' power of Dulness, the kind of 'all-composing' power it actually embodies, the creative power of human 'wit', remains to confront the triumph of Dulness with a very different kind of composure, energy, and integrity.

WILLIAM HOGARTH

V. DE S. PINTO

The place of William Hogarth is certainly with the great English Augustan writers, Defoe, Swift, Pope, Gay, and Fielding, rather than with the elegant eighteenth-century portrait painters such as Reynolds and his successors. More clearly perhaps than any other Englishman of his period Hogarth saw that his age needed a new kind of art to express the spirit of a new kind of civilization. About a hundred years after the beginning of Hogarth's career as an artist William Blake wrote

> May God us keep
> From Single vision & Newton's sleep.[1]

'Single vision' for Blake was the vision of the 'Enlightenment' produced by the scientific thinkers of the seventeenth century, a 'universe of death' consisting of abstract, colourless, soundless, tasteless atoms obeying rigid mathematical laws. Blake himself aspired to the 'fourfold vision' of the prophet or seer. The English artistic heritage was, however, saved by the men of the Augustan age who explored with fearless energy the world revealed by the 'twofold vision' of the common sensuous observer illuminated by occasional flashes of the 'threefold vision' of the poet. These men re-created the English artistic tradition after the dissolution of the old Court culture in the reigns of the last Stuart kings, and produced new forms such as the realistic painting, the novel and the ballad opera, which embodied the lusty, vigorous, social and intellectual life of the young 'bourgeois' civilization of which England was now the chief representative in Europe. In this work William Hogarth, painter, draughtsman, engraver, and dramatic, realistic, and comic artist, played a decisive part.

The history of pictorial art in England has been very different from that of literature. English literature has a continuous history since the Middle Ages, but in the history of English pictorial art there is a great

gap extending for about two hundred years from the beginning of
the sixteenth till the beginning of the eighteenth century. Medieval
English craftsmen had a European reputation.[2] Their art was anonymous like the medieval lyrics and ballads, and it seems to have been
the product of the great religious houses.[3] When they were dissolved
at the Reformation, the tradition came abruptly to an end. From the
time of Henry VIII to that of William III, pictorial art in England
was mainly an upper-class luxury purveyed to wealthy patrons by
foreign artists such as Holbein and Zuccaro in the sixteenth century
and Rubens and Van Dyck in the seventeenth, as well as numerous
lesser men such as the admirable Czech engraver Wenceslaus Hollar,
who has provided us with our most vivid pictorial records of the
England of Cromwell and Charles II.[4] Of course, there was some
English painting in these two centuries. There were the delicate Elizabethan miniature portraits of Nicholas Hillyard and Isaac Oliver[5] and
the works of Van Dyck's English pupils such as Dobson and Cooper
in the seventeenth century, and at the other end of the social scale
the rough but sometimes spirited and vigorous woodcuts found in
many of the broadsides and chapbooks. Taken as a whole, however,
it can be said that there was no real English tradition of pictorial art
in this period. English noblemen, following the example of Charles I,
bought Italian, Spanish, Dutch, Flemish, and French pictures, and
there grew up the cult of the Old Masters, the snobbish, dilettante
adoration of everything in art that was old and foreign and covered
with dirt and brown varnish. The whole of Hogarth's career was a
protest against this sort of culture-snobbery. In a letter printed in *The
St James's Post* in June 1737, he attacked the picture-dealers who

depreciate every English work, as hurtful to their trade, of continually
importing shiploads of dead Christs, holy families, Madonnas, and other
dismal dark subjects, neither entertaining nor ornamental; on which they score
the terrible cramp names of some Italian masters, and fix on us poor Englishmen the character of *universal dupes*. If a man, naturally a judge of Painting,
not bigoted to those empirics, should cast his eye on one of their sham
virtuoso-pieces, he would be very apt to say, 'Mr Bubbleman, that grand
Venus (as you are pleased to call it) has not beauty enough for the character
of an English cook-maid.'[6]

Hogarth was more interested in English cook-maids than Italian
Venuses and he learnt to paint not in Italy but in London. He de-

livered English painting from the dilettanti and turned it into a living, popular art, using it to express the abounding vitality and bursting energy of the England of his day and also to expose its folly, its hypocrisy, and its cruelty with a satiric force not inferior to that of his great contemporaries Swift, Pope, and Fielding.

The son of a poor schoolmaster and literary hack from Westmorland, William Hogarth was born in London in 1697, when Dryden still had three years to live, Pope was a boy of nine, Swift in his thirtieth year and still unknown, and Defoe a man of thirty-six, who had already published several pamphlets, failed in business, and held a minor government post. Like William Blake about seventy years later, Hogarth left school when he was still a boy and was apprenticed to an engraver. He appears to have taught himself drawing in the first instance and to have deliberately trained his visual memory. At first he designed and engraved shop bills and coats of arms, then he passed to the drawing and engraving of illustrations to books (including a notable set for *Hudibras*), and original satiric designs.

It was in the third decade of the eighteenth century that Hogarth really began his career as a great popular artist re-establishing in England the tradition of popular satiric and moralizing art: it was the tradition that goes back to the marginal illustrations in medieval manuscripts, grotesque ornamental features in Gothic architecture, and the satirical carvings on misericord seats.[7]

A good example of the satiric work of Hogarth is the print called *Masquerades and Operas* (1724), a vigorous attack on the bad taste of his day and especially on that of the aristocracy. This plate, though it does not show the profound knowledge of life and insight into the human comedy of Hogarth's later pictures, is nevertheless the starting-point for much of his subsequent satire. It is a kind of pictorial parallel to *A Tale of a Tub* and *The Dunciad*. We see in it crowds of people flocking to Italian Opera, a Pantomime of Doctor Faustus and Heidegger's Masquerades, while the neglected volumes of Shakespeare, Otway, Dryden, and Congreve are wheeled away to be pulped. On a show-cloth hung from the Opera, the Earl of Peterborough is seen on his knees before Francesca Cuzzini (Ambrose Philips's 'Little Siren of the Stage'[8]), while in the background rises the façade of Burlington House, the mansion of the Earl of Burlington, the famous aristocratic dilettante and collector of

Italian pictures. It is labelled 'Academy of Arts' (a curious prophetic stroke, for it actually became the headquarters of the Royal Academy later on) and is surmounted by an effigy of William Kent, a showy, conceited English painter (but an architect of some merit) who had been trained in Italy and was a favourite of Lord Burlington. It was probably Hogarth's attack on Kent that recommended him to the notice of Kent's mortal enemy Sir James Thornhill (1678–1734), a painter of considerable ability, not an empty-headed imitator of continental fashions, but an intelligent student of the baroque style of contemporary Italy, which he adapted with some success in his mural paintings at St Paul's Cathedral, Greenwich Hospital, and elsewhere. He is also notable for starting the first regular school of painting in England since the dissolution of the monasteries. Hogarth attended this school and learnt much from Thornhill, particularly in the way of composition, grouping, and the painting of interiors. Thus he was now in a position to unite the popular, satiric realistic tradition, descending from Bosch, Breughel, Callot, and the Dutch engravers with the grace and distinction of the aristocratic baroque tradition, transmitted by Thornhill and Thornhill's Italian masters. As a painter in oils Hogarth first made his reputation by his 'conversation pieces', little paintings of figures in natural attitudes and groupings either in rooms or in the open air.[9] They correspond to the periodical essays of Steele, Addison, and their successors, and have the same virtues of urbanity, informality, and civilized ease. Hogarth's genius, however, was too strong and exuberant to be confined for long in such narrow limits. His kinship was to the authors of *A Tale of a Tub*, *The Dunciad*, *Moll Flanders*, and *Jonathan Wild*, not to those of *The Tatler*, *The Spectator*, and the *Guardian*.

From satiric prints and conversation pieces in oils Hogarth passed to that peculiar type of realistic, satiric, and moralizing painting which made him the most famous English artist of his day and gave him a European reputation.[10] The most memorable part of this work is to be found in the four great series of pictures which David Garrick in his Epitaph on Hogarth called his 'pictur'd Morals'.[11] They are *A Harlot's Progress* (1731/2), *A Rake's Progress* (1735), *Marriage à la Mode* (1745), and *Industry and Idleness* (1747). With them can be classed also the shorter sequences, such as *The Four Stages of Cruelty* and *The Four Times of the Day* (1738), *Beer Street* and *Gin Lane* (1751), and the

Election series (1754–66), as well as a number of single pictures of a similar character such as *A Modern Midnight Conversation* (1733), *The Distressed Poet* (before 1736), and *Taste à la Mode* (1742). In these works Hogarth invents a new kind of popular pictorial art very closely analogous to the English realistic, moralizing novel of the early eighteenth century, which was certainly profoundly influenced by his example. It is highly significant that the second of the two decades in which Hogarth's four great 'pictur'd Morals' appeared also saw the publication of the four major novels of Richardson and Fielding: *Pamela* (1740), *Joseph Andrews* (1742), *Clarissa* (1748), *Tom Jones* (1749).

Hogarth's 'pictur'd Morals' are a remarkable anticipation of the modern art of the film: the telling of a dramatic story in a series of pictures. The difference between the Hogarthian picture-sequence and the modern popular film is that, unlike the directors of Hollywood dramas, Hogarth does not aim primarily either at thrills or wish-fulfilment but at unflinching realism combined with a penetrating criticism of moral and social conditions. He describes his aims in a famous passage:

> I therefore turned my thoughts to a still more novel mode, *viz*. painting and engraving modern moral subjects, a field not broken up in any country or any age ... I wished to compose pictures on canvas, similar to representations on the stage; and further hope they will be tried by the same test, and criticized by the same criterion ... I have endeavoured to treat my subjects as a dramatic writer; my picture is my stage, and men and women are my players ... This I found was most likely to answer my purpose, provided I could strike the passions, and by small sums from many, by the sale of prints I could engrave from my own pictures, thus secure the property to myself.[12]

This important statement was actually made by Hogarth when he was petitioning for an Act of Parliament to protect his copyrights. It shows that Hogarth regarded himself as a popular dramatist who taught by 'striking the passions', and that he aimed at reaching a wide audience by making engravings from his own paintings to be sold at a low price. This was a revolutionary aim in an age when painters usually depended on aristocratic patrons. Hogarth certainly achieved it. Engravings of these famous sets of pictures (often pirated in spite of the Act of Parliament) very soon found their way all over England and became as familiar to Englishmen and Englishwomen as *The Pilgrim's Progress*, *Robinson Crusoe*, and *Gulliver's Travels*. Probably they were more widely known than any of those books, because even the illiterate could read Hogarth's 'pictur'd Morals', if only in poor engravings hung on the walls of innumerable inns, coffee-houses, shops, schools, and private houses, and few middle-class households in the eighteenth and nineteenth centuries were without a copy of one of the many books containing them, from which a very large number of people, like the present writer, derived some of their earliest impressions of pictorial art.

This meant that Hogarth became widely known less as the great painter which he undoubtedly is than as a popular moralist. In 1768, four years after his death, the Rev. John Trusler with the help of Mrs Hogarth published a collection of engravings of his pictures called *Hogarth Moralized*. The letterpress of this collection consists of unctuous expositions of Puritan middle-class morality, which show Hogarth's picture sequences in the light of tracts inculcating the virtues of hard work, thrift, and prudence, and showing the terrible fates which overcome the idle, the profligate, and the improvident. Hogarth, of course, was a moralist, but his pictures have a much deeper meaning than the copybook lessons which lie on the surface and are so easily measured by Dr Trusler's little yardstick. Every picture in the famous sequences is at once a vivid portrayal of the lusty, vigorous life of contemporary England and a powerful exposure of the cruelty, the heartlessness, and the stupidity of a society in which all human and moral values are being threatened by the power of money. Hogarth's harlots and rakes are not shown as naturally evil; they are pathetic, helpless figures who seem to be caught up and mangled by a pitiless mechanism of commercialized greed and vice.

Marriage à la Mode is the finest of the 'pictur'd Morals'. It is a satiric commentary on contemporary society as powerful as that of Pope's *Moral Essays*. The marriage of the depraved young nobleman with the daughter of the rich citizen typifies the alliance between the aristocracy and the commercial magnates which was the keystone of the Augustan social and political system. This masterly sequence has many meanings: one certainly is that the new money power was fundamentally hostile to human values. The pretty doll-like countess and the corrupted boy earl are like spoilt children who drift to their ruin amid sinister figures like the Quack and the Procuress in Plate

III. There is extraordinary pathos in the famous scene (Plate II)[13] in which the newly married pair sit yawning on opposite sides of the fireplace, their boredom and spiritual emptiness contrasted with the beauty and dignity of the noble eighteenth-century room where they are sitting.

The Four Stages of Cruelty is a great pictorial manifestation of humanitarianism. 'The prints,' Hogarth wrote, 'were engraved with the hope of, in some degree correcting that barbarous treatment of animals, the very sight of which renders the streets of our metropolis so distressing to every feeling mind.'[14] Here the story is a much simpler one, the 'progress' of Tom Nero, who starts by torturing dogs and horses, advances to rape and murder, and ends his career on the gallows, after which his corpse is dissected at Surgeons' Hall. Again we are confronted by something far bigger than a mere Cautionary Tale. The sequence is an outburst of bitter indignation against the brutality of the age. Hogarth, the lover of life, who delighted in children and animals, joins hands here with the Blake of *Auguries of Innocence*, whose burning lines may well have been inspired by these terrible prints:

> A dog starv'd at his Master's Gate
> Predicts the ruin of the State.
> A Horse misus'd upon the Road
> Calls to Heaven for Human blood.
> Each outcry of the hunted Hare
> A fibre from the Brain does tear.[15]

If *The Four Stages of Cruelty* is the fiercest of the 'pictur'd Morals', *The Four Times of the Day* is the gentlest. Here there is no connecting thread of dramatic narrative, but simply four brilliant 'shots' of street scenes in Augustan London, full of delight in the comedy, the vitality, and ironic contrasts of contemporary English life. More typical of the Hogarthian spirit are the twin pictures *Beer Street* and *Gin Lane*. They were often used for temperance propaganda, but they have a much profounder significance than the truism that beer is a healthier drink than gin. Actually these two pictures are revelations of eighteenth-century slum life, a powerful comment on the condition of the proletariat in the early period of capitalism. In *Beer Street* the atmosphere is one of fuddle and fatuous cheerfulness: in *Gin Lane*, perhaps Hogarth's most penetrating social satire, it is sordid, hopeless misery.

Here Hogarth is certainly not preaching a sermon against drink. He is showing that, in a world dominated by the power of money, the poor are left to rot in the gutter and drink themselves to death. Dickens in his comment on this picture puts his finger on its true meaning:

> I think it a remarkable trait in Hogarth's picture [Gin Lane], that, while it exhibits drunkenness in its most appalling forms, it also forces on attention a most neglected wretched neighbourhood, and unwholesome, indecent, abject condition of life ... There is no evidence that any of the actors in the dreary scene have ever been much better than we see them there. The best are pawning the commonest necessaries, the tools of their trade; and the worst are homeless vagrants, who give us no clue as to their having been otherwise in bygone days. All are living and dying miserably. Nobody is interfering for prevention or for cure in the generation going out before us, or the generation coming in ... The church is indeed very prominent and handsome; but ... quite passive in the picture as it coldly surveys these things in progress beneath its tower.[16]

Dickens is right; this is a picture of a world in which the Church has forgotten its duty towards the poor and the helpless, and the State has not yet learnt to take care of them. It is the beginning of the great age of *laissez-faire* and 'free enterprise', which reached its culmination in the time of Dickens. Again Hogarth is prophetic of Blake, the poet who wrote:

> The Harlot's cry from Street to Street
> Shall weave old England's winding Sheet.
> The Winner's Shout, the Loser's Curse,
> Dance before dead England's Hearse.[17]

Hogarth is by no means always a moralist or satirist of social conditions. The *March to Finchley* (1750), one of his most popular prints, is simply a piece of comic realism, which is also, incidentally, good-humoured deflation of heroics. The *Strolling Actresses Dressing in a Barn* (1738) has no satiric or moral intention at all; it is as Horace Walpole said,[18] 'a work of wit and imagination without any other end', a splendid and exuberant impression of the lawless, bohemian element of the population of eighteenth-century England, not the hopeless misery of *Gin Lane* or the 'High Life' of *Marriage à la Mode* or the *bourgeois* respectability of Frank Goodchild, but the world of the folk who lived by their wits on the fringe of society and snapped their fingers at convention and decorum. These strolling players (the predecessors of Vincent Crummles and his troupe), drinking, declaiming, dressing, and preparing for a performance of a farce called *The Devil to Pay in Heaven*, are portrayed with a breadth, a gusto, and an Aristophanic gaiety that recalls the only other great eighteenth-century work of art which deals effectively with the same world of vagrants, Burns's *The Jolly Beggars*:

> What is title, what is treasure,
>   What is reputation's care?
> If we lead a life of pleasure,
>   'Tis no matter how or where!
>
> With the ready trick and fable
>   Round we wander all the day,
> And at night in barn or stable
>   Hug our doxies on the hay.

Coleridge is reported by Charles Lamb to have said of Hogarth that in his work 'the satirist never extinguished that love of beauty which belonged to him as a poet'.[19] Hogarth's poetry is to be found throughout his works, in the delicate childlike head of the petulant girl countess in the second plate of *Marriage à la Mode*, in the saturnalia of the third plate of *A Rake's Progress*, and many other places in the famous sequences. The purest manifestations of it, however, are to be found in his portraits and figure studies such as the gay and brilliant picture of Mrs Elizabeth Salter in a yellow silk dress that sets off her dashing figure and pure complexion so admirably. Above all, it is to be found in that miracle of light, colour, and fresh sensuous girlhood, the sketch of *The Shrimp Girl*, the most lyrical of all Hogarth's paintings, which has the spontaneous, birdlike quality of a Shakespearian song.[20]

Hogarth went on painting and engraving till his death in 1764. He lived long enough to design some vigorous illustrations for *Tristram Shandy* and to produce a splendid satiric portrait of Jack Wilkes.

In his last years he seems to have been haunted by the idea of Time. The figure of Time as a kind of humorous, old winged God is seen in the strange print 'Time smoking a picture',[21] a humorous lamentation of an ageing painting and a comment on the snob-worship of dark, smoky, heavily varnished 'Old Masters'. It is also a painter-poet's conception of Mortality. The same figure of the old winged Time-god appears in Hogarth's strangest and most enigmatic production *The Bathos or Finis* (1764).[22] This print was designed as a tail-piece for a collection of his pictures. In it the great realist, the painter of the solid three-dimensional eighteenth-century world governed by the laws of Newtonian physics, shows us a prophetic vision of that world in ruins. Here Time is seen lying propped on a broken column with his broken scythe under his arm. The sign of the inn called 'The World's End' is collapsing on one side of the picture while smoke pours out of a ruined town on the other. In the foreground are various broken objects, including a cracked hourglass, and in the background a landscape with a corpse on a gallows lit by a lurid sky where Apollo, the Sun God, lies dead in his chariot. The title of the picture could be the words of Hotspur in *Henry IV*, Part I, 'Time . . . must have a stop', and it might be called Hogarth's surrealist master-piece. Here for once he has transcended realism, by creating a world of vision, a haunting vision of ruin and madness like that which Pope shows us at the end of *The Dunciad*. *The Bathos or Finis* is the epilogue to the Augustan age, the pictorial parallel to the madness of Collins and Smart, the work of an artist who remained sane but saw in a prophetic flash an image of the terror which sent poets to the mad-house and their graves in the mid-eighteenth century. When Hogarth engraved this picture, Blake was a child of six. His art began where Hogarth's left off. For a moment at the end of his career, Hogarth had a glimpse of the Fourfold Vision, the region in which Blake was to live and move and have his being.

Hogarth is a literary artist, not in the sense that he borrowed many of his themes from literature like the pre-Raphaelites, but in the sense that his aims were similar to those of the chief contemporary English writers and that his influence on literature was quite as im-portant as his influence on painting.[23] When he was young the English literary scene was dominated by the famous group of Queen Anne wits, Swift, Pope, Gay, Addison, and Steele. Hogarth seems to have had little personal connection with this group. He certainly knew Pope's work and Gay's *The Beggar's Opera* and was probably considerably influenced by both these writers. Swift does not seem to have heard of Hogarth till he was an elderly man in Dublin in the

1730s. Probably he enjoyed the prints of *A Harlot's Progress* (1731/2) and *A Rake's Progress* (1735); he certainly recognized in Hogarth a kindred spirit, for, in that terrific denunciation of human stupidity and depravity, *The Legion Club* (1736), he actually envisages a collaboration between himself and the painter:

> How I want thee, humorous *Hogart*?
> Thou I hear, a pleasant Rogue art;
> Were but you and I acquainted,
> Every Monster should be painted;
> You should try your graving Tools
> On this odious Group of Fools;
> Draw the Beasts as I describe 'em,
> Form their Features, while I gibe them;
> Draw them like, for I assure you,
> You will need no *Car'catura*;
> Draw them so, that we may trace
> All the Soul in every Face.[24]

Hogarth's most significant literary relationships were, however, as I have already suggested, with the new art of the English novel as it developed in the fourth and fifth decades of the eighteenth century. He was personally acquainted with both the great pioneers of this art, Samuel Richardson and Henry Fielding. The prim, fastidious, puritanical Richardson with his hatred of anything 'low' and his narrow *bourgeois* morality seems at first glance to have very little in common with the painter of *A Modern Midnight Conversation* and *Strolling Actresses Dressing in a Barn*. Yet we know from Boswell[25] that Hogarth was on intimate terms with Richardson, and R. E. Moore has shown convincingly that *Familiar Letters* (1741), the book on which Richardson was at work when he conceived the plan of *Pamela*, is full of reminiscences of *A Harlot's Progress* and *A Rake's Progress*.[26] *Pamela* itself has none of the broad humour and full blooded exuberance of Hogarth, but it certainly owes much to his pictures. Mrs Jewkes, the wicked old tool of Mr B— in Richardson's novel, bears a strong resemblance to Hogarth's procuress in Plate I of *A Harlot's Progress*, and the description of Colbrand, Mr B—'s Swiss valet, is extremely Hogarthian.[27] This vivid, realistic word-painting is found both in Richardson and Fielding, and it was something new in prose fiction. Even Defoe does not often give clear visual impressions of his scenes and characters, and much of the difficulty which a modern reader finds in getting through the stories of Aphra Behn and, still worse, the 'heroic' romances of the seventeenth century is due to the fact that those writers are incapable of visualizing, and when we read their books we seem to be moving through a world of formless and colourless abstractions. One of Hogarth's great services to English prose fiction was that he made our novelists use their eyes.

Hogarth's relationship to Henry Fielding, Richardson's rival, was certainly very close indeed, and can be described without exaggeration as a collaboration between two artists of equal stature and ability. R. E. Moore has shown that Fielding's dramatic burlesques (1730–37) are considerably influenced by Hogarth's early satiric prints, and there is no doubt that Hogarth and Fielding were working in close co-operation at this time.[28] The pattern of Fielding's career closely resembles that of Hogarth's. His first successes, the dramatic satires of the 1730s, correspond closely to Hogarth's early, topical satiric prints. Like Hogarth he found his true strength when he turned to comic, realistic narrative, and Hogarth undoubtedly helped to show him the way to the new art of *Joseph Andrews*. By 1742, when Fielding published his first novel, Hogarth had already produced *A Harlot's Progress*, *A Rake's Progress*, *The Four Times of the Day*, and the *Strolling Actresses Dressing in a Barn*, as well as such minor masterpieces as *A Modern Midnight Conversation* and *The Laughing Audience*. Already in 1740 in his periodical *The Champion*, Fielding had praised 'the ingenious Mr Hogarth' as one of the most 'useful *Satyrists* that any Age hath produced'. Of course, all sorts of ingredients went to make the delicious compound of *Joseph Andrews*. The influence of Hogarth, however, was certainly one of the determining factors in Fielding's new art of fiction. It seems to have been Hogarth who taught him not, indeed, the critical commonplace that there was a difference between burlesque and comedy, but the inward meaning of that difference and the immeasurable superiority of comedy:

Now what Caricatura is in painting, Burlesque is in writing; and in the same manner the comic writer and painter correlate to each other . . . He who should call the ingenious Hogarth a burlesque painter, would, in my opinion, do him very little honour; for sure it is much easier, much less the subject of admiration, to paint a man with a nose, or any other feature, of a preposterous size, or to expose him in some absurd or monstrous attitude, than to express the affections of men on canvas. It has been thought a vast commendation of a painter, to say his figures seem to breathe; but surely it is a much greater and nobler applause, that they appear to think!

These words from Fielding's Preface to *Joseph Andrews* are full of significance. He undoubtedly had a strong tendency to burlesque and caricature. It was the example of his friend Hogarth which taught him to restrain that tendency and create three-dimensional characters that not only 'breathe' but 'think', such as Joseph Andrews, Parson Adams, Mrs Slipslop, and the rest. Although there are few specific borrowings from Hogarth's pictures in *Joseph Andrews*, it is clear from references throughout the book that Fielding had them constantly in mind and pictures his scenes as they would have appeared to the painter. The famous scene in which Joseph, after being robbed, is found naked by the stagecoach, where the lady shrieks with horror, but nevertheless looks at the naked man through the sticks of her fan, comes straight from the last plate of *A Rake's Progress*, where she is seen ogling a naked Bedlamite through the sticks of a fan.

Tom Jones is, perhaps, even more indebted to Hogarth than *Joseph Andrews*. Three important characters, Mrs Bridget Allworthy, Partridge, and Square, are lifted (with generous acknowledgements) straight out of pictures by Hogarth. Again, throughout the story, we are constantly shown scenes and characters in terms of Hogarth's painting. 'O, Shakespeare! had I thy pen! O, Hogarth! had I thy pencil!'[29] Fielding exclaims, and then promptly, as it were, takes up Hogarth's 'pencil' and paints 'the pale countenance, staring eyes, chattering teeth, faltering tongue, and trembling lips' of the servant who comes to tell Squire Western of Sophia's disappearance. But Fielding's debt to Hogarth in *Tom Jones* is not merely to be found in detailed borrowings. The breadth, the vigour, the delight in every aspect of life, the crowded scenes, and the genial but unsentimental humour of *Tom Jones* are exactly the qualities of Hogarth's great picture. *Joseph Andrews* and *Tom Jones* are, in fact, Hogarthian 'progresses' in literary form. It would be a slight exaggeration to call them the 'books' of Hogarth's 'films', but to study them without reference to the 'pictur'd Morals' is like studying Shakespeare without reference to the Elizabethan theatre.

A writer in *The Times Literary Supplement*[30] has described the relationship between the great painter and the great novelist in words that can hardly be bettered:

Hogarth and Fielding revelled in the human medley. There is such a temperamental and intellectual bond between them that it can be said that Hogarth's pictures give a more exact idea of Fielding's attitude to life than the novelist does in the theories propounded in the celebrated preface to *Joseph Andrews*.

Hogarth was not only a major influence on the new English art of prose fiction; he was also the progenitor of a line of English cartoonists. F. D. Klingender has given an admirable description of his relationship to Rowlandson, Gillray, and their successors.[31] But Hogarth should not be studied merely as an 'influence'. An appreciation of his work is the best possible corrective to the still commonly held belief that the eighteenth century in England was a period of dry formalism and pedantic neo-classicism. Hogarth's pictures are the expression of the spirit of a great age of dynamic and revolutionary thought and imagination.

He is the one great popular English pictorial artist, the sensual, humorous, realistic, moralizing, poetic, illogical English genius expressing itself in colour, line, and form as it expresses itself in words in Chaucer, Ben Jonson, Fielding, and Dickens.

NOTES

1. *The Complete Writings of William Blake*, ed. G. Keynes (1957), 818.

2. See Joan Evans, *English Art, 1307–1361* (1949), 102–4.

3. See R. H. Wilenski, *English Painting*, 37–43, and, for more elaborate accounts, Talbot Rice, *English Art, 871–1100*, and Joan Evans, *English Art, 1307–1361*.

4. See Arthur M. Hind, *Wenceslaus Hollar* (1922).

5. See Wilenski, as above, 44–58; Carl Winter, *Elizabethan Miniatures* (Penguin), and J. Pope Hennessy, *A Lecture on Nicholas Hilliard* (1949).

6. Austin Dobson, *William Hogarth* (1891), 69, 70.

7. See F. D. Klingender, *Hogarth and English Caricature* (1944), iv. 1, 6.

8. See *The Poems of Ambrose Philips*, ed. M. G. Segar (1937), 107, 179.

9. For examples, see R. B. Beckett, *Hogarth* (1949), 22–4 and plates 19, 20, 24–30.

10. As early as 1746 Jean Rouquet, a French critic, published *Lettres de Monsieur XX à un de ses Amis à Paris, pour lui expliquer les Estampes de Monsieur Hogarth*.

11. Quoted by R. E. Moore in *Hogarth's Literary Relationships* (1948), 68.

12. Austin Dobson, *William Hogarth*, 42, 43.

13. See the original painting in the National Gallery, London, reproduced in R. B. Beckett, *Hogarth*, plate 143.

14. John Ireland, *Hogarth Illustrated*, III, 355.

15. See G. Keynes (ed.), 433.

16. See John Forster, *The Life of Charles Dickens*, II (1873), 382, 383.

17. See G. Keynes (ed.), 433.

18. H. Walpole, *Anecdotes of Painting*, IV (1827), 133.

19. *The Works of Charles and Mary Lamb*, ed. E. V. Lucas, I, 91.

20. Both the pictures mentioned in this paragraph are reproduced in R. B. Beckett's *William Hogarth*. The original paintings of both are in the National Gallery, London.

21. Austin Dobson, *William Hogarth*, 160, 161.

22. *The Works of William Hogarth*, II (1833), 278. The original drawing is reproduced in *The Drawings of William Hogarth*, ed. A. P. Oppé (1948), plate 91.

23. See R. E. Moore, *Hogarth's Literary Relationships*, 107–95.

24. *Swift's Poems*, ed. H. Williams, 839. Further evidence for Swift's admiration of Hogarth is given in a note by A. Dobson, *William Hogarth*, 53.

25. Boswell's *Life of Johnson*, ed. Powell (1934), I, 145, 146.

26. R. E. Moore, *Hogarth's Literary Relationships*, 187, 188.

27. See the quotations from *Pamela* on pp. 289–93 of this volume.

28. See R. E. Moore, *Hogarth's Literary Relationships*, 77–102.

29. H. Fielding, *Tom Jones*, Book X, ch. viii.

30. *The Times Literary Supplement*, 4 November 1949 (review of R. E. Moore's *Hogarth's Literary Relationships*).

31. See F. D. Klingender, Introduction to *Hogarth and English Caricature* (1944).

SAMUEL RICHARDSON

FRANK W. BRADBROOK

The novels of Samuel Richardson (1689–1761) present an almost impossible problem for the student of literature, who is not likely to have the time, interest, or stamina to read the nineteen bulky volumes of the standard edition. 'The father of the English novel' is curiously neglected. If read at all, he is usually dipped into in abridged versions. Yet it has been argued that Richardson was so exactly correct in his proportions that any attempt at abridgement must fail, and that it is therefore much better never to read *Clarissa* than to read it clipped. Certainly, it is better to read *Clarissa* in full than to read *Pamela*, *Clarissa*, and *Sir Charles Grandison* in snippets. For it is generally agreed that of Richardson's three novels *Clarissa* is the greatest, thought not, perhaps, the most influential. The difficulty, however, is not only one of bulk. From this point of view, Richardson presents no greater obstacle than many of the Victorian novelists, the Russians, or Proust in *À la recherche du temps perdu*. Coleridge, in one of his brief and brilliant critical asides in *Anima Poetae*, described his response to the novels, and it is a fairly typical one: 'I confess that it has cost, and still costs, my philosophy some exertion not to be vexed that I must admire, aye, greatly admire, Richardson. His mind is so very vile, a mind so oozy, so hypocritical, praise-mad, canting, envious, concupiscent.' Richardson combines a daunting bulk, with extreme unevenness of quality, and several quite repellent characteristics. Coleridge's response to the novels, the mingled fascination and repulsion, is a common one. An entertaining anthology might be compiled recording the horror and disgust aroused by this most moral of writers.

It was in middle age and by accident that Richardson became a novelist, though his profession of master-printer made him naturally interested in books. Compared with Fielding, his great rival, however, Richardson was not a cultured man. He was incapable of writing a great 'comic epic in prose', such as *Tom Jones*, since he was without any deep first-hand knowledge of the classics and almost completely humourless. Yet he querulously criticized his contemporaries, while resenting any criticism of himself. Surrounding himself with sycophantic women of second-rate intellect, he was treated by them as if he was the hero of one of his own novels. Despite all his limitations, however, this vulgar, complacent little bookseller gained a reputation in his own country and on the Continent second to none, and his influence can be seen in the novels of Fanny Burney, Jane Austen and George Eliot. How was it done?

Richardson's first approach to fiction (though not a novel) was *The Familiar Letters on Important Occasions*. These letters were intended to show young ladies how to think and act justly and prudently in the common concerns of human life. The combination of the letter and the didactic moral intention was to be characteristic of Richardson's fiction. A voluminous correspondent himself, he lived in an age that regarded letter-writing as an art. One of the few foreign writers whom he recommended was Mme de Sévigné. She is praised in *Clarissa* for giving 'a faithful and chaste copy of real life and manners'. In the novel, the letter form heightens and sustains dramatic tension and introduces variety, subtlety, and complication, owing to the illusion it creates that the reader is sharing in the events described, and because of the variety of points of view that is given of each situation that arises. It is both more intimate and more objective than the ordinary narrative method, and lends itself to the creation of ironic effects. Henry James saw the advantages of this technique, and after recording in his notebook the possibility of writing 'a story told in letters written alternately by a mother and her daughter and giving totally different accounts of the same situation', he produced in less than a year *A Bundle of Letters*.[1] The complex interweaving of comments by different groups of people, the sense that the reader has of individuals working at cross-purposes and according to different standards, the sudden dramatic and ironic contrasts that occur, are typical of the novels of Henry James. They are equally characteristic of the apparently clumsy epistolary method of Richardson.

The transition from *The Familiar Letters* to Richardson's first novel *Pamela* was simple. He himself said in one of his letters 'I almost slid into the writing of *Pamela*'. But once having done so, the novel took him only three months to write. The first two volumes were published in 1740, and later two further volumes, *Pamela in her Exalted Condition*, were added. The aim of the novel was to show virtue rewarded, and it consisted (in the words of the title-page) of 'a series of Familiar Letters from a Beautiful Young Damsel to her parents. Now first published in order to cultivate the Principles of Virtue and Religion in the Minds of the Youth of Both Sexes.' The theme of the novel, the resistance of the virtuous servant to the attempts at seduction made by her master, was familiar in Puritan literature, and not one that was confined to prose. In the Elizabethan age it had been the subject of *Willobie His Avisa. Or, The True Picture of a modest Maid, and of a chaste and constant Wife*. This moral and allegorical poem was as popular in its time as Richardson's novel, and for the same reasons. In the words of one critic 'the heroine is precisely the sort to appeal to the bourgeoisie, then and now. Resisting all improper advances of noble suitors, she exemplifies Puritan virtue and provides a warning, patly stated, for other maids.'[2] The heading of Canto II of the poem, 'The first triall of Avisa, before she was married, by a Noble man: under which is represented a warning to all young maids of every degree, that they beware of the alluring intisements of great men', might serve as a motto for *Pamela*. Both works were the object of satire and parody. Avisa was described as a wanton minion, and Pamela, rechristened Shamela, was depicted as a feigned innocent against whom all gentlemen should be cautioned. It was even maintained that Richardson, under the pretence of cultivating the principles of virtue, had conveyed 'the most artful and alluring Ideas'. He certainly provided the inspiration for the early part of Fielding's burlesque *Joseph Andrews*, where the adventures of Pamela's brother are described.

The earlier part of *Pamela*, which is the most powerful, forms a complete contrast to the later volumes, which show a more placid and detached interest in the social scene. The atmosphere of these early volumes is unreal in the manner of a fairy-story. Pamela acts the role of heroine locked in the castle of the villain Mr B— and threatened by his two ogre-like servants Mrs Jewkes and Monsieur Colbrand. Her enemies are described with a wealth of detail and have the reality of figures seen in a nightmare. These characters and the main part of the action are seen through the eyes of the heroine, and the picture that Pamela gives of Mrs Jewkes might have served as a model for one of Hogarth's paintings:

> She is a broad, squat, pursy, fat thing, quite ugly, if anything human can be so called; about forty years old. She has a huge hand, and an arm as thick as my waist, I believe. Her nose is fat and crooked, and her brows grown down over her eyes; a dead, spiteful, grey, goggling eye to be sure she has. And her face is flat and broad; and as to colour, looks like it had been pickled a month in saltpetre: I daresay she drinks ...
>
> (I, 119³)

The portrait of Monsieur Colbrand is equally macabre:

> He is a giant of a man for stature; taller by a good deal than Harry Mow-bridge, in your neighbourhood, and large boned and scraggy; and has a hand! – I never saw such an one in my life. He has great staring eyes, like the bull's that frightened me so; vast jaw-bones sticking out; eye-brows hanging over his eyes; two great scars upon his forehead, and one on his left cheek; and two large whiskers, and a monstrous wide mouth; blubber lips; long yellow teeth, and a hideous grin ...
>
> (I, 180)

Such gusto and vivid detail are what one normally associates with Elizabethan prose rather than with Richardson, but if one compares such passages with a typical piece of, say, Nashe, one can, while noting resemblances, also recognize the subtler ingenuity that has been lost:

> A bursten belly inkhorne orator called *Vanderhulke*, they pickt out to present him with an oration, one that had a sulpherous big swolne large face, like a Saracen, eyes lyke two kentish oysters, a mouth that opened as wide every time he spake, as one of those old knit trap doores, a beard as though it had been made of a birds neast pluckt in peeces, which consisteth of strawe, haire, and durt mixt together. He was apparelled in blacke leather new licourd, and a short gowne without anie gathering in the backe, faced before and behinde with a boistrous beare skin, and a red night-cap on his head.
>
> (*The Unfortunate Traveller*)

It was from Defoe that Richardson probably directly inherited his firm grasp of realistic detail. He had certainly read Defoe's *Robinson Crusoe* and *The Family Instructor*, and in both writers the tendencies towards realism and didacticism naturally go together. But Richardson was much more interested in analysing feelings and mental processes than Defoe. He brought to such analysis the same passion for precision that Defoe showed when describing external details, while his predecessor's influence was sufficiently strong to act as a restraining guard against his own particular weakness and vice, sentimentality.

In the company of the two vividly evoked henchmen and of the inevitable Mr B—, Pamela's virtue is tried. Many readers find both her character and the long-drawn-out tale of attempted seduction repulsive and tedious. Yet one cannot but admire the exactness and thoroughness with which her fluctuating feelings and states of mind are described, the psychological insight shown into the reactions of the frightened and fascinated victim. For Pamela, despite her protests (and some would say that she protests too much and does too little), is fascinated at the same time that she is frightened. She, herself, naïvely records her feelings:

> What is the matter, that with all his ill usage of me, I cannot hate him? . . . I could not in my heart forbear from rejoicing at his safety; though his death would have ended my afflictions . . .
>
> (I, 194)

After several attempts have been made to break down her resistance by force and intimidation, she is allowed to escape. Before reaching her home she receives a letter from Mr B— inviting her back. The description of her conflicting impulses that follows is all the more effective as self-revelation and confession because of its ingenuousness and apparent lack of subtlety:

> Oh my exulting heart! how it throbs in my bosom, as if it would reproach me for so lately upbraiding it for giving way to the love of so dear a gentleman! – But take care thou art not too credulous neither, oh fond believer! Things that we wish, are apt to gain a too ready credence with us. This sham marriage is not yet cleared up; Mrs Jewkes, the vile Mrs Jewkes! may yet instigate the mind of this master: his pride of heart, and pride of condition, may again take place: and a man that could in so *little* a space, first love me, then hate, then banish me his house, and send me away disgracefully; and now send for me again, in such affectionate terms, may *still* waver, may *still* deceive thee. Therefore will I not acquit thee yet, oh credulous, fluttering, throbbing mischief! that art so ready to believe what thou wishest! and I charge thee to keep better guard than thou hast lately done, and lead me not to follow too implicitly thy flattering and desirable impulses. Thus foolishly dialogued I with my heart; and yet, all the time, this heart is Pamela.
>
> (I, 276)

Pamela's own lack of insight into her thoughts and feelings does not prevent her from presenting them clearly. The reader is encouraged to supply the extra comment and analysis that are needed. The moment when she recognizes her own feelings for what they are is more attractive for being artless and unaffected:

> I know not *how* it came, nor *when* it began; but crept, crept it has, like a thief, upon me; and before I knew what was the matter, it looked like love.
>
> (I, 272)

After all the attempts of Mr B——, Pamela can still exclaim, as marriage draws nearer – 'Oh! what halcyon days are these', and record her final naïve confession:

> I hope he loves me! – But whether he does or not, I am in for it now, over head and ears I doubt, and can't help loving him; 'tis folly to deny it.
>
> (II, 42)

Unfortunately, the character of Pamela does not create the impression of pure and injured innocence that Richardson intended. The weakness of Richardson as a moralist is that he appears to be unconscious of the implications of the situations that he describes. There are elements of hypocrisy and coarse-grained vulgarity in his heroine. What repels the reader is not merely the inconsistency of a supposedly chaste maiden 'whose dreams are filled with ideas of rape, but whose waking moments resound to prate about her honour',[4] nor the ridiculousness of a situation where, in the words of a French critic, 'une fille qu'on veut séduire, qui en est persuadée, se résout tranquillement à rester exposée: et quel important motif la détermine? Une veste à broder.'[5] By some perverse obliquity of the writer the intended moral is reversed. Instead of showing virtue rewarded Richardson has written an apologia for a self-righteous equivalent of Roxana or Moll Flanders. And in describing how she defended her 'honour' Richardson dwells with a lingering relish on scenes that are supposed to be the prerogative in English literature of the more pornographic playwrights of the Restoration. D. H. Lawrence remarked that 'Boccaccio at his hottest seems to me less pornographical than *Pamela* or *Clarissa Harlowe*'.[6] So far as *Pamela* is concerned, he erred on the side of understatement. For, like Swift's broom-stick, Richardson is 'sharing all the while in the very same pollutions he

pretends to sweep away'. *Pamela* is sentimental and obscene: its
obscenity is a direct result of its sentimentality.

The comments of Mr B— occasionally introduce a wholesome
note of satire, which contrasts with what Pamela calls 'the naked
sentiments of my heart'. For him she is 'an artful young baggage',
'a subtle artful gipsy' who 'has a lucky knack of falling into fits, when
she pleases' and 'has wit at will, when she has a mind to display her
own romantic innocence, at the price of other people's characters'.
But Mr B— has exactly the same mixture of hypocrisy, vulgarity,
and (strangely enough!) of innocence and unawareness as Pamela
herself. After attempting for two volumes (and occasionally with
success) to put his hand into her bosom, he can still, when they are
reconciled and the marriage arranged, blithely refer to 'our innocent
enjoyments', and express the wish to 'pour my whole soul into your
bosom'. He, too, prates of honour as much as she does. The combination of triteness and indecency with pious professions is not
limited to any one character, but pervades the whole novel. Pamela's
father, to whom she has written constantly describing Mr B—'s
conduct, has a dream after the alliance has been put on a nominally
respectable basis. He sees 'nothing but Jacob's ladder, and angels
ascending and descending to bless him and his daughter' (II, 53).

By this time Pamela's prison has become her palace and 'the dear,
once naughty assailer of her innocence, by a blessed return of Providence, is become the kind, the generous protector and rewarder of it'
(II, 105). As she herself remarks, 'sure nobody was ever so blessed
as I!' She visits the summer-house again, where she had previously
been assaulted, prays and thanks God, then 'whips out again, so that
Mr B— hardly missed me' At this point Mr B— discovers that she
has a mind, and praises it. Later the marriage guests join in approval
of her blasphemous rewriting of the one hundred and thirty-seventh
Psalm to suit her own case while she was Mr B—'s prisoner. The
clergyman, Mr Williams, himself lectures her on the right use of
riches, quoting Proverbs: 'The liberal soul shall be made fat: and he
that watereth, shall be watered himself.' Unconscious irony could
hardly go farther than this.

Where Richardson is most successful is in catching the tone and
manner of Pamela's speech. Her talk, too, is full of proverbs and
colloquialisms. She refers to 'God, whose graciousness to us we have

so often experienced at a pinch'; she is so confounded at something that Mr B— says that 'you might have beat me down with a feather'; 'What I do, must be at a jerk, to be sure', she remarks. This habit was characteristic of Richardson himself, and the novels are full of a similar kind of moral aphorism: 'a man who has sons brings up chickens for his own table, whereas daughters are chickens brought up for the tables of other men'; 'those who will bear much, shall have much to bear'; 'the coyest maids make the fondest wives'. In the character of Pamela, Richardson was dealing with something that he knew and could cope with. Her language is his language, and her exchanges with Mrs Jewkes have a genuine dramatic liveliness:

'Pray, Mrs Jewkes,' said I, 'don't *madam* me so: I am but a silly poor girl, set up by the gambol of fortune, for a Maygame; and now am to be something, and now nothing, just as that thinks fit to sport with me: And let you and me talk upon a foot together; for I am a servant inferior to you, and so much the more as I am turned out of place.'

(I, 114)

It is when Richardson has to deal with characters from 'high life' that his touch fails. In the following conversation between Pamela, Mr B—, and Lady Davers, his sister, one notes how the style of the writing gradually degenerates into melodramatic fustian:

Not considering anything, I ran out of the closet, and threw myself at my dear master's feet, as he held her hand, in order to lead her out; and I said, Dearest sir, let me beg, that no act of unkindness, for my sake, pass between so worthy and so near relations. Dear, dear madam, said I, and clasped her knees, pardon and excuse the unhappy cause of all this evil; on my knees I beg your ladyship to receive me to your grace and favour, and you shall find me incapable of any triumph but in your ladyship's goodness to me.

Creature, said she, art *thou* to beg an excuse for me? Art *thou* to implore my forgiveness? Is it to *thee* I am to owe the favour, that I am not cast headlong from my brother's presence? Begone to thy corner, wench! begone I say, lest thy paramour kill me for trampling thee under my foot!

Rise, my dear Pamela, said my master; rise, dear life of my life; and expose not so much worthiness to the ungrateful scorn of so violent a spirit. And so he led me to my closet again, and there I sat and wept.

(II, 190)

The crudeness of this needs no emphasizing. Yet it was such raw material that Jane Austen refined to create the scenes between Elizabeth Bennet, Mr Darcy, and Lady Catherine de Bourgh in *Pride and*

Prejudice. Elizabeth Bennet is, of course, a gentleman's daughter, and aware of the fact. The nearest that Jane Austen ever got to depicting a Pamela was in the satirical portrait of Lucy Steele in *Sense and Sensibility*. She adopts the same tone of ignominious flattery towards Mrs Ferrars as Pamela does to Lady Davers. The description given of Lucy Steele's character is perhaps as good a summary of Pamela as one could hope to find:

> the active, contriving manager; uniting at once a desire of smart appearance with the utmost frugality, and ashamed to be suspected of half her economical practices; pursuing her own interest in every thought; courting the favour of Colonel Brandon, Mrs Jennings, and of every wealthy friend ... a most encouraging instance of what an earnest, an unceasing attention to self-interest, will do in securing every advantage of fortune, with no other sacrifice than that of time and conscience.
>
> (chs xlviii and l)

By her gratitude for the unkindness she receives, Lucy Steele becomes necessary to Mrs Ferrars as Pamela does to Lady Davers. The interest in social distinctions, in manners and morals, is common to Richardson and Jane Austen, though the discriminations of the later novelist are so much more delicate as to make the efforts of the pioneer read like a burlesque. But the sentiments of Lady Davers are essentially those of Lady Catherine de Bourgh. The one says:

> Thou'rt almost got into a fool's paradise, I doubt! And wilt find thyself terribly mistaken in a little while, if thou thinkest my brother will disgrace his family to humour thy baby-face!
>
> (II, 146)

Lady Catherine de Bourgh is equally violent:

> The upstart pretensions of a young woman without family, connections, or fortune. Is this to be endured? But it must not, shall not be. If you were sensible of your own good, you would not wish to quit the sphere, in which you have been brought up.
>
> (*Pride and Prejudice*, ch. lvi)

The reactions of Pamela and Elizabeth Bennet to the formidable challenge are, of course, completely different, the one passively retiring to her closet, the other, after utterly annihilating her enemy, politely escorting her to her carriage. The difference in response accords with the difference in social standing of the two characters, and this, in its turn, reflects the widely different interests of the two writers.

Despite the number of parodies of it that were made, *Pamela* won immediate popularity. In January 1741, two months after the publication of the book, *The Gentleman's Magazine* stated that it was 'judged in Town as great a Sign of Want of Curiosity not to have read *Pamela* as not to have seen the *French* and *Italian* Dancers'.[7] 'It was usual for ladies to hold up the volumes of *Pamela* to one another, to shew they had got the book that every one was talking of,' said Mrs Barbauld, and a later female admirer, Clara Reeve, noted that 'the person that had not read *Pamela* was disqualified for conversation, of which it was the principal subject for a long time.' Six years after its publication in England it had been translated into French, German, and Italian, and the younger Crébillon wrote from France to Lord Chesterfield that 'Without *Pamela* we should not know what to say or do here.'[8] Its popularity continued for a long time. In 1820 Leigh Hunt drew a picture of the maidservant of his day. Her property includes 'an odd volume of *Pamela*, and perhaps a sixpenny play, such as *George Barnwell* or Mrs Behn's *Oroonoko*'.[9]

Richardson, however, was not satisfied. He was concerned lest his first novel should appear to encourage the idea that 'a reformed rake makes the best husband'. *Clarissa* (1747–8), his second novel, was written partly to disprove this. It was intended, according to the preface,

to warn the inconsiderate and thoughtless of the one sex, against the base arts and designs of specious contrivers of the other, and to caution parents against the undue exercise of their natural authority over their children in the great article of marriage.

The actions and conduct of the worthy characters were to exemplify the highest and most important doctrines not only of morality, but of Christianity.

The first part of the novel is concerned with the efforts of Clarissa's family to persuade her to marry a certain Mr Soames, whom she detests. Here Richardson was dealing with a problem relevant to his day, when women were only just beginning to emerge from a position of subservience. Clarissa recognizes the right of her parents to forbid a marriage of which they disapprove. But she opposes their attempts to force her to marry against her will. Clarissa's situation is similar to that of Dorothy Osborne and of many others in real life, though Dorothy's attitude was the more obsequious.

The novel really comes to life from the moment that Clarissa is tricked into putting herself under the protection of Lovelace, a character that Richardson took from a play, *The Fair Penitent*, by Nicholas Rowe. Comparing Lovelace with Lothario in his *Life of Rowe*, Dr Johnson remarked 'it was in the power of Richardson alone to teach us at once esteem and detestation, to make virtuous resentment overpower all the benevolence which wit, elegance, and courage naturally excite; and to lose at last the hero in the villain'. In Richardson's second novel the villain is a much more complex character than Mr B— in *Pamela*, and he is successful in his attempt at seduction. The heroine gains a moral triumph over her disaster instead of a material reward. Many of the situations that occur in *Pamela* are repeated in *Clarissa*: it is in the more subtle manner of treatment that the difference lies.

After quoting a passage from *Clarissa* in which the heroine speaks of 'one half of humanity tormenting the other, and being tormented themselves in tormenting', E. M. Forster compares Richardson and Henry James as two writers who are 'looking at life from the same angle', psychologists sensitive to human suffering who appreciate self-sacrifice and whose work is characterized by 'a sort of tremulous nobility'.[10] Tremulous nobility describes perfectly the impression that Clarissa makes on the reader, and she does so without becoming at all unreal or unduly self-righteous. Her friend Miss Howe strikes this note at the beginning of the novel. It is sustained throughout, and only emphasized by the ignobility of her family, Lovelace, and his appalling associates:

So steady, so uniform in your conduct: so desirous, as you always said, of sliding through life to the end of it unnoted; and, as I may add, not wishing to be observed even for your silent benevolence; sufficiently happy in the noble consciousness which attends it: *Rather useful than glaring*, your deserved motto; though now, to your regret, pushed into blaze, as I may say: and yet blamed at home for the fault of others...

(I, Letter I, 2)

Lovelace, who 'was always as mischievous as a monkey', is, in a sense, merely a means to bring out the essential nobility of the heroine. He is the conventional stage villain who, as he himself says, 'had been a rogue, had I been a plough-boy'. Yet his description of Clarissa is as rapturous and glowing as Tom Jones's paean to Sophia. He compares himself to Milton's Satan: but he is also an eighteenth-century Leander who can celebrate the beauty of his Hero in prose that almost rivals the Elizabethan richness of Marlowe's poetry:

Thou hast often heard me launch out in praise of her complexion. I never beheld in my life a skin so illustriously fair. The lily and the driven snow it is nonsense to talk of: her lawn and her laces one might indeed compare to those: but what a whited wall would a woman appear to be, who had complexion which would justify such unnatural comparisons? But this lady is all glowing, all charming flesh and blood; yet so clear, that every meandering vein is to be seen, in all the lovely parts of her which custom permits to be visible.

Thou hast heard me also describe the wavy ringlets of her shiny hair, needing neither art nor powder; of itself an ornament, defying all other ornaments; wantoning in and about a neck that is beautiful beyond description.

Her head-dress was a Brussels-lace mob, peculiarly adapted to the charming air and turn of her features. A sky-blue riband illustrated that. But, although the weather was somewhat sharp, she had not on either hat or hood . . .

. . . Her morning-gown was a pale primrose-coloured paduasoy; the cuffs and robings curiously embroidered by the fingers of this ever-charming Arachne, in a running pattern of violets and their leaves; the light in the flowers silver; gold in the leaves. A pair of diamond snaps in her ears. A white handkerchief wrought by the same inimitable fingers concealed – O Belford! what still more inimitable beauties did it not conceal! – And I saw, all the way we rode, the bounding heart (by its throbbing motions I saw it!) dancing beneath the charming umbrage.

Her ruffles were the same as her mob. Her apron a flowered lawn. Her coat white satin, quilted: blue satin her shoes, braided with the same colour, without lace; for what need has the prettiest foot in the world of ornament? Neat buckles in them: and on her charming arms a pair of black velvet glove-like muffs, of her own invention; for she makes and gives fashions as she pleases. – Her hands velvet of themselves, thus uncovered the freer to be grasped by those of her adorer.

(III, Letter V, 29–30)

Clarissa's beauty and nobility, thus evoked, are set against the background of Mrs Sinclair, the procuress, the brothel in which she lives, and the house of the sheriff's officer in which she is later arrested for debt and lodged. Mrs Sinclair is described with the same realism as Mrs Jewkes had been in *Pamela*: 'The old dragon straddled up to her, with her arms kimboed again, her eye-brows erect, like the bristles upon a hog's back, and, scowling over her shortened nose, more than half-hid her ferret eyes.' Tormented physically and mentally, subjected to every sort of humiliation and victimization, Clarissa's spirit never breaks. The accompanying abuse that she has to suffer from her family is shown to be as criminal as the physical humiliations inflicted, and to be, in fact, the direct cause of them. Clarissa's greatness is that, while resisting and defending herself to the uttermost, she accepts her fate as just. In cutting herself off from her family, however unjust they are, she cuts herself off from society of the normal kind, but not from God. The situation is a genuinely tragic one.

The agonies and atrocities are relentlessly piled on and culminate in the final physical outrage, after which, for Clarissa, there only remains death. There must, it is suggested, be a world after this to do justice to injured merit and to punish such barbarous perfidy. But this is hinted rather than directly stated. For the reader who has followed the story closely, Clarissa's death comes as a positive relief. The idea of some sort of retribution is merely dramatically suggested in the contrast of the death-scenes of Clarissa and Mrs Sinclair. It is here, in its dramatic presentation of what Christian fortitude and resignation can achieve when the world has done its worst, that this almost completely masochistic novel transcends itself. After all that Clarissa has undergone, Richardson is still able to show, as in *Pamela* he had failed to do, virtue triumphant. Lovelace's description of her on her death-bed, his realization that essentially she is untouched, contains the implicit compliment paid by vice to her nobility; while the reformed accomplice, Belford, gives the last turn of the screw in his account of the end of Mrs Sinclair. After this, the inevitable duel and the death of Lovelace at the hands of Clarissa's single, though ineffective, family supporter, Colonel Morden, appears as a matter of comparatively minor importance, though it does result in the story ending on a note of just retribution.

Richardson's last novel, *Sir Charles Grandison* (1754) was an attempt to present, in contrast to Lovelace, a picture of the ideal gentleman. Though Sir Charles's Italian admirer, Clementina, goes mad, the novel is, generally speaking, lacking in the more melodramatic type of incident. The attempt at the seduction of the heroine, Harriet Byron, by Sir Hargrave Pollexfen, is a very tame affair compared with the activities of Mr B— and Lovelace. Because of the more placid interest in manners and morals, this appears to have been Jane Austen's favourite among the novels.

The characters, divided into men, women, and Italians, are taken almost exclusively from 'high life'. Harriet Byron is the most beautiful woman in England: Clementina, her rival for the hand of the perfect gentleman, is the noblest lady on the Continent. Harriet prefers Clementina to herself. Yet despite this façade, the tone and attitude of the novelist inevitably reflect his middle-class origins. C. L. Thomson remarked with justice that the description of Grandison Hall sounds like a passage from an auctioneer's catalogue. The characters similarly betray their origin. Harriet Byron, for instance, 'is one of the best economists, and yet one of the finest ladies in the country'. Her life is one of 'orderliness, method, harmony, observance ... ease, dignity, condescension ... she hardly ever was heard to direct twice the same thing to be done or remembered.' An ideal domestic manager like Pamela, she believes in method and early hours, 'ease without hurry will do anything'. Prudence is as much her characteristic as Pamela's too. She even confesses to be a prude and a Puritan 'in the best senses of those abused words'.

Sir Charles Grandison himself is a quite impossible figure of perfection. Honour and punctilio direct all his actions, and Clementina goes so far as to entreat him to forgive her for preferring God to himself. Not merely the perfect gentleman, he is also the perfect butler. While waiting on the bride and the company at his own wedding feast he makes the waiters look awkward. He is also the embodiment of sentiment, in the best sense, 'Imitating the Divinity, he regards the heart, rather than the head.' A perfect courtier, he disarms two of his enemies, Major O'Hara and Captain Salmonet, but cannot forgive himself for violating the sanctity of his own house. On another occasion, when he refuses to fight his enemies, he can still succeed in extracting admiration from them for his magnanimity. He also possesses the supreme gift of making a compliment to one lady without depreciating the others who are present (for he is, of course, perpetually surrounded by women). As one of them says, 'You are Sir Charles Grandison. Sir, I need not say more.'

A few attempts are made to introduce some human traits into this effigy. He confesses himself that he is naturally choleric, 'subject to sudden gusts of passion', and that he is proud and ambitious. Yet he convinces both the ladies who love him that he is too good for them to accept. He is threatened by another with a poniard, but succeeds in subduing her by his bearing. Even the villain is rescued by Sir Charles late on in the story, and kneels to his deliverer. In Italy, the bishop asserts that if he were one of them he might expect canonization: 'His Holiness Himself would receive you with blessings at the footstool of his throne.' Since, in fact, Sir Charles can put himself in everyone's situation and can forget his own interest so completely, no one can hold out against him. His conduct to his horses, even, is impeccable, for he refuses to dock their tails. Only once is he guilty of trickery. Harriet Byron is persuaded to sign a letter which he has doubled down so that she does not see that she is agreeing to hasten the marriage. But this merely confirms his perfection, since he has forestalled her own wishes. He is, in fact, an example of unbounded charity and universal benevolence to people of all professions, though he is no leveller but believes that rank or degree entitles a man, who is not utterly unworthy, to respect. Amidst all the infection of fashionable vice and folly, his only weaknesses are the few that have been mentioned. But among readers he has not been a universally popular character. Leslie Stephen unkindly described him as a spinner out of indefinite twaddle of a superior kind, and recalled Becky Sharp's famous reflection upon the moral effect of five thousand a year.[11]

Clementina's family, the Porrettas, have also all the English middle-class virtues. They are affectionate to one another, sharing each other's suffering. For as Richardson remarks, 'in Italy, as well as in other countries, there are persons of honour, of goodness, of generosity, and who are above reserve, vindictiveness, jealousy, and those other bad passions by which some mark indiscriminately a whole nation'. Clementina, in particular, has the delicacy which distinguishes the woman of true honour. After all her troubles, she gains glory after her death, for a temple is erected to her in the garden of the Grandisons.

The ideal standards of manners and morals are the same for all the characters. Modesty, good sense, and amiable temper – the Addisonian ideals, in fact – are taken as normal for both sexes, for all ranks of society, in all civilized countries. Wit is reconciled with politeness, and humour restrained by decorum. There is a certain Dr

Bartlett, to whom Sir Charles addresses much of his correspondence, and who embodies these standards even more completely than Sir Charles himself. He is described as 'a saint and at the same time a man of true politeness'. Sir Charles recommends his example to Mr Grandison, a reformed rake, who will, he says, be civilized, 'when you can be serious on serious subjects, yet so cheerful in your seriousness, as if it sat easy upon you'. Exactly the same words had been used in *The Tatler*, 5. Here a religious work is praised because

it is written with the Spirit of one who has seen the World enough to under-value it with good Breeding. The Author must certainly be a man of Wisdom as well as Piety, and have spent much Time in the Exercise of both. The real Causes of the Decay of the Interest of Religion are set forth in a clear and lively manner, without unseasonable Passions; and the whole Air of the Book, as to the Language, the Sentiments, and the Reasonings, shews it was written by one whose Virtue sits easy about him, and to whom Vice is thoroughly contemptible. It was said by one of this Company, alluding to that Knowledge of the World the Author seems to have, the Man writes much like a Gentleman, and goes to Heaven with a very good Mien.

Such a work might well have been written by Sir Charles Grandison himself. For he makes it a tacit rule never to begin a journey on Sunday, nor, except when in pursuit of works of mercy or necessity, to travel in time of Divine service. In the absence of a clergyman, he himself says grace at the table, and in church he edifies everybody by his cheerful piety. We can well imagine that both Sir Charles Grandison and Dr Bartlett 'would go to Heaven with a very good Mien'.

It is Richardson's achievement in this novel to have dramatized the ethical and social principles of *The Tatler* and of *The Spectator* so that they could be used by later novelists, such as Fanny Burney and Jane Austen, who had come under other influences, particularly that of Dr Johnson. Jane Austen found the manner and matter of *The Spectator* disgusting to a person of real taste:

the substance of its papers so often consisting in the statement of improbable circumstances, unnatural characters, and topics of conversation, which no longer concern any one living; and their language too frequently so coarse as to give no very favourable idea of the age that could endure it.

(*Northanger Abbey*, ch. v)

On the other hand, 'every circumstance narrated in *Sir Charles Grandison*, all that was ever said or done in the cedar parlour was familiar to her; and the wedding days of Lady L. and Lady G. were so well remembered as if they had been among living friends'.[12] There is an upstart called Captain Anderson in *Sir Charles Grandison*, who pays court to Harriet Byron's friend, Charlotte Grandison, who might be the model for Willoughby in *Sense and Sensibility* or Wickham in *Pride and Prejudice*. The style of the writing itself, with its subtlety and delicacy of touch, its crispness tending naturally towards epigram, recalls Jane Austen's:

> Captain Anderson appeared to me at first a man of sense, as well as an agreeable man in his person and air. He had a lively and easy elocution. He spoke without doubt, and I had therefore the less doubt of his understanding. The man who knows how to say agreeable things to a woman in an agreeable manner has her vanity on his side, since to doubt his veracity would be to question her own merit. When he came to write, my judgement was even still more engaged in his favour than before. But when he thought himself on a safe footing with me, he then lost his handwriting, and his style, and even his orthography.
>
> (II, Letter xxxv, 225)

The theme of the father who is nearly responsible for the ruin of his daughters inevitably reminds the reader of Mr Bennet in *Pride and Prejudice* and of Sir Thomas Bertram in *Mansfield Park*:

> Thus had Sir Thomas Grandison with all his pride like to have thrown his daughter, a woman of high character, fine understanding, and an exalted mind, into the arms of a man who had neither fortune nor education, nor yet good sense nor generosity of heart, to countenance his pretensions to such a lady, or her for marrying beneath herself.
>
> (II, Letter xxxvi, 267)

A complete account of the influence of Richardson's novels would require a volume in itself. In England, France, and Germany his works fundamentally altered and shaped the course of the development of fiction. His influence in England was particularly strong on the women writers and readers who patronized the new circulating libraries. In France, Prévost, his translator, said that *Clarissa* had to be softened and watered down to adapt it to the more delicate taste of the French. But Diderot, in his famous *Éloge*, expressed unrestrained admiration:

> O Richardson, Richardson, first of men in my eyes, you shall be my reading at all times! Pursued by pressing needs; if my friend should fall into poverty; if the limitations of my fortune should prevent me from giving fit attention to the education of my children, I will sell my books; but you shall remain on the same shelf as Moses, Euripides, and Sophocles, and I will read you by turns.

Such different writers as Rousseau in *La Nouvelle Héloîse*, and Choderlos de Laclos, the author of *Les liaisons dangereuses* (who called *Clarissa* 'un chef d'oeuvre des hommes'), acknowledged their debt. The influence on the early Goethe, particularly on *Werther*, is well known.

But perhaps it is only right that the last word on Richardson should be with that discriminating English reader, who, while admiring his power of creating and preserving the consistency of his characters, and whose knowledge of his works was 'probably such as no one is likely again to acquire', could yet still see his faults. In Jane Austen's unfinished novel, *Sanditon*, there is a satirical portrait of a typically enthusiastic admirer of Richardson. Sir Edward Denham had read more sentimental novels than agreed with him:

his fancy had been early caught by all the impassioned, & most exceptionable parts of Richardson; & such Authors as have since appeared to tread in Richardson's steps, so far as Man's determined pursuit of Woman in defiance of every opposition of feeling and convenience is concerned.

These works had since 'occupied the greater part of his literary hours, & formed his character'. The result of his addiction is shown in the later part of the story. Jane Austen both appreciated Richardson's virtues and was one of his keenest critics. Her mockery was all the more effective because of its delicacy. She owed much to him, but her six slim major novels also contain the final implied comment on his prolix art with its curious mixture of coarseness and distinction.

NOTES

1. See *The Notebooks of Henry James*, ed. F. O. Matthiessen and Kenneth B. Murdock (1947), 11–12.

2. Louis B. Wright: *Middle Class Culture in Elizabethan England* (Chapel Hill, North Carolina, 1935), 476–7.

3. The references are to the edition of the complete works with a prefatory note by Austin Dobson and a Life and Introduction by Prof. W. M. Lyon Phelps (London, 1902). In the case of *Pamela*, references are to the volume and page only, since a large proportion of the novel is taken up with her journal. In quotations from *Clarissa* and *Sir Charles Grandison* the number of the letter is also given, for the convenience of readers of other editions.

4. B. W. Downs, *Samuel Richardson* (*The Republic of Letters Series*), 112.

5. *Lettre sur Pamela*, quoted by Prof. B. W. Downs, *Samuel Richardson,* 101.

PART THREE

6. D. H. Lawrence, *Pornography and Obscenity*. See *Phoenix: The Posthumous Papers of D. H. Lawrence*, ed. with an introduction by Edward D. McDonald (1936), 174.

7. Quoted by F. S. Boas in 'Richardson's Novels and their Influence', in *Essays and Studies of the English Association*, II, 46.

8. Quoted by C. L. Thomson, *Samuel Richardson. A Biographical and Critical Study* (1900), 272.

9. Quoted by M. Phillips and W. S. Tomkinson, *Women's Education in the Eighteenth Century* (1926), 162.

10. E. M. Forster, *Aspects of the Novel* (1949), 18.

11. Leslie Stephen, *Hours in a Library*, I, 57 and 73 (new edn, 1909). This excellent essay is by far the best brief introduction to Richardson's novels.

12. J. E. Austen-Leigh, *Memoir of Jane Austen*, ed. R. W. Chapman (1951), 89.

FIELDING AND SMOLLETT

JOHN PRESTON

Fielding and Smollett, close contemporaries, masters of the picaresque, followers of Cervantes, seem to invite comparison. But what comparison inevitably brings out is the many ways in which they are quite unalike. A close look in the first place at two comparable episodes from the novels will make it clear that a description of their work has to follow two quite different routes.

In *Ferdinand Count Fathom* (1753), the third of Smollett's fictional works, there is a celebrated episode in which a lonely, benighted traveller falls into the hands of robbers and murderers. The scene, as Damian Grant points out in his introduction to the novel, has its precedents in many earlier works, and particularly in Fielding's first novel, *Joseph Andrews*, published about a decade earlier in 1742. Joseph and his two travelling companions, Fanny and Parson Adams, are likewise benighted and fearful of being attacked by murderers; but in this episode the 'murderers' turn out to be sheep-stealers and the travellers soon find a welcome in a friendly house. Behind both episodes can be traced the example of two writers whose influence was definitive, Cervantes and Le Sage. Both Fielding and Smollett could be said to be aware that in these episodes as elsewhere they were continuing a literary tradition. But this is the point at which we can begin to see how they diverge.

Smollett was certainly quite deliberate and explicit in aligning himself with Le Sage – he published a translation of *Gil Blas* in 1748 and of *Le Diable Boiteux* in 1750 – and with Cervantes, whose *Don Quijote* he imitated in *Sir Launcelot Greaves* (1760–62) and translated between 1748 and 1751. His first novel *Roderick Random* (1748) was modelled, he tells us in the Preface, on Le Sage's plan in *Gil Blas*. And the episode in *Fathom* follows roughly the same lines as the first of Gil Blas's picaresque adventures. Fathom finds himself alone, deserted by his guide, in a forest at night:

... the darkness of the night, the silence and solitude of the place, the indistinct images of the trees that appeared on every side, 'stretching their extravagant arms athwart the gloom,' conspired with the dejection of spirits occasioned by his loss to disturb his fancy, and raise strange phantoms in his imagination.

(ch. xx)

Like Gil Blas he thinks he is about to get help, and makes his way to a cottage where an old woman receives him 'with great hospitality'. But, again like Gil Blas, he finds he is actually worse off than before: chapter xxi is headed, 'He falls upon Sylla, seeking to avoid Charybdis.' He finds he is locked into his bedroom, yet unable to lock the door on his side against intruders:

... [he] began to be seized with strange fancies, when he observed that there was no bolt on the inside of the door, by which he might secure himself from intrusion. In consequence of these suggestions, he proposed to take an accurate survey of every object in the apartment, and in the course of the inquiry, had the mortification to find the dead body of a man, still warm, who had been lately stabbed, and concealed beneath several bundles of straw.

(ch. xxi)

Eventually he escapes and flees in panic through the forest with the old woman as hostage.

Yet, in spite of its literary origins (and even its use of literary allusion in the quotation, 'stretching their extravagant arms . . .', from John Armstrong's *The Art of Preserving Health* (1744), the episode is surely striking above all for its underivative, unliterary immediacy. It is a direct evocation, for its own sake, and in an unusual way, of an extreme state of mind: it is a study in terror. In dedicating the novel to his own alter ego, 'Doctor . . .', Smollett writes of the effect that 'a deep impression of terror' might have on anyone 'not confirmed in the pursuit of morality and virtue'. Terror can be potent: 'the impulses of fear which is the most violent and interesting of all the passions, remain longer than any other upon the memory'. Such impulses as these fascinate Smollett. They do not need the rather strained moral justification he provides for them. And indeed Smollett, far from trying to explain them away, does enforce their objective reality. We might have been encouraged to dismiss them as Fathom's 'disagreeable reveries', 'strange phantoms in his imagination ... that gradually prevailed over all the consolations of reason and philosophy'. Yet no such consolations are forthcoming. Reason and philosophy cannot argue away the 'unspeakable horror' of coming on the corpse. Fathom is pushed beyond his fearful imaginings: 'his heart began to palpitate, his hair to bristle up, and his knees to totter; his thoughts teemed with presages of death and destruction ...'. Smollett is measuring the limits of fear. He is exploring at the extremities of experience. When Fathom makes his final flight in terror through the forest he is 'haunted by the most intolerable apprehensions': 'Common fear was a comfortable sensation to what he felt in this excursion.' This was one of the passages that led Scott to call Smollett 'sublime'. He found here the Smollett who was a 'searcher of dark bosoms', who loved 'to paint characters under the strong agitation of fierce and stormy passions'.

Yet this view, cogent as it is, does not exactly describe Smollett's genius. For one thing he does not achieve the kind of psychological inwardness suggested by 'a searcher of dark bosoms'. It is very striking that the entire episode is carried on purely in terms of descriptive narrative. Mental states have the same dimension as events in the external world. 'Fathom ... listened with the most fearful attention; but his sense of hearing was saluted with nought but the dismal sighings of the trees ...' It is not that the sighings seem 'dismal' as registered by his 'fearful' attention: it is not through his consciousness that we approach the scene. *Both* adjectives refer to a matter of fact. Everything in the episode is external to the narrator's understanding of it: Fathom's terror gets its massive reality from the fact that the narrator is unable or unwilling to inhabit it. In fact there is something strange about this kind of detachment. It suggests that Smollett is in some way more involved in his material than he can say, as if his stylistic medium is at odds often with his essential purpose. There is something characteristic of him, an inner contradiction of style, or separation of styles, that further weakens the force of 'sublime'.

This is something that Damian Grant explains as 'the permeation of Smollett's style by the new mood and movement we associate with romanticism'. The 'recognizable syntactic balance' of Smollett's 'Augustan' sentences is, he maintains, 'qualified by the content, which, as it were, stands out against the declarative temptations of the style'.[1] This gives the impression that the emergence of a new sensibility is the important thing; but what is really interesting in Smollett is the embarrassment of a style pulled apart by contradictory impulses. It is always blowing hot and cold. It courts excess and cancels it. A characteristic manoeuvre is the double negative, which enforces an extreme assertion by denying its opposite. It is a device which might serve the purposes of a thoroughly Augustan irony, but in Smollett the irony is very often forestalled. Fathom, we read, 'was by no means a man to set fear at defiance!' The exclamation mark signals Smollett's recognition that this would be the form of an ironic deflation of Fathom; but the context forbids it. The 'many concurring circumstances of danger and distress', the tempest, the torrents of rain by which Fathom is 'actually invaded to the skin', are too powerfully evoked to accommodate the reservations of irony.

Indeed the formula is habitually used without even a gesture in the direction of irony: 'the conversation of his guide did not at all tend to the elevation of our hero's spirits'; 'nor was his breast free from the terrors of assassination'; 'such a discovery could not fail to fill the breast of our hero with unspeakable horror'. These are statements which sound simultaneously reserved and emphatic, both cautious and extreme. And the same effect is felt through the diction of the whole episode. Words suggesting intense reactions ('unspeakable', 'transports', 'dread', 'palpitate', 'paroxysm') are treated as part of a rational, even predictable sequence devoid of personal involvement. 'Such a discovery could not fail to fill the breast of our hero, with unspeakable horror; for he concluded that he himself would undergo the same fate before morning, without the juxtaposition of a miracle in his favour.' It is not only that the syntax leans on negatives ('could not fail', 'without'), and hinges on a rationalizing conjunction ('for he concluded'): it is notably dependent on abstractions (a discovery fills with horror, without a juxtaposition). The protagonist himself is reduced to a grammatical inflection ('of our hero', 'in his favour'); there is a split between him and his functions ('his heart began to palpitate, his hair to bristle up, and his knees to totter'). *His* role is to carry forward the reasoning that seems at odds with the feeling ('for he concluded'). There is a disjunction between feelings and having the feelings. The intense subjectivity of the experience is objectified; excessive emotion becomes separated from the capacity to respond to it. The style is hectic and cool at the same time. There is both an overwhelming closeness and a great distance in the rendering. The moment when Fathom discovers the corpse is both stunningly sensational and remotely abstracted and detached: he 'had the mortification to find the dead body of a man, still warm, who had been lately stabbed, and concealed beneath several bundles of straw'. The sentence veers away from what is done (the finding of a body) to what is felt, or rather to the having of feelings (he 'had the mortification to find'). The clarity of this style is the clarity of nightmare and derangement.

The parallel episode, from Fielding's *Joseph Andrews* (III, ii) is quite of a different kind, both in detail and in overall conception. This too is a scene of darkness and fear; but in this case the darkness is metaphorical, the fear part of an existential game, and the whole episode a profoundly literary conception. Like Smollett Fielding draws on literary allusion and quotation, but unlike Smollett he does so not incidentally but as part of a total organization of literary relationships. The whole episode is shot through with an awareness of literary values and the sense of literature as a vital presence. Joseph Andrews, his sweetheart Fanny and their unworldly mentor Parson Abraham Adams are benighted on their journey home to the West Country. They are in complete darkness and therefore beset by irrational and unnerving fears, of ghosts, or 'apparitions' or murderers. But Fielding has not Smollett's interest in extreme emotional states. In this narrative of an encounter with 'murderers' who are in fact sheep-stealers he is imitating Cervantes' description of the encounter between Don Quijote and the priests escorting a dead body to Segovia (I, xix). And just as in *Don Quijote* the point of the story is not to be found in Sancho's terror at coming across them but in Don Quijote's imagining that 'this was one of the adventures out of his books', so in Fielding's version the interest centres on questions about the reality of imagined things.

The very darkness of this 'Night Scene', the one thing that seems unequivocal in it, is presented as though it were an imagined condition. 'It was, indeed, according to *Milton*, Darkness visible', not merely *like* it but actually the thing itself, as he imagined it. In this night that is nearly unimaginable (darkness visible) yet as real as if Milton was imagining it, everything becomes equivocal. Adams

'laments the loss of his dear Aeschylus', yet he is in a darkness in which
the idea of a book is meaningless: he 'was a little comforted, when
reminded, that if he had it in his possession, he could not see to read'.
Yet this darkness in which things are illegible contains things which
can be 'read'. Joseph and Fanny embrace in the darkness as if, being
invisible to Adams, they do not reveal themselves to him. Yet he
seems to be aware of them and of what they are doing: '*Adams* sat
at some distance from the lovers, and being unwilling to disturb
them, applied himself to Meditation.' After the scare of the supposed
murderers the travellers decide to 'take the opportunity of the dark' to
escape unseen. Adams, leading the way, slips and falls down hill.
Joseph and Fanny are frightened but, 'if the light had permitted them
to see it, they would scarce have refrained from laughing to see the
Parson rolling down the Hill, which he did from top to bottom,
without receiving any harm'. There was a comedy, a harmless fall.
Yet the comedy was precisely what could not be seen, and in that
sense could not happen; and yet, in Fielding's narrative it can and
does happen. Indeed the whole scene is made visible in his narrative.
The 'murderers' are known to the travellers only as 'unsubstantial
Beings', 'Voices' which Adams thought 'almost at his Elbow, tho' in
fact they were not so extremely near'. 'In fact': the 'fact' is made
perfectly legible to the reader of the narrative, as are the 'facts' that
'Adams fell on his knees', Fanny embraced Joseph, 'Joseph drew his
Penknife'; none of these actions is invisible to us. We see the darkness
and we see also the things that cannot be seen in the darkness.

The whole of this 'Night Scene' examines the way things can be
known to exist. For the participants the way is speech. The darkness
is a place of voices, and the most declarative voice is the most literary.
Surrounded as he thinks by murderers, Adams declaims verses from
the *Aeneid*: '*Est hic, est animus lucis contemptor . . .*' (Here is a soul that
disdains the light). Later in the chapter, when the travellers have
found a welcoming fireside and a hospitable family, they have still
to establish their bona fides. Adams does so by again invoking
the support of literature. He breaks into an extended critique of
Homer concluding with a celebration of the poet's creative imagination: 'But did ever Painter imagine a scene like that in the 13th and
14th Iliads? where the Reader sees at one View the Prospect of *Troy*,
with the Army drawn up before it; . . . This is Sublime! This is

Poetry!' Adams gains credence from his confidence in the power of poetry to make things exist.

What he is celebrating (it occurs to the reader sharing his experience) is the power by means of which he himself is made to exist. Like Joseph and Fanny in this episode he has been placed at the very edge of non-being, illegible in the darkness yet capable of being imagined into life and particularly into the kind of life manifest in language, into the life of a work of literature. The chapter ends with him telling his 'story', and in return expecting to hear their host's story: 'if it be not too troublesome, Sir, your History, if you please.' The whole episode, which is pivotally placed at the mid-point of the novel, just after a discussion about fiction and truth, and a tribute to Cervantes and Le Sage, is in effect a reflection on the conditions of its own kind of reality. It is profoundly involved with questions about literary experience and, quite appropriately therefore, is closely modelled on another night scene (I, xx) from *Don Quijote*. Don Quijote and Sancho Panza have found themselves benighted, terrified of the noise of the fulling-mills, almost persuaded that what happens in their profound darkness could be thought not to have happened at all, yet aware in some way that even this episode is part of a 'story' and therefore likely to be recorded and read. They have both depended on 'utterances' in order to defend themselves against the dark, Quijote on his noble speech proclaiming chivalric courage and defiance, Sancho on his self-generating story of the goatherd ferrying his goats across a river; both begin to understand that the story through which they have come into being cannot now be untold. These two night scenes enforce both the precariousness and the irrevocability of the world of fiction.

At this point, where Fielding is closely aligned with Cervantes, he is paradoxically at his furthest remove from Smollett, who also aligns himself with Cervantes. The two writers diverge at the point where they have most in common, Smollett drawing from Cervantes images of alienation and a dislocated subjectivity, Fielding discovering in him the equivocal and complex images of the real world reflected in an imagined one.

Fielding's art is one that reflects on itself. It is the art, that is, of a narrator. All narration depends on a continuing process of reflection and mediation. Fielding must be the first English writer to project onto this narrative process an image of himself as narrator. He defines himself as narrator and thus, in effect, duplicates himself. He becomes not only the shaping consciousness of the told story, but the consciousness of that consciousness. He tells the story and at the same time listens to the telling of the story. This is what he must have learnt from Cervantes. The multiplying of narrators in *Don Quijote* (Cide Hamete Benengeli, the translator of Hamete's text, 'Cervantes-as-narrator') is a way of exposing the layers of self-consciousness latent in the narrative process. Fielding drew on Cervantes for something that had not been negotiable in the hundred and more years that *Don Quijote* had been available in English translation. With the publication in 1742 of *Joseph Andrews*, 'Written in imitation of the manner of Cervantes, Author of *Don Quixote*', he made the self-conscious novel accessible to the English tradition.

In a sense he found in Cervantes what he had no need to look for. From the beginning his art had indulged the possibilities of self-reflection. In his first work, his writings for the theatre in his twenties, he developed a vigorous talent for parody and burlesque. Many of his most characteristic productions are plays about what plays are like, or rather what they are not like. They are concerned, many of them, with the forms of drama: *The Author's Farce* (1730), *The Grub-Street Opera* (1731), *The Covent-Garden Tragedy* (1732); and many of these forms are malformed. *Tom Thumb: A Tragedy* (1730) is a strutting devaluation of tragedy. When Fielding revised it in 1731 he called it *The Tragedy of Tragedies*: the tragedy of Tragedies is that they are now conformable to the ratio denoted by the sub-title, 'Tom Thumb the Great'. Fielding's most notable successes in this vein deal not just with the subversion of dramatic forms but with the disintegration of the very idea of drama. *Pasquin* (1736), following the example of Buckingham's play, *The Rehearsal*, and many subsequent 'rehearsal' plays, enacts first a rehearsal of 'a comedy called The Election' and then 'a tragedy called *The Life and Death of Commonsense*'. Trapwit rehearses his comedy in the presence of Fustian, the author of the tragedy, who in turn presents his tragedy before Sneerwell, the critic. All the normal functions of the theatre are displaced: writer and critic change roles; actors, indeed characters, rebel ('the author and Common Sense are quarrelling in the green-room'); spectators become the centre of the action; the plays, unable to define their subjects, become themselves the subject of a play; 'performance' is inept, the comedy and the tragedy reside in the 'play' of responses to that non-performance. Fielding's play, *Pasquin*, is no play; it consists of the presentation of two non-plays; it is nothing itself and its theme is the nothing that drama now is. It is energized by the vacuum at its centre. If it is, according to the sub-title, 'a dramatic satire on the times', it is so because the evacuation of the drama is itself a satire on the times. There is a kind of manic hilarity in this ballooning process of reflection without a centre. It is self-consciousness operating under the conditions of farce.

In none of his other works does Fielding come as close as this to the creation of a form so self-reflexive as to question its own existence. Indeed it is notable that in *Jonathan Wild* (first published in the *Miscellanies* of 1743, but begun as early, perhaps, as 1737 when the Licensing Act ended Fielding's career as a dramatist) Fielding aims at a much more direct presentation. The 'satire on the times' has the same objectives and strategies as it had in the plays. Hostility to the Walpole administration and disgust at the whole scandal of political corruption still find expression in the bitter ironies by which 'greatness' is brought into conjunction with the squalid 'Covent Garden' world of pimps and crooks, or with the trivialities of a dwarfish world. The moral vacuity exposed by the plays now hardens into what Bernard Harrison, in a brilliant analysis of *Jonathan Wild*, calls 'an overpowering vision of the desolation, vacuity and death of spirit on which these neat clicking mechanisms (i.e. of successful villainy) feed and to which they lead'.[2] This desolating vision is generated by the unrelenting logic with which the book redefines the concepts of 'great' and 'low'. As a 'great' man Wild is 'entirely free from those low vices of modesty and good-nature'; his greatness should not be confused with goodness, 'for greatness consists in bringing all manner of mischief on mankind, and goodness in removing it from them. It seems very unlikely therefore that the same person should possess them both.' The whole inverted system of moral values is sustained by a total inversion of language. This was a recurring concern for Fielding. More than ten years later and only two years before his death, he encapsulated it in the mordant redefinitions of *A Modern Glossary* (in the *Covent Garden Journal*, 14 January 1752): 'PATRIOT', for instance, now signifies 'A Candidate for a Place at Court';

'POLITICS, The Art of getting such a Place'; 'GREAT, Applied to a Thing, signifies Bigness, when to a Man, often littleness, or Meanness.' Evidently Fielding wanted to make sure that, in *Jonathan Wild*, subverted meanings of this kind should be plainly and uncomfortably visible. For once, therefore, though he adopts that mode of direct address to 'my reader', 'our reader', that was to be central to the concept of a self-reflexive narrative he refuses its offered possibilities. It is as if in putting the language of politics and power to the test of his irony he is shocked to see how vulnerable it really is. There is no play in it. He has exposed a numbing unreality, and for once seems to have no option but to let it reveal itself.

In *Joseph Andrews* he confronts what is recognizably the same world of arrogance, stupidity, suspicion and brutality; but now he releases himself by creating an alternative world, 'a rehearsal of civilization' as one critic puts it,[3] a medium for detachment, reflection, self-knowledge. It is not so much that Fielding offers an alternative *kind* of world, the world (say) of comedy, as a refuge from reality, but rather that he asks the reader to enter the world of reflection which will allow him to 'read' life and not be coerced by it. It is true that his own description of the book makes more of its moral intention than of any Cervantean play with the relations between literature and life. He maintains that its form, the 'Comic Romance' or 'comic Epic-Poem in Prose', will allow both for truth to nature and for the exposure of affectation and vanity to ridicule. And elsewhere he appears to be claiming that if the book provokes the reader into self-consciousness it will not be in a spirit of play but in order to enforce this moral design: readers will see their unflattering reflection in the novel's ridiculous pictures of vanity and selfishness, which will 'hold the Glass to thousands in their Closets, that they may contemplate their Deformity' (III, i). Yet Fielding does reckon with the possibility that if a book reflects its readers it must in some way be taken to be reflecting them *as* readers. In an essay in the Opposition paper the *Champion*, which Fielding was editing in 1739–41, very shortly before writing *Joseph Andrews*, he quotes from the opening chapter of Locke's *Essay Concerning Human Understanding*:

> *The Understanding, like the Eye* (says Mr Lock), *whilst it makes us see and perceive all other things, takes no Notice of itself; and it requires Art and Pains to set it at a Distance and make it its own Object.*

(1 March 1739–40)

Fielding adds: 'no *Narcissus* hath hitherto discovered any Mirrour for the Understanding.' Yet what is it that Cervantes has discovered by standing back from his own narration (in effect telling the story by 'reading' the way in which Cide Hamete tells it) but a 'mirrour' for the understanding? And in *Joseph Andrews* Fielding picks up exactly this capacity to reflect the process of reflection.

The book is to be a book shaped by its own awareness of other books: it begins in parody, of Cibber's autobiography and of Samuel Richardson's *Pamela*, and it reflects on the 'great Good that Book is likely to do' by showing Joseph as the reader of his sister Pamela's life and as 'keeping the excellent Pattern of his Sister's Virtue before his Eyes'. It is also a book shaped by its awareness of *being* a book: its narrator reflects on 'our ensuing History', on the difficulty of 'seeing through' it ('he is a sagacious Reader who can see two Chapters before him'), on the business of writing it (a digression is introduced 'for no other Purpose than to lengthen out a short Chapter') and the process of reading it. What is more, the story actually turns out on occasions to be the story of other, interpolated, stories, and on those occasions the actors in the story take on the roles of storytellers or listeners. The story of Joseph Andrews and Parson Adams, like the story of Don Quijote, is the story of a journey: it takes the form of a repeated movement into the unknown, of meetings with strangers and of the assembling of all these into knowledge. And in the same way the reader journeys through the book: the 'reader' may 'proceed to the Sequel of this our true History', or 'travel to the next chapter'; and at nearly the mid-point of this journey he comes on an argument between Parson Adams and an innkeeper about the rival advantages of travelling by sea and travelling in books, 'the only way of travelling', in Adams's opinion, 'by which any Knowledge is to be acquired'. That opinion is not, in fact, entirely endorsed: after all Adams is conspicuously deficient in knowledge of the real world. In any case the argument is never brought to a conclusion; it is interrupted by Joseph and Fanny and, as the chapter ends, 'all together renewed their Journey'. Yet that renewed journey, at the end of Book II, continues at the beginning of Book III, not with news of their next encounter but with the narrator's reflections, which he addresses to the reader, on the relation between fiction and reality. He invokes the example of Cervantes and Le Sage (the reader must take this book in the light of his reading of other books), and then he points to the self-knowledge that may be acquired by readers of his own book, which will 'hold the Glass to thousands in their Closets ...' The moral reflection is more closely bound up with the whole sequence of reflective activities than was at first evident.

It is, in fact, of the essence of Fielding's art that it should return us to itself. What is *Joseph Andrews* about? There is a sense in which it has to be said to be 'about' the writing and the reading of *Joseph Andrews*. The book is called *The History of the Adventures of Joseph Andrews*. It is the story of a story. This is not to say that, as with some of the plays, the tendency of Fielding's narrative art is self-consuming. But there is certainly the possibility that it will seem unable to lead to anything beyond itself. The books will be 'about' books, the novels will be about stories, reading them will entail reading about reading.

Fielding himself was able to countenance just this possibility. In an important essay, written for the *Covent Garden Journal* of Tuesday 4 February 1752, he broaches the whole question of the 'Scope and End of Reading'. It cannot be for 'Amusement only', but for 'a much more noble and profitable Purpose ... to recommend wholesome Food to the Mind'. Reading 'a great and good Author' should be thought of as 'searching after Treasures' which can be stored in the mind to be used 'on sundry Occasions in our lives'. But we shall first need to know how to distinguish 'the great and good' from 'such Scriblers as Tom Brown, Tom D'Urfy, and the Wits of our Age'. To do so calls for taste, and taste ('a nice Harmony between Imagination and the Judgment') is notably lacking in the 'Bulk of Mankind'. Yet taste can be acquired. 'There are very few who have not in their Minds some small Seeds of Taste'; and this latent sense 'surely it is in the Power of Art very greatly to improve'. 'I shall therefore,' Fielding concludes, 'in a future Paper, endeavour to lay down some Rules' for acquiring good taste. Meanwhile, abstain from all bad books!

The value of reading derives from taste, taste develops under the influence of Art, that influence must be mediated through books and writing. Read me, says Fielding, and I will help you to read well. With finer taste we will be better readers; we must become better readers in order to refine our taste. This is a circle which actually seems to exclude the 'sundry occasions' on which we might put to use the 'treasures' derived from reading. What are we to make of this? What can we say, for instance, about the experience of reading *Tom Jones*? Are we to say that what we get from *Tom Jones* is the ability to be better readers of *Tom Jones*?

In fact that is one of the things that should be said about it. It is something that is implicit, for instance, in the ironic double meaning of its plot. The plot of *Tom Jones* (1749) has always attracted attention and has for that reason come to seem very hard to swallow. It seems to stand for a failure to invest the characters and their lives with a significance of their own, and to offer instead an ingenious mechanism for sustaining the reader's interest. But in fact the plot does not make that kind of effect, or at least it does not do so on a first reading. Its first effect is to lead the reader through a series of unpredictable events in which the only shaping force appears to be Fortune: characters are frustrated in their attempts to shape events to their will, and the reader is obliged to share their sense of confusion and hazard. Yet, on a second reading, our knowledge of the *whole* plot gives us a privileged access to many episodes: we can now see them as clues to a meaning which was not available before. The temptation now is to treat this privileged view of the plot as the reliable one; the improved reading is the only 'reading'; the book will be thought not to have been read at all until after it has been read. But can we discount that first reading? When Allworthy is ill, apparently fatally ill, he deputes his nephew Blifil to leave the sick room where all are assembled and to speak to a stranger whose arrival has just been announced. We shall not know until the story is concluded that this visitor is the lawyer Dowling, that he brings news of the death of Tom's mother, and that Blifil is keeping the news to himself. But we need to discover not only what was hidden from us but also that we did not know it was hidden. The pleasure we get from the second 'privileged' reading is that of knowing that it *is* privileged, and of setting against it our experience of being in the dark. In short the second reading has to *be* the second reading, making us *realize* our ignorance of what is going on, and revealing the way the clues are concealed. The better reading to which the novel leads us is that in which the simultaneous presence of two readings generates an ironic double plot, both clear and obscure, rational and irrational, confused and orderly.

In the same kind of way Fielding's constant reminders to his readers that they *are* readers may demonstrate that what they are acquiring is the ability to read *Tom Jones*. In setting up a relationship with the reader Fielding is in effect 'foregrounding' the process of reading. It is not that he is clumsily constrained to explain what he could not successfully project imaginatively. He is making the reader conscious all the time of what is involved in the writing and reading, the collaborative imagining into existence, of a fictional story. Thus, whilst this novel must in one way be thought of as reflecting on itself, and educating its reader to be *its* readers, it is also to be seen as 'laying bare' the conventions by which meanings are created in all fictional narratives. And the value of this activity can be seen as opening up an alternative version of the conventions under which our perceptions of the ordinary world operate. Our heightened consciousness of the formal devices of literature, deriving from our 'education' as readers, is a contribution to our total capacity for understanding the processes by which we organize the meanings of our world. Reading *Tom Jones* defines us as readers of *Tom Jones*, but that definition need not be thought limiting. The self-reflexive novel reflects the conditions of all our interpretation of experience.

Fielding opens up a route for a formalist description of his work when, as in *Joseph Andrews* and *Tom Jones*, he brings into focus the usually diffused and invisible processes involved in their creation. In two late works he explores in more immediately personal terms the relations between literary experience and the experience of life. In *Amelia* (1751) Fielding turns from the Epic (or Romance) strategies of developed plotting, pursuits, voyages, encounters to a more enclosed, intimate narrative. Or, more exactly, he turns the attributes of epic inside out, presenting the inner personal meaning of epic situations. Booth, the unheroic, flawed hero is first introduced in a compromising relationship with Miss Matthews. They are a kind of Dido and Aeneas; their clandestine association in a prison cell is a shabby modern parody of Virgil, and it leads not to a hero's visible confrontation with his destiny but to the private awareness of a guilt which seeps into all his dealings with himself and others. Whereas Tom Jones, seen from the outside, can be treated generously, Booth is viewed unsparingly as one would view one's own deficiencies. Now the novel has ceased to reflect itself and seems to have become a vehicle for self-reflection. Its version of an epic narrative trains the light of literary experience onto the inadequacies of life.

In his last work, the autobiographical *Journal of a Voyage to Lisbon* published posthumously in 1755, the year after his death, Fielding tells the story of his last journey to a warmer climate in the futile hope of recovering his health. He is in effect making literature out of the remaining days of his life. A decade earlier he had seen such a process as the cue for parody: in chapter I of *Joseph Andrews* he ridicules Colley Cibber as the 'great Person ... who lived the life he hath recorded, and is by many thought to have lived such a life only in order to write it'. Now Fielding is prepared to acknowledge in himself the embarrassment and the privilege of living simultaneously both in the real and the reflected worlds. In the process he both creates and destroys himself: he it is, as the reflective intelligence, who shapes and inhabits the whole book; yet he cannot allow his own reflection to appear in the book. His scruples as a writer are reinforced by his recognition that, incapacitated by dropsy, he is now 'as dead a luggage as any'. The intelligence which has brought everything else into living reality wills itself into non-existence. The act of writing prefigures his actual death, his no longer being there. At the same time it is he who creates the narrative from which he must be absent. Writing allows him to commit himself to reality by detaching himself: he enters the world by writing about it, that is by vacating it. The *Lisbon Voyage* is the last stage in Fielding's remarkable exploration of the relations between literature and life.

Fielding can be friendly with the world because his art, aware of itself, is aware of its separation from the world. Tobias Smollett is an artist fighting against the world, which has a suffocating and oppressive proximity. He cannot afford to play, as Fielding does, with the reflective ambiguities of fictive existence and non-existence. He is beset. His art is for fending off the world. It cannot relax: it has to keep itself intact under assault. It seems Swiftian in its violence, but it is not in fact fuelled by disgust so much as by an almost desperate need to define its own independence and identity. In an age dominated by the notion of satire it must have looked as if it should be defined as satire, its energy the energy of anger and opposition, 'The strong antipathy of good to bad'. And indeed Smollett himself seemed willing to promote this view. In *The Adventures of Sir Launcelot Greaves* (1760–62) Smollett creates his own version of a quixotic hero, alienated from the world, not by *his* insanity but by the world's. 'I quarrel with none but the foes of virtue and decorum, against whom I have declared perpetual war, and them I will everywhere attack as the natural enemies of mankind.' This is the stance that he in fact discerned in *Don Quijote* and which he invoked in trying to define his own art as a novelist. In the preface to his first novel, *Roderick Random* (1748), he praises Cervantes not only for having overthrown Romance but for having converted it to 'purposes far more useful and entertaining, by making it assume the sock, and point out the follies of ordinary life'. Like Fielding Smollett seems to take it for granted that comic Romance will have a corrective purpose: it will be the most effective kind of satire, 'that which is found, occasionally, in the course of an interesting story'.

Yet Random does not, like Greaves, proclaim himself a scourge of folly. His story has very little to do with correction. It is really about a state of war, and about war as some kind of token of the authenticity of experience. Random recognizes himself only through the extremes of conflict and the intensity of his reactions to it. 'I was incensed'; and then, I was 'severely punished'; then, 'far from being subdued . . . my indignation triumphed'. 'I sallied out in a transport of rage and sorrow', 'I was extremely mortified', 'I enjoyed this triumph', and so on. He knows therefore that he exists, but he never understands the meaning of his existence. He is as much a victim of Fortune at the end of his story as at the beginning. There can be no question of development in his character. He is located at the heart of a conflict but the conflict is not one that can progress through complication and crisis to resolution. There is no 'history' of Random to relate. The conflict he is in is an existential one. He is fighting for his life.

He is, that is to say, competing for attention. Like the hero of *Peregrine Pickle* (1751) he must dominate or cease to exist. This is why the mode of these novels has to be exaggeration, visual caricature, exclamation, verbal distortion. There can be no movement but from one extreme to another, from shock to shock, from terror to hysterical laughter or from sexual excitement ('my cheeks glowed, my nerves thrilled, and my knees shook with ecstasy!') to disgust ('Heaven and earth! ... I found Miss Sparkle converted into a wrinkled hag turned of seventy! I was struck dumb with amazement, and petrified with horror!'). The writing has to be overloaded; each new event, each statement is in competition with all the other statements; there is no remission from the struggle for attention.

Fighting for life can also mean fighting to save oneself from being overwhelmed. The people in Smollett's novels are perpetually in danger of losing their immunity and privacy, of being contaminated, infected, invaded. They are assaulted by voices, by oaths, by blows, and, most nauseatingly, by smells. Smells do invade the body; we breathe them in and we cannot choose not to breathe them in. The actor Quin, on his brief appearance in *Humphry Clinker*, puts the matter succinctly: 'life,' he says, 'would stink in his nostrils, if he did not steep it in claret.' 'The very air we breathe,' says Matt. Bramble in the same novel, 'is loaded with contagion. We cannot even sleep, without risque of infection. I say, infection!' Of course, Quin and Bramble are, as Jery Melford says, 'cynic philosophers': Bramble acknowledges his growing misanthropy. Yet it is the case that the people in Smollett's novels are faced with a choice: they maintain their separateness, their sense of individuality, or they risk infection. The one point at which Roderick Random has room in his life for another individual is when, his body 'infected with a distemper contracted in the course of an amour', he meets a prostitute who is likewise infected. He listens to and is moved by her story and stays with her till both are cured.

Smollett's characters are isolated individuals; companionship, let alone love, would expose them to the disease of humanity. Even in *Humphry Clinker*, published in 1771, the year of Smollett's death, the people are insulated from each other. The device of building the novel out of a series of letters goes a long way towards lifting it out of the obsessive monomania that governs the behaviour of so many of his characters. At the same time this very form cuts the characters off from each other. Not only do they render separate and incompatible accounts of places, people and events, so that they can hardly be said to be writing about shared experiences even, still less sharing their reactions to them, but they each in turn as they write become spectators of the others. They become separated not only from each other

but from their own actions, which emerge most clearly when objectified in someone else's account.

Smollett's work is charged throughout with a clamorous assertive-
ness, as if defending a territory. Paul-Gabriel Boucé, seizing on
Smollett's manifold assaults on the language, his inexhaustible versatility in creating comic distortions of speech, as one of his most
characteristic activities, finds in it the underlying motive and clue to
Smollett's nature. He sees in it 'the ultimate refuge of the individual
who feels himself menaced by the pressures of society and attempts
under cover of an idiolect, to stave off his own annihilation and the
death of a civilization'.[4] In Fielding there was play, 'a rehearsal of
civilization'; in Smollett the play is either manic or desperate, and
civilization is under siege.

NOTES

1. Damian Grant, *Tobias Smollett* (1977).
2. Bernard Harrison, *Henry Fielding's* Tom Jones: *The Novelist as Moral
Philosopher* (Sussex University Press, 1975), 131.
3. Andrew Wright, *Henry Fielding: Mask and Feast* (1965).
4. Paul-Gabriel Boucé, *The Novels of Tobias Smollett* (1976), 350.

TRISTRAM SHANDY AND THE ARTS
OF FICTION

D. W. JEFFERSON

Tristram Shandy is one of the most fruitful of all works for those who are interested in the possibilities of fiction. Sterne's inveterate preoccupation with methods and theories might seem to provide us with plenty of clues to the nature of his contribution, though his humorous manner is liable to disguise its full importance. His game frequently has the effect of understating the implications of his art, but in other places he makes a comedy of over-elaborating his structures. This elusiveness affects every aspect of his work. There are few books that demand of the reader more reconsideration, or that treat him more often to the pleasure of new discoveries.

We could quite usefully begin at the beginning – no novel opens with a more piquant statement of the author's intentions – but there are other beginnings, and perhaps the most rewarding introduction to Sterne is the passage where he enters upon an account of Uncle Toby, and in particular of his hobby-horse, in one of his most beautifully designed digressions. The view of characterization stated here and illustrated in the chapters that follow is much more valuable than one would expect from his playful style, and is one of his great gifts to the novel:

> A man and his HOBBY-HORSE, though I cannot say that they act and re-act exactly after the same manner in which the soul and body do upon each other: Yet doubtless there is a communication between them of some kind, and my opinion rather is, that there is something in it more of the manner of electrified bodies, – and that, by means of the heated parts of the rider, which come immediately into contact with the back of the HOBBY-HORSE – By long journies and much friction, it so happens that the body of the rider is at length filled as full of HOBBY-HORSICAL matter as it can hold; – so that if you are able to give but a clear description of the nature of the one, you may form a pretty exact notion of the genius and character of the other.
>
> (I, ch. 24)

This is superior to the Jonsonian theory of humours, though Sterne uses this old idiom too, and to ideas of the ruling passion, because it does not emphasize excessively the individual's psychological isolation (though there is a solipsist element, amiably recognized, in Toby's condition) but rather his relations with something outside himself. The principle may be applied to any pursuit that can dominate sensibility, with occasions for fantasy but also with a structure of objective facts. The imagination can appropriate and transform facts so that they become part of the personality. In Toby's case the need for fantasy is especially great because the facts have gone. Owing to a wound received at the siege of Namur he has been invalided at quite an early age out of the army and deprived of the profession to which he was and remains utterly devoted. The wound itself is disaster enough, as we learn from the brief reference to four years of 'unspeakable miseries', which are mitigated in some measure by the kindness of his brother, who gives him the best apartment in his London house and brings his friends in to chat by his bedside. But with his literary good manners, for which no novelist had a finer instinct, notwithstanding the transgressions which have alienated some critics, Sterne does not overstress the intensely painful aspects of this situation. There is some wry surgical gossip about the wound and how Toby got it, and the friendly inquiries are treated with true eighteenth-century decorum, in keeping with his simple stoicism and freedom from self-pity:

> The history of a soldier's wound beguiles the pain of it; – my uncle's visitors at least thought so, and in their daily calls upon him, from the courtesy arising out of that belief, they would frequently turn the discourse to that subject . . .
>
> (I, ch.24)

But Toby has difficulty in assembling the facts of the siege, and volume II begins with his attempt to overcome his vexation: his attempt, as it were, to reconstruct the world he has lost. The facts are resistant and idiosyncratic. They have their terminology, with rhetorical potentialities, and the narrator makes a work of art of Toby's confusion; but if the effect is light the frustration is real:

> What rendered the account of this affair the more intricate to my uncle Toby, was this, – that in the attack of the counter-scarp before the gate of St Nicolas, extending itself from the bank of the Maes, quite up to the great waterstop; – the ground was cut and cross-cut with such a multitude of

dykes, drains, rivulets, and sluices, on all sides, – and he would get so sadly bewildered, and set fast amongst them, that frequently he could neither get backwards or forwards to save his life; and was oft-times obliged to give up the attack upon that very account only.

(II, ch. 1)

Annoyance and agitation hinder his convalescence. His immediate problem is solved by a map, which enables him to give his visitors a clear account of where 'he had the honour to receive his wound;' though the fortnight's work with it did the wound itself no good. 'But the desire of knowledge, like the thirst of riches, increases ever with the acquisition of it ... The more my uncle Toby drank of this sweet fountain of science, the greater was the heat and impatience of his thirst.' Thus, in words that give a flourish to Toby's addicted state, the narrator in fact traces a man's fight for the restoration of his spirit. And when he turns to the manifestations of the struggle, rhetoric again enables him to remain within the comic convention, which is so very much the best preservative:

> Oh my uncle!, ... is it fit, good-natured man! thou should'st sit up, with the wound upon thy groin, whole nights baking thy blood with hectic watchings? – Alas! 'twill exasperate thy symptoms, – check thy perspirations, – evaporate thy spirits, – waste thy animal strength, – dry up thy radical moisture, – bring thee into a costive habit of body, impair thy health, – and hasten all the infirmities of thy old age, – O my uncle! my uncle Toby!
>
> (II, ch. 3)

Finally comes Trim's solution and Toby's response to it: 'My uncle Toby blushed as red as scarlet as Trim went on, – but it was not a blush of guilt, – of modesty, – or of anger; – it was a blush of joy ...' And in an incomparable passage of dialogue Trim builds up his prospects of 'good air, and good exercise, and good health', with the delightful details of their future undertakings on the bowling green, until Toby is 'overcome with rapture'. Then, on the last page of this sequence: 'Never did lover post down to a beloved mistress with more haste and expectation, than my uncle Toby did, to enjoy this self-same thing in private ...' (II, ch. 5), words which point to another aspect of his case, but with a grace that calls for no comment.

The early history of the hobby-horse ends here, but it is a recurring motif throughout the book, and in a wonderful sequence of chapters beginning with volume VI, chapter 22, it appears in all its glory. We have now moved on into the next century, and Marlborough's wars provide ample scope for Toby and Trim. The picture is one of great happiness:

> When the town, with its works, was finished, my uncle Toby and the corporal began to run their first parallel – not at random, or any how – but from the same points and distances the allies had begun to run theirs; and regulating their approaches and attacks, by the accounts my uncle Toby received from the daily papers, – they went on, during the whole siege, step by step with the allies.
>
> When the Duke of Marlborough made a lodgment, – my uncle Toby made a lodgment too. – And when the face of a bastion was battered down, or a defence ruined, – the corporal took his mattock and did as much, – and so on; – gaining ground, and making themselves masters of the works one after another, till the town fell into their hands.
>
> To one who took pleasure in the happy state of others, – there could not have been a greater sight in the world, than, on a post-morning, in which a practicable breach had been made by the Duke of Marlborough, in the main body of the place, – to have stood behind the horn-beam hedge, and observed the spirit with which my uncle Toby, with Trim behind him, sallied forth; – the one with the *Gazette* in his hand, – the other with a spade to execute the contents. – What an honest triumph in my uncle Toby's looks, as he marched up to the ramparts! What intense pleasure swimming in his eye as he stood over the corporal, reading the paragraph ten times over to him, as he was at work, lest, peradventure, he should make the breach an inch too wide, – or leave it an inch too narrow. – But when the *chamade* was beat, and the corporal helped my uncle up it, and followed with the colours in his hand, to fix them upon the ramparts – Heaven! Earth! Sea! – but what avails apostrophes? – with all your elements, wet or dry, ye never compounded so intoxicating a draught.
>
> (VI, ch. 22)

This art of entering into Toby's intimate relationship with his cherished pursuit is of course the novelist's; but within the economy of the novel it is the narrator who performs this function, and the character of whom he writes is always 'my uncle Toby'. Strictly, direct knowledge of his uncle, as of his father, could only have been based on what he observed in the years following the 5 November 1718, when he was born, and he could only have reported effectively on their declining years. But by an admirable artistic licence he has direct access to a remoter past. In the first chapter he picks up words exchanged by his father and mother just before he was begotten, and, in a later chapter, words exchanged by his father and Uncle Toby on the day when his birth becomes imminent; but, as we have seen, he also has access to conversations between Toby and Trim that took place twenty years before he was born. It would be difficult to say how Sterne makes this so irresistibly appealing; but part of the magic is in the ease and audacity with which, without establishing credentials or stating a narrative policy, he just causes voices from the past to be heard. It suggests, if we thought about it, a hovering invisible presence of infinite responsiveness and resourcefulness. Sometimes the narrator is an historian, but in many places he is very much a witness, who shares with us his special feeling for the principal characters and also his pleasure as an artist in presenting them with a play of style and a variety of techniques of enhancement or disguise. In the last quotation Toby is presented most lovingly, but the tone of the early passage announcing the hobby-horse would seem to promise something of much less human importance. The word 'hobby-horse' itself trivializes what the narrator knows perfectly well is not trivial. So his policy at this point is to adopt an attitude to his reader which is the very reverse of an appeal to sentiment; and this recalls chapter 6 of the first volume, where he first introduces himself as the companionable narrator, offering a playful image, with references to 'a fool's cap with a bell on it' and the prospect of some trifling on the road. This gives no indication of the delicacy of feeling he is to show four chapters later in his portrait of Yorick, himself an incorrigible jester but also with 'spiritual and refined sentiments'. And here follows his affectionate tribute to the 'peerless knight of La Mancha' (I, 10). There was an abundance of examples before Sterne of the narrator who establishes a personal rapport with the reader and claims some kind of access, direct or indirect, to the characters, but *Tristram Shandy* is a new phenomenon. Pretending at first to be mainly humorous in his intentions, with his talk of fools' caps and hobby-horses, and maintaining throughout the rhetorical devices that can turn heartfelt speeches into set pieces, so that there is always something to amuse: by means of these and other artifices Sterne achieves freedom to cherish a character and bestow the wealth of his sensibility upon him.

There was never a novel in which so much is shared. The narrator shares himself with us, and also his father and uncle, who as excellent brothers share many an amicable silence with each other and also some misunderstandings which do not disrupt their affection. The relationship of the brothers has the value almost of a narrative structure, so much of the one being revealed in his response to the other and in the other's response to him, in conversations that give shape and form to their mutuality. There is a fine moment (III, 10) when unobtrusively and apparently by an instinctive rapport, but also with the narrator's appreciative handling of the dialogue, they aid and abet each other at Dr Slop's expense. Mr Shandy, annoyed by Dr Slop's cursing of Obadiah, solemnly and with insidious urbanity persuades him to profit by the Ernulphus curse. The notation here is of a quiet sophistication that expresses well their fraternal understanding and the narrator's appreciation of them.

The seven chapters beginning with the theory of hobby-horses and concluding with Trim's inspired suggestion are part of a parenthesis, a digression, which contains also a statement of his theory of digressions. The point of departure for the digression as a whole is in chapter 21 of the first volume, which is of crucial importance to the main narrative in that if it does not actually take us a stage further it comes very near to doing so, and is only prevented by the digression we are considering:

– I wonder what's all that noise, and running backwards and forwards for, above stairs, quoth my father, addressing himself, after an hour and a half's silence, to my uncle Toby, – who you must know, was sitting on the opposite side of the fire, smoking his social pipe all the time, in mute contemplation of a new pair of black-plush-breeches which he had got on, – What can they be doing, brother? – quoth my father, – we can scarce hear ourselves talk. I think, replied my uncle Toby, taking his pipe from his mouth, and striking, the head of it two or three times upon the nail of his left thumb, as he began his sentence, – I think, says he ...

But the narrator intervenes. The conversation must be suspended and Uncle Toby's comment withheld until we come to know him better. A Victorian reader of novels would have seen nothing unusual in an orderly digression designed to provide background to a character who had just been introduced on the point of his taking up an important role. The eccentricity here lies in the sudden break in the dialogue, the cutting short of Toby's speech at the crucial point when he is about to say something relevant to the situation that looms ahead. What that situation is we shall not know for some time, but it is no other than the fact that Mrs Shandy is in labour, so that with the birth of the hero (the narrator himself) the story may have yet another beginning, though not very soon. The point of technique here is the manner in which the digression disrupts the main narrative, if 'main narrative' is an appropriate term for a development so recent and so fragile. The impression is one of collision between rival claims upon our attention.

Tristram Shandy from the outset is a novel in which people interrupt each other, and here the narrator interrupts himself. The effect is comic, but it dramatizes and gives shape to untidy realities which we recognize. Real life does not always respect distinctions between the main theme and the digression, nor can a neat new chapter always be set aside for the latter. In real life a major theme might be completely lost, whereas in Sterne's best planned digressions we return with felicitous precision to the point where the narrative was broken. So, after Toby has responded with rapture to Trim's idea, the purpose of the digression has been achieved and we can come back to the brothers at the fireside:

– What can they be doing, brother? said my father – I think, replied my uncle Toby, – taking, as I told you, his pipe from his mouth, and striking the ashes out of it as he began his sentence; – I think, replied he, – it would not be amiss, brother, if we rung the bell.
Pray, what's all that racket over our heads, Obadiah? – quoth my father; – my brother and I can scarce hear ourselves speak. Sir, answered Obadiah, making a bow towards his left shoulder, – my Mistress is taken very badly; – and where's Susannah running down the garden there, as if they were going to ravish her? – Sir, she is running the shortest cut into the town, replied Obadiah, to fetch the old midwife. Then saddle a horse, quoth my father, and do you go directly for Dr Slop, the man-midwife, with all our services . . .

(II, ch. 6)

After so much delay even so small a development is like a leap forward. But the matter that caused the delay, as we have seen, is of the richest. The narrator claims that digressions 'are the sunshine, – they are the life, the soul of reading; – take them out of this book for instance, – you might as well take the book along with them . . .' (I, 22). The truth is that the protagonists of the 'main narrative' will continue to sit by the fireside, waiting, which is all the male members of the household are in a position to do at this time when the real action is supplied, unseen and in another place, by the women. The main narrative is largely a stagnant narrative, calling out for digressions.

On the subject of digressions the narrator makes elaborate claims for the ingenuity of his system:

> ... the machinery of my work is of a species by itself; two contrary motions are introduced into it, and reconciled, which were thought to be at variance with each other. In a word, my work is digressive, and it is progressive too, – and at the same time.
>
> (I, ch. 22)

This heightens our sense that method is at work, and we can take pleasure in the author's genial concern that we should be aware of it. Method certainly is present but its triumphs are not always specifically those on which he dwells with most satisfaction. Sterne likes to see his own methods, and also the world he depicts, in terms of ingenious mechanisms, and when he enjoys a playful exaggeration of their complexity there is a likelihood that another kind of artistic accomplishment is present to which he does not call attention. There is one such mechanism in the Shandy home:

> Though in one sense, our family was certainly a simple machine, as it consisted of a few wheels; yet there was thus much to be said for it, that these wheels were set in motion by so many different springs, and acted one upon the other from such a variety of strange principles and impulses, – that though it was a simple machine, it had all the honour and advantages of a complex one, – and a number of as odd movements within it, as ever were beheld in the inside of a Dutch silk-mill.
>
> (V, ch. 6)

From such a description we might expect rather more than we get. The point of the 'machine' is simply that 'whatever motion, debate, harangue, dialogue, project, or dissertation' was being put forward in the parlour, there was another to the same purpose at the same time in the kitchen; and the reason is traceable to the bad hinge on the parlour door, which provided an excuse for leaving the door slightly ajar for the eavesdropping Obadiah. The passage it left was 'indeed not as wide as the Dardanells, but wide enough, for all that, to carry on as much of this windward trade as was sufficient to save my father the trouble of governing his own house'. This is elementary enough. Complexity is present perhaps when Trim's oratory in the kitchen on the theme of Bobby's death (and the mourning that must ensue) is examined in detail in its effect on Susannah, the scullion and others, with their different interests and fantasies; but much of this is literary play, comic inflation of a point about diversity of motive. The complexities of the Dutch silk-mill are a joke, but the idiosyncratic Shandy household depicted here is an advance on previous households in fiction, and Mr Shandy's idiosyncratic failure to get the hinge mended is one of those small strokes of characterization such as Fielding, with his concern for the most general features of human nature, would never have thought of. The creaking hinge invariably robs Mr Shandy of his nap, and of course it wakes him up in the splendid episode where Trim enters with the two 'mortars' (III, 22). It inspires a rhetorical outburst from the narrator:

> By all that is good and virtuous, if there are three drops of oil to be got, and a hammer to be found within ten miles of Shandy Hall, – the parlour door hinge shall be mended this reign.
>
> (III, ch. 21)

Another thing that is achieved here is a sense of localization; not of course the realistic local colour of later fiction, but we have the impression of an intensely domestic existence, and it is produced with a minimum of specific references to household objects. As Mr Shandy and Toby sit by the fireside the details we can visualize best are a few personal ones: Toby's black plush breeches and his pipe; but the scene of habitual ease is unforgettable. This is where the brothers belong, where we shall always imagine them. Again, to use Fielding as the touchstone: no conversation or other event in Mr Allworthy's home has associations of this kind. Characters in fiction before Sterne might occupy a bedroom, a closet, a kitchen as the action required, but this sense of the habitual, of belonging, is new.

Something similar is true of the other dimension, time. In all fiction events need time in which to develop, but our concern may be exclusively with the events. Sterne gives us a feeling of time itself, with the events sometimes hardly sufficient to fill it. This is a philosopher's subject, and becomes the theme for one of the most entertaining exchanges between Mr Shandy and his brother. The former's observation that 'it is two hours and ten minutes – and no more ... since Dr Slop and Obadiah arrived ... but to my imagination it seems almost an age', produces the unexpected reply from Toby that ''tis owing, entirely ... to the succession of our ideas', which irritates Mr Shandy because his sole motive for the remark was his intention to follow it up with a 'metaphysical dissertation' on this same theme.

Toby's admission that he knows 'no more than his horse' about this Lockeian principle clears the way for a truly formidable exposition. But after further evidence of Toby's incomprehension Mr Shandy begins to ponder, and this has the effect of causing his succession of ideas to be entirely suspended: he falls asleep, and so does his brother, and it is at this moment, what with Dr Slop's being occupied elsewhere, that the narrator seizes his opportunity to write his preface! This is good comedy, and an amusing example of Sterne's way with philosophical ideas, but more important is the awareness he creates in us of time as the medium in which the characters must occupy themselves somehow. When time is wasted, when there are virtually no events, time comes into its own as an essential part of experience. As the three characters sit waiting for events outside their control, they must kill time, which Yorick's sermon and the Ernulphus curse enable them to do. By a curious paradox, in this novel where the characters for much of the time do little more than breathe, they are exceptionally convincing as human presences. They have time in fact to be themselves.

Sterne does not, as Jane Austen does in *Emma* and Virginia Woolf in *Mrs Dalloway*, give us a day or any other stretch of time in the life of a character, a realistically conceived period containing important events or routine or near-vacancy. There is no such thing as a day in the life of Mr Shandy or his brother. Time is rhetorically rather than realistically conceived. The two brothers are together by the fireside, and we are told that they have been sitting in silence for an hour and a half, but the length of time has no relation to the kind of sequence of events that would include breakfast and dinner. It is a tableau, a set piece. If meals were depicted in *Tristram Shandy* they too would be rhetorically conceived, not part of a daily round as Mrs Ramsay's great event is in *To the Lighthouse*, though this has plenty of rhetoric too. There is no overt concern with realism in the modern sense in Sterne's treatment of time or of place. All is rhetoric and play, but the result does in fact bring the art of the novel nearer to the kind of reality, in these two respects, that a modern writer might wish for, and Sterne has been an important influence in the twentieth century.

There is no nicer illustration of this play than the episode in which Mr Shandy and Toby are on the stairs (IV, 9–13). The disaster of his child's nose has caused Mr Shandy to lie prostrate for some time with Toby at his side; but now he has recovered his composure sufficiently to concentrate his hopes on his son's name. The disaster of the name is to follow swiftly, but meanwhile he philosophizes with Toby as they proceed downstairs. Getting them downstairs while doing justice to all that happens in act or word on the way is a slow business, and he prolongs it by reflecting on the slowness and on the thought that if every day of his life is to be as busy as this one (the first) the more he writes the more he will have to write and the more 'your worships' will have to read ('Will it be good for your worships' eyes?'). An infinite amount can be said about everything, and this is an issue for theories of realism. The adventure on the stairs could have been handled with great effect by Joyce with the elaborate technique of the catechism adopted in the Ithaca episode of *Ulysses*. The details are of delay:

> We shall bring all things to rights, said my father, setting his foot upon the first step from the landing – This Trismegistus, continued my father, drawing his leg back, and turning to my uncle Toby – was the greatest (Toby) of earthly beings ...
>
> (IV, ch. 11)

Susannah passing by provides an occasion for more talk and more delay, so that the narrator is obliged to send for a 'day-tall critic', who solves the problem by dropping a curtain at the foot of the stairs, thus applying the convenient guillotine of stage convention. But the prolonging of the episode is largely a joke and the problem of getting the brothers off the stairs exists mainly in the realm of comic rhetoric. Not much of the detail of delay is in fact used, but with it Sterne captures familiar features of human behaviour: the fatal tendency to pause, to be arrested, interrupted, deflected from one's purpose, so that the simplest operation – a leave-taking, for example – can be indefinitely protracted. Part of the effect here depends on our recognition that the setting – the landing, the stairs – is familiar territory to the two brothers, and their movements or pauses habitual.

The opening of *Tristram Shandy* can be best discussed in the light of our knowledge of what follows. Characteristically, the book begins with an incident that we need not take seriously. In chapter 2, where he introduces the homunculus, the little creature already completely shaped as a human being according to early biological theorists,[1] and dwells upon the shock to his system caused by the unfortunate interruption of the act of intercourse and the danger of his arriving at his destination in a disabled state, we accept all the pathos and the Whig politics (the homunculus has *rights*) as comedy. This exploitation of the theory is a piece of Shandean licence. So the necessity for beginning his story *ab ovo*, by way of calling attention to the responsibilities of parents even in the moment of generation, is a joke, it is comic pre-science fiction. Serious issues relating to parenthood are not raised. This way of beginning, his rhetorical insistence on the moment of begetting as the only correct starting point, establishes the style of comedy within which he will later refer to something quite different: the disastrous irresponsibility of Mr Shandy's insistence on the terms of the marriage agreement, which, because of a false alarm on a previous occasion, exposes his wife to the hazards of a confinement in the country, when she might have had the best treatment in London.

Rueful comedy is the note from the outset. Tristram was born 'into this scurvy and disastrous world of ours', and fortune, 'ungracious Duchess, has pelted [him] with a set of as pitiful misadventures and cross accidents as ever small HERO sustained'. 'Sport of small accidents, Tristram Shandy! that thou art, and ever will be!' is his exclamation as he focuses later upon the role of Obadiah, who tied the knots which impeded Dr Slop and was therefore instrumental in causing the 'depression' of his, the hero's, nose (III, ch. 8), and the note is much the same as at the opening of the book, though Obadiah's error would never have been committed had Mr Shandy not committed the much graver one which caused Dr Slop to be involved in the first place. The narrator handles Mr Shandy's action with a mixture of humour and filial forbearance. There was a 'hobby-horsical' side to it. Mr Shandy was against visits to the metropolis, for political reasons. As in the body natural so in the body national blood and spirits 'driven up into the head faster than they could find their ways down' were dangerous. But the false alarm had occurred at the time of year when his wall-fruit and greengages especially 'in which he was very curious' were just ready for picking, and he was also vexed about the expense; and this is somehow accepted along with his other Shandean foibles, so that the words 'he peremptorily insisted upon the clause' do not come over to us as gross tyranny, and this is partly because Mrs Shandy, the immediate victim of the decision, scarcely exists as a character in this totally male-dominated comedy. It would hardly operate so easily as comedy if it were less male-dominated and if she were not almost entirely absent from the scene. We are accustomed to outrageous male domination in the novels of this period, usually at the expense of daughters, notably Clarissa Harlowe and Sophia Western, and here the fathers are openly tyrannical. In *Tristram Shandy* tyranny never emerges as a theme. In fact the fatal clause was added to the marriage settlement at the suggestion of none other than the benign Toby. The two brothers are sublimely unconscious of injustice in such matters, nor is there the slightest hint of protest or social satire on the male prerogative in this novel. Yet it is within the framework created by this particular kind of arbitrary male behaviour that the comedy takes its shape.

At one stage in Mr Shandy's career as a speculative philosopher he arrived at the conviction that the best way of ensuring the well-being of a child was to arrange for a Caesarian section. He mentioned this to his wife 'merely as a matter of fact, but seeing her turn pale as ashes . . . he thought it was well to say no more of it' (II, ch. 19). But when things go wrong the image upon which the narrator lavishes his rhetorical resources is that of the stricken father, who on learning of the breaking down of the bridge of his child's nose by the edge of a pair of forceps, throws himself prostrate across his bed 'in the wildest disorder imaginable, but at the same time, in the most lamentable attitude of a man borne down with sorrows, that ever the eye of pity dropped a tear for' (III, ch. 29). Mr Shandy's predicament is absurd, but the absurdity is seen in a Cervantic light. His tragedy is that of a philosopher, and, in the chapters that follow, his theory of noses, to which he had attached so much importance, is expounded with an eloquence that equals anything in the old pre-scientific literature of the previous age:

Now Ambrose Paraeus convinced my father that . . . the length and goodness of the nose was owing simply to the softness and flaccidity in the nurse's breast, – as the flatness and shortness of *puisne* noses was, to the firmness and elastic repulsion of the same organ of nutrition in the hale and lively, – which, though happy for the woman, was the undoing of the child, inasmuch as his nose was so snubbed, so rebated, and so refrigerated thereby, as never to arrive *ad mensuram suam legitimam*; – but that in case of the flaccidity and softness of the nurse or mother's breast, – by sinking into it, quoth Paraeus,

as into so much butter, the nose was comforted, nourished, plumped up,
refreshed, refocillated, and set a-growing for ever.

(III, ch. 38)

As we have seen, an obvious reason why so much of the novel seems
uneventful, with the main characters sitting in silence or killing time
in various ways, their minds occupied with cherished obsessions, is
that most of our attention is upon the male figures who, of course,
have no function when a child is being born. Life is not uneventful
for Mrs Shandy. 'Above stairs' important things are happening, but
her side of the story is not represented. But we detect a pointedness in
the behaviour of the women. They take no notice of Mr Shandy, and
Susannah's mission to fetch the old woman goes ahead without a
word of information to him until he rings for Obadiah. In the episode
with Mr Shandy and Toby on the stairs, Susannah trips by 'without
looking up', and gives an offhand reply to Mr Shandy's question.
The brothers react in different ways to this female behaviour, and this
is a good comic scene; yet what is taking place above stairs is a glaring
consequence, were the novel so focused, of a male dispensation.

If the stricken father is the central figure in those parts of the book
where Toby is not central, the main story of *Tristram Shandy* concerns
the narrator himself and the unfortunate manner of his entrance into
the world. This provides the theme from the first sentence onwards.
The book could be described as his 'complaint', though a humorous
one, and his presence as the hovering witness of those crucial early
scenes might be said to dramatize his need to press his case. Drama
and rhetoric are present at every stage of the unfortunate sequence of
events, but always in the interests of comedy. The book has no place
in the literature that deals with the wrongs of children. Sterne does
not begin to be a precursor of Blake or Dickens, any more than he
is to be cited in the cause of the victimized woman. The warmth and
humanity of *Tristram Shandy* is in the hero's affectionate understanding of his uncle Toby, his humorous forbearance towards his father,
his sense of the relationship between the brothers and his portrait of
Yorick. The extraordinary artistry of the book, and Sterne's capacity
to turn so much of life into a joke, leave the reader entirely content
with and probably unaware of these limits. It is in the nature of
comedy to ignore some things in order to appreciate others, and the
art with which they are ignored contributes to the effect. With its

continual reminders, though in absurd terms, of the hazards of child-birth and the vulnerability of the very young, familiar realities in that age, the comedy is frequently tinged with black but as comedy it is enjoyed. All this is in keeping with the spirit of the whole book in which, even at its most generous, the absurd is always present.

NOTE

1. This topic is treated by Louis A. Landa in 'The Shandean Homunculus: The Background of Sterne's "Little Gentleman"', *Restoration and Eighteenth-Century Literature: Essays in Honour of Alan Dugald McKillop*, edited by Carroll Camden (University of Chicago Press, 1963), 49–68.

AUGUSTAN REFLECTIVE POETRY

NORMAN CALLAN

> Grant me, indulgent Heaven! a rural seat
>   Rather contemptible than great!
> Where, though I taste life's sweets, I still may be
>   Athirst for immortality!
> I would have business; but exempt from strife!
>   A private, but an active life!
> A conscience bold, and punctual to his charge!
>   My stock of health; or patience large!
> Some books I'd have, and some acquaintance too;
>   But very good, and very few!
> Then (if a mortal two such gifts may crave!)
>   From silent life I'd steal into the grave.

To anyone reflecting casually on Augustan poetry it is not perhaps these unassuming verses by Nahum Tate (1652–1715) that comes first to mind: rather he would recall as typical of the age such poems as *Hudibras, Absalom and Achitophel, The Rape of the Lock, The Dunciad* – satirical masterpieces, manifesting an exclusive, if disapproving, interest in life as lived in cities. Yet the list would contain exceptions – Gray's *Elegy*, certainly, Thomson's *Seasons*, and perhaps some of Collins's odes. And if this train of thought were pursued it would quickly become evident that the view of Augustan poetry as predominantly satirical is altogether one-sided. In mere quantity the line of poetry which runs from such late-seventeenth-century writers as Charles Cotton through Lady Winchilsea, Pope (before 1717), Thomson, Gray, Collins, Shenstone and so on to Goldsmith and Cowper is probably preponderant; and if its masterpieces do not seem able to compete with those of satire, this is perhaps because (as Milton found) the depiction of actual evil is more spectacular than that of ideal good. To see in this line (as so many do) a trend which is untypical of the age, or even unrelated to satire, is to miss its significance. In presenting an idealized picture of rural peace (Tate's poem affords an undistinguished but compact example), and using this as the starting-point for reflection, it is clearly the counterpart of satire, and springs from the impulse to comment on human existence which is the mark of all Augustan poetry. To put the point more briefly, there is no great gulf between *The Vanity of Human Wishes* and the *Elegy Written in a Country Churchyard*: and it is no accident that the predominating literary influence of the age is that of the Roman Horace, a poet who excelled both in urban satire and in the poetry of rural meditation.

If at first it seems surprising that an age noted for its urbanity and social sense should devote so much of its energies to the praise of solitude, this is largely because of the way the Augustans have been treated by literary critics and historians, who have mostly taken the line that if Augustan rural solitude is not the rural solitude of the Romantics it is negligible; if it is not negligible, then it is not Augustan. The Romantics themselves fostered the attitude, especially Wordsworth who wrote in the *Essay Supplementary*:

> Now it is remarkable that, excepting the *Nocturnal Reverie* of Lady Winchilsea and a passage or two in the *Windsor Forest* of Pope, the poetry intervening between the publication of *Paradise Lost* and *The Seasons* does not contain a single new image of rural nature; and scarcely presents a familiar one from which it can be inferred that the eye of the poet had been steadily fixed upon his object, much less that his feelings had urged him to work upon it in a spirit of genuine imagination . . .

Because he is attempting to create the taste by which his poetry is to be enjoyed, Wordsworth has some justification for these sweeping generalizations: but critically they are misleading, since they are based on assumptions which the Augustans never made. It is comment of this kind which has rendered appreciation of the non-satirical poetry of the period so difficult.

Nor has appreciation been advanced by well-intentioned criticism which, in answer to Wordsworth and Arnold, claims to find in a poet like Matthew Green the dawn of the Romantic movement. 'Green's aim is still self-regarding, but it does not prevent him from entering into the green, liquescent world about him. His senses have thawed, and the genial warmth of the sun-steeped earth has passed through him to his mind and melted its chilly decorum.' From this it would appear that in so far as Green is self-regarding he is a bad poet, but in so far as he is trying to anticipate Keats he is a good one. The fact that it is his self-regarding wit which makes him the peculiar

poet that he is has been totally ignored, while the fact that he has a
sensitivity to external nature closely akin to that of many of his contemporaries is made to suggest that he has escaped from the conventions of his age. To such wishful thinking a more perceptive critic's
verdict on Shenstone provides sufficient answer:

... that Shenstone wrote of his own jasmines and harebells does not prove
that he was nearer to Wordsworth than to Horace, or perhaps Virgil. That his
friends thought of the Leasowes [Shenstone's elaborately landscaped estate] as
Gothic – which it was not – does not ally him with Romance rather than
with Reason. That he chose his fashions to suit himself does not remove him
from the heart of the eighteenth century. ... [1]

Indeed, when one comes to look closely, it is the pertinacity of critics in
decrying the absence of something that was never meant to be there,
or in praising the presence of something equally absent that is so
surprising. Of no other age has the poetry been so little read for its
own sake, or so much for the sake of comparison with other ages.

Tate's poem belongs to what may be called the poetry of rural contentment, a strain descending from antiquity, and appearing in such
sixteenth-century lyrics as Dekker's *Sweet Content* and Shakespeare's
Under the Greenwood Tree. In the two succeeding centuries this strain
mingles with that of solitary contemplation, thereby taking in such
pieces as Milton's *L'Allegro* and *Il Penseroso*, and Marvell's *Garden*. Here,
too, may be included Vaughan's *Retreat* and Traherne's *Solitude*. Thus,
in some measure, the poetry to be treated in this chapter derives from a
tradition extending far beyond the Augustan period. But within
the period the tradition undergoes certain modifications which
distinguish the poetry from that which precedes and that which
follows; and with the most important of these modifications it would
be as well to begin.

The cadences of Tate's poem are those of the seventeenth century: in
them may be heard a rather feeble echo of *The Garden* or *The Retreat*.
The same is even more true of the much finer poem on a similar theme
– Charles Cotton's (1630–87) *The Retirement*,[2] addressed to Izaak
Walton:

> Farewell thou busy world, and may
>   We never meet again:
> Here can I eat and sleep and pray,
> And do more good in one short day
> Than he who his whole age outwears

Upon thy most conspicuous theatres,
　　Where nought but vice and vanity do reign.

Good God! how sweet are all things here!
How beautiful the fields appear!
How cleanly do we feed and lie!
Lord! what good hours do we keep!
　　How quietly we sleep!
What peace! What unanimity!
How innocent from the lewd fashion,
Is all our business, all our conversation.

Oh how happy here's our leisure!
Oh how innocent our pleasure!
Oh ye valleys, oh ye mountains,
Oh ye groves and crystal fountains,
　　How I love at liberty
By turn to come and visit ye!

O Solitude, the soul's best friend,
That man acquainted with himself dost make,
And all his Maker's wonders to intend;
　　With thee I here converse at will,
　　And would be glad to do so still;
For it is thou alone that keep'st the soul awake.

How calm and quiet a delight
　　　it is alone
To read, and meditate, and write,
By none offended, and offending none;
To walk, ride, sit, or sleep at one's own ease,
And pleasing a man's self, none other to displease!

The conversational rise and fall of this is in sharp contrast to an early
poem by Pope (1688–1744):

　　　Happy the man whose wish and care
　　　　　A few paternal acres bound,
　　　Content to breathe his native air
　　　　　In his own ground.

　　　Whose herds with milk, whose fields with bread,
　　　　　Whose flocks supply him with attire;
　　　Whose trees in summer yield him shade,
　　　　　In winter fire.

　　　Blest, who can unconcern'dly find
　　　　　Hours, days and years slide soft away,
　　　In health of body, peace of mind,
　　　　　Quiet by day.

Sound sleep by night; study and ease
    Together mix'd; sweet recreation;
And innocence which does most please
    With meditation.

Thus let me live, unseen, unknown,
    Thus unlamented let me die,
Steal from the world, and not a stone
    Tell where I lie.

Here the perfect organization of the poem's cadences carries an air of
assurance which is not present in the more hesitant rhythms of its
seventeenth-century counterparts: and this measured emphasis perhaps forms a line of demarcation between the poetry of the two
centuries. It can be seen, for instance, separating Cotton from Gray:

Beside some water's rushy brink
With me the muse shall sit and think
    (At ease reclin'd in rustic state)
How vain the ardour of the crowd,
How low, how little are the proud,
    How indigent the great!

But such differences, which spring at least to some extent from the
individual temper of the poet, only serve to underline the essential
unity of all these pieces when they are compared with such poems as
The Garden or *The Retreat*. For Marvell and Vaughan 'nature' is a
symbol in whose weaker glories may be spied some glimpses of
eternity – in fact, a mystical symbol. For Cotton or Pope, on the
other hand, if it is a symbol at all, it is a social one, standing for what
is sincere and unpretentious, as opposed to what is affected and
grandiose.

   In some degree all the poems from which I have quoted achieve a
compromise which is typical of the age. In the earlier part of the
seventeenth century, retreat to nature meant retirement from practical business to ideal contemplation: the typical ring of the poetry
is other-worldly – 'a green thought in a green shade', 'like stars upon
some gloomy grove'. For the Augustans such a retreat meant a turning
from ambition to usefulness. Parnell's hermit (in the poem of that
name) is not fully equipped for his vocation until he has come out
into the world and learned that apparent injustices are all part of God's
purpose for mankind. The ring of Tate's poem – like so many of its

kind, it derives directly from Horace's second Epode – is markedly
practical: he asks for the best of both worlds –

> Where, though I taste life's sweets, I still may be
> Athirst for immortality!

This compromise resolves the old conflict between nature and art:
nature is still the antithesis of the artfulness of the courtier and the
man of affairs; but she is now 'nature methodiz'd', or perhaps
'nature taught art' – either the useful rural arts of the ploughman and
husbandman (as in Pope's poem), or else (a later version) the arts of
the landscape gardener, as in Shenstone's (1714–63) *Rural Elegance*:

> Whether we fringe the sloping hill
>   Or smooth below the verdant mead;
> Whether we break the falling rill
>   Or through meand'ring mazes lead;
> Or in the horrid bramble's room
> Bid careless groups of roses bloom;
> Or let some shelter'd lake serene
> Reflect flowers, woods, and spires, and brighten
>   all the scene.

When Pope (*Moral Essays*, IV) prophesies the end of Timon's lavish
villa, the 'nature' which succeeds it is not that of awe-inspiring
desolation, but of the cultivated cornfield:

> Another year shall see the golden ear
> Embrown the slope, and nod on the parterre,
> Deep harvests bury all his pride had plann'd,
> And laughing Ceres reassume the land.

The main strength of Augustan poetry about rural nature lies in its
contact with human values. At its best there is nothing trivial or cosy
about it. When this contact begins to weaken, the poetry sometimes becomes dilettante and emasculated; but the best of it has a
dignity and a detachment which make it both worthy of respect and
attractive.

One of the chief reasons for this is its freedom from selfishness.
Tate –

> ... would have business, but exempt from strife!
> A private, but an active life –

and John Pomfret (1667–1703), whose poem *The Choice* is another typical Augustan elaboration on Horace's second Epode, makes the point more explicitly:

> I'd have a clear and competent estate,
> Where I might live genteely, but not great:
> As much as I could moderately spend;
> A little more, sometimes, t'oblige a friend.
> Nor should the sons of poverty repine
> Too much at fortune, they should taste of mine...

This benevolent note, which echoes through the period in Pope's 'man of Ross' (*Moral Essays*, III) –

> He feeds yon alms-house, neat but void of state,
> Where Age and Want sit smiling at the gate,
> Him portion'd maids, apprentic'd orphans blest,
> The young who labour, and the old who rest –

and in Goldsmith's (1730–74) village parson (*The Deserted Village*, 159ff.) –

> Pleas'd with their tales, the good man learn'd to glow,
> And quite forgot their vices in their woe;
> Careless their merits or their faults to scan,
> His pity gave ere charity began –

is a reflection of the spirit of the age which saw the beginnings of most of the great philanthropic movements. It rings true, so long as it is not heard with the ear of the twentieth-century welfare state. Philanthropy does not, of course, make poetry; but false sentiment mars it. And it is worth noting that few Augustan poems can be described as sentimental.

To suppose, however, that the Augustan poets never contemplated the more forbidding aspects of nature, or that they were moved only by a field of ripening grain or a hillside dotted with sheep, would be quite wrong. On the contrary, throughout the period there runs a cult of nature's more awful solemnities, clearly distinguishable in such poems as Parnell's *Night Piece*, Gray's *Bard*, and Collins's *Ode on the Superstitions of the Scottish Highlands*. Some of the best poetry of Thomson's *Seasons* is inspired by the lonelier aspects of Teviotdale, and works such as Dyer's *Ruins of Rome* and Blair's *Grave* are meditations upon scenes of desolation. Some of these lie outside the scope of this chapter, but enough of their characteristics will be found in the poems which do come within our compass to make it clear that the range of sensitiveness was indeed as wide as the famous passage from *The Castle of Indolence* suggests:

> Sometimes the pencil, in cool airy halls
> Bade the gay bloom of vernal landskips rise,
> Or Autumn's varied shades imbrown the walls:
> Now the black tempest strikes the astonish'd eyes;
> Now down the steep the flashing torrent flies;
> The trembling sun now plays o'er ocean blue,
> And now rude mountains frown amid the skies;
> Whate'er Lorrain light touch'd with softening hue,
> Or savage Rosa dash'd, or learned Poussin drew.

Nevertheless, whatever the theme, the Augustan poet was always writing within the social context of his age. Whether the reflections he offers are the minute, practical ones of Green, or the vaster, more nebulous ones of Dyer, they are of a kind which the reader himself will have experienced. He does not aim at shocking his audience into awareness by insisting on his own individuality; he merges himself in the general consciousness of his readers, pointing to what they have in common and ignoring what separates them. This, rather than peculiarities of sensitivity or style, is what separates the Augustan poet from his Romantic successor.

The literary complement of this social awareness is a strong sense of tradition, and a genius for perceiving the relevance of past literature to contemporary themes. The Augustans valued their poetry as much for the literature from which it was derived as for anything novel the writer had to impart. Indeed, the newness of a poem like the *Elegy* or the *Ode to Evening* consists in the subtle relationship which the poet establishes between the experience of the past and that of his own day, creating thereby a sense of timelessness which is 'new' only in the sense that it is unique. In a way, therefore, it is true to say that Augustan poets looked at life through literature. But the description 'literary' which is so often bestowed on them takes no account of the 'literature' in question or of the intensity with which that literature was felt. As a term of critical reproach, 'literary' is useful to describe the kind of writer who takes refuge in the idiom of another age because he wishes to escape from the responsibilities of his own. So far from doing this, the Augustans turned to the poetry of Horace and Virgil – and of Horace in particular – because it seemed supremely significant for their own age, and because it did so well what, in their opinion, poetry ought to do – namely, express in memorable terms the community of ideas and feelings which alone made civilized existence possible. If, in our day, we find the poetry of Donne and Marvell most intensely apposite to our own experience because it stresses individuality of perception, the Augustans felt the poetry of Horace no less strongly because it did exactly the opposite.

The fact that they singled out Horace is, in itself, evidence of more than a merely dilettante intention. He is a poet whose style is essentially the product of his temper – a temper which is balanced, mature and manly. He lacks (or it might be truer to say he avoids) the poignancy of a poet such as Catullus; but this does not mean that he lacks feeling. The pathos of Catullus –

> cum semel nobis brevis occidit lux
> nox est una perpetua dormienda –

is intense because it is personal*: that of Horace –

> pallida mors aequo pulsat pede pauperum tabernas
> regumque turres† –

more diffused because more widely applicable. It is this balanced temper, and the grave, generalized phrasing which flows from it that the Augustans admired and attempted to reproduce in their own poetry.

Horace is pre-eminently the poet of general themes. His odes, apart from those on political subjects, treat of the pleasures of friendship, of rural solitude, the transience of human happiness, the folly of ambition, and so on – themes which have formed the common stock of reflection for the ordinary man in every age. These themes he touches with a remarkable delicacy of language and clarity of definition, giving to casual rumination the stamp of permanence. Thus, unlike the Romantic, he is a poet in accord with society, rend-

---

* Cf. Herrick, *Corinna*:

> So when or you or I are made
> A fable, song, or fleeting shade,
> All love, all liking, all delight
> Lies drowned with us in endless night.

† Shirley gives the sense, though with different imagery:

> Sceptre and crown must tumble down,
> And in dust be equal made
> With the poor crooked scythe and spade.

ering what is potentially poetic in others actually so. He is, in fact, the best exponent of his own maxim that the poet's task is to handle a common subject in a personal way.

The key to Horace's odes lies in their perfect decorum: not a stilted adherence to a critical code, but a delicate adjustment between language, metrical emphasis, thought, and feeling, which creates in turn the sense of harmony between poet and reader wherein the effect of such poetry generally lies. To pin this power of adjustment down to any particular function of poetic genius is impossible. Clearly it depends on a special kind of sensitiveness in the poet: equally it implies lively critical intelligence. Further, it is more likely to appear in an age in which the reader is willing to be pleased than in one in which he prefers to be shocked: in fact, an age in which the reader looks for what he knows in poetry rather than what he does not know. Above all, it demands on the part of both reader and poet an understanding of how much personal emotion a poem can bear without disturbing the balance. All these conditions are best summed up in the Augustan critical term 'judgement'.

Augustan insistence on proportion allows, it is true, little scope for that presentation of the unique nature of an emotional experience which is often so moving in other poetry. But if the range of sensitivity is thus limited in one way, it is extended in another. In Gray's *Elegy* or Horace's poem on the death of Varus (*Odes*, I, 24) the expression of bereavement may be less personally poignant than in Donne's *Nocturnal* or Wordsworth's 'Lucy' poems; but this is because the expression has been framed to imply all such situations, and not simply the poet's own. The poet's sense of loss is held in balance against his awareness of himself as a member of his own audience. And the same attitude enables poetry whose most obvious characteristic is an elegant lightheartedness to include also a strain of genuine sadness. This is the case, for instance, with Horace's 'Quis multa gracilis...' and with some of Matthew Prior's (1664–1721) occasional pieces, whose tone though essentially that of polished irony can yet include an unaffected sadness:

> My bloom of life, my little flower
> Of beauty quickly lost its pride:
> For sever'd from its native bower
> It on thy glowing bosom died.

Yet car'd I not what might presage
Or with'ring wreath or fleeting youth:
Love I esteem'd more strong than age,
And time less innocent than truth.

Largely because of a mistaken division which has been made between
light and serious poetry, we have come to notice in poems like these
only the elegance, forgetting that elegance can be part of a valid
poetic attitude. In both these poems the elegance holds the balance
between the 'two ways of looking at things' which are opposed to
each other. That the movement of the verse is not dramatic, like the
movement of Donne's or Herbert's verse, is true enough; but this
again is part of the poet's attitude, for drama necessarily stresses one
emotion at the expense of others. Horace's poetry and the poetry of
the eighteenth-century Horatian tradition is not dramatic: it is essentially reflective. That is to say, the experiences which it treats are
not presented for the sake of their immediate impact, but for the
sake of generalized reflections (whether formulated or implied)
which flow from a balanced presentation of different emotional
states. The remoteness of their presentation is thus intentional. If there
is no agony or exaltation in these poems, this is not because the poet
does not understand agony or exaltation, but because he is concerned
with seeing these states in relation to others.

A good deal of space has been devoted to the poetry of Horace
because it is necessary to understand what is at the root of the
Augustan tradition of reflective verse. The Augustans modified the
Horatian approach to suit their own circumstances, but the habit of
observation for the sake of general reflection persists. It is to be seen
very clearly in Lady Winchilsea (1661–1720) who, partly because of
Wordsworth's commendation of the *Nocturnal Reverie*, is sometimes
regarded as an exception to the Augustan tradition:

In such a night when every louder wind
Is to its distant cavern safe confin'd;
And only gentle Zephyr fans its wings,
And lonely Philomel, still waking, sings;
Or from some tree, fam'd for the owl's delight,
She, hollowing clear, directs the wand'rer right;
In such a night, when passing clouds give place,
Or thinly veil the heaven's mysterious face;
When in some river overhung with green,

The waving moon and trembling leaves are seen;
When freshen'd grass now bears itself upright,
And makes cool banks to pleasing rest invite,
Whence springs the woodbine and the bramble-rose,
And where the sleepy cowslip shelter'd grows;
Whilst now a paler hue the foxglove takes,
Yet chequers still with red the dusky brakes,
When scatter'd glow-worms, but in twilight fine,
Show trivial beauties watch their hour to shine;
. . . .
When the loos'd horse, now as his pasture leads,
Comes slowly grazing thro' th' adjoining meads,
Whose stealing pace, and lengthen'd shade we fear,
Till torn-up forage in his teeth we hear;
When nibbling sheep at large pursue their food,
And unmolested kine rechew the cud;
When curlews cry beneath the village walls,
And to her straggling brood the partridge calls;
Their short-liv'd jubilee the creatures keep,
Which but endures whilst tyrant man does sleep;
When a sedate content the spirit feels,
And no fierce light disturbs, whilst it reveals,
But silent musings urge the mind to seek
Something too high for syllables to speak;
Till the free soul, to a compos'dness charm'd,
Finding the elements of rage disarm'd,
O'er all below, a solemn quiet grown,
Joys in th' inferior world and thinks it like her own:
In such a night let me abroad remain,
Till morning breaks, and all's confus'd again:
Our cares, our toils, our clamours are renew'd,
Or pleasures, seldom reach'd, again pursued.

The lines about the foxglove and the horse undoubtedly have the kind of sensitivity which characterizes, let us say, the *Ode to a Nightingale*. But this sensitivity is to be found in individual poets of every age: to stress it unduly here is to ignore the pervading tone and intention of the poem, which is that of moral generalization and not the crystallization of a unique experience. The point may be clearer if we set Lady Winchilsea's poem alongside another Augustan 'nocturnal reverie', Parnell's (1679–1718) *Night Piece on Death* . . .

How deep yon azure dyes the sky
Where orbs of gold unnumber'd lie,
While thro' their ranks in silver pride

349

The nether crescent seems to glide!
The slumb'ring breeze forgets to breathe,
The lake is smooth and clear beneath,
Where once again the spangl'd show
Descends to meet our eyes below.
The grounds which on the right aspire,
In dimness from the view retire:
The left presents a place of graves,
Whose wall the silent water laves.
That steeple guides thy doubtful sight
Among the livid gleams of night.
There pass, with melancholy state,
By all the solemn heaps of fate,
And think, as softly-sad you tread,
Above the venerable dead,
'Time was, like thee they life possess'd,
And time shall be, that thou shalt rest.'

Parnell is the more disciplined poet: the line of his thought moves with more certainty and his work is more obviously composed. Lady Winchilsea is more naïve, and perhaps more physically sensitive than Parnell, with the result that her poem has the effect of greater spontaneity, Parnell's of greater poise. But the temper of the two poems, evident in the firmness with which 'observation' is subordinated to 'reflection', is essentially the same. It springs from the belief that particular reactions can only be given significance in general reflections, and it is this attitude which stamps the whole Augustan tradition.

Within the tradition, as will become increasingly evident, there is scope for great variety. Indeed, it is one of the pleasures of reading this poetry to see the way in which the personalities of different poets emerge. Lady Winchilsea's *Petition for an Absolute Retreat*, for instance, is obviously in the tradition of the poems examined so far, yet it shows evidence of a personality markedly different from Pomfret's or Pope's:

Give me, Oh indulgent fate!
Give me yet, before I die,
A sweet, but absolute retreat,
'Mongst paths so lost, and trees so high,
That the world may ne'er invade,
Thro' such windings and such shade,
My unshaken liberty . . .

Lady Winchilsea is an example of a writer of poetry with a strong, lively, and well-stored mind, who is only intermittently a complete poet. At times she can be moving, as in the *Nocturnal Reverie*, or in the opening passages of her elegy for Sir William Twisden:

> But Oh! in vain; things void of sense we call,
> In vain implore the murmuring sound
> Of hollow groans from underneath the ground,
> Or court the loud lament of some steep water's fall;
> On things inanimate we would force
> Some share of our divided grief,
> Whilst Nature (unconcern'd for our relief)
> Pursues her settl'd path, her fixt and steady course...

But even in such passages it is the strength of the understanding which makes them impressive. For the most part she holds her reader by the quickness of her intelligence, and it is worth noting that she is able to do so because she is writing within the framework of a tradition where intelligence plays a major part. In any other she might have been a pedestrian versifier; as it is, she is eminently readable.

No poem could better illustrate this point about intelligence than Matthew Green's (1696–1737) *The Spleen*, in the direct line of Horatian retirement descending from Horace's second Epode and embracing both Pope's 'Happy the man' and Pomfret's *Choice*:

> A farm some twenty miles from town,
> Small, tight, salubrious and my own;
> Two maids; that never saw the town,
> A serving-man not quite a clown,
> A boy to help to tread the mow,
> And drive, while t'other holds the plough;
> A chief, of temper form'd to please,
> Fit to converse, and keep the keys;
> And better to preserve the peace,
> Commission'd by the name of niece;
> With understandings of a size
> To think their master very wise.
> May heaven (it's all I ask for) send
> One genial room to treat a friend,
> Where decent cupboard, little plate,
> Display benevolence, not state...

But, once again, it is obvious that we have here quite a different kind of personality from anything we have met so far. This is retorting

Horace on Horace, and Pomfret on Pomfret. There are signs of a
quick irony which show the writer on guard against the dangers of
mere wishfulness always lurking in this kind of writing. His reaction
to the natural scene is sensitive and vivid; but quite unlike that of
Lady Winchilsea:

> And may my humble dwelling stand
> Upon some chosen spot of land:
> A pond before full to the brim,
> Where cows may cool and geese may swim;
> Behind, a green like velvet neat,
> Soft to the eye, and to the feet;
> Where odorous plants in evening fair
> Breathe all around ambrosial air;
> From Eurus, foe to kitchen ground,
> Fenced by a slope with bushes crown'd,
> Fit dwelling for the feather'd throng
> Who pay their quit-rents with a song;
> With op'ning views of hill and dale,
> Which sense and fancy too regale,
> Where the half-cirque, which vision bounds,
> Like amphitheatre surrounds:
> And woods impervious to the breeze,
> Thick phalanx of embodied trees,
> From hills through plains of dusk array
> Extended far, repel the day.
> Here stillness, height, and solemn shade
> Invite, and contemplation aid:
> Here nymphs from hollow oaks relate
> The dark decrees and will of fate,
> And dreams beneath the spreading beech
> Inspire, and docile fancy teach;
> While soft as breezy breath of wind,
> Impulses rustle through the mind ...

This could almost be used as a catalogue of the external marks of
Augustan reflective poetry – retirement to the 'Horatian' farm, the
Virgilian beech tree as an aid to contemplation, the Horatian allusive-
ness, the 'Roman' vocabulary, and so on. But, as a counterbalance,
there is also a different, almost colloquial vocabulary which, with the
lively verse-movement, seems to mock the solemnities of 'half-
cirque' and 'amphitheatre'. Green is not a satirist: that he feels
directly the attraction of his theme is evident in his *Apology for the
Quakers:*

> O Contemplation! air serene
> From damps of sense and fogs of spleen!
> Pure mount of thought! thrice holy ground,
> Where grace, when waited for, is found . . .

But he is too subtle and mercurial a poet to be absolutely single-minded; and too honest to pretend to be so. The passage goes on:

> Well-natur'd, happy shade, forgive!
> Like you I think, but cannot live.
> Thy scheme requires the world's contempt,
> That, from dependence life exempt;
> And constitution fram'd so strong,
> This world's worst climate cannot wrong.
> Not such my lot, not Fortune's brat,
> I live by pulling off the hat,
> Compell'd by station every hour
> To bow to images of power;
> And in life's busy scenes immers'd
> See better things, and do the worst.

The few poems Green wrote provide a lively diversion within the Horatian tradition, and leave the reader always wishing he had lived longer and written more.

Another example of such variety is found in John Dyer (1700–58). His two poems *Grongar Hill* and *The Country Walk* are instances of what Johnson christened 'local poetry, of which,' he goes on to say, 'the fundamental subject is some particular landscape, to be poetically described, with addition of such embellishments as may be supplied by historical retrospection or incidental meditation'.[3]

To quote in order to demonstrate the common characteristics of Augustan reflective poetry would now be merely repetitive: *Grongar Hill* has all the customary landmarks – the praise of contentment, rural solitude as a stimulus to contemplation, the 'gothic' ruin which inspires sombre thoughts on human greatness, and so on. But unlike Lady Winchilsea and Matthew Green, Dyer's strength does not rest in his reflective powers: it lies in his power to record a visual experience:

> About his chequer'd sides I wind,
> And leave his brooks, and meads behind,
> And groves, and grottos where I lay,
> And vistas shooting beams of day:

Wider and wider spreads the vale
As circles in a smooth canal . . .
Still the prospect wider spreads,
Adds a thousand woods and meads,
Still it widens, widens still,
And sinks the newly risen hill . . .

The verse and the manner of description here clearly owe something to *L'Allegro*: but Dyer's eye is the eye of Wordsworth rather than of Milton:

Where am I, Nature? I descry
Thy magazine before me lie!
Temples! – and towns! – and towers! – and woods!
And hills! – and vales! – and fields! – and floods!
Crowding before me, edg'd around
With naked wilds, and barren ground . . .

Yet before hailing these and other lines from *The Country Walk* as one more manifestation of pre-Romanticism, it would be as well to note how Augustan they are. It is not just that Dyer is a lesser poet than Wordsworth and lacks 'a sense of something far more deeply interfused'; his whole attitude is Augustan. 'Nature' is the source of temples and towns, quite as much as of hills and vales. The whole picture is systematically composed, with orderly nature ringed about by the chaos of naked wilds and barren ground. It is a picture to be found repeatedly in Augustan poetry – in Matthew Green's poem *The Spleen*, for instance, or in Pope's *Windsor Forest*:

And mid the desert fruitful fields arise,
That, crown'd with tufted trees and waving corn,
Like verdant isles the sable waste adorn . . .

Especially it appears in the work of the eighteenth-century landscape gardener. Dyer's individual contribution to the tradition is his peculiar visual awareness – it might almost be called the technique of the expanding prospect – and of this something more will be said below. But his poetry is rooted in the Augustan tradition, and whoever fails to recognize this will miss much of its quality.

So far, an attempt has been made to indicate the general nature of the Augustan tradition of reflective poetry, and to show something of the scope which the tradition afforded for the expression of in-dividual genius. In what remains of the chapter I propose to look in some detail at four poems, namely Collins's *Ode to Evening*, Thomson's *Castle of Indolence*, Gray's *Elegy Written in a Country Churchyard*, and Shenstone's *Rural Elegance*. Of these, the *Elegy* represents the highest achievement of the Augustan reflective tradition, while each of the others illustrates at least some aspect of the tradition in its most notable form.

Nothing could better illustrate the diversity of effect to be found within the tradition than to read, one after the other, Dyer's *Grongar Hill* and Collins's (1721–59) *Ode to Evening*. These poems, whose material facts and literary sources are much alike, reveal two entirely different kinds of poetic communication. As has already been indicated, Dyer's impulse is to record the effect of what he sees. To avoid misunderstanding it would be as well to stress the word *effect*. *Grongar Hill* is no versified ordnance survey. The reader is always conscious of the poet's eye transmuting visual facts –

> How close and small the hedges lie,
> What streaks of meadow cross the eye –

into an aesthetic experience; and it is in the successful communication of the experience that the value of the poem lies. *Grongar Hill* is, indeed, a very personal poem. Its weakness, as well as its strength, rests in this – that one is continually being reminded of the duality of what is seen and the person seeing it.

With the *Ode to Evening* one is no longer conscious of the poet as an individual, or of some particular scene that is being observed, but only of separately recognizable elements coalescing in Collins's slow modulations to create a unique poem. Superficially the literary elements derive chiefly from Milton. Much of the vocabulary echoes *Lycidas*, and the solitude of

> ... the hut
> That from the mountain's side
> Views wilds and floods ...

is that of *Il Penseroso* rather than of Horace's Sabine farm. But the influence which informs the poem more deeply is that of such odes; as the fourth, ninth, and seventeenth of Horace's first book. Particularly the unfolding of the poem, with each stanza drifting into the next, recalls Horatian forms and is quite unlike the sharp transitions of *Il Penseroso* and *L'Allegro*. But the hold which this poem has on the reader lies in the way it gives permanence to a mood; a permanence which is achieved by the poet's power of realizing abstractions. Much nonsense has been written, even by Coleridge, about the Augustan habit of personification, a habit which is closely connected with the Aristotelian maxim that poetry should speak of general truths. While it is of course true that in some Augustan poetry personification offers a poor substitute for imagination, the effectiveness of the practice is completely vindicated by the strength and assurance of the poetry of Gray or Johnson or Goldsmith. With Collins, however, as with Horace, personification is much more than a means of vigorous generalizing: it is a mode of thought and feeling as inherent in his mind as paradox is in the mind of Donne. With him an abstraction at the opening of a poem gradually accumulates (usually through echoes of other poetry) wider and wider implications of feeling, until, at the poem's close, it is realized, not as an intellectual counter, but as the symbol of a state of mind. This process is to be seen at its finest in the *Ode to Simplicity*, in 'How sleep the brave', and best of all, in the *Ode to Evening*.

Despite its strong literary affinities, to analyse Collins's poetry in terms of such things is dangerous. The echoes of the *Ode to Evening* (like those of Milton's *Comus*) have been so altered by the poet's sensibility that their sources are of little more than historical importance. All that can be said with safety is that the poem is a perfect example of 'imitation', in which literary materials have been absorbed and recreated to suggest at once a continuing tradition and a unique awareness.

Compared with Collins's poetry, that of Thomson[4] (1700–48) presents fewer difficulties. Collins's mind is inward turning: his poetry, though it never loses touch with human values, has no strong practical bent. Thomson's bent is always social. *The Castle of Indolence*, a poem which uses the *Faerie Queene* stanza, was begun as a private Spenserian joke about the poet's friends. But like others (Gay and Shenstone among them), Thomson became the captive of an enchantment he had set out to deride.

The Augustans were two-minded about Spenser: they tended to regard his vocabulary as material for parody, but at the same time they recognized in him the strain of 'fancy' or 'imagination' which Johnson so well analyses in *Rasselas* and the Life of Collins. The strain of fancy, however, was never exclusively predominant in Augustan poetry at its best. Even in Collins's most 'fanciful' poem, the *Ode on the Superstitions of the Scottish Highlands*, it mingles with a strain of social reflection. Gray's *Bard*, despite its fantastic visioning, is concerned with English history, and it is this concern (as one realizes after long acquaintance with the poem) that holds the work together, giving it the measured progression which Gray's more flamboyant effects at first obscure. In *The Castle of Indolence* the two strains of fancy and social preoccupation are to be seen in their clearest form. The first canto, which describes the enchanted land of Indolence, gives full scope for Thomson's remarkable sensuousness and fantasy:

> And up the hills, on either side, a wood
> Of black'ning pines, ay waving to and fro,
> Sent forth a sleepy horror through the blood;
> And where this valley winded out, below,
> The murmuring main was heard, and scarcely heard, to flow.
>
> A pleasing land of drowsyhead it was:
> Of dreams that wave before the half-shut eye;
> And of gay castles in the clouds that pass,
> For ever flushing round a summer sky...

It would be difficult to find many parallels to this before *The Lotus Eaters*, and it is perhaps not surprising (though disheartening) that even Thomson's chief editor should say of the poem: 'There is poetry in the first canto; the second is mainly didactic.' Whatever 'didactic' may imply, the second canto, telling of the destruction of the enchanter by the Knight of Industry, forms the essential complement of the first, which, by itself, would be a freak, however delightful. The reader who is looking for surprises will prefer the first canto: the reader who values Augustan poetry for its own sake will sense that a piece of writing such as the one above needs something to complete it:

> Nor from his deep retirement banish'd was
> The amusing cares of rural industry.
> Still, as with graceful change the seasons pass,
> New scenes arise, new landskips strike the eye,
> And all the enliven'd country beautify:
> Gay plains extend where marshes slept before;

O'er recent meads the exulting streamlets fly;
Dark frowning heaths grow bright with Ceres' store;
And woods imbrown the steep, or wave along the shore.

As nearer to his farm you made approach,
He polish'd nature with a finer hand:
Yet on her beauties durst not art encroach;
'Tis art's alone these beauties to expand.
In graceful dance immingl'd, o'er the land
Pan, Pales, Flora and Pomona played...

Collins and Thomson represent, as it were, the introversive and extraversive poles of the poetic temperament; and it is evidence of the strength and flexibility of the Augustan tradition that it is able to accommodate both without distortion. In Gray's *Elegy*[5] the extremes merge to produce both an epitome and the masterpiece of the tradition. The occasion of the poem may have been the death of a friend, and the pattern may have been the 24th ode of Horace's first book: yet never do personal sorrow or pedantry intrude. Gray (1716–71) meditates on great general themes – mortality, humility, contentment – and the universality of his themes is reinforced by echoes from earlier literature – Horace, Ovid, Chaucer, Sir Thomas Browne, Milton, Waller all contribute. But the echoes are never verbal copies. Where Horace wrote 'What if you sang a strain more soothing than Thracian Orpheus, would the blood return to the empty face?...', Gray echoes him in such a way that one is aware only of the pressure of great poetry of the past, not of a specific instance:

Can storied urn, or animated bust,
Back to its mansion call the fleeting breath?
Can honour's voice provoke the silent dust,
Or flattery soothe the dull, cold ear of death?

Similarly, though the vocabulary is classical, words like 'rugged' and 'rude' implying their Latin as well as their more general English sense, the esoteric meaning is there only to strengthen the significance, never to display the poet's scholarship, or startle the reader.

The development of the poem is a movement from landscape images that are the common property of the Augustan tradition to philosophical musings which are no less prevalent; yet in no other poem does meditation flow from image with such naturalness. Gray's poetic temper is so perfectly adapted to this kind of writing that it would almost seem to have been evolved for him. In all his poetry the power of his imagination to endow a local setting with significant forms is evident. The figures which people the landscape of the *Elegy* have their counterpart in the 'idle progeny' of the Eton College ode and the 'insect youth' of the *Ode on the Spring*. In these, however, the effect is perhaps more strained. In the *Elegy* it is not until one looks closely that one realizes how much the strength of the poem owes to the way in which, after a passage of musing, the 'local' element returns, to lead to yet further comment. The effect of the poem is of a series of waves, each growing with almost imperceptible power, then sinking back to the original starting-point.

To isolate characteristics of style and thought is inevitably to falsify the view of this poem; for the triumph of the *Elegy* is the triumph of what I. A. Richards has called 'an exquisitely adjusted tone ... the perfect recognition of the writer's relation to the reader in view of what is being said and their feelings about it'.[6] And to say this is to say that the secret of the poem lies in the age as well as the poet. Only within the Augustan tradition (unless one should include Chaucer's age) could a poet's delicate perception of the contemporary intellectual and emotional atmosphere have found such complete expression.

The *Elegy* marks the culmination of the Augustan reflective tradition: its influence persists, notably in *The Deserted Village*, until the close of the century. But from 1750 onwards the main stream of the tradition – which runs from Shenstone, the landscape artist of the Leasowes and editor of Dodsley's *Collection*, to Cowper – shows a change of temper. Shenstone did not turn his back on Horace:

> From plains and woodlands; from the view
>> Of rural nature's blooming face,
>> Smit by the glare of rank and place,
> To courts the sons of fancy flew ...
>> Paternal acres please no more;
> Adieu the simple and sincere delight –
>> Th' habitual scene of hill and dale,
>> The rural herds, the vernal gale,
>> The tangl'd vetch's purple bloom,
>> The fragrance of the bean's perfume,
> Be theirs alone who cultivate the soil,
> And drink the cup of thirst, and eat the bread of toil.

With certain reservations this might have been written by Lady Winchilsea; and it is no more helpful to look for the germs of Romanticism in *Rural Elegance* than in her *Petition for an Absolute Retreat*. Nevertheless, even here a significant shift of emphasis is evident. For Lady Winchilsea, retirement was to afford scope for moral reflection:

> Thus from noise and crowds remov'd,
> Let each moment be improv'd;
> Every object still produce
> Thoughts of pleasure and of use ...

For the owner of Leasowes it was scope for the expression of sensibility:

> And sure there seem, of human kind
>   Some born to shun the solemn strife;
> Some for amusive tasks design'd,
>   To soothe the certain ills of life;
> Grace its lone vales with many a budding rose,
>   New founts of bliss disclose,
> Call forth refreshing shades, and decorate repose.

By comparison with Lady Winchilsea's tough intellectual fibre there is a languor about this which points to more than a difference between individual poets. It is part of a shift of emphasis which marks all forms of literature in the second half of the century – a shift from moral and social issues towards the cultivation of feeling for its own sake.

'Sensibility' is not, of course, the discovery of the poets of the later eighteenth century; but in the earlier poets it was incidental, in the later ones it is paramount. In Shenstone's Arcadia, moral and social values are of secondary importance to feeling:

> Why brand these pleasures with the name
> Of soft, unsocial toils, indolence and shame?
> Search but the garden, or the wood,
>   Let yon admir'd carnation own
> Not all was meant for raiment or for food,
>   Not all for needful use alone;
> There, while the seeds of future blossoms dwell,
> 'Tis colour'd for the sight, perfum'd to please the smell.

Johnson's most frequently quoted comment on Shenstone is both unkind and untrue. 'Shenstone's pleasure,' he says, 'was all in the eye;

he valued what he valued merely for its looks; nothing raised his indignation more than to ask if there were fish in his water.' Nevertheless, it puts a finger on an important point.

The qualities of Shenstone's poetry – selective simplicity of language and a sense of appositeness in the use of traditional forms – are essentially Augustan and classical. His classicism, however, is not Chesterfield's rigid subservience to 'the modes'; it is of a kind in which it is possible to be familiar and at ease because not entirely dependent on external standards: and in this Shenstone contributes something to the Augustan tradition of which it was perhaps in need. Yet the gain is offset by a loss. Poetry which has no strong intellectual content is seldom emotionally vigorous. By his preference of 'feeling' to 'understanding' Shenstone paradoxically robs Augustan poetry of much of its robustness. The air of Arcadia is more rarefied, and so more delicate, than that of Grongar Hill. But it is also less fortifying.

NOTES

1. A. R. Humphreys, *William Shenstone* (Cambridge, 1937).

2. For an eighteenth-century modification of this kind of poem, see John Gay's *Rural Sports* (*Gay's Poetical Works*, Oxford, 1926).

3. *Lives of the Poets* (Life of Denham). Johnson makes Denham's *Cooper's Hill* (q.v.) the first of this type of poem. See also Samuel Garth's *Poem of Claremont* and Pope's *Windsor Forest*. Nearly all the poems mentioned in this chapter have some 'local' characteristics – especially Gray's *Elegy* and Goldsmith's *Deserted Village*.

4. Thomson's *The Seasons* is the great achievement of the Augustan 'Georgic' tradition. 'Winter', at least, should be read. See also the same poet's *Solitude*.

5. For the growth of this poem, see *The Augustan Reprint Society: Publication No. 31* (1951). This contains the 1751 text and a facsimile of the Eton College MS., as well as a valuable introduction by George Sherburn.

6. *Practical Criticism* (1929), 207. See the whole passage, and also the further discussion at 252f.

OLIVER GOLDSMITH

BORIS FORD

In his last, unfinished poem, *Retaliation*, Oliver Goldsmith (*c.* 1730–74) looks round the feast and sees each guest as choice dish: 'Our Dean shall be venison . . . Our Burke shall be tongue . . .' And himself he sees as 'Magnanimous Goldsmith, a goosberry fool'. The line, taken from that minor masterpiece of magnanimous satire, could serve as his epitaph: Goldsmith was indeed such an incongruous mixture and therein perhaps lies the clue to his quizzical success. He himself thought poorly of his chances with posterity, yet though he was constantly depressed by the reception he received in his lifetime, he has enjoyed a steady popularity from his own day to the present. Unostentatious as a writer and gauche as a social being, he found himself exclaiming more than once that 'the public will never do me justice; whenever I write anything, they make a point to know nothing about it'. And yet he became a close friend of Dr Johnson and Sir Joshua Reynolds, of Burke and Garrick; and as a member of the Literary Club of nine, which met every Monday night at the Turk's Head in Soho, he was an accepted figure in his own right (Boswell, by contrast, was admitted to the Club long after Goldsmith, and then only at the insistence of Johnson).

In spite of all he said and expected, Goldsmith's main works, when they eventually appeared, were immediately acclaimed: first, *The Traveller* (1764), which Johnson declared the finest poem since Pope; then *The Vicar of Wakefield* (1766), which in five months went into three editions; next, the immediately popular *The Deserted Village* (1770); and finally, his comedy *She Stoops to Conquer* (1773), which he had so long struggled to have performed. These four works earned him a contemporary reputation second only to that of Dr Johnson himself, and since then, he has seldom been out of favour. He and his writings survived from an age that was subsequently thought artificial and even superficial; and they may have survived because of the seemingly un-Augustan qualities with which they are imbued. It is significant that the word most commonly used to characterize Goldsmith's writings is 'charm'.

Nonetheless, though some of his more renowned anthology-pieces, such as the Lamb-like *A City Night-Piece*, undoubtedly tend to disguise the fact, Goldsmith was essentially an Augustan and his virtues as well as his weaknesses are those of his age. In his life as a hack who turned his hand from Ancient to Natural History and back again, he was a typical author of the London of his time. Always struggling against the clock to put together new work for the press, Goldsmith presents a wretched picture of a considerable native talent squandered on ephemeral work. As he himself wrote in his *Enquiry into the Present State of Polite Learning in Europe* (1759):

> The author, when unpatronized by the Great, has naturally recourse to the bookseller. There cannot be, perhaps, imagined a combination more prejudicial to taste than this. It is the interest of one to allow as little for writing, and of the other to write as much, as possible; accordingly, tedious compilations, and periodical magazines, are the result of their joint endeavours. In these circumstances, the author bids adieu to fame, writes for bread, and for that only. Imagination is seldom called in; he sits down to address the venal muse with the most phlegmatic apathy; and, as we are told of the Russians, courts his mistress by falling asleep in her lap. His reputation never spreads in a wider circle than that of the trade, who generally value him, not for the fineness of his compositions, but the quantity he works off in a given time.

He spoke feelingly: for instance his name as author nowhere appeared in the *Enquiry* when it was first published. For years he was accustomed to a life of hardship and poverty and, above all, of indignity, and this was only aggravated by his inability to keep any money in his pockets for longer than a few hours, through his excessive generosity or his weakness for magnificent clothes. The Rev. Thomas Percy, who was later to become celebrated for his 'relics' and ballads, visited Goldsmith at the age of thirty:

> I called on Goldsmith at his lodgings in March, 1759, and found him writing his *Enquiry* in a miserable dirty-looking room, in which there was but one chair; and when, from civility, he resigned it to me, he himself was obliged to sit in the window. While we were conversing together, some one tapped gently at the door, and being desired to come in, a poor ragged little girl, of a very becoming demeanour, entered the room, and dropping a courtesy, said, 'My mamma sends her compliments and begs the favour of you to lend her a chamber-pot full of coals.'

For all his awkwardness in company, he was liable among friends to be irresponsibly gay, just as, among the needy, he was certain to be irresponsibly generous. Towards the end of his life, a young countryman of his came to him for help and Goldsmith, who was as usual much harassed at that time, gave him work as his amanuensis. Later this M'Donnell wrote: 'I saw him only in his bland and kind moods, with a flow, perhaps an overflow, of the milk of human kindness for all who were in any manner dependent upon him.' In the end, for all the recognition that came his way, Goldsmith's health collapsed under the strain, and he died miserably and in poverty at the young age of about forty-four.[1]

The wonder is that his writings remained so free of bitterness – so little 'schooled by continued adversity into a hatred of their kind'. Even in *The Vicar of Wakefield*, which is a tale of unending woe if ever there was one, there is no recrimination and the tone is not particularly personal in its pressure. Indeed, the character in that novel most closely modelled on Goldsmith himself is the elder son, George, who introduces his long account of misfortune on the Continent (much of it is autobiographical) with the comment that 'the less kind I found fortune at one time, the more I expected from her another, and being now at the bottom of her wheel, every new revolution might lift, but could not depress me.'

The basis of Goldsmith's distinction as a writer is his straightforward simplicity and the unassuming elegance of his style. These qualities, though they may have come to him easily, were nonetheless quite deliberately cultivated. His *Enquiry* ends with a clear statement of his beliefs on the nature of good writing:

As our gentlemen writers have it therefore so much in their power to lead the taste of the times, they may now part with the inflated stile that has for some years been looked upon as fine writing, and which every young writer is now obliged to adopt, if he chuses to be read. They may now dispense with the loaded epithet, and dressing up of trifles with dignity. For to use an obvious instance, it is not those who make the greatest noise with their wares in the streets, that have the most to sell. Let us, instead of writing finely, try to write naturally. Not hunt after lofty expressions to deliver mean ideas; nor be for ever gaping, when we only mean to deliver a whisper.

This could have been written in no other age than Goldsmith's: it has the easy deportment that bespeaks the Augustan virtues. And though it closely accords with Johnson's advice to a budding writer – that he should go through his work and whenever he came on a passage that struck him as uncommonly fine, he should strike it out – yet one feels that Goldsmith followed his own precepts more successfully than his great contemporary. Partly, no doubt, this was due to his own temperament. But also, Goldsmith had the advantage, from the stylistic point of view, of not being much given to speculation or deep self-searching, so that he seldom needed to strike a profound any more than a sublime note. He pursued, and most notably in his essays, an even and genial tone that makes him nearly always easy, if seldom exciting, to read. For instance:

Whatever may be the merits of the English in other sciences, they seem peculiarly excellent in the art of healing. There is scarcely a disorder incident to humanity, against which they are not possessed of a most infallible anti-dote. The professors of other arts confess the inevitable intricacy of things; talk with doubt, and decide with hesitation, but doubting is entirely unknown in medicine; the advertising professors here delight in cases of difficulty; be the disorder never so desperate or radical, you will find numbers in every street, who, by leveling a pill at the part affected, promise a certain cure without loss of time, knowledge of a bedfellow, or hindrance of business.

(It is an irony to reflect that Goldsmith, himself a doctor of sorts, almost certainly hastened his own end by insisting on 'leveling a pill' at his own affected system, a pill of quite the wrong character for his purpose.) This passage, which is chosen pretty well at random from *The Citizen of the World* (1762), is typical of Goldsmith's Grub-Street manner. Its graceful flow is unmistakable. The irony is gentler and less complex than Pope's or Swift's, perhaps because Goldsmith was generally less involved in his subject-matter than they were. It is an irony founded upon a conception of life reverting to, or at least implying, good sense as the true basis of polite manners and social decorum.

It is this, perhaps, that attracted him so much to Beau Nash and that makes his *Life of Richard Nash* (1762) so sympathetic, albeit so judicious, a study. Partly, of course, Goldsmith was envious of the creator and monarch of fashionable Bath who, though he 'was clumsey, too large and awkward, and his features harsh, strong, and peculiarly irregular; yet even, with these disadvantages, he made love, became an universal admirer of the sex, and was universally admired'.

In fact, however, Goldsmith's own lack of brilliance or cleverness made his writings all the more limpid, and his good sense is carried without any flourish of self-importance or self-approbation. The essay which touched genially on affairs of the day ideally suited his style, and if his writings in this manner are not much read now, that is essentially a tribute to the good journalism that they are: they attempted no more than was appropriate, and Goldsmith would have been the last to suppose that they might be read centuries after they were written.

The Vicar of Wakefield is, without doubt, the work on which Goldsmith's popularity rests. It has been successful from the day of publication until the present – though interestingly enough it lay for two years in the hands of his bookseller and was only brought out after the triumph of his poem *The Traveller*: and Johnson, who had not thought very much of its prospects, observed that sixty guineas was 'no mean price' for Goldsmith to receive for it. The novel's great strength is its quality of stoical resignation. Washington Irving's wholly sympathetic account is probably typical of most people's reactions, when he writes that Goldsmith 'has given them [his scenes and characters] as seen through the medium of his own indulgent eye, and has set them forth with the colourings of his good head and heart.'

But if this prescription was capable of producing great art in the case of Dickens, it was less successful in the case of Goldsmith himself. For it is his very goodness of head and heart that makes it hard to be altogether satisfied with the novel today. Or rather, the goodness portrayed in the Vicar and his family is of too naïve a character; one might almost say that the book suffers for want of the Augustan poise that Goldsmith reveals elsewhere. In the first place, the novel is unusually short, and this has the effect of making its sequence of tumultuous calamities seem rushed and thus superficial. Within a few pages, for instance, the Vicar, who is lodged in jail, learns that one of his daughters has died; then word is brought that his other daughter has been 'carried off by ruffians'; and lastly his son George, whom he had supposed safe with his regiment, is suddenly brought in 'all bloody, wounded, and fettered with the heaviest irons'. This wealth of incident is both underprepared and underdeveloped, and it calls forth yet more of the resignation with which the Vicar has met his previous misfortunes; except that on this occasion the Vicar treats the assembled prisoners, who 'loved to hear my counsel', to a lengthy 'exhortation' on the 'equal dealings of providence', a sermon which is tedious even by his standards.

This is not, as it may at first appear, a trifling criticism, for the radical weakness of the novel lies in Goldsmith's ambiguous attitude towards the Vicar himself. The novel, because it is related by him in the first person, is never able to present the Vicar with the gentle irony that he deserves. The 'exhortation', for example, is tedious but without any suggestion that the reader need wonder at tediousness spun out to such a length. Elsewhere, the Vicar reveals an unbearable smugness: on one occasion he finds his daughters dressed for church in what seems to him unbecoming splendour and 'frippery', and he therefore protests strongly, remarking that ' "the nakedness of the indigent world may be cloathed from the trimmings of the vain" ' He continues:

This remonstrance had the proper effect; they went with great composure, that very instant, to change their dress; and the next day I had the satisfaction of finding my daughters, at their own request, employed in cutting up their trains into Sunday waistcoats for Dick and Bill, the two little ones, and what was still more satisfactory, the gowns seemed improved by this curtailing.

This note is pervasive, and in this respect the novel is strangely unlike Goldsmith's other writings, which are seldom solemn-faced and decorous – and incidentally this un-ironic passage comes oddly from Goldsmith, who could never resist decking himself out in fine clothes and never appeared to suffer any pangs of conscience on this account.

The other element in the novel that jars today is its note of romantic artificiality. Consider, for instance, the Vicar and his family enjoying a picnic:

On these occasions, our two little ones always read for us, and they were regularly served after we had done. Sometimes, to give a variety to our amusements, the girls sung to the guitar; and while they thus formed a little concert, my wife and I would stroll down the sloping field, that was embellished with blue-bells and centaury, talk of our children with rapture, and enjoy the breeze that wafted both health and harmony.

This picture of what the Vicar later calls 'vacant hilarity' is innocent enough, no doubt; yet it has about it too much of the set-piece, of the formal group-portrait in costume, where Nature is painted in to suit the occasion. Moreover, the words themselves – 'embellished', 'rapture', 'wafted' – tend to be cloying, so that though one knows well enough that the confection is only meant to be simple and innocent, to the palate it tastes altogether too sweet. Moreover the concert is described as lending *'variety'*, yet within a dozen lines we read that 'our young musicians began their *usual* concert', and this lack of precision blurs the picture of the reality that Goldsmith clearly intended it to have. Because of this, the Vicar's family remains two-dimensional. His two daughters are differentiated, to be sure, but one finds oneself having to turn back to their first introduction to remind oneself which is which, and then concluding that it does not matter much anyway. Similarly, when the daughters are abducted, one notes the horror and sorrow of the Vicar and his wife without feeling moved to share it. And this is inevitably a blemish, because de-tachment, even disinterest, is not at all what Goldsmith intended, even though one must add, in all fairness, that he did not intend indulgence either. In *The Vicar of Wakefield*, Goldsmith failed to work out the appropriate mode for his story, with the result that the characters are too generalized and they develop with all too little convincing life – especially when compared with the palpable and yet lively impostures of the cast of *She Stoops to Conquer*, a play which may not be much in the way of literature but at least has an abundance of negative virtues. Compared with Fielding or Jane Austen, between whom Goldsmith the novelist seems to stand in an unsuccessful sort of way, this novel is ultimately a slight, if 'charming', creation: it is, as Henry James aptly described it, 'the spoiled child of our literature'.

If this seems a severe judgement, it is one that helps to define the distinction of Goldsmith's major poems, particularly his *The Deserted Village*, for they succeed where the novel fails. Early on in the novel, there is a passage that is unusually apt, though without thrusting itself out of context. After losing their money, the Vicar and his family move to a simpler and more modest living, and this new home is introduced thus:

The place of our retreat was in a little neighbourhood, consisting of farmers, who tilled their own grounds, and were equal strangers to opulence and poverty. As they had almost all the conveniences of life within themselves, they seldom visited towns or cities in search of superfluity. Remote from the polite, they still retained the primaeval simplicity of manners; and frugal by habit, they scarce knew that temperance was a virtue. They wrought with cheerfulness on days of labour; but observed festivals as intervals of idleness and pleasure. They kept up the Christmas carol, sent true love-knots on Valentine morning, eat pancakes on Shrovetide, shewed their wit on the first of April, and religiously cracked nuts on Michaelmas eve. Being apprized of our approach, the whole neighbourhood came out to meet their minister, drest in their finest cloaths, and preceded by a pipe and tabor: A feast also was provided for our reception, at which we sate chearfully down; and what the conversation lacked in wit, was made up in laughter.

The feeling and manner of this description is very close to *The Deserted Village*. It is particularized, and yet the detail does not crystallize into sharp individuality, but rather tends to suggest a generalized reality. The 'they' of this passage, though ostensibly the Vicar's new parishioners, seem mainly to be embodiments of a way of life amidst which he and his family will live. One feels no need to have them introduced by name, or even to see them as distinct people. It is this quality of elegiac generalization that one finds in *The Deserted Village* and it is what gives the poem a strength that it shares, in many respects, with Gray's great *Elegy*.

Goldsmith was a most assured poet, and it is no wonder that *The Traveller* should have been so well received. It was the first of his works to appear under his own name, and it established him as an author in his own right.[2] Above all, it established him as a great Augustan poet, revealed in the judicious tone, the unruffled movement, the urbane and fluent control of the couplet:

> To men of other minds my fancy flies,
> Embosom'd in the deep where Holland lies,
> Methinks her patient sons before me stand,
> Where the broad ocean leans against the land,
> And, sedulous to stop the coming tide,
> Lift the tall rampire's artificial pride.
> Onward methinks, and diligently slow
> The firm connected bulwark seems to grow;
> Spreads its long arms amidst the watry roar,
> Scoops out an empire, and usurps the shore.
> While the pent ocean rising o'er the pile,
> Sees an amphibious world beneath him smile;
> The slow canal, the yellow blossom'd vale,
> The willow tufted bank, the gliding sail,
> The crowded mart, the cultivated plain,
> A new creation rescued from his reign.

This could not be done better, or more exactly. Its imagery, in particular, is so fitting as to draw no attention to itself, and yet it wonderfully conveys the sense of the 'diligently slow', patient creation of the amphibious world of Holland, carved, as it were, out of the sea and yet still part of it, an impression of the 'broad ocean' transformed into the 'slow canal' much as wild nature was being transformed and landscaped in contemporary England. At the same time, Roger Lonsdale is surely right when he describes the poem's survey of various nations as 'essentially imaginative' and its true concerns as being with 'moral landscapes'.

The theme of *The Deserted Village* is related to some lines towards the end of *The Traveller*, lines which come very close, as does the whole of the later poem, to Goldsmith's sense of being himself an exile:

> . . . Seen opulence, her grandeur to maintain,
> Lead stern depopulation in her train,
> And over fields where scatter'd hamlets rose,
> In barren solitary pomp repose?
> Have we not seen at pleasure's lordly call,
> The smiling long-frequented village fall?
> Beheld the duteous son, the sire decay'd,
> The modest matron, and the blushing maid,
> Forc'd from their homes, a melancholy train,
> To traverse climes beyond the western main;
> Where wild Oswego spreads her swamps around,
> And Niagara stuns with thund'ring sound?

Goldsmith was a voluntary exile, of course, and he apparently had no overwhelming urge to return to his own village of Lissoy in Ireland, which some of his biographers have diligently identified as the source of the Village in the poem. But this is, on the whole, rather beside the point, for what counts is Goldsmith's *sense* of the idealized village community and of the exile inevitably brought about by the 'barren solitary pomp' (a line of great and measured denunciation). Though *The Deserted Village* seems in many ways to continue and complete *The Traveller*, in that the earlier poem relates the poet's wanderings in search of more congenial modes of life and the later poem presents us with the intimate 'long-frequented' world from which he first set out and to which there can be no return because

it has fallen into waste and decay, its tone is notably more secure
and its mode is more clearly established.

The poem opens with an evocation of the Village as it once had
been, or ideally might have been. The poet picks out the details in
these lines:

> How often have I paused on every charm,
> The sheltered cot, the cultivated farm,
> The never failing brook, the busy mill,
> The decent church that topt the neighbouring hill,
> The hawthorn bush, with seats beneath the shade,
> For talking age and whispering lovers made;
> How oft have I blest the coming day,
> When toil remitting lent its turn to play,
> And all the village train from labour free
> Led up their sports beneath the spreading tree;
> While many a pastime circled in the shade,
> The young contending as the old surveyed;
> And many a gambol frolicked o'er the ground,
> And slights of art and feats of strength went round;
> And still as each repeated pleasure tired,
> Succeeding sports the mirthful band inspired;
> The dancing pair that simply sought renown
> By holding out to tire each other down;
> The swain mistrustless of his smutted face,
> While secret laughter tittered round the place;
> The bashful virgin's side-long looks of love,
> The matron's glance that would those looks reprove:
> These were thy charms, sweet village; sports like these,
> With sweet succession, taught even toil to please;
> These round thy bowers their chearful influence shed,
> These were thy charms – But all these charms are fled.

The adjectives in the first few lines have an effect less of precision
than of generalization: if they are exact, it is with the exactness of the
familiar rather than, as with Donne, of the previously unperceived.
Similarly with the life of the village, 'When toil remitting lent its
turn to play': the sports, though detailed indeed, are less the sports
of a distinctively individual village (such as Lissoy) than of the
idea of a village, of an ideally familiar village. If this generalizing
tendency of the words seemed to weaken the novel, because there the
narrative needed a greater fullness of personal detail, in the poem the

371

same tendency emerges as a strength, because here Goldsmith is not concerned with narrative but with recalling to his readers a common heritage, a scene bred in the bone.

The poem progresses – though, in fact, its total impact is less one of progress than of a picture of past and present perceived all at once – in a series of ebbings and flowings. The village is recalled in its old perfection, and then seen in its present 'shapeless ruin'; recalled again in fresh detail, as 'Remembrance wakens with all her busy train' – a memory above all of sound, of the milk-maid singing, the herd lowing, the gabbling geese, the watchdog's baying voice, the loud laugh, all interleaved with the nightingale's song; and then again banished in the face of today's reality – today when 'the sounds of population fail', when there are 'No cheerful murmurs' but only 'yon widowed, solitary thing', who in her present wretchedness of life is become 'The sad historian of the pensive plain'. The change is felt in the shift from noise to silence, and in the way the movement of the lines slows down to a heavy inertia.

Thus are evoked, like bastions of common virtue and worth from a bygone age, the village preacher and village schoolmaster and the village inn. Again the precise details of the scene evoke a hallowed familiarity; Goldsmith's personal memories of his father and his teacher undoubtedly provided the undercurrent of regret, but he has not left us with individual portraiture. Because of this, the verse is able to move without transition into the lines of general denunciation, in which the poet speaks with a full-dress Augustan weight and poise:

> Yes! let the rich deride, the proud disdain,
> These simple blessings of the lowly train;
> To me more dear, congenial to my heart,
> One native charm, than all the gloss of art;
> Spontaneous joys, where Nature has its play,
> The soul adopts, and owns their first born sway;
> Lightly they frolic o'er the vacant mind,
> Unenvied, unmolested, unconfined.
> But the long pomp, the midnight masquerade,
> With all the freaks of wanton wealth arrayed,
> In these, ere triflers half their wish obtain,
> The toiling pleasure sickens into pain;
> And, even while fashion's brightest arts decoy,
> The heart distrusting asks, if this be joy.

This denunciation, recalling Pope's *Epistle to Boyle* on 'the Use of Riches', is founded on a conviction that the natural order, which consists of Nature cultivated into fruitfulness by Man, has been despoiled by 'the freaks of wanton wealth':

> The robe that wraps his limbs in silken sloth,
> Has robbed the neighbouring fields of half their growth.

– the word 'sloth' comes suddenly in place of the expected 'cloth', with a hissing, despising force. And the passage ends with the terse epitaph:

> The country blooms – a garden, and a grave.

Goldsmith's verse moves, almost always, at a deceptively even pace. The shifts of tone and emphasis are all but imperceptible, and they only seldom startle. Yet, within this even tenor, the verse mounts in intensity and then sinks back as the poet's vision moves between past and present. Only very occasionally does a single line stand out, like a sudden unassimilable protest, as in the lines where the poet is rejecting the city as a possible refuge for the dispossessed peasantry:

> The dome where Pleasure holds her midnight reign,
> Here, richly deckt, admits the gorgeous train;
> Tumultuous grandeur crowds the blazing square,
> The rattling chariots clash, the torches glare.
> Such scenes like these no troubles e'er annoy!
> Sure these denote one universal joy!
> Are these thy serious thoughts? – Ah, turn thine eyes
> Where the poor houseless shivering female lies.
> She once, perhaps, in village plenty blest,
> Has wept at tales of innocence distrest.

The long-drawn open-vowelled words of the earlier lines, the thick opulence that is conveyed through the sound of 'gorgeous' and 'grandeur', are brought up short in the line 'Where the poor houseless shivering female lies', whose emphatically slow concentration seems to prevent any eye escaping the harsh human tragedy before it. And the 'village plenty' of the following line seems to acquire from the earlier passages of the poem a deep-rooted richness, a harvest richness of life and humanity, that contrasts damningly with the callous opulence of the pleasure dome. But this suddenly vivid detail gives way again to the more generalized picture of the earlier sections of the poem, as the poet sees the 'poor exiles' leaving the village: the 'good old sire', his 'lovely daughter', and her 'fond husband' are not clichés, not lay-figures so much as symbols of a lost order. Indeed, within a few more lines the poet speaks of seeing 'the rural virtues leave the land', the abstract virtues of 'contented toil', 'hospitable care', 'kind connubial tenderness', 'piety', 'steady loyalty', 'faithful love'; and yet, such a felt reality do these abstractions now have in the poem, that the poet is able to imbue them, in a couplet that echoes the earlier rhyme, with a shadowy solidity:

> Downward they move, a melancholy band,
> Pass from the shore, and darken all the strand.

So, by the end, the evoked scene of the village has given way to the virtues it was felt to embody, and 'sweet Poetry' is summoned to

> Teach erring man to spurn the rage of gain;
> Teach him, that states of native strength possess,
> Tho' very poor, may still be very blest.

The moral does not seem out of place, even though it may well seem unnecessary, for the poem has all along revolved implicitly around just such a generalized statement of its theme.

Ultimately *The Deserted Village* represents a triumph of manner, but one has immediately to add that it was a manner that was the product of a settled attitude to life. In other hands, the hands of some of his contemporaries as well as of most of his successors, the theme might have been sentimentally done, its nostalgia overlaid with a coating of wistful sentiment. But Goldsmith was not in the least of a melting disposition, though he was of an intensely sympathetic one. If he wrote nothing of the very first quality and a good deal that was trivial, he comes down to us as one of the central writers of his age, of a geniality and humanity that single him out among his contemporaries. 'Let not his frailties be remembered, he was a very great man': what is significant about Johnson's verdict is not that he was, of course, exaggerating, but that there was something about magnanimous, gooseberry fool Goldsmith that impelled him so to do.

NOTES

1. Washington Irving, in his sympathetic biography, relates that when Goldsmith died, he was mourned not only by his peers but also by 'the

lamentations of the old and infirm, and the sobbing of women, poor objects of his charity to whom he had never turned a deaf ear, even when struggling himself with poverty'.

2. Tom Davis, in his introduction to his edition of the poems and plays (1975) notes that 'the literary elite of the day paid him the interesting tribute of refusing to believe he wrote it: it was so good, they thought, it must be Johnson's'.

SHAKESPEARE CRITICISM

P. A. W. COLLINS

'Till of late years,' wrote Thomas Rymer in 1674, 'England was as free from critics as it is from wolves.' Rymer was exaggerating, but during this period criticism does increase in bulk and quality. In formal treatises and (more often) in essays and prefaces to new poems and plays and to reprints of old ones, ideas on the principles of writing were set forth, defined, and clarified, and a determined effort was made to assess both current literature and the inheritance from the past; for England now had a literature which could stand comparison with the other great modern literatures, Italian and French, and even (some claimed) with the Ancient. Shakespeare was the writer most generally considered our champion against the masters of other literatures, and the present essay will take most of its examples from Shakespeare-criticism from Dryden to Johnson. When a large subject is to be discussed in a short space, some drastic selection is necessary, and Shakespeare is (as Pope wrote) 'of all English poets ... the fairest and fullest subject for criticism'. All the major critics discuss him, and their critical principles and methods are exemplified in and may be inferred from what they say of him. And it is during this period that Shakespeare was first systematically criticized and accorded the rank he has since retained. By 1765, Johnson could claim for him 'the dignity of an ancient'; veneration for him was, as another critic wrote in the same year, part of the national religion. A century before, Dryden was being adventurous in asserting that Shakespeare 'of all modern, and perhaps ancient poets, had the largest and most comprehensive soul', and at his best towered 'high above the rest of poets'.

Dryden's *Essay on Dramatic Poesy* (1668), where this remark appears, was not an academic exercise: Dryden wrote dramas besides criticizing them, and his judgement of Shakespeare had implications for his practice as a dramatist. The theatres had reopened in 1660, after nearly twenty years, and during this time a good deal of theorizing about the drama and its 'Rules' had been produced in France. As Pope wrote later, in 1711,

> ... Critic-learning flourish'd most in France.
> The rules a nation, born to serve, obeys ...
> But we, brave Britons, foreign laws despis'd ...
> (*Essay on Criticism*, 712–15)

The political analogy used here was often invoked, and the chauvinism which Pope displays makes his praise, a few lines later, for 'the sounder few [who] here restor'd Wit's fundamental laws' sound half-hearted. These 'Rules' had been known, but little regarded, in Shakespeare's England; by 1660, however, Corneille had shown that they worked, and his success, together with the prestige of France as the centre of European civilization, presented a challenge to the English native dramatic tradition. The most prominent Rule of drama was that the 'three Unities' should be observed: the plot should develop one action, with no irrelevancies or sub-plots, and this action should be completed in one day and one place. This Rule was not so arbitrary and pedantic as many Englishmen then, and since, have thought it, though a scrupulous and unimaginative 'working to rule' could be, in drama then as in Trades Unions now, awkward rather than effective. But, properly understood, the discipline of the Unities was a wholesome reaction against laxity and incoherence of construction, and could help a Racine to economy of means and concentration of effect.[1]

This notion of having 'Rules' for writers is alien to us now, and so is another practice of the time – looking to the literature of the past for 'models'. Some explanation may be helpful. To Dryden, as to his fellows, it seemed self-evident, that 'if nature is to be imitated [and this was the aim of drama], then there is a rule for imitating nature rightly; otherwise there may be an end, and no means conducing to it'. Ancient Greek and Latin literature was still the common standard of reference for modern Europe; to emulate it, and the civilization which produced it, was the height of achievement. Not implausibly, many critics recommended more or less direct imitation of the Ancients. Horace, in his *Ars Poetica*, an influential document at this time, had advised the ancient Romans to imitate the Greeks, and Virgil's success had shown what could be done by following in

Homer's footsteps. But the poet need not confine himself to imitating particular writers or works, which inevitably had some faults: he could follow the 'Rules', a set of which existed for every form or 'Kind' (e.g. epic, tragedy, comedy, ode, pastoral, satire). The Rules were formulae abstracted by critics from a study of the admitted successes of the past, perhaps supplemented by an 'exercise of right reason'. This process of formulating Rules is analogous to the scientist's generalizing after observing many particular instances, and indeed it owed something of its prestige to science. It had been one of the preoccupations of seventeenth-century philosophers, such as Bacon and Descartes, to find and formulate a correct 'method' of investigation, the use of which would make the discovery of truth an easier, and almost a mechanical, task. No literary critics denied that poets needed 'Nature' (inborn abilities) as well as Art (which included a knowledge of the Rules), but they thought that in poetry as in science 'well begun is half done'.

In drama, there was little direct imitation of the Ancients; the modern stage and audience, it was agreed, made this impossible. But drama had its Rules which, according to the common account, were derived ultimately from Aristotle's *Poetics*, which, in its turn, had been derived from Aristotle's 'observation of those things in which Euripides, Sophocles, and Aeschylus pleased' (as Dryden asserted). Now, Shakespeare had notoriously broken all the Rules: he lived in 'a barbarous age', and either did not know them or had been forced by his barbarous audience to ignore them. And not only his dramatic structure, but also his language, versification, and often his subject-matter offended against the critical principles developing in the 1660s. The critics had, then, to decide whether respect for these new principles of writing should modify or destroy their respect for Shakespeare, or *vice versa*; or whether the Shakespearian mode of writing, and the one now favoured, should both be recognized as valid. In fact, all three things happened, and often in the mind of the same critic. Critics differed as to the balance between Shakespeare's 'beauties' and 'faults', the tendency being for the faults to seem less important to each succeeding generation and eventually to be adjudged not faults at all. In the earlier stages of this discussion, a favourable judgement upon Shakespeare was often justified by an appeal to the authority of Longinus, whose *On the Sublime* had recently been translated from the Greek and popularized. Longinus' criticism was enthusiastic rather than judicial. He did not go fault-finding, but 'surveyed the Whole' (the words are Pope's, who is paraphrasing Longinus) and warmly praised those poems which, even though faulty, displayed great genius and 'transported' the reader. His example was important for the eighteenth century, and was 'methodized' by those critics who referred literary judgements to their 'taste' – the emotional impact which a poem made on them – rather than to formal principles. By this test, Shakespeare succeeded with all but the most prejudiced: for as Addison said,

> Our inimitable Shakespeare is a stumbling-block to the whole tribe of these rigid critics. Who would not rather read one of his plays, where there is not a single rule of the stage observed, than any production of a modern critic, where there is not one of them violated!
>
> (*The Spectator*, 592)

The walls of the critical Jericho did not fall at once, however, and there was some justice in the critics' continuing to recommend obedience to the Rules rather than imitation of Shakespeare's form. Shakespeare is 'inimitable' in a stricter sense than Addison intends: if great writers are to be regarded, as they were then, as potential 'models', few are more disastrous than Shakespeare. The poetical-dramatic unity of his plays is not obvious or easily defined; for most imitators, his freedom of time and place, his double-plots and mixture of tragedy and comedy, only gave authority for a chaos that was euphemistically called 'variety'. Even those critics who defended Shakespeare's mode of construction thought him a bad precedent.[2] Critics were in a similar dilemma over Spenser and Milton, who by early in the eighteenth century had been recognized as our greatest poets after Shakespeare. Neither of them conformed to current ideals of vocabulary and versification; Spenser's form, too, offended against the epic Rules. Both of them did prove, in fact bad models, and again critics were torn between admiration for their sublime and imaginative qualities (of a kind rare in the first half of our period) and dislike of their faults and their imitators.

Shakespeare, Spenser, and Milton were alike, too, in 'going beyond Nature', in the sense that they did not confine themselves to the naturalistic reproduction of ordinary human experience. It was a critical commonplace that it is impossible for any thought to be beautiful which is not just, and has not its foundation in the nature of things; that the basis of all wit is truth; and that no thought can be valuable, of which good sense is not the groundwork.

(ADDISON: *The Spectator*, 62)

One agrees that poetry, to be significant, must be 'truthful', in some sense of the word; but 'truth' could be very narrowly conceived. The works of Rymer (1641–1713), one of the most discussed and influential critics of his time, are a good example of what may happen then (translation of Rapin 1674, *Tragedies of the Last Age* 1678, *Short View of Tragedy* 1692). Spenser had great genius but, in *The Fairie Queene*, 'all is fanciful and chimerical, without any uniformity, without any foundation in truth; his poem is perfect Fairy-land'; *Paradise Lost* is only what 'some are pleased to call a poem'; and Shakespeare fares no better. Rymer examines the tragedies of the last age 'by the Practice of the Ancients and by the Common Sense of All Ages'; but he does not often invoke the Rules, for 'there is no talking of Beauties when there wants Essentials'. Learning is superfluous, even 'women-judges' can detect the faults of the Elizabethans: 'common sense suffices'. Rymer's very literal and prosaic common sense demonstrates that 'the tragical part [of *Othello* is] plainly none other than a Bloody Farce, without salt or savour'. Shakespeare's language was as Bedlam-like as his plots: 'In a play one should speak like a man of business.' Not that Rymer wanted photographic realism in drama; he quotes with approval Aristotle's claim (*Poetics*, 1451) that the poet, by limiting himself to the typical and essential, is 'more philosophical' than the historian, who must record also the exceptional and accidental in human affairs. Thus, soldiers have for centuries been notoriously 'open-hearted, frank, plain-dealing': yet Shakespeare has offended against the 'decorum' for this type in creating his Iago –

... to entertain the audience with something new and surprising, against common sense and Nature, he would pass upon us a close, dissembling, false, insinuating rascal.

(*Short View of Tragedy*)

Rymer invented and popularized the phrase 'poetical justice'; in life, the wicked may sometimes flourish like the bay-tree, but this is not typical, and the unfortunate exception to the rule is not a properly instructive spectacle for the stage.

The rationalism represented by Rymer was an important ingredient in the criticism of the period. It was, of course, a literary manifestation of the dominant philosophy; well might Boileau complain that 'Descartes had cut the throat of poetry'.[3] For Rymer, as for others, 'enthusiasm', whether poetical or religious, was suspect. 'Reason' should control poetical Fancy and religious faith: 'Those who object against reason are the Fanatics of poetry, are never to be saved by their good works.' Rymer was an able and intelligent man, but it was clear even to most of his admirers that his critical equipment was inadequate. Nevertheless, even a century later he was still being referred to as a prominent adversary of Shakespeare. At least, as Spingarn notes, Rymer inaugurated the detailed study of literary texts, and thus aided the movement away from general to concrete criticism.

Despite Rymer, Shakespeare became recognized as the greatest of English, and perhaps of all, dramatists. In 1660 Jonson was commonly regarded as greater, and Beaumont and Fletcher were more popular, but Dryden decisively asserted Shakespeare's superiority.[4] Jonson was 'the more correct poet ... I admire him, but I love Shakespeare'. Dryden's *Essay* was written 'chiefly to vindicate the honour of our English writers, from the censure of those who unjustly prefer the French before them', and quotations have already been made from his famous passage on Shakespeare, which Johnson later called 'a perpetual model of encomiastic criticism': to write it in 1668 was a major critical achievement. The *Essay* is the best critical piece of its generation. It traverses most of the current controversies over drama: the relative merits of the Ancient, the French and the Elizabethan plays, of Shakespeare, Jonson, and Fletcher, of blank verse and rhyme, the validity of the Rules and of Imitation, the necessity of verisimilitude. Dryden adulates Shakespeare and the other Elizabethans, though he declines to imitate them, chiefly because they cannot be equalled on their own ground; but in other essays (for Dryden's criticism is almost all occasional, and fluctuates) he sometimes patronizes them. They lived in a barbarous age, and lack the wit, polish, and refined language now demanded of dramatists; but still —

Theirs was the Giant Race before the Flood ...
Our Age was cultivated thus at length,
But what we gain'd in skill we lost in strength.
(*To Mr Congreve*)

This assessment of the relation between his and 'the last age' came
more easily to Dryden and his fellows, because similar comparisons
had long been made between the Golden and Silver Ages, between
Homer, the earlier and 'the greater genius', and Virgil, 'more correct' but inferior. Only occasionally is this idea modified or sup-
planted by literary analogies with scientific 'progress', and then most
commonly it is only asserted that progress has been made in limited
respects, of 'skill', 'wit', and versification, not of total greatness.

A more serious limitation in Dryden's criticism, which he shared
with his contemporaries and successors, is suggested by such remarks
as that he agrees with Jonson's (apocryphal?) horror at 'some bombast speeches of Macbeth, which are not to be understood', and that
Shakespeare's 'whole style is so pestered with figurative expressions,
that is is as affected as it is obscure'. He admits elsewhere that 'it is
almost a miracle that much of [Shakespeare's] language remains so
pure'; but a man and an age which cannot understand, let alone
approve, Shakespeare's use of language are clearly prevented from
anything approaching a full appreciation of him. Dryden's complaint
is repeated by all the major critics for a century.[5] Shakespeare's
earlier poetry was most congenial. Dryden, to 'do justice to that
divine poet', quotes him at his best – in *Richard II*. Pope makes the
illuminating remark that the style of *Two Gentlemen of Verona* 'is
less figurative, and more natural and unaffected, than the greater part
of this author's [plays] though supposed to be one of the first he
wrote'. Gray illustrates his famous assertion that 'Shakespeare's language is one of his principal beauties ... Every word in him is a
picture' by quoting *Richard III*. The effectiveness of Shakespeare's
poetry was often *felt*, and the striking passages, or 'beauties', were
distinguished in some eighteenth-century editions, and collected into
anthologies. Dr Johnson, while criticizing the 'mean words' which
provoked his 'risibility' in Lady Macbeth's 'Come, thick night!'
speech, recognizes that here 'is exerted all the force of poetry, that
force which calls new powers into being, which embodies sentiment,
and animates matter': but 'perhaps scarce any man now peruses it

without some disturbance of his attention from the counteraction of the words and the ideas' (*Rambler*, 168). No eighteenth-century critics could read Shakespeare – any more than they could read Donne[6] – without experiencing this counteraction; the new ideals of correctness, smooth versification, clear expression, and simple imagery were too potent. One of the few points of agreement for all four participants in Dryden's dialogue on *Dramatic Poesy* is that 'the sweetness of English verse was never understood or practised by our fathers'; only recently had English poets learned 'to mould their thoughts into easy and significant words; to retrench the superfluities of expression', and to master rhyme. Waller and Denham were usually credited with this achievement; Denham's *Cooper's Hill*, said Dryden, 'is, and ever will be, the exact standard of good writing'. Shakespeare's versification was as licentious, by this standard, as his imagery was imperfect by Johnson's definition of the perfect simile: it 'must both illustrate and ennoble the subject; must show it to the understanding in a clearer view, and display it to the fancy with greater dignity'. Shakespeare's plays were generally acted in 'adapted' versions during this period: not only is the structure often simplified and 'regularized', but so is the verse, to the point of emasculation.[7]

The great eighteenth-century exemplar of correctness in verse is, of course, Pope, and the neatness of his couplets in the *Essay on Criticism* contributes much to its tone and implies something of its critical attitude. The *Essay* is not original in its ideas, as Addison noted with approval in *The Spectator*, 253. It is well-phrased and typical rather than profound, and typical not least in its muddled eclecticism, its rejection of any one orthodoxy. Thus, the Rules are at one point an inference from the practice of the Ancients, at another they existed before the Ancients wrote and the Ancients grandly broke them, at another they were delivered to the hitherto 'un-confin'd' poets by Aristotle. Modern writers should 'beware' of breaking the Rules, but modern critics should not judge mechanically by them. Pope variously advises the poet to imitate the Ancients, obey the Rules, and 'follow Nature'; these three prescriptions are reconciled by the identification – a commonplace of the time – of Nature and the Rules (which are 'Nature methodized') and Nature and the Ancients ('To copy Nature is to copy them', 'Nature and Homer were, he [Virgil] found, the same'). Again, Pope fluctuates between recommending the reserve of the man of sense ('For fools admire, but men of sense approve'*), and acclaiming 'the generous pleasure to be charm'd with Wit' when 'rapture warms the mind'. Pope does not clarify this when he says that the ideal critic is 'Blest with a taste exact, yet unconfin'd'. These inconsistencies, though they are signs of the weakness of Pope's critical position, are at least also evidence of his wish to tolerate and enjoy literature of various sorts.

This allowance for 'rapture', and for the 'grace beyond the reach of art', and the recognition that 'Applause, in spite of trivial faults, is due', owe something to Longinus, and Pope's *Preface* to his *Iliad* (1715) is an excellent example of criticism inspired by the Longinian spirit and style. Pope praises Homer, as elsewhere he praises Spenser and Shakespeare, for that 'unequalled fire and rapture', which can 'over-power criticism, and make us admire even while we disapprove', and he shrewdly remarks that

perhaps the reason why most critics are inclined to prefer a judicious and methodical genius to a great and fruitful one, is because they find it easier for themselves to pursue their observations through an uniform and bounded walk of Art, than to comprehend the vast and various extent of Nature.

Actually, the major critics did not, in general, reject or depreciate the 'great and fruitful' geniuses. Dryden had written admirably of Chaucer, who was not, by the standards of the day, 'judicious and methodical', and Shakespeare and Spenser were generally extolled. The critics did fail, however, to give a satisfactory account of the kind of poetic unity which the works of the immethodical geniuses possessed. 'To judge of Shakespeare by Aristotle's rules,' said Pope, 'is like trying a man by the laws of one country, who acted under those of another.' This historical approach sounds promising, and was to be a useful development in the criticism of Shakespeare and other by-gone writers, during the course of the century; but here it is inadequate. As Professor Butt has remarked, 'Pope does not take the further step of discovering what the rules of Shakespeare's country were.' Pope does hazard an analogical justification for Shakespeare's plan: his plays resemble a Gothic cathedral as more regular plays resemble a 'neat modern building'.

* 'Admire' is here used in the Latin sense of 'to feel astonishment' (cf: Horace's 'nil admirari'), and 'approve' means 'put to the test'.

The latter is more elegant and glaring, but the former is more strong and more solemn ... [The Gothic] has much the greater variety, and much the nobler apartments; though we are often conducted to them by dark, odd and uncouth passages. Nor does the whole fail to strike us with greater reverence, though many of the parts are childish, ill-placed, and unequal to its grandeur.

(Preface to Shakespeare)

This Gothic analogy had already been used by Hughes, and was later to be used by Hurd, with reference to Spenser; but not until Coleridge wrote (and again used it) do we find the beginning of a full understanding of the Shakespearian form. Pope is still at the stage of finding too 'many of the parts' faulty.

Long before Coleridge's time, however, Shakespeare was generally exonerated from breaking the Unities: Johnson, in his *Rambler*, 156 (1751) and his Shakespeare *Preface* (1765), had made the final statement of his century's case for Shakespeare, in this respect. Johnson rightly insists that the Unities are not an essential in drama, though the arguments he uses are not altogether convincing. There is no reason why the scene should not be altered in a play, he urges: for 'the spectators are always in their senses, ... and where is the absurdity of allowing that place to represent first Athens, and then Sicily, which was always known to be neither Sicily nor Athens, but a modern theatre?' This is an inadequate account of stage-illusion, and does not grapple with the cases for and against changes of scene in plays of various kinds. When it comes to the point, Johnson cannot find 'any art of connexion or care of disposition' in *Antony and Cleopatra*. Similarly, Johnson's defence of tragi-comedy is inadequate. 'When Shakespeare's plan is understood, most of the criticisms of Rymer and Voltaire vanish away' – but an understanding of 'Shakespeare's plan' is not much furthered by suggestions that these plays exhibit 'the real state of sublunary nature, which partakes of good and evil, joy and sorrow', that they are doubly instructive because they may 'convey all the instruction of tragedy or comedy', and that anyway 'all pleasure consists in variety' – and least of all by the assertion that Shakespeare's 'disposition ... led him to comedy ... In tragedy he is always struggling after some occasion to be comic.' Shakespeare's 'variety', both in his whole canon and within each play, Johnson appreciated; but neither he, nor any of his contemporaries, understood the unity-in-complexity of either his plotting or his poetry, let alone the interrelation between his plotting, his poetry and his characterization.

If neither Shakespeare's poetry nor his 'plan' could be understood or heartily approved, inevitably he was praised chiefly for his characterization (rather as Chaucer, today, is rarely praised for any specifically poetic qualities, but for his 'warm humanity'). Thus Dryden claims that 'no man ever drew so many characters, or generally distinguished 'em better, excepting only Jonson'; Pope asserts that Shakespeare is 'not so much an imitator, as an instrument, of Nature ... he seems to have known the world by Intuition, to have looked through human nature at one glance'. Such general praises of Shakespeare's characterization abounded, and were followed in the second half of the eighteenth century by a number of detailed studies of particular characters in Shakespeare, of which Morgann's *Dramatic Character of Falstaff* (1777) is the most elaborate.[8] So for Johnson, 'the praise of Shakespeare is that his drama is the mirror of life', it contains 'human sentiments in human language'. Johnson is, as T. S. Eliot said, 'a mature if limited critic', and the strength of his Shakespeare-criticism is that he judges Shakespeare by his mature and profound sense of the human situation. Shakespeare, he insists, shows us, not the phantoms and impossible heroes so common in literature, but *men*: and Shakespeare's men are not so particular and unique, such 'individuals', that we can learn little from their conduct, but are 'the genuine progeny of common humanity, such as the world will always supply, and observation will always find'. Shakespeare's picture of life is just, and his observation both wide and subtle. Johnson continually points to the 'strokes of nature' in Shakespeare: Lady Macbeth's arguments are those of any wicked wife to any husband, the difference between the effects of grief on Leonato in *Much Ado* and Constance in *King John* shows Shakespeare's 'knowledge of the passions'. This knowledge and wisdom Shakespeare sometimes makes explicit in 'practical axioms and domestic wisdom' which, if collected, would form 'a system of civil and economical prudence'; but it is for the picture, not for the wise saws and modern instances, that he is most to be valued.

Shakespeare has, however, his faults, which Johnson will not ignore; for the business of a critic, he said, is not (as Addison and other Longinian critics had asserted) to 'point out beauties rather than faults' – nor was it the opposite: rather, 'to hold out the light of reason, whatever it may discover' (*The Rambler*, 93). Moreover, it was expedient as well as honest to 'confess the faults of our favourite, to gain credit to our praise of his excellencies'. There is justice in some of Johnson's criticisms: Shakespeare's plotting and climaxes are sometimes loose and careless, some of his bawdry and word-play is tedious and otiose. But some of the 'faults' are rather Johnson's than Shakespeare's.

He sacrifices virtue to convenience, and is so much more careful to please than to instruct, that he seems to write without any moral purpose.

While one agrees with Johnson's claim – and it is part of his strength as a critic that he insists on it – that 'he that thinks reasonably must think morally', one is forced to recognize, as F. R. Leavis puts it in an excellent essay on Johnson, that 'he cannot appreciate the ways in which not only Shakespeare's drama but all works of art *act* their moral judgements. For Johnson a thing is stated, or it isn't there.' Nor can Johnson see how truth may be stated in myth or symbol, how *The Tempest* and *A Winter's Tale*, for instance, are more than pleasant romantic pieces: significantly, he says of the latter that 'with all its absurdities, it is very entertaining', but praises specifically only 'the character of Autolycus, ... very naturally conceived, and strongly represented'.

Johnson's Shakespeare-criticism shows the strengths and the weaknesses of his sensibility, and of the critical tradition he had inherited. This tradition he did not accept inertly, as an authoritative substitute for independent judgement: for him, 'Reason wants not Horace to support it', 'there is always an appeal open from criticism to nature', and no respect is due to those who 'draw their principles of judgement rather from books than from reason'. Johnson was independent about the letter of his tradition but not rebellious against its spirit. Mrs Thrale noted 'his extreme distance from those notions which the world has agreed, I know not very well why, to call romantic'. Johnson, she explained, admires Shakespeare for his 'just representation of human manners', but the romantic critics expatiate rather on his 'creative powers and vivid imagination'. The second half of the eighteenth century had critics, as well as poets, who have later been described as 'Romantic precursors': the most interesting are the brothers Warton, both minor poets too, and Bishop Hurd (Joseph Warton, 1722–1800, *Adventurer* papers on Shakespeare 1753–4, *Essay on the Genius and Writings of Pope*, volume I, 1756, volume II, 1782; Thomas Warton, 1728–90, *Observations on the Fairy Queen*, 1754, *History of English Poetry*, 1774–81, *Preface* to Milton's Minor Poems, 1785; Richard Hurd, 1720–1808, *Letters on Chivalry and Romance*, 1762).[9] These critics were all dissatisfied with the poetry of Pope and the like, who seemed to them to lack the 'nobler' qualities of our earlier masters. They suggested that poetry had declined in force and depth because the climate of opinion was uncongenial: science and philosophy had impoverished the imagination, and poets had languished under a literary-critical reign of terror. 'The Sublime and the Pathetic,' Joseph Warton asserted, 'are the two chief nerves of genuine poesy. [Warton's archaism is symptomatic.] What is there transcendently sublime or pathetic in Pope?'* 'Sublimity', like 'Imagination', was becoming an important critical notion by now; in the same year as volume I of Warton's *Essay on Pope*, there appeared Burke's *Philosophical Enquiry into the Origin of our Ideas of the Sublime and the Beautiful*, the best of a series of such inquiries beginning with Addison's *Spectator* papers (411–21) on the Pleasures of the Imagination. The 'sublime' – a term taken from Longinus, but expanded beyond his meaning – was often used to describe those great effects that could not be accounted for in terms of Rules and correctness. But this new 'cant of criticism' could be as limiting as the old. If the cant of correctness and regularity had led to an overestimation of Waller and Denham and their inheritors, and an injustice to Shakespeare, the cant of sublimity and imagination too often justified an indulgence, fundamentally frivolous, in poetic fancies and fairylands, and in manifestations of emotion, however chaotic or factitious. Thus, Joseph Warton was too readily impressed by *Otranto* and *Udolpho*, and the 'sublime' poetry of Young, Akenside, and Gray.

Here Johnson is sounder. His *Lives of the Poets* (1779–81) is his finest work, and the finest piece of criticism in our period. On Cowley and Milton, two of the earliest poets discussed there, he

---

*Pathetic in the eighteenth century sometimes means simply *moving*: it is significant that, just about the mid-century, it begins to take on its later, more specialized, meaning – conducive to *sorrowful* or *pitiful* emotion.

betrays some of the limitations which affected his Shakespeare-criticism, the same inability to appreciate uses of language outside his tradition, and indirect or symbolical ways of conveying truths. But in his discussions of the poets nearer his own time, his limitations are less exposed: Joseph Warton's swans, for instance, he rightly sees are half goose. Warton had enthused over Gray's *Odes* ('the most exquisite pieces of *pure poetry* in our language') and particularly his *Bard* ('truly sublime'). Johnson sees through this notion of 'pure poetry': his insistence that poetry, in Arnold's phrase, 'is at bottom a criticism of life' is more responsible and rewarding. 'I do not see that *The Bard* promotes any truth, moral or political' – this, as Leavis remarks, is Johnson's way 'of saying that for a mature, accomplished, and cultivated mind such as Gray's to be playing this kind of game and exhibiting itself in these postures is ridiculous'. None of the 'Romantic precursor' critics had this strength and seriousness of approach, and we should beware, in literary as in political history, of what Professor Butterfield has called 'the Whig interpretation' – valuing, say, the Wartons because they 'anticipated' later critical developments, such as those of Wordsworth and Coleridge, which we esteem: in fact, these Romantics were little helped by, or respectful of, their 'precursors', and it was the weakness rather than the strengths of Romantic aesthetic and criticism that were 'anticipated'. They are, for the most part, interesting historically, as straws in the wind, rather than intrinsically. Johnson, as an unfriendly contemporary, Thomas Twining, admitted, with all his faults 'is always entertaining, never dull or trite ... he has his originalities of thought, and making you see things ... There is in him no echo.' For this reason, if for no other, Johnson still deserves the praise given him by his eminent friend and follower, Sir Joshua Reynolds,[10] that he has 'the faculty of teaching inferior minds the art of thinking'.

NOTES

1. See W. P. Ker's discussion of the Unities in his *Essays of John Dryden*, I, xxxix–xlix (Oxford, 1900).

2. See W. P. Ker, as above 176–7; *Taste and Criticism in the 18th Century*, ed. H. A. Needham (London, 1952); and Johnson, *Rambler*, 156.

3. Basil Willey's *Seventeenth Century Background* (London, 1934) is useful on this point; see especially 86–92, 205–40, 290–5.

4. See W. P. Ker, as n. 1, 79–82; and G. E. Bentley, *Shakespeare and*

Jonson: Their Reputations in the 17th Century Compared (Chicago, 1945). Suggestions about the significance of the great popularity of Beaumont and Fletcher will be found in T. S. Eliot's *Selected Essays* (2nd edn, 1934), 155, 194, 211, and in L. C. Knights's *Drama and Society in the Age of Jonson* (London, 1937), 292–300.

5. See, e.g., W. P. Ker, as n. 1, 167–72, 201, 202–4, 224–6; *Shakespeare Criticism: a Selection (1623–1840)*, ed. D. Nichol Smith (World's Classics, 1916), 28, 58, 60; *Johnson on Shakespeare*, ed. Walter Raleigh (London, 1925); and *Spectator*, 39, 285.

6. On the rejection of Metaphysical 'wit', see *The Spectator* 58–63, Pope's *Essay on Criticism* 11. 289–304, and Johnson's *Life of Cowley*. Cf. Pope's *Satires of Dr Donne versified* (1733).

7. See examples on Montagu Summers's selected *Shakespeare Adaptations* (Boston, 1922), and F. R. Leavis's comparison between *Antony and Cleopatra* and Dryden's *All for Love* in *Scrutiny*, V (1936).

8. D. Nichol Smith, as n. 5, 173–214; see also 143–72, and L. C. Knights's notes on the development of Shakespeare-criticism in his 'How Many Children Had Lady Macbeth?', in *Explorations* (London, 1946).

9. Selections from some of these works can be found in *English Critical Essays, 16th–18th Centuries*, ed. E. D. Jones (World's Classics, 1922), 365–80, 451–60; D. Nichol Smith, as n. 5, 60–79; and H. A. Needham, as n. 2, 112–17, 144–9.

10. See Blake's marginalia (c. 1808) on Reynold's *Discourses* (1769–90) for a stimulating criticism of assumptions which Reynolds shared with Johnson: Nonesuch *Blake* (1939 edn), 770–812.

WILLIAM COWPER

D. J. ENRIGHT

Although a good deal has been written about Cowper (1731–1800),
the larger part of it relates either to his life or to the religious and
social movements of his time. Detailed studies of his connection with
Evangelicalism and of the part which he played in the various
humanitarian activities of the last quarter of the eighteenth century
are thus available, but his admirers have made no great attempt to
justify Cowper the poet as distinct from Cowper the critic of society.
Admittedly it is not easy to find much to say about Cowper's poetry
itself: for the greater part its virtues are as obvious as its weaknesses.
While his work contains something to recommend it both to
admirers of Pope and to admirers of Wordsworth, it can arouse
neither as much hostility nor as much enthusiasm as both of these
writers have done at one time or another. The aim of this essay is to
suggest that, uneven as his poetry is, Cowper speaks with an individual, if quiet, voice, and that although he is unlikely to enjoy any
great vogue, he has something to offer which will never fall entirely
out of fashion or out of date.

Between the self-assured work of the Augustans and the energetic
and diverse movements of the Romantic Revival came a period of
half-hearted, characterless writing, when the poets, looking backwards and forwards at the same time, drifted on a slow current of
change which they could neither govern nor understand. T. S. Eliot's
comment on the age is illuminating: 'Instead of working out the
proper form for its matter, when it has any ... it merely applies the
magniloquence of Milton or the neatness of Pope to matter which
is wholly unprepared for it; so that what the writers have to say
always appears surprised at the way in which they choose to say it'
(see p. 232). On occasion these poets achieved work which, lacking in
direction and power, yet wins respect by its honesty and decency.
One such monument of 'transition' is Gray's *Elegy Written in a*

Country Churchyard, but more of this kind of writing is offered by Cowper than by any of the other poets with whom he is commonly associated.

The poets whom Eliot describes strained their talents in an attempt to achieve effects utterly beyond those talents; when they have the words, the subject seems inadequate, and when they have the subject, the words seem to be the wrong ones. The tedium of reading poets who roll in the trough between two creative waves deters us from seeing tragedy in their efforts to visualize the nature of the wave which should carry them to some undesignated shore. In this period grandiloquent gestures commonly end in bathos. But bathos, though not absent from Cowper, is comparatively rare; his concern to see that justice was done to God and to man at least gave him something to write about, and when he was writing about nothing in particular a customary modesty prevented his deluding himself. At such moments he would say:

> But no prophetic fires to me belong;
> I play with syllables, and sport in song.

There was always an endearing consciousness of his 'amateur status' about Cowper; it was not a false modesty, but rather a happiness to be of use and an acceptance of his limitations which make him one of the very few poets of his time of whom we do not complain that they should have written either quite differently or not at all. His modesty, together with recognition of the serious nature of his occupation, finds expression in the *Epistle to Lady Austen* —

> I, who scribble rhyme,
> To catch the trifles of the time,
> And tell them truths divine and clear.

He merely 'scribbles rhyme' — yet those rhymes can 'tell truths'. And for a minor poet to be more interested in 'truths' than in 'rhymes' is no bad thing, for only the major genius can afford to dedicate himself to art.

The 'transitional' nature of Cowper's writing is clearly brought out by *The Sofa* (the first book of *The Task*, 1784). This begins with ninety lines, in an informative and serio-comic style, on the history of seating:

> Thus first necessity invented stools,
> Convenience next suggested elbow-chairs,
> And luxury th' accomplished S O F A last.

After a gently satirical passage on those who sleep when they should be awake, the argument takes a personal turn, remaining humorous still —

> The S O F A suits
> The gouty limb, 'tis true; but gouty limb,
> Though on a S O F A, may I never feel . . .

The verse then becomes much more personal and the humour drops away:

> For I have lov'd the rural walk through lanes
> Of grassy swarth, close cropt by nibbling sheep . . .

In a short passage we move from a diluted form of the Augustan-social mode to an anticipation of the Romantic-natural. The rest of the book meanders from topic to topic: description of landscape, the life of the country poor, 'artificial' gardening, the virtues of rural life, Nature preferred to Art, the 'spleen' in cities, an anecdote which reminds us of Wordsworth's Ruth or Margaret, gipsies, the way of life of the 'gentle savage', London, and the preference for a country life.

In the aspect of 'transitional' poet it may be interesting to examine Cowper's attitude towards Pope, the great figure of the last great poetic school, and Milton, the great influence on this 'Transition', who offered something so unlike Pope that imitation of it seemed not merely reaction but progress. Where Pope is concerned, Cowper's feelings are mixed:

> Then Pope, as harmony itself exact,
> In verse well disciplin'd, complete, compact,
> Gave virtue and morality a grace . . .

No poet (apart from the author of *Don Juan*) will concede so much for a long time to come; we observe that Cowper allows Pope more than social satire – he 'gave virtue and morality a grace'. The passage (which occurs in *Table Talk*) continues thus, however:

> But he (his musical finesse was such,
> So nice his ear, so delicate his touch)

Made poetry a mere mechanic art;
And ev'ry warbler has his tune by heart.

Though the criticism is directed against his followers, the phrase 'mechanic art' looks forward to Matthew Arnold's verdict on Pope ('the splendid high priest of our age of prose and reason'); and certainly some of Cowper's letters suggest that he really preferred the verse of Prior. All the same, *Table Talk* is written in heroic couplets, and a comparison with Pope's use of the form indicates less a greater imaginative force or liberty of expression in Cowper than a blurring of point and a tendency towards wordiness. Of the difference in tone (should one compare the portrait of Addison in the same passage with Pope's Atticus) we shall say more later.

Cowper's admiration for Milton (whom he undertook to edit in 1791) is wholehearted, and in a letter (31 October 1779) he rushes to defend the poet against Johnson's criticisms. He makes no attempt to excuse the 'childish prattlement of pastoral compositions', it is interesting to note, but picks out for praise in *Lycidas* 'the liveliness of the description, the sweetness of the numbers, the classical spirit of antiquity'. It is, however, the music of *Paradise Lost* – 'like that of a fine organ' – which draws his eloquence.

Cowper's attitude towards a third poet, Homer, is instructive in a different way. In 1793, when he was working on a second edition of his translation of the *Iliad* and *Odyssey*, he wrote *To John Johnson, on his presenting me with an antique bust of Homer*. The opening expresses a decent pride in his work on 'my old fav'rite bard', which suddenly gives way to a grim self-castigating sestet –

> The grief is this, that sunk in Homer's mine
> I lose my precious years, now soon to fail,
> Handling his gold, which, howso'er it shine,
> Proves dross, when balanc'd in the Christian scale

– lines which strike us as the heavy labouring of what for Christians is a self-evident truth. The sonnet ends on a curious note:

> Be wiser thou – like our fore-father DONNE,
> Seek heav'nly wealth, and work for God alone.

We cannot believe that Donne's style of poetry would appeal to Cowper; what weighs with him here, apart perhaps from his mother's kinship with Donne, is the fact that the latter became Dean of St

Paul's and a famous and powerful preacher. Cowper is more self-consciously Christian than Donne (whose genius was as apt for love-poetry as for religious); in his attitude towards writing he is closer to George Herbert. The latter's lines,

> A verse may find him, who a sermon flies,
> And turn delight into a sacrifice,

are echoed by Cowper, for his preoccupation was with Christian truth, and poetry recommended itself as an acceptable means of conveyance. In *The Task* (Book III) he assures us of his concern to drive his mind 'To its just point – the service of mankind'. The nature of that service is described more than once; for example, in a letter, 18 February 1781 – 'I am merry that I may decoy people into my company, and grave that they may be better for it. Now and then I put on the garb of a philosopher, and take the opportunity that disguise procures me, to drop a word in favour of religion.'

But if Cowper bears much the same relation to a somewhat Calvinistic Methodism as Herbert bears to seventeenth-century Anglicanism, the fact remains that Methodism and its related movements loom larger in his work or more specific than does Anglicanism in that of Herbert. Occasional similarities of mood – Cowper's

> Perhaps the self-approving haughty world,
> That as she sweeps him with her whistling silks
> Scarce deigns to notice him

reminds us of Herbert's

> Then came brave Glory puffing by
> In silks that whistled, who but he?
> He scarce allow'd me half an eye –

yield to a greater dissimilarity. For while the earlier poet can hardly be described as an artist for art's sake, yet the question of intellectual agreement or otherwise raises itself far more frequently with Cowper. The reason perhaps is that Herbert, quietly assuming fundamental intellectual consent, presents us with sheer experience, and we have experienced the poem before the question of agreement can arise. Cowper, on the other hand, customarily attacks from outside, often exaggerating the opposition which the reader is likely to put up, and thus constructing an argument which will find agreement only where agreement already exists. None the less, that argument is helped along by simple and telling metaphor, and we can well believe that Cowper's influence was effective both in helping the inarticulate to understand their emotions and in fostering emergent religious feeling. If we postulate a contrast between the poetry which creates experience and forces it upon the reader and the poetry which describes and discusses experience, then it is to the latter class that most of Cowper's work belongs.

On several occasions Cowper gives a second reason for writing poetry: 'Amusements are necessary, in a retirement like mine, especially in such a state of mind as I labour under. The necessity of amusement makes me sometimes write verses; it has made me a carpenter, a birdcage maker, a gardener . . .' (letter, 6 April 1780). Innate modesty and a tendency to apologize for his authorship discounted, such remarks seem appropriate to the leisurely pace and comparatively mild emotional drive of much of his verse. His Miltonics, for instance, are garrulous by comparison with Milton. At times we suspect that he is deliberately making his 'task' last as long as possible: compression, economy, and vividness of point were not virtues at which he aimed. He rarely takes a leap in his poetical progress, but rather leads by slow and steady – and often predictable – steps up to the issue at stake. The long reflective poem seems his natural medium, and as a representative passage we may take these lines from *The Task* (Book II):

> Oh, popular applause! what heart of man
> Is proof against thy sweet seducing charms?
> The wisest and the best feel urgent need
> Of all their caution in thy gentlest gales;
> But swell'd into a gust – who then, alas!
> With all his canvas set, and inexpert,
> And therefore heedless, can withstand thy pow'r?

The theme is announced in language which cannot fail to be understood, and to which 'every bosom returns an echo', for the echo has not ceased sounding since the words were last used. The metaphor of sail and wind (part of Cowper's recurrent imagery) is then brought into play, and the antithesis between 'the wisest and the best' and 'inexpert, and . . . heedless' is reinforced by the parallel contrast between 'gentlest gales' and 'gust'. The reader is not made to see anything in a new light, but Cowper displays his meaning clearly and with little fuss.

Much of his reflective verse is concerned with contemporary abuses – social, political, moral, and religious. In the last hundred lines of the first book of *The Task* the theme is country versus city. The first twenty-five lines generalize in favour of the former. London, Cowper then says, is

> by taste and wealth proclaim'd
> The fairest capital of all the world,
> By riot and incontinence the worst.

The next twenty-five lines are spent in demonstrating London's 'fairness' – her arts, science, and commerce – while the following twenty-five are allotted to her 'riot and incontinence' – injustice, peculation, deference to fashion instead of to God's laws. This deliberate, carefully balanced picture is followed by twenty-five lines in praise of country life, culminating in the judgement that the folly of sophisticated city dwellers

> Has made, what enemies could ne'er have done,
> Our arch of empire, steadfast but for you,
> A mutilated structure, soon to fall.

The whole passage is extremely readable, but it cannot be said that the situation is clarified by any brilliant image or the point driven home with a truly poetic intensity. The consistently easy flow of the verse does not hide the presence of a good deal of padding – tautology as in 'Rank abundance breeds / In gross and pamper'd cities sloth and lust, / And wantonness and gluttonous excess' – which detracts from its impact; the rhythm verges at times on a rather unctuous oratory; the metaphor is largely of a conventional kind, perhaps too decent to deserve the epithet 'cliché' – philosophy's 'eagle eye', 'yon burning disk', 'queen of cities'. On the other hand, Cowper occasionally introduces the aphoristic line which sums up in memorable form the gist of the matter. Two good examples are adjacent in this passage – 'knees and hassocks are well-nigh divorc'd' and the household words, 'God made the country, and man made the town'.

But the prime characteristic of the passage is its generality. The very largeness and abstractness of 'London' leaves the virtues and vices ascribed to her rather vague and not particularly convincing.

Cowper is moralizing, not satirizing, and we shall be disappointed if we look for the type of satirical art achieved by Pope, with its vivid particularity, its pungency and bite. For Cowper,

> An individual is a sacred mark,
> Not to be pierc'd in play, or in the dark.

He offers nothing comparable to Pope's Sporus or Atticus; we respect his gentleness as a man, but may wish that, as a poet, he had felt fewer compunctions. His concern to be scrupulously fair works rather ambiguously in this sphere. Earlier in the same book of *The Task*, among descriptions of natural beauties, he has held up to view the unromantic aspects of country life ('So farewell envy of the *peasant's nest*!'), and we incline in the end to feel that Cowper's chief reason for preferring the country is a negative one – the country is less dangerous to health and virtue. Great poetry operates in ways less *directly* just than this, and Cowper's legalistic procedure brings him near to saying nothing at all, in terms of poetic procedure.

But it is unfair to emphasize the negative aspects of his work and unsafe to generalize about him, for Cowper's style is rather more versatile than it at first seems, and his greatest successes are frequently found in a context of dull conventional versifying. Book II of *The Task* contains a grim passage on preaching in which ponderous parentheses and thumping repetition of the magical word ('The pulpit ... The pulpit ... I say the pulpit') lead up to a pompous climax –

> There stands the messenger of truth: there stands
> The legate of the skies!

Its manner is, in fact, of the bullying, 'pulpiteering' type. Yet a little later comes a vividly dramatic skit on fashionable preachers:

> The things that mount the rostrum with a skip,
> And then skip down again; pronounce a text;
> Cry – hem: and, reading what they never wrote,
> Just fifteen minutes, huddle up their work,
> And with a well-bred whisper close the scene!

Similarly, to take the group of long poems known as the *Moral Satires*, *The Progress of Error* issues in somewhat shrill tones such trite and unconfirmed generalizations as

> Peace follows virtue as its sure reward;
> And pleasure brings as surely in her train
> Remorse, and sorrow, and vindictive pain;

yet we find in *Truth* lively passages, exemplified by the picture of 'sanctimonious pride':

> Yon ancient prude, whose wither'd features show
> She might be young some forty years ago ...
>
> (l. 131 *et seq.*)

And whereas *Expostulation*, verbosely living up to its title, contains much protracted moralizing – here we sympathize with Leslie Stephen's remark that 'Cowper is an instance of a thinker too apart from the great world to apply the lash effectually' – *Conversation* proves how agile Cowper could be in handling the lesser vices:

> Some men employ their health, an ugly trick,
> In making known how oft they have been sick ...
> They thought they must have died they were so bad –
> Their peevish hearers almost wish they had.
>
> (l. 311 *et seq.*)

With Stephen's comment in mind, we should take note of Cowper's several poems on slavery, varying from the mischievous *Pity for poor Africans* ('I pity them greatly, but I must be mum, / For how could we do without sugar and rum?') to *The Negro's Complaint* which, concerning itself with those to whom the lash was literally applied, shows no shameful remoteness from one sort of 'great world':

> Still in thought as free as ever,
>   What are England's rights, I ask,
> Me from my delights to sever,
>   Me to torture, me to task?
> Fleecy locks, and black complexion
>   Cannot forfeit nature's claim;
> Skins may differ, but affection
>   Dwells in white and black the same.

Among his fables, *The Moralizer Corrected* and *The Needless Alarm* are mountains which give birth to mice, while on the other hand *The Retired Cat* demonstrates its 'moral' in a manner altogether charming. And if Cowper sometimes offers such arrant 'poetic diction' as 'the feather'd tribes domestic' and 'public hives of puerile

resort' (i.e. schools), he is nevertheless capable of this fine apostro-
phizing of an oyster:

> You, shapeless nothing in a dish —
> You that are but almost a fish

while, on a higher level, his vision of the Earthly Paradise Regained
in Book VI of *The Task* is suddenly brought alive and made radiant
by the brilliant image in which the child, caressing the 'azure neck'
of 'the crested worm', receives 'the lambent homage of his arrowy
tongue'.

There is no need to dwell long on Cowper as a precursor of
romanticism. A certain similarity to Wordsworth is obvious on occasion (e.g. *The Task*, Book I, 'For I have lov'd the rural walk
through lanes ...'), but the earlier poet neither rises to the later's
direct and powerful vision nor sinks to the cloudy portentousness of
which he was capable at times. For sharp and appreciative observation
of nature, Cowper is often excellent; but he exclaims against the man
who

> views it, and admires; but rests content
> With what he views

and takes extreme care to point out that

> Nature is but a name for an effect,
> Whose cause is God.

The constant acknowledgement of God as the power behind the
scenery reminds us that a greater poet, dispensing with such explicit
warnings, would have put God *into* the description instead of rele-
gating him to a moralizing footnote.

Happily the greater part of Cowper's work (in which we include
his attractive letters) bears little obvious relation to his spiritual torments. The latter may be detected behind the incongruous severity
of his diatribe against the workman's pint (*The Task*, Book IV), for
instance, or his gloomy misgivings about Handel's popularity (Book
VI, 'Man praises man'). Elsewhere his personal anguish emerges in
the recurrent image of the storm-tossed sailor or the wrecked ship.
To take but a few examples: *Truth* begins thus,

> Man, on the dubious waves of error toss'd,
> His ship half founder'd, and his compass lost ...

The mariner in *The Task*, Book I, in his yearning for 'Nature in her green array', throws himself overboard 'and is seen no more'. In a fairly conventional way shipwreck provides the setting for *Temptation*, one of the Olney Hymns (1779), while something similar, but personally felt, occurs in *To Mr Newton on his return from Ramsgate*:

> I, tempest-toss'd and wreck'd at last,
> Come home to port no more,

and is repeated, more potently, in *On the Receipt of My Mother's Picture*:

> Always from port withheld, always distress'd –
> Me howling winds drive devious, tempest-toss'd ...

Related imagery is used in *Tirocinium* to describe the plight of a boy handed over to the care of a 'public nursery': 'left upon so wild a beach' and 'adrift upon a rolling sea'. The boy cannot trust to his own moral powers, he needs his father's guidance – just as man needs the direct guidance of God, or Salvation. *Human Frailty* reminds us,

> ... oars alone can ne'er prevail
> To reach the distant coast,
> The breath of heav'n must swell the sail,
> Or all the toil is lost.

Thus, in the vicinity of what might seem a banal metaphor, we find Cowper's most personal poetry – the poetry of one who is convinced of his own damnation. It, and the image, culminate in his last original poem – and his most powerful – *The Castaway*:

> No voice divine the storm allay'd,
> No light propitious shone;
> When, snatch'd from all effectual aid,
> We perish'd, each alone:
> But I beneath a rougher sea,
> And whelm'd in deeper gulfs than he.

To sum up, Cowper's original work falls into five groups: the eight *Moral Satires*; the six books of *The Task*; *Tirocinium, or A Review of Schools*; the Olney Hymns; and, lastly, the many miscellaneous shorter poems. While his moral preoccupations naturally drew him to the long reflective poem, it is in the shorter poems that he has preserved the gentler pleasures of his life. The verses on his pets and those of his friends are particularly charming: tender and unsophisticated without being sentimental – *Epitaph on a Hare*, *The Colubriad*, *On the Death of Mrs Throckmorton's Bullfinch*, and *Epitaph on Fop*, for example. Animals quietened the raw nerve of Calvinism in him, for he did not feel obliged to teach them morality. And when, forgetting, he upbraids his spaniel for killing a bird, Beau's retort is lively and effective –

> If killing birds be such a crime,
> (Which I can hardly see)
> What think you, Sir, of killing Time
> With verse address'd to me?

The Task would benefit from selective abridgement, but, together with some of the shorter pieces – *Alexander Selkirk* (with its moving reference to the 'shocking' tameness of the animals), *Lines Written during a period of insanity*, *The Poplar Field*, *To Mary*, *On the Receipt of My Mother's Picture*, *On the Loss of the 'Royal George'*, *The Castaway*, the perennial *John Gilpin* and others – it ensures Cowper's place as one of the most pleasant and most individual of our minor poets, one of the few 'transitional' poets whose work has integrity and is not nullified by what went before or came after.

SAMUEL JOHNSON

ARTHUR HUMPHREYS

Thanks mainly, though far from solely, to Boswell, Johnson as a person is the best-known of the Augustans. His fame is that of stalwart character and common sense, opinionative and independent, blunt and dogmatic, holding fast by a robust Tory patriotism. Such a reputation, while neither discreditable nor untrue, is far from an adequate estimate of him, and happily, as the bases of Augustan culture are better understood, the admiration for his written work which the wiser critics and scholars have traditionally felt is spreading. With many readers, it is true, the rational controls and critical disciplines of Augustanism still suggest a denial of the full life of man, but the better opinion is gaining ground that within whatever necessary limitations the Augustans' vigour and enlightened seriousness achieved a constructive and not merely restrictive civilization such as only sound intelligence, healthy instinct, and a fundamental sense of tradition could accomplish.

Of that civilization Johnson is the strongest representative; to express it was his instinctive and his deliberate aim.[1] A century later Matthew Arnold, equally impressive as critic and critical influence, and like Johnson the spokesman of classically rooted Christian humanism, was far less favourably placed; he had to speak against the whole trend of his time, for culture was ceasing to hold anarchy in check. On the one hand, Johnson's excellence is personal, the excellence of superlative moral power, and of wit and intellect massive, surprising, sensitive, and subtle: Mrs Thrale's guests once pleasantly compared his mind to an elephant's trunk, 'strong to buffet even the tiger, and pliable to pick up even the pin'. But, on the other hand, it is an excellence also of the time. Culture was quite aware of anarchy, which had so prevailed a century earlier, but it was sure that it could keep anarchy in check, that reason and discipline in faith and morals, good taste and practice in the arts, and social care in matters of daily life were the intended expressions of human nature. These ambiguous terms were defined by the Christian, rational, and humanistic traditions in which Augustanism worked, and they amounted to a thoroughly mature and responsible sense of values.

Johnson was supported (even so vigorous a mind is the better for support) by the strong general ethos of his time, and one of the most significant things about him is his perpetual reference to the open air of public assent. Assertions that 'every reader' likes this or dislikes that, that 'every man' believes this or disbelieves that, are refreshingly abundant – refreshingly not because the postulated unanimity has always worn well (though often it has), but because its attitude is that of frank confident spokesmanship for the ordinary man, though with the important proviso that the ordinary man is assumed to embody sound taste and considered judgement. Johnson's thought has fine, wide publicity; he seeks the truth which (he thinks) all men can know, and he expresses it with a wit which makes it memorable. This truth is not a cynical or tarnished worldly wisdom; it is concerned with the central moral needs of human life, and the generic workings of human nature. It is not peculiar and individual truth, but the truth of a tradition, of which Anglicanism was the presiding faith, the humane arts the exemplars, and human nature within that tradition the norm. Johnson, incidentally, like most Augustan humanists, elevates moral philosophy far above the new fashion for physical science; 'men more frequently require to be reminded than informed', he observes, and whereas information is a function of the growing materialism, reminding is a function of an accepted philosophy, recalling the things needful to the proper conduct of life. The more we know of the Augustans, and of Johnson, the more enviable seems this relationship by which in the most serious matters of life and letters he can refer to the public ('the common sense of readers uncorrupted by literary prejudices'). This is by no means to say that he is a critical demagogue, or eager for general assent in universal *bonhomie*. The case is precisely the opposite; he does not lower the standards of judgement to those of the average man – he expects the average man to rise to the standards of a large sanity and reason.[2] His sense of responsibility is great – 'I am now writing this,' he tells Boswell in a letter, 'and you when you read this are reading, under the Eye of Omnipotence'; he recognizes that responsibility and instinctively bears it, and part of his sense of it is his reference of particular judgements to large grounds of general principle, grounds which are both the bases of his civilization and also personal convictions rooted in his own experience. It is that basis of principle, the belief that truth can be rationally sought and must be expounded plainly, and that men can agree on all important matters, that gives Johnson's thought such amplitude and representative strength.

That amplitude and strength as well as more specifically poetic qualities are prominent in his major poems, *London* (1738) and *The Vanity of Human Wishes* (1749), whose exceptional distinction is the product of strength, subtlety, and, often, a serious wit. The words that spring to mind for them – 'monumental', 'grave', 'deliberate', and so on – are insufficient; they recognize weight or volume, but not the verbal vitality which animates what might otherwise be a mere simulacrum of grandeur. Since poetry cannot be interesting without at the very least sounding interesting, it is proper to insist first on the masterly grandiloquence, based partly (though not as a mere decorative trick) on simple sound mechanics like assonance and alliteration –

> While yet my steady Steps no Staff sustains,
> And Life still vig'rous revels in my Veins . . .

> Explain their Country's dear-bought Rights away,
> And plead for Pirates in the Face of Day –

and partly on astute variations of rhythm:

> For who would leave, unbrib'd, *Hibernia's* Land,
> Or change the Rocks of *Scotland* for the Strand?

> O'er Love, o'er Fear, extends his wide Domain,
> Unconquer'd Lord of Pleasure and of Pain.

This recalls Dryden's manner, but there are melodies here both stronger and subtler than Dryden's vigorous tunes, the products of an excellent ear serving an excellent mind and evolving an almost voluptuous interplay of vocables to recommend to the attention not merely the expression's sense but its complex of feelings too:

> Obsequious, artful, voluble and gay . . .

> Diffuse the tuneful Lenitives of Pain . . .

The March begins in Military State,
And Nations on his Eye suspended wait

An Age that melts with unperceiv'd Decay,
And glides in modest Innocence away.

The sound is sound not for its own sake, as the imagery is imagery
not for its own sake, but for the sake of the meaning. The collaboration of sound and meaning gives at once one of the full pleasures of
poetry, a sensory enrichment of a content in itself interesting. In
such a passage as the following the half-caught alliterations and
assonances, the echoes and onomatopoeia ('snarling Muse', 'brisker
Air', 'silken Courtiers gaze', 'turn the varied Taunt') realize the meaning and, as it were, present it to the mind through the ear:

By Numbers here from Shame or Censure free,
All Crimes are safe, but hated Poverty,
This, only this, the rigid Law pursues,
This, only this, provokes the snarling Muse.
The sober Trader, at a tatter'd Cloak
Wakes from his Dream, and labours for a Joke;
With brisker Air the silken Courtiers gaze,
And turn the varied Taunt a thousand ways.

This vital significance of sound is found too in Johnson's prose,
which is not always credited with phrasing as fine in auditory as in
intellectual quality. In the verse it is important as providing its own
kind of 'body' to themes that in their morality-manner, with generalized categories of idea and example, need as much substantializing
as they can get. The complaint is often heard, indeed, that Johnson's
large meditations on moral themes are too general, too oracular and
insufficiently personal, yet as one comes to know his work it is clearly
the product of a mind both weighty and intelligent which, when it
generalizes (as it often does in writing, though less so in conversation),
does so merely as a broadening of its own experience, and expresses
its idea with a particularly individual stamp of style.[3] General, then,
the poems are, as public utterance with words as the firm counters
of broad moral points of view; but they have a sweep and comprehension which save the attention from distracting particularities and
are guaranteed not to be vacuous by the full harmony and the flexible
significance of sound.

The guarantee extends further. Johnson's phrasing looks as though it is the simple elements of meaning – 'hated Poverty', 'rigid Law', 'snarling Muse', 'sober Trader', 'tatter'd Cloak', 'labours for a Joke', or

> Unnumber'd Suppliants croud Preferment's Gate,
> Athirst for Wealth, and burning to be great;
> Delusive Fortune hears th'incessant Call,
> They mount, they shine, evaporate, and fall.

But though simple elements of meaning are here, there is more than simplicity in them. There is economy, relevance, adequacy. The epithets are not novel or, at first, striking, but they are something better; they are in their descriptive definiteness absolutely right. Of the nouns they accompany one aspect only is to be characterized, and characterize it they do. They are cogent and precise, and any impression that Johnson's phrasing disperses on inspection into *mere* generalization is untenable. The first lines of *The Vanity of Human Wishes* have been thought vulnerable:

> Let Observation with extensive view
> Survey Mankind, from *China* to *Peru*;
> Remark each anxious Toil, each eager Strife,
> And watch the busy scenes of crouded Life.

Yet these do what is wanted – they open a broad morality-panorama (the whole poem depends on broad sweeps and general categories – even its historical figures are there as types and symbols), and they indicate the required aspect of each word. 'Busy scenes', 'crouded Life' – like 'Unnumber'd Suppliants', 'Athirst for Wealth, and burning to be great', 'delusive Fortune' and 'incessant Call' – are directly defined in the one necessary aspect. As for lines like 'Obsequious, artful, voluble and gay', 'And Sloth effuse her opiate fumes in vain', or 'They mount, they shine, evaporate, and fall', auditory pleasure and precise relevant meaning are perfectly united in them: idea, image, attitude, and moral comment are conveyed simultaneously by Johnson's clear and subtle undissociated sensibility. Part of their precision is the fact that words like 'obsequious', 'voluble', 'effuse', and 'evaporate', though naturalized in English and therefore, unlike many Augustan Latinisms, easily digested, have a peculiar aptness arising from their derivation. Johnson was, in fact, keenly aware of this subtle language-flavour deriving from the complex origins of

English; prefacing the *Dictionary* he says he has aimed at giving both
Latin and Teutonic equivalents to improve his readers' awareness of
the language.

The poems bring into view both large extents and particular
instances, both the generic and the specific, and play the one against
the other. The suspicion of vague rhetoric in

> Has Heav'n reserv'd, in pity to the Poor,
> No pathless Waste, or undiscover'd Shore?
> No secret Island in the boundless Main?

is dispelled by the pungency of

> No peaceful Desert yet unclaim'd by *Spain*?

And a famous passage in *The Vanity of Human Wishes* extends its
vast remote panorama and then actualizes the theme by a sharp
decisive reference:

> But few there are whom Hours like these await,
> Who set unclouded in the Gulphs of Fate.
> From Lydia's Monarch should the Search descend,
> By Solon caution'd to regard his End,
> In Life's last Scene what Prodigies surprise,
> Fears of the Brave, and Follies of the Wise?
> From Marlb'rough's Eyes the Streams of Dotage flow,
> And Swift expires a Driv'ler and a Show.

There is harmony in this alternation; the writer uses all his knowledge
easily, expanding into large perspectives and also concentrating
down to particular persons. The result is so consonant partly because
Johnson has found the right mental world for these reflections which
are at once moral generalities and particular experience (so particular,
indeed, that Johnson burst into tears over the scholar's poverty in
The Vanity of Human Wishes), and yet so general that such a passage
partakes of the nature of parable.[4] This mental world finds a middle
ground on which the general and the personal marry, from which
the mind easily opens to broad sweeps of idea and as easily focuses
on the detail of life.

Such a way of putting it is perhaps not very lucid, and a reference
to Gray's *Elegy* may help. In that poem the general notion of humble
worth and obscure destinies is embodied in the picture of the churchyard tombs, and extends outwards into the pattern of country work

and life, ploughing, herding, homecoming, parenthood, and faith. The reader hardly reflects that this is all a *general* theme; the mind is occupied by the churchyard scene, the household (blazing hearth, and children), cockcrow and hunting-horn, the harvesting of crops and the cutting of timber, then (by contrast) the splendour of Church and State which the villagers cannot rival, and then again the humble churchyard. The *Elegy* is a series of images, not an abstraction. Yet its images are not, as it were, particular atoms; the elms and yews symbolize country tradition and peaceful death; the swallow's nest and the housewife's hearth symbolize fruitful life; the cockcrow and the horn, the sickle and ploughing-teams symbolize active energy. Johnson's praise of the *Elegy* as abounding 'with images which find a mirror in every mind, and with sentiments to which every bosom returns an echo' — itself an example of this unobtrusive yet direct use of the generic image — is a recognition of this representative quality, and though the sentiments of his own longer poems (based on classical satire) by being more sombre are perhaps less universal than Gray's they have a broad acceptable truth of which the images are emblems. In *The Vanity of Human Wishes* the portraits of Wolsey and Charles of Sweden are like this; the characters do not interest us particularly as persons, but their names touch off the notion of splendour ending in defeat and their descriptions have, in grandiose impetus and volume, both the generality of large ideas and the concreteness of real figures. Wolsey in his 'full-blown Dignity', with 'Law in his Voice, and Fortune in his Hand', with the stream of honour flowing at his nod and jealous courtiers ('the Train of State') waiting to desert him, surrounded by the generic symbols of power — 'the Pride of aweful State, / The golden Canopy, the glitt'ring Plate' — is a person embodying a concept, and so is Charles, 'Unconquer'd Lord of Pleasure and of Pain', with peace courting his hand, war sounding the trumpet, nations suspended on his glance, and the dramatic ignominy of his fall conveyed by three simple generic images — 'a barren Strand, / A petty Fortress, and a dubious Hand'.

One concludes that Johnson felt life strongly as a union of fact and idea, that all life, physical and conceptual, was forcibly real to him. Indeed, thoughts and morality have for him an impressive force which weighs on actual life (his written and spoken aphorisms make almost a physical impact; Mrs Thrale records that 'he was more strongly and more violently affected by the force of words representing ideas' than anyone she knew). In these rich, resonant, witty, and massive poems Johnson provides more than the 'good sense in good metre' which a contemporary saw in them (though there is that too): he provides discourses charged with controlled passion, which steep life in thought and thought in life, and resound with a grandeur which does not exclude intimacy. *London* is the more uneven of the two major works, though its best passages are admirable; *The Vanity of Human Wishes* is among the few very great Augustan poems.

The shorter poems include the well-phrased *Epitaph upon Claudy Philips*, brief and deeply moving; the *Prologue at the opening of the Theatre in Drury Lane* (1747), so apt that much of it has become almost proverbial; and the two quatrain-poems, *A Short Song of Congratulation* (1780) and *On the Death of Dr Robert Levet* (1783). Both are in the central Augustan manner – social in substance, decisive in phrase, mature in vigour, and open-eyed in the light of common day. The disciplined movement and trochaic tune of the former were in A. E. Housman's mind as he started *The Shropshire Lad*, but the character is different – is pungent and downright instead of poignant and troubling; it is the idiom not of nostalgia and sentiment but of judgement and audacity. The elegy on Dr Levet is one of the century's most impressive things – grave, concentrated, and final. The images are few, conventional, and general – 'hope's delusive mine', 'sudden blasts', 'misery's darkest caverns'; the vocabulary is plain, with an undertone of Latin usage (words like 'officious' and 'innocent' have their original, not their modern, sense); the aim is simply to tell the truth. Nothing calls attention to itself, everything to its subject: the obscure, devoted servant of the neediest poor is portrayed decisive phrase by phrase in simple patterns of idea ('sudden blasts, or slow decline'; 'Of ev'ry friendless name the friend'; 'The pow'r of art, without the show'; 'The busy day, the peaceful night'); each item stands in steady relationship to the others. The voice observes the brief significant lingerings needed for reminiscence ('Yet still he fills affection's eye'), for careful definition ('Obscurely wise, and coarsely kind'), and for earnestness ('And sure th'Eternal Master found . . .'). The only moment that startles is the almost metaphysical particularity (dramatically justified) of the last stanza:

Then with no throbbing fiery pain,
    No cold gradations of decay,
Death broke at once the vital chain,
    And free'd his soul the nearest way.

No restrictive praise – control, balance, good taste, and the like – is adequate; the tone, as in all Johnson's major work, is exactly right; he serves ends so much greater than himself that blemishes of self-display or superiority are simply not to be found, and the Christian gravity and the strength of his nature display themselves here in charity, integrity, and tenderness.

On 20 March 1750, Johnson emerged, in Boswell's words, 'in the character for which he was eminently fitted – a majestic teacher of moral and religious wisdom'. In other words, he issued the first number of *The Rambler*, a periodical paper to be followed twice weekly for the next two years by 207 successors, of which he wrote all but five. From 1758 to 1760 it was followed, in a lighter tone and brisker style, by the weekly *Idler*, in 103 numbers of which Johnson wrote ninety-one. After a reign of forty years Addison's fashion of essay received not a deliberate but still a real challenge, for Johnson's nature could not be harnessed to the urbane social commentary which *The Spectator* had popularized, and if he fell short of *The Spectator*'s animation he surpassed in grandeur even its more solemn moments, as also those of Berkeley's religious papers in *The Guardian*. If the qualities of Addison and Johnson are to be compared, it is reasonable to do so by putting side by side the end of the 26th *Spectator* on the tombs in Westminster Abbey, and the end of the last *Idler*:

When I look upon the tombs of the great, every emotion of envy dies in me; when I read the epitaphs of the beautiful, every inordinate desire goes out; when I meet with the grief of parents upon a tombstone, my heart melts with compassion; when I see the tomb of the parents themselves, I consider the vanity of grieving for those whom we must quickly follow. When I see kings lying by those who deposed them, when I consider rival wits placed side by side, or the holy men that divided the world with their contests and disputes, I reflect with sorrow and astonishment on the little competitions, factions, and debates of mankind. When I read the several dates of the tombs, of some that died yesterday and some six hundred years ago, I consider that great day when we shall all of us be contemporaries, and make our appearance together.

(*The Spectator*, 26)

That, in its calculated rise and fall of rhythm, in the careful curve and undulation of each sentence, in its parallelism and symmetry, is an artful masterpiece of construction, but the pseudo-grandeur and profundity with which it treats a severe simple truth are positively distasteful. Put beside its complacency the following, and Johnson's own treatment of a severe simple truth appears immeasurably superior in tone and appropriateness:

> As the last *Idler* is published in that solemn week which the Christian world has always set apart for the examination of the conscience, the review of life, the extinction of earthly desirès, and the renovation of holy purposes; I hope that my readers are already disposed to view every incident with seriousness, and improve it with meditation; and that, when they see this series of trifles brought to a conclusion, they will consider that, by outliving the *Idler*, they have passed weeks, months, and years which are no longer in their power; that an end must in time be put to everything great, as to everything little; that to life must come its last hour, and to this system of being its last day, the hour at which probation and repentance will be in vain; the day in which every work of the hand, and imagination of the heart, shall be brought to judgement, and an everlasting futurity shall be determined by the past.

Nothing in Johnson's journalism became him like the leaving it, and it may seem unfair to match him at his strongest with Addison who here is not at his best (though he gives signs of thinking he is). Johnson, indeed, would have strongly deprecated any attempt to promote him over his predecessor's head; his *Life of Addison* ends with one of the most notable tributes ever paid by one writer to another. Posterity, as Macaulay observes, has traditionally decided in Addison's favour and it is Johnson's own aphorism that 'about things on which the public thinks long it commonly attains to think right'. Yet even in his own day there were those who preferred his strength to Addison's smoothness; he himself found Steele 'too thin for an Englishman's taste', and Mrs Thrale formed the impression that really, despite his praise, he felt much the same about Addison.[5] Perhaps it is fairest to conclude, with Arthur Murphy, an early biographer, that 'Addison lends grace and ornament to truth; Johnson gives it force and accuracy'. But for one reader at least, Johnson at his best is so superior to Addison at his best (the 'bests' being admittedly in very different kinds of work) as to render insignificant the question whether average Addison is better than average Johnson; average Johnson may lack Addison's vivacity, but the best Johnson adds nobility to life. That *The Rambler*, after a cool initial reception, came by Johnson's death to achieve ten editions in its collected form is a tribute to developing Augustan taste.

For while Johnson's immediate incentive was his living ('No man but a blockhead ever wrote except for money'), characteristically he earned it not by coaxing or flattering, but by firm concentration on truth. This truth was not the daily realism of life; that, he protested in the 4th *Rambler*, is already 'promiscuously described' in the novel. His theme is 'those parts of nature which are most proper for imitation'; he enlists under the Christian-humanist banner of conduct and faith.[6] He is sometimes too didactic, often too sweeping, and by no means always interesting. But impending always over these venial faults are the virtues of wit and grandeur; ever and anon the morality-subjects are sharpened by aphorism (indeed, typically they begin and end in aphorism, with a masterful survey of the territory in between) raising them into the air of permanent truth, or are deepened by personal contact with the moral realities behind them. As for grandeur, the eighteenth century produced no finer prose than the end of *The Rambler* No. 77 on the duties of authors, or No. 185 (Christmas Eve, 1751) on forgiveness, or *The Idler* No. 41 on his mother's death, or No. 103 already quoted.

The sense of life as probation stirred Johnson's deepest emotions. The *Prayers and Meditations* he composed for his private use, steeped in an earnest Anglican idiom, are full of this theme; so, indeed, is much of his work and not least the periodical-writing. Man he defines as 'a being placed here only for a short time, whose task it is to advance himself to a higher and happier state of existence, by unremitted vigilance of caution and activity of virtue' (*Idler* 43). Periodical essays have seldom been inspired by deeper feelings than these; his sense of his own indolence, arising from intermittent constitutional languor and melancholia, was like a conviction of sin, no more to be dispelled by the counter-evidence of his massive output than the sinner's sense of guilt is dispelled by evidence of his virtues, and he lived under a pressure which none but his intimates knew and which, with ill health, accounted for much of his testiness.

It accounted likewise, however, for his charity and his passion for truth. His judgements on moral problems are movingly wise and tolerant, and as for truthfulness, he imposed on his whole circle, says

Boswell, 'perpetual vigilance against the slightest degree of false-hood'. Factual truth was to be told just as it happened; moral truth was to be forwarded both by reiteration of moral principles and by the removal of illusion. In his removal of illusion he may be compared with Swift, but instead of Swift's angry passion in the exposure of human ignominy he dissipates the smoke-screen of distractions which conceal the morality by which one should live. Swift's main intention is, no doubt, constructive and reasonable, but he strips off so much pretension as to leave mankind naked and sore; the process, if in some sense just, is the justice of revenge, not of mercy. Johnson's proceedings are different; Mrs Thrale speaks of 'his truly tolerant spirit and Christian charity', and Boswell of his being 'never querulous, never prone to inveigh against the present times'. His sense of moral truth is one which operates on life to help mankind in its basic soundness and its daily struggle: he does not seek to make things seem easier than they are, yet he discountenances the rigour which demands too much of human kind. His sense of human fallibility (his own, in particular) leads him to sympathy, not to condemnation; he checks conventional judgements by his own experience and is prepared to defend, for instance, those who rise in the world and forget their friends, those who think better of themselves than circumstances warrant, those who are generous through vanity, and those who write better than they live.

Dryden's phrase about Shakespeare is true of Johnson – 'he is always great, when some great occasion is presented to him'. This is apparent in the periodicals and also in the letters, which deserve more comment than can be offered here (their substance and manner are strikingly interesting),[7] where space allows only the suggestion that nothing better reflects his stature than his letters on bereavements. To James Elphinston on his mother's death, to Mrs Thrale on those of her son and husband, to Bennet Langton on those of his uncle and Thrale and Levet, to Dr Thomas Lawrence on that of his wife, and, above all, to Dr William Dodd on his approaching execution (an epistolary situation of truly appalling difficulty) – in all such cases there can be no rival to the impeccably phrased sympathy and strength with which his readers are reminded (mankind, as we have seen, more often needs reminding than informing) of the deep moralities of life and death.

Rasselas (1759), which has been called a prose *Vanity of Human Wishes*, is, like the journals and letters, an occasional piece, hurried through to pay his mother's funeral expenses. But like the journals and letters its substance is anything but occasional. To call it the most distinguished English-Oriental moral tale, to compare and contrast it with Voltaire's contemporary *Candide*, is not to touch its essence; its essence is that it is the concentration of Johnson's greatness. Its harmony has the massive and subtle music of the poems; there are modulated melodies – 'Why should not life glide quietly away in the soft reciprocations of protection and reverence?'; there are orchestrated grandeurs like the compelling dignity of the first sentence, or Imlac's meditation on the Pyramid (chapter xxxii). Its moral quality is a notable triumph for Augustan humanism; since the recipe for happiness proves elusive, it is the practice of virtue that emerges, not at all platitudinously, as the end of life.

Rasselas is a parable, and on that fact depends its method. Its characters are representatives, not individuals; its incidents are diagrams, not events; its imagery, like that of the poems, is of general types, and its illustrations are simple. As Imlac the philosopher observes in a famous dissertation on poetry, 'the business of a poet is to examine not the individual but the species, to remark general properties and large appearances: he does not number the streaks of the tulip'. The tale, though as impressive and important as all but the best of Augustan novels, does not proffer itself as realistic fiction. An inventor devises artificial wings: he drops into a lake. A philosopher preaches stoicism: he is overwhelmed by his daughter's death. A pasha is at the height of prosperity: he is deposed by the Sultan: the Sultan himself is murdered by his Janissaries. Such events are demonstrative, not realistic. The point is worth making only because unless one consciously resolves to tolerate formal allegory the virtues of *Rasselas* may go unrecognized; a willing suspension of impatience is required for this unrealistic, parabolic narrative, in which the complexities of life are generalized by schematization. Johnson gets simplicity of outline from large propositions which ignore the streaks of the tulip, but by his sacrifice of detail he secures large compensations. Principally he gains clarity of pattern and boldness of mass, and this is appropriate to his needs since his aim as always is to reveal the large outlines of fundamental duty ('As the mind of Dr Johnson was greatly expanded,' remarks Mrs Thrale, 'so his first care was for general, not particular or petty morality'). The simplification is a concentration, not an enfeeblement; distractions are discarded, and the central meaning clarified.

Yet to overstress the general and abstract would be misleading. Like the poems, the tale chooses a middle ground between abstract and concrete, on which morality can be embodied and an impression of real life adequately yet unobtrusively maintained. The landscape on which Rasselas meditates (chapter iv) is that of a moralist, not an artist, and it serves to prompt his self-criticism:

> The moon by more than twenty changes admonished me of the flux of life; the stream that rolled before my feet upbraided my inactivity. I sat feasting on intellectual luxury regardless alike of the examples of the earth, and the instructions of the planets.

Yet with its tree-shaded rivers, lake, and fantastic mountains, its playing fish, singing birds, and browsing animals, the book has a quiet charm appropriate to its oriental exoticism. Scenes and places are, for their purposes, sufficiently indicated – the Happy Valley, the Nile, Cairo, the Pyramids, and the desert; the persons, though they talk a *Rambler* idiom, are suitable inhabitants of these representative settings and suitable recipients of moral experience; and the images are easily illustrative:

> Distance has the same effect on the mind as on the eye, and while we glide along the stream of time whatever we leave behind us is always lessening, and that which we approach increasing in magnitude. Do not suffer life to stagnate; it will grow muddy for want of motion; commit yourself again to the current of the world. (ch. xxxv)

Such imagery obeys the harmony of the book; it reveals the meaning with a quiet and satisfactory illumination.

The tone varies between dignity, sombreness, irony, and wit. The dignity and sombreness stress endurance instead of joy, knowledge instead of fancy, honesty instead of illusion; the irony is a simple and strong quality which never (it may be noted) indicates on Johnson's part any self-congratulation on superior wisdom; the wit generates aphorisms and curiously concentrated (almost 'metaphysical') effects on occasion, like Pekuah's comment on the needlework she did when a prisoner – 'you know that the mind will easily straggle from the fingers, nor will you suspect that captivity and absence from Nekayah could receive solace from silken flowers'. It also, by shrewd analysis and shaping, disciplines and patterns the ragged material of life, for though Johnson did not suppose life to be orderly he did serve a code of letters which elicited unity and definiteness from its confusions, as in his social views he maintained the ideal of social order. This is his style of mind, evinced in mastery of material and in a firm placing of every detail (even his earliest surviving work, his first letter, already shows it). To illustrate this adequately in a short space is impossible, but it may be seen, for example, in the impeccable organization of the second chapter – 'The discontent of Rasselas in the Happy Valley'. Each item is interrelated with the others, but the effect is not factitious; it is that of a mind creating symmetry and coherence, and improving on what Johnson calls 'mere obvious nature'.

One last point is related to wit and subtlety: it concerns Johnson's handling of commonplaces. They abound in his own writing, and the point of interest is to see him dealing with those of other people, as he does in the tales of two specious philosophers (chapters xviii and xxii) and as, elsewhere, he does with the opinions of the criticasters Dick Minim and Tom Steady (*The Idler*, 60, 61, 78), of readers who wanted *The Rambler* merely to repeat *The Spectator* (*The Rambler*, 23), and, most forcibly, of Soame Jenyns, a gentleman-philosopher whose *Free Inquiry into the Nature and Origin of Evil* (1757) provoked Johnson to one of the most trenchant of all book reviews. In *Rasselas* the first philosopher is exposed by his remorseless accumulation of clichés and by his desiccated and theoretical manner – 'he shewed ... he compared ... he communicated ... he enumerated ... he exhorted'. The second philosopher is exposed by his failure to define; his axioms – 'to live according to nature' and so on – could come from a *Rambler* individually, but never in this bland abundance unrelieved by the precisions of wit. Johnson knows when generalizations convey and when they avoid a meaning; his own are not intellectual 'proofs' but the warm deductions of experience. He exposes the specious by irony which works sometimes (as with Soame Jenyns) by open assault and sometimes by subtly slanted phrase and by parodic verbiage replacing wit.

The *Journey to the Western Islands of Scotland* (1775), briefer and less lively than Boswell's *Journal of a Tour to the Hebrides* (1785) though it is, and sometimes depreciated because Johnson is supposed not to enjoy scenery sufficiently, nevertheless commands admiration. Along with it should be read the very similar letters to Mrs Thrale from Scotland. Its origin was less in a thirst for Hebridean beauty than in curiosity about 'savage virtues', and the longest section is a dissertation on customs. But the result is broader and deeper than simple sociology. In the first place, as one might expect, Johnson takes to the sublime almost as to his own element − to that sense of grandeur and mystery which the vogue of the Bible and Milton, of Longinus and the new aesthetics of Burke[8] was impressing on the Augustan mind (Shakespeare, he once said, surpassed Young as the ocean a tea-kettle, and Corneille as the forest a clipped hedge). Slanes Castle, on its Aberdeenshire cliff, suggests 'all the terrific grandeur of the tempestuous ocean'; he tries to imagine the winter spate at the Falls of Fiers; he finds delight in the loneliness of Glen Moriston; the moonlit sea from Mull to Iona is 'a solemn and pleasing scene', and even a violent storm between Oban and Inverary is praised as 'a nobler concert of the rough music of nature than it had ever been my chance to hear before'. History has its own sublimity; he laments the ruins of St Andrews, Aberbrothick, and Elgin, and the meditation on Iona is one of the best things in the book. In the second place, such comments are not the casual embroidery of sentiment. Scenery and history evoke reflections, which come with all Johnson's spacious gravity, on the paradoxical grandeur and weakness of man. Wild landscape, he observes, displays 'one of the great scenes of human existence', and confronts us with the precarious condition of life. No paraphrase does justice to the severe passion with which Johnson enforces this common reflection, but the paragraph towards the end of the 'Anoch' section, beginning 'We were in this place at ease and by choice' and ending 'Yet what are these hillocks to the ridges of Taurus, or these spots of wildness to the deserts of America?' has in full measure his unique impressiveness.

Another section of this volume treats of criticism, and to discuss critical principles here would be redundant. But to avoid the critical documents altogether would be a sin of omission and a lapse in proportion, for Johnson without the *Preface to the English Dictionary* (1755), the *Preface* to Shakespeare (1765), and the *Lives of the Poets* (1779–81) would lose markedly in achievement. The first of these, characteristically, is a masterly mixture of general principles and personal experience; intellectually commanding and ingenious amidst all the complications of lexicography, Johnson impresses (as he impressed Boswell) by comprehensive and analytic power. The second, together with the notes on the plays, shows his best power in epitome, the vigour with which he represents the sane and unidolatrous tradition of Augustan criticism, his conclusive and happy boldness of phrase, and his broad and intimate humanity. To have his say on Shakespeare was for him, as for most critics, a supreme challenge and opportunity, never better taken. As for the *Lives*, 'the biographical part of literature is what I love most,' he told Boswell, who in another connection observed that 'Johnson loved business, loved to have his wisdom actually operate on real life.' No form could better express his sense of literature as emerging from and reflecting on life than literary biography, already evolved in Izaak Walton's *Lives* (1640–70), Thomas Sprat's *Cowley* (1668), Gilbert Burnet's *Passages of the Life and Death of the Earl of Rochester* (1680), William Oldys's *Life of Sir Walter Ralegh* (1736), and Johnson's own *Life of Richard Savage* (1744), but still hardly significant as criticism. Johnson's commentaries blossom naturally and pervasively into annotations on life; his subjects are not writers only but men, and his praise of Samuel Butler applies to himself:

> The most valuable parts of his performance are those which retired study and native wit cannot supply. He that merely takes a book from books may be useful, but can scarcely be great. Butler had not suffered life to glide beside him unseen or unobserved. He had watched with great diligence the operations of human nature, and traced the effects of opinion, humour [i.e. disposition], interest, and passion. From such remarks proceeded that great number of sententious distichs which have passed into conversation and are added as proverbial axioms to the general stock of practical knowledge.

All Johnson's criticisms, and even some of his occasional petulances, are prompted by his sense of truth. This truth is, mainly, the recognizable substance of life, with its normal passions and activities in their due proportions; Shakespeare is praised for allowing love no more preponderance in his plays than it has in life, the metaphysical poets are blamed for their eccentric images and ideas. But behind this quotidian truth is the other truth, of religion, allying his criticisn. with his deepest intuitions and giving it a dimension which other critics seldom approach. This does not appear often; many subjects hardly admit of it. But in the last resort it is there to provide its own scale of judgement. This metaphysical fact, the existence of religious truth guaranteeing a series of moral truths, is Johnson's ultimate authority; its reality for him is the incentive to a certain kind of critical demand – too narrow (we should say) when it requires direct ethical improvement, but bracingly large and generous when it insists on a discipleship not of current vogue or private vision but of life in its permanent and communal reality, held to be recognizable by every man and to be described in terms all recognize as true. The aim of such discipleship, however, is not (it may be repeated) mere realism but a concern for an understanding of life into which enters moral conduct; Johnson's criticism is steeped in the ethos of Christian humanism and it holds, with the astronomer in *Rasselas*, that 'to man is permitted the contemplation of the skies, but the practice of virtue is commanded' (ch. xl).

To speak too much in terms of a general ethos, however, is as one-sided as to stress too much the abstract or general in Johnson. That ethos is there, like a sounding-board to give resonance to what he says; one is never far from that other dimension. Still, it is of actual life that Johnson always thinks, and all his thought opens directly into it. 'The highest pleasure that the drama can give' lies in engrossed, uncritical reading of Shakespeare's 'just representations of general nature' (i.e. of life in its common truth), for 'his drama is the mirror of life'. And this, finally, seems the place for a word about Johnson's idea of literary originality, since the originality that he (like his contemporaries) most valued is that which Shakespeare showed in securing his 'just representations' – that function of the imagination which does not merely mirror life but brings it home to the reader with both novelty and familiarity. Shakespeare does this abundantly; in Shakespeare, not only the 'practical axioms and domestic wisdom' which Johnson praises in a curious but characteristic phrase, but innumerable other perceptions also are minted from raw experience and added to the stock of recognized truths. Such imagination works not by that 'perverseness of ingenuity' which beset the metaphysical poets but by seeming to remind us, in an improved form, of what we already sense to be true of life. This reminding is Johnson's whole intention in creative as well as critical work; it is concentrated into his comment on a passage he repeatedly praised in Congreve's *Mourning Bride*:

> He who reads these lines enjoys for a moment the powers of a poet; he feels what he remembers to have felt before, but he feels it with great increase of sensibility; he recognizes a familiar image, but meets it again amplified and expanded, embellished with beauty and enlarged with majesty.
>
> (*Life of Congreve*)

There is, indeed, nothing unusual in this; most readers of most poetry want recognition-plus-revelation, though at different times the proportions of familiar and novel will differ, and demands for beauty and ennoblement may change, according to the spirit of the time, into those for realism and intensity. The point is that while Johnson's mind naturally encompasses religion and moral philosophy, it is none the less vigorously and variously interested in the daily spectacle of society, and accords the highest praise to writers who best bring to mind the common experience of man, felt as imaginatively transcending commonplaceness.

Johnson was fortunate, in the short run, in that he had a shared code of intelligent taste to express, and, in the long run, in that that code was concerned centrally and thoughtfully with what the common sense (the conjoined form of those words is too slight in meaning) of the Christian-humanist tradition indicated to be important about man. An acceptance of duty to God and truth, a discipline of imagination and reason by which eccentricity and whim submit to the large authority of 'things as they are' ('We may take Fancy for a companion,' he wrote to Boswell, 'but must follow Reason as our guide'), and a wish to assert human community in serious and intelligent interests, the whole done within a tradition but with striking personal wit and independence – these qualities, exercised through the whole range of mind from vigorously grasped detail to comprehensive sanity about mankind at large, render the criticism (despite its limitations) thoroughly bracing and encouraging. Johnson is a great critic because while he works in a tradition his judgements are not those of tradition merely; they are judgements of tradition from which most of what is superficial has been pruned off by his unsurpassed power of looking at a subject for himself.

No one writing on Johnson can feel happy unless he has set him vividly in the context of his London life, surrounded by friends and acquaintances and reacting to the events of his time. This essay, not being another Boswell's *Life*, has clearly not done that, and may well be accused of having disembodied its subject. To refer the reader to other biographical treatments is, though necessary, no real amends; perhaps, instead, one ought to recall how varied, and how consciously enjoyed, was the Augustans' social world. Not all of it was enjoyable: Johnson's own experience, and the *Life of Richard Savage* (humanly speaking the finest of the *Lives*), are among the abundant evidence that makes that clear. But social enjoyment abounds in Augustan letters, and the zest of Johnson's participation in it is prominent in any portrait of him. Moreover, as Joseph Wood Krutch has remarked, the eighteenth century was 'the golden age of the amateur'. The intelligent man might speculate, not indeed on everything (for Augustan orthodoxy was timid about fundamentals, and Johnson himself was infuriated by deists or 'infidels'), but about a wide variety of acceptable subjects – the classics, the arts, history and current affairs, social life, personalities, the sciences, and so on. Even with John Wilkes, that provocative Whig, Johnson soon found common ground – 'classical learning, modern literature, wit and humour, and ready repartee' (Boswell's *Life*, III, 79). Common ground there was, in that fortunate Augustan culture of the non-specialist, where the availability of current knowledge enabled and encouraged any intelligent man to pursue an active breadth of interests. The vivacity of Johnson's conversation, Krutch suggests, was partly a safeguard against the onset of depression, but it was partly a sign of his confidence in his company, in the currency of knowledge and ideas – though again with the proviso that fundamentals were not to be shaken. The Augustan unity could not last long, but while it did last it produced a society confident, animated, and coherent, and Johnson, a central figure if ever there was one, was in ideas, personality, and social experience its best embodiment.

NOTES

1. Besides contemporary evidence, such as Boswell's *Life*, and the Piozzi and Murphy reprints in *Johnsonian Miscellanies*, ed. G. B. Hill (London, 1897), see J. W. Krutch, *Samuel Johnson* (London, 1948) and F. R. Leavis's 'Johnson and Augustanism' in *The Common Pursuit* (London, 1952).

2. See F. R. Leavis, as above, 97, 103.

3. See Walter Raleigh, *Six Essays on Johnson* (London, 1910).

4. The lines are 135–64. For comment, see *Poems*, ed. D. Nichol Smith and E. L. McAdam (Oxford, 1941), 46; and *Johnsonian Miscellanies*, ed. G. B. Hill, I, 180. A similar incident is in Hill, as above, I, 284.

5. For contemporary opinion, see Boswell's *Life*, ed. G. B. Hill and L. F. Powell (London, 1934–50), I, 224, and G. B. Hill, as above, I, 283.

6. See in particular the last *Rambler*, No. 208.

7. See introduction to *Selected Letters of Samuel Johnson*, ed. R. W. Chapman (London, 1925). The letters of condolence referred to are those (to Elphinston) of 25 September 1750; (to Mrs Thrale) of 25 March 1776, and 5 and 12 April 1781; (to Langton) of 21 September 1758, and 20 March 1782; (to Lawrence) of 20 January 1780; and (to Dodd) of 26 June 1776.

8. Longinus, *On the Sublime*; and Burke, *The Origin of our Ideas of the Sublime and the Beautiful* (1757).

ARCHITECTURE AND LANDSCAPE

ARTHUR HUMPHREYS

The quality of a civilization shows itself in its arts. This is notably true of the Augustan age, convinced as it was of the ethical-intellectual content of its art-forms: the Renaissance belief that a new philosophical era demanded a new literature and aesthetic was as deep-rooted in England as in Italy or France. This was a deliberate movement in civilization, an allegiance no longer to the medieval but to the humanism of Rome and Italy: the arts which had hitherto subconsciously (though no less effectively) expressed the spirit of their age now did so consciously, and with such success that architecture is the Augustans' mistress-art; in the arts of the whole period there are few experiences comparable in value with the sight of St Paul's, Blenheim, Kedleston, Syon, or the Royal Crescent at Bath.

The arts related themselves not only to aesthetic but also to political, ethical, and educational codes. They had a political bearing because they were held to express the national spirit: as Wren wrote:

> Architecture has its political uses; Public Buildings being the Ornament of a Country; it establishes a Nation, draws People and Commerce; makes the People love their native Country, which Passion is the Original of all great Actions in a Commonwealth.
>
> (*Parentalia, or Memoirs of the . . . Wrens*, 1750, Tract I)

A patriot like Defoe could confidently refer the new triumphs of building to the country's growing prosperity. Incidentally, politics could have a bearing on design; the great dining-rooms of the wealthy, Robert Adam explains in commenting on his scheme at Syon, were meant for those influential dinner-parties in which 'every person of rank' could 'enter with ardour into those discussions to which [politics] give rise'.[1] The great houses were not, as in France, merely country retreats; they were centres of political manoeuvre. But Augustan architecture had its ethical basis too; its churches have been called the most considerable body of religious art ever produced for a Protestant community up to that time, and its styles, both ecclesiastical and secular, paid homage to an ideal antiquity, to the harmony and order which humanism asserted. Its ideals of balance, lucidity, and controlled power were those that Augustan literature looked to as the standard of human nature.[2] Moreover, as Addison said, though beauty is a quality not objectively 'in' its source but subjectively interpreted from it, the faculty of interpretation is a particular sign of God's beneficence, and a man of a cultured taste, Addison asserts, enjoys not merely dilettante pleasure but the highest qualities of his nature (*The Spectator*, 411–13). And finally the arts had their educational bearing because knowledge of them was indispensable to the educated man, nourished not only on classical reading but on connoisseurship at home and preferably on the Grand Tour abroad, where with often obsequious regard he cultivated Renaissance painting, classical Roman and Italian building (later, Greek and Syrian), and

> ... vases bossed and huge inscriptive stones,
> And intermingling vines and figured nymphs,
> Floras and Chloes of delicious mould.
>> (DYER: *The Ruins of Rome*)

It is less possible with architecture than with literature to start about 1660. Much of Augustan inspiration goes back straight to Inigo Jones (1573–1652), the genius who collaborated and quarrelled with Ben Jonson and who, by a single act of innovating power, transplanted from Italy to England the Palladian style.[3] Andrea Palladio (1518–80) was not, like Brunelleschi or Michelangelo, one of the supreme Italian originators; his style is more 'classical' and scholarly. But it is full of grace and power, and it suited the English spirit better than anything more grandiose; with some modification (Inigo Jones, for instance, spaced the details of his façades more widely and so tranquillized them towards that serenity that characterizes English Palladian) it proved the happiest of models. Palladio, says Colen Campbell's *Vitruvius Britannicus* (1715), 'arrived to the *Ne plus ultra* of his art'; and Inigo Jones, in becoming his disciple, also had 'out-done all that went before'. Jones's masterpieces fall between the years 1615 and 1650, and include the Greenwich Queen's House, the Whitehall Banqueting Hall, St Paul's in Covent Garden, and the superb house at Wilton near Salisbury with its double-cube room designed for Van Dyck portraits. Architecture, he said, should be 'solid, proportional according to the rules, masculine and unaffected', and so for nearly two centuries it remained, with the important additions of richness and grace. But besides grander compositions he initiated, in laying out Covent Garden and Lincoln's Inn Fields, that 'terrace' fashion which blossomed into the disciplined order of Augustan streets, squares, and crescents. The Augustans credited his contemporary Peter Mills (c. 1600–70) with having provided London's first regular façade, and having pointed away from Tudor individualism, in designing the adjacent Great Queen Street (c. 1640). However much is said in the following pages of the major churches and country houses, it should never be forgotten that the decent order of modest street architecture, often carefully controlled by by-laws (as with much of London's eighteenth-century development, or Warwick's after the fire of 1694), is, if less spectacular, quite as significant a sign of taste. Not all building was good: not all poets were Popes or all prose-writers Johnsons. But the disciplined craftsmanship which proliferated in capable couplets and orderly sentences made an even greater contribution to English civilization in ordinary domestic architecture and design.

Between Inigo Jones and Wren there were able architects, like Mills already mentioned, who also built the notable Thorpe Hall, near Peterborough;[4] Sir Roger Pratt, architect of Coleshill, Berkshire (burnt down in 1952 and, most regrettably, immediately demolished); and John Webb – 'Inigo Jones's man', Evelyn called him – who oversaw various of his master's commissions, worked on Jones's designs for Whitehall Palace, and himself built great houses at Lamport in Northamptonshire for Sir Giles Isham (1654–7), Amesbury in Wiltshire (1661), Gunnersbury in Middlesex (1663), and the King Charles block at Greenwich Hospital (1665). But the next great stage is that of Wren (1632–1723), one of those who, with Newton, Boyle, Locke, Milton, Dryden, Purcell, and Grinling Gibbons, remind us that the late seventeenth century, prolifically fertile and imaginative, was among the greatest periods of English genius. His bent was towards science, and his early posts were precocious professorships in astronomy. His architecture is indeed intellectual, though not in a chill or negative sense, intellectual rather as Milton is intellectual, with classical scholarship assimilated in the

Wren: St Paul's Cathedral, London, from the west

Renaissance way to original genius, and made to glow into grandeur and beauty by sheer splendour of imagination. Whatever the scale of Wren's work, from moderate parish church or college chapel to palace or cathedral, it always suggests immense and wonderful power, harmoniously informing and enriching its volumes and surfaces. By a fortunate circumstance Wren was assistant to Sir John Denham, poet and Surveyor-General of Works, when Denham died in 1669; he thereby became responsible for designing London's public buildings after the Great Fire, and his City churches, inventively varied in adaptation to their awkward sites, are subtly modulated through all stages of their interiors and exteriors up to their crowning obelisks, lanterns, balls and cones, with a tough reasonableness underlying the lyric grace which reminds us to which century they belong. These, with the smaller masterpieces like the Pembroke and Emmanuel Chapels and Trinity Library at Cambridge, the Sheldonian Theatre and Trinity Chapel at Oxford, and Morden College at Blackheath, and with the greater masterpieces at Greenwich Palace, Hampton Court, Chelsea Hospital, and St Paul's Cathedral, are intellectually and imaginatively among the richest and strongest of English achievements and make Wren one of the supreme architects of the world.

Greatly as he outshines his contemporaries, six others deserve mention with him, since their combined work marks England's nearest approach to 'baroque' taste – taste expressing not the accuracy and poise of the strict classic but using a classical language to express dramatic energy and emotion in varied outline and ebullient forms. They are William Talman (1650–1720), Nicholas Hawksmoor (1661–1736), Sir John Vanbrugh (1664–1726), Thomas Archer (1668–1743), John James (1672–1746), and James Gibbs (1682–1754). Labels are crude expedients; 'baroque' here means no great formal resemblance between these men but a sharing of imaginative energy which has its counterpart in Restoration literature. Talman, Archer, and James are less important than Hawksmoor, Vanbrugh, and Gibbs. The first of them did some of the City halls after the Fire (the Fishmongers', Haberdashers', Drapers', and Tailors'), but is best remembered for the grandeur of Chatsworth. James's best work is St George's in Hanover Square, with fine bravura in its Corinthian portico and a tower full of spring and vigour. Archer is more

Archer: St Philip's Cathedral, Birmingham

interesting than either: he designed St Philip's, Birmingham (the cathedral), and two astonishingly fine London churches in St Paul's, Deptford, and St John's, Westminster. His elevations are strongly modelled and his towers and spires vigorously conceived. St Philip's gratifies the eye with curves vitally related between its portico, its tower walls (which, surprisingly concave, curl outward to buttress-like double pilasters at each corner), and its dome and cupola. St Paul's, Deptford, is a powerful and handsome composition, with bold square nave and a circular tower rising through a semicircular portico; St John's is one of London's most remarkable buildings, conventionally reckoned ungainly but in fact strikingly successful in its command over dramatically interrupted lines, a refreshing and invigorating conception.

Much greater than these men, however, were Hawksmoor and Vanbrugh, located at the centre of the movement, for Hawksmoor spent thirty years in Wren's office and also worked with Vanbrugh on Castle Howard. The baroque, it has been said, 'intellectualized the picturesque', and the phrase fits both men. Besides the handsome Queen's Library and quadrangle at Oxford (where he also fitted All Souls with its Gothic quad), and the boldly fine Easton Neston house in Northamptonshire, Hawksmoor did six remarkable London churches – St Alphege, Greenwich, where James added the tower; St Anne, Limehouse, and St George-in-the-East; St Mary Woolnoth with grandiosely-masonried walls and strange double-peaked front; St George, Bloomsbury; and Christ Church, Spitalfields, with perhaps the finest feature of all, a west front with columned porch whose barrel-vault and horizontal wings are brilliantly echoed in successive curves and horizontals up the tower and steeple, which soars at last into a virtual Gothic spire. These churches are signalized by their force and emotional daring, which risk ugliness yet save themselves by grandeur. The same thing, more dramatically, is true of Vanbrugh, playwright-architect, whose work was for two centuries the butt of satire (with, however, some generous eulogies), and is now rightly extolled. The reason is not its habitable convenience; in this respect Blenheim, though perhaps better than often supposed, is unconvincingly organized, and Seaton Delaval strikes one as completely and brazenly preposterous. But Vanbrugh was a modeller rather than a planner, and his successes are not those of domestic efficiency.

Castle Howard, in Yorkshire, with a Corinthian order reinforcing the main block beneath a dominating pediment, with a sweep of round-headed but strongly keystoned windows from end to end (the effect has the vitality of multiplied Gothic ogives), with a picturesque enrichment of urn-like finials sprouting along the skyline, and a theatrical lantern tower and dome dominating everything, is a spectacle of captivating spirit. In Vanbrugh's work, Reynolds per-

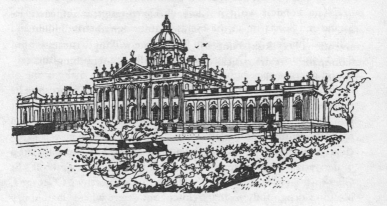

Vanbrugh: Castle Howard, Yorkshire

ceived, 'there is a greater display of imagination than we shall find perhaps in any other'.[5] The grandeur of the much-visited and well-known Blenheim needs no emphasis: the scale and audacity of its composition are breath-taking: here again Vanbrugh has no British rival. As for Seaton Delaval, if not more astonishing than Blenheim (nothing could be), it is quite unforgettable. Vanbrugh once referred to 'the tame, sneaking south', and this Northumbrian house seems designed to express the opposite qualities of the north. Along with his other compositions it has the quality of 'movement', which Reynolds defined in him and later architects like Robert Adam sought successfully to imitate, as the eye is carried back from the forecourt's great projecting wings to the fortress-like and almost castellated main block, with heavy rustication* of its front wall and grouped columns, and superhuman keystones over its arches. Van-

*Masonry of large blocks with roughened surface and sunken joints.

brugh did other buildings elsewhere and his signature is of a severe and generally spectacular grandeur – 'baroque without ornament', it has been called. Here the severity and spectacle are more than merely grand; they are in the highest degree dramatic, and the sight of them is one of the great architectural experiences of life.

As for Gibbs, with less distinctive energy than Hawksmoor and Vanbrugh and more scholarly training (he had studied in Paris and Rome), he is not inferior in accomplishment, since he fixed a splendid mark on London with St Clement Danes's steeple, St Mary-le-Strand and St Martin-in-the-Fields. Cambridge's Senate House and Fellows' Building at King's, and Oxford's Radcliffe Camera, are not less prominent: at Derby he built All Saints (the cathedral), whose internal open lightness and fluency of curve make it one of the finest of neo-classic churches, and at Ditchley in Oxfordshire he replaced the Earl of Lichfield's antiquated seat by a house of that refined opulence which Lord Burlington and William Kent soon made the century's dominant fashion. In church design he was particularly influential; his *Book of Architecture* (1728) bore fruit in a crop of derivative Gibbsian spires, one of the best being on Flitcroft's St Giles-in-the-Fields which, with Hawksmoor's nearby St George's, blossoms delightfully in the architectural desert where Shaftesbury Avenue meets Holborn. Others occur, for instance, in Kent (Mereworth), Worcester (St Nicholas), Wolverhampton (St John), and in the transatlantic colonial style from New England to South Carolina. Gibbs carries on the line of Wren with all the Augustan virtues of a Roman power and richness, and it is hard to think that the visual dramas of Trafalgar Square or the Strand, of Oxford or Cambridge, would not have been diminished if any contemporary other than Wren had been substituted for him.[6]

The phase of taste which brings Augustan domestic building to the height of its splendour is, however, the next, that associated with the man whom Gay calls 'Burlington, belov'd of ev'ry Muse', Pope's friend, and a great patron-connoisseur. Lord Burlington (1694–1753) gathered round him, in more or less close association, a group who turned from Wren's baroque tradition to the stricter beauties of Palladianism – or, more truly, from what was often (especially in the provinces, and despite the greater architects' example) a rather stolid style of heavy plasterwork, coarse orders, and dark wainscoting, to an ordered opulence.[7] Among Burlington's aides and disciples were most of the best men before Robert Adam – Colen Campbell (d. 1729), the Venetian Giacomo Leoni (1686–1746), Henry Flitcroft ('Burlington Harry', 1697–1769), James Paine (1725–89), and pre-eminently William Kent (1685–1748). Pope put their aims in a couplet –

> Jones and Palladio to themselves restore,
> And be whate'er Vitruvius* was before.

On an illuminating Grand Tour to Italy (1714–15) Burlington drew Palladio's buildings and bought Palladio's sketches. He sponsored Leoni's two magnificent volumes, lavish with text and plates, of *The Architecture of A. Palladio in Four Books* (1715), and also Kent's *Designs of Inigo Jones* (1727), which included some by John Webb and by Burlington and Kent themselves. Among the most handsome of Augustan publications, and historically of great importance, is Colen Campbell's *Vitruvius Britannicus, or the British Architect* (3 vols: 1715–25), which deplores the ornateness of Italian baroque, holds Palladio and Inigo Jones to be supreme, and still has praises for contemporaries from Wren to Hawksmoor and James. 'Vitruvius Britannicus' was traditionally a design for Inigo Jones, but Campbell applies it generically to the major English classicists. As one more (not the last) of Burlingtonian volumes there is Robert Castell's splendid *Villas of the Ancients Illustrated* (1728), dedicated to the Earl with a confident tribute:

When I again reflect that many works of Inigo Jones's and Palladio's had perish'd but for your Love to Architecture, I lay aside my Fears, and the rather as this Work is wholly founded on the Rules of the Ancients, for whom your Lordship has on all Occasions manifested the greatest Regard.

More now begins to be heard of 'the Ancients'; the Burlingtonians were great revivalists, and set a fashion for archaeological research. The results were of extreme aesthetic importance – Robert Wood brought back the styles of Roman Syria (*The Ruins of Palmyra*, 1753; *The Ruins of Balbec*, 1757), James Stuart and Nicholas Revett's famous *Antiquities of Athens* (1762) launched the severe correctness of a

---

*Marcus Pollio Vitruvius, born about 80 B.C., is noted for his work *De Architectura*, rediscovered in St Gall monastery in the fifteenth century and highly influential throughout the Renaissance.

'Greek' fashion, and Robert Adam proved his scholarship (encouraged to do so, he said, by the welcome given to Wood's volumes) with *The Ruins of the Palace of the Emperor Diocletian at Spalato* (1764). Ultimately the central tradition was dispersed in imitation and eclecticism. Yet we need not anticipate; English Palladian is full of character, and not at all academically decadent. From the 1710s to about 1780 one great building after another rose in a style of rich dignity – Burlington's own Chiswick House, modelled on a Palladian villa, and his York Assembly Rooms, which have been handsomely restored, with the noble perspective of its Corinthian-columned Egyptian Room glowing with harmonious colour;[8] Leoni's Clandon Park at Guildford, with a fine sense of space and enrichment, Moor Park in Hertfordshire, its loftiness emphasized by Corinthian pilasters and engaged columns rising the whole height of its elevation, and Lyme Hall in Cheshire; Campbell's new front to Burlington House, Piccadilly, Mereworth in Kent, Wanstead in Essex (since demolished), Houghton in Norfolk, built for Walpole (the interior by Kent), and Stourhead in Wiltshire; Flitcroft's Woburn Abbey in Bedfordshire and Wentworth Woodhouse in Yorkshire; and Kent's Devonshire House in Piccadilly (demolished), Holkham in Norfolk, a notable house in Berkeley Square (No. 44) with a spectacularly-modelled staircase, and the universally familiar Horse Guards. Kent designed or shared in many other buildings, as painter, architect, furniture designer, or, most famously, landscapist (he was the man, in Horace Walpole's phrase, who 'leaped the fence and saw that all Nature was a garden'), and he has consequently been disparaged as a universal dabbler. More properly, a recent (and the only adequate) study of him suggests,[9] he is the strongest candidate for an empty niche between Wren and Reynolds. The spirit of the eighteenth century is in Kent as much as any man; in architecture he has the power of the central tradition and in his 'natural' gardening the confidence of the innovator who thinks himself (in this case rightly) to be moving in a happy direction. His work implies the cultural strength of the oligarchy – wealth, zest, and the disciplined harmony of ordered power. For all its refinements Palladianism is still an idiom of strength; its lordly disposition of mass, its rich decoration, its bold mouldings and pediments, its commanding Corinthian columns, these inherit the full genius of Augustanism. It steered

Kent: 44 Berkeley Square, London

English architecture clear of the floridity which afflicted the Continent.

As the age of Pope is dominated by Burlington, so, though a shade less completely, is that of Johnson by Robert Adam (1728–92) and his subordinate brother James (1730–94).[10] As the Burlingtonians evolved their style out of baroque but also reacted from it, so the Adams evolved theirs out of the Burlingtonian (their father William was an early and distinguished Scots Palladian) but sought greater refinement and a more elegant serenity. The early Georgians' sturdy woodwork, the Palladians' compartmented ceilings and strongly-moulded walls and doorways, gave way before delicate plaster arabesques, silk damask hangings, and glowing colour. Robert Adam carried to perfection the Palladian fashion of rooms *en suite*, each related to its neighbours, with symmetrical alignments giving vistas and perspectives, shaping his spaces with coved ceilings or curved apses round which the eye flows with the utmost sense of grace. His masterpieces are such conceptions as the series of rooms which surround the great alabaster-columned hall of Kedleston, or that sequence – entrance hall, anteroom, dining-room, drawing-room, and long gallery, each of exquisite splendour – which he devised at Syon. 'The parade, the convenience, and social pleasures of life,' he said, were in his plans 'more strictly attended to in the arrangements and disposition of apartments' than ever before: connoisseurs, he hoped,

will easily perceive within these few years a remarkable improvement in the form, convenience, arrangement, and relief of apartments; a greater movement and variety in the outside composition, and in the decoration of the inside an almost total change.

(*Works in Architecture of Robert and James Adam*, 1778, preface)

And a footnote on 'movement' (for which he admired Vanbrugh) is prophetic:

Movement is meant to express the rise and fall, the advance and recess, with other diversity of form, in the different parts of a building, so as to add greatly to the picturesque of the composition. For the rise and fall, advancing and receding, with the convexity and concavity and other forms of the great parts, have the same effect in architecture that hill and dale, foreground and distance, swelling and sinking, have in landscape; that is, they serve to produce an agreeable and diversified contour that groups and contrasts like a picture.

Kenwood: Adam room or Lord Mansfield's Library

He clearly looked on his style as a matter not only of elegantly adorning surfaces (he, and more especially his imitators, have been accused of reducing architecture to decoration) but of handling masses with a dynamic sense of all three dimensions and producing what might well be called a romantic effect. His terms, perhaps, are misleading; they suggest a painter who has strayed into architecture, a designer of plastic forms rather than of habitable structures, and indeed 'the picturesque' in the romantic sense was not at all beyond him; his numerous 'Gothic' and Piranesian drawings of ruins are evidence, and so, spectacularly, is his astonishing Culzean Castle, that vast crenellated and turreted pile which crowns an Ayrshire cliff and whose exterior vies in romantic feeling with the confronting Firth of Clyde and mountains of Arran. An upheaval in sensibility is not far away. But Adam is far more than a designer of architectural scenery; Culzean itself internally is a fine classical house, with all of Adam's harmony of volume and grace of line, particularly in a circular salon and oval staircase, and like the rest of his work it is the expression by genius of that phase when the early vehemence of Augustan culture had been directed into an admirably ordered civilization. Adam decorated or adapted far more houses than he built; still, in whatever capacity he worked, in places like Shardeloes, Harewood, Kedleston, Osterley, Syon, Kenwood, Nostell Priory, and Mersham-le-Hatch, he and his brilliant executants developed the most exquisite elegances of colour and line that England has to show, displayed in interiors both lavish and refined behind façades of serene distinction.

To touch on the other main names perfunctorily is hardly fair to them; however, it is better than to imply that the whole eighteenth-century achievement was that of a few leaders. In furniture, too, the fame of Chippendale, Sheraton, and Hepplewhite has until recently unjustly obscured the many designers who, in London and the provinces, and indeed across the Irish Sea, worked with excellent invention and taste.[11] The major architects, then, include John Vardy, whose Spencer House presents its quintessentially Palladian façade to Green Park in London; the elder George Dance, with London's Mansion House, and the younger with a formidably severe Newgate Prison (demolished); William Chambers, whose great monument – an unquestioned masterpiece – is Somerset House, and Chambers's pupil James Gandon, whose Dublin Custom House recalls his master.

These three last mentioned have been called the finest public buildings in Britain since the time of Wren. There are also Lancelot ('Capability') Brown, whom Chambers tartly disliked for carrying off the commission to build Claremont House in Surrey for Clive of India, and who, though principally famous for landscape gardening, was an attractive Palladian;[12] James Paine, who was much in favour before the Adam vogue, and whose great houses at Kedleston and Nostell Priory[13] Adam took over and completed; and James Wyatt, who sprang into fame at twenty-six with the Oxford Street Pantheon (1772) and immediately began to divert fashion from the Adams. The Pantheon, the universal theme of society talk, did not last long, but Wyatt left great classical houses, at Heaton Park near Manchester, Heveningham Hall in Suffolk, and Dodington in Gloucestershire, in a brilliant style, closely resembling yet cooler and chaster than the Adams' – and then turned his tastes with the time and plunged into Gothic, though by no means abandoning the classical.

And finally, there are the sterling architects of the provinces,[14] chief among them the John Woods, father and son, of Bath, who created some of Georgian England's finest compositions in the Palladian terraces of that city – in the North and South Parades, Queen Square, the Circus, the Royal Crescent, and the Assembly Rooms – and nearby at Prior Park, Titanbarrow, and Belcombe Court. Not far behind comes John Carr of York, engaged on several of the great country houses, like Harewood, and on town buildings like the handsome Crescent at Buxton. Elsewhere there were Henry Bell of King's Lynn, with his picturesque and Wren-like Custom House there (an object-lesson on how to be delightful on a site about sixty feet square) and perhaps the almost-Continental-baroque Duke's Head; Thomas White of Worcester, who may have worked for Wren and whose Guild Hall and St Nicholas are thoroughly pleasing; and William and John Bastard, who did good street houses and an admirable church in Blandford, Dorset, after a fire in 1731. There were many others – Warwickshire and the Bath-Bristol area were particularly rich in local talent – but to particularize would be to enter too much into detail. What is necessary here is not to investigate the minutiae of architectural history (though, indeed, research into provincial building is paying rewarding dividends of interest) but to stress how the steady and thoughtful evolution of Augustan literature, and its percolation through a more closely united society to every part of the land, were paralleled by the same process in architecture, and accompanied by a similar ability to perform well in visual design, according to the standards of good craftsmanship and accepted models. Even when provincial towns have nothing to show of the first rank, they provide some of the eighteenth century's most enduring satisfactions in their churches, parsonages, public buildings, and dwelling-houses. The triumphal mansions are, in a way, less significant; having behind them all that money can buy they represent a specialized taste. The sound-

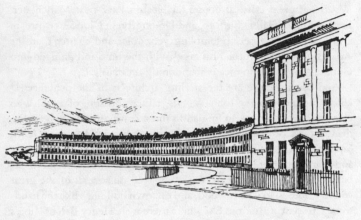

The Woods: Royal Crescent. Bath

ness of Augustan instinct is more reliably shown by those thousands of buildings it produced almost without thinking, for the common purposes of life.

The lifespan of English neo-classicism is about fifty years longer at each end in architecture than in literature. Its first triumphs are the early ones of Inigo Jones; its last, the great Regency schemes of John Nash, in Carlton House Terrace and Regent's Park, Sir John Soane's Bank of England, and, indeed, much later buildings in the nineteenth century, like Elmes's St George's Hall in Liverpool. But the story becomes one of multiplying models and dispersed effort, and the spirit anything but Augustan. It is necessary rather to return to the eighteenth century to mention two signs of that eclecticism which was to disrupt the settled (though never static) tradition; they are *chinoiserie* and the Gothic. The former[15] arose from the importation, with expanding trade, of Eastern products; it made itself felt first in applied design, particularly of lacquer work, on late seventeenth-century furniture, and thereafter the gay asymmetrical unperspectived decoration of Chinese figures and scenes held its place throughout the eighteenth century, to be amplified in the nineteenth by a rash of pseudo-exotic imitations from all over Asia. Augustan

The Woods: The Palladian Bridge, Prior Park, Bath

chinoiserie is often, though not always, charming; it was simultaneously satirized and cultivated; it produced a crop of eccentric yet gay and elegant furniture and picturesque latticed bridges and summer-houses; delicately bizarre wall-papers were imported from the Orient and hung in classical mansions like Moor Park and Woburn, or town houses like Mrs Elizabeth Montagu's in Portman Square; the more adventurous aristocrats and gentry indulged their tastes in a 'Chinese' room, as the Duke of Beaufort did at Badminton, the Duke of Bedford at Woburn, and Richard Lord Verney at Claydon. Drawings of Chinese structures and furniture appeared in pattern-books, and William Chambers, whose youthful travels in the East enabled him to figure as an expert, produced two remarkable books – *Designs of Chinese Buildings* (1757) and *A Dissertation on Oriental Gardening* (1772) – as well as the Pagoda at Kew. The Chinese were, incidentally, credited by many enthusiasts with sublime virtue, but that is beside the point: their decorative arts would have been quite as influential had they been supposed as iniquitous as other men.

For with Gothic, *chinoiserie* was a glimpse of the strange and unclassical, free from 'the rules of the Ancients', a decorative revelry if not a solid repast. It was the contrasting element of the grotesque in an age of enlightened good sense. Sometimes it was very grotesque, and then it was bad; some eighteenth-century *chinoiserie* furniture is hideous. But sometimes it was only slightly grotesque, and then it provided a kind of English rococo, fanciful and gay. And often, in the richly and charmingly ornate designs applied to lacquered furniture, it was not grotesque at all but enchanting. It was a minor mode, until it merged into the larger exoticism of the Romantic Revival; it diversifies the field of Augustan taste most engagingly; and it suggests the puckish readiness of taste to escape from the reasonable into the fantastic.

As for the Gothic,[16] that never quite vanished from favour. Lovers of the past dwelt fondly on the veneration old buildings inspired in them, and at Oxford Wren designed Christ Church's Tom Tower in a noble Gothic style. The popular levels of Augustan taste as reflected in Defoe's *Tour* could still be enthusiastic – Defoe himself not infrequently commends the venerable grandeur of Gothic buildings; and in 1742 the antiquary William Stukeley suggested that Glastonbury should be preserved because of 'that great concourse of strangers that comes to see it'. Men of intelligence like Vanbrugh, Gay, Pope, and Hogarth could admire the Gothic style, though perhaps only half-comprehending it, and provincial builders could still build in it; St Mary's tower at Warwick (1697–1704) has been called the final flourish of English Perpendicular architecture. Gothic was never, therefore, quite submerged. Yet fashionable taste certainly relegated it to a subordinate role, either as a pleasing reminder of outlived barbarism, or as a piquant ingredient in a view. In these dubious guises it broke out as a craze towards the middle of the century: the first sham ruins – those pointed reminders that Augustan taste could be odd – appeared in Lord Bathurst's park near Cirencester about

Bell: The Custom House, King's Lynn

1733; Kent put up a ruin for Lord Cobham at Stowe (1742), and then did Gothic screens at Gloucester and Beverley; Batty Langley's *Gothic Architecture Improved by Rules and Proportions* (1742) tried to discover from medieval buildings an aesthetic system; Sanderson Miller made his name as a Gothicist with a ruin at Hagley in 1746; and in 1747 Horace Walpole bought Strawberry Hill and set about the battlementing, pinnacling, fenestrating, and cluttering which his letters so rapturously describe. Strawberry Hill is elaborate and enthusiastic dilettantism, 'architecture' in terms of decorative application within and romantic asymmetry without, in the quintessential spirit of the oncoming 'picturesque' vogue. A great deal of archaeological investigation went into it, much of it in a spirit which may not unfairly be called 'innocent foolery with Gothic patterns',[17] but some of it showing a serious desire for Gothic form. 'Walpole,' it has been said, 'demonstrated for the first time a loyalty to medieval precedent which appeared, on the face of it, to be as fastidious as that of any classical architect to the precedents of Rome.'[18] Strawberry Hill is the most famous portent of an earthquake in taste; Gothic (or, rather, Gothick) was promoted from the recesses of the park to be not only light decoration but the very spirit of a fashionable house. In the later eighteenth century Gothick imitations abound, some deriving from Walpole's example, others from other 'Gothick' practitioners such as William Kent (1685–1748). There are many pleasing churches, humbly aspiring to the spiritual resonance of medieval Christianity, many charming villas and cottages, and, increasingly, houses and (at the turn of the century) show places on a grand scale – James Wyatt's Lee Priory in Kent (1782) for instance – of which Walpole wrote to its owners, 'My house is . . . but a sketch by beginners, yours is finished by a great master', and the same architect's Fonthill, Wiltshire, for William Beckford (1790), which soon collapsed, and Ashridge, Hertfordshire (1806). And, of course, there is Robert Adam's Culzean Castle, Ayrshire (1780–90) (see p. 438).

The connections of this with literary taste are clear; it is all part of that mixed medievalizing and naturalizing which were soon to transform European aesthetics. While the Gothick vogue was encouraging an artificial sense of the past, its twin-brother of 'natural' gardening was simultaneously producing some of the most delightful and original works of art the English imagination has ever achieved. The evolution of the 'natural' garden, briefly, meant the abandonment of geometrical plans, of straight walks and avenues, of symmetrical terraces, balustrades, and waterworks, in favour of lawns and park-land.[19] Man's control over Nature was exercised not by that domi-nance which levels hill and valley, regularizes pools and flower-beds, and sets out trees in rows, but by that subtler process which takes advantage of natural features, the slopes of ground, the varying shapes of copses, and the natural flow of water. The stages of transformation at Stowe, for instance, can be followed in successive maps showing the work done in turn by Bridgeman, Kent, and 'Capability' Brown: the geometrical parterre goes first, then by degrees the formal walks focusing on statues and temples, then the canalized stream and the straight-edged lake, until finally (the saplings being given time to grow) the scene extends as at present, with an immense sweep of lawn down to and beyond a 'natural' lake, and screens of trees advanc-ing and receding on either hand to lead the eye easily away – a scene of paradisal serenity. The result is, of course, much better than Nature herself could do – a remark which applies to the whole of pastoral England under its careful regimen of planting and farming, but pre-eminently to estates such as Kent and Brown, and later Hum-phrey Repton, developed. Subsequently, towards the end of the century, coincidentally with the fuller fervour of Romanticism, opinions were divided; was Nature to be treated in Brown's gentle and placid manner, which might be insipid, or should she be as shaggy and 'picturesque' as possible? But that is really too late a topic for treatment here; its solution, approximately, was to reserve the mild treatment for landscape gardening (fortunately), and to go un-kemptly wild in painting or to tour in search of the natural grandeurs of romantic scenery. The vogue of the picturesque enthusiast, like William Gilpin (1724–1804), whose numerous books on the subject[20] are important documents in taste, affected rather landscape at large than in the garden.

To connect Augustan literature and the visual arts is not difficult. In the case of landscape and the Gothic no more need be said in the brief compass here available than to stress how strongly, from both aesthetic and philosophical quarters the current set towards the subtler intuitions, the irrational perceptions, a reverence for natural beauty, and the senses of mystery, and of humility before the countryside and the past. Apparently contradicting the intellect's scientific triumphs, there began an aesthetic distrust which dissociated the aesthetic from the rational. But the contradiction was only apparent: the more Nature's processes seemed great, harmonious, and organic, the less right man seemed to have to impose his own discipline upon her, unless he imposed it so discreetly as to make his discipline seem her own work.

But the central Augustan mode is different, for it inherits the authority of the humanist tradition. In all the arts respect was due to the great and acknowledged masters: in literature, neo-classic criticism is founded not on subservience to but certainly on admiration for classical precedent; in painting, the influential critics of the eighteenth century, Jonathan Richardson and Sir Joshua Reynolds,[21] derive the idealizing principles of their art from classical statuary and the Renaissance masters; in architecture, the discipleship is clear. 'The buildings of the Ancients,' Robert Adam observes in prefacing *The Ruins of the Palace of the Emperor Diocletian*,

are in Architecture what the works of Nature are with repect to the other Arts; they serve as models which we should imitate, and as standards by which we ought to judge.

The closeness of this imitation varied, and as the century advanced the increase in archaeological verisimilitude tended to subject original invention to scholarly derivation. Only as long as architecture maintained a parallel with literature in invigorating its classical devotion with native boldness and invention did the tradition find new things to say.

Why should a Mediterranean architecture have been so cultivated in (as satirists indefatigably reiterated) an unkind English climate? The answer is partly aesthetic; the style was the handsomest English architects had ever seen, and, however unsuited they were to British weather, vast porticoes and detached pavilions looked superb. But more deeply the answer is in terms of the intellectual clarification and social ideals of the day. Classical styles reflected the great Whig confidence in a 'free', wealthy, and oligarchical society; the lines of classical architecture, palatial or humble, reminded the proprietor that his age had outgrown the obscure chaos of former ages and, with the added advantages of Christian faith and British enterprise, was sharing the cultural light which had shone in Virgil and Horace and had brightened again in the Italy of the Renaissance. Whiggism, with its doctrine of enlightened liberty, had much to do with this spirit. But it was not a Whig monopoly; it belonged to the whole state of society. Augustan literature and art typically find their support in social life; Augustan paintings, instead of rendering a personal vision, fit into Augustan rooms as pieces of furniture to be lived with, part of the décor of that kind of life. Nor was it merely an English aristocratic code. The states of the Atlantic seaboard of America shared with Britain the sense that classical styles were as 'masculine and un-affected' as Inigo Jones said they should be, and spoke for the spirit of enlightened reason and manly good sense; here, in pure and un-ornate form, were styles which particularly suited both the vigorous and enterprising colonials before the Revolution and the independent and liberated republicans after it. Back in Britain, as with literature, the public participated ever more widely in art; it bought reproductions; it quarrelled in the press over the style and siting of statues; and from 1768 it had the Royal Academy to flock to. Better than any-where else society saw its ideals of enlightenment, amenity, progress, classical discipline, and 'polite imagination' expressed in its architecture, and of serene pastoralism realized in its parks.

NOTES

John Summerson's *Architecture in Britain 1530 to 1830* (Pelican History of Art, 1953) is an invaluable guide to the whole subject.

1. See Christopher Hussey, 'Syon House, Middlesex', in *Country Life*, 1 December 1950.

2. A good analysis of these ideals is in Geoffrey Scott, *The Architecture of Humanism* (London, 1914), ch. 8.

3. On Inigo Jones, Wren, Vanbrugh, Hawksmoor, Gibbs, and Adam, see John Summerson, *Architecture in Britain 1530–1830* (1953).

4. See Howard Colvin, 'The Architect of Thorpe Hall', *Country Life*, 6 June 1952.

5. See Reynolds, *Discourse XIII*.

6. A good many evidences of Gibbs's influence are collected in *Stuart and Georgian Churches outside London*, by Marcus Whiffen (1947).

7. For Burlington's ideals, see Pope, *Epistle to Burlington*, and Christopher Hussey's introduction to *The Work of William Kent*, by Margaret Jourdain (1948).

8. See R. A. Alec-Smith, 'The York Rooms Restored', *Country Life*, 22 June 1951.

9. See Christopher Hussey, as above.

10. The standard study is A. T. Bolton, *The Architecture of Robert and James Adam* (1922), but *The Age of Adam* by James Lees-Milne (1947) and *The Work of Robert Adam* by Geoffrey Beard (1978) are more easily available and are highly effective.

11. See R. Edwards and M. Jourdain, *Georgian Cabinet Makers*, 1946.

12. His buildings (and gardens) are well studied in Dorothy Stroud, *Capability Brown* (rev. edn, 1957).

13. For Nostell, see Christopher Hussey, 'Nostell Priory, Yorkshire', in *Country Life*, 16, 23, and 30 May 1952.

14. Marcus Whiffen, as above, has much incidental information on provincial architects; e.g. White of Worcester, the Bastards, Strachan of Bristol, the Patys of Bristol, the Hiorns and Smiths of Warwick, and the Wings of Leicester. For the Woods, see Bryan Little, *The Building of Bath* (1947), and Gordon Nares, 'Belcombe Court, Wiltshire', in *Country Life*, 22 December 1950. For Henry Bell, see Arthur Oswald, 'King's Lynn, Norfolk, III', in *Country Life*, 20 July 1951; for the Smiths of Warwick, Arthur Oswald, 'Georgian Warwick, I and II', in *Country Life*, 19 and 26 October 1951, and 'Davenport House, Shropshire', in *Country Life*, 27 June and 11 July 1952. For the Woodwards of Chipping Campden, see Howard Colvin, in *Architectural Review*, March 1948, and C. W. Beard and J. A. Piper, 'An Architectural Discovery', in *Country Life*, 9 March 1951. For the Bastards of Blandford, see Arthur Oswald, 'Blandford', in *Old Towns Revisited* (1952), an informative and well-illustrated study of eight country towns.

15. Sir William Chambers's *Designs for Chinese Buildings* (1757) and *Dissertation on Oriental Gardening* (1772) are fascinating but hard to obtain. More available are B. Sprague Allen, *Tides in English Taste* (Harvard, 1937), ch. ix; W. W. Appleton, *A Cycle of Cathay* (New York, 1951); J. Steegman, *The Rule of Taste* (1936); A. O. Lovejoy, 'The Chinese Origin of a Romanticism', in *Essays in the History of Ideas* (Johns Hopkins, 1948); and A. R. Humphreys, 'Lords of Tartary', in *The Cambridge Journal*, III, 1, and *The Augustan World* (1954), ch. vi. There are some interesting pages also in Sacheverell Sitwell, *British Architects and Craftsmen* (1945), 116–18.

16. See B. Sprague Allen, as above, ch. xiv, and Lovejoy, as above, 'The First Gothic Revival', also K. Clark, *The Gothic Revival* (rev. edn 1950).

17. See John Summerson, *Architecture in Britain 1530–1830* (1953), 242ff.

18. *ibid.*, 243.

19. See Horace Walpole, 'Of Modern Gardening', in *Anecdotes of Painting*; Christopher Hussey, *The Picturesque* (1927); H. Repton, *The Theory and Practice of Landscape Gardening* (1805) and *An Enquiry into the Changes of Taste in Landscape* (1806); A. R. Humphreys, *William Shenstone* (1937), Part II; Margaret Jourdain, as above, and Dorothy Stroud, *Capability Brown* (1950).

20. See *Observations relative chiefly to ... Cumberland and Westmorland* (1787), *Observations on the River Wye* (1782), *The Highlands of Scotland* (1789),

Remarks on Forest Scenery (1791), and *Observations on the Western Parts of England* (1798). Also, as satire, W. Combe and T. Rowlandson, *The Tours of Dr Syntax in Search of the Picturesque* (1809).

21. See Richardson, *Theory of Painting* (1715), *The Art of Criticism* (1719), and *The Science of a Connoisseur* (1719): and Reynolds, *Discourses, passim.*

PART IV

APPENDIX

COMPILED BY C. J. HORNE
REVISED BY VICTORIA OWENS

E.L.	Everyman's Library edition
E.L.H.	*English Literary History*
M.L.R.	*Modern Language Review*
M.P.	*Modern Philology*
N.C.B.E.L.	*New Cambridge Bibliography of English Literature*
O.S.A.	Oxford Standard Authors
P.M.L.A.	*Publications of the Modern Language Association of America*
P.Q.	*Philological Quarterly*
S.P.	*Studies in Philology*
W.C.	World's Classics edition
abr.	abridged
b.	born
c.	circa
ed., eds	edited, editor(s)
edn.	edition
facs.	facsimile
pub.	published
repr.	reprinted
rev.	revised
trans.	translated
?	probably

Under each author, the aim has been to list first the standard biographies (if any), second, standard editions, and third a selection of books and articles for further study.

FOR FURTHER READING
AND REFERENCE

The Social and Intellectual Setting

I. HISTORIES: GENERAL AND POLITICAL

Ashley, M. *England in the Seventeenth Century*, 1952
Beaglehole, J. C. *The Exploration of the Pacific*, 1934; 1966
Beddard, R. (ed.) *The Revolutions of 1688*, 1991
Black, J. (ed.) *Britain and the Age of Walpole*, 1984
Clark, G. N. *The Later Stuarts, 1660–1714*, 1934: rev. 1956
Goodwin, A. (ed.) *The American and French Revolutions, 1763–93*, 1965.
Gregg, E. *Queen Anne*, 1980
Holdsworth, W. S. *A History of English Law*, 12 vols., 5th edn 1931
Horn, D. B. and Ransome, M. *English Historical Documents*, vol. x, *1714–83*, 1957
Hutton, R. *The Restoration: A Political and Religious History of England and Wales, 1658–1667*, 1985
Jones, J. R. (ed.) *The Restored Monarchy 1660–1688*, 1979
    Liberty Secured? Britain Before and After 1688, 1992
Langford, P. *A Polite and Commercial People: England 1727–1783*, 1989
Macaulay, T. B. *History of England from the Accession of James II*, 5 vols., 1849–61; ed. T. F. Henderson, 5 vols., 1931
Ogg, D. *England in the Reign of Charles II*, 2 vols., rev. 1962
    England in the Reign of James II and William III, 1955
Plumb, J. H. *England in the Eighteenth Century*, 1950; rev. 1963
Trevelyan, G. M. *England under Queen Anne*, 3 vols., 1930–34
Watson, J. S. *The Reign of George III, 1760–1815*, 1960
Williams, B. *The Whig Supremacy, 1714–1760*, 1939; rev. 1962
Williams, J. A. *Cook and the Opening of the Pacific*, 1946

Alden J. R. *The American Revolution 1775–1783*, 1954
Biddle, S. *Bolingbroke and Harley*, 1975
Brooke, J. *King George III*, 1972
Butterfield, H. *George III, Lord North and the People, 1779–80*, 1949
Colley, L. *In Defiance of Oligarchy. The Tory Party 1714–60*, 1982
Dickinson, H. T. *Walpole and the Whig Supremacy*, 1973
Feiling, K. G. *A History of the Tory Party, 1640–1714*, 1924; 1951

The Second Tory Party, 1714–1832, 1938

Goldgar, B. A. *Walpole and the Wits: The Relations of Politics to Literature, 1722–1742*, 1976

Hanson, L. W. *Government and the Press, 1695–1763*, 1936

Harris, T. *Politics Under the Later Stuarts: Party Conflict in a Divided Society 1660–1715*, 1993

Kramnick, I. *Bolingbroke and his Circle*, 1968

Monod P. K. *Jacobitism and the English People 1688–1788*, 1989; 1993

Namier, L. B. *The Structure of Politics at the Accession of George III*, 2 vols., 1929; 1957

Plumb, J. H. *Sir Robert Walpole*, 2 vols., 1956–60

Rea, R. R. *The English Press in Politics, 1760–1774*, 1963

Reed, M. *The Georgian Triumph, 1700–1830*, 1983

Rudé, G. *Wilkes and Liberty*, 1962

Trevelyan, G. M. *The English Revolution, 1668–1689*, 1938

II. THE SOCIAL AND ECONOMIC BACKGROUND

Brown, T. *Amusements Serious and Comical*, 1700–1702; ed. A. L. Hayward, 1927

Defoe, D. *The Compleat English Tradesman*, 1725–7
  An Essay upon Projects, 1697; ed. H. Morley, 1889
  A Plan of the English Commerce, 1782; 1927

Fielding, H. *An Enquiry into the Causes of the Late Increase in Robbers*, 1751; ed. M. R. Zirker, 1988

Howard, J. *The State of the Prisons*, 1784; ed. K. Ruck, 1929

Smith, A. *The Wealth of Nations*, 1776; ed. E. Cannan, 2 vols., 1904

Ward, E. *The London Spy*, 1698–1700; ed. A. L. Hayward, 1927

Allen, R. J. *The Clubs of Augustan London*, 1933

Ashton, J. *Social Life in the Reign of Queen Anne*, 2 vols., 1882; 1925

Ashton, T. S. *An Economic History of England*, 1955
  The Industrial Revolution, 1948

Baugh, D. A. (ed.) *Aristocratic Government and Society in Eighteenth-Century England*, 1975

Beattie, J. M. *The English Court in the Reign of George I*, 1967

Black, J. *The British and the Grand Tour*, 1985
  The English Press in the Eighteenth Century, 1987

Boucé, P.-G. (ed.) *Sexuality in Eighteenth-Century Britain*, 1982

Browne, A. *The Eighteenth-Century Feminist Mind*, 1987

Bucholz. R. O. *The Augustan Court. Queen Anne and the Decline of Court Culture*, 1993

Clapham, J. H. *The Bank of England*, 1, 1944

Clark, G. N. *The Idea of the Industrial Revolution*, 1953

Clarke, J. C. D. *English Society 1688–1832: Ideology, Social Structure and Political Practice during the Ancien Regime*, 1985

Cole, G. D. H. and Postgate, R. *The Common People, 1746–1946*, 4th edn 1949

Collins, A. S. *Authorship in the Days of Johnson*, 1927
The Profession of Letters, 1928

Cranfield, G. A. *The Development of the Provincial Newspaper, 1700–1760*, 1962

Cruickshank, D. and Burton, N. *Life in the Georgian City*, 1990

Cunnington, C. W. and P. *Handbook of English Costume in the Eighteenth Century*, 1957; rev. 1972

Darby, H. C. (ed.) *An Historical Geography of England before 1800*, 1963

Deane, P. *The First Industrial Revolution*, 1965

Ellis, A. *The Penny Universities. A History of the Coffee-Houses*, 1956

Ernle, Lord [R. E. Prothero] *English Farming, Past and Present*, 1912; rev. 1927

Feather, J. *The Provincial Book Trade in Eighteenth-Century England*, 1985

George, M. D. (ed.) *England in Transition*, 1931; 1953
English Social Life in the Eighteenth Century, 1923

Habbakuk, H. J. 'English Population in the Eighteenth Century', in *Econ. Hist. Review*, 2nd series, VI, 1953
Marriage, Debt and the Estates System. English Landownership, 1650–1950, 1995

Halsband, R. *Lord Hervey: Eighteenth-Century Courtier*, 1973

Hamilton, H. *The Industrial Revolution in Scotland*, 1932

Hay, D. *et al.* (eds.) *Albion's Fatal Tree: Crime and Society in Eighteenth-Century England*, 1975

Holmes, G. *The Making of a Great Power: Late Stuart and Early Georgian Britain, 1660–1722*, 1993

Holmes, G. and Szechi, D. *The Age of Oligarchy: Pre-Industrial Britain, 1722–1783*, 1993

Humphreys, A. R. 'The Rights of Woman in the Age of Reason', in *M.L.R.*, XLI, 1946

Marshall, D. *Dr Johnson's London*, 1967
English People in the Eighteenth Century, 1956

Mingay, G. E. *English Landed Society in the Eighteenth Century*, 1963

Myers, S. M. *The Bluestocking Circle: Women, Friendship and the Life of the Mind in Eighteenth-Century England*, 1989

Porter, R. *English Society in the Eighteenth Century*, 1982

Quinlan, M. J. *Victorian Prelude: A History of English Manners, 1700–1830*, 1941

Reed, M. and Wells, R. (eds.) *Class, Conflict and Protest in the English Countryside, 1700–1880*, 1990

Rousseau, G. S. and Porter R. (eds.) *Sexual Underworlds of the Enlightenment*, 1988

Rudé, G. *Hanoverian London, 1714–1808*, 1971

Sambrook, J. *The Eighteenth Century: The Intellectual and Cultural Context of English Literature, 1700–1789*, 1986; 1993

Saunders, J. W. *The Profession of English Letters*, 1964

Schucking, L. L. *The Sociology of Literary Taste*, 1931; trans., 1966
Schwartz, R. B. *Daily Life in Johnson's England*, 1983
Spadafora, D. *The Idea of Progress in Eighteenth-Century Britain*, 1989
Stone, L. *Uncertain Unions: Marriage in England, 1660–1753*, 1992
    Broken Lives: Separation and Divorce in England, 1660–1857, 1993
Sutherland, J. *The Restoration Newspaper and Its Development*, 1986
Thomson, G. S. *Life in a Noble Household, 1614–1700*, 1937
    The Russells in Bloomsbury, 1669–1771, 1940
Trevelyan, G. M. *Illustrated English Social History*, II–III, 1950–55; 1964
Warner, W. J. *The Wesleyan Movement in the Industrial Revolution*, 1930
Whiteley, J. H. *Wesley's England*, 1938
Williams, R. *The Country and the City*, 1973
Wordsworth, C. *Social Life at the English Universities in the Eighteenth Century*, 1874

III. DIARIES, LETTERS, MEMOIRS, TRAVEL

See under *Authors:* Boswell, Burney, Chesterfield, Cowper, Defoe, Evelyn, Gibbon, Gray, Johnson, Pepys, Swift, Walpole
Anson, G. *A Voyage round the World*, 1748; ed. G. Williams, 1974
Aubrey, J. *Brief Lives*, ed. A. Clark, 2 vols., 1898; ed. A. Powell, 1949, rev. 1963
Burnet, G. *Bishop Burnet's History of his Own Time*, ed. M. J. Routh, 7 vols., 1823
Byrom, J. *Private Journals and Literary Remains*, ed. R. Parkinson, 2 vols., 1854–7; selections ed. H. Talon, 1950
Cook, J. *The Journals of Captain James Cook on His Voyages of Discovery*, ed. J. C. Beaglehole, 5 vols., 1955–74
Crabbe, G., Jun. *Life of the Rev. George Crabbe*, 1834; 1932
Dampier, W. *Voyages*, ed. J. Masefield, 2 vols., 1906
Fiennes, C. *The Journeys of Celia Fiennes*, ed. C. Morris, 1947; rev. 1949; illus. edn, 1982
Fielding, H. and S. *The Correspondence of Henry and Sarah Fielding*, ed. C. T. Probyn and M. C. Battestin, 1993
Fox, G. *The Journal of George Fox*, 1694; 1924; ed. J. Nickalls, 1952
Hearne, T. *Collections* [Diary, etc., 1705–35] ed. C. E. Doble and H. E. Salter, 11 vols., 1885–1918
Hervey, Lord J. *Memoirs of the Reign of King George II*, ed. R. Sedgwick, 3 vols., 1931, rev. 1963
Hickey, W. *Memoirs*, ed. A. Spencer, 4 vols., 1923; 1949
Montagu, Lady M. W. *Complete Letters*, ed. R. Halsband, 3 vols., 1965–7; selection in E.L.; *Essays and Poems etc.*, ed. R Halsband and I. Grundy, 1977. See *Life* by R. Halsband, 1956
Moritz, C. P. *Travels in England in 1782*, 1795; ed. P. Matheson, 1924
Percy, T. (Bishop) *The Percy Letters*, ed. D. Nichol Smith, C. Brooks, *et al.*, vols. 1–5, 1944–57; vols. 6 *et seq.*, 1977–in progress

Ryder, D. *Diary 1715–1716*, ed. W. Matthews, 1939

Spence, J. *Observations, Anecdotes, etc.*, ed. J. M. Osborn, 2 vols., 1966

Thrale, Mrs H. L. *Thraliana. The Diary of Mrs Hester Lynch Thrale (later Piozzi)*, *1776–1809*, ed. K. C. Balderston, 2 vols., 1942
    The Piozzi Letters: Correspondence of Hester Lynch Piozzi, ed. E. A. and L. D. Bloom, 1991–in progress

Walpole, H. *Memoirs of the Reign of King George II*, ed. J. Brooke, 3 vols., 1985
    Memoirs of the Reign of King George III, ed. Sir D. Le Marchant, 4 vols., 1845

Wendeborn, G. F. A. *A View of England towards the Close of the Eighteenth Century*, 2 vols., 1791

Wesley, J. *Journal*, ed. N. Curnock, 8 vols., 1909–16; 6 vols., 1902;
    Letters, ed. J. Telford, 8 vols., 1931

White, G. *The Natural History and Antiquities of Selbourne*, 1789;
    The Writings, ed. H. J. Massingham, 2 vols., 1938

Wood, A. à, *Life and Times, 1632–95*, ed. A. Clark, 5 vols., 1891–1900

Woodeford, J. *The Diary of a Country Parson, 1758–1802*, ed. J. D. Beresford, 5 vols., 1924–31; repr. 1981

Young, A. *The Farmer's Tour through the East of England*, 4 vols., 1771
    A Six Months' Tour through the North of England, 4 vols., 1770
    A Six Weeks' Tour through the Southern Counties of England and Wales, 1768; 1772

IV. PHILOSOPHY, RELIGION AND EDUCATION

See under *Authors:* Berkeley, Hume, Law, Locke, Mandeville, Shaftesbury

Butler, J. *The Analogy of Religion*, 1736

Becker, C. L. *The Heavenly City of the Eighteenth-Century Philosophers*, 1932

Bradley, J. E. *Religion, Revolution and English Radicalism*, 1990

Bredvold, L. I. *The Intellectual Milieu of John Dryden*, 1934; 1956
    The Natural History of Sensibility, 1962

Cassirer, E. *The Philosophy of the Enlightenment*, 1951; 1960

Cragg, G. R. *Reason and Authority in the Eighteenth Century*, 1964

Fairchild, H. N. *The Noble Savage*, 1928

Fox, C. (ed.) *Psychology and Literature in the Eighteenth Century*, 1988

Gay, P. *The Enlightenment*, 2 vols., 1967–70

Grimsley, R. (ed.) *The Age of Enlightenment*, 1980

Hazard, P. *European Thought in the Eighteenth Century*, 1954; 1965

Johnson, J. W. *The Formation of Neo-Classical Thought*, 1967

Jones, R. F. *Ancients and Moderns. A Study of the Background of the Battle of the Books*, 1936

Laski, H. J. *Political Thought in England: Locke to Bentham*, 1920

Lovejoy, A. O. *Reflections on Human Nature*, 1961

MacLean, K. *John Locke and the English Literature of the Eighteenth Century*, 1936

Macpherson, C. B. *The Political Theory of Possessive Individualism: Hobbes to Locke*, 1962

Mazzeo, J. A. (ed.) *Reason and the Imagination: Studies in the History of Ideas, 1600–1800*, 1962

Morrill, J. et al. (eds.) *Public Duty and Private Conscience in Seventeenth-Century England*, 1993

Mossner, E. C. *Bishop Butler and the Age of Reason*, 1936; 1990

Price, M. *To the Palace of Wisdom: Studies in Order and Energy from Dryden to Blake*, 1964

Richetti, J. J. *Philosophical Writing: Locke, Berkeley, Hume*, 1983

Rosenbaum, S. P. (ed.) *English Literature and British Philosophy*, 1971

Røstvig, M.-S. *The Happy Man: Studies in the Metamorphoses of a Classical Ideal*, 2 vols., 1954–8

Stephen, L. *History of English Thought in the Eighteenth Century*, 2 vols., 1876–80

Weinbrot, H. D. *Augustus Caesar in 'Augustan' England: The Decline of a Classical Norm*, 1978

Willey, B. *The Seventeenth-Century Background*, 1934; 1962
    The Eighteenth-Century Background, 1940; 1961

Baumer, F. L. *Religion and the Rise of Scepticism*, 1960

Bell, G. C. *The Rediscovery of John Wesley*, 1935; 1983

Champion, J. A. I. *The Pillars of Priestcraft Shaken: The Church of England and its Enemies 1660–1730*, 1992

Clarke, W. K. L. *Eighteenth-Century Piety*, 1944

Coomer, D. *English Dissent under the Early Hanoverians*, 1946

Cragg, G. R. *The Church and the Age of Reason, 1648–1789*, 1970

Grell, O. P. et al. (eds.) *From Persecution to Toleration: The Glorious Revolution and Religion in England*, 1991

Hayden, C. *Anti-Catholicism in Eighteenth-Century England*, 1993

Hill, C. *The English Bible and the Seventeenth-Century Revolution*, 1992

Rupp, G. *Religion in England, 1688–1791*, 1985

Semmel, B. *The Methodist Revolution*, 1974

Shepherd, T. B. *Methodism and the Literature of the Eighteenth Century*, 1940

Sher, R. B. *Church and University in the Scottish Enlightenment: The Moderate Literati of Edinburgh*, 1985

Tyerman, L. *Life and Times of John Wesley*, 3 vols., 1870–71

Davis, H. *Stella. A Gentlewoman of the 18th Century*, 1942

Douglas, D. C. *English Scholars, 1660–1730*, 1939; rev. 1951

Hans, N. *New Trends in Education in the Eighteenth Century*, 1951

Jones, M. G. *The Charity School Movement*, 1938

McDowell, R. B. and Webb, D. A. *Trinity College Dublin 1592–1952. An Academic History*, 1982

Mallet, C. E. *History of the University of Oxford*, II–III, 1924–7
Sutherland, L. S. *The History of the University of Oxford. The Eighteenth Century*, 1986
Winstanley, D. A. *The University of Cambridge in the Eighteenth Century*, 1922
Wordsworth, C. *Scholar Academical. Some Accounts of the Studies at the English Universities in the Eighteenth Century*, 1877; 1910

V. SCIENCE

Boynton, H. F. (ed.) *Beginnings of Modern Science: Scientific Writings of the 16th, 17th and 18th Centuries*, 1948
Burke, J. G. (ed.) *The Uses of Science in the Age of Newton*, 1983
Bush, D. *Science and English Poetry*, 1950
Butterfield, H. *The Origins of Modern Science*, 1949; rev. 1957
Clark, G. N. *Science and Social Welfare in the Age of Newton*, 1937; rev. 1949
Dampier, W. C. *A History of Science and its Relations with Philosophy and Religion*, 1929; rev. 1966
Davie, D. *The Language of Science and the Language of Literature, 1700–1740*, 1963
Espinasse, M. *Robert Hooke*, 1956; 1962
Grafton, A. *Defenders of the Text: The Tradition of Scholarship in an Age of Science*, 1991
Hall, A. R. *The Revolution in Science 1500–1750*, 1983
Hartley, H. (ed.) *The Royal Society. Its Origins and Founders*, 1960
Hunter, M. *Science and Society in Restoration England*, 1981
     Science and the Shape of Orthodoxy: Intellectual Change in Late Seventeenth-Century Britain, 1995
Jacob, M. C. *The Newtonians and the English Revolution 1689–1720*, 1976
Jones, W. P. *The Rhetoric of Science: A Study of Scientific Ideas and Imagery in Eighteenth-Century Poetry*, 1966
Kearney, H. F. *Science and Change, 1500–1700*, 1971
Kuhn, T. S. *The Structure of Scientific Revolutions*, 1960; 1962
Nicolson, M. H. *Pepys's Diary and the New Science*, 1965
     Newton Demands the Muse, 1946
Raven, C. E. *John Ray, Naturalist*, 1942
Singer, C. et al. (eds.) *A History of Technology*, III, *From the Renaissance to the Industrial Revolution*, 1957
Sprat, T. *A History of the Royal Society*, 1667; ed. J. I. Cope and H. W. Jones, 1958
Stewart, L. *The Rise of Public Science: Rhetoric, Technology and Natural Philosophy in Newtonian Britain, 1660–1760*, 1992
Vickers, B. (ed.) *English Science, Bacon to Newton*, 1987
Westfall, R. S. *Science and Religion in Seventeenth-Century England*, 1958
Willey, B. *The Seventeenth-Century Background*, 1934; 1962
     The Eighteenth-Century Background, 1940; 1961

VI. ·ARTS AND ARCHITECTURE

See under *Authors:* Burke, Hogarth

Campbell, C. *Vitruvius Britannicus; or, the British Architect,* 3 vols., 1717–25

Denvir, B. (ed.) *The Eighteenth Century: Art, Design and Society, 1689–1789,* 1983

Gilpin, W. *Three Essays: on Picturesque Beauty; on Picturesque Travel; and on Sketching Landscape,* 1792

Repton, H. *Observations on the Theory and Practice of Landscape Gardening,* 1803

Reynolds, Sir J. *Discourses on Art,* 1769–91; ed. A. Dobson, 1907; ed. R. W. Wark, 1959; 1975, 1981; ed. P. Rogers, 1992

Richardson, J. *Essays on the Theory of Painting,* 1715; 1725

Appleton, W. W. *A Cycle of Cathay. The Chinese Vogue in England,* 1951

Barrell, J. *Painting and the Politics of Culture: New Essays on British Art, 1700–1850,* 1992

Clark, Lord, *The Romantic Rebellion: Romantic versus Classic Art,* 1973

Ford, B. (ed.) *The Cambridge Guide to the Arts,* Vol. 5, *The Augustan Age,* 1991
The Cambridge Cultural History of Britain, Vol. 5, *Eighteenth-Century Britain,* 1992

Hardy, J. and McGredie, A. (eds.) *The Classical Temper in Western Europe,* 1983

Lipking, L. *The Ordering of the Arts in Eighteenth-Century England,* 1975

Macaulay, J. *The Gothic Revival, 1745–1845,* 1975

Malek, J. S. *The Arts Compared: An Aspect of Eighteenth-Century British Aesthetics,* 1974

Solkin, D. H. *Painting for Money: The Visual Arts and the Public Sphere in Eighteenth-Century England,* 1993

Burke, J. *English Art, 1714–1800,* Oxford History of English Art, IX, 1976

George, M. D. *English Political Caricature,* 2 vols., 1959

Hayes, J. *The Landscape Painting of Thomas Gainsborough,* 2 vols., 1982

Herrmann, L. *British Landscape Painting of the Eighteenth Century,* 1973

Klingender, F. D. *Art and the Industrial Revolution,* 1947; rev. 1968

Paulson, R. *Emblem and Expression: Meaning in English Art of the Eighteenth Century,* 1975

Tinker, C. B. *Painter and Poet. Studies in the Literary Relations of English Painting,* 1938

Waterhouse, E. K. *Painting in Britain, 1530–1790,* 1953; rev. 1978
Reynolds, 1941

Wendorf, R. *The Elements of Life: Biography and Portrait Painting in Stuart and Georgian England,* 1990

Bold, J. *John Webb: Architectural Theory and Practice in the Seventeenth Century,* 1989

Bolton, A. T. *The Architecture of Robert and James Adam*, 2 vols., 1922
Downes, K. *The Architecture of Wren*, 1982
    Hawksmoor, 1959
Friedman, T. *James Gibbs*, 1984
Lees-Milne, J. *The Age of Adam*, 1947
Richardson, A. E. *An Introduction to Georgian Architecture*, 1949
Scott, G. *The Architecture of Humanism*, 1914
Summerson, J. N. *The Architecture of the Eighteenth Century*, 1986
    Georgian London, 1945; rev. 1988
    Sir Christopher Wren, 1953
Whiffen, M. *Stuart and Georgian Churches*, 1948
Wilson, M. I. *William Kent*, 1984
Worsley, G. *Classical Architecture in Britain: The Heroic Age*, 1995

Hinde, T. *Capability Brown: The Story of a Master Gardener*, 1986
Hunt, J. D. *The Figure in the Landscape: Poetry, Painting and Gardening during the Eighteenth Century*, 1976
    Garden and Grove: The Italian Renaissance Garden in the English Imagination 1600–1750, 1986
Hunt, J. D. and Willis, P. (eds.) *The Genius of the Place: The English Landscape Garden 1620–1820*, 1975
Hussey, C. *English Gardens and Landscapes, 1700–1750*, 1967
Jacques, D. *Georgian Gardens: The Reign of Nature*, 1983
Manwaring, E. W. *Italian Landscape in Eighteenth-Century England*, 1925
Turner, R. *Capability Brown and the Eighteenth-Century English Landscape*, 1985

Edwards, R. and Jourdain, M. *Georgian Cabinet-Makers*, 1944
Jourdain, M. and Rose, F. *English Furniture. The Georgian Period, 1750–1830*, 1953
Jourdain, M. *English Interior Decoration, 1500–1830*, 1950
MacQuoid, P. A. *A History of English Furniture*, II–IV, 1938

Grant, S. K. *Dr Burney as Critic and Historian of Music*, 1983
Hadow, W. (ed.) *The Oxford History of Music*, III–V, 1902–4
Lonsdale, R. *Dr Charles Burney: A Literary Biography*, 1965
Scholes, P. A. *The Great Dr Burney*, 2 vols., 1948
Smith, R. *Handel's Oratorios and Eighteenth-Century Thought*, 1995

The Literature

VII. GENERAL BIBLIOGRAPHIES

Alston. R. C. *The Eighteenth-Century Short Title Catalogue*, 1983
Bibliography of English Language and Literature, annually since 1920
The Eighteenth Century: A Current Bibliography, annually since 1978, formerly in P.Q.

Foxon, D. F. *English Verse 1701–1750: A Catalogue of Separately Printed Poems with Notes on Contemporary Collected Editions*, 2 vols., 1975

Harbage, A. (ed.) *Annals of English Drama 975–1700*, 1940; rev. 1964; rev. S. S. Wagonheim, 1989

Horne, C. J. in the *New Pelican Guide to English Literature*, IV, 1982

Marcuse, M. J. *A Reference Guide for English Studies*, 1990

Mell, D. C. *English Poetry, 1660–1800. A Guide to Information Sources*, 1982

MLA International Bibliography of Books and Articles on the Modern Languages and Literatures, annually since 1922

Oxford History of English Literature, VI–VIII, 1959–79; 1990

Restoration: Studies in English Literary Culture, 1660–1700, biannually
    The Scriblerian and the Kit-Cats, biannually

Stratman, C. J. et al. (eds.) *Restoration and Eighteenth-Century Theatre Research: A Bibliographical Guide, 1900–1968*, 1971 and annually

Studies in English Literature, 1500–1900, 'Recent Studies in the Restoration and Eighteenth Century' annually

Sullivan, A. *British Literary Magazines: The Augustan Age and the Age of Johnson*, 1983

Todd, J. (ed.) *A Dictionary of British and American Women Writers, 1660–1880*, 1984

Watson, G. (ed.) *The New Cambridge Bibliography of English Literature*, II, 1971

Wing, D. G. *Short-Title Catalogue of English Books 1641–1700*, 3 vols., 1945–51; rev. 1994

The Year's Work in English Studies, annually since 1919

VIII. GENERAL STUDIES

Atkins, G. D. *Reading and Deconstruction: Deconstructive Reading*, 1983

Barrell, J. *English Literature in History, 1730–80*, 1983

Battestin, M. C. *The Providence of Wit: Aspects of Form in Augustan Literature and the Arts*, 1974

Bell, I. A. *Literature and Crime in Augustan England*, 1991

Browning, J. D. (ed.) *Satire in the Eighteenth Century*, 1983

Butt, J. and Carnall, G. *The Age of Johnson, 1740–1789*, Oxford History of English Literature, VIII, 1979; 1990

Byrd, M. *London Transformed: Images of the City in the Eighteenth Century*, 1978

Carnochan, W. B. *Confinement and Flight: An Essay in English Literature of the Eighteenth Century*, 1977

Craig, D. *Scottish Literature and the Scottish People 1680–1830*, 1961

De Porte, M. V. *Nightmares and Hobbyhorses: Swift, Sterne and Augustan Ideas of Madness*, 1974

Dobrée, B. *The Early Eighteenth Century, 1700–1740: Swift, Defoe and Pope*, History of English Literature, VII, 1959; 1990

Ehrenpreis, I. *Acts of Implication. Suggestion and Covert Meaning in the Works of Dryden, Swift, Pope and Austen*, 1981
    Literary Meaning and Augustan Values, 1974

Empson, W. *Seven Types of Ambiguity*, 1930; rev. 1963
    Some Versions of Pastoral, 1935; 1966
    The Structure of Complex Words, 1951; 1977
Erskine-Hill, H. *The Augustan Idea in English Literature*, 1983
Folkenflik, R. (ed.) *The English Hero, 1660–1800*, 1982
Fussell, P. *The Rhetorical World of Augustan Humanism: Ethics and Imagery from Swift to Burke*, 1965
Greene, D. *The Age of Exuberance: Backgrounds to Eighteenth-Century English Literature*, 1970
Hagstrum, J. H. *Sex and Sensibility. Ideal and Erotic Love from Milton to Mozart*, 1980
    Eros and Vision: The Restoration to Romanticism, 1989
Hilles, F. W. and Bloom, H. (eds.) *From Sensibility to Romanticism*, 1965
Hilson, J. C. *et al.* (eds.) *Augustan Worlds: Essays in Honour of A. R. Humphreys*, 1978
Humphreys, A. R. *The Augustan World*, 1954
Kenny, V. C. *The Country-House Ethos in English Literature 1688–1750: Themes of Personal Retreat and National Expansion*, 1984
King, B. *Seventeenth-Century English Literature*, 1982
Lonsdale, R. (ed.) *Dryden to Johnson*, Sphere History of Literature in the English Language, IV, London 1971, rev. 1986
MacLean, K. *John Locke and the English Literature of the Eighteenth Century*, 1985
Nichols, J. *Illustrations of the Literary History of the Eighteenth Century*, 6 vols., 1817–31
    Literary Anecdotes of the Eighteenth Century, 9 vols., London, 1812–1815
Nicholson, C. *Writing and the Rise of Finance: Capital Satires of the Early Eighteenth Century*, 1994
Novak, M. E. (ed.) *English Literature in the Age of Disguise*, 1977
    Eighteenth-Century English Literature, 1983
Paulson, R. H. *The Fictions of Satire*, 1967
Rawson, C. *Satire and Sentiment, 1660–1830*, 1994
Rivers, I. *Books and their Readers in Eighteenth-Century England*, 1982
M. M. Roberts and R. Porter (eds.) *Literature and Medicine during the Eighteenth Century*, 1993
Rogers, P. *Grub Street*, 1977
    The Augustan Vision, 1974
    Literature and the Popular Culture in Eighteenth-Century England, 1985
Sitter, J. *Arguments of Augustan Wit*, 1991
Stephen, L. *English Literature and Society in the Eighteenth Century*, 1904; 1963
Studies in the Eighteenth Century, ed. R. F. Brissenden and J. C. Eade, 4 vols., 1968–79; ed. J. P. Hardy and J. C. Eade, 1983; ed. C. Duckworth and H. Le Grand, 1989
Summerfield, G. *Fantasy and Reason: Children's Literature in the Eighteenth Century*, 1985
Sutherland, J. R. *Restoration Literature: Dryden, Bunyan, Pepys*, Oxford History of English Literature, VI, 1969; 1990

Tillotson, G. *Augustan Studies*, 1961

Wedgwood, C. V. *Seventeenth-Century English Literature*, 1950

Weinbrot, H. *Eighteenth-Century Satire: Essays on Text and Context from Dryden to Peter Pindar*, 1988
    Britannia's Issue: The Rise of British Literature from Dryden to Ossian, 1993

Wilson, J. H. *The Court Wits of the Restoration*, 1948

Wittig, K. *The Scottish Tradition in Literature*, 1958

IX. THE LANGUAGE

Arthos, J. *The Language of Natural Description in Eighteenth-Century Poetry*, 1949

Baugh, A. C. *A History of the English Language*, 1935

Boulton, J. T. *The Language of Politics in the Age of Wilkes and Burke*, 1963

Dobson, E. J. *English Pronunciation, 1500–1700*; 2 vols., 1957; rev. 1968

Hawes, C. *Mania and Literary Style: The Rhetoric of Enthusiasms from the Ranters to Christopher Smart*, 1996

Johnson, S. *A Dictionary of the English Language*, 2 vols., 1755; 1967 (facs.); *Selection*, ed. E. L. McAdam and G. Milne, 1963
    Preface to the English Dictionary, 1755; repr. in *Prose and Poetry*, ed. M. Wilson, 1950

Knowlson, J. *Universal Language Schemes in England and France 1600–1800*, 1975

McIntosh, C. *Common and Courtly Language: The Stylistics of Social Class in Eighteenth-Century English Literature*, 1986

Mullan, J. *Sentiment and Sociability. The Language of Feeling in the Eighteenth Century*, 1988

Reddick, A. *The Making of Johnson's Dictionary, 1746–1773*, 1990

Rivers, I. *Reason, Grace and Sentiment: A Study of the Language of Religion and Ethics in England, 1660–1786*, 1991

Serjeantson, M. S. *A History of Foreign Words in English*, 1935

Tillotson, G. *Augustan Poetic Diction*, 1964

Tucker, S. I. *Protean Shape: A Study in Eighteenth-Century Vocabulary and Usage*, 1967
    Enthusiasm: A Study in Semantic Change, 1972

Vallins, G. H. *The Wesleys and the English Language*, 1957

X. POETRY

Aubin, R. A. *Topographical Poetry in Eighteenth-Century England*, 1936

Barash, C. *English Women's Poetry, 1649–1714*, 1996

Bate, W. J. *The Burden of the Past and the English Poet*, 1970; 1971

Bond, R. P. *English Burlesque Poetry, 1700–1750*, 1932

Brown, W. C. *The Triumph of Form. A Study of the Later Masters of the Heroic Couplet*, 1948

Bush, D. *Mythology and the Romantic Tradition in English Poetry*, 1937; 1957
    Science and English Poetry, 1950
Chapin, C. F. *Personification in Eighteenth-Century English Poetry*, 1955
Davie, D. *Articulate Energy: An Inquiry into the Syntax of English Poetry*, 1955
    Purity of Diction in English Verse, 1952
    The Eighteenth-Century Hymn in England, 1993
Doody, M. A. *The Daring Muse: Augustan Poetry Reconsidered*, 1985
Erskine-Hill, H. *The Poetry of Opposition and Revolution: Dryden to Words-
    worth*, 1996
Foxon, D. F. *English Verse 1701–1750: A Catalogue of Separately Printed Poems
    with Notes on Contemporary Collected Editions*, 2 vols., 1975
Goodridge, J. *Rural Life in Eighteenth-Century English Poetry*, 1996
Hamilton, K. G. *The Two Harmonies: Poetry and Prose in the Seventeenth
    Century*, 1963
Jack, I. *Augustan Satire, 1660–1750*, 1952; 1966
Johnson, S. *Lives of the English Poets*, 1779–81; ed. G. B. Hill, 3 vols., 1905; in
    w.c.
Leavis, F. R. *Revaluation*, 1936; 1964
Lewis, J. E. *The English Fable: Aesop and Literary Culture*, 1996
Miner, E. *The Restoration Mode from Milton to Dryden*, 1974
Pinto, V. de S. *The Restoration Court Poets*, 1965
Piper, W. B. *The Heroic Couplet*, 1969
Pittock, M. G. H. *Poetry and Jacobite Politics in Eighteenth-Century Britain and
    Ireland*, 1994
Snyder, E. D. *The Celtic Revival in English Literature, 1700–1800*, 1923
Sowerby, R. *The Classical Legacy in Renaissance Poetry*, 1994
Spacks, P. M. *The Poetry of Vision*, 1966
Sutherland, J. R. *A Preface to Eighteenth-Century Poetry*, 1948
Tillotson, G. *Augustan Poetic Diction*, 1964
Trickett, R. *The Honest Muse: A Study in Augustan Verse*, 1967
Wasserman, E. R. *Elizabethan Poetry in the Eighteenth Century*, 1947

XI. THE NOVEL

Alter, R. *Rogue's Progress: Studies in the Picaresque Novel*, 1964
Baker, E. A. *The History of the English Novel*, III–V, 1929–34; 1957
Battestin, M. C. (ed.) *British Novelists, 1660–1800*, 2 vols., 1985
Booth, W. C. *The Rhetoric of Fiction*, 1961
Brissenden, R. F. *Virtue in Distress: Studies in the Novel of Sentiment from
    Richardson to Sade*, 1974
Castle, T. *Masquerade and Civilization: The Carnivalesque in Eighteenth-
    Century English Culture and Fiction*, 1986
Conant, M. P. *The Oriental Tale in the Eighteenth Century*, 1908
Gove, P. *The Imaginary Voyage in Prose Fiction, 1700–1800*, 1941
Hahn, H. G. and Behrn, C. *The Eighteenth-Century British Novel and Its
    Background: An Annotated Bibliography and Guide to Topics*, 1985

Hazlitt, W. 'On the English Novelists' in *The English Comic Writers*, 1819; in E.L. and W.C.

Hunter, J. P. *Before Novels: The Cultural Contexts of Eighteenth-Century Fiction*, 1990

Kettle, A. *An Introduction to the English Novel*, I, 1951; 1967

Leavis, F. R. *The Great Tradition*, 1948; 1962

Leavis, Q. D. *Fiction and the Reading Public*, 1932

McKeon, M. *The Origins of the English Novel 1600–1740*, 1987

Paulson, R. H. *Satire and the Novel in Eighteenth-Century England*, 1967

Preston, J. *The Created Self: The Reader's Role in Eighteenth-Century Fiction*, 1970

Raven, J. *British Fiction 1750–1770: A Chronological Check-List of Prose Fiction Printed in Britain and Ireland*, 1987

Scheuermann, M. *Her Bread to Earn: Women, Money and Society from Defoe to Austen*, 1993

Spacks, P. M. *Imagining a Self: Autobiography and Novel in Eighteenth-Century England*, 1976

Spencer, J. *The Rise of the Woman Novelist*, 1986

Tompkins, J. M. S. *The Popular Novel in England*, 1932; 1961

Uphaus, R. W. (ed). *The Idea of the Novel in the Eighteenth Century*, 1988

Van Ghent, D. *The English Novel: Form and Function*, 1953; 1967

Varma, D. P. *The Gothic Flame: Being the History of the Gothic Novel in England*, 1957

Watt, I. *The Rise of the Novel: Studies in Defoe, Richardson and Fielding*, 1957; 1987

Weinstein, A. *Fictions of the Self, 1500–1800*, 1981

XII. PROSE

Anderson, H. *et al.* (eds.) *The Familiar Letter in the Eighteenth Century*, 1966

Bond, R. P. (ed.) *Studies in the Early English Periodical*, 1957

Bourne, H. R. F. *English Newspapers*, 2 vols., 1887

Carlson, C. L. *The First Magazine. A History of the 'Gentleman's Magazine'*, 1938

Crane, R. S. and Kaye, F. B. *A Census of British Newspapers and Periodicals, 1620–1800*, 1927; 1967

Cranfield, G. A. *The Development of the Provincial Newspaper, 1700–1760*, 1962

Downey, J. *The Eighteenth-Century Pulpit*, 1969

Dyson, A. E. *The Crazy Fabric: Essays in Irony*, 1965

Graham, W. *The Beginnings of English Literary Periodicals*, 1926
    English Literary Periodicals, 1930

Hazlitt, W. 'On the Periodical Essayists', in *The English Comic Writers*, 1819; in E.L. and W.C.

Lessenich, R. P. *Elements of Pulpit Oratory in Eighteenth-Century England (1660–1800)*, 1972

Nangle, B. C. *The Monthly Review (1749–1789)*, 1934
Sullivan, A. (ed.) *British Literary Magazines: The Augustan Age and the Age of Johnson, 1698–1788*, 1983
Werkmeister, L. *The London Daily Press, 1772–1792*, 1963
Wiles, R. M. *Freshest Advices: Early Provincial Newspapers in England*, 1965

Daghlian, P. B. (ed.) *Essays in Eighteenth-Century Biography*, 1968
Shumaker, W. *English Autobiography*, 1954
Stauffer, D. A. *The Art of Biography in Eighteenth-Century England*, 2 vols., 1941
 English Biography before 1700, 1930
Wendorf, R. *The Elements of Life: Biography and Portrait Painting in Stuart and Georgian England*, 1990

Millar, J. H. *Scottish Prose of the Seventeenth and Eighteenth Centuries*, 1912
Thomson, J. A. K. *Classical Influences on English Prose*, 1956

XIII. DRAMA

Anthony, R. *The Jeremy Collier Stage Controversy*, 1937
Avery, E. L. *et al.* (eds.) *The London Stage, 1660–1800. A Calendar of Plays, etc.*, 12 vols., 1960–79
Barnett, O. *The Art of Gesture: The Practice and Principles of Eighteenth-Century Acting*, 1987
Bateson, F. W. *English Comic Drama, 1700–1750*, 1929
Bernbaum, E. *The Drama of Sensibility, 1696–1780*, 1915
Bevis, R. W. *English Drama: Restoration and Eighteenth Century*, 1988
Boas, F. S. *An Introduction to Eighteenth-Century Drama*, 1953
Brown, L. *English Dramatic Form, 1660–1760*, 1981
Burns, E. *Restoration Comedy: Crises of Desire and Identity*, 1987
Cibber, C. *An Apology for the Life of Mr Colley Cibber*, 1740; ed. R. W. Lowe, 2 vols., 1889; in E.L.
Craik, T. W. (ed.) *The Revels History of Drama in English*, V–VI, 1975–6
Dobrée, B. *Restoration Comedy*, 1924
 Restoration Tragedy, 1929
Donaldson, I. *The World Upside-Down: Comedy from Jonson to Fielding*, 1970
Fiske, R. *English Theatre Music in the Eighteenth Century*, 1973, 1986
Fujimura, T. H. *The Restoration Comedy of Wit*, 1952
Genest, J. *Some Account of the English Stage from 1660 to 1830*, 10 vols., 1832
Harbage, A. (ed.) *Annals of English Drama 975–1700*, 1940; rev. 1964; rev. S. S. Wagonheim, 1989
Highfill, P. H. *et al.* (eds.) *A Biographical Dictionary of Actors, Actresses, Musicians, Dancers, Managers and Other Stage Personnel in London, 1660–1800*, 1973–in progress
Hogan, C. B. *Shakespeare in the Theatre, 1701–1800*, 2 vols., 1952–7

Holland, N. The First Modern Comedies: The Significance of Etherege, Wycherley and Congreve, 1959

Holland, P. The Ornament of Action: Text and Performance in Restoration Comedy, 1979

Hughes, D. English Drama 1660–1700, 1996

Hughes, L. A Century of English Farce, 1956
    The Drama's Patrons. A Study of the Eighteenth-Century London Audience, 1971

Hume, R. D. The Development of English Drama in the Late Seventeenth Century, 1976
    The Rakish Stage: Studies in English Drama, 1660–1800, 1983

Kenny, S. S. (ed.) British Theatre and the Other Arts, 1660–1800, 1984

Langbaine, G. An Account of the English Dramatic Poets, 1691

Leech, C. 'Restoration Comedy. The Earlier Phase', in Essays in Criticism, I, 1951

Loftis, J. Comedy and Society from Congreve to Fielding, 1959
    The Politics of Drama in Augustan England, 1963

MacMillan, D. (ed.) Catalogue of the Larpent Plays in the Huntington Library, 1939

Maguire, N. K. Regicide and Restoration: English Tragicomedy, 1660–1671, 1992

Masters, A. The Play of Personality in the Restoration Theatre, 1992

Meredith, G. An Essay on Comedy, 1877; 1897

Milhous, J. and Hume, R. D. Producible Interpretation: Eight English Plays 1675–1707, 1985

Miner, E. (ed.) Restoration Dramatists: A Collection of Critical Essays, 1966

Nicoll, A. A History of Early Eighteenth-Century Drama, 1700–1750, 1925; rev. 1952
    A History of Late Eighteenth-Century Drama, 1750–1800, 1927; rev. 1952
    A History of Restoration Drama, 1660–1700, 1923; rev. 1952

Powell, J. Restoration Theatre Production, 1984

Price, C. A. Henry Purcell and the London Stage, 1984

Price, C. J. L. Theatre in the Age of Garrick, 1973

Roberts, D. The Ladies: Female Patronage of Restoration Drama, 1989

Rosenfeld, S. Strolling Players and Drama in the Provinces, 1660–1765, 1939

Sherbo, A. English Sentimental Drama, 1957

Stone, G. W. and Kahl, G. M. David Garrick. A Critical Biography, 1979

Stratman, C. J. et al. (eds.) Restoration and Eighteenth-Century Theatre Research: Bibliographical Guide, 1900–1968, 1971 and annually

Styan, J. L. Restoration Comedy in Performance, 1985

Uphaus, R. W. (ed.) The Idea of the Novel in the Eighteenth Century, 1988

Weber, H. The Restoration Rake-Hero: Transformation in Sexual Understanding in Seventeenth-Century England, 1986

Wilcox, J. The Relation of Molière to Restoration Comedy, 1938

Wilson, J. H. The Influence of Beaumont and Fletcher on Restoration Drama, 1928

Zimbardo, R. A. A Mirror to Nature: Transformation in Drama and Aesthetics, 1660–1732, 1986

XIV. CRITICISM AND THEORY

Anderson, H. and Shea, J. S. (eds.) *Studies in Criticism and Aesthetics, 1600–1800*, 1967

Atkins, J. W. H. *English Literary Criticism: 17th and 18th Centuries*, 1951

Babcock, R. W. *The Genesis of Shakespeare Idolatry, 1766–1799*, 1931

Bate, W. J. 'The Sympathetic Imagination in Eighteenth-Century English Criticism', in E.L.H., XII, 1945

Bentley, G. E. *Shakespeare and Jonson: Their Reputations in the Seventeenth Century Compared*, 2 vols., 1945

Bronson, B. H. and O'Meara, J. (eds.) *Johnson on Shakespeare*, 1986

Clark, A. F. B. *Boileau and the French Classical Critics in England, 1660–1830*, 1925

Congleton, J. E. *Theories of Pastoral Poetry in England, 1684–1798*, 1952

Dennis, J. *The Critical Works*, ed. E. N. Hooker, 2 vols., 1939–43
    Grounds of Criticism in Poetry, 1704, ed. J. V. Price, 1994 (facs.)

Dryden, J. *Of Dramatic Poesy and Other Essays*, ed. G. Watson, 2 vols., 1962
    Essays, ed. W. P. Ker, 2 vols., 1900

Durham, W. H. (ed.) *Critical Essays of the Eighteenth Century, 1700–1725*, 1915; 1961

Elkin, P. K. *The Augustan Defence of Satire*, 1973

Engell, J. *Forming the Critical Mind: Dryden to Coleridge*, 1989

Elledge, S. (ed.) *Eighteenth-Century Critical Essays*, 2 vols., 1961

Fussell, P. *The Rhetorical World of Augustan Humanism*, 1965
    Theory of Prosody in Eighteenth-Century England, 1954

Green, F. C. *Minuet: A Critical Survey of French and English Literary Ideas in the Eighteenth Century*, 1935

Hagstrum, J. H. *The Sister Arts. The Tradition of Literary Pictorialism and English Poetry from Dryden to Gray*, 1958

Henn, T. R. *Longinus and English Criticism*, 1934

Johnson, J. W. *The Formation of English Neo-Classical Thought*, 1967

Johnson, S. *Lives of the English Poets*, 1779–81; ed. G. B. Hill, 3 vols., 1905 in E.L. and W.C.

Kernan, A. B. *The Plot of Satire*, 1965

Levine, J. M. *The Battle of the Books: History and Literature in the Augustan Age*, 1991

Monk, S. H. *The Sublime: A Study of Critical Theories in XVIII-Century England*, 1960

Nicolson, M. *Mountain Gloom and Mountain Glory: The Development of the Aesthetics of the Infinite*, 1959; 1963

Noel, T. *Theories of the Fable in the Eighteenth Century*, 1975

Nussbaum, J. and Brown, L. (eds.) *The New Eighteenth Century: Theory, Politics, English Literature*, 1988

Rymer, T. *Critical Works*, ed. C. A. Zimansky, 1956

Simon, I. (ed.) *Neo-Classical Criticism 1660–1800*, 1971

Smith, D. Nichol (ed.) *Eighteenth-Century Essays on Shakespeare*, 2nd edn, 1963

   Shakespeare in the Eighteenth Century, 1928

Spingarn, J. E. (ed.) *Critical Essays of the Seventeenth Century*, II–III, 1908–9; 1957

Steiner, T. R. *English Translation Theory 1650–1800*, 1975

Sutherland, J. R. *English Satire*, 1958

Swedenburg, H. T. *The Theory of the Epic in England, 1650–1800*, 1944

Vickers, B. (ed.) *Shakespeare: The Critical Heritage*, 6 vols., 1974–1981

Wellek, R. *A History of Modern Criticism*, I, 1955

   The Rise of English Literary History, 1941

AUTHORS AND WORKS

Collections and Anthologies

The Augustan Reprints: a series of facsimiles, 1946–in progress
George, M. D. (ed.) *England in Johnson's Day*, 1928
Myers, W. (ed.) *Restoration and Revolution*, 1986
Price, M. (ed.) *The Restoration and the Eighteenth Century*, Oxford Anthology of English Literature, III 1973

Anderson, R. (ed.) *The Works of the British Poets*, 13 vols., 1792–1795
Ault, N. (ed.) *Seventeenth-Century Lyrics*, 1928
Barrell, J. and Bull, J. (eds.) *The Penguin Book of English Pastoral Verse*, 1974
Chalmers, A. (ed.) *The Works of the English Poets*, 21 vols., 1810
Davie, D. *The Late Augustans*, 1958
Davison, D. (ed.) *The Penguin Book of Eighteenth-Century Verse*, 1973
Dodsley, R. (pub.) *A Collection of Poems*, 3 vols., 1748; 6 vols., 1758
Fowler, A. (ed.) *The New Oxford Book of Seventeenth-Century Verse*, 1991
Grierson, H. and Bullough, G. (eds.) *The Oxford Book of Seventeenth-Century Verse*, 1934
Holloway, J. and Black, J. (eds.) *Later English Broadside Ballads*, 2 vols, 1975
Johnson, S. (ed.) *The Works of the English Poets*, 68 vols., 1779–81; 75 vols., 1790
Lonsdale, R. (ed.) *The New Oxford Book of Eighteenth-Century Verse*, 1984; 1989
   Eighteenth-Century Women Poets, 1989
Lord, G. de F. (ed.) *Anthology of Poems on Affairs of State: Augustan Satirical Verse, 1660–1714*, 1975
Lord, G. de F. *et al.* (eds.) *Poems of Affairs of State: Augustan Satirical Verse, 1660–1714*, 7 vols., 1963–75
Pinto, V. de S. and Rodway, A. E. (eds.) *The Common Muse. An Anthology of Popular British Ballad Poetry*, 1957
Pollard, A. (ed.) *Silver Poets of the Eighteenth Century*, 1976
Smith, D. Nichol (ed.) *The Oxford Book of Eighteenth-Century Verse*, 1926
Wilson, J. H. (ed.) *Court Satires of the Restoration*, 1976

Aitken, J. (ed.) *English Letters of the XVIII Century*, 1946

Allott, K. *The Pelican Book of English Prose*, II–III, 1956

Simon, I. (ed.) *Three Restoration Divines: Barrow, South, Tillotson. Selected Sermons*, 2 vols., 1967–76

Trawick, L. M. (ed.) *Backgrounds of Romanticism: English Philosophical Prose of the Eighteenth Century*, 1967

Chalmers, A. (ed.) *The British Essayists*, 45 vols., 1817

Lynam, R. (ed.) *The British Essayists*, 30 vols., 1827

Segar, M. G. (ed.) *Essays from Eighteenth-Century Periodicals*, 1947

Bell's British Theatre, 21 vols., 1776–81; 36 vols., 1791–1802

Booth, M. R. (ed.) *Eighteenth-Century Tragedy*, 1965

Cordner, M. (ed.) *Four Restoration Marriage Plays*, 1995

Cumberland, R. (ed.) *The British Drama*, 14 vols., 1817

Danchin, P. (ed.) *The Prologues and Epilogues of the Restoration (1660–1700)*, 1981

Dobrée, B. (ed.) *Five Heroic Plays*, 1960
     Five Restoration Tragedies, 1928

Inchbald, E. (ed.) *The British Theatre*, 25 vols., 1808, 1824

Kendall, K. (ed.) *Love and Thunder: Plays by Women in the Age of Queen Anne*, 1988

Lawrence, R. G. (ed.) *Restoration Plays*, 1976

McMillin, S. (ed.) *Restoration and Eighteenth-Century Comedy*, 1973

Maidment, J. and Logan, W. H. (eds.) *Dramatists of the Restoration*, 14 vols., 1872–9

Nettleton, G. H. and Case, A. E. (eds.) *British Dramatists from Dryden to Sheridan*, 1939; rev. 1969

Salgado, G. (ed.) *Three Restoration Comedies*, 1968

Sutherland, J. (ed.) *Restoration Tragedies*, 1977

Taylor, W. D. (ed.) *Eighteenth Century Comedy*, 1929

Trussler, S. (ed.) *Burlesque Plays of the Eighteenth Century*, 1969; 1995

Authors

ADDISON, JOSEPH (1672–17190): Essayist, poet and statesman; son of Dean of Lichfield; educated Charterhouse (with Steele), Queen's College, Oxford; fellow of Magdalen, 1697–1711; Latin poems attracted Dryden's notice, 1693; toured Europe with pension, preparing for diplomatic service, 1699–1703; celebrated victory of Blenheim in poem, *The Campaign*, 1705; friendship with Swift, Steele, etc.; under-secretary of state, 1706; M.P. 1708–1719; to Ireland, chief secretary to Lord Wharton, 1709; lost office on fall of Whigs, 1711; collaborated with Steele in *The Tatler* (1709–11); *The Spectator* (1711–12); great success of tragedy, *Cato*, 1713; contributed to *The Guardian* (1713) and new *Spectator* (1714); unsuccessful comedy, *The Drummer*, 1715; again chief secretary for Ireland; political newspaper, *The*

Freeholder, 1715–16; a lord commissioner of trade, married Countess of Warwick, 1716; retired with £1,500 pension, 1718, estrangement from Steele; buried Westminster Abbey.

Life by L. Aikin, 2 vols., 1843; P. Smithers, 1954
Works ed. R. Hurd, 6 vols., 1811; 1854–6; 1883
Miscellaneous Works in Verse and Prose ed. A. C. Guthkelch, 2 vols., 1914
The Freeholder ed. J. Leheny, 1980
The Guardian ed. J. C. Stephens, 1982
The Spectator ed. D. F. Bond, 5 vols., 1965; 1987
The Tatler ed. D. J. Bond, 3 vols., 1987
Addison and Steele: Selections from 'The Tatler' and 'The Spectator' ed. R. J. Allen, 2nd edn, 1970; 1982
Letters ed. W. Graham, 1941
See bibliography under *Prose* (pp. 468–9)
E. A. and L. D. Bloom, *Joseph Addison's Sociable Animal*, 1971
   (eds.) *Addison and Steele: The Critical Heritage*, 1980
L. A. Elioseff, *The Cultural Milieu of Addison's Literary Criticism*, 1963
S. Johnson, *The Lives of the Poets*, ed. G. B. Hill, vol. II, 1905
J. Lannering, *Studies in the Prose Style of Joseph Addison*, 1951; 1970
C. S. Lewis, 'Addison', in *Essays on the Eighteenth Century Presented to David Nichol Smith*, 1945
T. B. Macaulay, 'The Life and Writings of Addison', in *Critical and Historical Essays*, II, 1907.

ARBUTHNOT, JOHN (1667–1735): Physician and wit; b. Scotland; M.D., St Andrews, 1696; taught mathematics in London; F.R.S., 1704; physician to Queen Anne, 1705; close friend of Swift and Pope; supported Tory ministry, 1710–14; political pamphlets, including *The History of John Bull*, 1712; member of Scriblerus Club with Swift, Pope, etc.. 1713; contributed largely to *Memoirs of Martinus Scriblerus* (pub. 1741); wrote many progressive medical works; popular for wit, humour and kind heart.

Life by L. M. Beattie, 1953; 1967; R. C. Steensma, 1980
Life and Works ed. G. A. Aitken, 1892
The History of John Bull ed. A. W. Bower and R. A. Erickson, 1976

BEHN, MRS APHRA (1640–89): Dramatist and novelist; b. Canterbury or Wye, daughter of (?) John Amis; obscure and probably improper early career; claimed to have lived as a child in Surinam, Guyana; returned to England, 1658; married city merchant, 1664; spy for Charles II in Antwerp, 1666–7, getting information from lover, William Scot; fifteen plays produced, 1670–1689, mainly coarse and amatory comedies of contemporary London life; also wrote poems and novels, notably *Oroonoko, or the Royal Slave*, c. 1678, romanticizing her supposed career in Surinam.

Life by V. Sackville-West, 1927; M. Duffy, 1977, A. Goreau, 1980
Works ed. J. Todd, 7 vols., 1992–6

Oroonoko, The Rover and Other Works ed. J. Todd, 1993
The Poems of Aphra Behn: A Selection ed. J. Todd, 1994
See:
M. A. O'Donnell, *Aphra Behn: An Annotated Bibliography*, 1986
S. Wiseman, *Aphra Behn*, 1996

BERKELEY, GEORGE (1685–1753): Philosopher, b. Ireland; educated Kilkenny and Trinity College, Dublin; *Essay towards a New Theory of Vision*, 1709; *Principles of Human Knowledge*, 1710; to England, 1713; friendly with Swift, Pope, Steele, Addison; Dean of Derry, 1724; missionary enterprise in America, 1728–32; popular philosophical dialogues, *Alciphron*, 1732; Bishop of Cloyne, 1734; d. Oxford. His philosophical immaterialism opposed to Locke's theory of external, material reality.

Life by A. A. Luce, 1949; 1992
Works ed. A. A. Luce and T. E. Jessop, 9 vols., 1948–57
Philosophical Works ed. M. R. Ayers, 1975; 1991
Select Writings, E.L., 1910
See:
D. Berman, *George Berkeley: Idealism and the Man*, 1994
J. Dancy, *Berkeley: An Introduction*, 1987
A. C. Grayling, *Berkeley: The Central Arguments*, 1986

BOSWELL, JAMES (1740–95): Biographer and diarist; b. and educated Edinburgh; son of judge, Lord Auchinleck; studied law at Edinburgh and Glasgow; desired literary fame and acquaintance of the great; visited London, met Dr Johnson, 1763; abandoned law studies at Utrecht, 1764, to make tour of Germany, France, Switzerland, Italy with variety of amatory escapades; introduced self to Rousseau and Voltaire; visited Corsica, met General Paoli; returned to England, 1766; *Account of Corsica* (1768) achieved European fame; married cousin, 1769; unwillingly practised law in Edinburgh; contributed frequently to newspapers, etc. (essays, *The Hypochondriack*, 1777–83); visited London and Johnson almost annually, 1772–84; led Johnson on tour of Scotland and Hebrides, elected to 'The Club', 1773; sought career in law and politics in London; *Journal of a Tour of the Hebrides*, 1785; settled in London, 1789; *Life of Johnson*, 1791; depression and ill-health in last years; d. London. Mass of manuscript journals discovered earlier this century at Fettercairn House and Malahide Castle.

Life by D. B. Wyndham Lewis, 1946; 1952; C. B. Tinker, 1922; F. A. Pottle, 1966; repr. 1984; J. Brady, 1984; R. Hutchinson, 1995
The Private Papers of James Boswell from Malahide Castle ed. G. Scott and F. A. Pottle, 18 vols., 1928–34
Yale Editions of the Private Papers ed. F. A. Pottle *et al.*, 1950–in progress
Boswell's London Journal, 1762–63 ed. F. A. Pottle, 1966
Tour to Corsica ed. S. C. Roberts, 1923, ed. M. Bishop, 1951
Tour to the Hebrides ed. R. W. Chambers, 1924; 1930; ed. L. F. Powell,

1950; ed. (from original MS.) F. A. Pottle and C. H. Bennett, 1936; in E.L.;

Life of Johnson and Journal of a Tour to the Hebrides ed. G. B. Hill, 6 vols., 1887; rev. and enlarged L. F. Powell, 1934–50, 1984

Life of Johnson and in numerous edns, including E.L. and O.S.A.

Letters ed. C. B. Tinker, 2 vols., 1924

See:

F. Brady, *Boswell's Political Career*, 1965

B. H. Bronson, 'Boswell's Boswell', in *Johnson Agonistes and Other Essays*, 1944; 1946

A. E. Brown, *Boswellian Studies*, 1972

J. L. Clifford (ed.) *Twentieth-Century Interpretations of Boswell's 'Life of Johnson'*, 1970

G. Clingham, *James Boswell. The Life of Johnson*, 1992
    (ed.) *New Light on Boswell*, 1992

P. A. W. Collins, *James Boswell*, 1956

R. Craik, *James Boswell: The Scottish Perspective*, 1994

D. L. Passler, *Time, Form and Style in Boswell's 'Life of Johnson'*, 1971

F. A. Pottle, *The Literary Career of James Boswell, Esq.*, 1929; 1965
    Pride and Negligence. The History of the Boswell Papers, 1982

J. A. Vance (ed.) *Boswell's 'Life of Johnson': New Questions, New Answers*, 1988

BOYLE, HON. ROBERT (1627–91): Natural philosopher and theologian; son of first Earl of Cork; studied in Europe; set up laboratory at Oxford, 1654; industrious experimenter, especially in chemistry; 'Boyle's Law' of gases, 1662; a founder of Royal Society, voluminous writer in science, morality, religion; influence in his day only less than that of Newton.

Life by L. T. More, 1944

Works ed. T. Birch, 5 vols., 1744; 6 vols., 1772

The Sceptical Chemist, 1661; 1911

See:

Hunter, M. (ed.) *Robert Boyle Reconsidered*, 1994

BURKE, EDMUND (1729–97): Statesman and political writer; son of Protestant Dublin attorney; educated Trinity College, Dublin and Middle Temple; frequented society of writers; *A Philosophical Enquiry into the Origin of our Ideas of the Sublime and the Beautiful*, 1757; started *The Annual Register*, 1759; member of 'The Club', 1763; private secretary to prime minister, and M.P., 1765; in speeches and pamphlets opposed attitude of North Ministry towards American colonies; speculations involved him in permanent financial difficulties; championed cause of Ireland and Catholic emancipation; Paymaster of Forces, 1782; joined in impeachment of Warren Hastings, from 1788; denounced French Revolution (*Reflections*, 1790) and broke with Fox and the Whigs; retired with government pension, 1794. Had devoted life to five 'great, just and honourable causes'.

Life by Sir J. Prior, 1824, etc.; Lord J. Morley, 1879; Sir P. Magnus, 1939; C. Cruise O'Brien, 1992

Works ed. W. Willis and F. W. Rafferty, 6 vols., 1906–7

Writings and Speeches ed. P. Langford and W. B. Todd, 1981–in progress

The Philosophy of Edmund Burke ed. L. I. Bredvold and R. G. Ross, 1960

A Philosophical Enquiry into the Origin of our Ideas of the Sublime and Beautiful ed. J. T. Boulton, 1958; rev. 1987; ed. A. Phillips, 1990

Pre-Revolutionary Writings, ed. I. Harris, 1993

Reflections on the Revolution in France ed. L. G. Mitchell, 1993

Correspondence ed. T. W. Copeland *et al.*, 10 vols., 1958–78

See:

C. B. Bone, *Burke and the Nature of Politics*, 2 vols., 1957–64

C. J. Gandy and P. J. Stanlis (eds.) *Edmund Burke: A Bibliography of Secondary Sources to 1982*, 1983

J. P. Locke, *Burke's Reflections on the Revolution in France*, 1985

C. B. Macpherson, *Burke*, 1980

B. T. Wilkins, *The Problem of Burke's Political Philosophy*, 1967

BURNEY, FRANCES, MADAME D'ARBLAY (1752–1840): Novelist and diarist; daughter of Dr Burney, the musician; novels, *Evelina*, 1778; *Cecilia*, 1782; *Camilla*, 1796; *The Wanderer*, 1814; friend of Dr Johnson and protégée of Mrs Thrale; second keeper of robes to Queen Charlotte, 1786–91; married French refugee general, 1793; in France, 1802–12; last part of long life in England. Diaries give account of Johnson's circle and life at Court.

Life by M. A. Doody, 1988

Early Diary, 1768–78 ed. A. R. Ellis, 2 vols., 1889; 1913

Diary and Letters of Madame d'Arblay, 1778–1840, ed. C. Barrett and A. Dobson, 6 vols., 1904; selections in E.L.

The Journals and Letters ed. J. Hemlow *et al.*, 12 vols., 1972–84

Camilla ed. E. A. and L. D. Bloom, 1972, 1983

Cecilia, ed. P. Sabor and M. A. Doody, 1988; in W.C.

Evelina ed. E. A. Bloom, 1968, 1982: ed. M. A. Doody, 1994

See:

E. Farr, *The World of Fanny Burney*, 1993

J. T. A. Grau, *Fanny Burney. An Annotated Bibliography*, 1981

K. M. Rogers, *Frances Burney: The World of 'Female Difficulties'*, 1990

BUTLER, SAMUEL (1612–80): Satirist; details of life obscure; son of prosperous Worcestershire yeoman; a censorious child; King's School, Worcester; possibly Gray's Inn; never at university, but greatly learned; in household of Countess of Kent; acquainted with Selden; considered painting as career; clerk to various county magistrates, possibly including fanatical Puritan, Sir Samuel Luke; secretary to Earl of Carbery and steward of Ludlow Castle, 1661; *Characters*, 1667–9 (pub. 1759); *Hudibras*, rhymed satire on Puritans, begun before Restoration (three parts, 1662, 1663, 1677) delighted Charles

II and Royalists; secretary to Duke of Buckingham, whom he probably helped with *The Rehearsal*; pension from King, 1677; died of consumption, though tradition of poverty is exaggerated.

Life by G. Wasserman, 1976; 1989
Works, ed. A. R. Waller and R. Lamar, 3 vols., 1905–28
Characters ed. C. W. Daves, 1970
Hudibras ed. J. Wilders, 1967
Hudibras Parts I and II and Selected Other Writings ed. J. Wilders and H. de Quehen, 1973
See:
D. Gibson, in *Seventeenth-Century Studies* ed. R. Shafter, 1933
I. Jack, *Augustan Satire*, 1952; 1966
G. Wasserman, *Samuel Butler and the Earl of Rochester: A Reference Guide*, 1986

CHATTERTON, THOMAS (1752–70): Poet; posthumous child of poor Bristol schoolmaster; 'the marvellous boy' pub. poems before age of twelve; through muniments of St Mary Redcliffe church became fascinated with Middle Ages; apprenticed to attorney, 1767; fabricated medieval documents and poems of monk Thomas Rowley; sent specimens to Dodsley and Walpole; controversy about genuineness; exposed by T. Tyrwhitt; reduced to despair by neglect, poisoned himself in London; 'Rowley' poems pub. 1778, 1782; belated recognition of his poetic genius.

Life by E. H. W. Meyerstein, 1930
The Complete Works ed. D. S. Taylor and B. B. Hoover, 2 vols., 1971
Selected Poems, ed. G. Lindop, 1986
D. S. Taylor, *Thomas Chatterton's Art: Experiments in Imagined History*, 1978

CHESTERFIELD, PHILIP DORMER STANHOPE, EARL OF (1694–1773): Statesman, wit, letter-writer; distinguished diplomatic and administrative career; ambassador to The Hague, 1728–32; successful Lord Lieutenant of Ireland, 1745–6; contributed to *The World*, 1753–6; generous patron of writers, rebuked by Johnson for belated recognition, 1755; concern for education of illegitimate son (d. 1768), writing to him almost daily; thereafter gave similar attention to godson. A master of manners and worldly wisdom.

Life by S. Shellaberger, 1935; W. Connely, 1939
Letters ed. B. Dobrée, 6 vols., 1932; ed. D. Roberts, 1992; Selections in E.L.
See:
R. Coxon, *Chesterfield and his Critics*, 1925

CHURCHILL, CHARLES (1731–64): Satirist; son of clergyman; educated Westminster and St John's College, Cambridge; dissipated clergyman;

notorious for personal satires, on actors in *The Rosciad* (1761), on Lord Bute and the Scots in *The Prophecy of Famine* (1763); associated with Wilkes, contributing to *The North Briton*; political and social satires against Smollett, Hogarth, Dr Johnson, and Wilkes's adversaries; depicted worst vices of the day, including own, in *The Times*, 1764; d. Boulogne. Wrote in couplets, preferring Dryden to Pope as model.

Life by W. C. Brown, 1953; R. J. Smith, 1977
Poems ed. J. Laver, 2 vols., 1933; ed. D. Grant, 1956
See:
T. Lockwood, *Post-Augustan Satire: Charles Churchill and Satirical Poetry, 1750–1800*, 1979

CIBBER, COLLEY (1671–1757): Actor and dramatist; son of Danish sculptor; Grantham School; actor, 1690; most important theatrical figure of his time; skilful comedies, *The Careless Husband* (1705) the best; as actor excelled in parts of fops and eccentric characters; controlled theatre in Drury Lane, *c.* 1710–33; poet laureate, 1730; ridiculed, especially his odes for New Year and King's birthday, by Pope, Swift, Fielding; 'hero' of Pope's revised *Dunciad*, 1743; his *Apology for the Life of Mr Colley Cibber, Comedian* (1740) contains irresistible self-portrait and valuable account of theatre and actors.

Life by L. R. N. Ashley, 1965; new edn 1989; H. Koone, 1986
Dramatic Works, 5 vols., 1777; Facsimile edn, 1966
Three Sentimental Comedies ed. M. Sullivan, 1973
An Apology, etc., ed. B. R. S. Fone, 1968; ed. J. M. Evans, 1987
See:
F. W. Bateson, *English Comic Drama, 1700–1750*, 1929
De W. C. Croissant, *Studies in the Work of Colley Cibber*, 1912

COLLIER, JEREMY (1650–1726): Non-juring clergyman and controversialist; educated Ipswich and Caius College, Cambridge; *A Short View of the Immorality and Profaneness of the English Stage*, 1698, attacking Congreve, Vanbrugh, etc; kept up attack in further pamphlets, 1699–1708.

A Short View, ed. B. Hellinger, 1987
See:
R. Anthony, *The Jeremy Collier Stage Controversy*, 1937
A. O. Beljame, *Men of Letters and the English Public in the Eighteenth Century*, 1881; trans. E. O. Lorimer, ed. B. Dobrée, 1948

COLLINS, WILLIAM (1721–59): Poet; b. Chichester, son of hatter; educated Winchester and Magdalen College, Oxford; *Persian Eclogues*, 1742, while still an undergraduate: *Odes*, 1746, including 'Ode to Evening' and 'How sleep the brave'; *Ode on the Popular Superstitions of the Highlands of Scotland* written 1749; saved from penury by legacy, 1749; suffered from nervous depression, at times insane; d. in sister's house at Chichester.

Life by E. G. Ainsworth, 1937; P. L. Carver, 1967
Works ed. R. Wendorf and C. Ryskamp, 1979
Poems ed. R. Lonsdale, 1969, rev. 1977; 1985; in *Silver Poets of the Eighteenth Century*, 1976
See:
S. Johnson, *Lives of the Poets*, ed. G. B. Hill, Vol. III, 1905
P. M. Spacks, *The Poetry of Vision*, 1967
R. Wendorf, *William Collins and Eighteenth-Century Poetry*, 1981
A. S. P. Woodhouse, 'The Poetry of Collins Reconsidered', in *From Sensibility to Romanticism* ed. F. W. Hilles and H. Bloom, 1965

CONGREVE, WILLIAM (1670–1729): Dramatist; b. Bardsey, Yorkshire; childhood in Ireland, father on military service there; fellow-student of Swift at Kilkenny and Trinity College, Dublin; studied law in London, 1691; pub. verse; novel *Incognita*, 1692; fame with first comedy, *The Old Batchelor*, 1693; *The Double Dealer*, 1694; *Love for Love*, 1695; tragedy, *The Mourning Bride*, 1697, censured by Jeremy Collier; *The Way of the World*, 1700, coolly received; held government sinecures; enjoyed friendship and admiration of Swift, Steele, Pope, intimately attached to Duchess of Marlborough; buried Westminster Abbey.

Life by D. C. Taylor, 1931; J. C. Hodges, 1941
Works ed. M. Summers, 4 vols., 1923; ed. B. Dobrée, 2 vols., 1925–8; ed. F. W. Bateson, 1930
Complete Plays ed. H. Davies, 1967
Comedies ed. E. S. Rump, 1985
The Double-Dealer ed. J. C. Ross, 1981
Love for Love ed. M. M. Kelsall, 1988
The Way of the World ed. B. Gibbons, 1971; 1994
Incognita and *The Way of the World* ed. A. N. Jeffares, 1966
Letters and Documents ed. J. C. Hodges, 1964
See under *Drama* studies by Dobrée, N. Holland, Meredith
L. Bartlett, *William Congreve: A Reference Guide*, 1979
M. Kelsall, *Congreve: 'The Way of the World'*, 1981
A Lindsay and H. Erskine-Hill, *William Congreve: The Critical Heritage*, 1989
H. Love, *William Congreve*, 1975
P. Lyons (ed.) *Congreve Comedies: A Selection of Critical Essays*, 1982
B. Mann (ed.) *A Concordance to the Plays of William Congreve*, 1973
D. Thomas, *William Congreve*, 1992
V. Woolf, 'Congreve's Comedies' in *The Moment, and Other Essays*, 1947

COWPER, WILLIAM (1731–1800): Poet; b. Great Berkhamstead, son of rector; bullied at boarding school; Westminster School; called to Bar, 1754; disappointed in love for cousin, temporary insanity; strain of preparing for examinations brought on second attack with attempted suicide; in retirement with Rev. Unwin at Huntingdon, 1765–7, then with his widow ('My Mary') at Olney; there came under strenuous evangelical influence of Rev. John Newton: *Olney Hymns*, 1779; more peaceful life after Newton's departure for London, though intermittent melancholia; verse satires, suggested by Mrs Unwin, in *Poems*, 1782; humorous ballad, *John Gilpin*, 1782; at prompting of Lady Austen, *The Task*, 1785; trans. Homer; Mrs Unwin d. 1796; stricken in mind and body; tragic lyric, *The Castaway*, 1798. Record of quiet delights of country and his own gentle nature in letters.

Life by T. Wright, 1892; rev. 1921; D. Cecil, 1929; M. J. Quinlan, 1953; C. Ryskamp, 1959; J. King, 1986
Works ed. R. Southey, 15 vols., 1853–7; 8 vols., 1853–5
Poems ed. J. D. Baird and C. Ryskamp, 3 vols., 1980–95
'The Task' and Selected Other Poems ed. J. Sambrook, 1994
Poetry and Prose ed. B. Spiller, 1968
Translation of the 'Odyssey', ed. P. Levi, 1992
Correspondence ed. T. Wright, 5 vols., 1904–25; selections in E.L. and W.C.
Letters and Prose Writings, ed. J. King and C. Ryskamp, 5 vols., 1979–86
See:
M. Golden, *In Search of Stability: The Poetry of William Cowper*, 1960
B. Hutchings, *The Poetry of William Cowper*, 1982
V. Newey, *Cowper's Poetry*, 1982

DEFOE, DANIEL (?1660–1731): Journalist and novelist; life of strange and varied adventures, details imperfectly known; wrote more than 500 pieces; b. London, son of dissenting tallow-chandler, James Foe; travelled on Continent; engaged in Monmouth's rebellion, 1685; joined William III's army, 1688; took up commerce; failed for £17,000; *Essay upon Projects*, 1697; *The True-born Englishman*, 1701; ironic attack on High Church principles, *The Shortest Way with the Dissenters*, 1702; as a result fined, pilloried, imprisoned; changed name to Defoe; political and economic *Review*, 1704–13; served cause of Nonconformists and Whigs as secret agent of Godolphin and Harley, largely in Scotland; served Tories, 1710–14; thereafter gave doubtful support to both parties; *Robinson Crusoe*, 1719; other fiction followed, including *Captain Singleton* (1720), *Moll Flanders* (1722), *A Journal of the Plague Year* (1722), *Roxana* (1724); observant traveller, *A Tour thro' the Whole Island of Great Britain*, 1724–7; writing for promotion of English commerce, 1725–31. A shrewd, shifty, ingenious man, much mistrusted and frequently imprisoned. Buried Bunhill Fields.

Life by J. R. Moore, 1958; J. Richetti, 1987; P. Backscheider, 1989
Romances and Narratives ed. G. A. Aitken, 16 vols., 1895
Novels and Selected Writings, 14 vols., 1927–8
Captain Singleton, 1969; *Colonel Jack* ed. S. H. Monk, 1989; *Journal of Plague*

Year, ed. P. R. Backcheider, 1992; *Memoirs of a Cavalier*, ed. J. T. Boulton, 1991; *Moll Flanders*, ed. D. Blewett, 1989; *Robinson Crusoe*, ed. M. Shinagel, 1975; 1994; ed. P. Rogers, 1980; 1981; *Roxana*, 1964; 1981; 1982

The Review ed. A. W. Secord, 22 vols., 1938

The Best of Defoe's 'Review' ed. W. L. Payne, 1951

Tour ed. G. D. H. Cole, 2 vols., 1927; repr. in E.L.

Robinson Crusoe and Other Writings ed. J. Sutherland, 1968

Selected Poetry and Prose ed. M. Shugrue, 1968

Selected Writings ed. J. T. Boulton, 1975

Letters ed. G. H. Healey, 1955

For extensive list of writings, see N.C.B.E.I., II, 883–905

See:

P. K. Alkon, *Defoe and Fictional Time*, 1979

M. Byrd (ed.) *Daniel Defoe: A Collection of Critical Essays*, 1976

F. H. Ellis (ed.) *Twentieth-Century Interpretations of 'Robinson Crusoe'*, 1969

L. B. Faller, *Crime and Defoe: A New Kind of Writing*, 1993

C. H. Flynn, *The Body in Swift and Defoe*, 1990

J. R. Hammond, *A Defoe Companion*, 1993

M. E. Novak, *Realism, Myth and History in Defoe's Fiction*, 1983

S. Peterson, *Daniel Defoe: A Reference Guide 1731–1924*, 1987

J. Richetti, *Defoe's Narratives: Situations and Structures*, 1975

P. Rogers (ed.) *Defoe: The Critical Heritage*, 1972

M. Schonhom, *Defoe's Politics: Parliament, Power, Kingship and 'Robinson Crusoe'*, 1991

G. A. Starr, *Defoe and Casuistry*, 1971

    Defoe and Spiritual Autobiography, 1965

J. A. Stoler, *Daniel Defoe: An Annotated Bibliography of Modern Criticism, 1900–1980*, 1984

J. R. Sutherland, *Daniel Defoe: A Critical Study*, 1971

E. Zimmermann, *Defoe and the Novel*, 1975

DRYDEN, JOHN (1631–1700): Poet, satirist, dramatist, critic; b. Aldwinkle, Northamptonshire; brought up in Puritan environment; Westminster and Trinity College, Cambridge; served Cromwell's chamberlain; *Heroic Stanzas* on death of Cromwell, 1659; settled in London; celebrated Restoration of Charles II in *Astraea Redux*, 1660; F.R.S., 1662; married Lady Elizabeth Howard, 1663; turned playwright for livelihood, averaging almost a play a year, 1663–81; defined his dramatic principles in prefaces, prologues, essays; *Essay of Dramatic Poesy*, 1668; poem, *Annus Mirabilis*, 1667; poet laureate, 1668; historiographer, 1670; his heroic plays burlesqued by Buckingham (?) in *The Rehearsal*, 1671; blank-verse tragedy, *All for Love*, 1678; political and personal verse satires, *Absalom and Achitophel* (1681–2), *The Medall* (1678–82), *MacFlecknoe* (1682, written 1678); didactic religious poems, *Religio Laici* (1682), *The Hind and the Panther* (1687), the latter after conversion to Roman Catholicism, 1686; lost offices after Revolution, 1688; in old age turned to writing again for a living; plays, odes, translations, with valuable critical prefaces; verse translation of Virgil (1697) said to have earned him £1,200, adaptations of Chaucer, Boccaccio, Ovid as *Fables, Ancient and Modern*, 1700, with distinguished preface; *Secular Masque*, hailing a new age, 1700; buried Westminster Abbey.

Life by C. E. Ward, 1961; J. A. Winn, 1987
See:
J. M. Osborn, *John Dryden. Some Biographical Facts and Problems*, 1940; rev. 1965
Works ed. E. N. Hooker *et al.*, 21 vols., 1956–in progress
Poetry, Prose and Plays ed. D. Grant, 1952
    Selections ed. D. Grant, 1985; ed. K. Walker, 1987, (in O.S.A.)
Poems ed., J. Kinsley 4 vols., 1958; one vol., 1961; ed. P. Hammond and D. Hopkins, 4 vols., 1995–in progress
Four Comedies; Four Tragedies ed. L. A. Beaurline and F. Bowers, 2 vols., 1967
All for Love ed. N. J. Andrew, 1975; ed. D. M. Vieth, 1972
Essays ed. W. P. Ker, 2 vols., 1900; 1926
Essay of Dramatic Poesy ed. D. Nichol Smith, 1900; ed. J. T. Boulton, 1964
Of Dramatic Poesy and Other Critical Essays ed. G. Watson, 2 vols., 1962
Selected Criticism ed. J. Kinsley and G. Parfitt, 1970
Translation of Virgil's 'Aeneid' ed. H. Clarke, 1989
Letters ed. C. E. Ward, 1942
See:
L. I. Bredvold, *The Intellectual Milieu of John Dryden*, 1934; 1956
D. Bywaters, *Dryden in Revolutionary England*, 1991
T. S. Eliot, *Homage to John Dryden*, 1924
    John Dryden. The Poet, the Dramatist, the Critic, 1932
W. Frost, *Dryden and the Art of Translation*, 1955
J. D. Garrison, *'Pietas' from Vergil to Dryden*, 1992
J. M. Hall, *John Dryden: A Reference Guide*, 1984
P. Hammond, *John Dryden*, 1991
P. Harth, *Contexts of Dryden's Thought*, 1968
    Pen for a Party: Dryden's Tory Propaganda in its Contexts, 1993
S. Johnson, *Lives of the Poets*, ed. G. B. Hill, I, 1905
B. King (ed.) *Dryden's Mind and Art*, 1969
J. and H. K. Kinsley (eds.) *Dryden: The Critical Heritage*, 1971, 1995
A. C. Kirsch, *Dryden's Heroic Drama*, 1965
D. B. Kramer, *The Imperial Dryden: The Poetics of Appropriation in Seventeenth-Century England*, 1994
E. Miner, *Dryden's Poetry*, 1967
    (ed.) *John Dryden*, 1972
E. Miner and J. Brady (eds.) *Literary Transmission and Authority: Dryden and Other Writers*, 1993
G. Montgomery (ed.) *Concordance to the Poetical Works*, 1967

H. T. Swedenberg (ed.) *Essential Articles for the Study of John Dryden*, 1966

M. van Doren, *The Poetry of John Dryden*, 1920; 1931; rev. 1946, 1960

J. A. Winn, *'When Beauty Fires the Blood': Love and the Arts in the Age of Dryden*, 1992

J. A. Zamonski, *An Annotated Bibliography of John Dryden: Texts and Studies, 1949–1973*, 1975

DYER, JOHN (?1700–1758): Poet and painter; b. Wales, lived most of life there; Westminster School; studied law and, in Italy, painting; became clergyman; *Grongar Hill*, a loco-descriptive poem, 1725 or 6; didactic poems in 'Georgic' tradition. *The Ruins of Rome* (1740), *The Fleece* (1757).

Life by B. Humfrey, 1980
Poems ed. E. Thomas, 1903; 1989; in *Minor Poets of the Eighteenth Century*, 1930
Grongar Hill ed. R. C. Boys, 1941

ETHEREGE, SIR GEORGE (?1634–?91): Dramatist; of good Berkshire family; brought up in France, travelled, studied law; man of the world in London; *The Comical Revenge, or Love in a Tub*, 1664; *She Wou'd if She Cou'd*, 1668; secretary to ambassador in Constantinople, 1668–71; married money and knighted; *The Man of Mode, or Sir Fopling Flutter*, 1676; envoy to Ratisbon, 1685–9; Jacobite exile in France; d. Paris.

Life by A. R. Husboe, 1987
Plays and Poems ed. A. W. Verity, 1888
Plays ed. H. F. B. Brett-Smith, 2 vols., 1927; ed. M. Cordner, 1982
The Man of Mode ed. J. Barnard, 1979
She Would If She Could, ed. C. M. Taylor, 1978
Poems ed. J. Thorpe, 1963
Letters ed. F. Bracher, 1974
See:
B. Dobrée, *Essays in Biography*, 1925
     Restoration Comedy, 1924
D. A. Mann, *A Concordance to the Plays and Poems of Sir George Etherege*, 1985
     Sir George Etherege. A Reference Guide, 1981
D. Underwood, *Etherege and the Seventeenth-Century Comedy of Manners*, 1957

EVELYN, JOHN (1620–1706): Virtuoso and diarist; b. Wotton, Surrey; educated Balliol College, Oxford, and Middle Temple; man of means, Royalist; travelled in Europe; settled at Sayes Court, Deptford, 1653, and laid out famous garden; unsuccessfully planned Restoration, 1659; assisted in founding Royal Society; served on public bodies; translations and writings on architecture, engraving, gardening, etc.; removed to Wotton, 1694, where he died. Chiefly remembered for *Diary*, describing travels, leading men and events.

Life by Lord A. Ponsonby, 1933; J. Bowle, 1981
Writings, ed. G. de la Bedoyère, 1995
Diary ed. E. S. de Beer, 6 vols., 1955; one vol., 1959; G. de la Bedoyère, 1994; selected J. Bowle, 1983; 1985
The Life of Mrs Godolphin ed. H. Sampson, 1939
See:
W. G. Hiscock, *John Evelyn and his Family Circle*, 1956
G. Keynes, *John Evelyn: A Study in Bibliography*, 1968
C. Marburg, *Mr Pepys and Mr Evelyn*, 1935

FARQUHAR, GEORGE (1677–1707); Dramatist; b. Londonderry, Ireland, son of clergyman; Trinity College, Dublin, 1694–5; worked for bookseller; became actor; to London, 1697; *Love and a Bottle* produced, 1698; *The Constant Couple or a Trip to the Jubilee*, 1699; with Army in Holland, 1700; *Sir Harry Wildair*, 1701; *The Inconstant* and *The Twin Rivals*, 1702; married young lady of pretended fortune, 1703; *The Stage-Coach*, 1704; *The Recruiting Officer*, 1706; *The Beaux' Stratagem*, 1707; died in poverty. Easy-going, genial character.

Life by W. C. Connely, 1949
Complete Works ed. C. A. Stonehill, 2 vols., 1930; ed. S. S. Kenny, 2 vols., 1988
The Beaux' Stratagem, in *Restoration Plays*, 1976; ed. M. Cordner, 1976; ed. C. N. Fifer, 1977
The Recruiting Officer etc. ed. J. Ross, 1977; 1991; ed. W. Myers, 1995
See under *Drama*, studies by Boas, Dobrée
E. N. James, *George Farquhar: A Reference Guide*, 1985

FIELDING, HENRY (1707–54): Dramatist, journalist, novelist; b. Sharpham Park, Somerset, of distinguished legal and military family; Eton, 1719; studied law, Leyden, *c.* 1728; struggle for livelihood in London; wrote plays, 1728–37; managed Little Theatre in Haymarket, conducting campaign against Walpole till muzzled by Licensing Act (1737); called to Bar, 1740; periodical *The Champion*, 1739–41; ridiculed Richardson's *Pamela* with *Joseph Andrews* (1742) and probably *An Apology for the Life of Mrs Shamela Andrews* (1741); anti-Walpole *Jonathan Wild*, 1743; anti-Jacobite periodicals; J.P. for Middlesex, 1748, concerned with poverty and suppression of crime; *Tom Jones*, 1749; *Amelia*, 1751; humanitarian writing in *Covent Garden Journal*, 1752; broken in health, went on voyage to Portugal; d. Lisbon; *Journal of a Voyage to Lisbon*, pub. 1755.
Life by F. Homes Dudden, 2 vols., 1952; P. Rogers, 1979; M. C. Battestin, 1989

Works ed. Sir L. Stephen, 10 vols., 1882; ed. G. Saintsbury, 12 vols., 1893; ed. W. E. Henley, 16 vols., 1903; 1967; ed. W. B. Coley and F. Bowers, Wesleyan edn, 1967–in progress

Novels, 10 vols., 1962

Joseph Andrews, ed. D. Nokes, 1987; ed. S. Copley, 1987; 1993; *Tom Jones*, ed. S. Baker, 1973; 1993; *Jonathan Wild*, ed. D. Nokes, 1982; *Shamela* ed. I. Watt, 1956; 1980; *Voyage to Lisbon* ed. T. Keymer, 1996

Covent Garden Journal ed. G. E. Jensen, 2 vols., 1915

See under *Drama*

R. Alter, *Fielding and the Nature of the Novel*, 1968

M. C. Battestin, *The Moral Basis of Fielding's Art: A Study of 'Joseph Andrews'*, 1959

   (ed.) *Twentieth-Century Interpretations of 'Tom Jones'*, 1968

I. A. Bell, *Henry Fielding: Authorship and Authority*, 1994

I. Ehrenpreis, *Fielding's 'Tom Jones'*, 1964

H. G. Hahn, *Henry Fielding: An Annotated Bibliography*, 1979

B. Harrison, *Henry Fielding's Tom Jones: The Novelist as Moral Philosopher*, 1975

R. D. Hume, *Henry Fielding and the London Theatre 1728–1737*, 1988

J. P. Hunter, *Occasional Forms: Henry Fielding and the Chains of Circumstance*, 1975

H. K. Miller, *Henry Fielding's 'Tom Jones' and the Romance Tradition*, 1976

E. J. Morrissey, *Henry Fielding: A Reference Guide*, 1980

R. Paulson (ed.) *Fielding: A Collection of Critical Essays*, 1962

R. Paulson and T. Lockwood (eds.) *Henry Fielding: The Critical Heritage*, 1969

C. J. Rawson, *Henry Fielding*, 1968

   Henry Fielding and the Augustan Ideal under Stress, 1972; 1991

K. G. Simpson (ed.) *Henry Fielding: Justice Observed*, 1985

A. J. Smallwood, *Fielding and the Woman Question*, 1989

D. Thomas, *Henry Fielding*, 1990

GAY, JOHN (1685–1732): Poet and dramatist; b. Barnstaple; apprenticed to London mercer; *Wine*, 1708, poem against water-drinkers; *Present State of Wit*, 1711; secretary to Duchess of Monmouth, 1712–14; serious and burlesque pastorals, *Rural Sports* (1713), *The Shepherd's Week* (1714); satirical farce, *What d'ye Call It*, 1715; mock heroic *Trivia, or the Art of Walking the Streets of London*, 1716; minor public employments, patronage of various nobles, friendship of Pope and Swift; unable to fend for himself, was cared for by Duke and Duchess of Queensberry; popularity of *Fables* (1727, 1738); *The Beggar's Opera*, 1728; sequel *Polly* banned on political grounds, 1729

Life by W. H. Irvine, 1940; P. M. Spacks, 1965; D. Nokes, 1995

Dramatic Works ed. J. Fuller, 2 vols., 1983

Poetry and Prose ed. V. A. Dearing, 2 vols., 1974

Poetical Works (and major plays) ed. G. C. Faber, 1926
The Beggar's Opera ed. F. W. Bateson, 1934; ed. P. E. Lewis, 1973; ed. E. V. Roberts, 1969, 1986
Letters ed. C. F. Burgess, 1966
See:
A. Forsgren, *John Gay, Poet 'of a Lower Order'*, 2 vols., 1964–71
P. Lewis and N. Wood (eds.) *John Gay and the Scriblerians*, 1989
Y. Noble (ed.) *Twentieth-Century Interpretations of 'The Beggar's Opera'*, 1975

GIBBON, EDWARD (1737–94): Historian; b. Putney, of good family; 'unprofitable' education at Westminster and Magdalen College, Oxford; owed precocious erudition to 'invincible love of reading'; turned Roman Catholic, 1753; under Calvinist pastor at Lausanne, 1753–8, abandoned Romanism; fluent in French; forced to break off engagement to Swiss girl; captain in Hampshire militia, 1761–3; in Rome formed plan of writing history of its decline, 1764; settled in London, 1772, proceeded with historical studies; M.P. and minor offices, 1774–83; first vol. of *History of the Decline and Fall of the Roman Empire*, 1776; replied to protests against his attitude to Christianity; vols. II–III, 1781; retired to Lausanne, 1783, completed *History*, 1788; returned to England, 1793, lived with Earl of Sheffield; buried Fletching, Sussex.

Life by D. M. Low, 1937; P. B. Craddock, 2 vols., 1983–8
Decline and Fall of the Roman Empire ed. J. B. Bury, 7 vols., 1896–1900; rev. 1926–9; 6 vols., 1910; 7 vols. 1903–4; abr. 1964; ed. D. Womersley, 3 vols., 1995
Miscellaneous Works ed. Lord Sheffield, 5 vols., 1814
Autobiographies ed. J. Murray, 1896; in E.L. and W.C.
Memoirs of My Life ed. G. A. Bonnard, 1966
The English Essays ed. P. B. Craddock, 1972
Letters ed. J. E. Norton, 3 vols., 1956
See:
H. L. Bond, *The Literary Art of Edward Gibbon*, 1960
G. W. Bowersock *et al.* (eds.) *Edward Gibbon and 'The Decline and Fall of the Roman Empire'*, 1977
J. W. Burrow, *Gibbon*, 1985
W. B. Carnochan, *Gibbon's Solitude: The Inward Worlds of the Historian*, 1987
L. Gossman, *The Empire Unpossess'd. An Essay on Gibbon's 'Decline and Fall'*, 1981
R. Porter, *Edward Gibbon: Making History*, 1988

GOLDSMITH, OLIVER (1730–74): Journalist, essayist, poet, novelist, dramatist; son of Irish clergyman; educated Trinity College, Dublin; studied medicine at Edinburgh, Leyden; piped and sang his way through Europe, 1755–6; returned destitute, failed as physician and teacher, became hack-writer of reviews, biographies, etc.; *Enquiry into the Present State of Polite Learning*, 1759; met Dr Johnson, 1761; member of 'The Club'; *Chinese Letters* (*The Citizen of the World*), 1760–62; *The Vicar of Wakefield*, 1762 (pub. 1766); *The Traveller*, 1764; removed from Islington to the Temple; *The Good-natur'd Man* at Covent Garden, 1768, after being rejected by Garrick; *She Stoops to Conquer* immensely successful, 1773; *The Deserted Village*, 1770; *Retaliation*, 1774; buried in Temple Church. Wrote and translated great diversity of works for booksellers; a man often foolish, always in debt, but generous, tender-hearted, and loved by all.

Life by Sir J. Prior, 2 vols., 1837; J. Forster, 1848; 2 vols., 1854; A. Dobson, 1888; R. M, Wardle, 1957
Poems; *Essays*; *Vicar of Wakefield*; *Plays*, in E.L., O.S.A., W.C.
Poems and Plays ed. T. Davis, 1993
She Stoops to Conquer ed. T. Davis, 1979; ed. N. King, 1985
The Vicar of Wakefield, ed. O. Doughty, 1928; 1974; 1982; ed. A. Friedman, 1974
Poems ed. R. Lonsdale, 1969; 1976
Collected Letters ed. K. C. Balderston, 1928
Selected Writings ed. J. Lucas, 1988
See:
M. Emslie, *Goldsmith: 'The Vicar of Wakefield'*, 1963
G. S. Rousseau (ed.) *Goldsmith: The Critical Heritage*, 1974
A. Swarbrick (ed.) *The Art of Oliver Goldsmith*, 1984
S. H. Woods *Oliver Goldsmith: A Reference Guide*, 1982

GRAY, THOMAS (1716–71): Poet and scholar; b. London, son of broker; at Eton formed 'quadrumvirate' with Horace Walpole, West, and Ashton; Peterhouse, Cambridge, 1734–8; travelled in France and Italy with Walpole, 1739–41, quarrelled, and returned alone; resided at Peterhouse, studying law; *Odes* and *Sonnet on the Death of West*, 1742; friendship with Walpole renewed, 1745; *Elegy in a Country Churchyard* completed, 1750; removed to Pembroke College, 1756, offended by a practical joke; *The Progress of Poesy* (1754) and *The Bard* printed by Walpole, 1757; declined laureateship, 1757; settled in London to read at British Museum, 1759–61; imitations of Icelandic and Celtic verse; professor of history and modern languages at Cambridge, 1768; interested in botany; visited Scottish Highlands, 1765; tour of Lake District, 1769, described in journal; buried at Stoke Poges, Buckinghamshire, the village usually associated with the *Elegy*.

Life by R. Martin, 1934; R. W. Ketton-Cremer, 1955; A. K. L. Sells, 1980
Works ed. Sir E. Gosse, 4 vols., 1884; rev. 1902–6
Complete Poems ed. H. W. Starr and J. R. Hendrickson, 1966
Poems ed. R. Lonsdale, 1969; rev. 1977; in *Silver Poets of the Eighteenth Century*, 1976
Correspondence ed. P. Toynbee and L. Whibley, 3 vols., 1935; rev. 1971

PART FOUR

Selected Letters ed. J. Beresford, 1925
See:
M. Arnold, *Essays in Criticism. Second Series*, 1888
R. S. Edgecombe, *'Wonted Fires': A Reading of Thomas Gray*, 1992
W. B. Hutchings and W. Ruddick (eds.) *Thomas Gray: Contemporary Essays*, 1993
S. Johnson, *Lives of the Poets*, ed. G. B. Hill, vol. III, 1905
S. Kaul, *Thomas Gray and Literary Authority*, 1992
F. R. Leavis, *Revaluation*, 1936
A. T. McKenzie, *Thomas Gray: A Reference Guide*, 1982
R. Martin, *Essai sur Thomas Gray*, 1934
H. W. Starr, *Gray as a Literary Critic*, 1941

GREEN, MATTHEW (1696–1737): Poet; remembered solely for his poem *The Spleen* (1737), admired by Pope and Gray.

Poems, in *Minor Poets of the Eighteenth Century*, 1930
The Spleen ed. W. H. Williams, 1936

HOGARTH, WILLIAM (1697–1764): Painter and engraver; b. London; apprenticed to silversmith and engraver; set up independently as engraver, *c.* 1720; began attending Thornhill's art school, *c.* 1724; illustrations to *Hudibras* 1726; married Jane Thornhill, 1729; painted 'conversation pieces', 1728–9; 'A Harlot's Progress' (first of the 'pictur'd Morals'), 1731–2; 'A Rake's Progress', 1735, 'Hogarth's Act' protecting engravers' copyright, 1735; letter on sham 'Old Masters', 1737; 'The Four Stages of Cruelty', 1738; 'Marriage à la Mode', 1745, 'Beer Street' and 'Gin Lane', 1751; pub. *The Analysis of Beauty*, 1753; 'The Election' series, 1754–66; serjeant-painter, 1757; quarrel with Wilkes and Churchill, 1762–3; d. at Leicester Fields, London. Attacked connoisseurs for neglect of native talent; excelled as sincere pictorial satirist, depicting both tragic and humorous scenes.

Life by R Paulson, 2 vols., 1971; 3 vols., 1995
The Analysis of Beauty ed. J. Burke, 1955
See:
F. Antal, *Hogarth and his Place in European Art*, 1962
J. Burke and C. Caldwell (eds.) *Hogarth: The Complete Engravings*, 1968
F. D. Klingender, *Hogarth and the English Caricature*, 1944
R. E. Moore, *Hogarth's Literary Relationships*, 1948
R. Paulson, *Hogarth's Graphic Works*, 2 vols., 1965; rev. 1970

HUME, DAVID (1711–76): Philosopher and historian; b. Edinburgh; Edinburgh University; in France, 1734–7; *Treatise of Human Nature*, 1739–40; in Europe, 1745–8; *Enquiry concerning Human Understanding*, 1748; *Enquiry concerning the Principles of Morals*, 1751; clerical opposition; *Political Discourses*

(1752) extended fame to Europe; Keeper of Advocates' Library, Edinburgh, 1752–7; leader in Edinburgh intellectual life; *History of Great Britain*, 1754–61; secretary of British Embassy in Paris, 1763–6; brought Rousseau back to England and quarrelled; under-secretary of state, 1767–8; retired to Edinburgh; *Dialogues concerning Natural Religion*, pub. 1779. Logical scepticism in religion and philosophy; demonstrated in his life that virtue is not dependent upon religion.

Life by E. C. Mossner, 1954; 1970; 1980

Philosophical Works ed. T. H. Green and T. H. Grose, 4 vols., 1875–8

Selected Essays ed. S. Copley and A. Edgar, 1993, in W.C.

Treatise of Human Nature ed. L. A. Selby-Bigge, 1888; 1941; ed. E. C. Mossner, 1969; in E.L.

Letters ed. J. Y. T. Greig, 2 vols., 1932; 1983

See:

J. L. Mackie, *Hume's Moral Theory*, 1980

D. F. Norton, *David Hume: Commonsense Moralist, Sceptical Metaphysician*, 1982

    (ed.) *The Cambridge Companion to Hume*, 1993

J. Noxon, *Hume's Philosophical Development: A Study of His Methods*, 1973

T. Penelhum, *David Hume: An Introduction to his Philosophical System*, 1992

J. V. Price, *The Ironic Hume*, 1965

W. B. Todd (ed.) *Hume and the Enlightenment*, 1974

JOHNSON, SAMUEL (1709–84): Lexicographer, critic, poet, essayist; son of Lichfield bookseller; ailing childhood; Pembroke College, Oxford, 1728; left after four terms because of poverty; intermittent country-schoolmastering; married much older widow, 1735; to London, 1737, with pupil, Garrick; contributed to the *Gentleman's Magazine* parliamentary reports, etc.; adaptation of Juvenal's satire, *London*, 1738; *Life of Savage* (1744), record of friendship shared in poverty; preparing edn of Shakespeare and dictionary; *The Vanity of Human Wishes* and production of tragedy *Irene* by Garrick, 1749; *The Rambler* twice weekly, 1750–52; wife died, 1752; contributed to *The Adventurer*, 1753–4; fame with *Dictionary of the English Language*, 1755, after rejecting Lord Chesterfield's belated offer of patronage; *The Idler* weekly, 1758–60; *Rasselas*, Abyssinian moral tale, 1759; government pension, 1762, brought leisure for company and conversation; met Boswell, 1763, and the Thrales, 1764, with whom he often stayed at Streatham; founded 'The Club', 1764; edn of Shakespeare, 1765; series of Tory pamphlets in 1770s; journey to Highlands and Skye with Boswell, 1773, recorded in *Journey to the Western Islands of Scotland* (1775) and in Boswell's *Tour* (1785); at request of London booksellers, 1777, wrote *Lives of the Poets* (1779–81); buried Westminster Abbey, after quarter-century of almost undisputed literary predominance.

Life by J. Boswell, 2 vols., 1791; ed. G. B. Hill, 6 vols., 1887; rev. L. F. Powell, 1934–50; in E.L. and O.S.A.; J. L. Clifford, 2 vols., 1955–79; D. J. Greene, 1970; W. J. Bate, 1977; R. de Maria, 1993

Works ed. A. Murphy, 12 vols., 1792, etc.; 11 vols., 1825

Yale Edition of the Works of Samuel Johnson, ed. H. W. Liebert, *et al.*, 1958– in progress

Prose and Poetry (selected) ed. R. W. Chapman, 1922; ed. M. Wilson, 1950; 1966; ed. W. K. Wimsatt and F. Brady, 1977; ed. P. Cruttwell, 1982; ed. D. Greene, 1984

Poems ed. D. Nichol Smith and E. L. McAdam, 1941; rev. 1974

The Complete English Poems ed. J. D. Fleeman, 1971; 1982

Rasselas 1927; ed. J. P. Hardy, 1968; 1988; ed. G. Tillotson and B. Jenkins, 1971; ed. D. J. Enright, 1976; ed. G. J. Kolb, 1991

Journey to the Western Islands ed. R. W. Chapman, 1924; ed. P. Levi, 1984; ed. J. D. Fleeman, 1985

Early Biographical Writings ed. J. D. Fleeman, 1973

Lives of the Poets ed. G. B. Hill, 2 vols., 1897; 3 vols. 1905

Johnsonian Miscellanies ed. G. B. Hill, 2 vols., 1897

Letters ed. R. W. Chapman, 3 vols., 1952; 1984; selections in W.C.; ed. B. Redford, 5 vols., 1992–94

See:

J. T. Boulton (ed.) *Johnson: The Critical Heritage*, 1971

O. M. Brack and R. E. Kelley (eds.) *The Early Biographies of Samuel Johnson*, 1974

J. Cannon, *Samuel Johnson and the Politics of Hanoverian England*, 1995

J. L. Clifford and D. J. Greene, *Samuel Johnson: A Survey and Bibliography of Critical Studies*, 1970

R. de Maria, *Johnson's 'Dictionary' and the Language of Learning*, 1986

W. Edinger, *Samuel Johnson and Poetic Style*, 1977

J. D. Fleeman, *A Bibliography of the Works of Samuel Johnson*, 2 vols., 1996

R. Folkenflik, *Samuel Johnson, Biographer*, 1978

J. Gray, *Johnson's Sermons: A Study*, 1972

D. J. Greene (ed.) *Samuel Johnson: A Collection of Critical Essays*, 1965

I. Grundy, *Samuel Johnson and the Scale of Greatness*, 1986

J. H. Hagstrum, *Samuel Johnson's Literary Criticism*, 1952; rev. 1967

J. P. Hardy, *Samuel Johnson: A Critical Study*, 1979

R. Holmes, *Dr Johnson and Mr Savage*, 1993

N. Hudson, *Samuel Johnson and Eighteenth-Century Thought*, 1988

H. H. Nangle, *A Concordance to the Poems of Samuel Johnson*, 1973

A. Reddick, *The Making of Johnson's Dictionary, 1746–1773*, 1990

P. Rogers, *Johnson*, 1993

R. B. Schwartz, *Samuel Johnson and the New Science*, 1971
    Samuel Johnson and the Problem of Evil, 1975

W. K. Wimsatt, *Philosophic Words: A Study of Style and Meaning in the 'Rambler' and the 'Dictionary' of Samuel Johnson*, 1948

The Prose Style of Samuel Johnson, 1941

LAW, WILLIAM (1686–1761): Theologian; b. King's Cliffe, near Stamford; fellow of Emmanuel College, Cambridge, 1711; refused oaths to George I; controversies with latitudinarians and deists; *A Serious Call to a Devout and Holy Life* (1728), manual of Christian behaviour, inspired the Wesleys; tutor in Gibbon family, 1728–40; centre of small spiritual community at King's Cliffe from 1740.

Life by J. H. Overton, 1881
Works ed. G. B. Morgan, 9 vols., 1892–3
A Serious Call in E.L.; ed. P. G. Stanwood, 1978; ed. H. C. Backhouse, 1987
Selected Mystical Writings ed. W. L. and S. H. Hobhouse, 1938
See:
H. Talon, *William Law: A Study in Literary Craftmanship,* 1948

LOCKE, JOHN (1632–1704): Philosopher, b. Somerset; educated Winchester, Christ Church, Oxford; lecturer on rhetoric and moral philosophy at Oxford; physician in house of Earl of Shaftesbury, 1667; *Essay concerning Toleration,* 1667; F.R.S., 1668; various official posts; in France, 1675–9; resided in Oxford, expelled for supposed complicity in Shaftesbury's plots, 1684; lived in Holland; restored to public offices by William III; *Essay concerning Human Understanding,* 1690; *Treatises of Government,* 1690; *On Education,* 1693; *Reasonableness of Christianity,* 1695. The great empirical rationalist of modern philosophy.

Life by H. R. Fox Bourne, 2 vols., 1876; M. Cranston, 1957
Works ed. P. H. Nidditch, 1975; 1979
Correspondence ed. E. S. de Beer, 1976–in progress
Some Thoughts Concerning Education ed. J. W. and J. S. Yolton, 1989
Essay concerning Human Understanding in E.L.; ed. P. H. Nidditch, 1975; 1979
Two Treatises of Government ed. P. Laslett, 1960; 1988; ed. M. Goldie, 1993; 1994
See:
J. C. Attig, *The Works of John Locke: A Comprehensive Bibliography,* 1985
C. Fox, *Locke and the Scriblerians: Identity and Consciousness in Early Eighteenth-Century Britain,* 1989
R. Hall and R. Woodhouse (eds.) *Eighty Years of Locke Scholarship: A Bibliographic Guide,* 1983
I. Harris, *The Mind of John Locke: A Study of Political Theory in its Intellectual Setting,* 1994
K. MacLean, *John Locke and English Literature of the Eighteenth Century,* 1936
E. L. Tuveson, *The Imagination as a Means of Grace. Locke and the Aesthetics of Romanticism,* 1960

MACKENZIE, HENRY (1745–1831): Novelist; b. and educated Edinburgh, a leader in its political, legal, literary life; novels of 'sensibility', *The Man of Feeling* (1771), a 'bosom favourite' of Burns, *The Man of the World* (1773); *Julia de Roubigné* (1777); also four plays; periodicals, *The Mirror* (1779–80) and *The Lounger* (1785–7); interested in German literature. Dubbed by Scott the 'Northern Addison'.

Life by H. W. Thompson, *A Scottish Man of Feeling*, 1931
Works, 8 vols., 1808
The Man of Feeling ed. B. Vickers, 1967; rev. 1987
Literature and Literari: The Literary Correspondence and Notebooks of Henry Mackenzie, ed. H. W. Drescher, 1989–in progress

MACPHERSON, JAMES (1736–96): 'Translator' of Gaelic poems, b. Scottish Highlands, son of farmer; Aberdeen and Edinburgh Universities; schoolteacher; *Fragments of Ancient Poetry . . . translated from the Gaelic or Erse Language*, 1760; followed up success with 'translations' of Gaelic poet Ossian, *Fingal* (1762), *Temora* (1763), largely his own invention; gratified current hunger throughout Europe for primitive national poetry; authenticity challenged by Dr Johnson and others; political posts in America and London; buried Westminster Abbey.

Life by T. B. Sanders, 1894
The Poems of Ossian ed. W. Sharp, 1896; ed. H. Gaskill, 1996
See:
J. S. Smart, *James MacPherson*, 1905
F. J. Stafford, *The Sublime Savage*, 1988
P. Van Tieghem, *Le Préromantisme*, II, 1930

MANDEVILLE, BERNARD (1670–1733): Physician, moral philosopher, controversialist; b. Holland; practised medicine in London from 1690s; satirical allegory in octosyllabic verse, *The Grumbling Hive: or, Knaves Turn'd Honest*, 1705; enlarged with prose essays, dialogues, commentary as *The Fable of the Bees; or Private Vices, Publick Benefits*, 1714–29. His sardonic paradox, that the luxury and vices of the individual contribute to the general welfare of the community, and that virtue is founded on selfishness, stirred up a long and vigorous controversy. Also wrote fables and discourses on religion and various social issues.

The Fable of the Bees, etc. ed., with commentary, F. B. Kaye, 2 vols., 1924; ed. P. Harth, 1970; 1989
See:
M. M. Goldsmith, *Private Vices, Public Benefits: Bernard Mandeville's Social Thought*, 1985
E. J. Hundert, *The Enlightenment's Fable. Bernard Mandeville and the Discovery of Society*, 1995
H. Munro, *The Ambivalence of Bernard Mandeville*, 1975
I. Primer (ed.) *Mandeville Studies*, 1975

NEWTON, SIR ISAAC (1642–1727): Mathematician and natural philosopher; b. Woolsthorpe, Lincs.; Grantham School; fellow of Trinity College, Cambridge; made numerous advances in mathematics and conceived idea of universal gravitation, 1665–6; F.R.S., 1672; laws of motion and theory of gravitation expounded in *Philosphiae Naturalis Principia Mathematica*, 1687; president of Royal Society, 1703–27; theories of light and colour in *Opticks*, 1704; quarrel with Leibniz over priority of invention of 'method of fluxions'; master of Mint, 1699; knighted, 1705; also wrote on theology and biblical chronology; buried Westminster Abbey.

Life by D. Brewster, 2 vols., 1855; 1866: F. E. Manuel, 1968; 1980; R. S. Westfall, 1981; 1994; A. R. Hall, 1992; 1996
Correspondence ed. H. W. Turnbull *et al.*, 7 vols., 1959–77
Newton: Texts. Backgrounds, Commentaries, ed. I. B. Cohen and R. S. Westfall, 1995
See:
F. E. Manuel, *The Religion of Isaac Newton*, 1974
M. H. Nicolson, *Newton Demands the Muse*, 1946
L. Stewart, *The Rise of Public Science: Rhetoric, Technology and Natural Philosophy in Newtonian Britain, 1660–1760*, 1992

OLDHAM, JOHN (1653–83): Poet and satirist; son of Gloucestershire dissenting minister; educated Tetbury and St Edmund Hall, Oxford; usher and private tutor, 1676–81; 'set up for a wit' in London, 1681; wrote amorous verse, pindaric odes, imitations of classical and French writers; chiefly remembered for ironical *Satyr against Vertue* (1679) and political *Satyrs upon the Jesuits* (1681); *Poems and Translations*, 1683; eulogized by Waller and Dryden.

Poems ed. H. F. Brooks and R. Selden, 1987
See:
H. F. Brooks, 'A Bibliography of John Oldham', with biographical and critical introduction, in *Oxford Bibliographical Soc. Proc.*, V, 1936
P. Hammond, *John Oldham and the Renewal of Classical Culture*, 1983

OTWAY, THOMAS (1652–85): Dramatist; b, Sussex; Winchester and Christ Church, Oxford; failed as actor; unrequited passion for Mrs Barry, the actress; success of rhymed heroic tragedy, *Don Carlos*, 1676; with army in Holland, 1678; adaptation of Racine and Molière and mediocre comedies; added sentimental pathos to heroic manner in blank-verse tragedies, *The Orphan* (1680), and *Venice Preserv'd* (1682), both frequently revived on stage; dissipated life; died destitute.

Life by R. G. Ham, *Otway and Lee*, 1931; 1974
Works ed. J. G. Ghosh, 2 vols., 1932
The Orphan ed. A. M. Taylor, 1977
The Soldier's Fortune, in *Four Restoration Marriage Plays*, ed. M. Cordner and R. Clayton, 1995

Venice Preserv'd in *Restoration Tragedies*, ed. J. Sutherland, 1977
J. M. Armistead, *Four Restoration Playwrights: A Reference Guide*, 1984
See:
B. Dobrée, *Restoration Tragedy*, 1929
S. Johnson, *Lives of the Poets*, I, ed. G. B. Hill, 1905

PEPYS, SAMUEL (1633–1703): Diarist and public servant; son of London tailor from Huntingdonshire; St Paul's School, Trinity Hall and Magdalene College, Cambridge; love-match with French girl, Elizabeth St Michel, 1655; served relative Edward Montagu (Earl of Sandwich), with whom brought Charles II from Holland, 1660; energetic official and reformer of abuses as Clerk of Acts in Navy Office, etc.; lover of wine, women, music, theatre, books, business, and money; record in cipher of private life and public events, 1660–69; in *Diary*; Secretary to Admiralty, 1672; imprisoned in Tower during Popish Plot, 1679; voyage to Tangier, 1683; president of Royal Society, 1684; again Secretary to Admiralty, 1684; deprived of office after Revolution, 1689; retirement at Clapham.

Life by A. Bryant, 3 vols., 1933–8; 1984–85; J. E. N. Hearsey, 1973; R. Ollard, 1974
Diary ed. R. Latham and W. Matthews, 11 vols., 1970–83; *The Shorter Pepys* ed. R. Latham, 1985; 1993
Private Correspondence, etc. ed. J. R. Tanner, 2 vols., 1926
Further Correspondence ed. J. R. Tanner, 1929
Letters and Secondary Diary ed. R. G. Howarth, 1932
The Letters of Samuel Pepys and his Family Circle ed. H. T. Heath, 1955
See:
C. Marburg, *Mr Pepys and Mr Evelyn*, 1925
M. H. Nicolson, *Pepys's Diary and the New Science*, 1965
J. H. Wilson, *The Private Life of Mr Pepys*, 1959

POPE, ALEXANDER (1688–1744): Poet; b. London, son of Roman Catholic linen-draper; precocious child, health ruined by early illness; lived in Windsor Forest, 1700–16; debarred by religion from universities; introduced by Wycherley to London life, *c.* 1704; already polished poet in *Pastorals*, 1709 (written earlier); quarrel with Ambrose Philips; *Essay on Criticism* (1711) brought him into Addison's circle; *Rape of the Lock*, 1712 (enlarged, 1714); political allusions in *Windsor Forest* (1713) appealed to Tories; lifelong friendship with Swift; breach with Addison, 1715; *Poems*, 1717; moved to Twickenham, 1719; friendship with Lady Mary Wortley Montagu and Martha Blount; fortune and fame with verse translations, *Iliad* (1715–20), *Odyssey* (1725–6); attacked for religion and incompetence in Greek; ed. of Shakespeare, attacked by Theobald, 1725; turned to ethical poems and satires; *The Dunciad*, with Theobald as mock hero, 1728 (enlarged, 1729; recast, 1742, Cibber replacing Theobald as 'hero'; complete, four books, 1743); *An Essay on Man*, 1732–4; four *Moral Essays*, 1731–5, on false taste, on avarice, on characters of men and women; *Imitations of Horace*, 1733–8, satirizing social follies, political corruption, with defence of own life and art; pub. private correspondence by devious methods, 1735–42; buried Twickenham.

Life by G. Sherburn, 1934; M. Mack, 1985
Poems (Twickenham Ed.) ed. J. Butt *et al.*, 11 vols., 1939–69; I vol., 1963; rev. 1983
Translation of the 'Iliad' ed. S. Shankman, 1996
Prose Works, vol. I, ed. N. Ault, 1936; vol. II, ed. R. Cowler, 1986
Selected Prose ed. P. Hammond, 1987
Correspondence ed. G. Sherburn, 5 vols., 1956, selections in w.c.
Poems and Prose ed. D. Grant, 1985; in o.s.a., ed. P. Rogers, 1993
See:
E. G. Bedford and R. J. Dillinger, *A Concordance to the Poems of Alexander Pope*, 1974
R. A. Brower, *Alexander Pope: The Poetry of Allusion*, 1959; 1986
M. R. Brownall, *Alexander Pope and the Arts of Georgian England*, 1978
L. D. Damrosch, *The Imaginative World of Alexander Pope*, 1987
P. Dixon, *The World of Pope's Satires*, 1968
   (ed.) *Alexander Pope*, 1972
H. Erskine-Hill, *The Social Milieu of Alexander Pope*, 1975
D. Fairer, *The Poetry of Alexander Pope*, 1989
   (ed.) *Pope: New Contexts*, 1990
D. H. Griffin, *Alexander Pope: The Poet in his Poems*, 1978
J. V. Guerinot (ed.) *Pope: A Collection of Critical Essays*, 1972
R. Halsband, *'The Rape of the Lock' and Its Illustrations, 1714–1869*, 1980
S. Johnson, *Lives of the Poets*, ed. G. B. Hill, vol. III, 1905
D. Knight, *Pope and the Heroic Tradition*, 1951
W. Kowalk, *Alexander Pope, An Annotated Bibliography of Twentieth-Century Criticism, 1900–1979*, 1981
F. R. Leavis, *Revaluation*, 1936; 1964
C. A. Lopez, *Alexander Pope: An Annotated Bibliography, 1945–1967*, 1970
M. Mack (ed.) *Essential Articles for the Study of Alexander Pope*, 1964; 1965
   The Garden and the City: Retirement and Politics in the Later Poetry of Pope, 1731–1743, 1969
   (ed.) *The Last and Greatest Art: Some Unpublished Poetical Manuscripts of Alexander Pope*, 1984
   Collected in Himself. Essays Critical, Biographical and Bibliographical on Pope and Some of His Contemporaries, 1982
M. H. Nicolson and G. S. Rousseau, *'This Long Disease, My Life': Alexander Pope and the Sciences*, 1968
F. Rosslyn, *Alexander Pope*, 1990
J. P. Russo, *Alexander Pope: Tradition and Identity*, 1972
P. M. Spacks, *An Argument of Images: The Poetry of Alexander Pope*, 1971
G. Tillotson, *On the Poetry of Pope*, 1938; 1950
   Pope and Human Nature, 1958

H. D. Weinbrot, *Alexander Pope and the Traditions of Formal Verse Satire*, 1982

A. L. Williams, *Pope's 'Dunciad': A Study of Its Meaning*, 1955

PRIOR, MATTHEW (1664-1721): Poet and diplomatist; b. Wimborne, son of joiner; Westminster and St John's College, Cambridge, under patronage of Earl of Dorset; wrote verses, Latin and English, from boyhood, Spenser his favourite poet; with Montagu burlesqued Dryden's *Hind and the Panther*, 1687; diplomat in Holland and France; as secret agent in Paris, 1711, negotiated Treaty of Utrecht for Tories; imprisoned by Whigs, 1715–16; magnificent subscription edn of *Poems*, 1718; with proceeds and £4,000 from Lord Harley purchased Down Hall, Essex; noted for epigrams, familiar, occasional, and narrative verse; also wrote long philosophical poems; buried Westminster Abbey.

Life by L. G. W. Legge, 1921; C. K. Eves, 1939; J. M. Rippy, 1986
Literary Works ed. H. B. Wright and M. K. Spears, 2 vols., 1959
Selected Poems ed. A. Dobson, 1889; ed. F. Bickley, 1923
See:
O. Doughty, 'The Poet of the "Familiar Style"' in *English Studies*, VII, 1925

RAY, JOHN (1627–1705): Naturalist; b. Essex, son of blacksmith; educated Braintree and Trinity College, Cambridge; met group of eager young scientists; influenced by Cambridge Platonists; during illness began study of plants; travelled extensively in Great Britain recording flora and fauna, 1658–62, and in Europe, 1663–6, visiting leading scientists; F.R.S., 1667; began scientific classification of species; the founder of modern biological science; wrote also on dialects, proverbs, religion.

Life by C. E. Raven, 1942
See:
B. Willey, *The Eighteenth-Century Background*, 1940; 1961

RICHARDSON, SAMUEL (1689–1761): Printer and novelist: b. Derbyshire, son of joiner; little education; apprenticed to London printer, whose daughter he married; set up printing business; compiled manual of letter-writing for uneducated people, with directions 'how to think and act justly and prudently in the common Concerns of Human Life', 1741; led to epistolary novels *Pamela* (1740–41), *Clarissa Harlowe* (1747–8); European fame; *Sir Charles Grandison* (1753–4); made many feminine friendships.

Life by A. D. McKillop, 1936; T. C. D. Eaves and B. D. Kimpel, 1971
Works ed. Sir L. Stephen, 12 vols., 1883–4
Novels, ed. A. Dobson and W. L. Phelps, 19 vols., 1902; 18 vols., 1929–31
Pamela ed. T. C. D. Eaves and B. D. Kimpel, 1971; in E.L. ed. P. Sabor, 1980

Clarissa ed. G. Sherburn, 1962; in E.L. ed. A. Ross, 1985
The History of Sir Charles Grandison ed. J. Harris, 1972
Selected Letters of Samuel Richardson ed. John Carroll, 1964
Familiar Letters, etc., 1941; ed. B. W. Downs, 1928
See:
R. F. Brissenden, *Virtue in Distress: Studies in the Novel of Sentiment from Richardson to Sade*, 1974
E. B. Brophy, *Samuel Richardson: The Triumph of Craft*, 1974
J. Carroll (ed.) *Samuel Richardson: A Collection of Critical Essays*, 1969
T. Castle, *Clarissa's Ciphers: Meaning and Dissension in Richardson's 'Clarissa'*, 1982
R. Cowler (ed.) *'Pamela': A Collection of Critical Essays*, 1969
M. A. Doody, *A Natural Passion: A Study of the Novels of Samuel Richardson*, 1974
T. Eagleton, *The Rape of Clarissa: Writing, Sexuality and Class Struggle in Samuel Richardson*, 1982
R. G. Hannaford, *Samuel Richardson: An Annotated Bibliography of Critical Studies*, 1980
J. Harris, *Samuel Richardson*, 1987
T. Keymer, *Richardson's 'Clarissa' and the Eighteenth-Century Reader*, 1992
M. Kinkead-Weekes, *Samuel Richardson: Dramatic Novelist*, 1973
B. Kreissman, *Pamela-Shamela: A Study of the Criticisms, Burlesques, Parodies and Adaptations of Richardson's 'Pamela'*, 1960
F. R. Leavis, *The Great Tradition*, 1948
S. W. R. Smith, *Samuel Richardson: A Reference Guide*, 1984
I. Watt, *The Rise of the Novel*, 1957
C. G. Wolff, *Samuel Richardson and the Eighteenth-Century Puritan Character*, 1972

ROCHESTER, JOHN WILMOT, EARL OF (1647–80): Poet, wit, satirist, courtier, libertine; b. Ditchley, Oxfordshire; succeeded to earldom, 1658; educated Burford, Wadham College, Oxford; travelled on Continent, 1661–5, studied at Padua; at Court, 1665; fought in war against Dutch, 1665–6; favourite of Charles II, by whom frequently banished from Court and pardoned; most notorious of group of noble rakes; Paris, 1669; patron of poets, including Dryden; *Satyr against Mankind, c.* 1675–6; wrote amorous lyrics; conversations with Burnet, 1679–80; seriously ill, 'conversion', public recantation, June, 1680; d. Woodstock.

Life by J. Prinz, 1927; V. De S. Pinto, 1935; rev. 1962; G. Greene, 1974; J. Lamb, *So Idle a Rogue*, 1993
Collected Works ed. J. Hayward, 1926
Complete Poems and Plays ed. P. Lyons, 1993 in E.L.
The Complete Works, ed. F. H. Ellis, 1994
Poems ed. D. M. Vieth, 1968; ed. K. Walker, 1984; 1988
Selected Poems ed. P. Hammond, 1982

Letters ed. J. Treglown, 1980
See:
D. Farley-Hills (ed.) *Rochester: The Critical Heritage*, 1972
M. Thormählen, *Rochester: The Poems in Context*, 1993
D. R. Vieth, *Rochester Studies, 1925–1982: An Annotated Bibliography*, 1984
    (ed.) *John Wilmot, Earl of Rochester*, 1988
G. Wasserman, *Samuel Butler and the Earl of Rochester: A Reference Guide*, 1986

SHADWELL, THOMAS (?1642–92): Dramatist and poet, b. Norfolk; educated Bury St Edmunds, Caius College, Cambridge, Middle Temple; travelled abroad; after 1668 produced dramatic pieces almost yearly, pictures of contemporary manners in tradition of Jonson's comedy of humours; feud with Dryden from 1682 and ridiculed by him in *MacFlecknoe* and *The Medall*; superseded Dryden as poet laureate and historiographer after the Revolution.

Life by A. S. Borgman, 1928; 1969
Complete Works ed. M. Summers, 5 vols., 1927
The Virtuoso, ed. M. H. Nicolson and D. S. Rodes, 1969
See:
J. M. Armistead, *Four Restoration Playwrights: A Reference Guide*, 1984
B. Dobrée, *Restoration Comedy*, 1924
C. J. Wheatley, *Without God or Reason: The Plays of Thomas Shadwell*, 1993

SHAFTESBURY, ANTHONY ASHLEY COOPER, THIRD EARL OF (1671–1713): Moral philosopher; pupil of Locke, whose philosophy he rejected; Winchester School; travelled in Europe; M.P., 1695–8; earldom, 1699; abandoned public life because of ill-health; *Characteristicks of Men, Manners, Opinions, Times*, 3 vols, 1711; d. Naples. Deist, Platonist, churchman; 'optimistic' philosophy, that man is naturally virtuous, the 'Moral Sentiment'.

Life by R. L. Brett, 1951; R. Voitle, 1984
Characteristics ed. J. M. Robertson, 2 vols., 1900; 1964
See:
L. E. Klein, *Shaftesbury and the Culture of Politeness: Moral Discourse and Cultural Politics in Early Eighteenth-Century England*, 1994
C. A. Moore, 'Shaftesbury and the Ethical Poets in England, 1700–1760', in *Backgrounds of English Literature, 1700–1760*, 1953

SHENSTONE, WILLIAM (1714-63): Poet, contemporary of Samuel Johnson at Pembroke College, Oxford; laid out estate, The Leasowes, Worcs., according to newer modes of gardening; Spenserian imitation, *The Schoolmistress* (1737–42–8) and *Pastoral Ballad* (1755), continuing tradition of descriptive poetry; also wrote elegies, odes, songs, ballads, essays, and lively letters.

Life by M. Williams, 1935; A. R. Humphreys, 1937
Poetical Works ed. G. Gilfillan, 1854
Letters ed. M. Williams, 1939; ed. D. Mallam, 1939
Shenstone's Miscellany 1759–63 ed. I. A. Gordon, 1952
See:
C. E. de Haas, *Nature and the Country in English Poetry*, 1928

SHERIDAN, RICHARD BRINSLEY (1751–1816): Dramatist and orator; son of actor-elocutionist; educated Harrow; moved to Bath; escorted beautiful singer, Elizabeth Linley, to France, fought two duels with her persecutor and married her, 1773; *The Rivals, St Patrick's Day, The Duenna* produced, 1775; acquired Garrick's share in Drury Lane Theatre, 1776; *A Trip to Scarborough* and *The School for Scandal* produced there, 1777; burlesque farce, *The Critic*, 1779; M.P., and government offices, 1780–1812; celebrated speeches impeaching Warren Hastings, 1787–8; confidential adviser to Prince of Wales; debts and brain disease in last years. A man of brilliant wit and charm, of gaiety and gallantry; splendid public funeral.

Life by W. Sichel, 2 vols., 1909; S. Ayling, 1985; J. Morwood, 1985
Plays and Poems ed. R. C. Rhodes, 3 vols., 1928
The Dramatic Works ed. C. Price, 2 vols., 1973
Plays ed. C. Price, 1975; in E.L. and W.C.
The Rivals ed. E. Duthie, 1979; 1991
The School for Scandal ed. F. W. Bateson, 1979
The Letters ed. C. Price, 3 vols., 1966
See:
P. Davison (ed.) *Sheridan: Comedies: A Casebook*, 1986
J. Loftis, *Sheridan and the Drama of Georgian England*, 1977

SMART, CHRISTOPHER (1722–71): Poet; Durham School and Cambridge; fellow of Pembroke Hall, 1740–49; convivial alehouse companion; journalist, wit, satirist in London; debts and religious mania; in madhouse, 1757–63; belated recognition of masterpiece, *A Song to David* (1763); *Jubilate Agno* composed during madness, which it imaginatively documents.

Life by A. Sherbo, 1967
Poems ed. N. Callan, 2 vols., 1949; ed. M. Walsh and K. Williamson, 6 vols., 1980–95
Selected Poems ed. K. Williamson and M. Walsh, 1990
Jubilate Agno ed. W. H. Bond, 1954
A Song to David ed. E. Blunden, 1924; ed. P. Searle, 1924; facsimile, 1926; ed. J. B. Broadbent, 1960
See:
M. Dearnley, *The Poetry of Christopher Smart*, 1968
H. Guest, *A Form of Sound Words*, 1989
R. Mahoney and B. W. Rizzo, *Christopher Smart: An Annotated Bibliography, 1743–1983*, 1984

A. Rodway, *The Romantic Conflict*, 1963
P. M. Spacks, *The Poetry of Vision*, 1966

SMITH, ADAM (1723–90): Political economist; b. Kirkcaldy; Glasgow University; Balliol College, Oxford; professor of logic, Glasgow, 1751, of moral philosophy, 1752; friend of Hume; *Theory of the Moral Sentiments*, 1759; visited France, met Voltaire, 1764; studious retirement at Kirkcaldy, 1767; originated scientific study of economics with *An Enquiry into the Nature and Causes of the Wealth of Nations*, 1776; member of Johnson's Literary Club.

Life by J. Rae, 1895; 1965
The Glasgow Edition of the Works and Correspondence, 6 vols., 1976–87
The Wealth of Nations ed. E. Cannan, 2 vols., 1904; 1991; in E.L. and W.C.
See:
V. Brown, *Adam Smith's Discourse*, 1995
R. H. Campbell and A. S. Skinner, *Adam Smith*, 1982
J. Z. Muller, *Adam Smith in His Time and Ours*, 1992
A. S. Skinner and T. Wilson (eds.) *Essays on Adam Smith*, 1975

SMOLLETT, TOBIAS GEORGE (1721–71): Surgeon, journalist, and novelist; b. Dumbartonshire of good family; studied medicine at Glasgow University; to London, 1739 (see *Roderick Random*); naval surgeon during warfare in West Indies, 1740–44 (see *Roderick Random*); London surgeon, 1744; *Roderick Random* (anon.) and trans. *Gil Blas*, 1748; *Peregrine Pickle*, 1751; *Ferdinand Count Fathom*, 1753; trans. *Don Quixote*, 1755; *Sir Launcelot Greaves*, 1760–62, in instalments; ed. *Critical Review*, 1756–63; popular *History of England*, 1757; fined, imprisoned for libel, 1759; ed. pro-government *The Briton*, 1762–3; from 1763 travelled widely in search of health; *Travels through France and Italy*, 1766; to Italy, 1769; *Humphry Clinker*, 1771; d. Leghorn.

Life by L. L. Martz, *The Later Career*, 1942; G. M. Kahrl, 1945; L. M. Knapp, 1949
Works ed. G. Saintsbury, 12 vols., 1895, etc.; ed. J. C. Beasley, *et al.*, 1979–in progress
Novels, 11 vols., 1925–6
Roderick Random, 1983; *Peregrine Pickle*, 1964; *Ferdinand Count Fathom*, 1971; *Sir Launcelot Greaves*, 1973, *Humphry Clinker*, 1966; ed. L. M. Knapp and P.-G. Boucé, 1984; ed. P. Miles, 1993; *Travels*, W.C. ed. J. L. Thorson, 1983
Letters ed. L. M. Knapp, 1970
See:
J. G. Basker, *Tobias Smollett: Critic and Journalist*, 1988
P.-G. Boucé, *The Novels of Tobias Smollett*, 1976
D. Grant, *Tobias Smollett: A Study in Style*, 1977

L. Kelly (ed.) *Tobias Smollett: The Critical Heritage*, 1987
R. D. Spector, *Tobias Smollett. A Reference Guide*, 1980
    Smollett's Women, 1995
M. Wagoner, *Tobias Smollett: A Checklist of Editions of his Work and an Annotated Secondary Bibliography*, 1984

STEELE, SIR RICHARD (1672–1729): Essayist, dramatist, and politician; b. Dublin; Charterhouse (with Addison) and Merton College, Oxford; captain in Life Guards; dissipated living but wrote edifying treatise, *The Christian Hero*, 1701; comedies produced, *The Funeral* (1701), *The Lying Lover* (1703), *The Tender Husband* (1705); official gazetteer, 1707; second wife, Mary Scurlock ('dear Prue'); heavy drinking and debts; *The Tatler*, 1709–11; lost gazetteership, 1710; *The Spectator*, with Addison, 1711–12; *The Guardian*, attacked by Tories, 1713; Whig M.P., 1713; pamphlets against Swift and government; *The Englishman*, 1713–14; expelled from parliament, 1714; new appointments under Hanoverians, and knighted, 1715; quarrelled with Addison, 1718; last comedy, *The Conscious Lovers*, 1722; driven from London by debts; d. Carmarthen.

Life by G. A. Aitken, 2 vols., 1889; C. Winton, 2 vols., 1964–70
Plays ed. S. S. Kenny, 1971
The Christian Hero ed. R. Blanchard, 1932
The Guardian ed. J. C. Stephens, 1982
The Tatler ed. D. J. Bond, 3 vols., 1987
The Spectator ed. G. G. Smith, 8 vols., 1897–8; E.L., 1907; ed. D. F. Bond, 5 vols., 1965; 1987
The Englishman ed. R. Blanchard, 1955
Periodical Journalism, 1714–16 ed. R. Blanchard, 1944
Tracts and Pamphlets ed. R. Blanchard, 1959
Addison and Steele: Selections, etc., ed. R. J. Allen, 2nd edn, 1970
Correspondence ed. R. Blanchard, 1941
See bibliography under *Prose* and *Drama*
E. A. and L. D. Bloom, *Addison and Steele: The Critical Heritage*, 1980; 1995
R. P. Bond, *'The Tatler': The Making of a Literary Journal*, 1971

STERNE, LAURENCE (1713–68): Novelist and clergyman; b. Clonmel, Ireland, son of poor lieutenant; school near Halifax; cared for by uncle; Jesus College, Cambridge; ordained 1737; vicar of Sutton-in-the-Forest, 1738; prebend of York Minster, 1741; married, 1741; first two vols. of *Tristram Shandy* (1760) denounced on moral and literary grounds; later vols., 1761–7; visited London, 1760, great social success; *Sermons of Mr Yorick*, 1760; because of ill-health travelled abroad, 1762–4, 1765–6; fell in love with Mrs Draper, 1767 (*Journal to Eliza*); separation from wife; *A Sentimental Journey through France and Italy*, 1768; d. London, in debt but not poverty-stricken.

Life by W. L. Cross, 1909; rev. 2 vols., 1925; 1929; A. H. Cash, 2 vols., 1975–86; 1992

Works ed. G. Saintsbury, 6 vols., 1894; ed. W. L. Cross, 12 vols., 1904; 7 vols., 1926–7; ed. M. and J. New, 1978–in progress

A Sentimental Journey ed. G. D. Stout, 1967; ed. I. Jack, 1968; 1984; ed. T. Keymer, 1994 in E.L.

Tristram Shandy ed. I. C. Ross, 1993 in W.C.; ed. M. New, 1992 in E.L.

Selected Works ed. D. Grant, 1950; 1970

Letters ed. L. P. Curtis, 1935

See:

M. Byrd, '*Tristram Shandy*', 1985

A. H. Cash and J. M. Stedmond (eds.) *The Winged Skull: Papers from the Laurence Sterne Bicentenary Conference*, 1971

M. V. De Porte, *Nightmares and Hobbyhorses: Swift, Sterne and Augustan Ideas of Madness*, 1974

H. Fluchère, *Laurence Sterne, From Tristram to Yorick*, 1965

L. Hartley, *Laurence Sterne in the Twentieth Century*, 1966

A. B. Howes (ed.) *Sterne: The Critical Heritage*, 1974

A. D. Nuttall, *A Common Sky: Philosophy and the Literary Imagination*, 1974

J. M. Stedmond, *The Comic Art of Laurence Sterne*, 1967

J. Traugott (ed.) *Laurence Sterne: A Collection of Critical Essays*, 1968

SWIFT, JONATHAN (1667–1745): Satirist, pamphleteer and poet; b. Dublin, posthumous child of English parents; Kilkenny School, Trinity College, Dublin; entered household of Sir William Temple, 1689, where he educated Esther Johnson ('Stella'), then a small child; prebend of Kilroot, near Belfast, 1695; returned to Temple at Moor Park, 1696; defended Temple against Bentley and Wotton in *The Battle of the Books*, pub. with a *A Tale of a Tub*, 1704; after Temple's death (1699), returned to Ireland; vicar of Laracor, etc., established Stella in Dublin; protracted visits to England during 1701–14; sought benefits for Irish clergy; friend of Addison, Arbuthnot, Steele, Pope; religious pamphlets and humorous pieces, *Miscellanies*, 1711; losing faith in Whigs on ecclesiastical issues, turned to Harley (Lord Oxford) and St John (Bolingbroke); political influence as Tory propagandist, *The Examiner* (1710–11). *The Conduct of the Allies* (1711), against prolongation of war with France; record of daily life in *Journal to Stella*; met Esther Vanhomrigh ('Vanessa'); Dean of St Patrick's, Dublin, 1713; on fall of Tories, returned to 'exile' in Ireland, 1714; began to write on behalf of oppressed Irish, 1720; *Drapier's Letters* against 'Wood's Halfpence', 1724; national hero of Irish; Vanessa died, 1723; *Gulliver's Travels* (1721–5) pub. 1726, during visit to England; death of Stella 1728; *Miscellanies*, 1727–8; attacked Irish bishops and Presbyterians, 1732; increasing ill-health and loss of memory, 1738; unsound in mind, 1742–5; buried St Patrick's.

Life by J. Forster, 1875; I. Ehrenpreis, 3 vols., 1962–83; D. Nokes, 1985

Prose Works ed. T. Scott, 12 vols., 1897–1909; ed. H. Davies *et al.*, 16 vols., 1939–74

Poems ed. H. Williams, 3 vols., 1937; rev. 1958

Poetical Works ed. H. Davis, 1967; ed. P. Rogers, 1983

A Tale of A Tub and *The Battle of the Books*, etc. ed. A. C. Guthkelch and D. Nichol Smith, 1920; rev. 1958; 1975

The Drapier's Letters ed. H. Davis, 1935

Gulliver's Travels ed. P. Dixon and J. Chalker, 1967; ed. C. T. Probyn, 1975; ed. P. Turner, 1986; ed. J. Riordan, 1992; ed. C. Fox, 1995

Gulliver's Travels and Other Writings ed. L. A. Landa, 1960; 1976; ed. R. A. Greenberg and W. B. Piper, 1973

J. H. Ellis (ed.) *Swift vs. Mainwaring: 'The Examiner' and 'The Medley'*, 1985

Swift on his Age. Selected Prose and Verse ed. C. J. Horne, 1953

Selections in O.S.A ed. A. Ross and D. Woolley, 1984

Correspondence ed. Sir H. Williams, 5 vols., 1963–5

Journey to Stella ed. Sir H. Williams, 2 vols., 1948; in E.L.

See:

H. Bloom (ed.) *Jonathan Swift's 'Gulliver's Travels': Modern Critical Interpretations*, 1984

R. I. Cook, *Jonathan Swift as a Tory Pamphleteer*, 1967

K. Craven, *Jonathan Swift and the Millennium of Madness*, 1992

D. Donoghue, *Jonathan Swift: A Critical Introduction*, 1969

A. B. England, *Energy and Order in the Poetry of Swift*, 1980

C. Fabricant, *Swift's Landscape*, 1983

O. W. Ferguson, *Jonathan Swift and Ireland*, 1962

J. I. Fischer, *On Swift's Poetry*, 1978

C. H. Flynn, *The Body in Swift and Defoe*, 1990

J. P. Forster, *Jonathan Swift: The Fictions of the Satirist*, 1991

R. Gravil (ed.) *Swift, 'Gulliver's Travels': A Casebook*, 1974

I. Higgins, *Swift's Politics: A Study in Disaffection*, 1994

A. N. Jeffares (ed.) *Fair Liberty Was All His Cry: A Tercentenary Tribute to Jonathan Swift*, 1967

A. C. Kelly, *Swift and the English Language*, 1988

L. A. Landa, *Swift and the Church of Ireland*, 1954

F. R. Leavis, 'The Irony of Swift' in *The Common Pursuit*, 1952; 1962

F. P. Lock, *The Politics of 'Gulliver's Travels'*, 1980

J. McMinn, *Jonathan Swift: A Literary Life*, 1991

W. Montag, *The Unthinkable Swift. The Spontaneous Philosophy of a Church of England Man*, 1995

F. Palmieri, *Critical Essays on Jonathan Swift*, 1993

R. Paulson, *Theme and Structure in Swift's 'Tale of a Tub'*, 1960

C. T. Probyn (ed.) *Jonathan Swift: The Contemporary Background*, 1979

C. J. Rawson (ed.) *The Character of Swift's Satire*, 1983

R. H. Rhodins, *Swift Studies, 1965–1980: An Annotated Bibliography*, 1984

M. Shinagel, *A Concordance to the Poems of Jonathan Swift*, 1972

M. K. Starkman, *Swift's Satire on Learning in 'A Tale of A Tub'*, 1950

J. J. Stathis, *A Bibliography of Swift Studies, 1945–1965*, 1967

H. Teerink, *A Bibliography of the Writings of Jonathan Swift*, 1937; 2nd edn, rev. A. H. Scouten

D. M. Vieth, *Swift's Poetry 1900–1980. An Annotated Bibliography of Studies*, 1982

   (ed.) *Essential Articles for the Study of Jonathan Swift's Poetry*, 1984

D. Ward, *Jonathan Swift: An Introductory Essay*, 1973

K. Williams, *Jonathan Swift and the Age of Compromise*, 1958

   (ed.) *Swift: The Critical Heritage*, 1970, 1995

D. B. Wyrick, *Jonathan Swift and the Vested Word*, 1988

TEMPLE, SIR WILLIAM (1628–99): Statesman and author; b. London; Emmanuel College, Cambridge; travelled abroad; met Dorothy Osborne, whom he married, 1655, after opposition of her Royalist family; in Ireland; diplomatic missions; declined political office; retired 1681; frequently visited at Moor Park by William III; employed Swift as secretary; wrote memoirs of diplomatic missions and essays on government, gardening, etc.; *Of Ancient and Modern Learning* (1690) set going in England Ancients *v.* Moderns controversy.

Life by C. Marburg, 1932; H. E. Woodbridge, 1940

Works, 4 vols., 1814

Early Essays and Romances ed. G. C. Moore, 1930

An Essay upon Ancient and Modern Learning and *Of Poetry* in *Critical Essays of the Seventeenth Century*, III ed. J. E. Spingarn, 1909

Five Miscellaneous Essays ed. S. H. Monk, 1963

See:

R. Faber, *The Brave Courtier, Sir William Temple*, 1983

K. H. D. Haley, *An English Diplomat in the Low Countries: Sir William Temple and John de Witt*, 1986

T. B. Macaulay, *Critical and Historical Essays*, I, 1843; in E.L.

THOMSON, JAMES (1700–48): Poet, b. Ednam, son of Scottish minister; Edinburgh University; abandoned theological training and moved to London, 1725; private tutor; *The Seasons*, 1726–30, reflecting interest in nature, science, theology; acquaintance of Arbuthnot, Gay, Pope; travelled in France and Italy as tutor to son of Lord Chancellor; *Liberty*, 1734–6; five tragedies; from 1736 lived retired at Richmond on pension, continually revising *The Seasons*; probably contributed 'Rule Britannia' to masque, *Alfred*, 1740; Spenserian allegory on his way of life, *The Castle of Indolence*, 1748; buried Richmond.

Life by L. Morel, 1895; G. C. Macaulay, 1908; D. Grant, 1951; J. Sambrook, 1991

Works ed. Lord Lyttelton, 4 vols., 1750, etc.

Poetical Works ed. J. L. Robertson, 1908

The Seasons ed. O. Zippel, 1908; ed. J. Sambrook, 1981

Liberty, The Castle of Indolence and Other Poems ed. J. Sambrook, 1986
Plays ed. J. C. Greene, 1987
Letters and Documents ed. A. D. McKillop, 1958
See:
R. Cohen, *The Art of Discrimination*, 1964
     The Unfolding of 'The Seasons': A Study of James Thomson's Poem, 1970
S. Johnson, *Lives of the Poets*, ed. G. B. Hill, vol. III, 1905
J. W. Mackail, *Studies of the English Poets*, 1926
D. Nichol Smith, *Some Observations on Eighteenth-Century Poetry*, 1937
P. M. Spacks, *The Varied God*, 1959

VANBRUGH, SIR JOHN (1664–1726): Dramatist and architect; son of London tradesman, grandson of refugee Flemish merchant; studied architecture in France, 1683–5; entered army, 1686; imprisoned in France, 1690–92; *The Relapse*, 1696; *The Provok'd Wife*, 1697; comptroller of board of works, 1702–12, 1715; manager of theatre in Haymarket, 1705–7; designed Castle Howard, Blenheim Palace, the original Haymarket Theatre, etc.; knighted, 1714; among other plays, mostly from the French, were *The Country House* (1703), *The Confederacy* (1705), *The Provok'd Husband* (completed by Cibber, 1728).

Life by G. H. Lovegrove, 1902; L. Whistler, 1938; M. Bingham, 1974; K. Downes, 1987
Complete Works ed. B. Dobrée and G. Webb, 4 vols., 1927–8
Four Comedies, ed. M. Cordner, 1989
The Relapse ed. C. A. Zimansky, 1970
The Provok'd Wife ed. A. Coleman, 1982; ed. J. L. Smith, 1974, 1993
The Provok'd Husband ed. P. Dixon, 1974; 1975
See under *Drama*, studies by Boas, Dobrée
B. Dobrée, *Essays in Biography*, 1925
F. McCormick, *Sir John Vanbrugh: A Reference Guide*, 1992

WALPOLE, HORACE, EARL OF ORFORD (1717–97): Author, politician and connoisseur; youngest son of Sir Robert Walpole; Eton and King's College, Cambridge; grand tour of France and Italy with Gray (*q.v.*), 1739–41; M.P., 1741–67; turned Strawberry Hill, Twickenham, into 'a little Gothic castle' and set up printing-press; wrote on noble authors, painting, engraving; 'Gothic romance', *The Castle of Otranto*, 1764; kept up lively, gossiping correspondence with friends, giving entertaining record of the age; 'the best informed gossip of his century'; succeeded to earldom, 1791.

Life by R. W. Ketton-Cremer, 1940; rev. 1946
Letters ed. Mrs P. Toynbee, 19 vols., 1903–5, 1918–25; selections in E.L.
Correspondence ed. W. S. Lewis *et al.*, 48 vols., 1937–83
Selected Letters ed. W. S. Lewis, 1973
The Castle of Otranto in E.L. and W.C.; ed. E. Clery, 1996
Memoirs of King George II ed. J. Brooke, 1985

See:
I. W. U. Chase, *Horace Walpole, Gardenist*, 1943
J. Gray, *Horace Walpole and William Beckford: Pioneers of the Gothic Revival*, 1994
P. Sabor, *Horace Walpole: A Reference Guide*, 1984
   (ed.) *Horace Walpole: The Critical Heritage*, 1987
W. H. Smith (ed.) *Horace Walpole, Writer, Politician and Connoisseur*, 1967

WARTON, JOSEPH (1722–1800): Critic and poet; educated Winchester, Oriel College, Oxford; clergyman; notably unsuccessful headmaster of Winchester, 1766–93; friend of poet Collins; *Odes*, 1744, 1747, avoiding didacticism and showing feeling for nature; *Essay on the Genius and Writing of Mr Pope*, 1756–82, admiring him but condemning imitators; friend of Johnson and circle; edited Pope, 1797

Life by J. Wooll, 1806
The Three Wartons: A Choice of their Verse ed. E. Partridge, 1927
See:
W. L. MacDonald, *Pope and his Critics*, 1951
J. Pittock, *The Ascendancy of Taste: The Achievement of Joseph and Thomas Warton*, 1973
H. Trowbridge, 'Joseph Warton on the Imagination', in M.P. XXXV, 1937
J. A. Vance, *Joseph and Thomas Warton. An Annotated Bibliography*, 1982

WARTON, THOMAS (1728–90): Critic and poet; Trinity College, Oxford; *Pleasures of Melancholy*, 1747; ed. collections of verse and classical texts; *Observations on the Faery Queen* (1754) the first adequate criticism of Spenser; professor of poetry, Oxford, 1757–67; pioneer *History of English Poetry*, 1774–81; professor of ancient history, Oxford 1785–90; poet laureate, 1785–90; ed. Milton's early poems, 1785; wrote humorous verse, sonnets, and poems inspired by antiquarian interests; friend of Dr Johnson.

Life by C. Rinaker, 1916
Poems ed. R. Mant, 2 vols., 1802
The Three Wartons. A Choice of their Verse ed. E. Partridge, 1927
See:
W. P. Ker, *Collected Essays*, I, 1925
D. Nichol Smith, 'Warton's History of English Poetry', in *Proc. of British Academy*, XV, 1929
J. Pittock, *The Ascendancy of Taste: The Achievement of Joseph and Thomas Warton*, 1973
R. Wellek, *The Rise of the English Literary History*, 1941

WINCHILSEA, ANNE FINCH, COUNTESS OF (1661–1720): Poet; neé Kingsmill, ancient Hampshire family; maid of honour at Court, 1683–4;

withdrew on marriage to Heneage Finch, later Earl of Winchilsea; Eastwell Park, Kent, from 1689; *Miscellany Poems by a Lady*, 1713; other poems remained in MS.; friend of Pope and Rowe; her *Nocturnal Reverie* noticed by Wordsworth for its new images of rural nature.

Life by B. McGovern, 1992
Poems ed. M. Reynolds, 1903; also in *Minor Poets of the Eighteenth Century*, 1930
Selected Poems ed. D. Thompson, 1987
See:
R. A. Brower, 'Lady Winchilsea and the Poetic Tradition of the Seventeenth Century', in S.P., XLII, 1945
C. H. Hinnant, *The Poetry of Anne Finch: An Essay in Interpretation*, 1994

WYCHERLEY, WILLIAM (?1640–1716): Dramatist; b. Clive, near Shrewsbury; became Roman Catholic in France; Inner Temple and Queen's College, Oxford; *Love in a Wood*, 1671; favoured by King's mistress, Duchess of Cleveland; *The Gentleman Dancing-Master*, 1672; commission in army, 1672; *The Country Wife*, 1672/3; *The Plain Dealer*, 1674; secret marriage to Countess of Drogheda displeased Charles II; imprisoned for debt; *Miscellany Poems* (1704) led to friendship with young Pope, who corrected his later verses and quarrelled; remarried just before death.

Life by C. Perromat, 1921; K. M. Rogers, 1972; B. E. McCarthy, 1979
Complete Works ed. M. Summers, 4 vols., 1924; 1965
Complete Plays ed. G. Weales, 1966
Plays ed. W. C. Ward, 1888; ed. G. Weales, 1966; ed. A. Friedman, 1979; ed. P. Holland, 1981
The Country Wife in *Restoration Plays*, E.L., 1976; ed. J. D. Hunt, 1973; ed. D. Cook and J. Swannell, 1975; ed. J. Ogden, 1973; 1991
The Plain Dealer ed. L. Hughes, 1967; 1968; ed. J. L. Smith, 1979
See under *Drama*, Studies by Dobrée, N. Holland
W. R. Chadwick, *The Four Plays of William Wycherley: A Study in the Development of a Dramatist*, 1975
B. E. McCarthy, *William Wycherley: A Reference Guide*, 1985
J. Thompson, *Language in Wycherley's Plays: Seventeenth-Century Language Theory and Drama*, 1984
R. Z. Zimbardo, *Wycherley's Drama*, 1965

YOUNG, EDWARD (1683–1765): Poet; b. Upham, near Winchester, son of clergyman; Winchester School; fellow of All Souls, Oxford; entered London literary circles; tragedies, 1719–21; satires, *The Universal Passion* (1725–8), much admired until outclassed by Pope; rector of Welwyn, 1730; failed to get expected bishopric; married daughter of Earl of Lichfield, 1731; her death inspired the 'pious gloom' of *The Complaint, or Night-Thoughts on Life, Death, and Immortality* (1742–5), which gained European fame; *Conjectures on Original Composition*, 1759.

Life by W. Thomas, 1901; H. C. Shelley, 1914
Complete Works ed. J. Doran, 2 vols., 1854; 1968
Poetical Works ed. J. Mitford, 2 vols., London, 1830, etc.
Night Thoughts ed. S. Cornford, 1989
Selected Poetry ed. S. H. Clark, 1994
Conjectures on Original Composition ed. F. J. Morley, 1918
Correspondence ed. H. Pettie, 1971
See:
I. St J. Bliss, 'Young's *Night Thoughts* in Relation to Contemporary
  Christian Apologetics', in P.M.L.A., XLIX, 1934
J. W. Mackail, *Studies of English Poets*, 1926

NOTES ON CONTRIBUTORS

FRANK W. BRADBROOK (d. 1983) Senior Lecturer in English, University College of North Wales, Bangor. Author of *Jane Austen: Emma* (1961) and *Jane Austen and her Predecessors* (1966); editor (with James Kinsley) of *Jane Austen: Pride and Prejudice* (1970).

NORMAN CALLAN (d. 1978) Emeritus Professor of English in the University of London. Author of *Poetry in Practice* and *The Collected Poems of Christopher Smart* (1949), etc. Was also Associate Editor for four volumes of the Twickenham Edition of *The Poems of Alexander Pope*.

A. S. COLLINS (d. 1959) Senior Lecturer in English at Leicester University. Author of *Authorship in the Days of Johnson* (1927), *Profession of Letters* (1928), and *Treasury of English Poetry* (1977).

P. A. W. COLLINS Emeritus Professor of English, University of Leicester. Author of *James Boswell* (1956), *Dickens and Crime* (1962), *Dickens and Education* (1963), and many other studies on Dickens and his period, including an edition of his public readings (1975) and the Dickens volumes in The Critical Heritage, and Interviews and Recollections, series.

T. S. ELIOT (d. 1965) Poet, critic and publisher. Editor of *The Criterion*. Awarded the Nobel Prize for Literature, 1948. His main critical works were *The Sacred Wood* (1920), *The Use of Poetry and the Use of Criticism* (1933), *What is a Classic?* (1945), *Selected Essays* (1951) and *Poetry and Poets* (1957).

D. J. ENRIGHT Writer, formerly university teacher. Publications include *Shakespeare and the Students* (1970), *The Alluring Problem: an Essay on Irony* (1986), and *Collected Poems* (1987). Editor of *A Choice of Milton's Verse* (1975), *Rasselas* (1976), *The Oxford Book of Contemporary Verse 1945–1980* (1980) and *The Oxford Book of Death* (1983).

S. L. GOLDBERG (d. 1991) Formerly Professor of English, University of Melbourne, and is now Senior Fellow, History of Ideas Unit, Australian National University, Canberra. Author of *The Classical Temper* (1961), *Joyce* (1962), *An Essay on 'King Lear'* (1974), and editor of the *Critical Review*.

COLIN HORNE is Emeritus Professor of English in the University of Adelaide. Fellow of the Australian Academy of the Humanities; formerly President of the Australasian and Pacific Society for Eighteenth Century Studies. He is the author of various publications on the eighteenth century, especially on Swift, Pope and Johnson.

ARTHUR HUMPHREYS (d. 1990) Professr of English at the University of Leicester. Author of *The Augustan World* (1954); editor of the Arden editions of 1 *Henry IV* (1960), 2 *Henry IV* (1966), *Much Ado About Nothing* (1981), and the new Penguin editions of *Henry V* (1968), *Henry VIII* (1971).

JANE JACK Fellow of St Anne's College, Oxford. Edited *Roxana* (1981), *Jane Eyre* (1969). Is engaged on a book, *The Uses of Pastoral*.

DOUGLAS WILLIAM JEFFERSON Emeritus Professor of English in the University of Leeds. Author of two books on Henry James and one on Jane Austen, and articles on Milton, Dryden, Scott, Dickens and other writers.

F. N. LEES (d. 1981) Reader in English Literature, University of Manchester. Author of *Christopher Marlowe: Edward II* (1954), *Gerard Manley Hopkins* (1966), *English Institute Essays* (1966). Contributed articles to *Scrutiny*, the *British Journal of Aesthetics*. *Gissing Newsletter*.

VIVIAN DE SOLA PINTO (d. 1969) Professor of English Literature at the University of Nottingham. His works of literary criticism ranged from the Restoration poets through William Blake to D. H. Lawrence. His last book, *The City that Shone* (1969), was an autobiography.

JOHN PRESTON was successively Professor of English and Comparative Literary Studies, University of Warwick and Professor of English Literature at Hong Kong University. Author of *The Created Self: The Reader's Role in Eighteenth-century Fiction* (1970), and chapters in *The Age of Enlightenment*, ed. R. Grimsley (1980).

PAT ROGERS DeBartolo Professor in the Liberal Arts, University of South Florida. Author of books on Grub Street, Pope, Defoe, Swift, Fielding, Reynolds and other eighteenth-century topics.

IAN P. WATT Professor of English and Director of the Humanities Centre, Stanford University, California. Author of *The Rise of the Novel* (1957), *Conrad in the Nineteenth-Century* (1980) and a study of *Nostromo* (1988).

INDEX